GREGG *Shorthand*

Functional Method

Diamond Jubilee Series
Second Edition

Shorthand written
by Charles Rader

Louis A. Leslie

Charles E. Zoubek

GREGG Shorthand

Functional Method

Gregg Division
McGraw-Hill Book Company

New York
St. Louis
Dallas
San Francisco
Düsseldorf
Johannesburg
Kuala Lumpur
London
Mexico
Montreal
New Delhi
Panama
Rio de Janeiro
Singapore
Sydney
Toronto

ACKNOWLEDGMENTS

The authors wish to express their appreciation to the following people for their valuable assistance in the preparation of *Gregg Shorthand, Functional Method, Diamond Jubilee Series, Second Edition:*

The teachers who have shared with the authors their experience with the first edition.

Mr. Charles Rader, for the beautiful shorthand and for the supervision of the production of the book.

Betty Binns, the designer, who was responsible for the physical attractiveness of the book.

Mrs. Mary Louise Intorrella and Mr. Jerome Edelman, members of the Gregg staff, who contributed so much to the production of the book.

Mr. Martin Bough of *Fundamental Photographs*, who took the cover, title, and chapter photographs.

Miss Bambi Hammil, who directed the taking of the pictures.

Mr. Syd Karson of *McGraw-Hill, Inc.*, who took the photographs for "Your Shorthand Practice Program" on pages 10, 11, and 12.

King Typographic Service Corp., which set the type, and R. R. Donnelley and Sons Company, which printed the book.

GREGG SHORTHAND, FUNCTIONAL METHOD, DIAMOND JUBILEE SERIES, SECOND EDITION

12 13 14 15 DODO 8 9 8 7 6

ISBN 07-037255-1

Preface

Gregg Shorthand, the universal system

Since its publication in 1888, Gregg Shorthand has been learned and used by millions of writers throughout the world not only in English but in many foreign languages as well. To most people the terms "shorthand" and "Gregg" are synonymous. Gregg Shorthand is truly the universal system of shorthand.

Gregg Shorthand is used by stenographers and secretaries as a vocational tool that enables them to obtain and hold interesting and rewarding positions in business. It is used by business and professional men and women who are relieved of the burden of writing cumbersome longhand when they must make notes, prepare important memoranda, and draft speeches and reports.

The success of any system of shorthand rests on the merits of its alphabet. The Gregg alphabet is the most efficient shorthand alphabet devised in more than 2,000 years of shorthand history. The fact that this alphabet, virtually without change, has been the basis of Gregg Shorthand for more than 80 years is indeed a tribute to the genius of its inventor, John Robert Gregg.

Functional Method

The Functional Method of teaching Gregg Shorthand has for many years been used with great success by thousands of teachers of the system. The Functional Method type of presentation, fundamentally a language-art type of teaching, allows much scope for the ingenuity of the individual teacher within the framework of language-art teaching. It is distinguished, in general, by the provision of a printed key to the shorthand plates, and by the absence of verbalization of rules or principles.

Diamond Jubilee Series, Second Edition

Objectives *Gregg Shorthand, Functional Method, Diamond Jubilee Series,* issued in 1963, the seventy-fifth anniversary of the invention of the system, has been well received by the shorthand teaching profession. Teachers found the system changes to be logical and the new teaching and learning devices helpful. The major objectives of that edition were:

1 To teach the student to read and write Gregg Shorthand rapidly and accurately in the shortest time possible.

2 To provide the student with transcription readiness by building his vocabulary and developing his ability to spell and punctuate accurately—all concurrently with the teaching of shorthand.

The objectives of *Gregg Shorthand, Functional Method, Diamond Jubilee Series, Second Edition,* remain the same as those of the First Edition.

Organization

In *Gregg Shorthand, Functional Method, Diamond Jubilee Series, Second Edition,* no word-building principles or outlines have been changed; nor have the organization of the textbook and the order of presentation of shorthand principles been changed.

Like the First Edition, the Second Edition is divided into three parts—Principles, Reinforcement, and Shorthand and Transcription Skill Building. These parts are subdivided into 10 chapters and 70 lessons. The last new theory is presented in Lesson 47.

New format

The first thing that will immediately impress the student and teacher is the new, modern format of the Second Edition. This Second Edition is without doubt the most attractive, eye-appealing shorthand textbook ever published.

This format makes it possible to present the shorthand practice material in two columns that are approximately the width of the columns of the student's shorthand notebook. The shorter lines make reading easier, for the eye does not have to travel so far from the end of one line of shorthand to the beginning of the next. The new format also makes it possible to highlight the words from the Reading and Writing Practice that are singled out for spelling attention. The words are placed in the margins rather than in the body of the shorthand.

Building transcription skills

This Second Edition continues to place great stress on the nonshorthand elements of transcription, which are taught concurrently with shorthand. It retains all the helpful transcription exercises of the First Edition, with slight, but very helpful, modifications. These include:

Business Vocabulary Builders Beginning with Chapter 2, each lesson contains a Business Vocabulary Builder consisting of several business words or expressions for which meanings are provided. The words and expressions are selected from the Reading and Writing Practice. The Business Vocabulary Builders help to overcome a major transcription handicap—a limited vocabulary.

Spelling—Marginal Reminders Words singled out from the Reading and Writing Practice for special spelling attention appear in the margins of the shorthand. Usually each word appears on the same line as its shorthand outline. These words appear in a second color in the shorthand so that they are easy to spot.

In the Second Edition, spelling is introduced in Chapter 4 rather than in Chapter 6, as in the First Edition.

Spelling—Families An effective device for improving spelling is to study words in related groups, or spelling families. In the Second Edition, the student studies six spelling families.

Similar-Words Drills These drills teach the student the difference in meaning between similar words that stenographers often confuse—*it's, its; accept, except; there, their.*

Punctuation Beginning with Lesson 31, nine frequent usages of the comma are introduced. Only one comma usage is presented in any given lesson. The commas appear in a square in the shorthand, and the reason for the use of the comma is shown above the square.

Common Prefixes An understanding of the meaning of common English prefixes is an effective device for developing the student's understanding of words. In the Second Edition, the student studies five common English prefixes.

Grammar Checkup In a number of lessons, drills are provided on rules of grammar that students often apply incorrectly.

Transcription Quiz Beginning with Lesson 57, each lesson contains a Transcription Quiz consisting of a letter in which the student has to supply internal punctuation. This quiz provides him with a daily test of how well he has mastered the punctuation rules presented in earlier lessons.

Reading and writing practice

In this Second Edition there are 41,868 words of shorthand practice material in the Reading and Writing Practice exercises. Much of the material is new. That which has been retained from the First Edition has been revised and brought up to date.

A new feature is the inclusion of a brief-form letter in *every* lesson of Part 1 (except the review lessons) beginning with Lesson 5. In the First Edition brief-form letters were provided only in those lessons in which a new group of brief forms was introduced.

Other features

Shorthand spelling helps When a new shorthand letter or abbreviating device is presented, the shorthand spelling is given. Formerly, this information had to be provided by the teacher.

Chapter openings Each chapter is introduced by a beautifully illustrated spread that not only paints for the student a vivid picture of the life and duties of a secretary but also inspires and encourages him in his efforts to acquire the necessary skills.

Student helps To be sure that the student gets the greatest benefit from each phase of his shorthand study, he is given step-by-step suggestions on how to handle it when it is first introduced.

Reading scoreboards At various points in the text, the student is given an opportunity to determine his reading speed by means of a scoreboard. The scoreboard enables him to calculate the number of words a minute he is reading. By comparing his reading speed from scoreboard to scoreboard, he sees some indication of his shorthand reading growth.

Recall charts In the last lesson of each chapter in Part 1, a unique recall chart is provided. This chart contains illustrations of all the theory taught in the chapter. It also contains illustrations of all the theory the student has studied up to that lesson.

Check lists To keep the student constantly reminded of the importance of good practice procedures, occasional check lists are provided. These check lists deal with writing shorthand, reading shorthand, homework, proportion, etc.

Gregg Shorthand, Functional Method, Diamond Jubilee Series, Second Edition, is published with pride and with the confidence that it will help teachers of Gregg Shorthand do an even more effective job of training rapid and accurate shorthand writers and transcribers.

The Publishers

Contents

Your shorthand practice program

The student studies the word lists by placing a card or a slip of paper over the type key and reading the shorthand words aloud.

How rapidly you develop skill in reading and writing shorthand will depend largely on two factors—the amount of time you devote to practice and the *efficiency* with which you practice. You will derive the greatest benefit from the material on which you practice if you practice efficiently. You will also be able to complete each lesson in the shortest possible time—a consideration that is no doubt of importance to you. The suggestions given here will help you to get the maximum benefit from the time you invest in shorthand practice.

Before you begin, select a quiet place in which to practice—and resist the temptation to turn on the radio or television set. Then follow the steps outlined below for each part of your shorthand practice.

Reading word lists

In each lesson there are a number of word lists that illustrate the principles introduced in the lesson. As part of your home practice, read these word lists in this way:

1 *With the type key exposed,* spell—aloud if possible—the shorthand characters in each outline in the list, thus: *"see, s-e; fee, f-e."* Reading aloud will help to impress the shorthand outlines firmly on your mind. Read all the shorthand words in the list in this way—with the type key exposed—until you feel you can read the shorthand outlines without referring to the type key.

2 Then *cover the type key* with a card or a piece of paper and read aloud from the shorthand, thus: *"s-e, see; f-e, fee."*

3 If the spelling of a shorthand outline does not immediately give you the meaning, move the card or piece of paper to expose the key and determine the meaning of the outline you cannot read. *Important:* Do not spend more than a few seconds trying to decipher an outline.

4 After you have read all the words in the list, read them a second time—perhaps even a third.

Note: In reading brief forms for common words and phrases, which first occur in Lesson 3, you need not spell the shorthand outlines.

Reading sentences, letters, and articles

Each lesson contains a Reading Practice (Lessons 1-20) or a Reading and Writing Practice (Lessons 21-70) in which sentences, letters, or articles are written in shorthand. Your practice on this material will help you develop your shorthand vocabulary. The first thing you should do is *read* the material in this way:

1 Place your left index finger under the shorthand outline you are about to read.

2 Place your right index finger on the type key to that shorthand outline. The key begins on page 364.

3 Read the shorthand, aloud if possible, until you come to a shorthand outline that you cannot read. Spell the shorthand strokes in the outline. If the spelling does not *immediately* give you the meaning, anchor your finger on the outline and turn to the key in the back, where your right index finger is resting near the point at which you are reading.

4 Determine the meaning of the outline you cannot read and place your right index finger on it.

5 Return to the shorthand from which you are reading—your left index finger has kept your place for you—and continue reading in this manner until you have completed the material.

By following this procedure, you will lose no time finding your place in the shorthand and in the key when you cannot read an outline.

6 If time permits, read the material a second time.

Remember, during the early stages your shorthand reading may not be very rapid. That is only natural, as you are, in a sense, learning a new language. If you do each day's lesson faithfully, however, you will find your reading rate increasing almost from day to day.

Writing the Reading and Writing Practice

Before you do any writing of shorthand, you should give careful consideration to the tools of your trade—your notebook and your writing instrument.

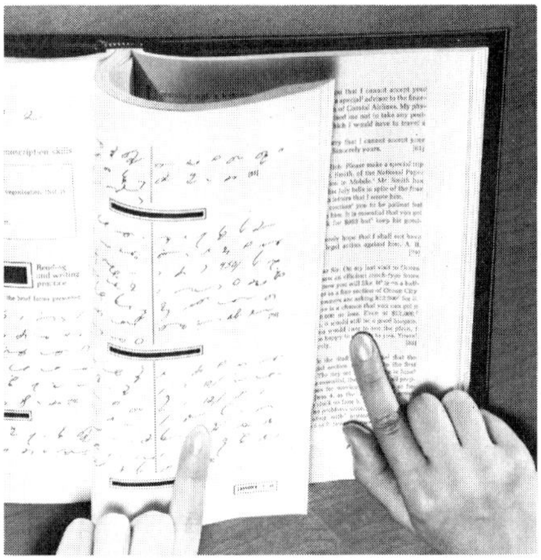

The student reads the Reading Practice, referring to the key whenever he cannot read an outline. Notice how the left index finger is anchored on the place in the shorthand; the right index finger, on the place in the key.

When copying, the student reads a convenient group of words aloud and then writes that group in her notebook. Notice how she keeps her place in the shorthand with her left index finger.

Your notebook The best notebook for shorthand writing is one that measures 6 x 9 inches and has a vertical rule down the center of each page. If the notebook has a spiral binding, so much the better, as the spiral binding enables you to keep the pages flat at all times. The paper should, of course, take ink well.

Your writing instrument A fountain pen is the most satisfactory instrument for writing Gregg Shorthand, but a fine ball-point pen will also do nicely. *A pencil is not recommended.* Because writing with a pen requires little pressure, you can write for long periods of time without becoming fatigued. A pencil, however, requires considerable pressure. In addition, the point quickly becomes blunt; and the blunter it gets, the more effort you have to expend to write with it. Pen-written notes remain legible almost indefinitely; pencil notes become blurred and hard to read. Pen-written notes are also easier to read under artificial light.

Having selected your writing tools, follow these steps in writing the Reading and Writing Practice:

1 Read the material you are going to copy, following the suggestions for reading shorthand on page 11. Always read everything before you copy it, referring to the key whenever you cannot read an outline after you have spelled it.

2 Place a card in the proper place in the key so that if you must refer to the key for an outline you cannot read, you will be able to do so with the minimum loss of time.

3 When you are ready to start writing, read a convenient group of words from the printed shorthand; then write the group, reading aloud as you write. Keep your place in the shorthand with your left index finger if you are right-handed, or with your right index finger if you are left-handed.

In the early stages your writing may not be very rapid, nor will your notes be as well written as those in the book. With regular practice, however, you will soon become so proud of your shorthand notes that you won't want to write any more longhand.

Good luck with your study of Gregg Shorthand.

1 PRINCIPLES

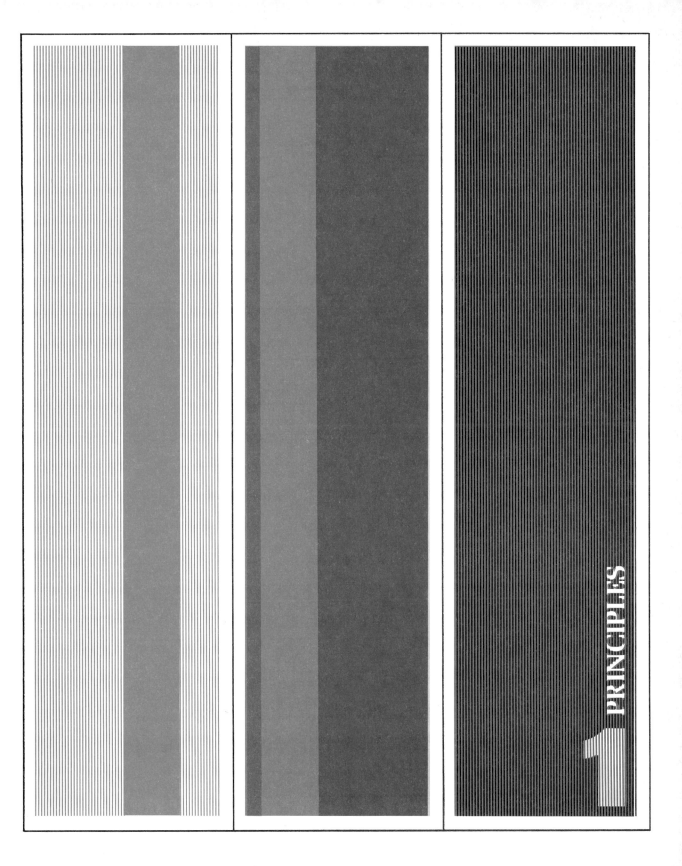

Chapter 1

Shorthand—stepping-stone to a career

There are many reasons why people decide to learn shorthand. No doubt you have your reasons. Perhaps the title of secretary appeals to you, and you realize that shorthand is a "must" if you are to earn that title. Perhaps you wish to acquire a skill that will help you earn your way through college. Or perhaps you have some personal reason for wanting to learn shorthand.

One very big reason why many people study shorthand is that they know that it opens doors to positions of responsibility that might otherwise be closed to them. In other words, they use shorthand as a stepping-stone to an interesting and profitable career.

How does shorthand open doors? How does it serve as a stepping-stone to a career? Let's cite the case of Janet Greene, a young lady who has considerable talent in art and is anxious to use this talent in the field of advertising.

Upon graduation from school Janet applied to several advertising agencies for a position in their art departments. She quickly found out that competition in this field is keen and that agencies were reluctant to hire young artists who have had no experience.

After being told by several personnel directors that they had no openings in which they could use her talent, Janet asked one of them, "How can

Dean
of

I get into the advertising field? I have my heart set on becoming a commercial artist." The personnel director's answer was direct: "Study shorthand and develop a good stenographic skill. You can always get a job as a stenographer—a well-paying job, too. Get your foot in the door of an advertising agency by working there as a stenographer. Then when you have made a niche for yourself, let it be known that you have artistic talents and ambitions. The chances are that you will be given an opportunity to demonstrate your talents." Good advice!

Every year countless young women—and many men—use their shorthand skill to open doors to varied and interesting careers. They may be careers in publishing, in advertising, in television, or in management. Competition is keen in these fields, and often the only way for a beginner to get into them is through the back door —the stenographic door!

Even the young lady who isn't really interested in a career—only in the title of "Mrs."—finds shorthand and stenographic training valuable. Thousands of young women continue to work after they are married to help earn money for a new home, to save for vacation travel, or to help meet unexpected expenses.

You have made a wise decision to learn shorthand!

LESSON 1

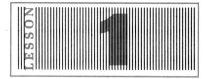

GREGG SHORTHAND IS EASY TO LEARN

Anyone who has learned to read and write longhand can learn to read and write Gregg Shorthand—it is as simple as that. The strokes you will write in Gregg Shorthand are the same strokes you are accustomed to writing in longhand.

Learning to write Gregg Shorthand is actually easier than learning to write longhand. Skeptical? Well, the following illustration should convince you of the truth of that statement.

In longhand, *f* may be expressed in many ways, all of which you had to learn. Here are six of them:

In addition, in many words the sound of *f* is expressed by combinations of other letters of the alphabet; for example, *ph*, as in *phase; gh*, as in *rough*.

In Gregg Shorthand there is only one way to express the sound of *f*, as you will learn later in this lesson.

With regular practice, your skill in Gregg Shorthand will develop rapidly.

Principles

GROUP A

1 **S-Z** The first stroke you will learn is the shorthand *s*, which is one of the most frequently used letters in the English language. The shorthand *s* is a tiny downward curve that resembles the longhand comma in shape.

Because in English *s* often has the sound of *z*, as in *saves*, the same downward curve is used to express *z*.

S-Z 

2 **A** The next stroke you will learn is the shorthand *a*, which is simply the longhand *a* with the final connecting stroke omitted.

A 

3 **Silent Letters Omitted** Many words in the English language contain letters that are not pronounced. In shorthand, these silent letters are omitted; only the sounds that are actually pronounced in a word are written. Examples:

The word *say* would be written *s-a;* the *y* would not be written because it is not pronounced. The word *face* would be written *f-a-s;* the *e* would not be written because it is not pronounced and the *c* would be represented by *s* because it is pronounced *s*.

What letters in the following words would not be written in shorthand because they are not pronounced?

day	*same*	*mean*	*tea*
save	*steam*	*dough*	*snow*

4 **S-A Words** With the strokes for *a* and *s*, you can form the shorthand outlines for two words.

say, s-a  *ace, a-s* 

▶ Notice that the *c* in *ace* is represented by the shorthand *s* because it has the *s* sound.

5 **F, V** The shorthand stroke for *f* is a downward curve the same shape as *s* except that it is larger—about half the height of the space between the lines in your shorthand notebook.

The shorthand stroke for *v* is also a downward curve the same shape as *s* and *f* except that it is very large—almost the full height of the space between the lines of your shorthand notebook. Note the difference in the sizes of *s, f, v.*

S  F  V 

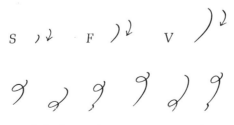

Safe, face, safes, save, vase, saves.

▶ Notice that the final *s* in *saves* has the *z* sound, which is represented by the *s* stroke.

6 **E** The shorthand stroke for *e* is a tiny circle. It is simply the longhand *e* with the two connecting strokes omitted.

E 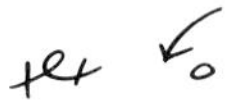

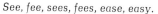

Be sure to make the *e* circle tiny and the *a* circle large.

Compare: E A 

See, fee, sees, fees, ease, easy.

▶ Notice that the *y* in *easy* is pronounced *e*; therefore, it is represented by the *e* circle.

> *Suggestion:* At this point take a few moments to read the procedures outlined for practicing word lists on page 10. By following those procedures, you will derive the greatest benefit from your practice.

GROUP B

7 **N, M** The shorthand stroke for *n* is a very short forward straight line. The shorthand stroke for *m* is a longer forward straight line.

N  M 

N

See, seen, say, sane, vain, knee.

▶ Notice that the *k* in *knee* is not written because it is not pronounced.

M

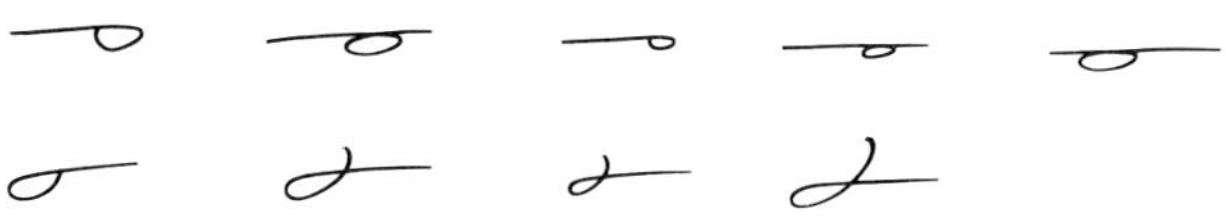

May, main, me, mean, name.
Aim, same, seem, fame.

8 T, D The shorthand stroke for *t* is a short upward straight line.
The shorthand stroke for *d* is a longer upward straight line.

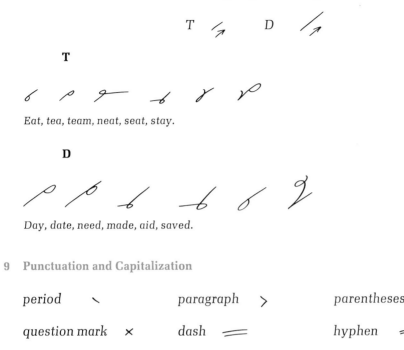

T
D

T

Eat, tea, team, neat, seat, stay.

D

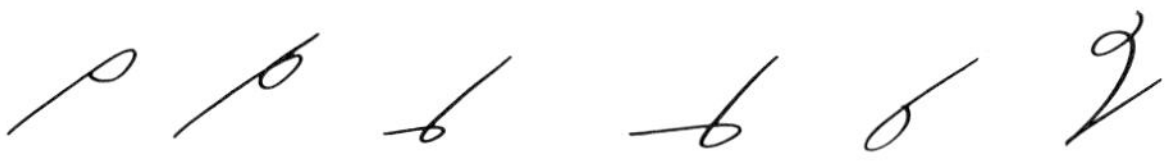

Day, date, need, made, aid, saved.

9 Punctuation and Capitalization

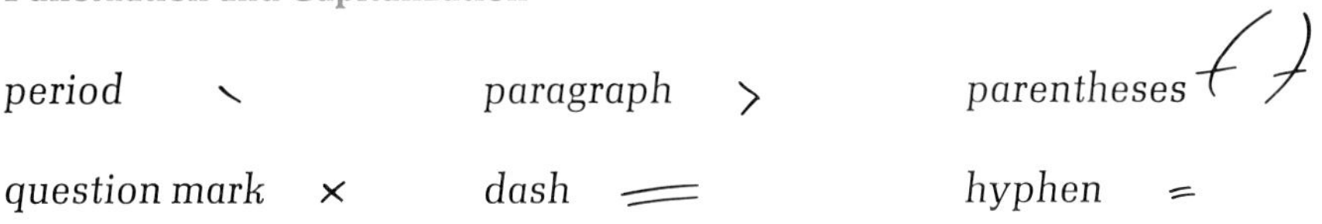
period
paragraph
parentheses
question mark
dash
hyphen

For all other punctuation marks, the regular longhand forms are used.

Capitalization is indicated by two upward dashes placed underneath the word to be capitalized.

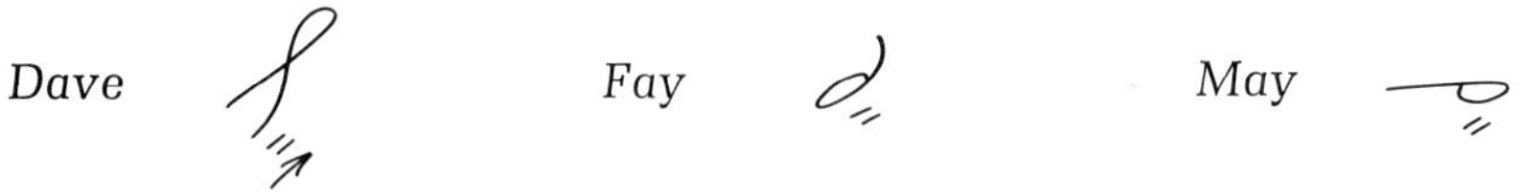
Dave
Fay
May

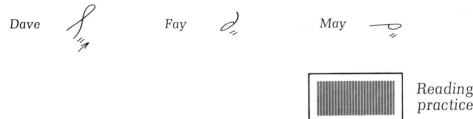

Reading practice

With the help of an occasional longhand word, you can already read complete sentences.

Read the following sentences, spelling each shorthand outline aloud as you read it, thus: *D-a-v-s, Dave's; f-e-t, feet.* If you cannot read a shorthand outline after you have spelled it, refer to the key.

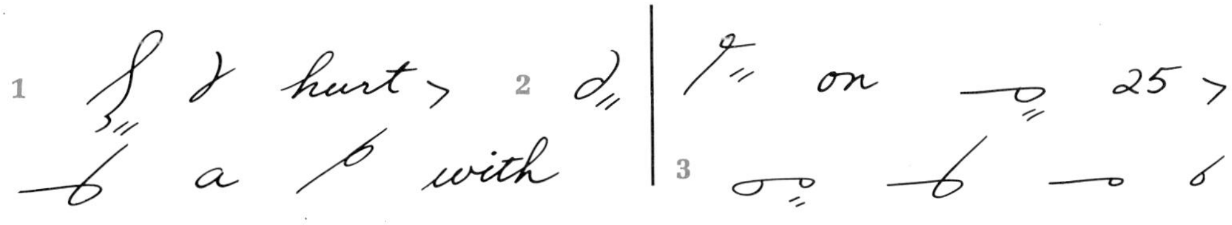
1
hurt
2
on
25
a
with
3

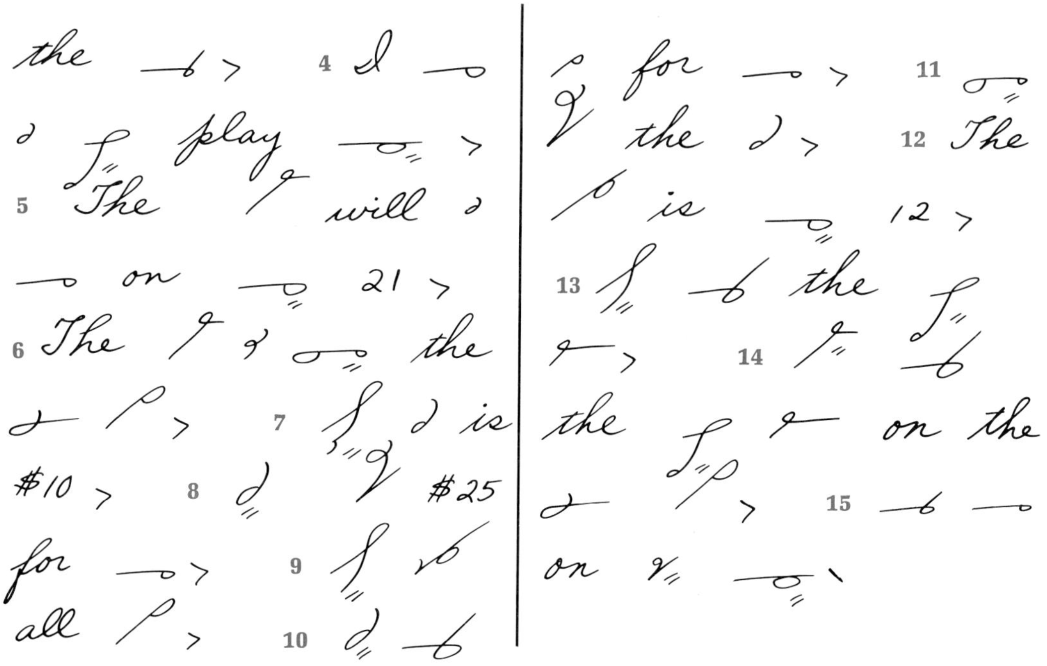

1. Dave's feet hurt. 2. Fay made a date with Dean on May 25. 3. Amy made me eat the meat. 4. I may see Navy play Maine. 5. The dean will see me on May 21. 6. The dean sees Amy the same day. 7. Dave's fee is $10. 8. Fay saved $25 for me. 9. Dave stayed all day. 10. Fay made tea for me. 11. Amy saved the fee. 12. The date is May 12. 13. Dave made the Navy team. 14. Dean made the Navy team on the same day. 15. Meet me on East Main.

LESSON 2

Principles

10 Alphabet Review In Lesson 1 you studied the following nine shorthand strokes. How quickly can you read them?

11 O, R, L The shorthand stroke for *o* is a small deep hook.

The shorthand stroke for *r* is a short forward curve.

The shorthand stroke for *l* is a longer forward curve about three times as long as the stroke for *r*.

▶ Note how these shorthand strokes are derived from their longhand forms.

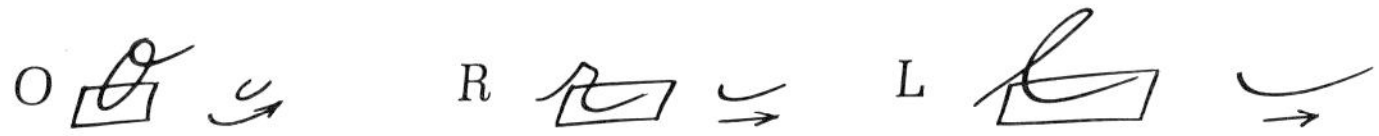
O
R
L

O

No, snow, tow, dough, sew, foe, phone.
Note, own, tone, dome, stone.

▶ Notice that in the last four words on the second line the *o* is placed on its side. By placing *o* on its side before *n* and *m* in these and similar words, we obtain smoother joinings than we would if we wrote the *o* upright.

R

Ray, rate, raid, trade, ear, dear.
Near, mere, store, more, fair, free.

L

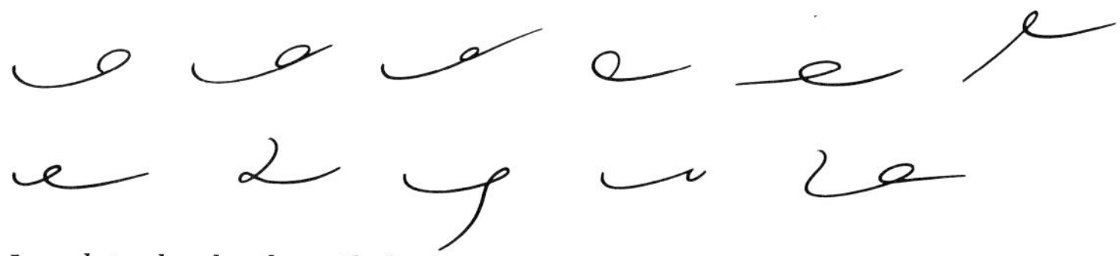

Lay, late, lead, ail, mail, deal.
Reel, feel, leave, low, flame.

▶ Notice that *fr*, as in *free*, and *fl*, as in *flame*, are written with one sweep of the pen, with no stop between the *f* and the *r* or *l*.

free  *flame* 

12 **H, -ing** The letter *h* is simply a dot placed above the vowel. With few exceptions, *h* occurs at the beginning of a word.

Ing, which almost always occurs at the end of a word, is also expressed by a dot.

He, hair, hole, heating, heeding, hearing.

13 **Long Ī** The shorthand stroke for the long sound of *ī*, as in *my*, is a large broken circle.

I 

My, might, tire, fine, vine, line.
Right, light, side, rely, mile.

14 **Omission of Minor Vowels** Some words contain vowels that are either not pronounced or are slurred in ordinary speech. For example, the word *even* is really pronounced *e-vn*; the word *meter* is pronounced *met-r*. These vowels may be omitted in shorthand.

Reader, meter, total, heater, later, even.

Reading practice

With the aid of a few words written in longhand, you can now read the following sentences. Remember to spell each shorthand word aloud as you read it and to refer to the key when you cannot read a word.

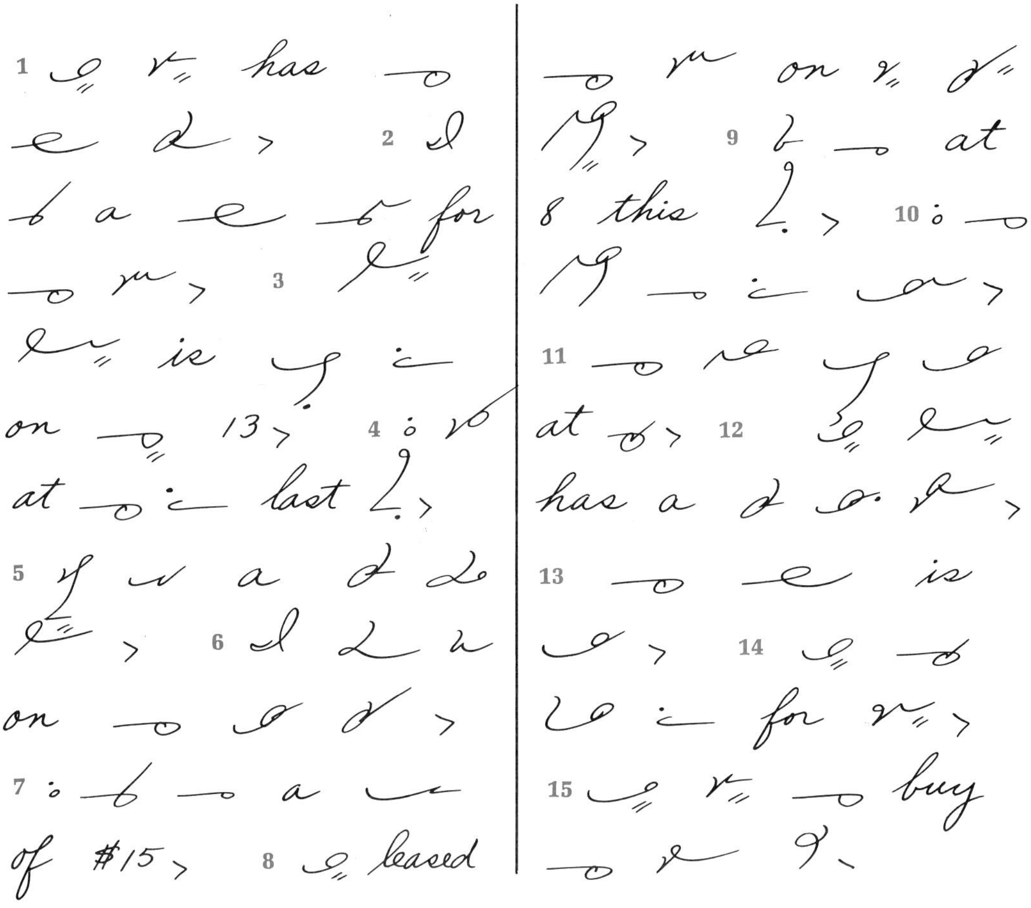

1. Ray Stone has my nail file. 2. I need a mail meter for my store. 3. Dale Taylor is leaving home on May 13. 4. He stayed at my home last evening. 5. Steven wrote a fine fairy tale. 6. I feel sore on my right side. 7. He made me a loan of $15. 8. Ray leased my store on East Side Drive. 9. Phone me at eight this evening. 10. He may drive me home later. 11. My train leaves late at night. 12. Ray Taylor has a fine writing style. 13. My mail is late. 14. Ray might fly home for Easter. 15. Lee Stone may buy my steel safe.

LESSON 3

Principles

15 Alphabet Review The strokes you studied in Lessons 1 and 2 are given here. How fast can you read them?

16 Brief Forms The English language contains many words that are used again and again in all the writing and speaking that we do.

As an aid to rapid shorthand writing, special abbreviations, called "brief forms," are provided for many of these common words. For example, we write *m* for *am*, *v* for *have*.

You are already familiar with the process of abbreviation in longhand—*Mr.* for *Mister*, *memo* for *memorandum*, *Ave.* for *Avenue*.

Because these brief forms occur so frequently, you will be wise to learn them well!

I, Mr., have, are-our-hour, will-well, a-an, am, it-at, in-not.

▶ Notice that some of the shorthand outlines have two or more meanings. You will have no difficulty selecting the correct meaning of a brief form when it appears in a sentence. The sense of the sentence will give you the answer.

17 Phrases By using brief forms for common words, we are able to save writing time. Another device that helps save writing time is called "phrasing," or the writing of two or more shorthand outlines together. Here are a number of useful phrases built with the brief forms you have just studied.

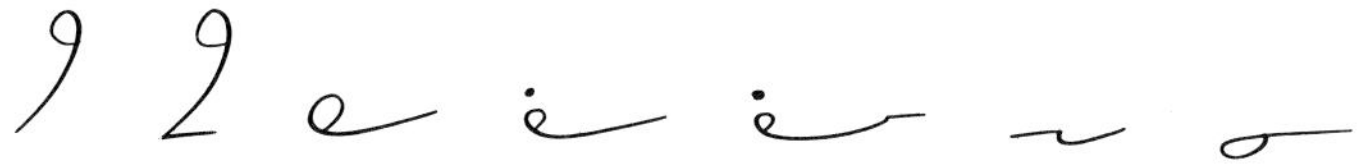

I have, I have not, I will, he will, he will not, in our, I am.

18 **Left S-Z** In Lesson 1 you learned one stroke for s and z. Another stroke for s and z is also used in order to provide an easy joining in any combination of strokes—a backward comma, which is also written downward. For convenience, it is called the "left s."

At this point you need not try to decide which s stroke to use in any given word; this will become clear to you as your study of shorthand progresses.

S-Z 

Eats, readers, files, ties, names, most, days.

19 **P, B** The shorthand stroke for *p* is a downward curve the same shape as the left s except that it is larger—approximately half the height of the space between the lines in your shorthand notebook.

The shorthand stroke for *b* is also a downward curve the same shape as the left s and *p* except that it is much larger—almost the full height of the space between the lines in your shorthand notebook.

▶ Notice the difference in the sizes of left *s*, *p*, and *b*.

S  P  B 

P

Pay, pays, pairs, price, please, people, hopes, opens, paid.

B

Bay, base, boats, brains, blames, blows, neighbors, beat.

▶ Notice that the combinations *pr*, as in *price; pl*, as in *please; br*, as in *brains;* and *bl*, as in *blames*, are written with one sweep of the pen without a pause between the *p* or *b* and the *r* or *l*.

price  please  brains  blames 

Reading practice

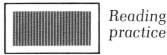

You have already reached the point where you can read sentences written entirely in shorthand.

> *Suggestion:* Before you start your work on this Reading Practice, read the practice procedures for reading shorthand on page 11. By following the procedures given there for using the Transcript of Shorthand, you will obtain the most benefit from your reading.

GROUP A

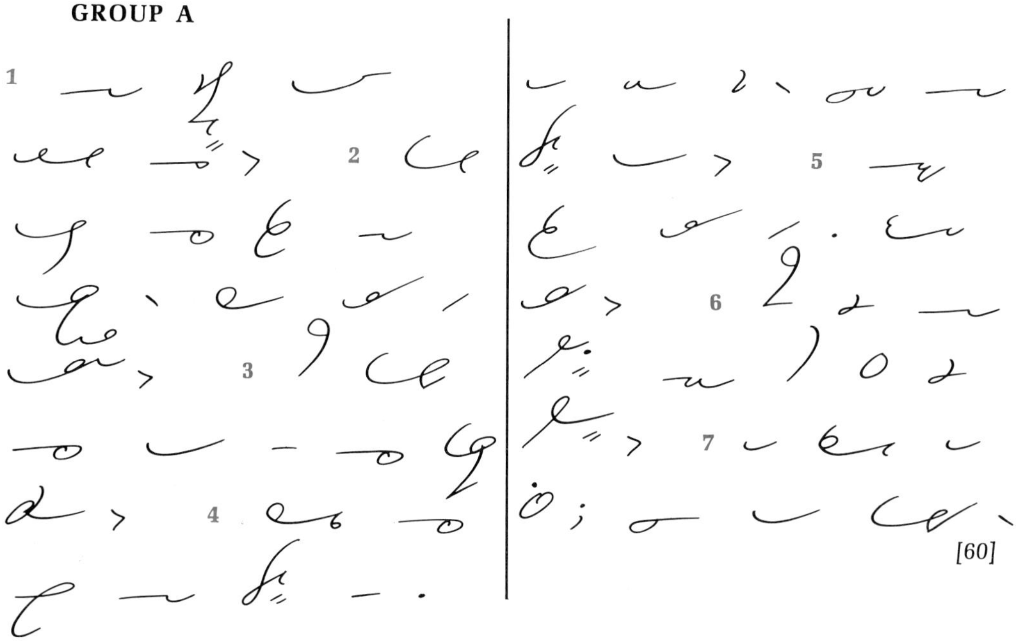

GROUP B

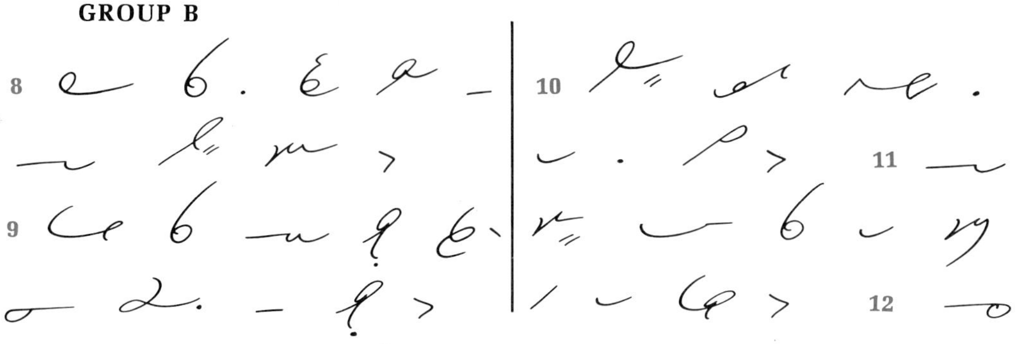

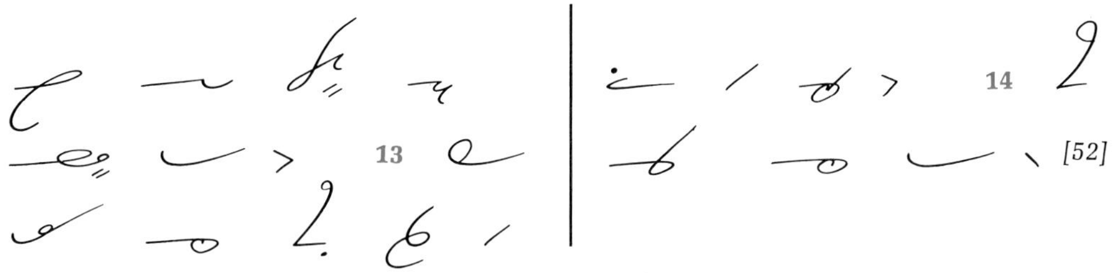
13
14
[52]

GROUP C

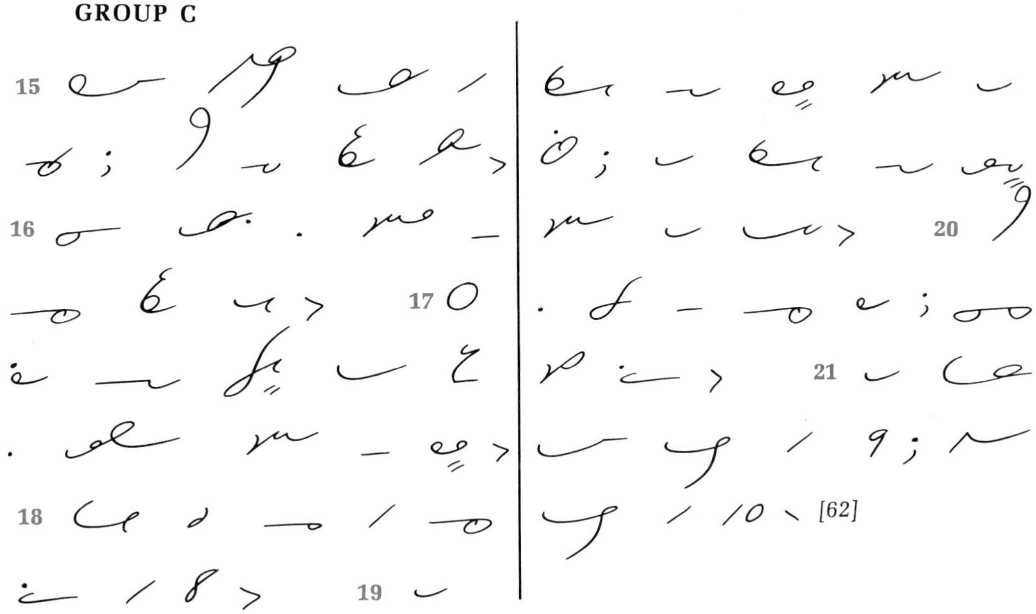
15
16
17
18
19
20
21
[62]

GROUP D

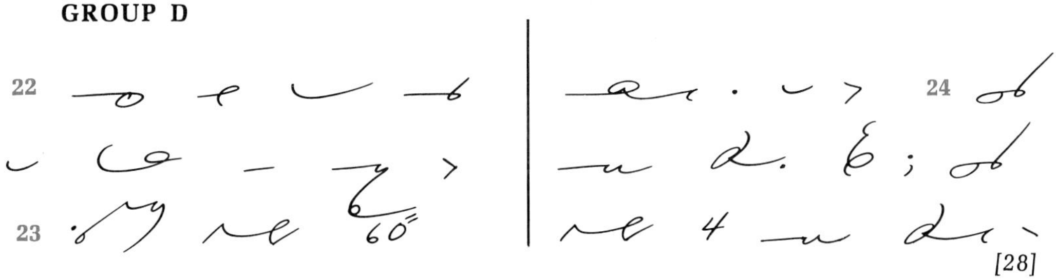
22
23
24
[28]

LESSON 4

Principles

20 Alphabet Review In Lessons 1 through 3, you studied 17 shorthand strokes. How rapidly can you read these strokes?

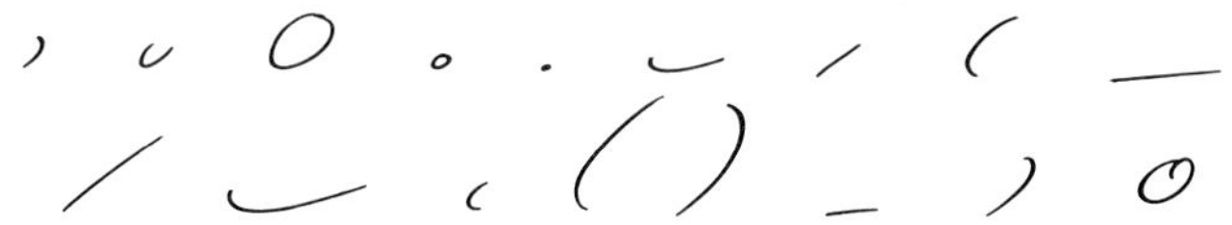

21 Sh, Ch, J The shorthand stroke for *sh* (called "ish") is a very short downward straight stroke.

The shorthand stroke for *ch* (called "chay") is a longer downward straight stroke approximately half the height of the space between the lines in your shorthand notebook.

The shorthand stroke for the sound of *j*, as in *jail* and *age*, is a long downward straight stroke almost the full height of the space between the lines in your shorthand notebook.

▶ Note carefully the difference in the sizes of these strokes.

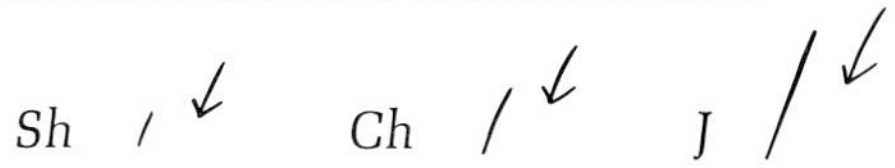
Sh
Ch
J

Sh

Spell: *ish-e, she*

She, showing, shows, showed, shades, shaped, shine, shore.

Ch

Spell: *e-chay, each; t-e-chay, teach*

Each, teach, reached, chains, chairs, cheaper, speech.

J

Spell: *a-j, age; j-a-l, jail*

Age, page, rage, stages, changed, jail, strange.

22 **OO, K, G** The shorthand stroke for the sound of *oo,* as in *to,* is a tiny upward hook.
The shorthand stroke for *k* is a short forward curve.
The shorthand stroke for the hard sound of g, as in *gain,* is a much longer forward curve. It is called "gay."

OO K G

OO

Spell: *t-oo, to; h-oo, who*

To-two-too, doing, shoe, who, fruit, room, true, noon, moved.

▶ Notice that the *oo* is placed on its side when it follows *n* or *m*, as in *noon* and *moved.* By placing the *oo* hook on its side in these combinations rather than writing it upright, we obtain smooth joinings.

K

Spell: *a-k, ache; t-a-k, take*

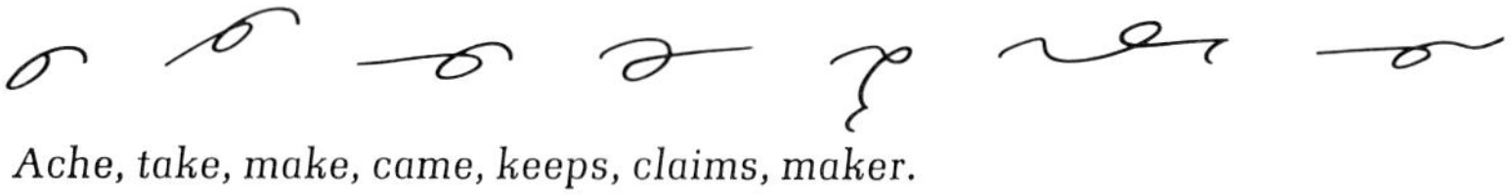

Ache, take, make, came, keeps, claims, maker.

G

Spell: *gay-a-n, gain*

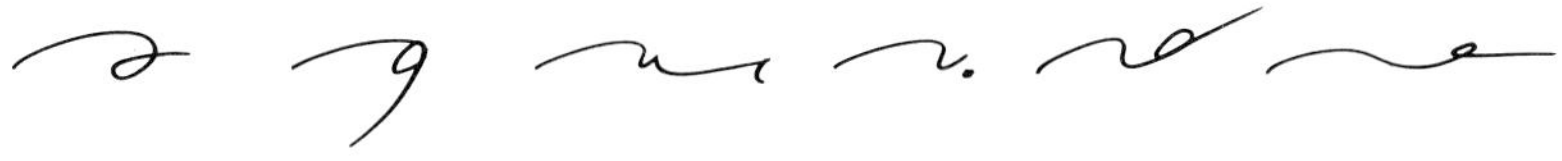

Gain, gave, goals, going, grade, gleam.

▶ Notice that *kr*, as in *maker*, and *gl*, as in *gleam*, are written with a smooth, wavelike motion. But *kl*, as in *claims*, and *gr*, as in *grade*, are written with a hump between the *k* and the *l* and the *g* and the *r*.

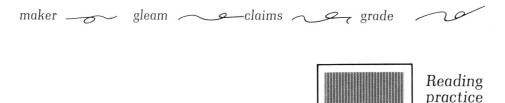

maker  *gleam*  *claims*  *grade* 

Reading practice

The following sentences contain many illustrations of the new shorthand strokes you studied in Lesson 4. They also review all the shorthand strokes, brief forms, and phrases you studied in Lessons 1 through 3.

Remember, you will get the most benefit from this Reading Practice and complete it in the shortest possible time if you follow the suggestions on page 11 for using the Transcript of Shorthand. Take a few moments now to reread those suggestions.

GROUP A

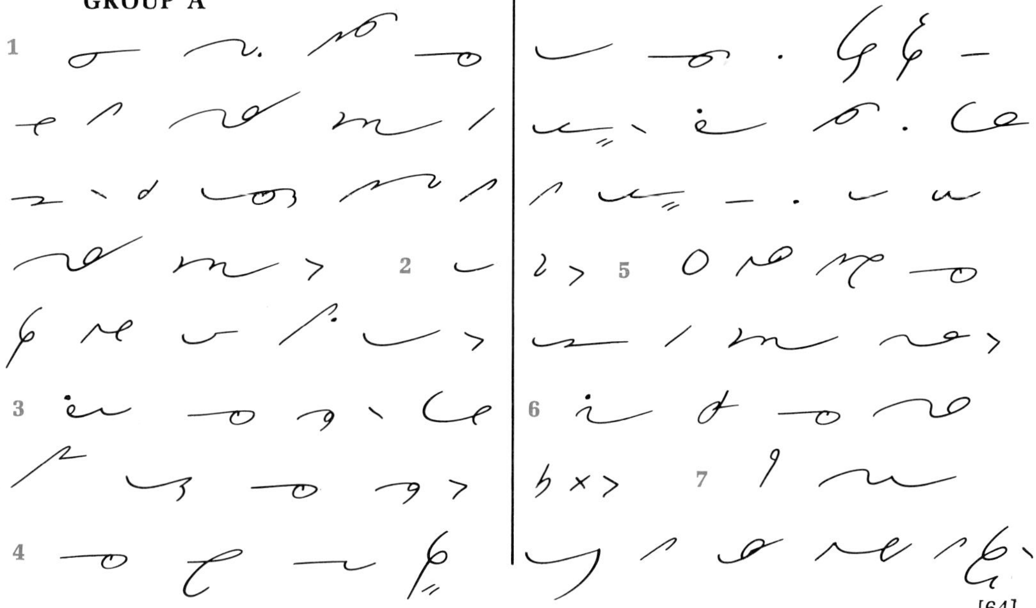

[64]

GROUP B

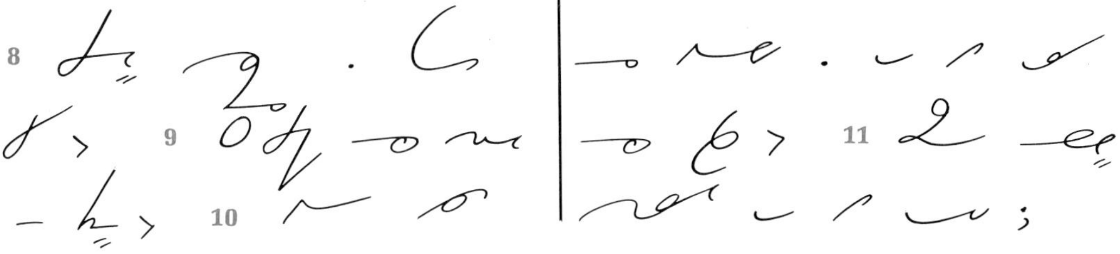

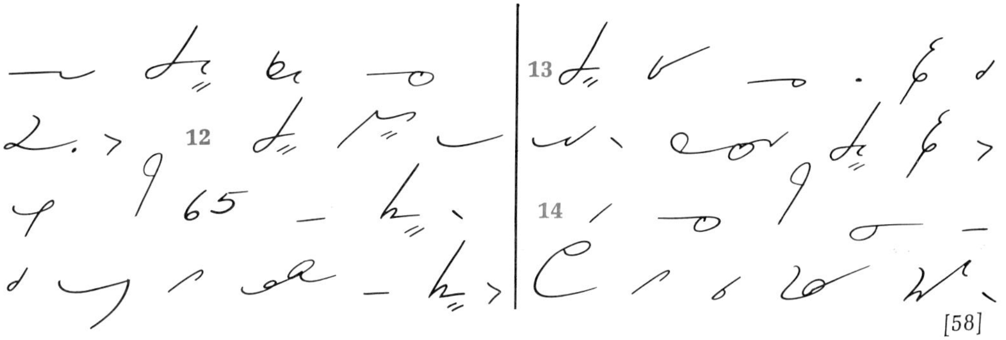

[58]

GROUP C

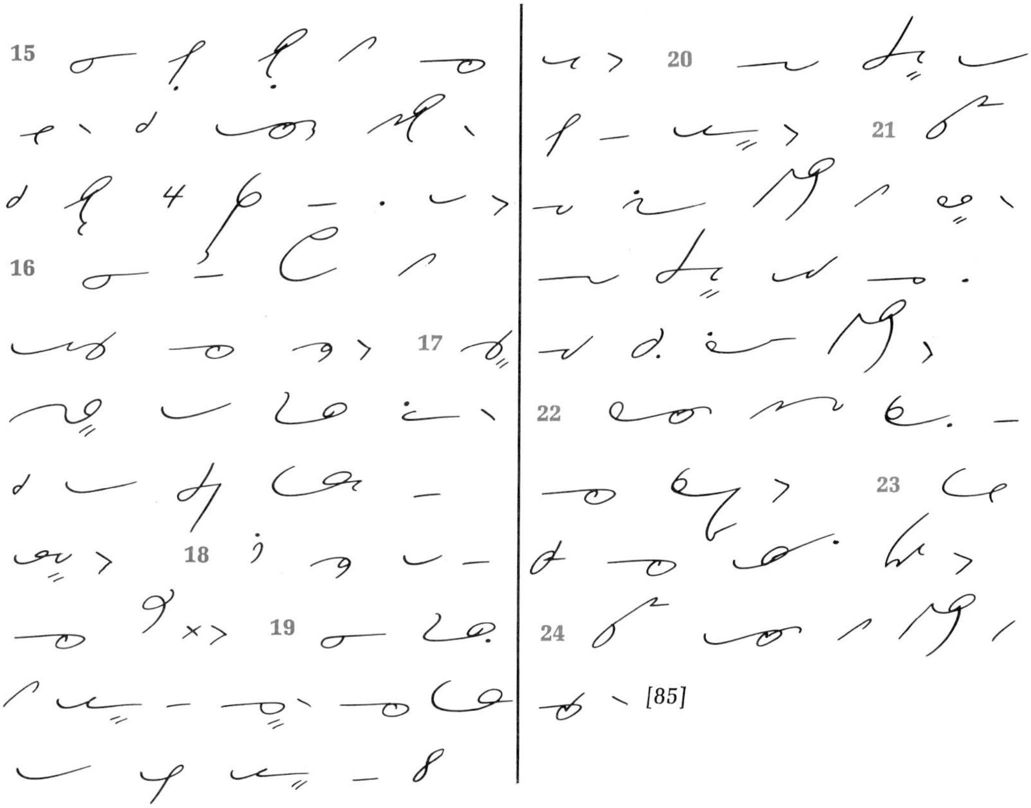

[85]

LESSON 5

Principles

23 **Alphabet Review** Here are all the shorthand strokes you have studied in Lessons 1 through 4. See how rapidly you can read them.

24 **A, Ä** The large circle that represents the long sound of ā, as in *main,* also represents the vowel sounds heard in *act* and *arm.*

A

Spell: *h-a-s, has*

Has, had, man, acting, facts, matters, fast, last.

Ä

Spell: *m-a-r-k, mark*

Mark, parked, large, far, cars, arm, start.

25 **E, I, Obscure Vowel** The tiny circle that represents the sound of ē, as in *heat,* also represents the vowel sounds heard in *let* and *trim,* as well as the obscure vowel heard in *her, church.*

E

Spell: *l-e-t, let*

Let, letter, any, telling, selling, checked, test, best.

I

Spell: *t-r-e-m, trim*

Trim, him, did, gives, bid, bills, ship.

Obscure Vowel

Spell: *h-e-r, her; e-r-j, urge*

Her, hurry, urge, earns, hurt, learn, church, search, served.

26 **Th** Two tiny curves, written upward, are provided for the sounds of *th.* These curves are called "ith."

At this time you need not try to decide which *th* stroke to use in any given word; this will become clear to you as your study of shorthand progresses.

Over Th  *Under Th* 

Spell: *ith-e-s, these; ith-o, though*

Over Th

These, thick, thicker, then, theme, bath, teeth, smooth.

Under Th

Though, throw, three, both, health, earth, clothing, thorough.

27 **Brief Forms** Here is another group of brief forms for very frequently used business words. Learn them well.

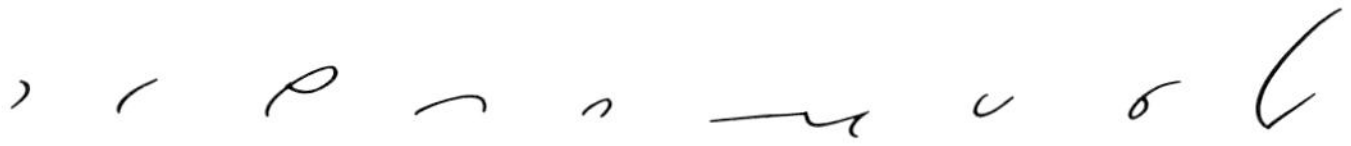

Is-his, the, that, can, you-your, Mrs., of, with, but.

Reading practice

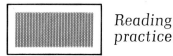

Your progress has been so rapid that you can already read business letters written entirely in shorthand.

28 **Brief-Form Letter** This letter contains one or more illustrations of all the brief forms you studied in this lesson.

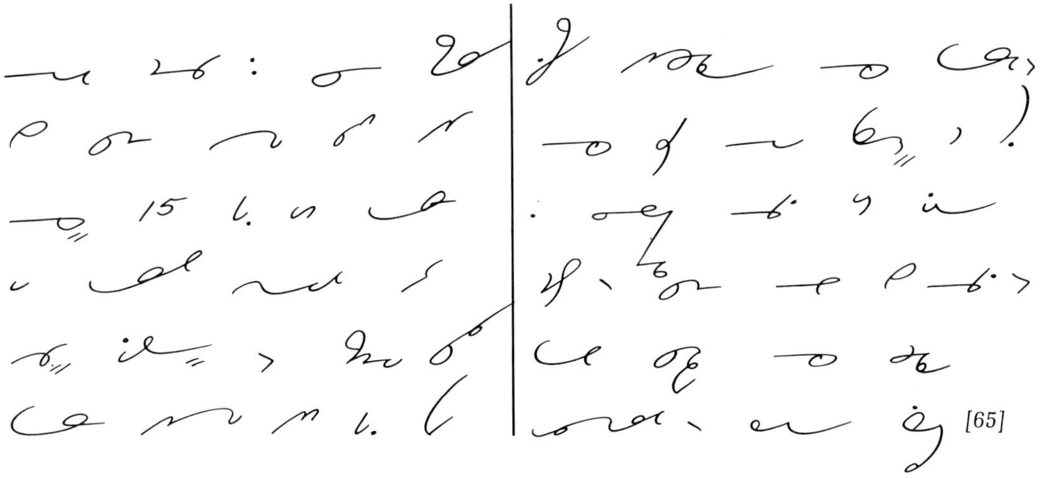

[65]

29

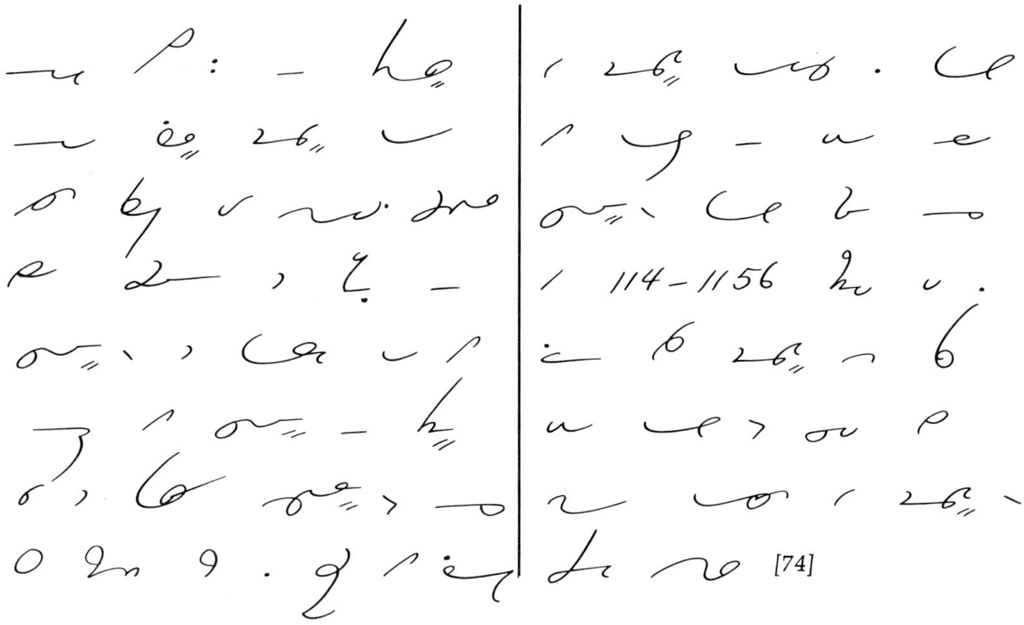

[74]

30

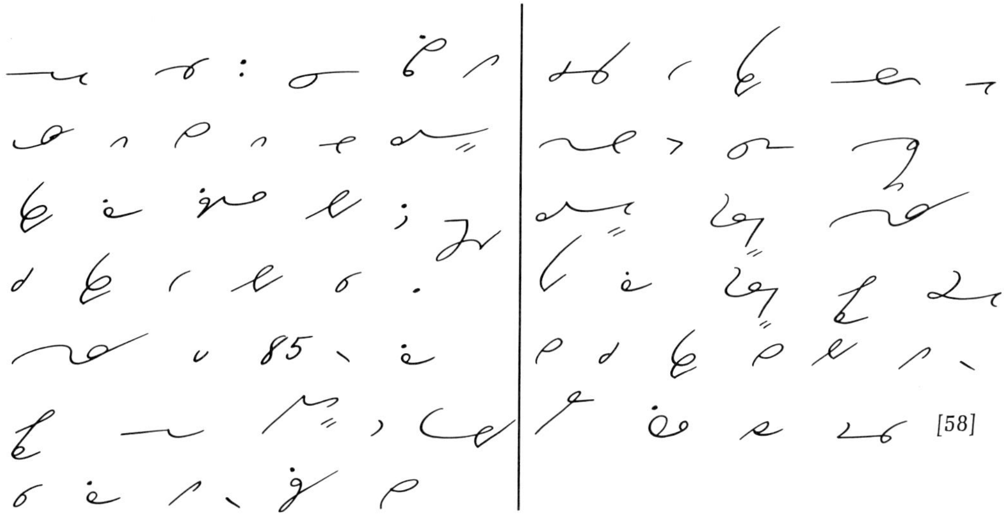

[58]

31

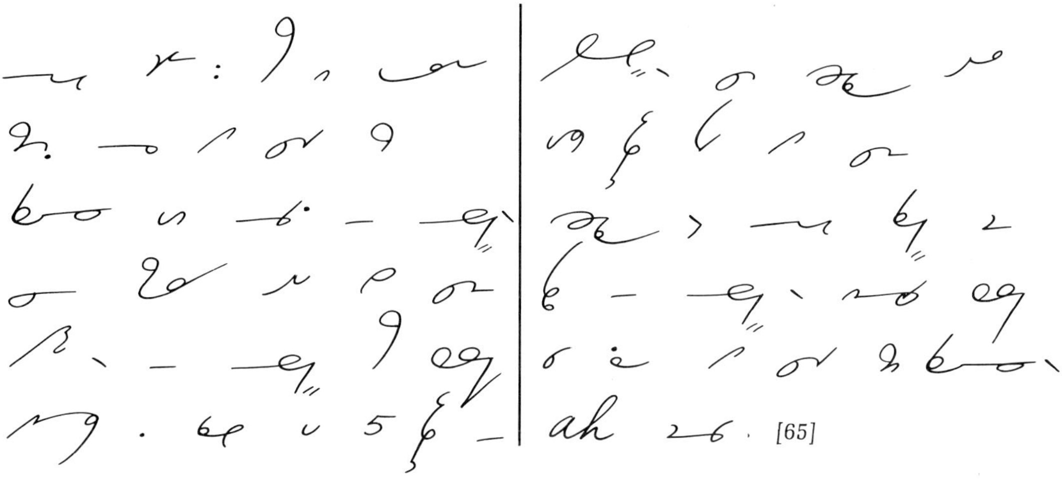

[65]

LESSON 6

Recall

Lesson 6 contains no new strokes for you to learn. In this lesson you will find an alphabet review, a Recall Chart, and a Reading Practice employing the shorthand devices of Lessons 1 through 5.

32 Alphabet Review Here are all the shorthand strokes you studied thus far. Can you read them in 20 seconds or less?

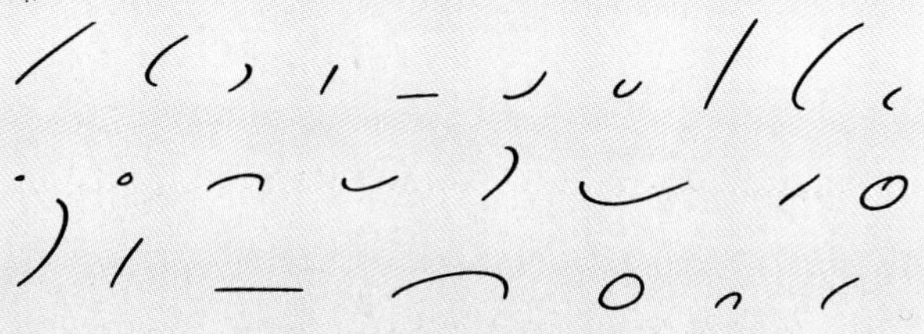

33 Recall Chart The following chart, which reviews the shorthand devices you studied in Lessons 1 through 5, is divided into three parts: (1) words that illustrate the principles, (2) brief forms, (3) phrases.

Spell out each word aloud, thus: *a-k-t, act.* You need not spell the brief forms and phrases.

The chart contains 84 words and phrases. Can you read the entire chart in 9 minutes or less? If you can, you are making good progress.

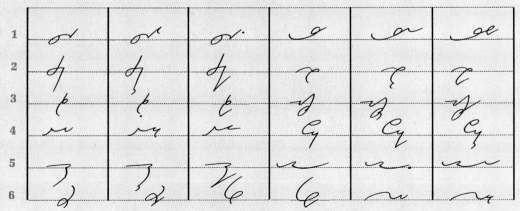

WORDS

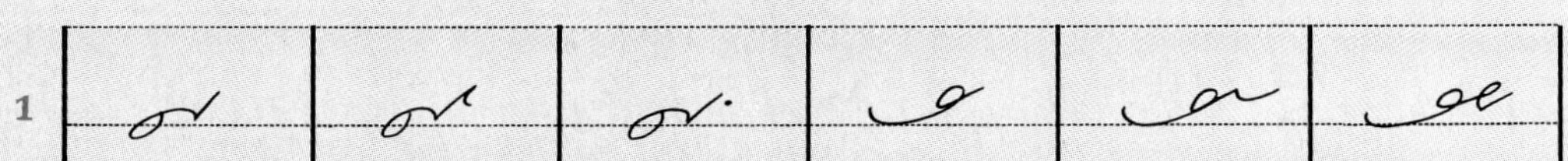

BRIEF FORMS

7, 8, 9

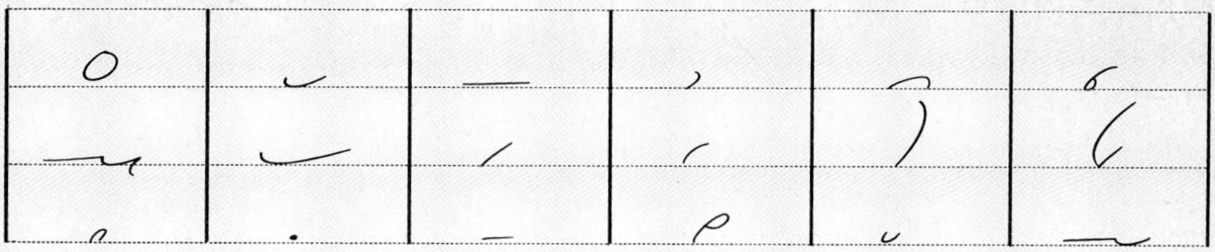

PHRASES

10, 11, 12, 13, 14

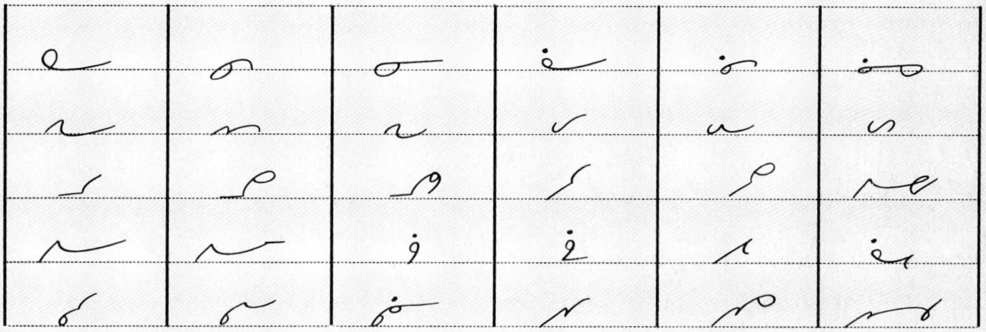

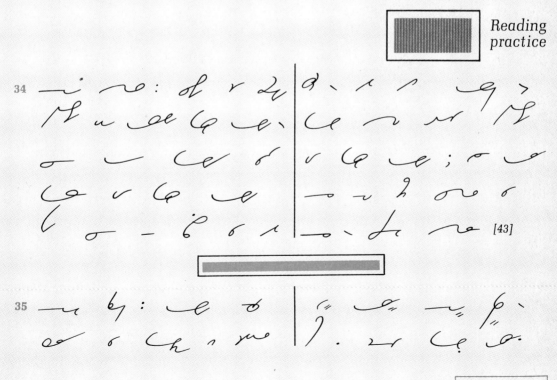

Reading practice

34

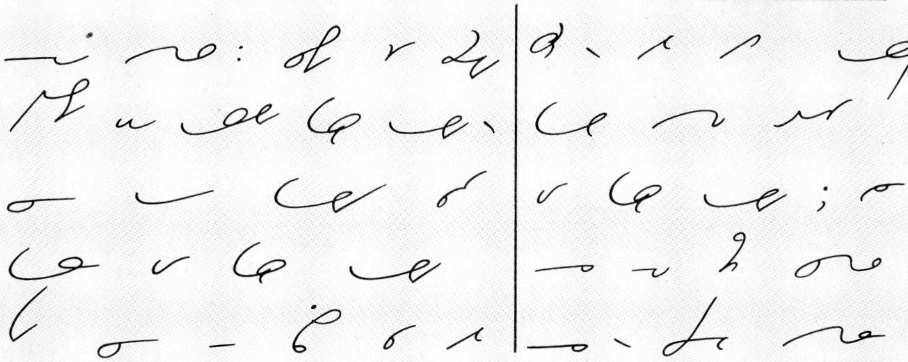

[43]

35

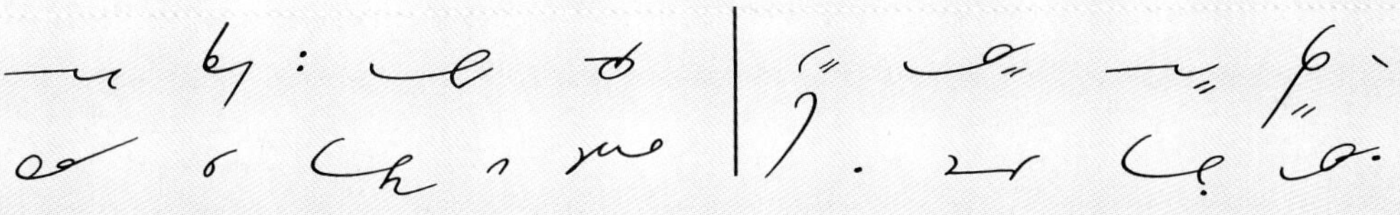

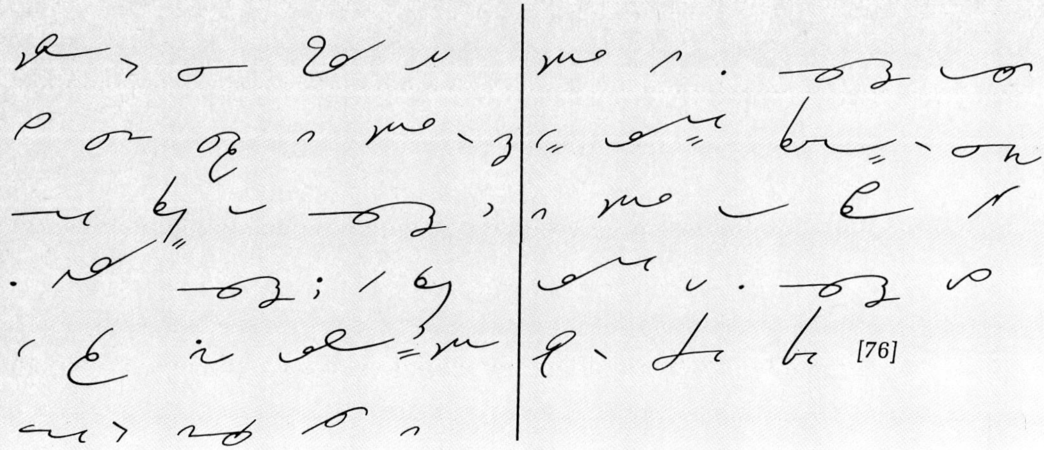

[76]

36

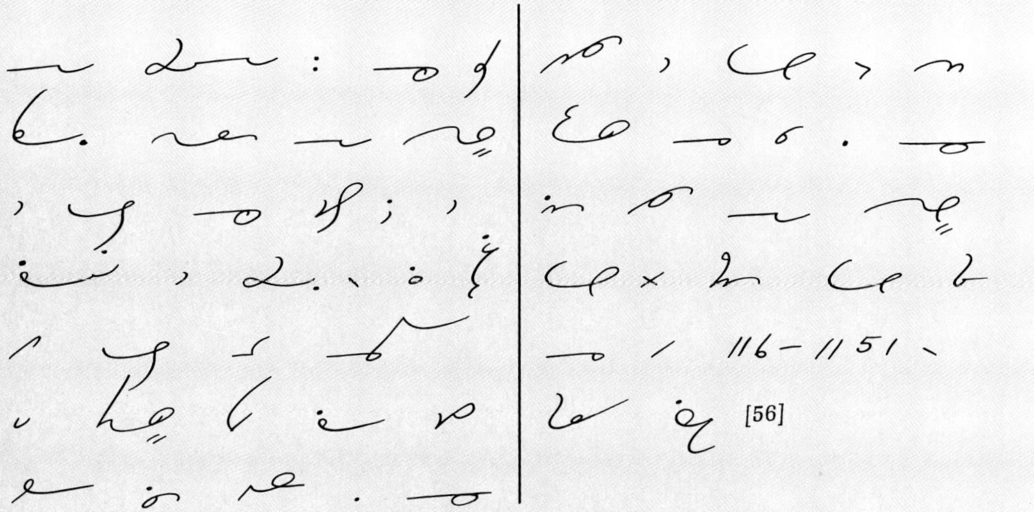

[56]

37

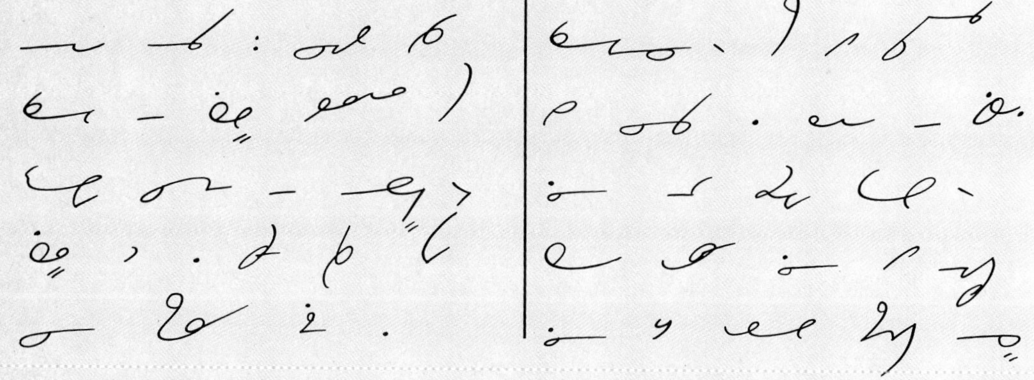

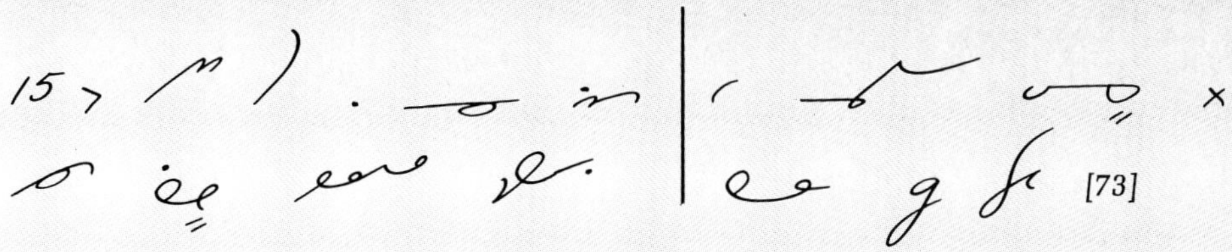

[73]

38

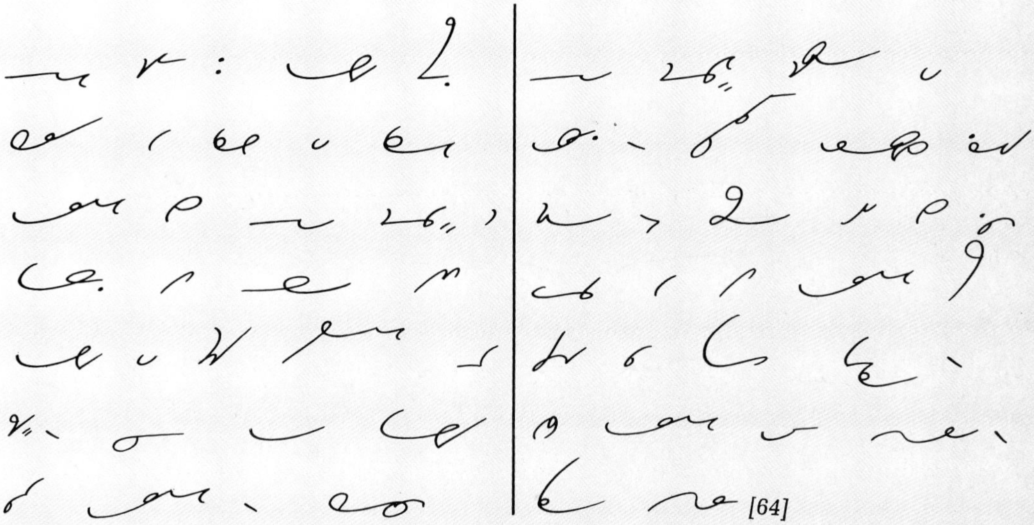

[64]

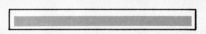

Chapter 2

Shorthand in the business office

Mr. Harding is general manager of a large manufacturing plant. If you were a fly on the wall in his office on a regular business day, this is what you might be likely to hear:

"Miss Phillips, please bring in your notebook. I want to dictate some letters . . . ."

". . . and, John, be sure to send a copy of that report to Mr. Castle in Denver and two copies to Ed Smith in Toledo—no, better send him three. By the way, when you send Smith's copies, include a list of our recent price changes. A copy of the report should go to Alison, too; I think he is in Miami this week. Be sure that everything goes airmail special. . . ."

"When Mrs. Cochran calls, tell her our group will meet her at the National Airport, South Terminal, at 3:30. Ask her to bring along the photographs and news releases on the Wilson project. Tell her she should plan to stay over in Wichita an extra day or two. Fred Toffi wants her to see the public relations people at Boeing. . . ."

If the employees to whom these instructions are directed

are to carry them out fully and accurately, they must listen carefully—and write the instructions down! Only if these employees can write shorthand rapidly can they be sure of getting all the facts on paper.

Studies show that almost half of our communicating time in the office is spent listening to others, and much of what the business employee hears must be recorded if he is to recall and act on it later.

Nearly all business employees have occasional need for a fast writing ability. For the stenographer or secretary, however, such a skill is a constant need. Shorthand is as important to her (or him) as the ability to type. Taking things down in shorthand is so much a part of her daily routine that when she is summoned by her boss—either directly or by buzzer or telephone—she automatically picks up her notebook and pen.

Every year hundreds of thousands of people in all parts of the world learn shorthand. Most of them study shorthand because they want to become secretaries. Secretarial work is perhaps the most popular—and frequently the most important—career in the world for young women.

More and more young men are learning shorthand, too. Some executives in such fields as transportation, engineering, and manufacturing hire men exclusively as secretaries. Frequently men who do not intend to become secretaries learn shorthand and find it a valuable skill in helping them to advance more rapidly in their chosen field. Thousands have found shorthand the open-sesame to administrative positions.

And speaking of business offices, the United States Government runs perhaps the largest "business office" in the world. The armed services alone need thousands of stenographers to record the many details of military activities. Many of these stenographers are civilians employed in the different branches of the armed forces. Other government installations, in Washington and throughout the free world, employ hundreds of thousands of civilian office personnel and offer an almost unlimited choice of fields of work for the skilled shorthand writer. The work is interesting and challenging.

LESSON 7

Principles

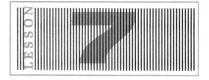

39 **O, Aw** The small deep hook that represents ō, as in *row*, also represents the sounds heard in *hot* and *drawing.*

O

Spell: h-o-t, hot

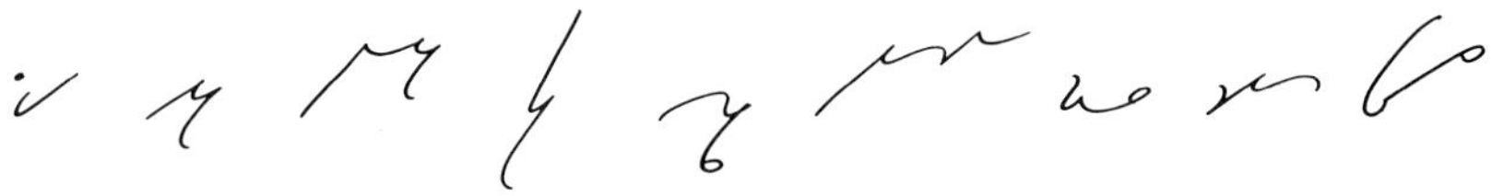

Hot, top, drop, job, copy, doctor, sorry, stock, body.

Aw

Spell: d-r-o-ing, *drawing*

Drawing, law, cause, ought, taught, brought, all, call.

40 **Common Business-Letter Salutations and Closings**

Dear Sir, Dear Madam, Yours truly, Sincerely yours, Yours very truly, Very truly yours.

► Note: While the expressions *Dear Sir, Dear Madam,* and *Yours truly* are considered too impersonal by experts in letter writing, they are still used by many businessmen. Therefore, special abbreviations are provided for them.

Building transcription skills

41 BUSINESS VOCABULARY BUILDER

Words are the stenographer's tools of her trade. The more words she knows and understands, the easier her task of taking dictation and transcribing will be.

To help you increase your knowledge and understanding of words, each lesson hereafter will contain a Business Vocabulary Builder consisting of words or expressions, selected from the Reading Practice, that should be part of your everyday vocabulary. A brief definition, as it applies in the sentence in which it occurs, will be given for each word or expression.

Before you begin your work on the Reading Practice, be sure that you understand the meaning of the words and expressions in the Business Vocabulary Builder.

Business vocabulary builder

marketing All activities involved in getting goods from the producer to the user.

semester A school term consisting, usually, of eighteen weeks.

abroad Outside the country.

bursar A treasurer of a school, such as a college.

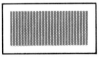

Reading practice

42 Brief-Form Review Letter This letter reviews all the brief forms presented in Lesson 5 as well as many presented in Lesson 3.

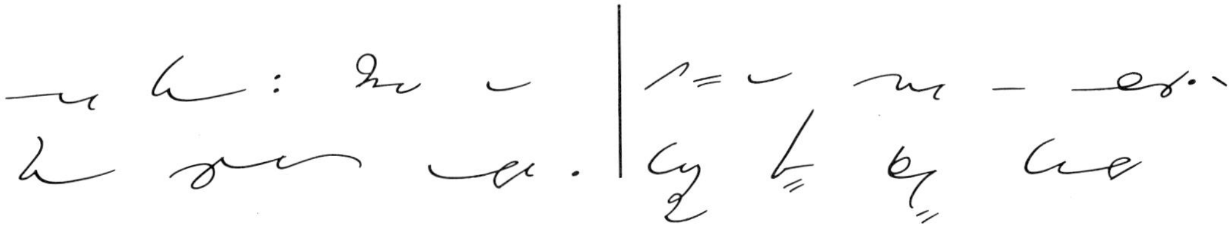

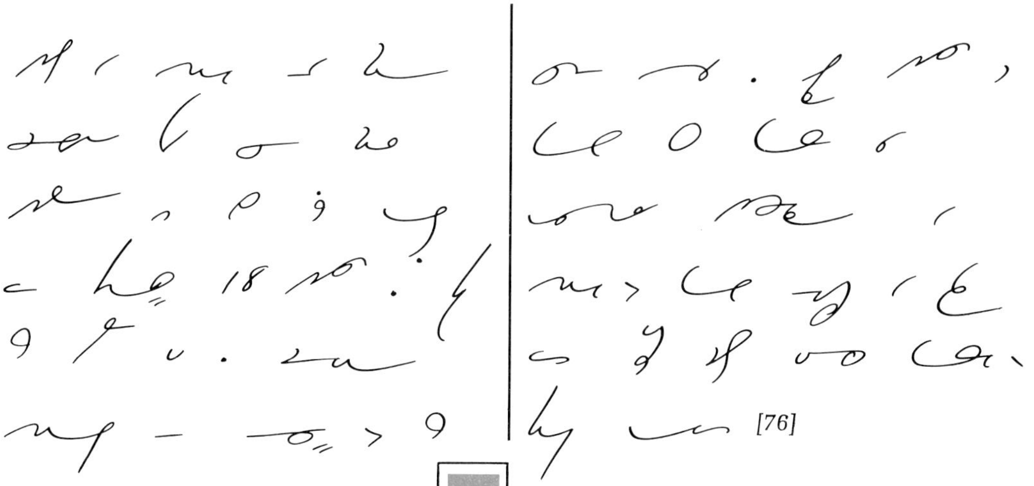

[76]

43

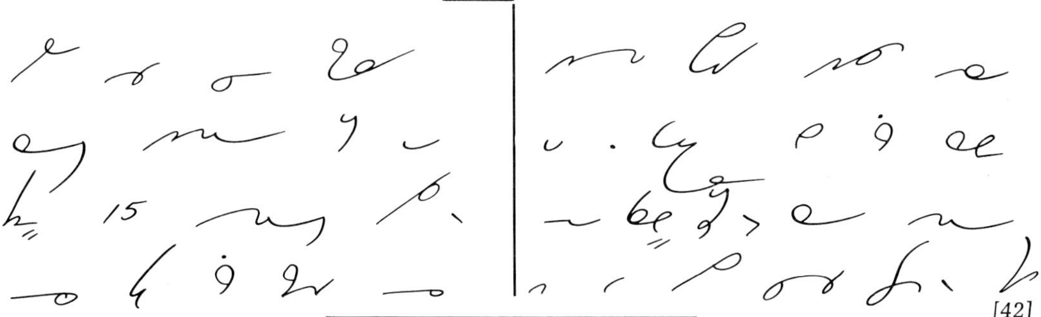

[42]

44

[54]

45

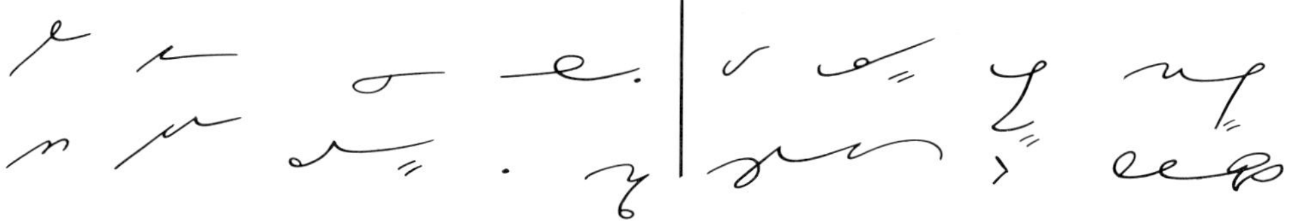

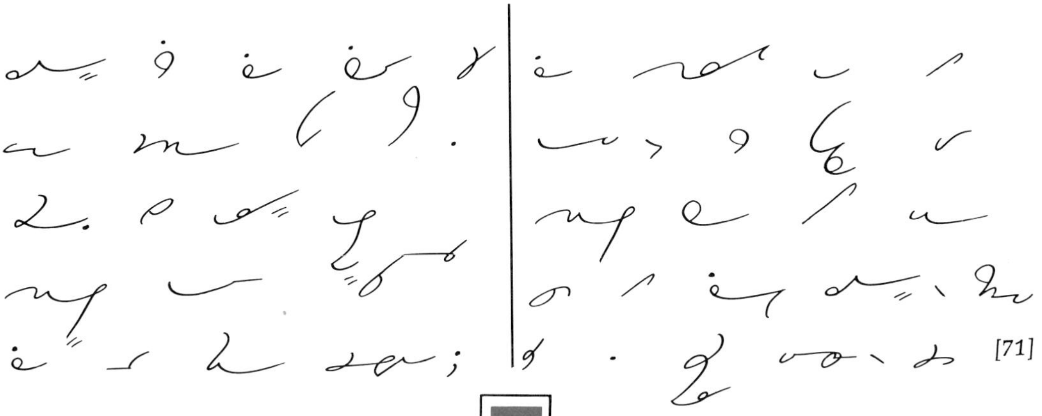

[71]

46

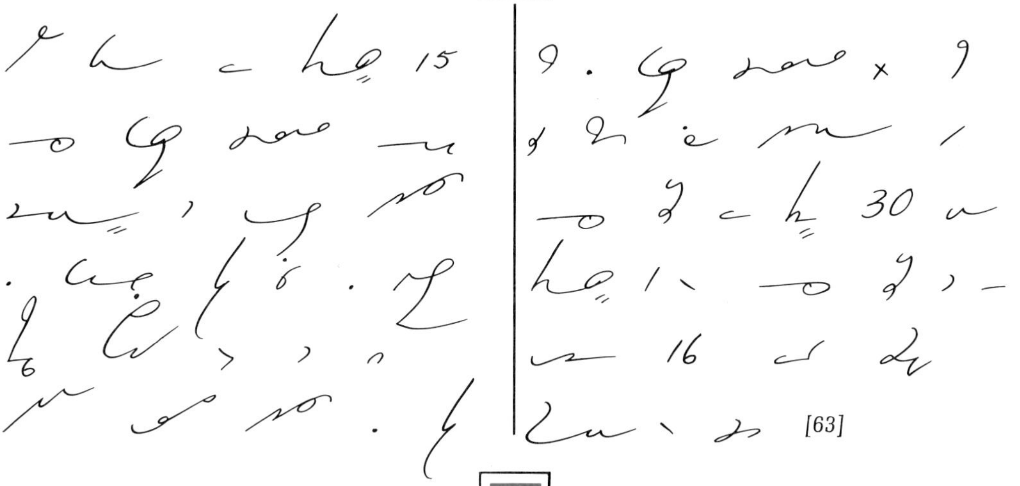

[63]

47

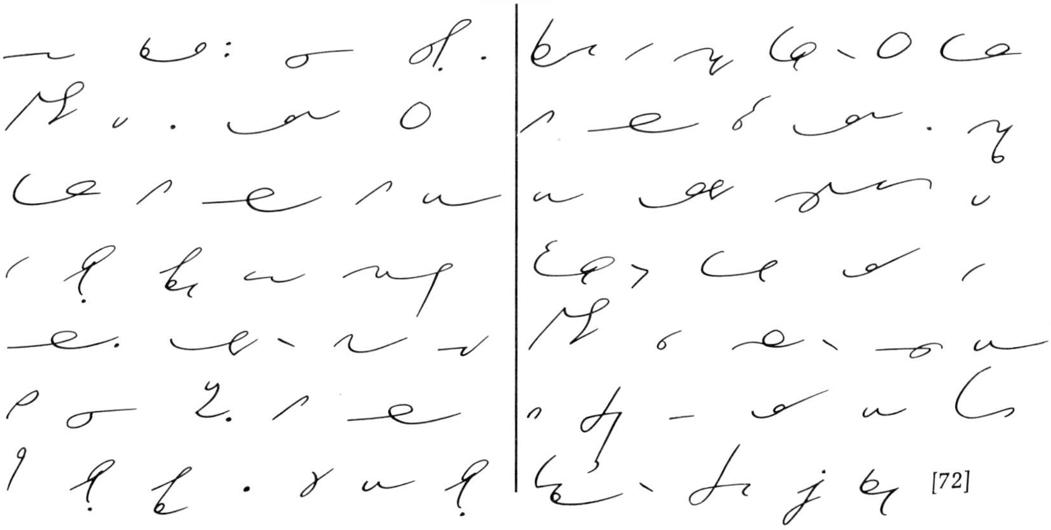

[72]

LESSON 8

Principles

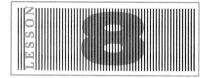

48 **Brief Forms** Here is the third group of brief forms for frequently used words.

For, shall, which, be-by, put, would, their-there, this, good.

49 **Word Ending -ly** The very common word ending *-ly* is expressed by the *e* circle.

Spell: b-r-e-f-le, *briefly*

Briefly, only, mostly, nearly, merely, highly, totally, daily.

▶ Notice how the circle for *-ly* in *daily* is added to the other side of the *d* after the *a* has been written.

50 **Amounts and Quantities** In business you will frequently have to take dictation in which amounts and quantities are used. Here are some devices that will help you write them rapidly.

400; 4,000; 400,000; $4; $4,000; $400,000; 4 o'clock; $4.50; 4 percent.

▶ Notice that the *n* for *hundred* and the *th* for *thousand* are placed underneath the figure.

Building transcription skills

51

Business vocabulary builder	
	goods Merchandise.
	earnestly Sincerely.
	billing machines Machines used in the preparation of bills and invoices.
	observe Inspect; watch.

Reading practice

52 **Brief-Form Letter** This letter contains one or more illustrations of the brief forms presented in this lesson.

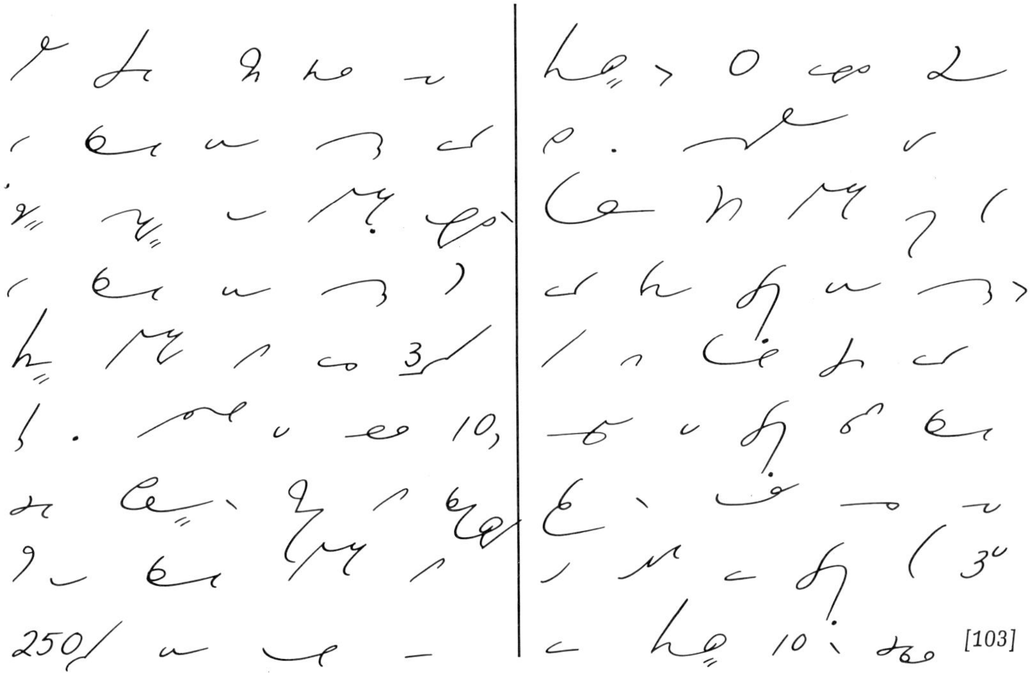

[103]

53

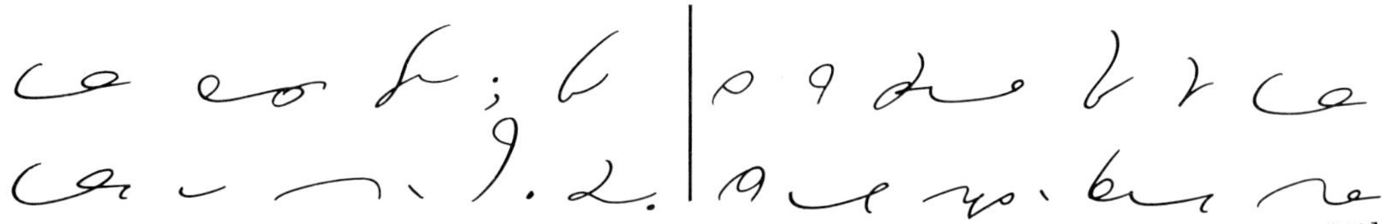

[40]

54

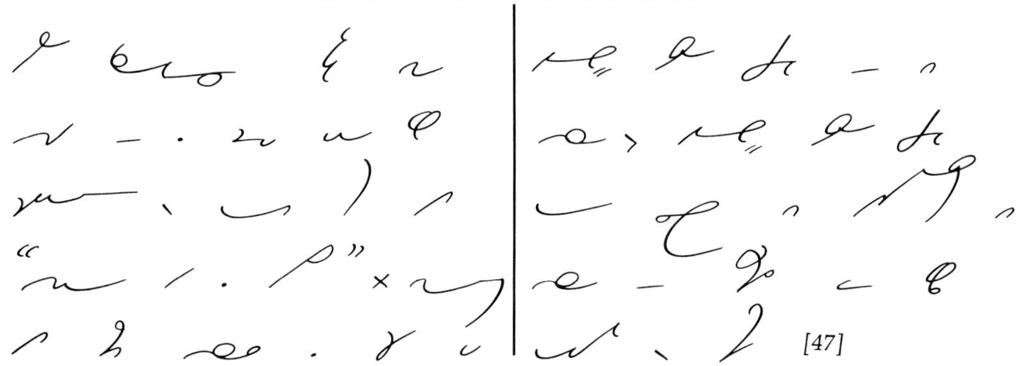

[47]

55

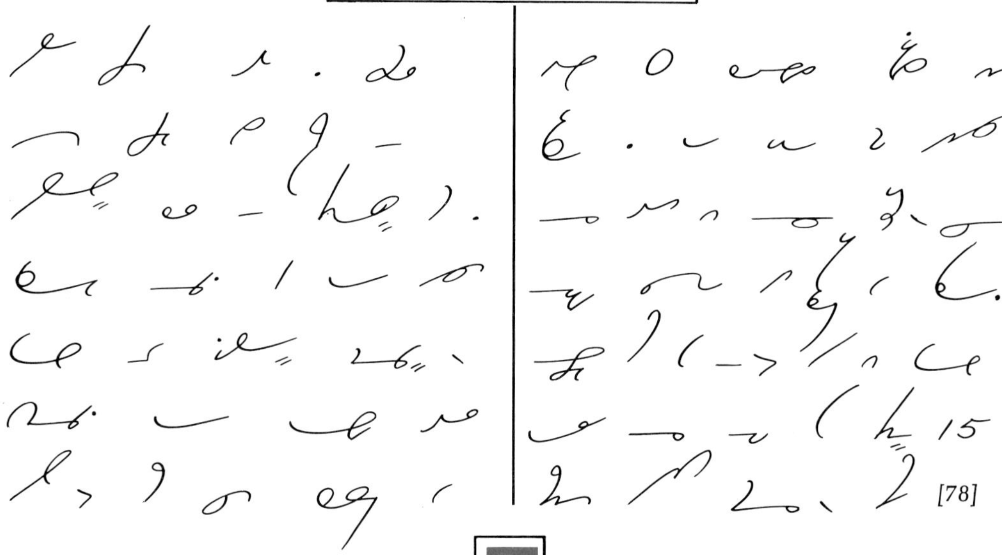

[78]

56

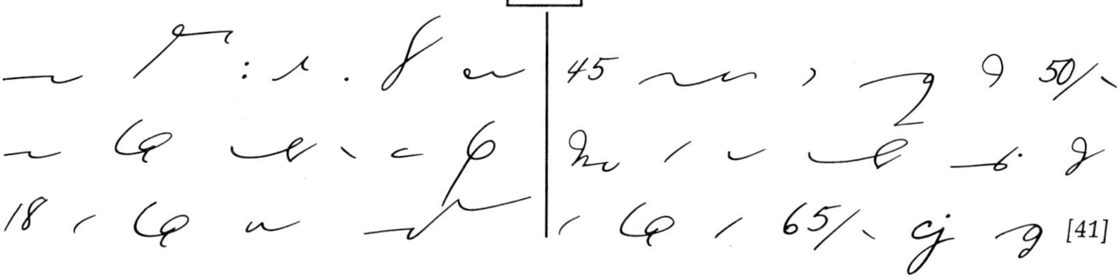

[41]

57 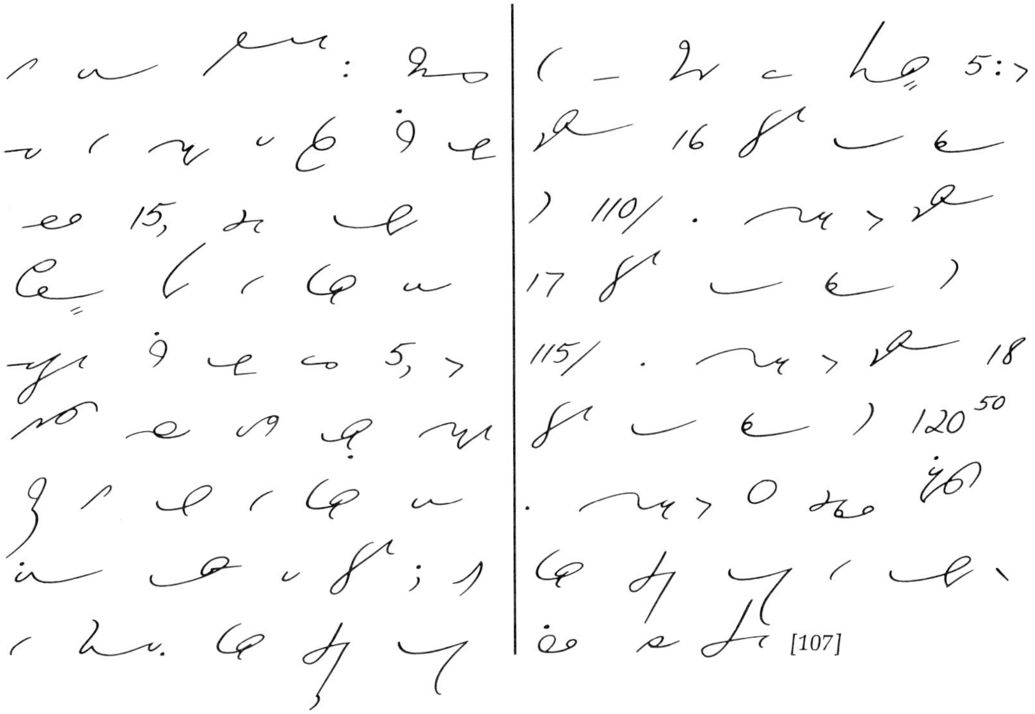
[107]

58 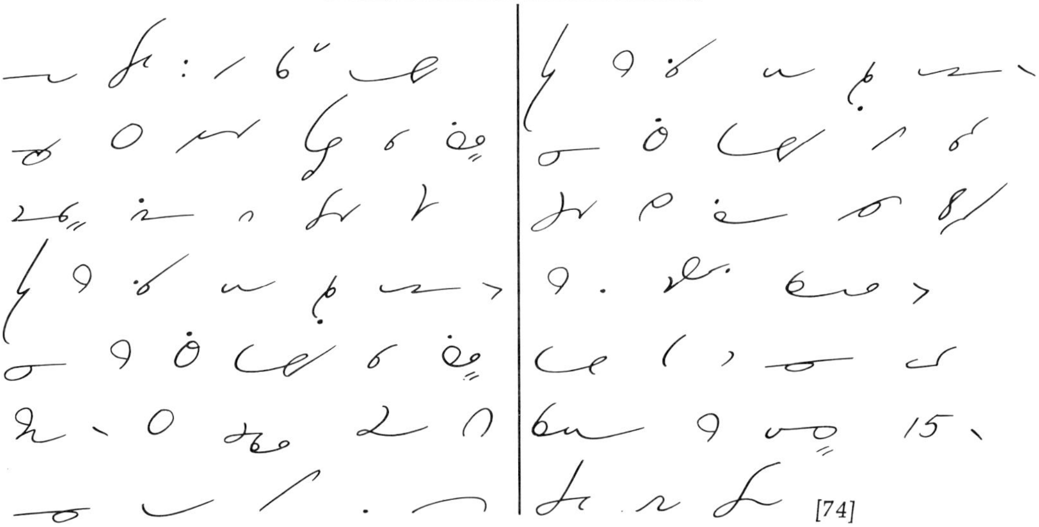
[74]

LESSON 9

Principles

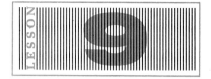

59 **Word Ending -tion** The word ending *-tion* (sometimes spelled *-sion*, *-cian*, or *-shion*) is represented by *sh*.

Spell: *a-k-shun, action*

Action, portions, position, occasion, physician, fashions, nation, national, cautioned.

60 **Word Endings -cient, -ciency** The word ending *-cient* (or *-tient*) is represented by *sh-t*; *-ciency*, by *sh-s-e*.

Spell: *p-a-shun-t, patient; e-f-e-shun-s-e, efficiency*

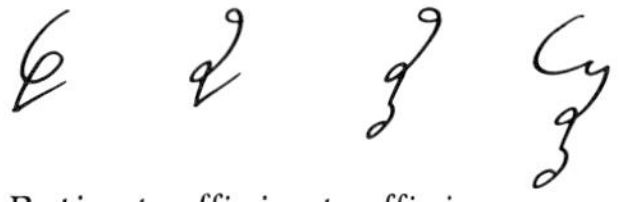

Patient, efficient, efficiency, proficiency.

61 **Word Ending -tial** The word ending *-tial* (or *-cial*) is represented by *sh*.

Spell: *o-f-e-shul, official*

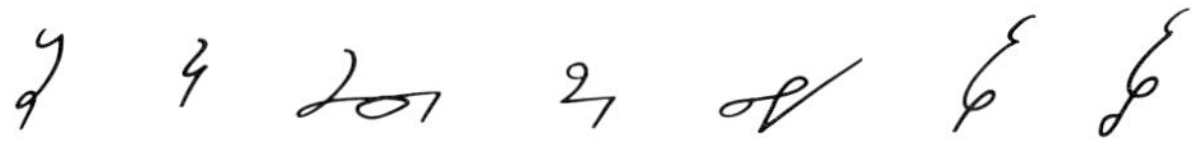

Official, social, financial, essential, initialed, special, specially.

62 **T for To in Phrases** In phrases, *to* is represented by *t* when it is followed by a downstroke.

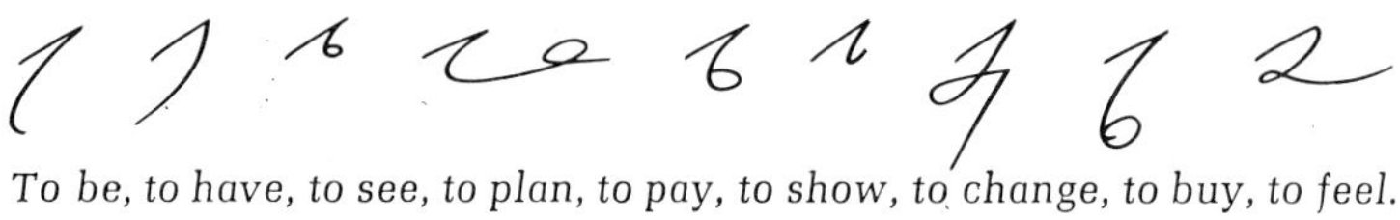

To be, to have, to see, to plan, to pay, to show, to change, to buy, to feel.

63

Business vocabulary builder	**financial** Having to do with money. **corporation** A type of business organization that is owned by stockholders. **essential** Necessary. **take legal action** Sue; take to court.

Reading practice

64 **Brief-Form Review Letter** The following letter reviews the brief forms presented in Lesson 8.

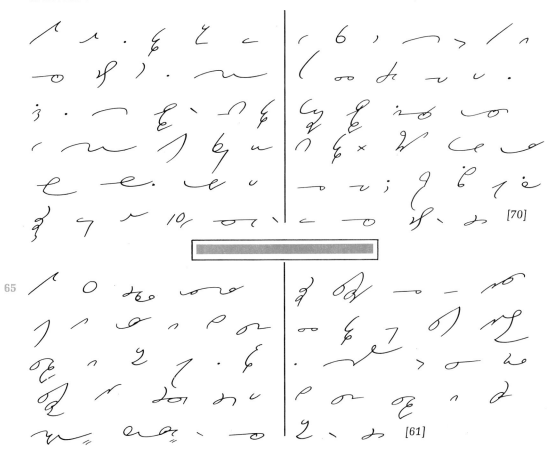

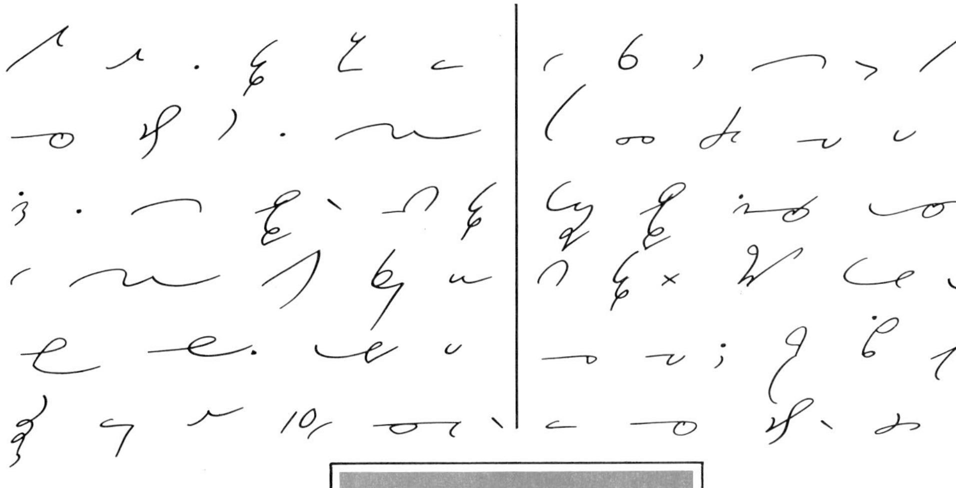

[70]

65

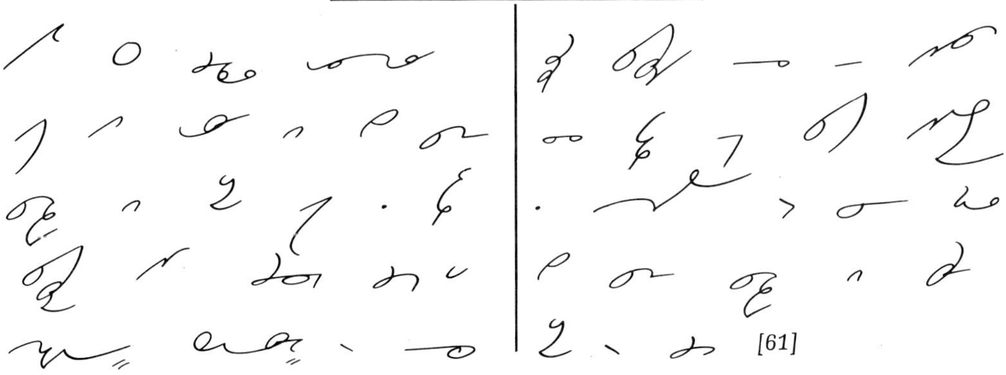

[61]

66

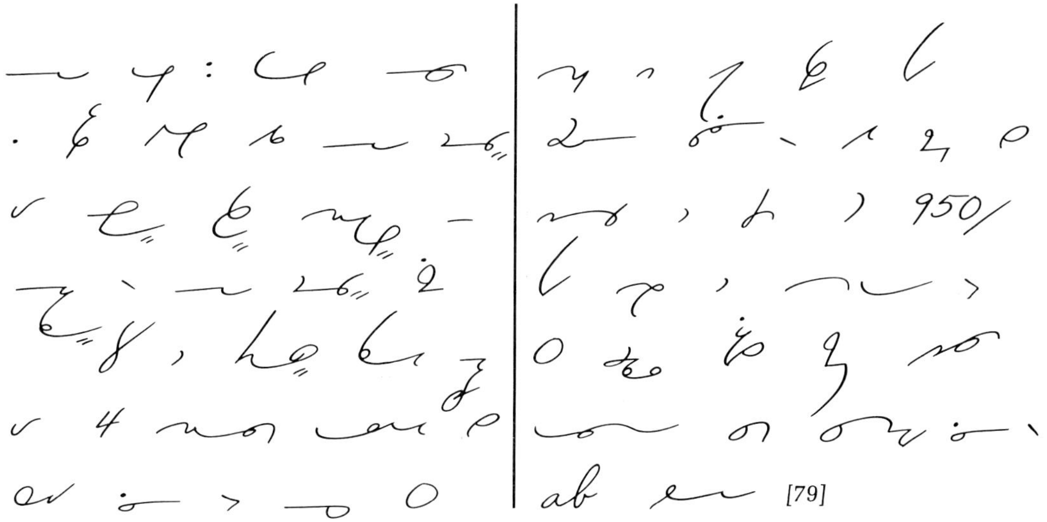

[79]

67

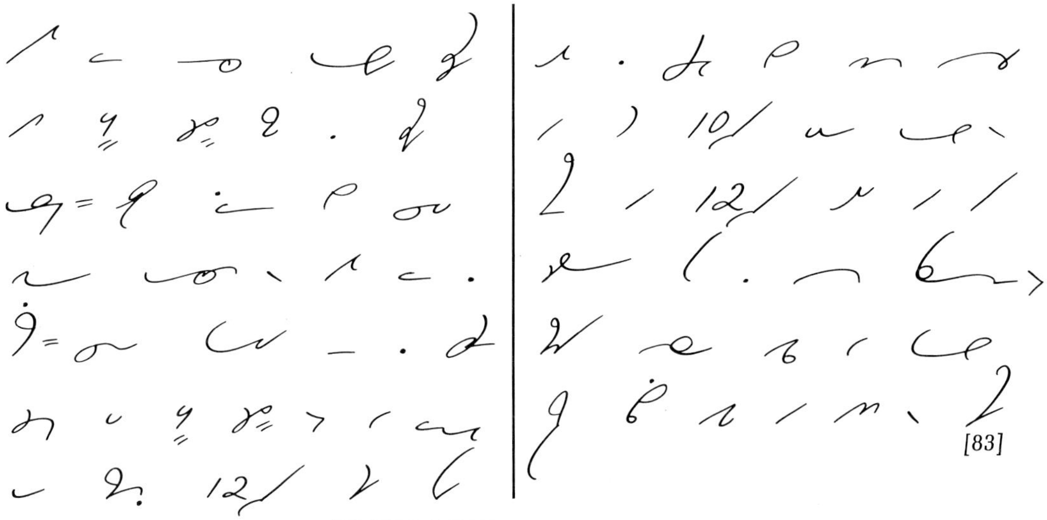

[83]

68

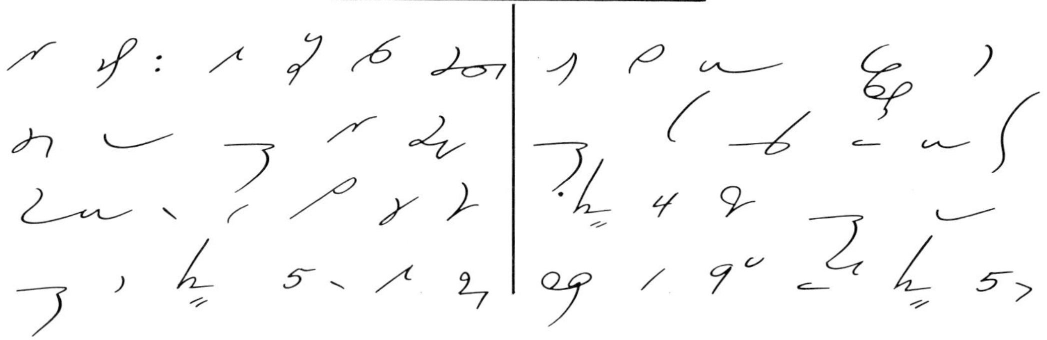

[71]

69

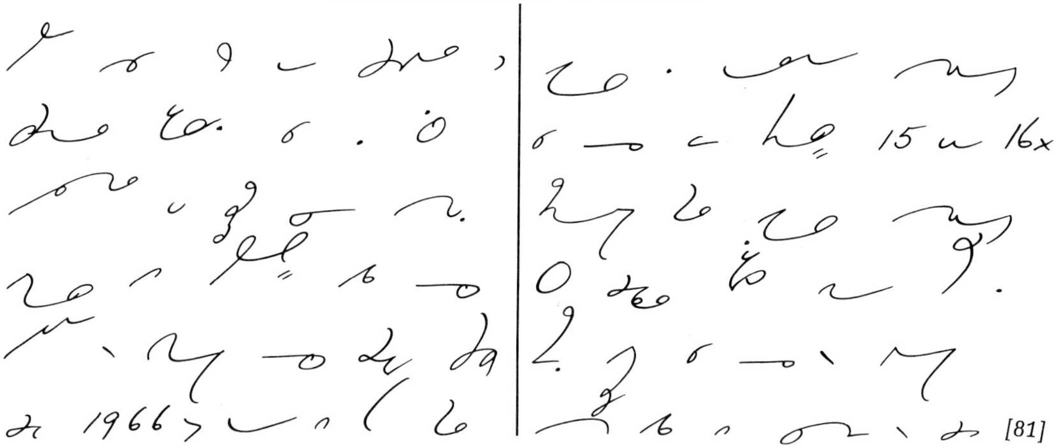

[81]

70

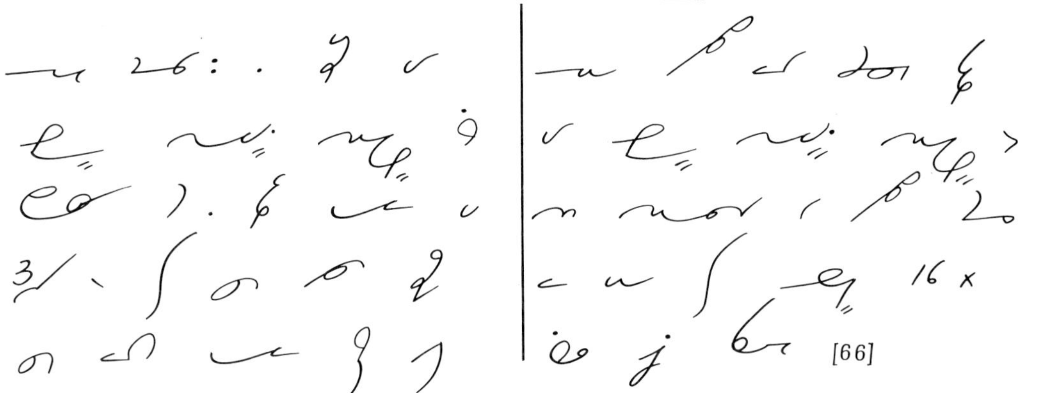

[66]

71

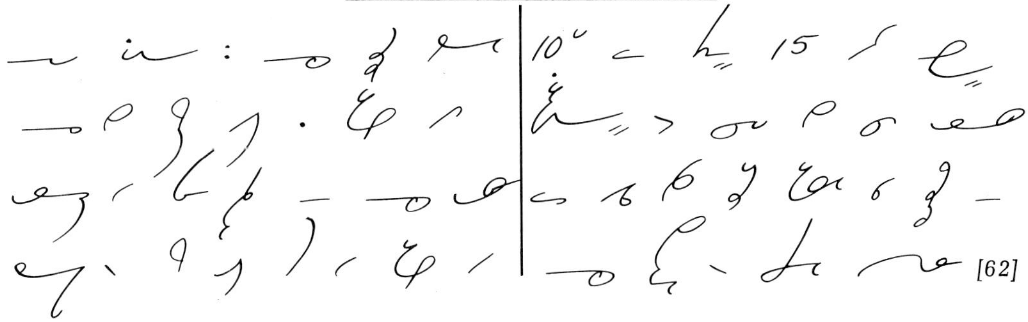

[62]

LESSON 10

Principles

72 **Nd** The shorthand strokes for *n-d* are joined without an angle to form the *nd* blend, as in *lined.*

Nd 

Compare: *line*  *lined* 

Spell: *l-ī-end, lined; l-a-end, land*

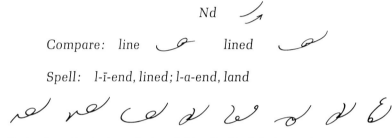

Trained, strained, planned, signed, friendly, kind, find, spend.

73 **Nt** The stroke for *nd* also represents *nt,* as in *sent.*

Spell: *s-e-ent, sent; ent-oo, into*

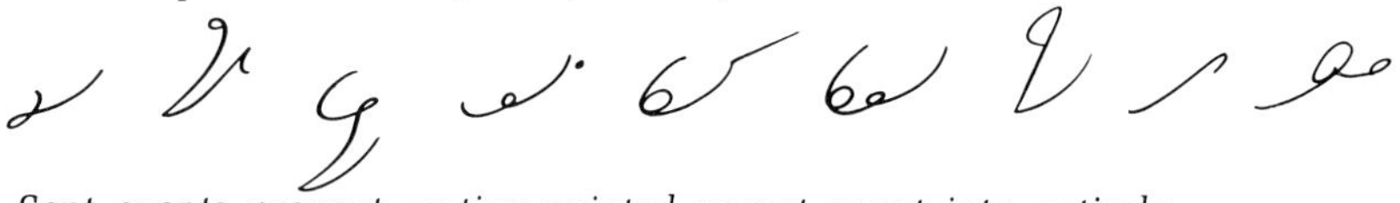

Sent, events, prevent, renting, painted, parent, agent, into, entirely.

74 **Ses** The sound of *ses,* as in *senses,* is represented by joining the two forms of *s.* The similar sounds of *sis,* as in *sister,* and *sus,* as in *versus,* are represented in the same way.

Compare: sense  senses 

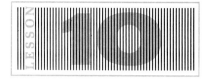

face  *faces* 

Spell: *s-e-n-sez, senses*

Addresses, promises, offices, cases, causes.
Places, necessary, losses, passes, sister, basis, versus.

Building transcription skills

75 **Business vocabulary builder**

firm (*noun*) Company

vacancy Opening.

mailing pieces Usually such items as circulars, booklets, and other advertising matter that are mailed to customers or possible customers.

current Belonging to the present time.

Reading practice

76 **Brief-Form Review Letter** This letter reviews all the brief forms you studied in Lesson 8.

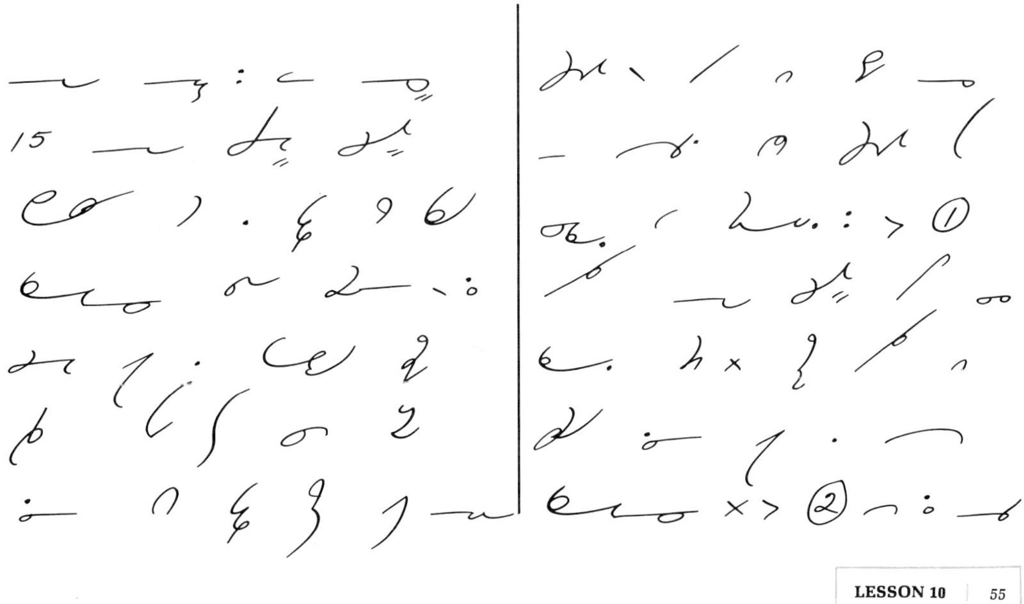

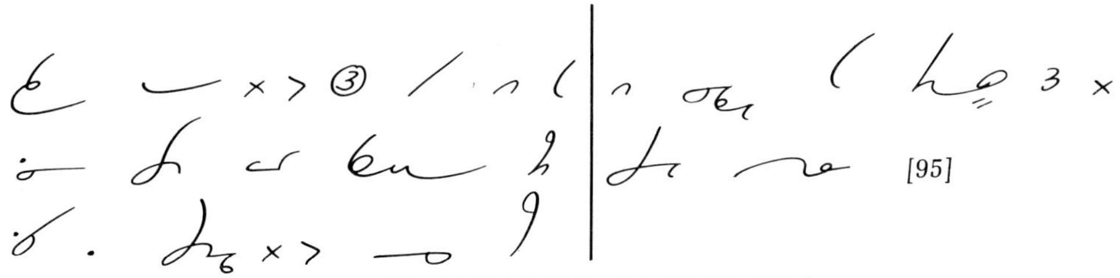

[95]

77

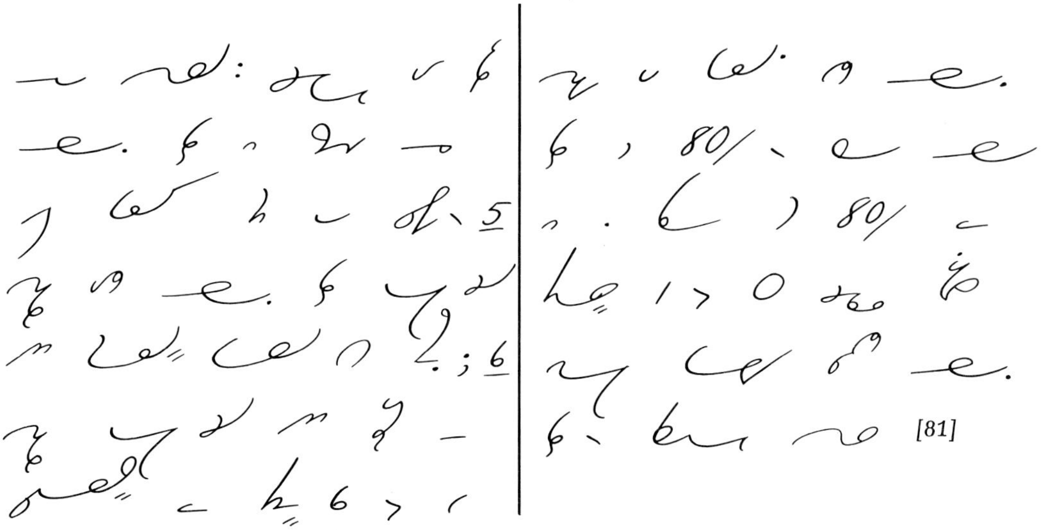

[81]

78

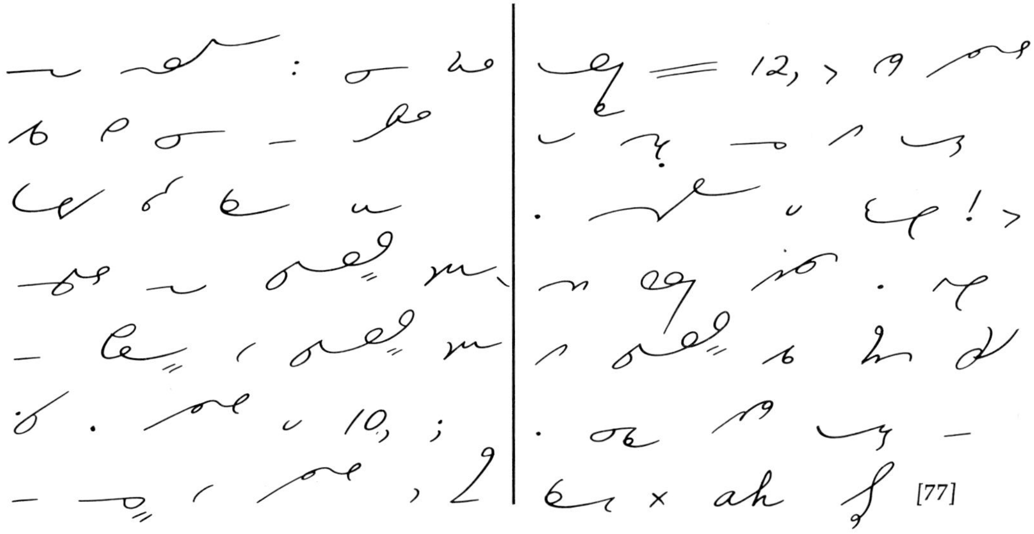

[77]

79

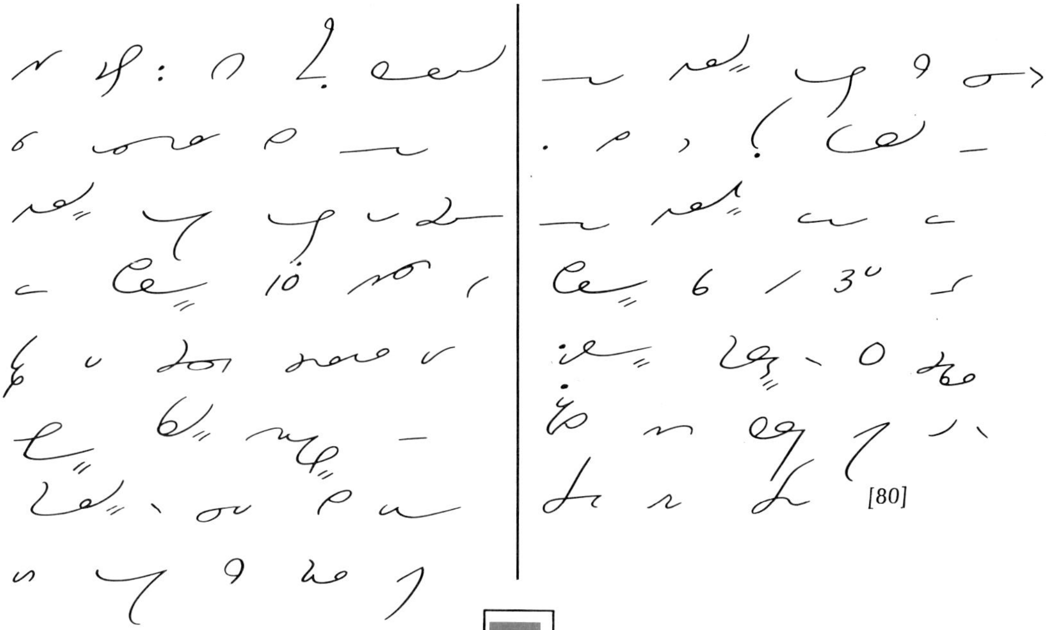

[80]

80

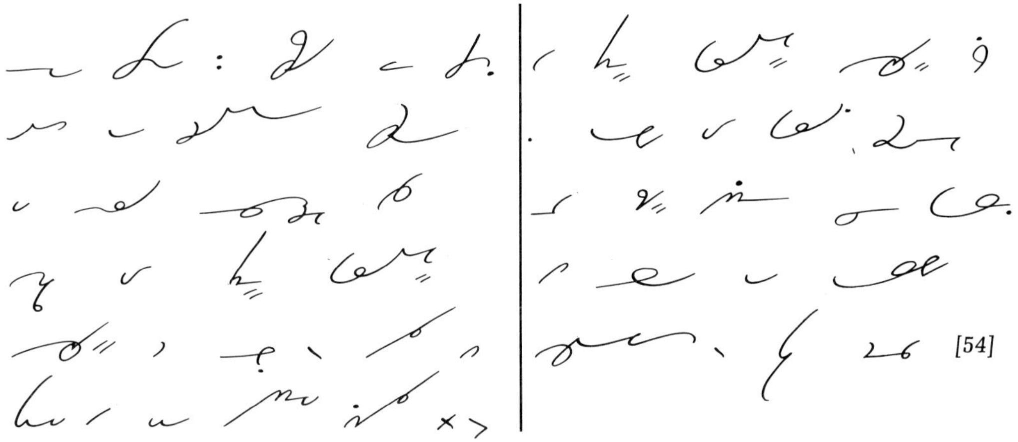

[54]

81

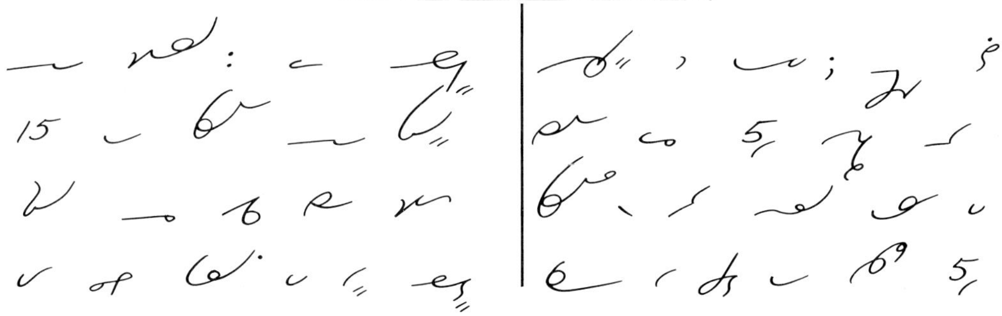

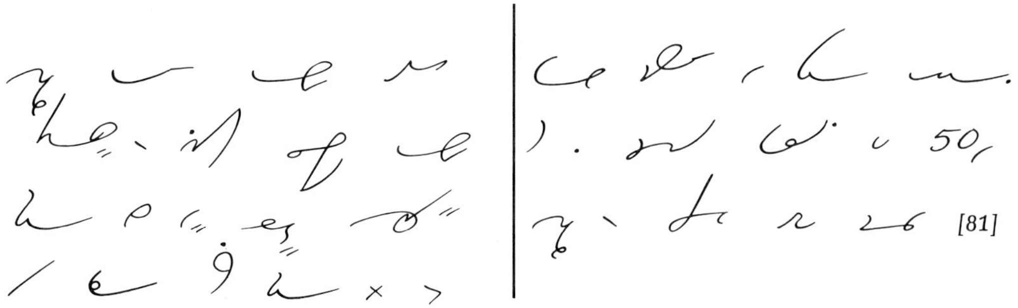

[81]

82

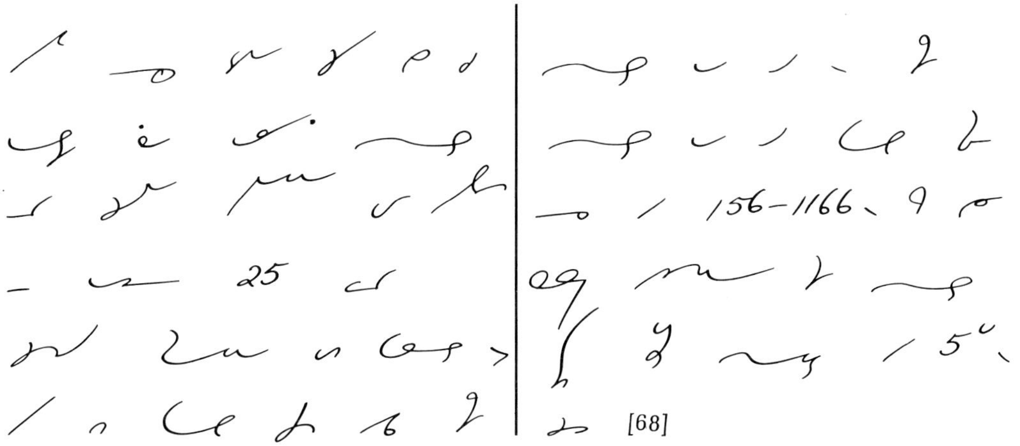

[68]

LESSON 11

Principles

83 **Brief Forms**

And, them, they, was, when, from, should, could, send.

84 **Rd** The combination *rd* is represented by writing *r* with an upward turn at the finish.

Compare: *fear*  *feared* 

Spell: *f-e-ärd, feared; h-e-ärd, heard*

Stored, tired, hired, appeared, record, heard, toward, harder.

85 **Ld** The combination *ld* is represented by writing the *l* with an upward turn at the finish.

Compare: *nail*  *nailed* 

Spell: *n-a-eld, nailed; o-eld, old*

Failed, old, settled, mailed, child, folded, billed.

86 **Been in Phrases** The word *been* is represented by *b* after *have, has, had.*

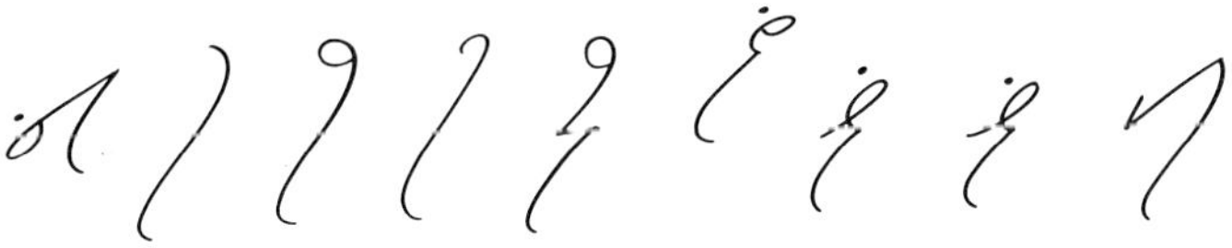

Had been, have been, I have been, you have been, I have not been, has been, it has been, there has been, should have been.

87 Able in Phrases The word *able* is represented by *a* after *be* or *been*.

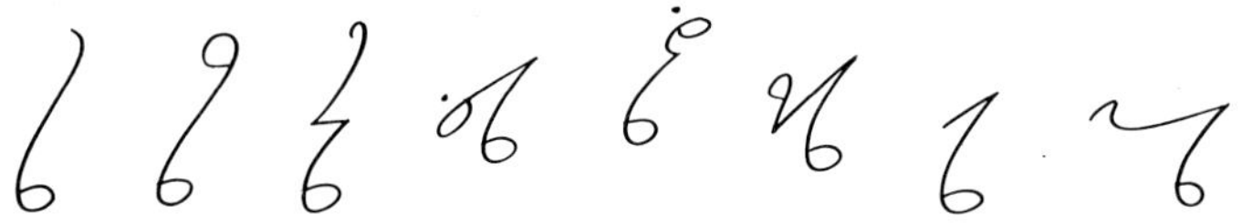

Have been able, I have been able, you have not been able, had been able, has been able, I should be able, to be able, you will be able.

Building transcription skills

88

Business vocabulary builder

parcel post A department of the post office that collects and delivers packages.

ignored Paid no attention to.

air travel card A card that enables a traveler to purchase a plane ticket on credit.

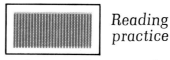

Reading practice

89 Brief-Form Letter The following letter contains at least one illustration of every brief form in paragraph 83.

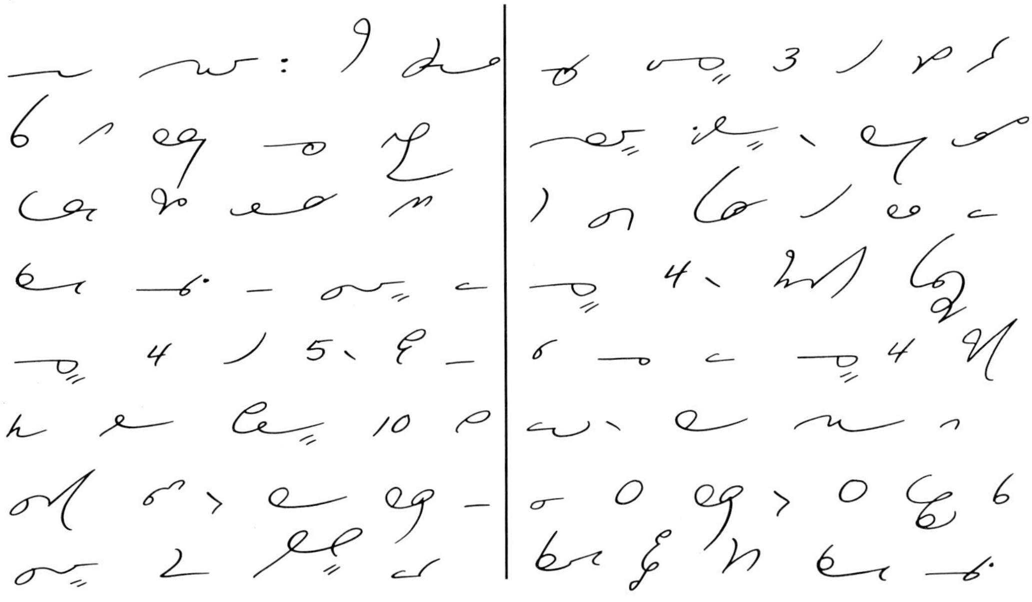

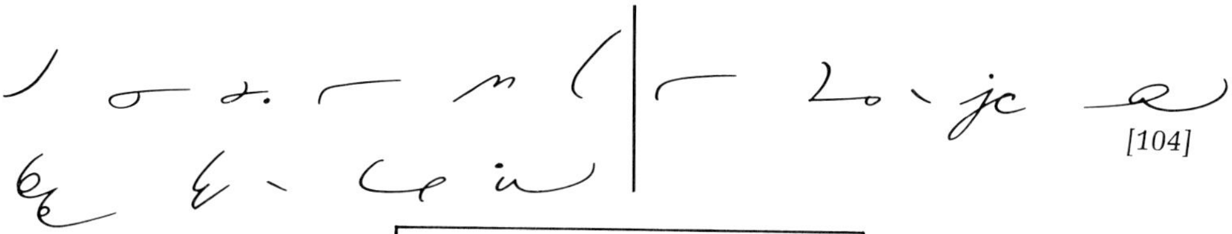

[104]

90

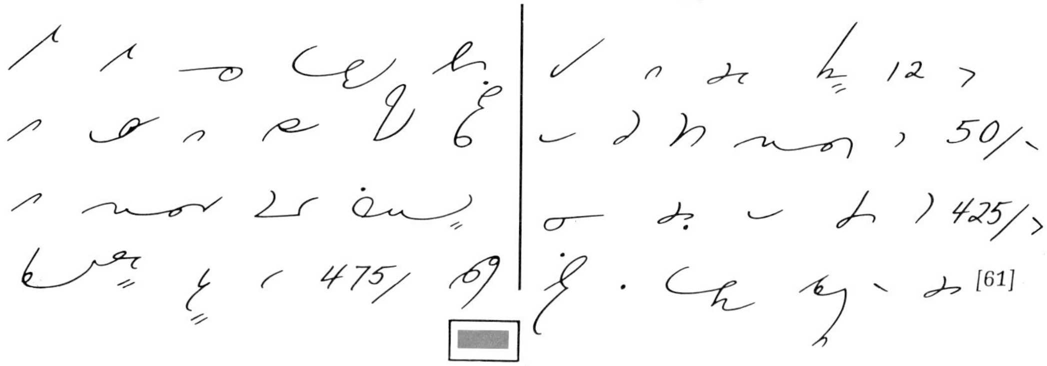

[61]

91

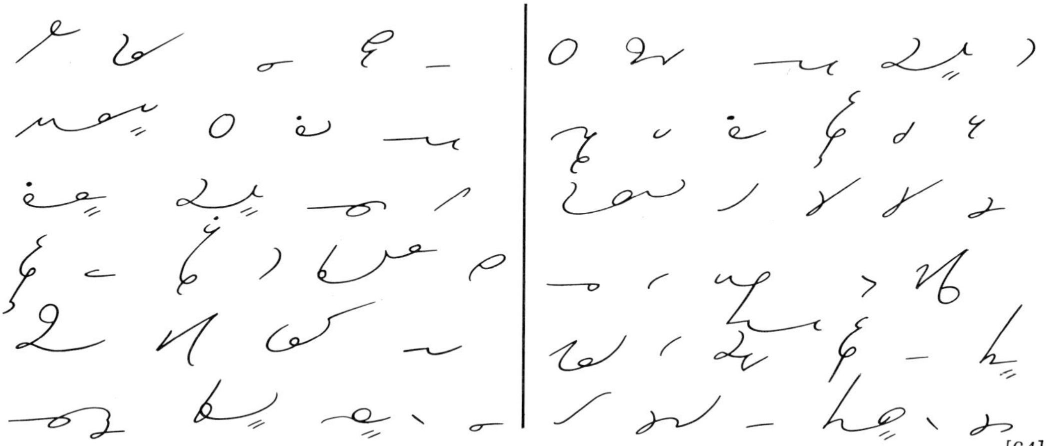

[64]

92

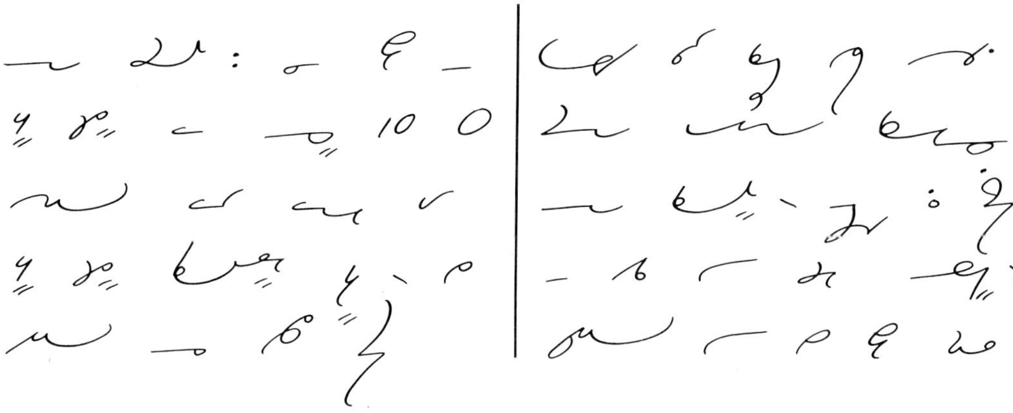

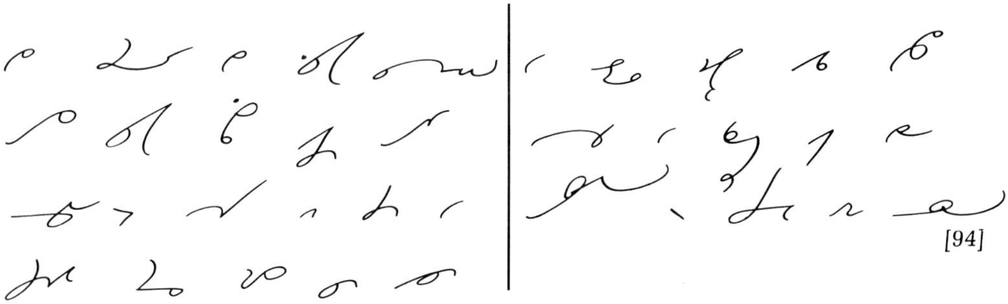

[94]

93

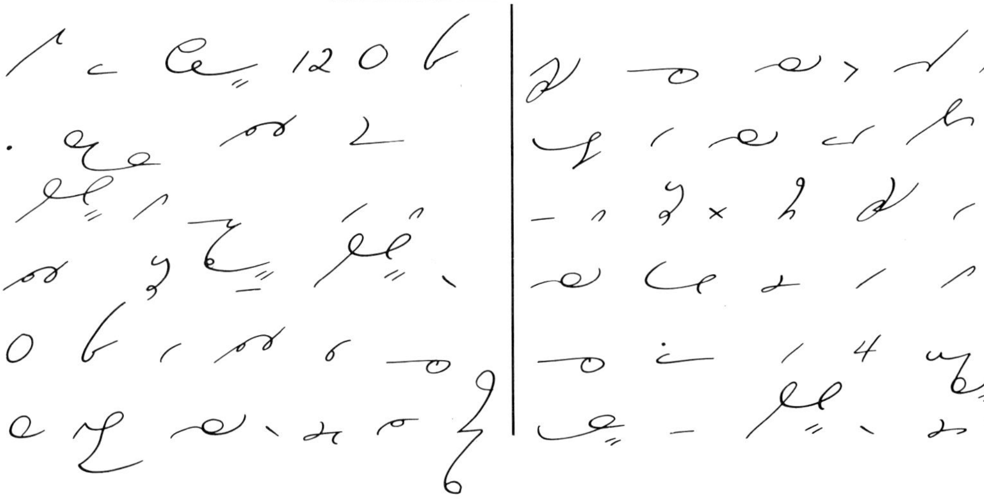

[61]

SHORTHAND READING CHECK LIST

When you read shorthand, do you—

☐ **1** Read aloud so that you know that you are concentrating on each outline that you read?

☐ **2** Spell each outline that you cannot immediately read?

☐ **3** Reread each Reading Practice a second time?

☐ **4** Occasionally reread the suggestions for reading shorthand given on pages 10 and 11?

LESSON 12

Recall

Lesson 12 is a "breather" for you; it presents no new shorthand devices for you to learn. It contains a helpful Recall Chart and several short letters that you should have no difficulty reading.

94 **Recall Chart** The following chart contains all the brief forms in Chapter 2 and one or more illustrations of all the shorthand devices you have studied in Chapters 1 and 2.

Can you read the entire chart in 9 minutes or less?

BRIEF FORMS

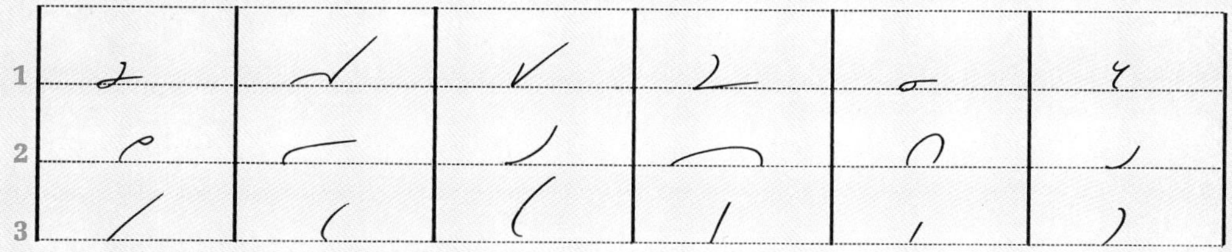

WORDS

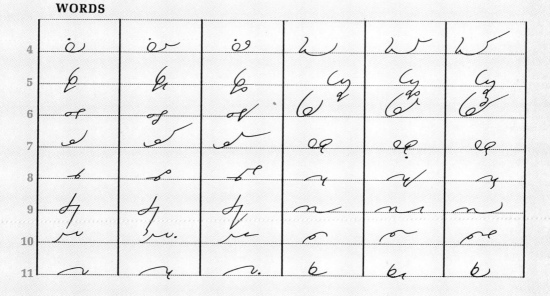

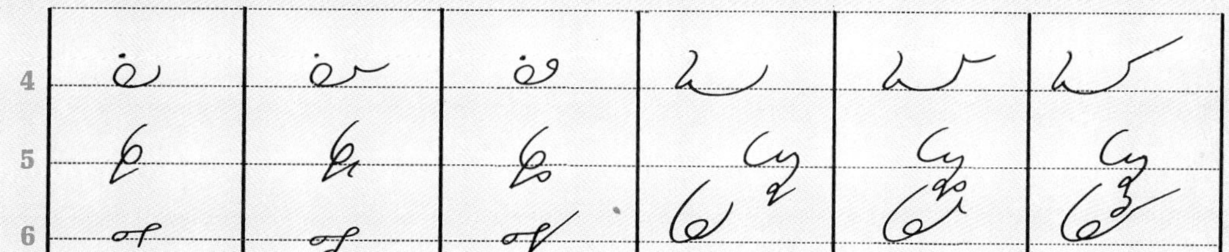

PHRASES AND AMOUNTS

12
13
14
15

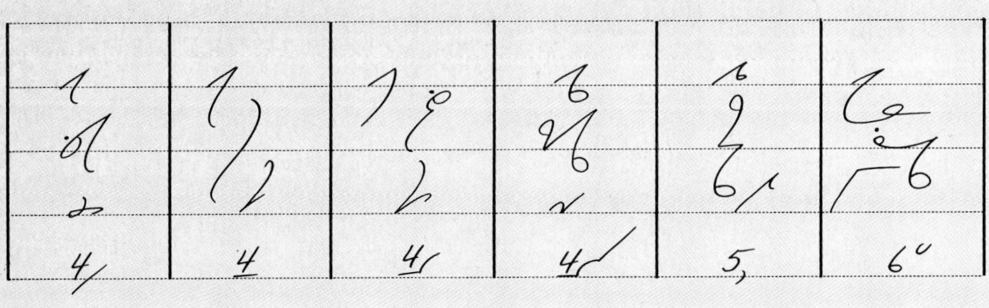

Building transcription skills

95

Business vocabulary builder	
	initial First.
	vacant Empty.
	admit Let in.

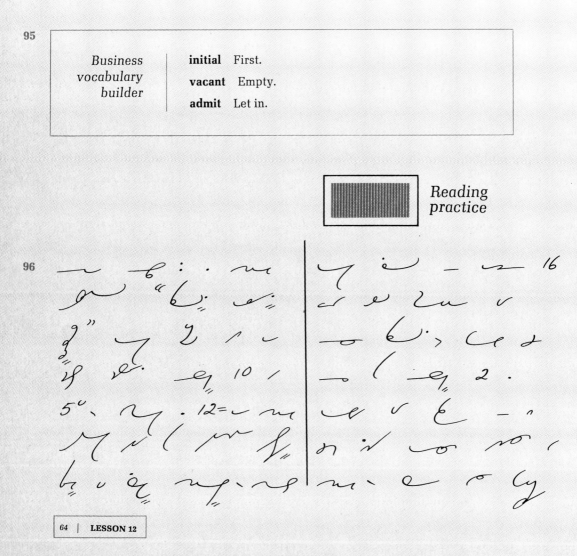

Reading practice

96

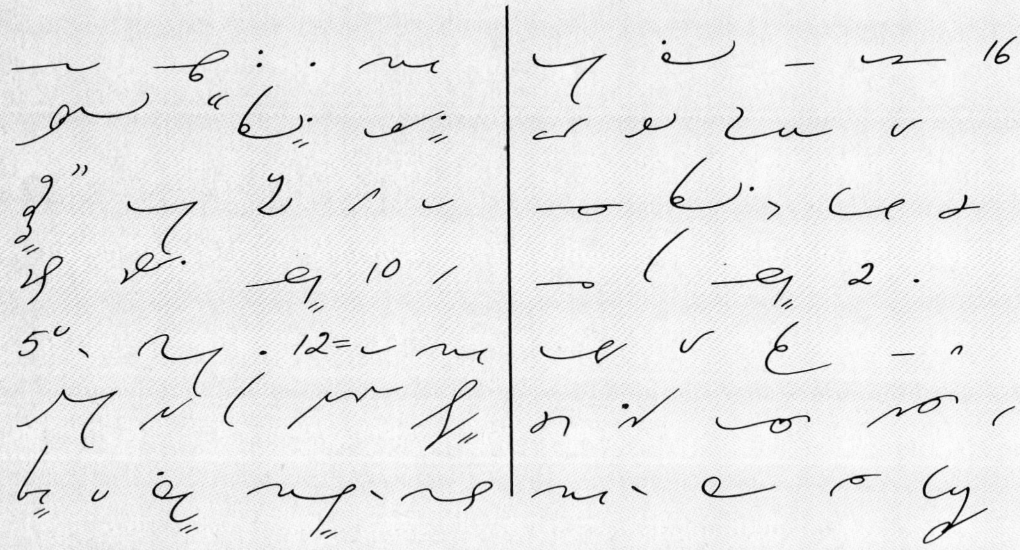

[84]

97 50/ 18 150/ [88]

98 15/ 15/ [57]

99 10/ 5

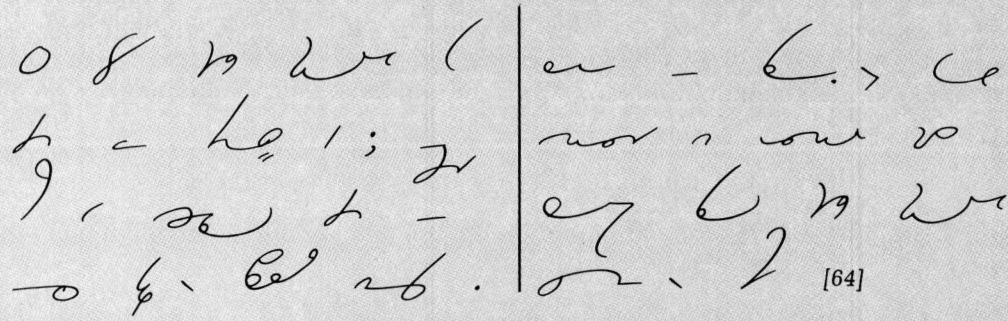

[64]

100

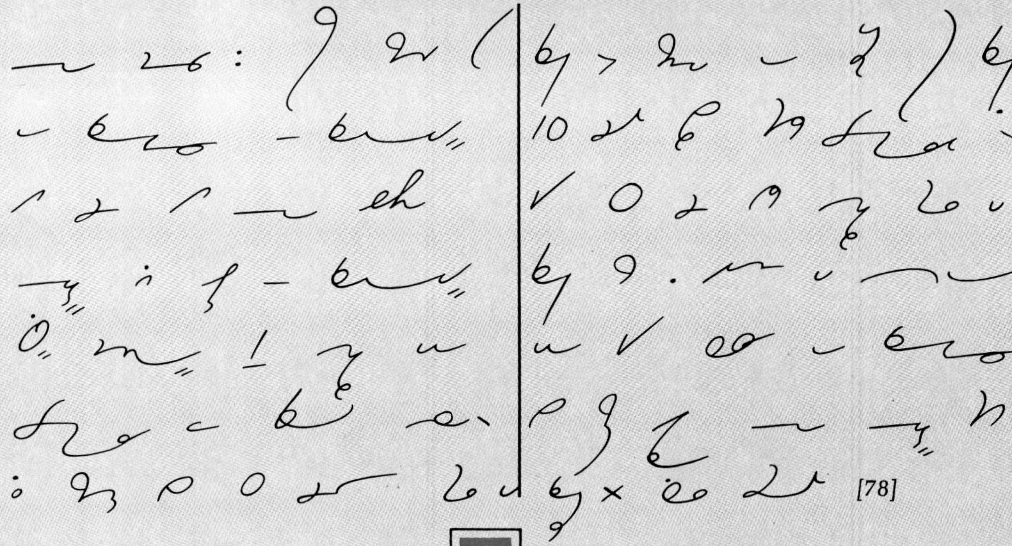

[78]

101

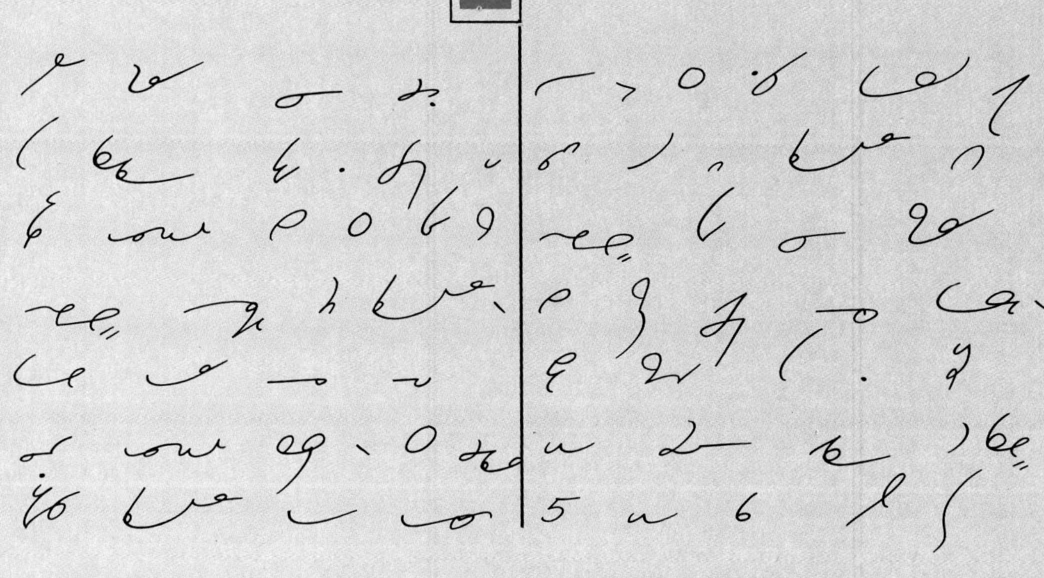

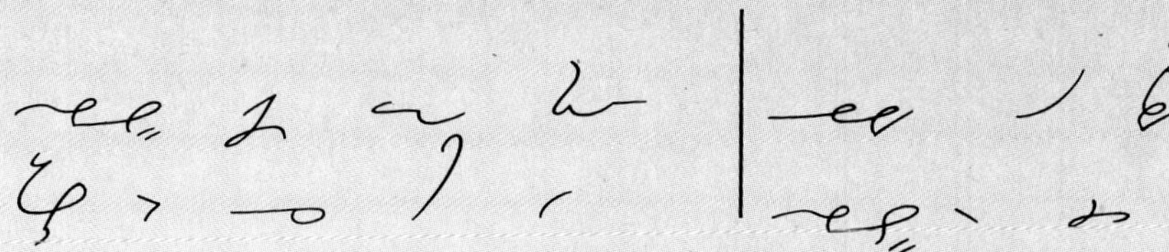

[94]

102

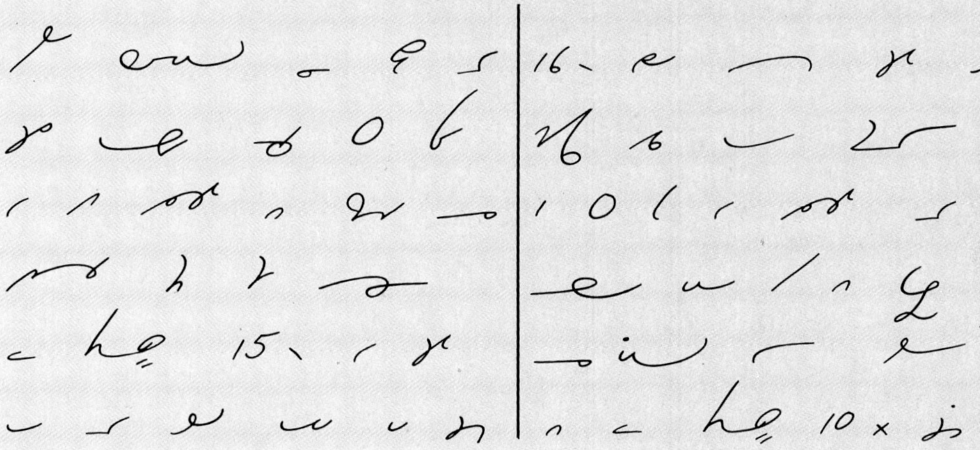

[65]

Chapter 3
Why be a secretary?

If you were to ask ten successful secretaries what they like about their jobs, you would no doubt obtain ten different answers. These answers, however, could be "capsuled" into five primary reasons why secretaries like their jobs:

1. "The work is interesting." The secretary in a travel-agency office gave this reason. Would you find it exciting to work in an organization that makes and sells phonograph records? broadcasts radio and television programs? produces advertisements for radio, TV, magazines, and newspapers?

operates an airline? These are only a few of the types of firms that need secretaries.

2. "A secretary often has dealings with important people." This was the reason given by a secretary to a lawyer. Secretaries do work for and with important people. These important people, and those with whom they come in contact, make the decisions that turn the wheels of industry, of business, of the professions, and of the arts. The secretary is brought into the "inner circle" of management, where she can observe big things happening.

3. "An office is a pleasant place in which to work." Does this sound like a strange reason for choosing secretarial work? Not if you consider the fact that more of a secretary's waking hours are spent in the office than at home. The important people in an office rate the best accommodations. If the executive for whom the secretary works has a choice location, she is likely to have one, too.

4. "The salary is good." The secretary who gave this reason works in an engineering firm that manufactures electronic devices for rockets. In comparison with general office employees the secretary receives excellent pay. Often the magic word "shorthand" makes the difference between a medium-paying job and a well-paying one!

5. "The work has variety." Most secretaries won't argue with the one who gave that reason. The secretary has dozens of opportunities for variety every day. The alert secretary will find all the variety she can possibly want; one day is never like another! In most business offices there is never a dull moment.

LESSON 13

Principles

103 **Brief Forms**

Glad, work, yesterday, very, thank, order, soon, enclose, were-year.

* In phrases, the dot is omitted from *thank. Thanks* is written with a disjoined left s in the dot position.

Thank you, thank you for, thanks.

104 **U, OO** The hook that expresses the sound of *oo*, as in *to*, also represents the vowel sounds heard in *does* and *foot*.

U

Spell: d-oo-s, *does*

Does, dozen, above, none, number, enough, us, precious, just.

▶ Notice that the *oo* in *none, number, enough* is turned on its side; that *oo-s* join without an angle in *us, precious, just.*

OO

Spell: *f*-oo-t, *foot*

Foot, book, full, looked, pulled, stood, took, pushed.

105 **W, Sw** At the beginning of words, the sound of *w* is represented by the *oo* hook; *sw*, by *s-oo*.

Spell: *oo-e, we; s-oo-e-t, sweet*

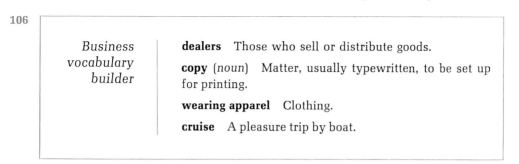

We, way, wait, week-weak, wash, wanted, wood, wool.
Sweet, swim, swell, swear.

Building transcription skills

106

Business vocabulary builder	
	dealers Those who sell or distribute goods.
	copy *(noun)* Matter, usually typewritten, to be set up for printing.
	wearing apparel Clothing.
	cruise A pleasure trip by boat.

Reading practice

107 **Brief-Form Letter** In the following letter all the brief forms presented in this lesson are used at least once.

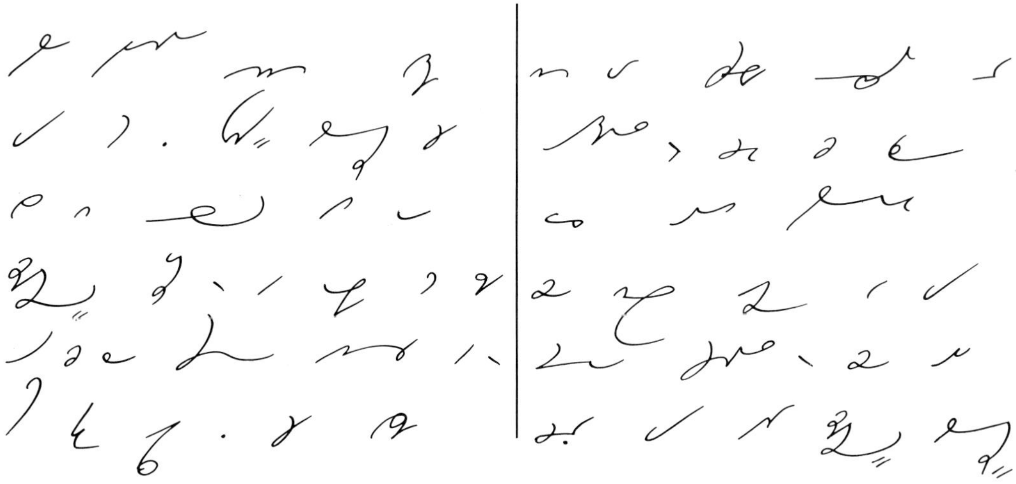

[93]

108

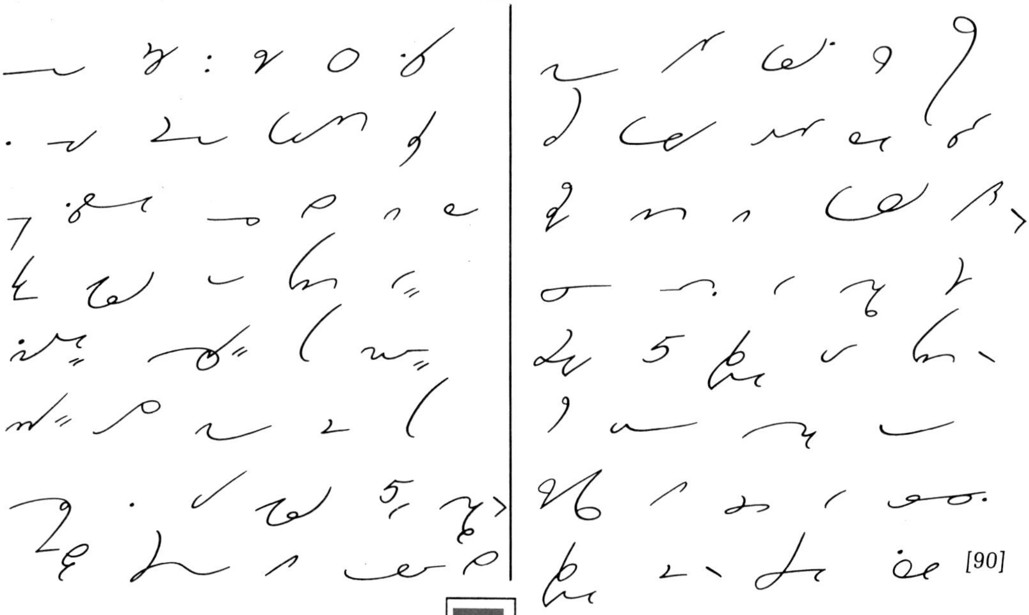

[90]

109

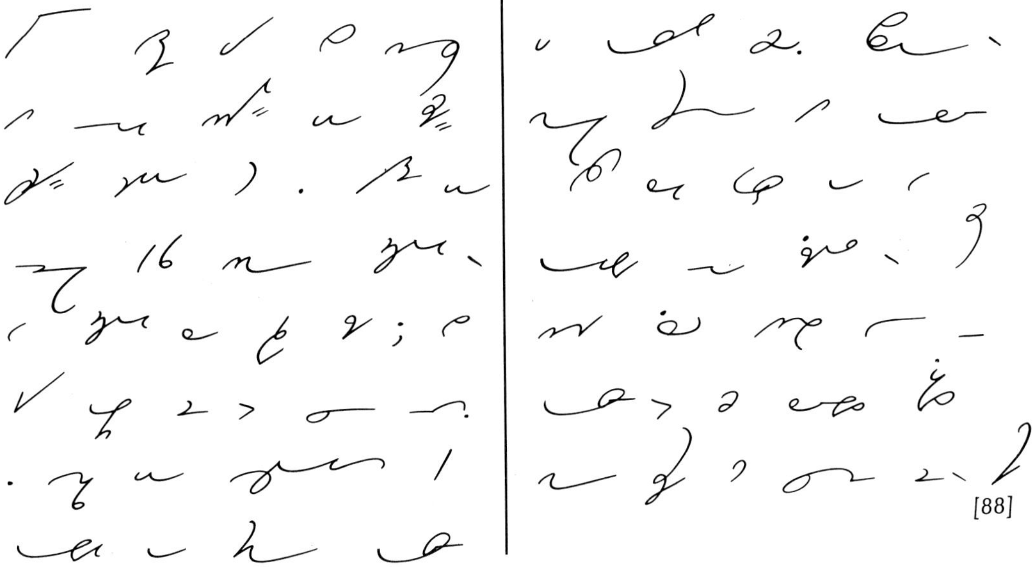

[88]

110

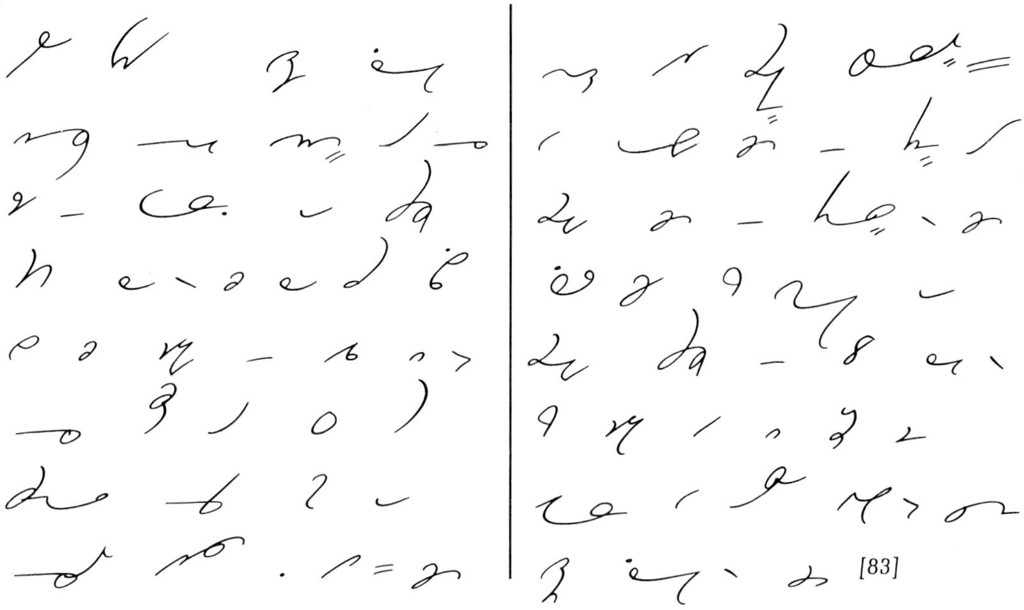

[83]

111

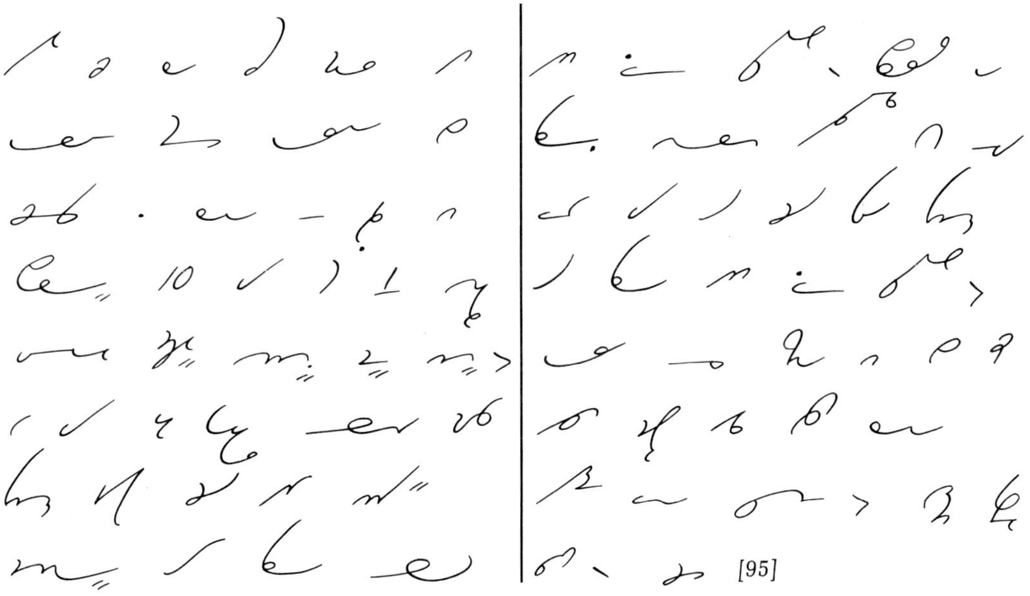

[95]

LESSON 14

Principles

112 **Wh** *Wh*, as in *white*, is pronounced *hw*—the *h* is pronounced first. Therefore, in shorthand, we write the *h* first.

Spell: *h-oo-ī-t, white*

White, while, wheel, whale, whip, wheat.

113 **W in the Body of a Word** When the sound of *w* occurs in the body of a word, as in *quick*, it is represented by a short dash underneath the vowel following the *w* sound. The dash is inserted after the rest of the outline has been written.

Spell: *k-oo-e-k, quick*

Quick, quit, quite, twice, equipped, always, roadway, Broadway.

114 **Ted** The combination *ted* is represented by joining *t* and *d* into one long upward stroke.

Ted 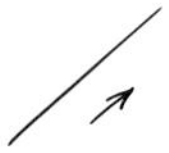

Compare: heat  heed  heated 

Spell: *h-e-ted, heated*

Acted, tested, rested, dated, rated, located, today, steady.

115 **Ded, Dit, Det** The long stroke that represents *ted* also represents *ded, dit, det.*

Spell: *t-r-a-ded, traded; o-ded, audit; ded-a-l-s, details*

Ded

Traded, needed, added, graded, deduct, deduction.

Dit, Det

Audit, edit, credited, creditor, details, debtor.

Building transcription skills

116

Business vocabulary builder	**frosted glasses** Glasses having a slightly roughened surface. **quote** Give a price on. **authorized** Having permission to. **survey** *(noun)* Inspection

Reading practice

117 **Brief-Form Review Letter** The following letter reviews the brief forms you studied in Lesson 13.

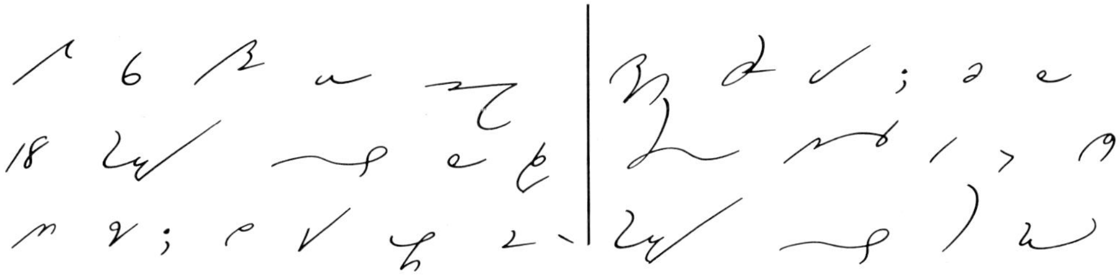

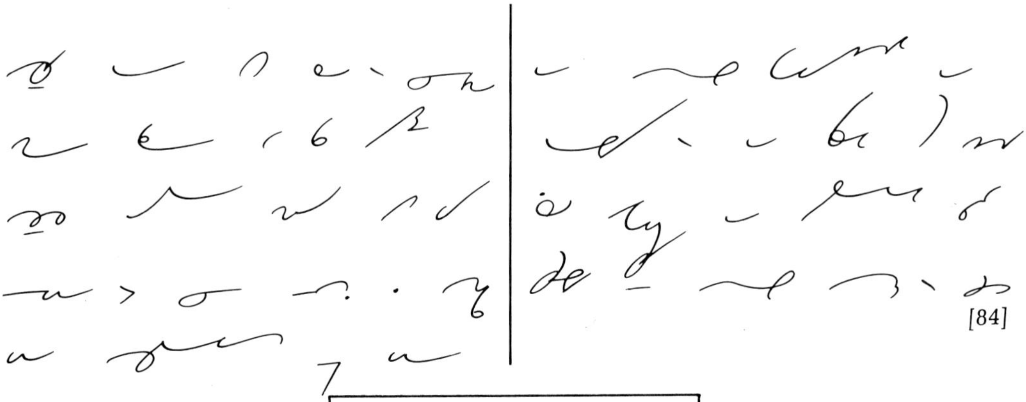

[84]

118

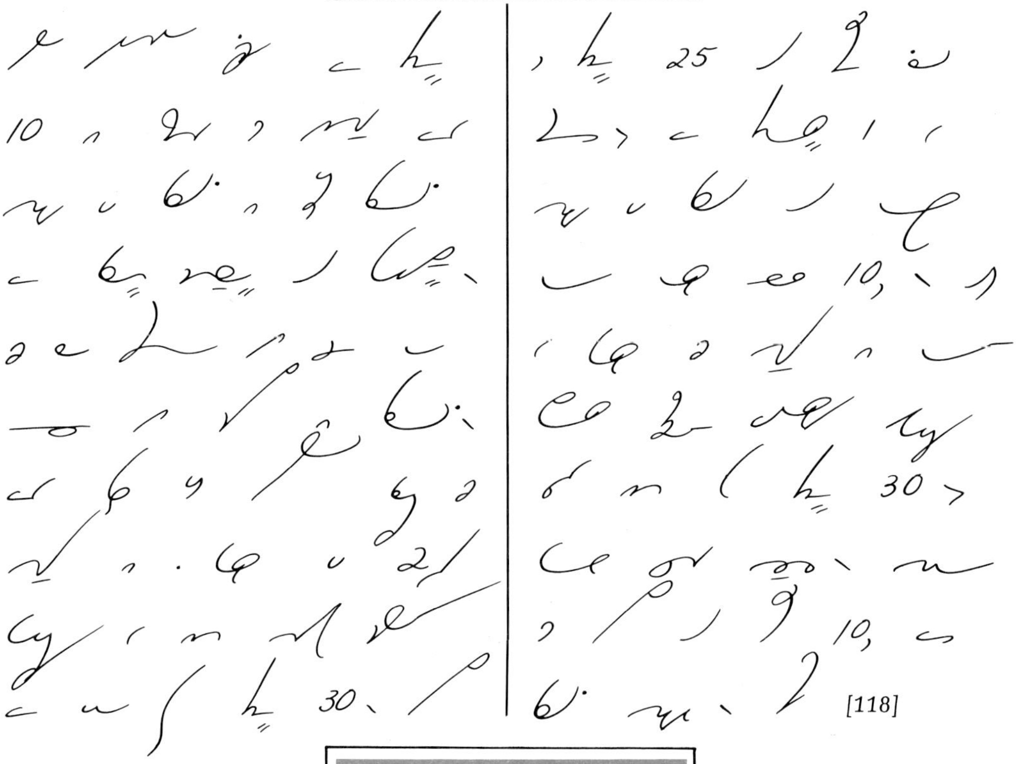

[118]

119

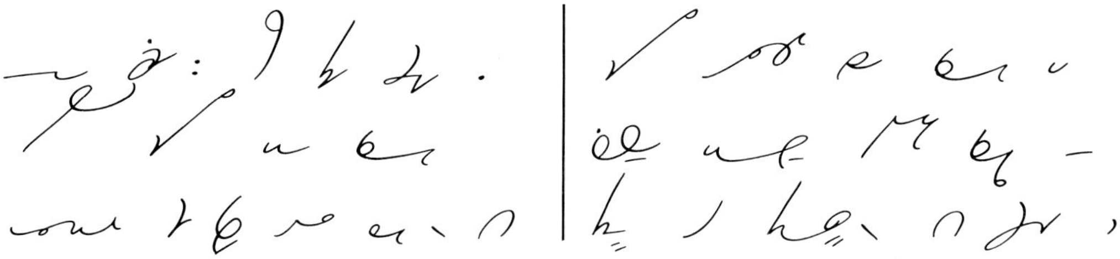

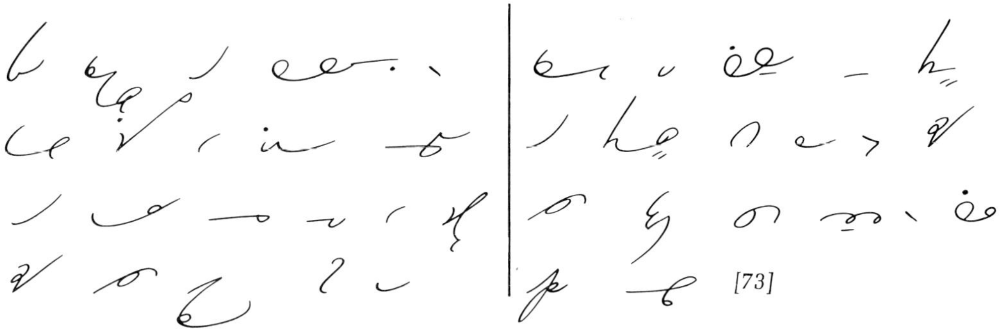
[73]

120

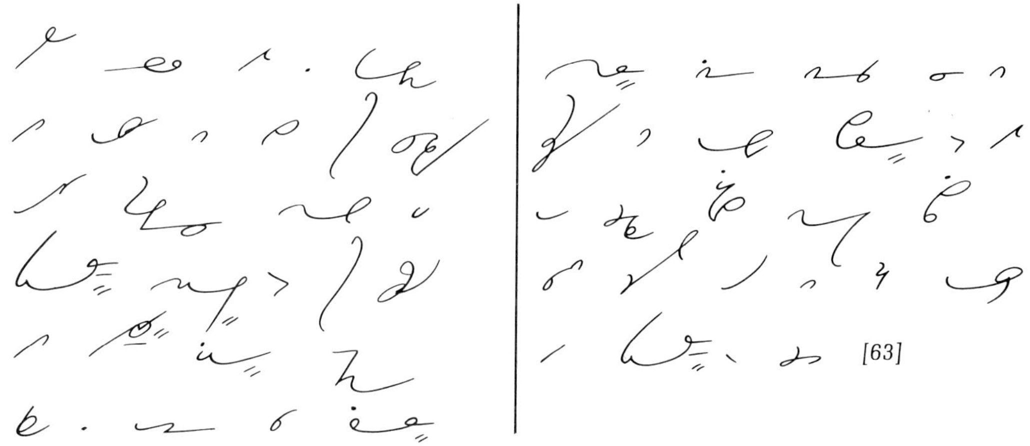
[63]

121

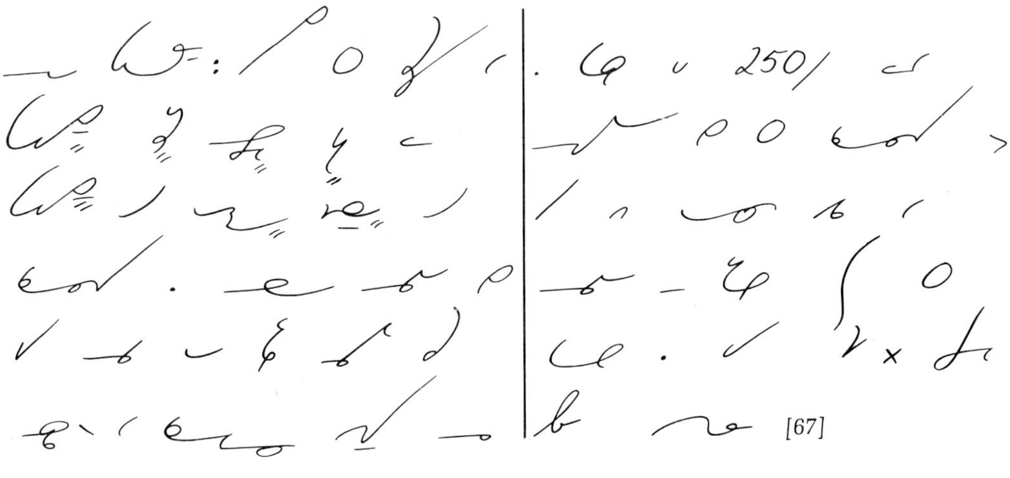
250
[67]

122

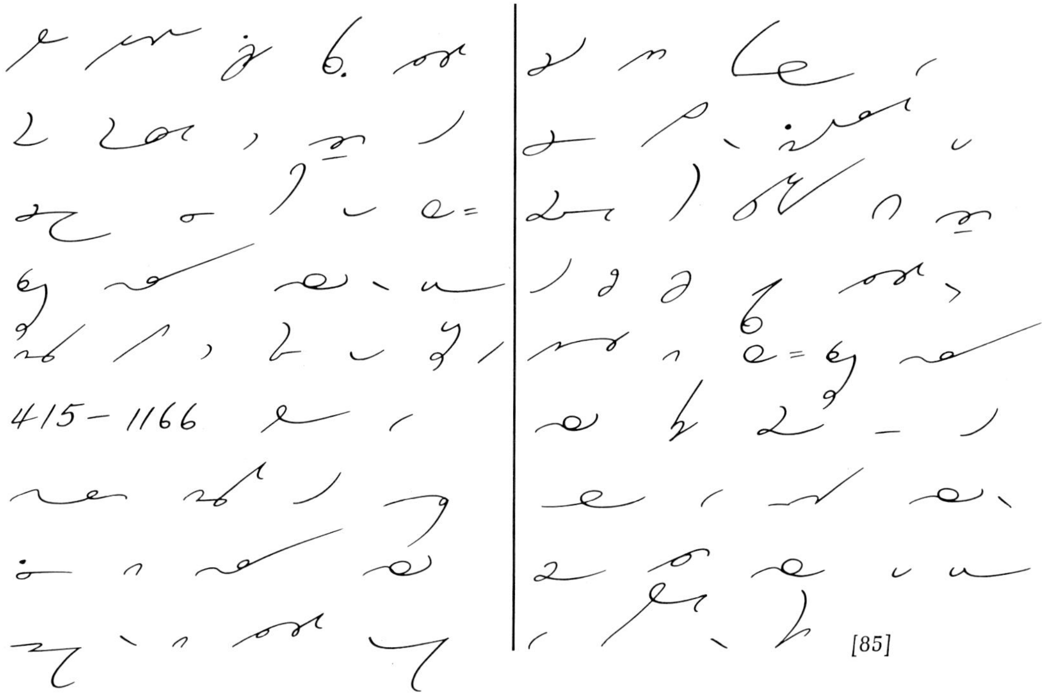
415-1166

[85]

STUDY-HABIT CHECK LIST

No doubt as a conscientious student you do your home assignments faithfully. Do you, however, derive the greatest benefit from the time you devote to practice?

☐ You *do* if you practice in a quiet place that enables you to concentrate.

☐ You *don't* if you practice with one eye on the television and the other on your practice work!

☐ You *do* if once you have started your assignment, you do not leave your desk or table until you have completed it.

☐ You *don't* if you interrupt your practice from time to time to call a friend or raid the refrigerator!

LESSON 15

Principles

123 **Brief Forms**

Value, than, one-won, what, about, great, thing-think, why, business.

124 **Brief-Form Derivatives**

Once, greater, things-thinks, thinking, businessman, businesses, values.

▶ Notice that a disjoined left s is used to express *things, thinks;* that the plural of *business* is formed by adding another left s.

125 **Word Ending -ble** The word ending *-ble* is represented by *b.*

Spell: p-a-bul, *payable*

Payable, available, reliable, sensible, terrible, possible, troubled, cabled.

126 **Word Beginning Re-** The word beginning *re-* is represented by *r.*

Spell: re-s-e-v-d, *received*

Received, revise, repaired, receipted, referring, research, reappear, reopen.

Building transcription skills

127

Business vocabulary builder	
racks	Equipment on which clothes are hung.
sites	Places, locations.
strive	Try hard.

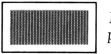

Reading practice

128 **Brief-Form Letter** All the brief forms presented in this lesson are used at least once in this letter.

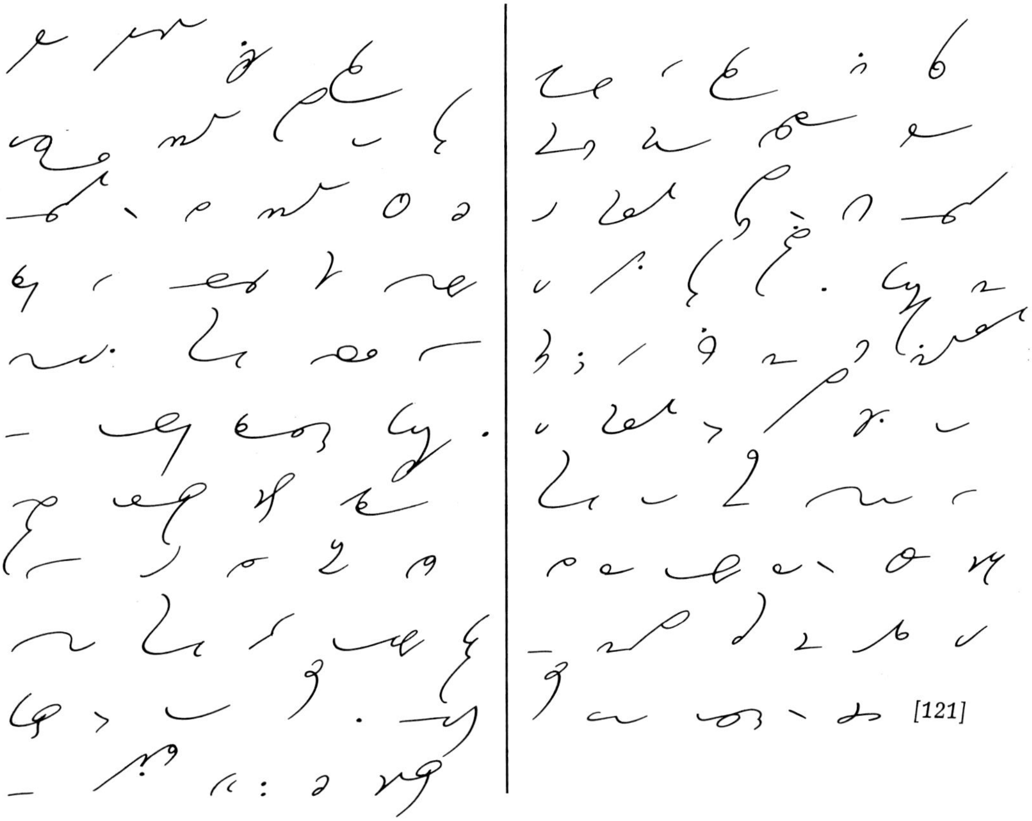

[121]

129

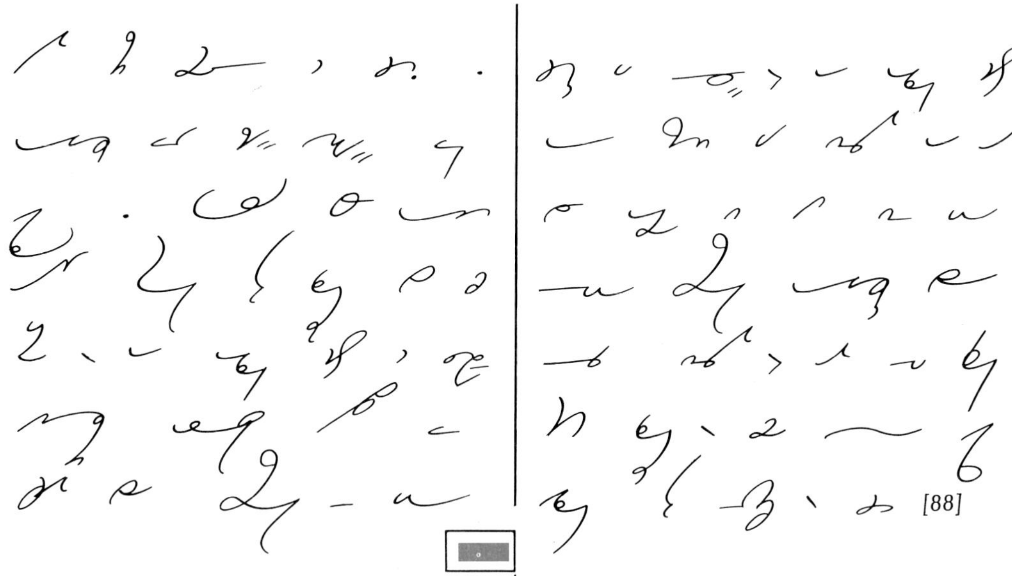

[88]

130

[95]

131

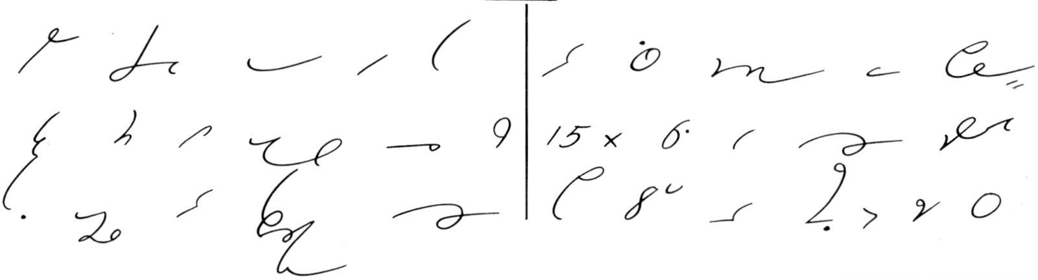

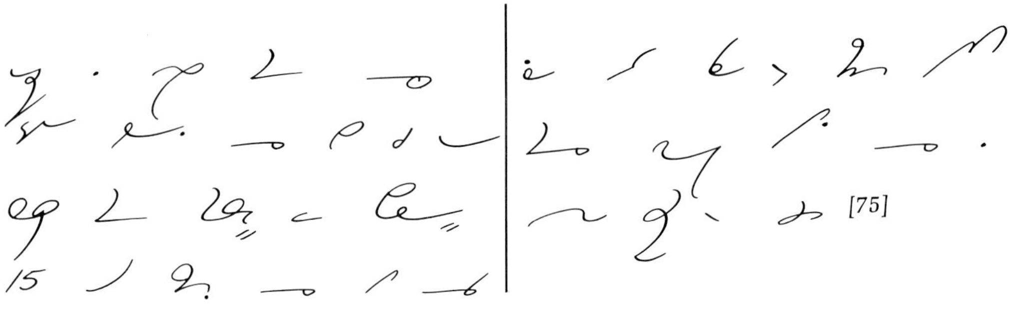
[75]

132

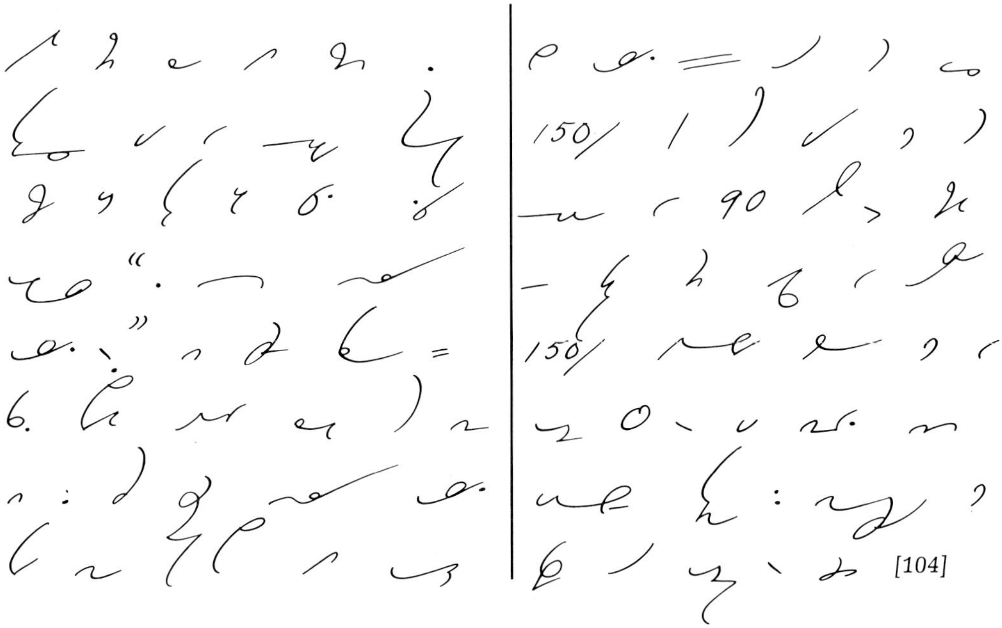
150
90
150
[104]

133

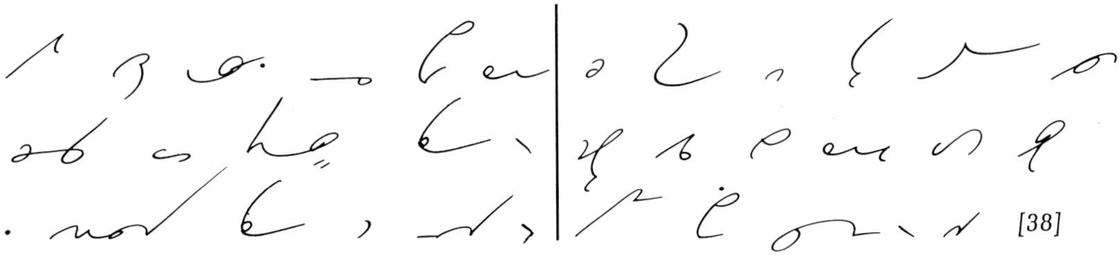
[38]

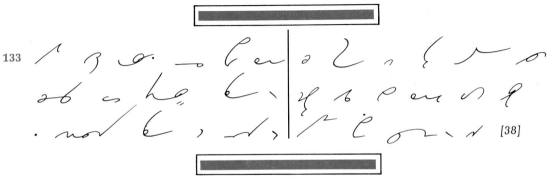

LESSON 16

Principles

134 Oi The sound of *oi*, as in *toy*, is represented by  .

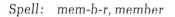

Spell: t-oi, toy

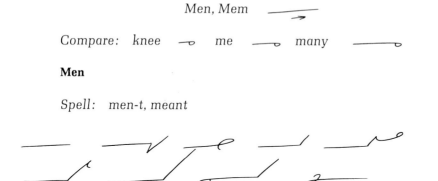

Toy, boy, join, annoy, oil, spoil, appoint, noise, voice.

135 Men, Mem The combinations *men, mem* are represented by joining *m* and *n* into one long forward stroke.

Men, Mem 

Compare: *knee* *me*  *many*

Men

Spell: men-t, meant

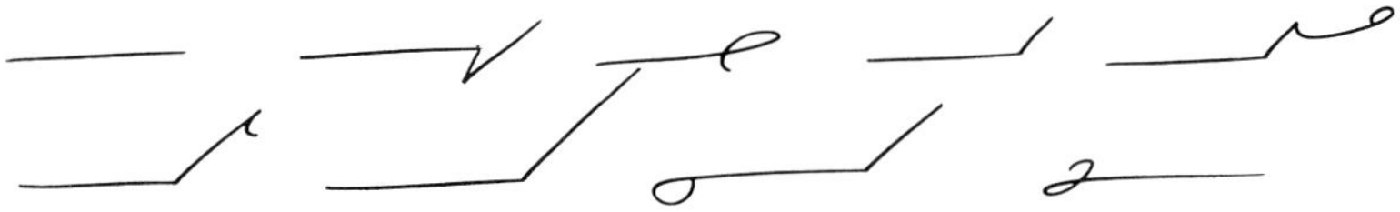

Men, mentioned, menace, meant, mentally.
Mends, mended, amend, women.

Mem

Spell: mem-b-r, member

Member, remember, memory, memorize.

136 Min, Mon, Mun, etc. The long forward stroke used for *men, mem* also represents *min, mon, mun,* etc.

Spell: *men-e-t, minute; men-r, manner*

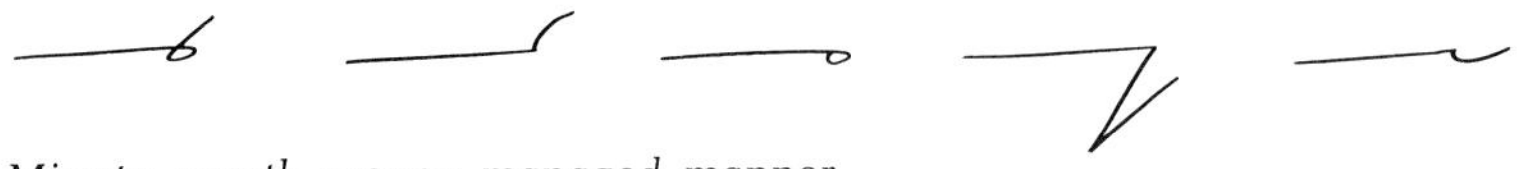

Minute, month, money, managed, manner.

137 Word Beginning Be- The word beginning *be-* is represented by *b.*

Spell: *be-k-a-m, became*

Became, begin, belief, believed, because, below, beneath.

Building transcription skills

138

Business vocabulary builder	
	asset Anything of value owned by a company—cash, equipment, etc.
	immensely Very much; greatly.
	treasurer An official in charge of the funds of a company or organization.
	succeeding Filling a job left by someone.

Reading practice

139 Brief-Form Review Letter This letter reviews the brief forms you studied in Lesson 15.

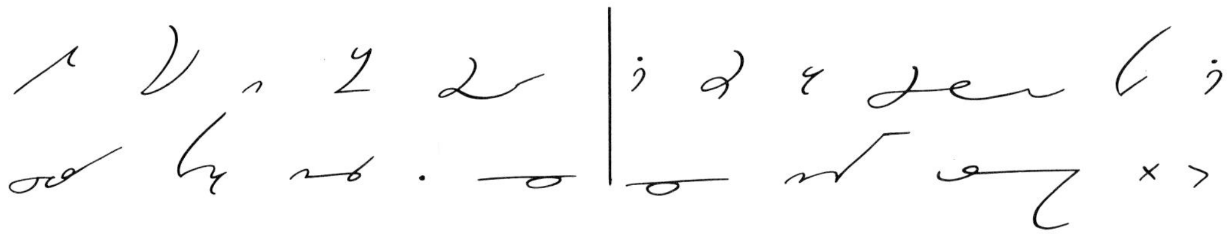

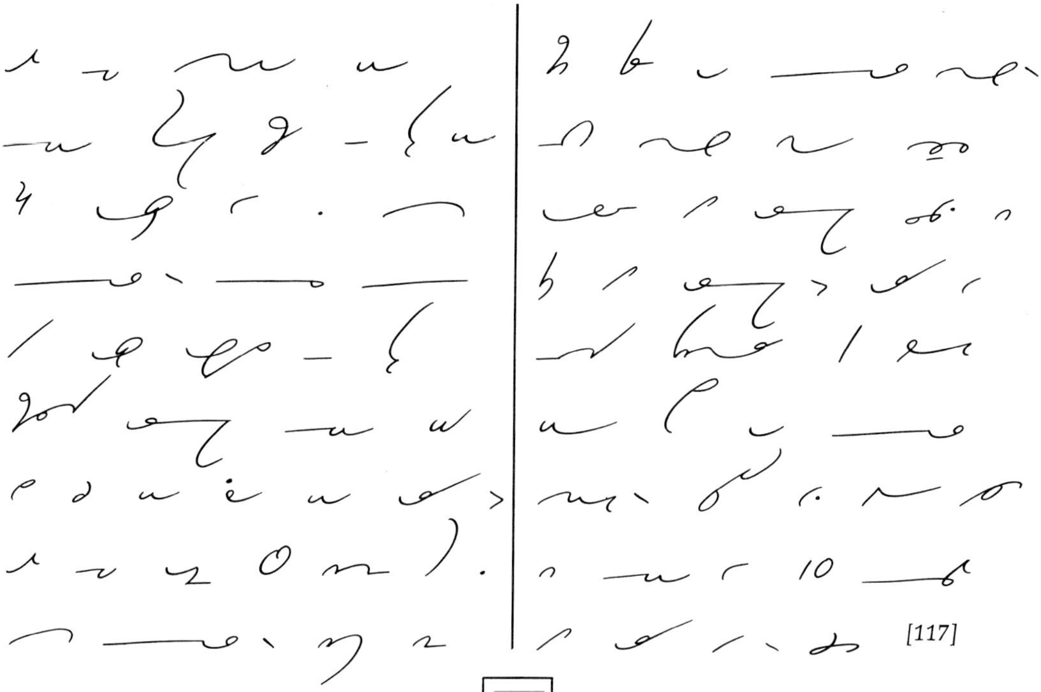

[117]

140 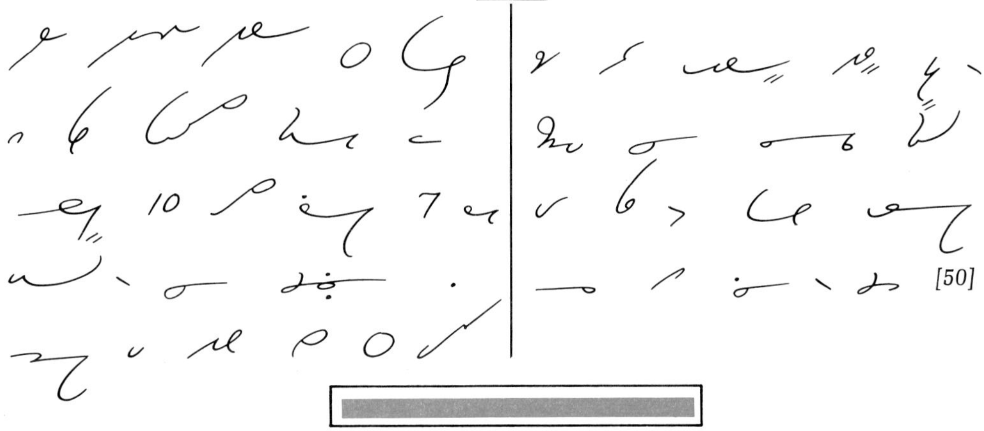

[50]

141 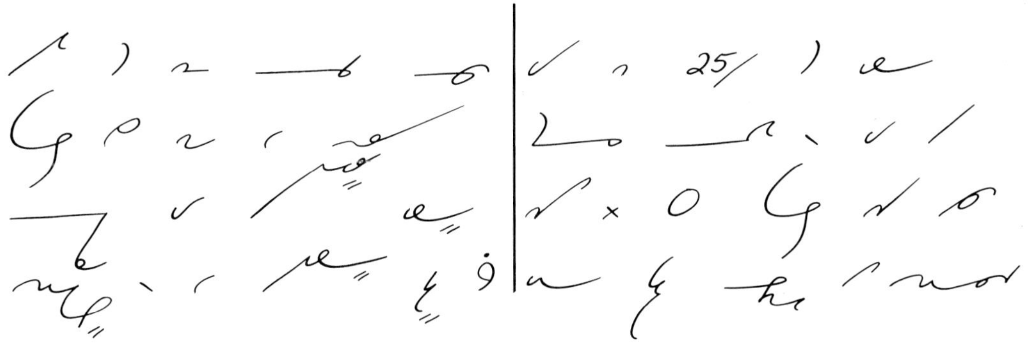

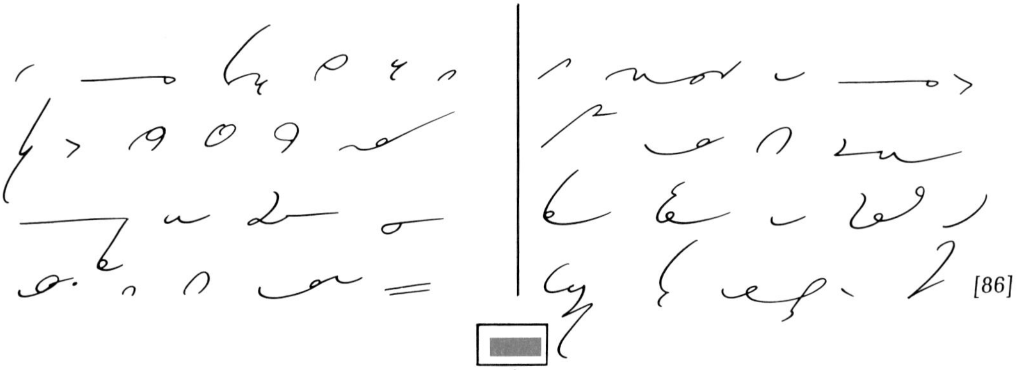

[86]

142

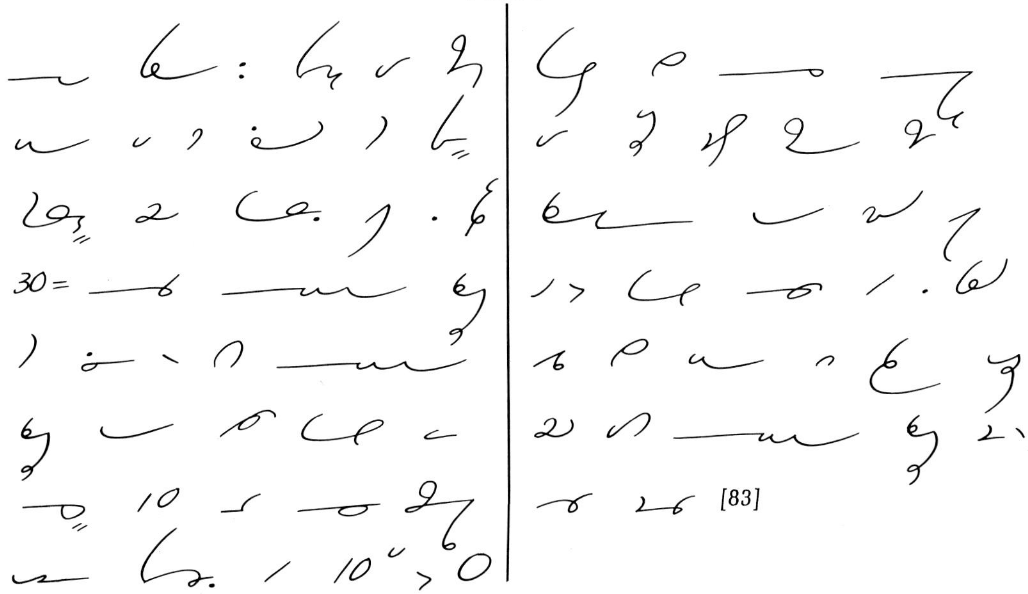

[83]

143

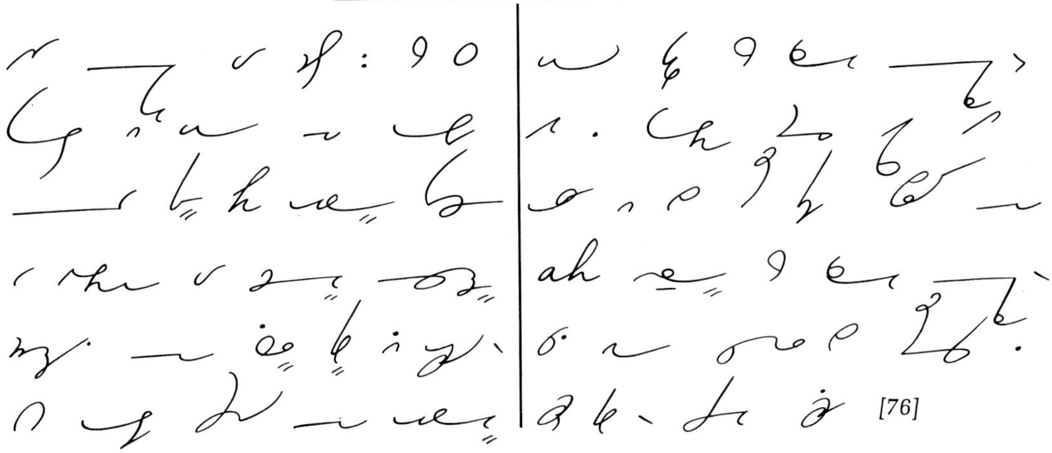

[76]

LESSON 17

Principles

144 Brief Forms When you have learned the following six brief forms, you will have learned more than half the brief forms of Gregg Shorthand.

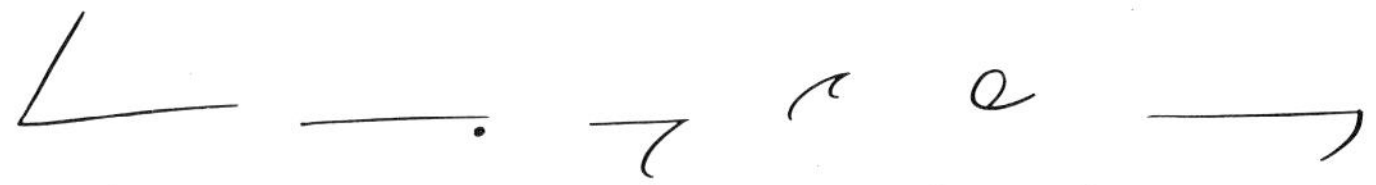

Gentlemen, morning, important-importance, those, where, manufacture.

145 Word Beginnings Per-, Pur- The word beginnings *per-, pur-* are represented by *pr.*

Spell: *pur-s-n, person; pur-chay-a-s, purchase*

Per-

Person, permit, perfect, persisted, personal, perhaps.

Pur-

Purchase, purchaser, purple, purse, purses.

146 Word Beginnings De-, Di- The word beginnings *de-, di-* are represented by *d.*

Spell: *de-s-ī-d, decide; de-r-e-k-t, direct*

De-

Decide, delay, desired, deserve, derive, deposit.

Di-

Direct, direction, diploma.

147 **Past Tense** As you have perhaps already noticed from your study of Lessons 1 through 16, the past tense of a verb is formed by adding the stroke for the sound that is heard in the past tense. In some words the past tense will have the sound of *t*, as in *baked;* in others, it will have the sound of *d*, as in *saved.*

Baked, saved, missed, changed, faced, showed, traced.

Building transcription skills

148 **SIMILAR-WORDS DRILL**

In the English language there are many groups of words that sound or look alike, but each member of the group is spelled differently and each has its own meaning.

Example: **sent** (dispatched), **scent** (a smell), **cent** (a coin).

There are many other groups of words that sound or look *almost* alike.

Example: **area** (space); **aria** (a melody).

The stenographer who is not careful will sometimes select the wrong member of the group when transcribing, with the result that her transcript makes no sense.

From time to time in the lessons ahead you will be given a similar-words exercise designed to help you select the correct word, so that when you become a stenographer you will not suffer the embarrassment of having your letters returned for correction.

Read carefully the definitions and the illustrative sentences in each similar-words exercise.

SIMILAR-WORDS DRILL | it's, its

it's The contraction of *it is.*

It's *a fine day.*

its (*no apostrophe*) Possessive form meaning *belonging to it.*

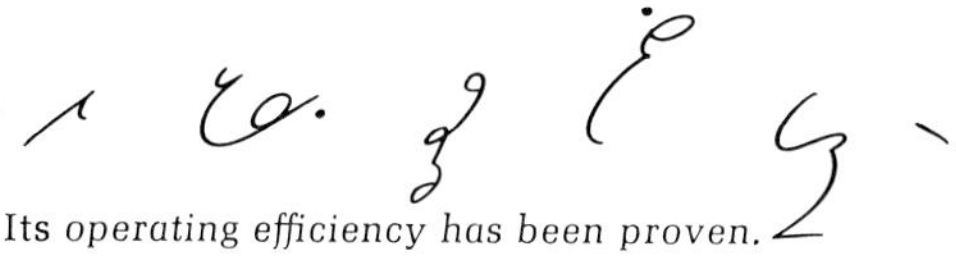

Its *operating efficiency has been proven.*

149

Business vocabulary builder	**board of directors** A group of people who run a company or organization. **minimum** The least (*maximum,* the most). **personnel records** Information concerning the people who work for a company. **proceed** Go ahead (do not confuse with *precede,* which means "come before").

Reading practice

150 **Brief-Form Letter** This letter contains one or more illustrations of all the brief forms you studied in this lesson.

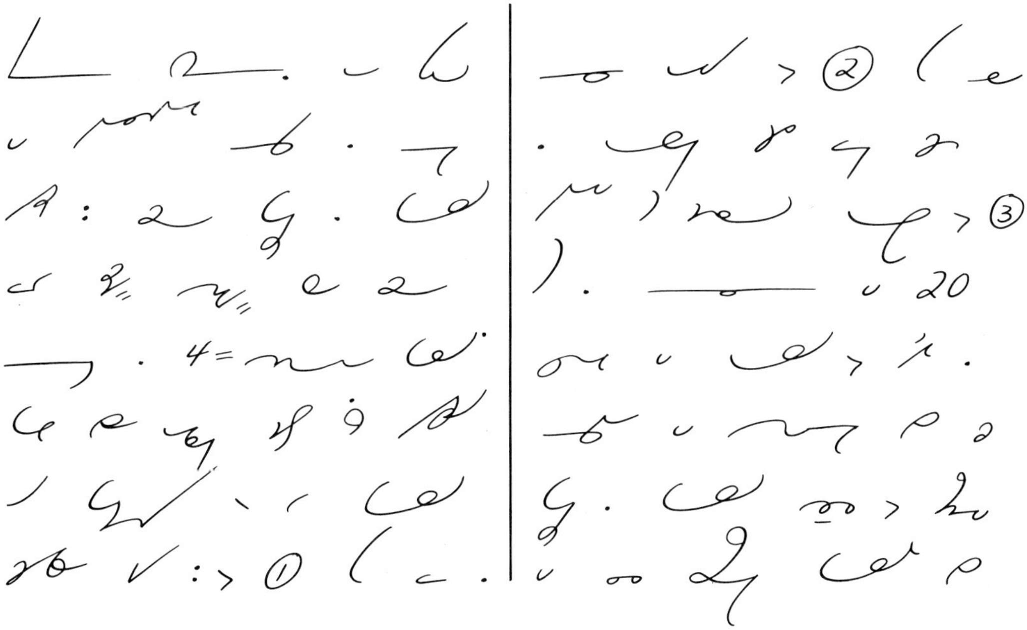

1185 [107]

213-116-

151

[103]

152

[81]

153

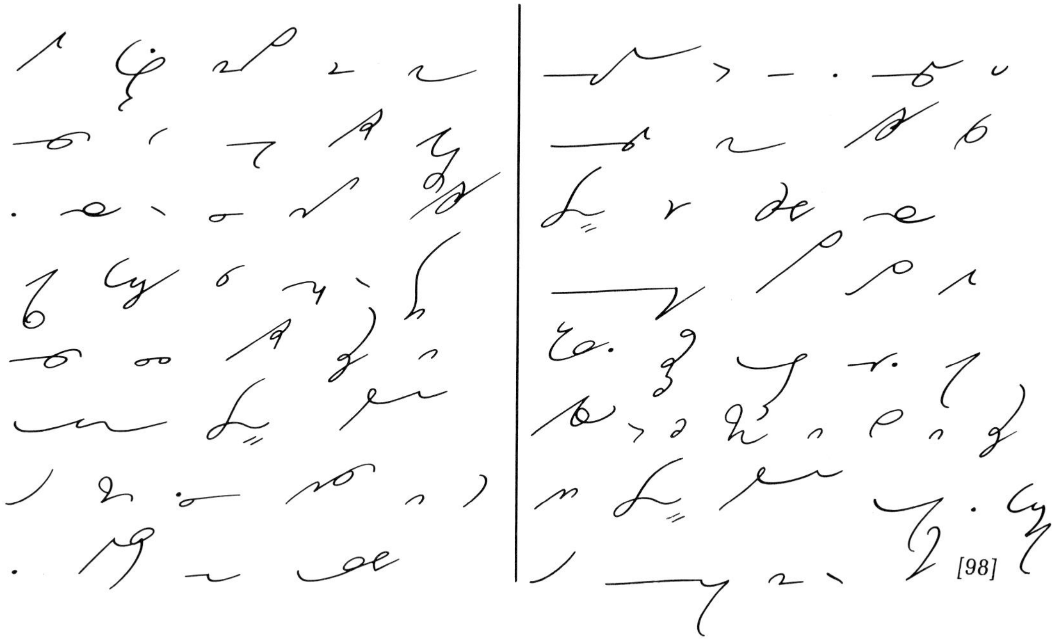
[98]

154

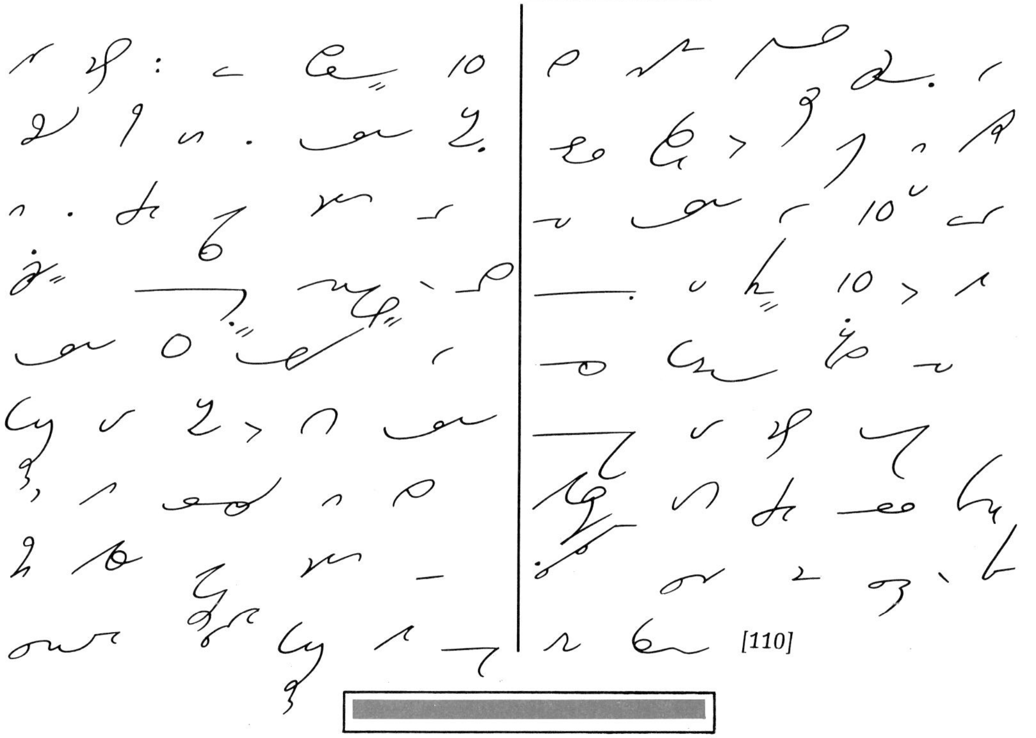
[110]

155

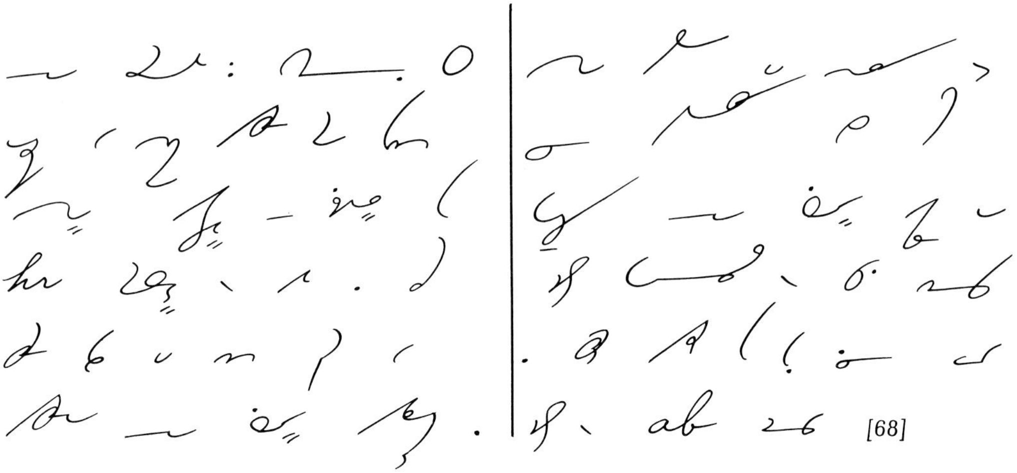

[68]

156 Coffee Break

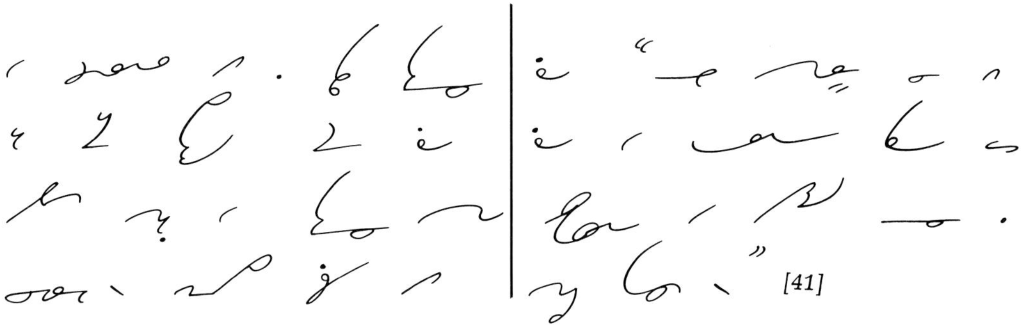

[41]

LESSON 18

Recall

Lesson 18 is another "breather" for you; it contains no new shorthand devices for you to learn. In this lesson you will find: a Recall Chart and a Reading Practice that you will find not only interesting but informative as well.

157 **Recall Chart** This chart reviews all the brief forms in Chapter 3 as well as the shorthand devices you studied in Chapters 1, 2, and 3.

The chart contains 90 words and phrases. Can you read the entire chart in 8 minutes or less?

BRIEF FORMS AND DERIVATIVES

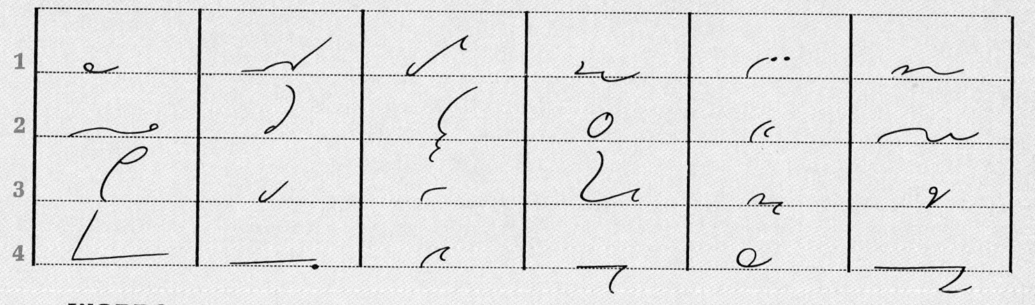

WORDS

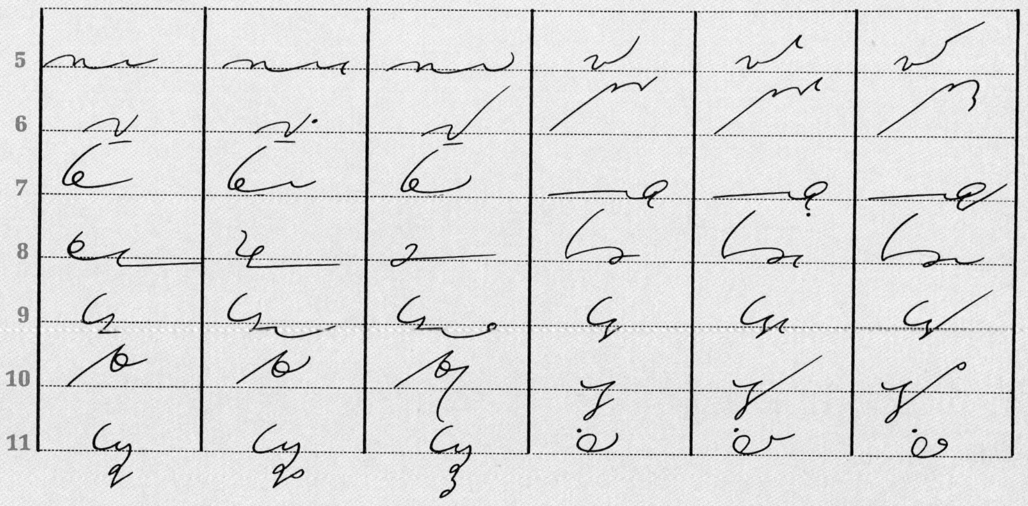

12
13

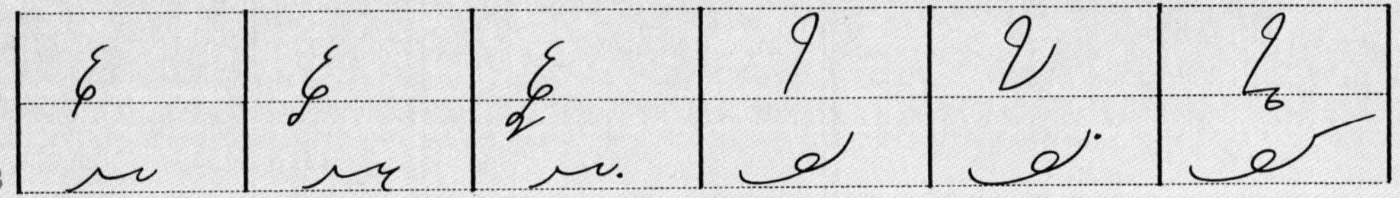

PHRASES AND QUANTITIES

14
15

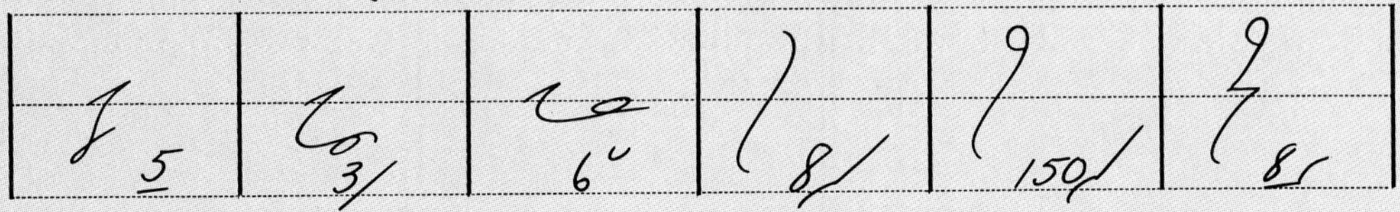

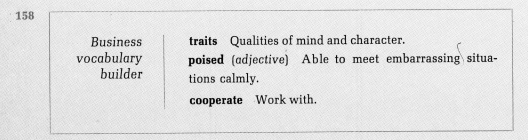

Building transcription skills

158

Business vocabulary builder	**traits** Qualities of mind and character. **poised** (*adjective*) Able to meet embarrassing situations calmly. **cooperate** Work with.

Reading practice

Reading Scoreboard One of the factors in measuring your progress in shorthand is the rate at which you read shorthand. Wouldn't you like to determine your reading rate on the *first reading* of the articles in Lesson 18? The following table will help you.

Lesson 18 contains 473 words.

If you read Lesson 18 in **19 minutes** *your reading rate is* **25 words a minute**
If you read Lesson 18 in **21 minutes** *your reading rate is* **23 words a minute**
If you read Lesson 18 in **23 minutes** *your reading rate is* **21 words a minute**
If you read Lesson 18 in **25 minutes** *your reading rate is* **19 words a minute**
If you read Lesson 18 in **27 minutes** *your reading rate is* **17 words a minute**
If you read Lesson 18 in **29 minutes** *your reading rate is* **16 words a minute**

If you can read Lesson 18 through the first time in less than 19 minutes, you are doing well indeed. If you take considerably longer than 29 minutes, here are some questions you should ask yourself:

1 *Am I spelling each outline I cannot read immediately?*

2 *Should I perhaps reread the directions for reading shorthand on page 11?*

After you have determined your reading rate, make a record of it in some convenient place. You can then watch your reading rate grow as you time yourself on the Reading Scoreboards in later lessons.

159 The Power of a Smile

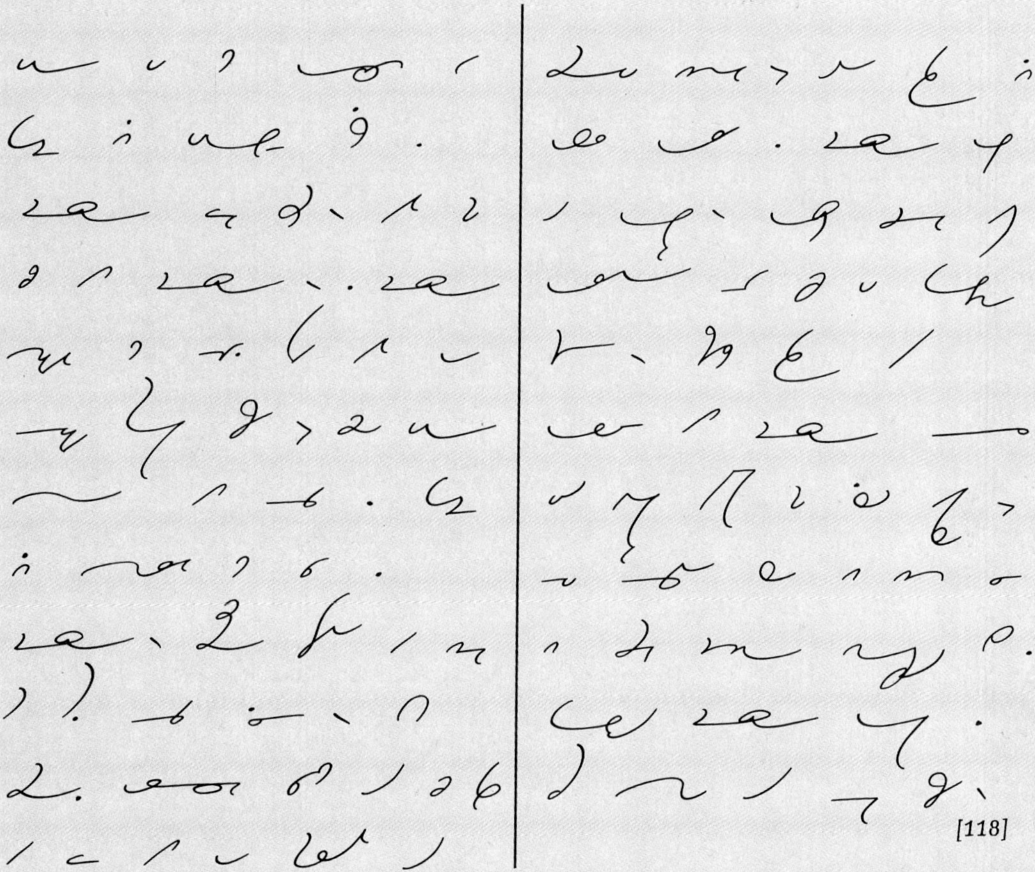

[118]

160 Desirable Traits

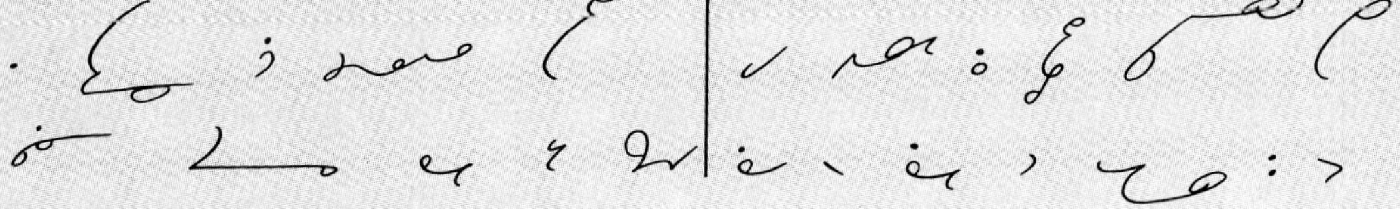

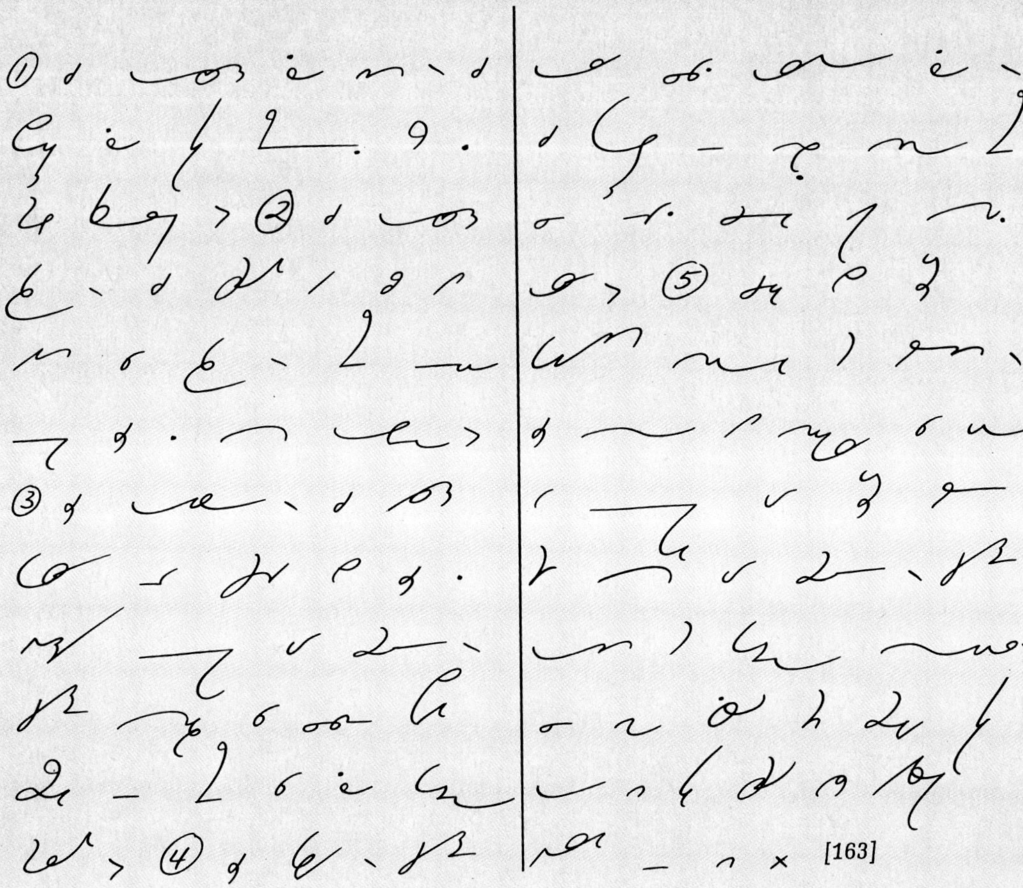

[163]

161 Good Health

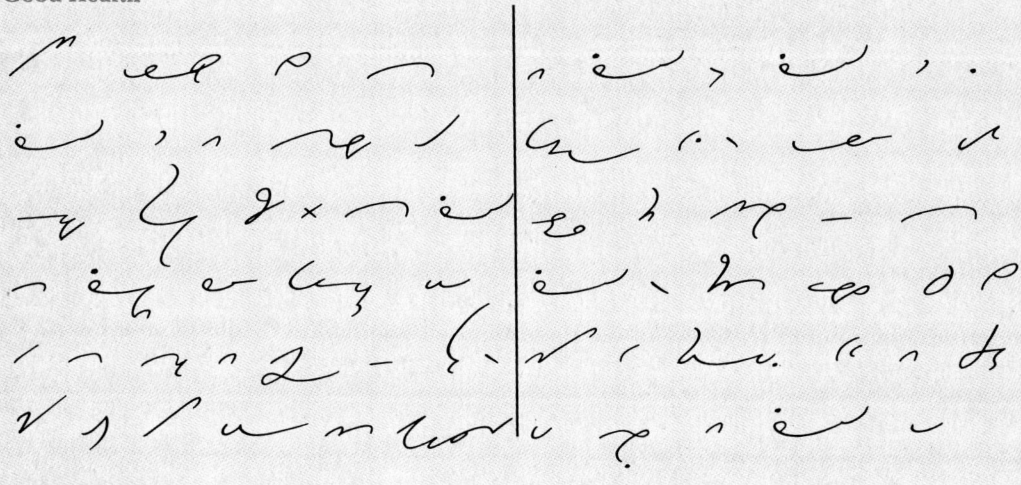

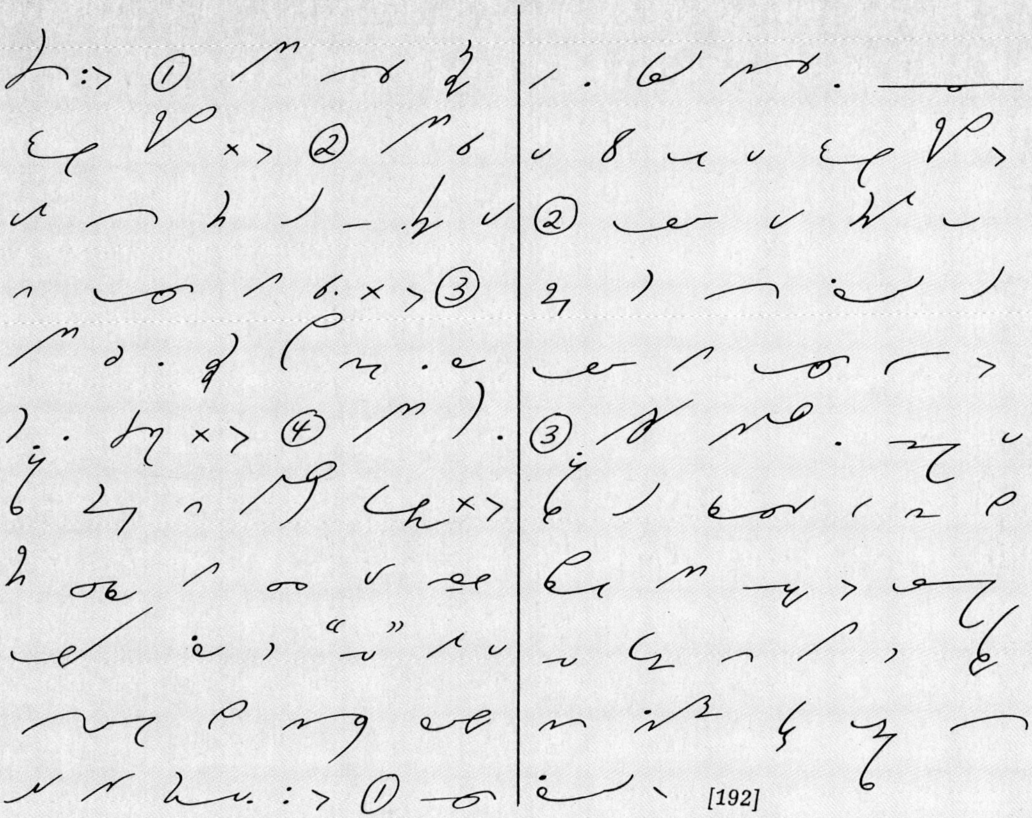

[192]

Chapter 4

The secretary's day

Some people think that all a secretary does is take and transcribe dictation. Nothing could be farther from the truth. While taking and transcribing dictation is an important part of a secretary's job, it is only one of the many duties she performs.

What is a typical day in the life of a secretary? Let's suppose you are secretary to Mr. C. G. Marsden, sales manager of a successful publishing company. Here is what your day might be like.

8:45 *Arrive at the office. Straighten and dust Mr. Marsden's desk. Check appointment calendar to be sure that his agrees with yours. You notice that he has made a 9:15 appointment with Mrs. Fuller. Get the correspondence you think he might need in talking with her.*

8:55 *Mr. Marsden arrives. Remind him of his 9:15 appointment and a luncheon date at 12:30 with Mr. Symond at the Belle Meade Restaurant. Ask him about arrangements for a 2:30 meeting of the advertising committee.*

9:05 *The mail arrives. Open all mail (except letters marked "Personal"). Read it and place it on Mr. Marsden's desk, along with any background correspondence he may need.*

9:15 *The receptionist calls you to say that Mrs. Fuller has arrived. You inform Mr. Marsden and then go out to the reception office to escort Mrs. Fuller in to see Mr. Marsden.*

9:35 *Mr. Marsden "buzzes" you on the intercom and tells you that Mrs. Fuller is leaving and asks you to get some papers that she is to take with her. You do so, bidding Mrs. Fuller good-bye at the elevator.*

9:40–10:15 *1. The telephone rings several times—company executives and outsiders asking for appointments and information.*
2. A messenger brings you a package of books c.o.d., and you take the money from petty cash to pay him.
3. Other executives call in person to speak to Mr. Marsden.

10:15 *Mr. Marsden calls you for dictation.*

11:00 *You return to your desk and begin transcribing.*

11:15 *Mr. Marsden asks for several papers that must be obtained from the files.*

11:30 *You call the receptionist*

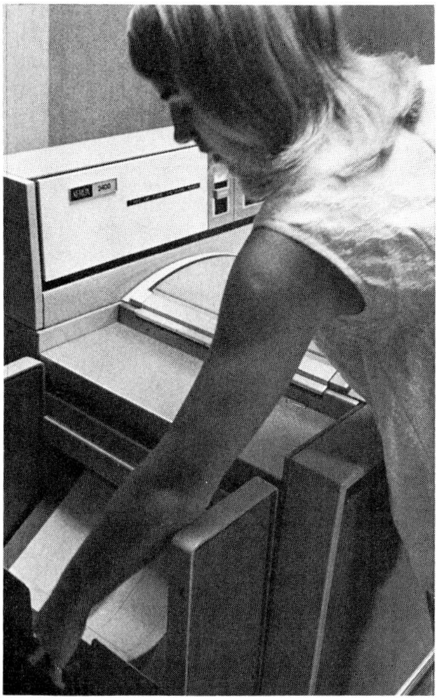

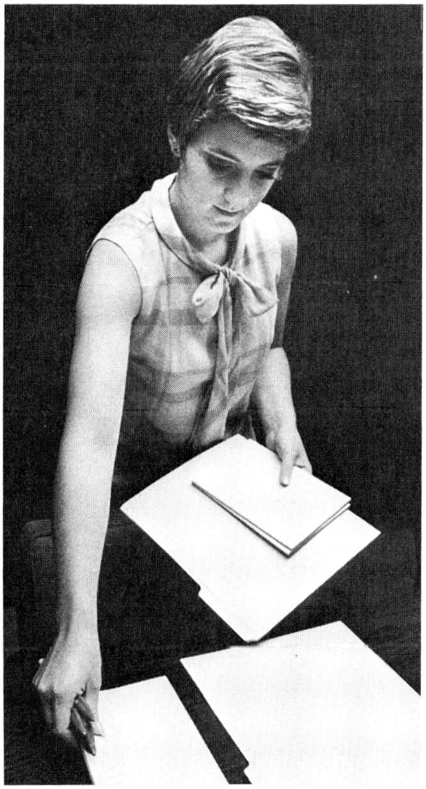

on the third floor to be sure that the conference room has been reserved for Mr. Marsden's 2:30 meeting.

12:00 You get ready to go to lunch with another secretary who works a few blocks away. Before leaving, you again remind Mr. Marsden about his luncheon date. You tell the relief receptionist that you are leaving for lunch.

12:55 Back from lunch, you return to your transcribing.

1:15-1:40 1. You answer several telephone calls.

2. You greet two callers who have come to see Mr. Marsden (neither has an appointment), and you persuade them to make an appointment for later in the week.

3. You duplicate the agenda for the advertising meeting and make photocopies of an advertising brochure to be discussed there.

4. You visit the conference room to see that there are enough chairs and that the room is in order. You distribute the materials for the meeting.

2:00 Mr. Marsden calls you in to dictate a short memo. He asks you to arrange to have a film and an operator in the conference room at three o'clock. You call the library for the film and office services to arrange for an operator.

2:25 You make sure that Mr. Marsden has all the necessary materials for the 2:30 meeting; then you return to your transcribing.

2:30-4:00 You get out two telegrams and finish transcribing Mr. Marsden's dictation. You telephone various people for information he needs for a report he is writing.

4:30 You prepare for Mr. Marsden's signature the letters that you have just typed and take them to him. After he has signed them, you get them ready for mailing.

5:00 You clear your desk, tell Mr. Marsden you are leaving (he is working late tonight), and then catch the first bus home.

As you think about the day's work, you are certain of only two things: (1) you did a good day's work, and (2) tomorrow's work schedule will be entirely different!

LESSON 19

Principles

162 Brief Forms Here is another group of nine brief forms for common words.

Present, part, after, advertise, company, wish, immediate, must, opportunity.

▶ Notice that there is no angle between the *k* and the *p* in the brief form *company.*

163 U The sound of u, as in *few*, is represented by  .

Spell: f-u, few

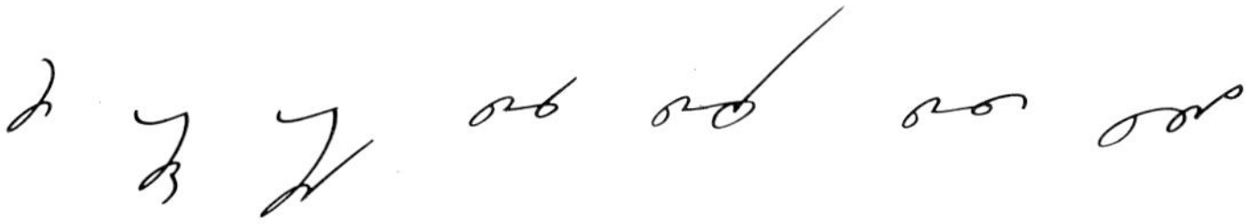

Few, refuse, reviewed, unit, united, unique, acutely.

164 Word Ending -ment The word ending -ment is represented by *m.*

Spell: a-r-a-n-j-ment, arrangement

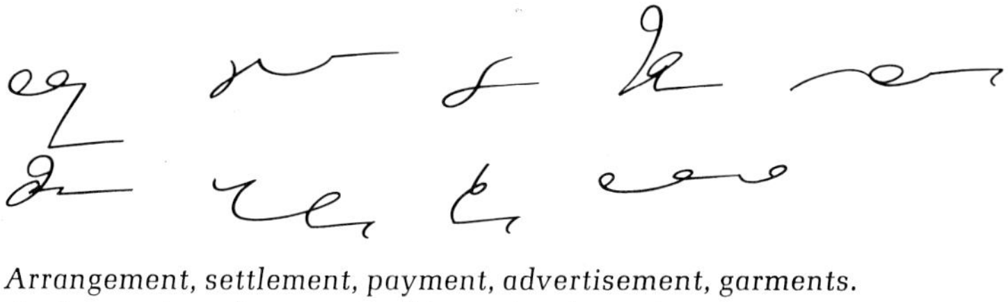

Arrangement, settlement, payment, advertisement, garments.
Assignment, replacements, shipments, elementary.

▶ Notice that in *assignment* the *m* for *-ment* is joined to the *n* with a jog.

Building transcription skills

165 SPELLING

The first impression you get of the letter on page 102 is a good one. It is positioned nicely; the margins are even; the date, inside address, and closing are all in their proper places. If you read the letter casually, you find that it makes good sense and apparently represents what the dictator said.

But if you read it carefully, you will quickly realize that the letter will never be signed; in fact, the dictator will no doubt have something to say to the stenographer who transcribed the letter. Why? It contains several misspelled words.

If you are to succeed as a stenographer or secretary, your letters must not only be an accurate transcript of what the dictator said, but they must also be free of spelling errors. A stenographer or secretary who constantly turns in transcripts with errors in spelling will not be welcome long in a business office!

To make sure that you will be able to spell correctly when you have completed your shorthand course, you will from this point on give special attention to spelling in each Reading Practice.

As you read the Reading Practice, you will occasionally find shorthand outlines printed in color. These outlines represent words that stenographers and secretaries often misspell. When you encounter an outline printed in color, finish reading the sentence in which it occurs; then glance at the margin, where you will find the word in type, properly syllabicated.

Spell the word aloud if possible, pausing slightly after each word division. (The word divisions indicated are those given in *Webster's Seventh New Collegiate Dictionary*.)

166

Business vocabulary builder	
	presentation A talk; a speech.
	taped Recorded on tape.
	tracer A follow-up investigation to locate a missing shipment of merchandise.

Reading practice

167 Brief-Form Letter

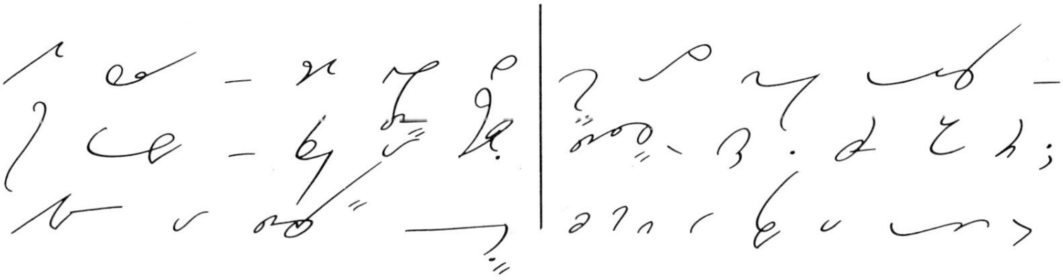

LUNN

LUNN INCORPORATED

245 PARK AVENUE

NEW YORK, NY 10035

CHARLOTTE
COLUMBUS
DENVER
DUBUQUE
ELGIN
FLINT
FT. WAYNE
FT. WORTH
HUNTINGTON
LEXINGTON
MADISON
MEMPHIS
NASHVILLE
NORFOLK
PORTLAND
ST. LOUIS
ST. PAUL
SANTA FE
SAVANNAH
SEATTLE
TEXARKANA
TUCSON
TULSA
WICHITA

September 22, 19--

Mr. John Case
2001 Huron Street
Seattle, Washington 98117

Dear Mr. Case:

It is a comfortible feeling to know that the heating system in your home does not have to depend on the elements. Snow and ice cannot leave you shiverring when you heat with gas. It travels under ground.

The dependability of gas is only one of its many virtues. A gas heat system costs less to instal and less to operate. It needs lots less serviceing, and it lasts longer. It has no odor and makes no filmy deposits that cause extra work.

No wonder more than 400,000 users of other feuls changed to gas last year.

Why not let us show you how easy it is to instal gas heat in your home.

Yours truely,

Thomas A. Frost
Sales Manager

TAF:re

Can you find all the errors in this letter?

fac·ing

mov·ing

sim·ply

re·view

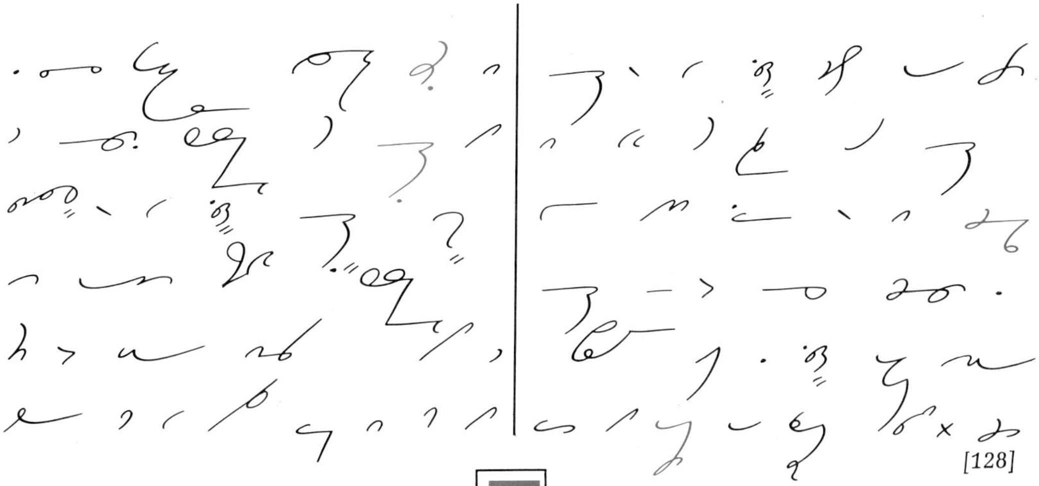

[128]

168

taped

Bu·reau

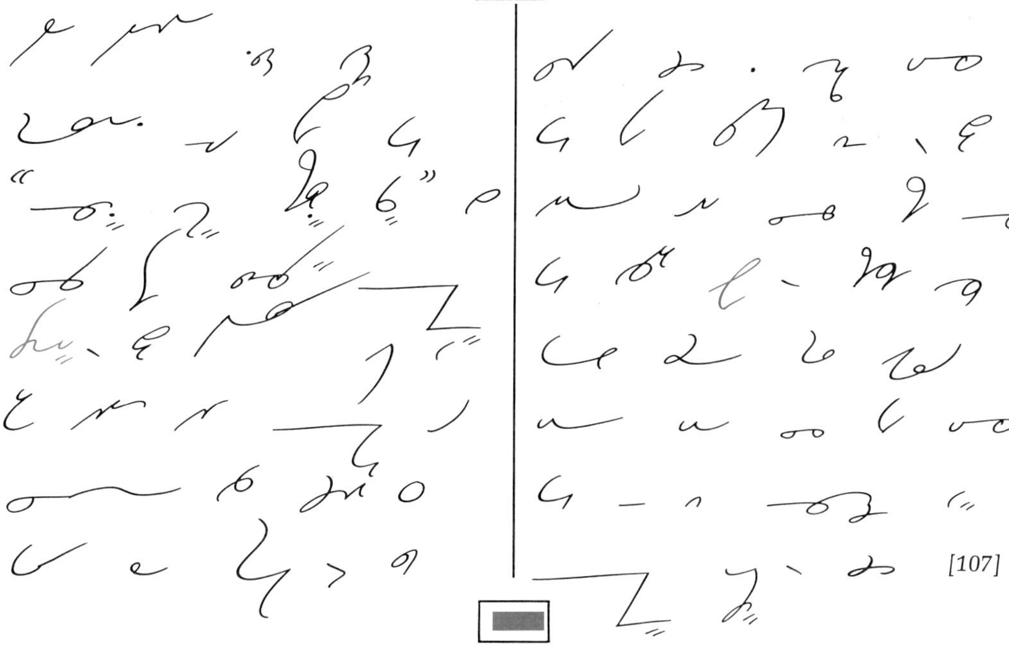

[107]

169

neph·ew

jew·el·ry

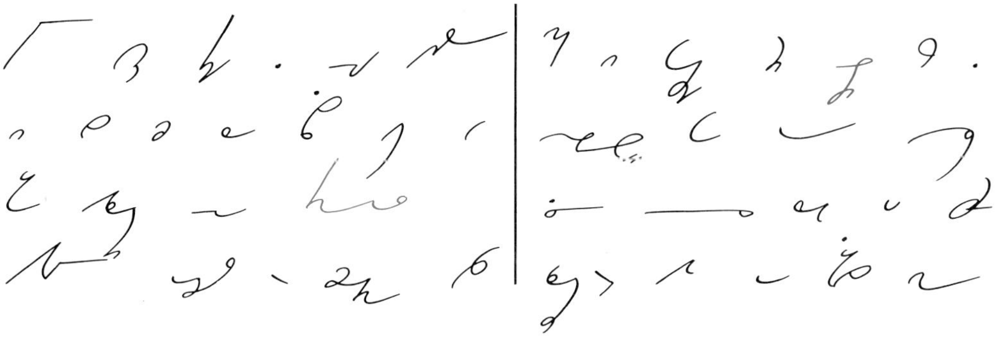

[71]

cat·a·log

170

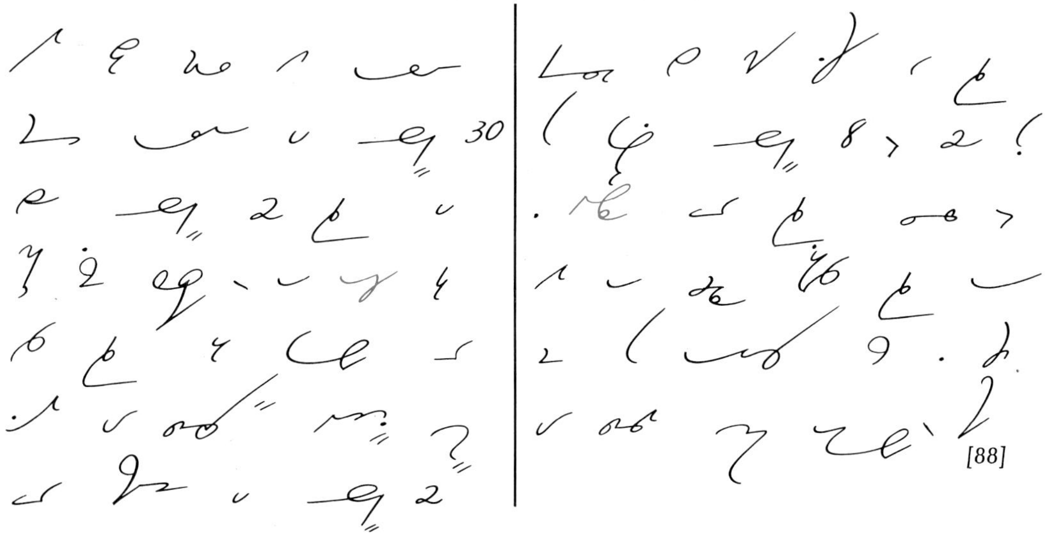

30
[88]

re·ceipt

trac·er

171

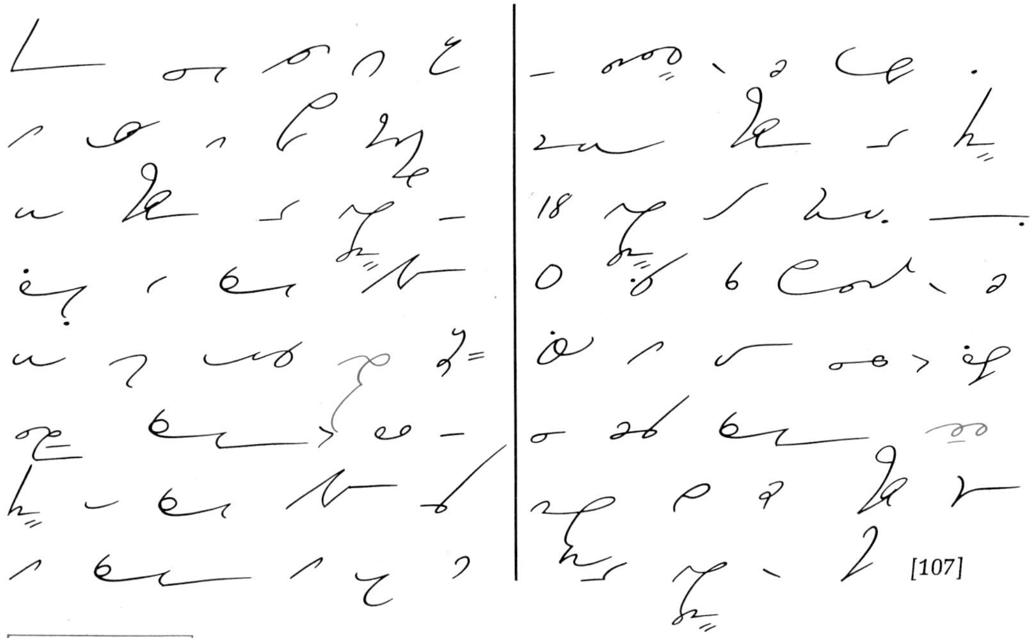

18
0
6
[107]

ca·pa·ble

quick·ly

172

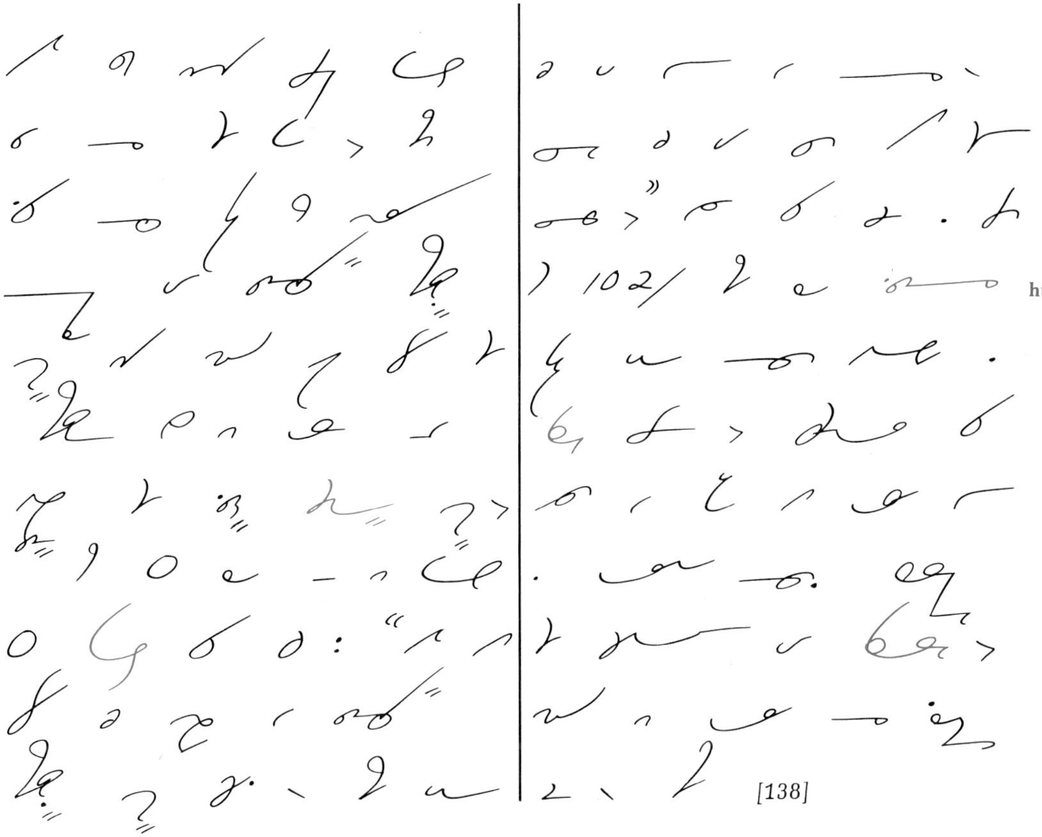

Fu·el

be·lieve

hu·man·ly

par·tial

bal·ance

[138]

TRANSCRIPT OF SHORTHAND CHECK LIST

Are you using the Transcript of Shorthand to best advantage?

☐ You *are* if you refer to it immediately when you cannot read a shorthand outline after you have spelled it.

☐ You *are not* if you spend several minutes trying to decipher an outline and refer to the transcript only as a last resort.

☐ You *are* if you keep your place in the shorthand with your left index finger each time you refer to the transcript.

☐ You *are not* if you must hunt for your place each time you return to the shorthand after referring to the transcript.

LESSON 20

Principles

173 Ow The sound of *ow,* as in *now,* is written  .

Spell: *n-ow, now*

Now, allow, doubt, proud, found, account, ounce, house.

174 Word Ending -ther The word ending *-ther* is represented by *th.*

Spell: *oo-ith, other*

Other, whether, neither, together, mother, either, rather, leather, bothered.

175 Word Beginnings Con-, Com- The word beginnings *con-, com-* are represented by *k.*

Con-

Spell: *con-s-e-r-n, concern*

Concern, confused, consisted, controlled, contract, considerable, connect.

Com-

Spell: *com-p-o-s, compose*

Compose, compare, completely, complain, commerce, committee.

176

Business vocabulary builder	**script** The written text matter of a play or movie or broadcast. **bid** (*noun*) Offer of a price to do something or provide something. **comment** (*verb*) Make a statement about.

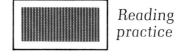

Reading practice

177 **Brief-Form Review Letter**

re·ceive

scripts

wheth·er
pro·ceed

178

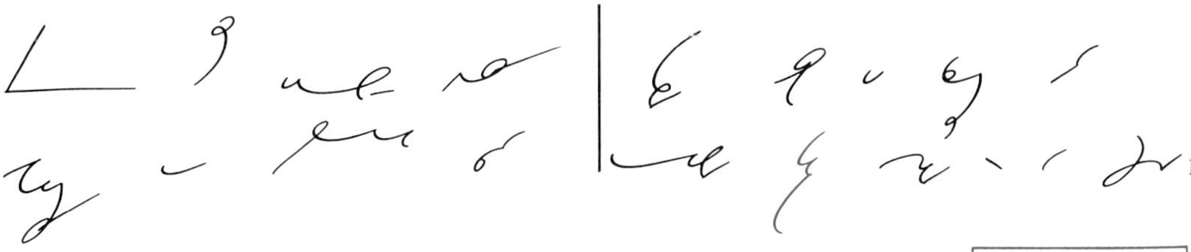

pos·si·ble

re·al·ize
leath·er

write

[110]

179

won't

rea·sons

al·ways

[108]

180

de·ci·sion

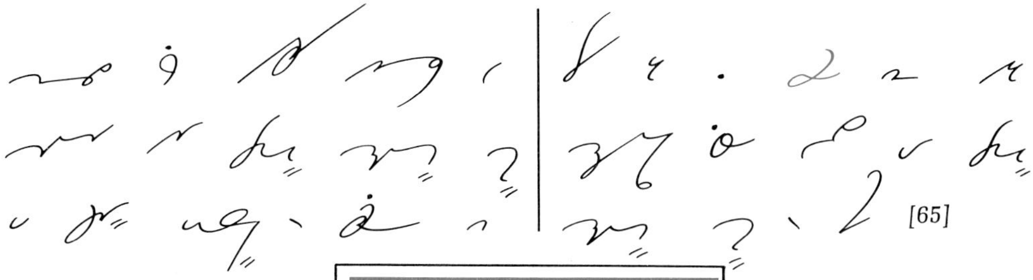

fair

[65]

181

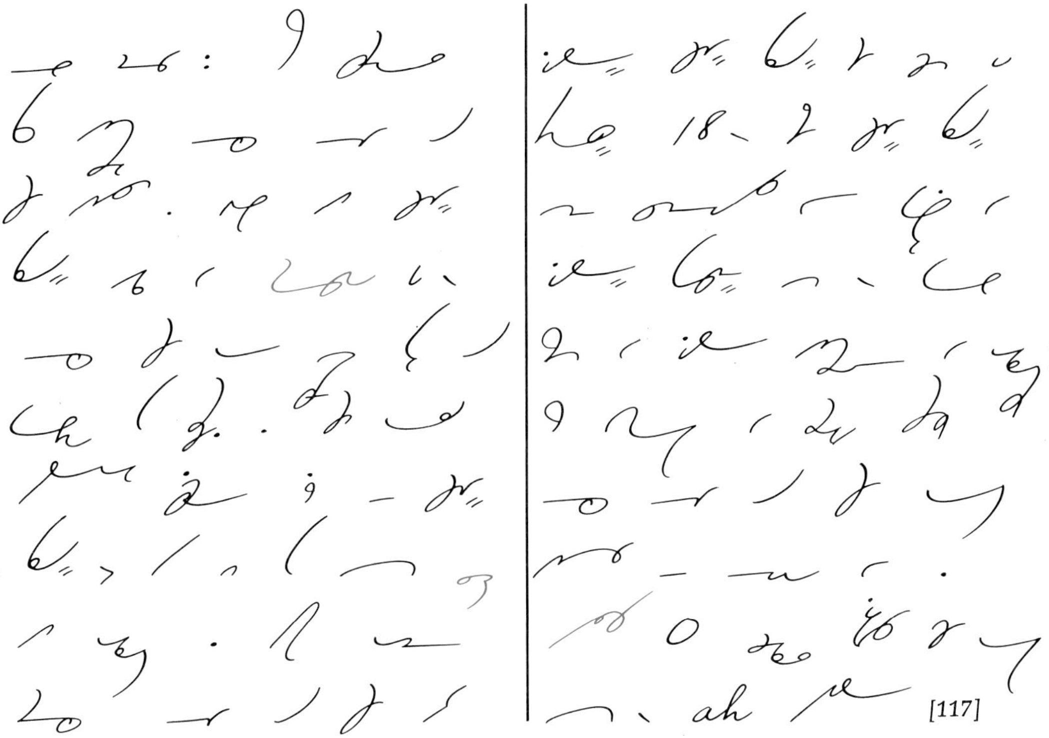

flow·er

enough

de·cade

[117]

182

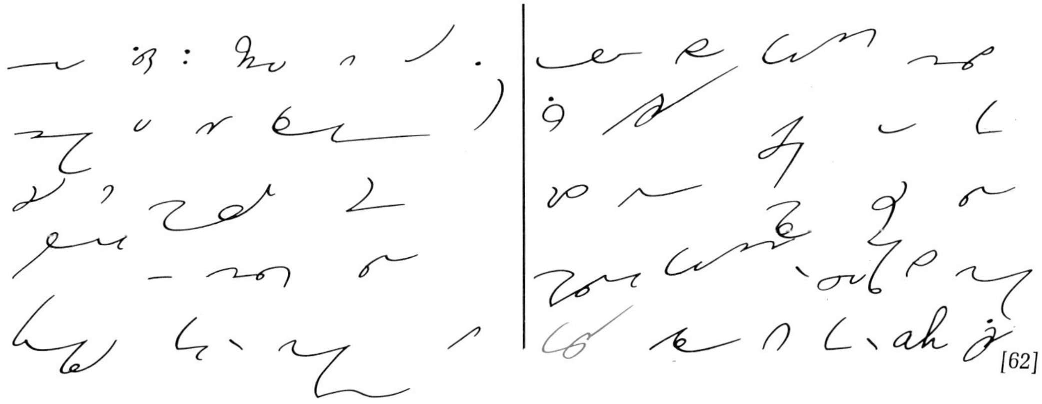

proud

[62]

LESSON 21

Principles

183 Brief Forms

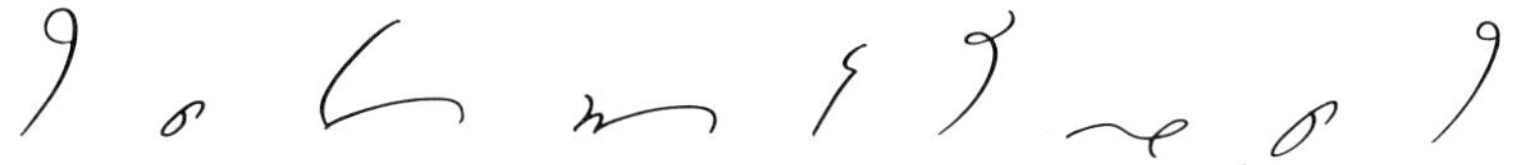

Advantage, use, big, suggest, such, several, correspond-correspondence, how-out, ever-every.

184 Den By rounding off the angle between *d-n,* we obtain the fluent *den* blend.

Den 

Spell: s-oo-den, sudden; den-r, dinner

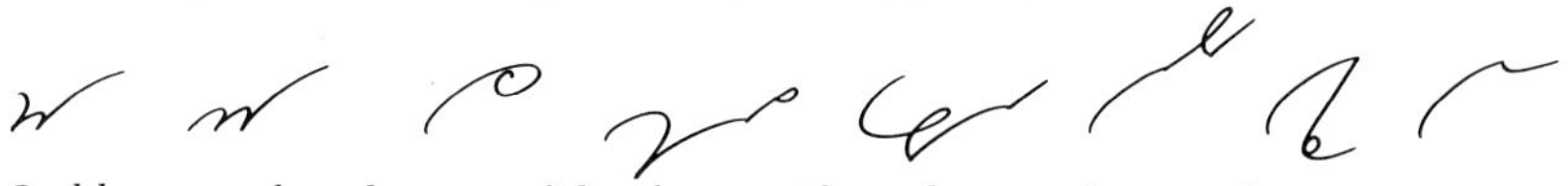

Sudden, wooden, deny, confidently, president, dentist, danger, dinner.

185 Ten The stroke that represents *den* also represents *t-n.*

Spell: a-ten-d, attend; k-o-ten, cotton

Attend, attention, written, sentences, gotten, competent.
Bulletins, cotton, tonight, stands, remittances, assistance.

186 Tain The stroke that represents *d-n, t-n* also represents *tain.*

Spell: o-b-tain, obtain

Obtain, contain, maintain, certain, attain, detain, obtainable, certainly.

187

Business vocabulary builder

accommodate Take care of.

correspondents Those who write or answer letters.

competence Ability.

unique Being the only one of its kind. (It is, therefore, incorrect to say "more unique" or "most unique.")

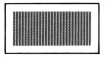

Reading and writing practice

Suggestion: Before you start your work on this Reading and Writing Practice, read the practice procedures for writing shorthand on page 11. By following these writing procedures, you will derive the most benefit from your practice and also complete your assignment in the shortest possible time.

188 Brief-Form Letter

wor·ry

enough

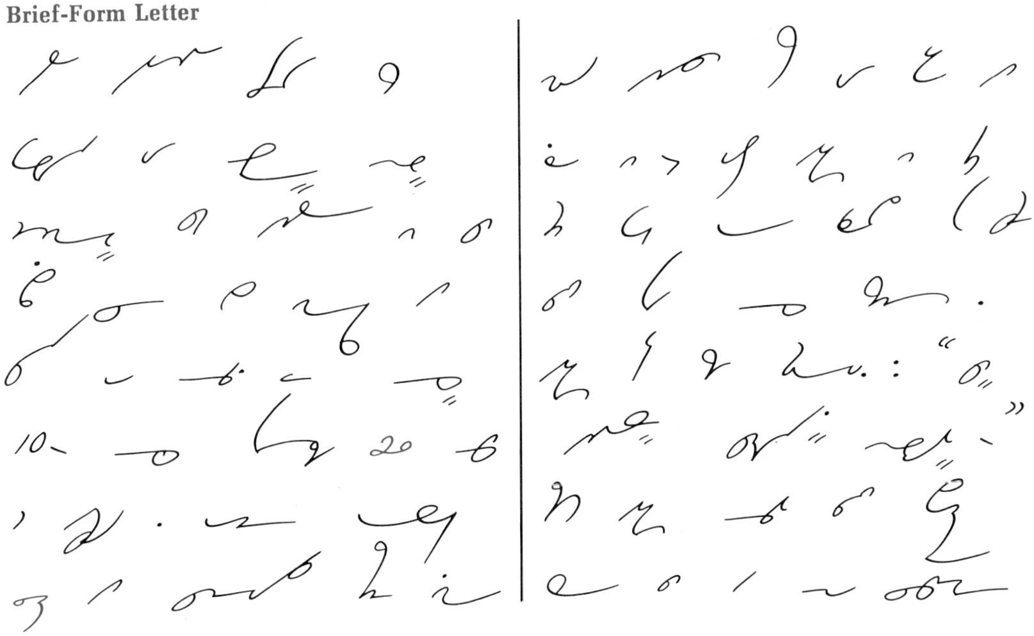

bul·le·tin

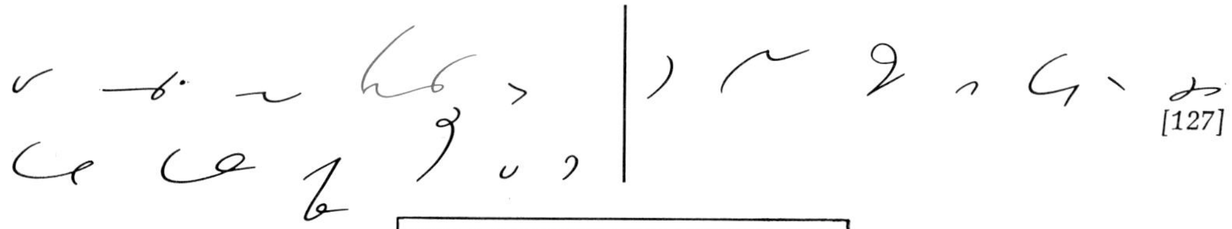

[127]

189

ap·ply·ing

sim·i·lar

of·fer

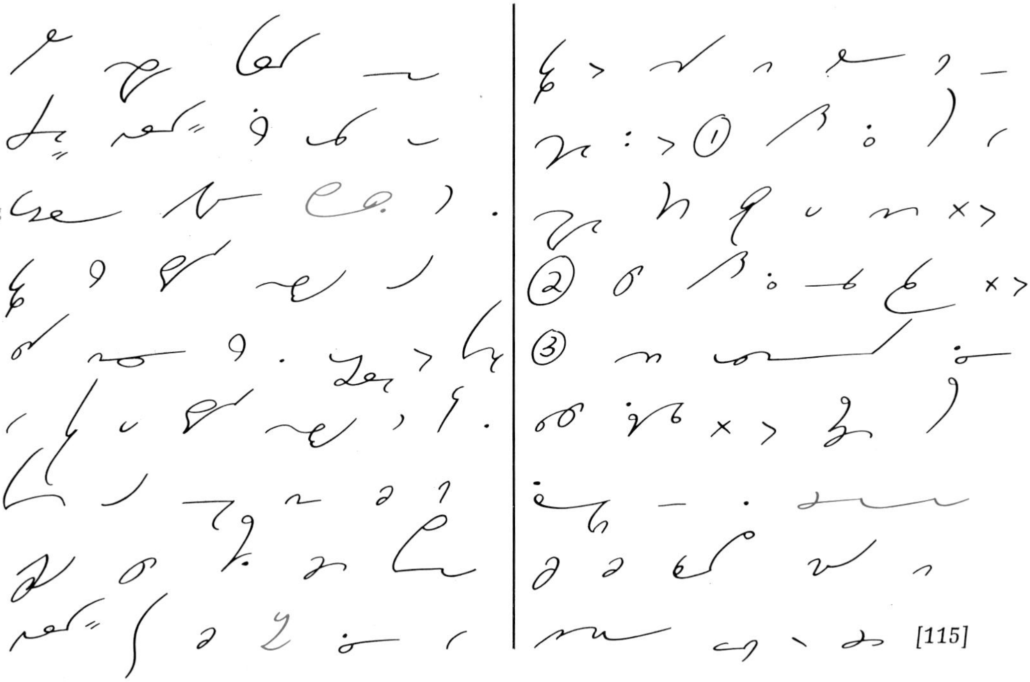

[115]

190

ac·ci·dent

nights

aban·don

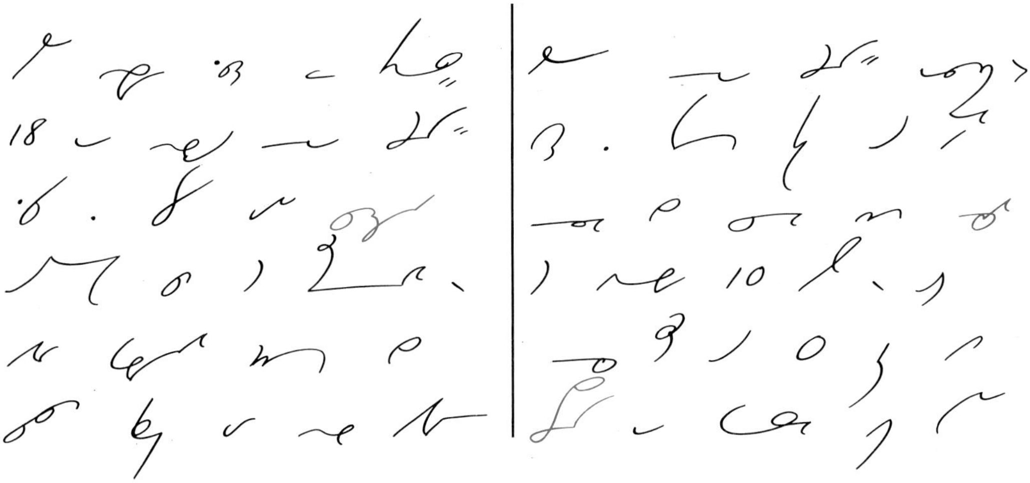

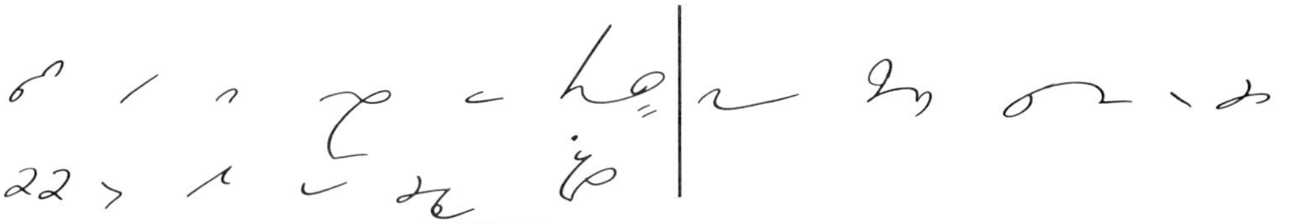

[93]

191

unique

samples

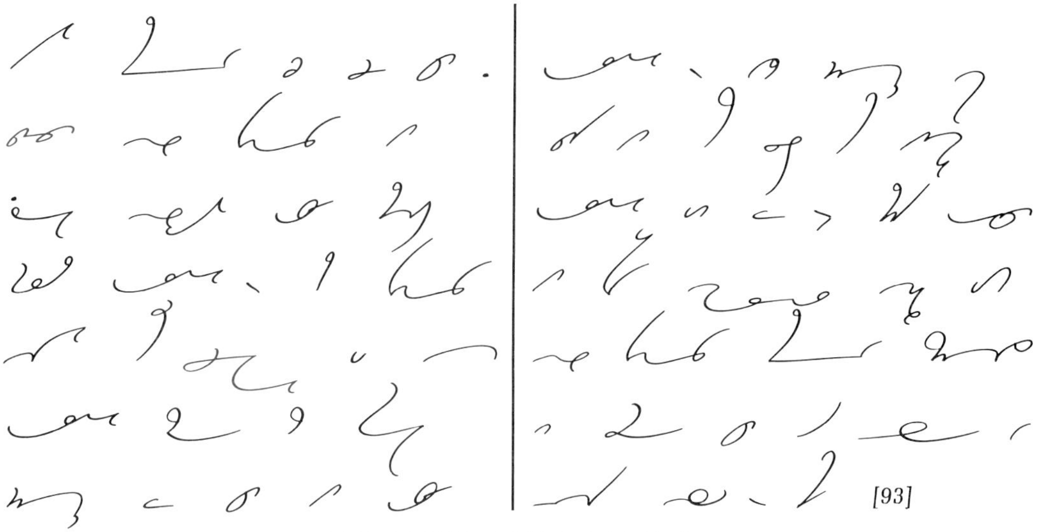

[93]

192

reason

cot·ton

es·caped

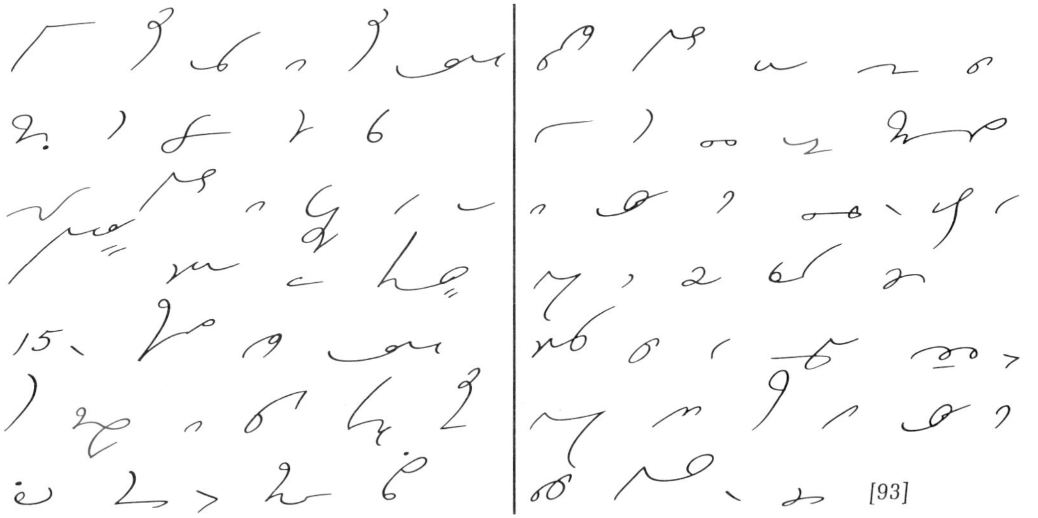

[93]

LESSON 22

Principles

193 **Dem** By rounding off the angle between *d-m,* we obtain the fluent *dem* blend.

Dem 

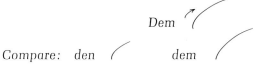

Compare: den  dem 

Spell: dem-a-end, demand; m-e-dem, medium

Demand, demonstrate, condemn, seldom, domestic, damage, medium.

194 **Tem** The stroke that represents *dem* also represents *t-m.*

Spell: tem-p-r, temper

Temper, temporary, attempt, system, item, tomorrow, customers.

195 **Business Abbreviations** Here are additional salutations and closings frequently used in business.

Dear Mr., Dear Mrs., Dear Miss, Yours sincerely, Cordially yours.

196 **Useful Phrases** With the *tem* and *ten* blends, we form these useful phrases.

To me, to know, to make.

197 Days of the Week

Sunday, Monday, Tuesday, Wednesday, Thursday, Friday, Saturday.

198 Months of the Year You are already familiar with the outlines for several of the months, as they are written in full.

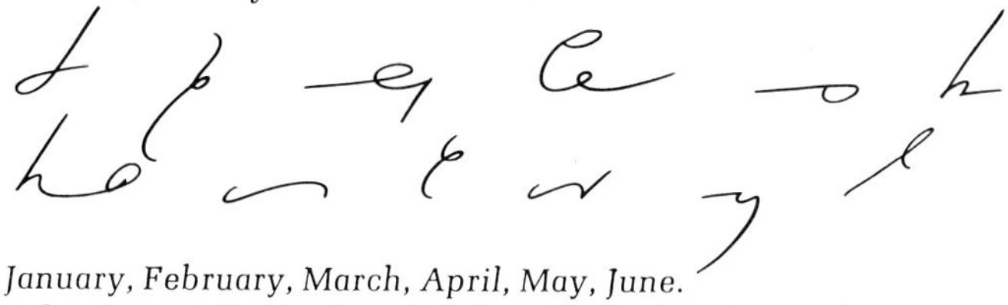

January, February, March, April, May, June.
July, August, September, October, November, December.

Building transcription skills

199

Business vocabulary builder	
	contemplate Intend to; consider doing.
	snuffs out Puts out; extinguishes.
	estimate *(noun)* An approximate calculation.

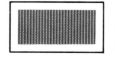

Reading and writing practice

200 Brief-Form Review Letter

growth

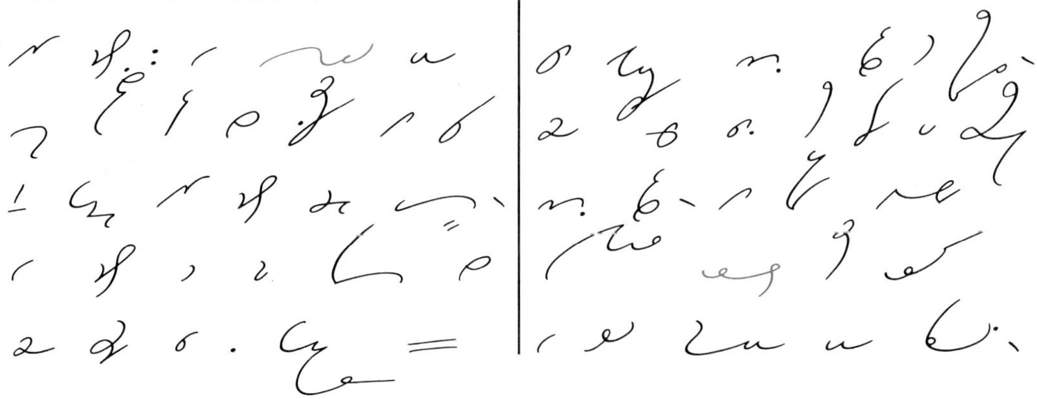

re·lief

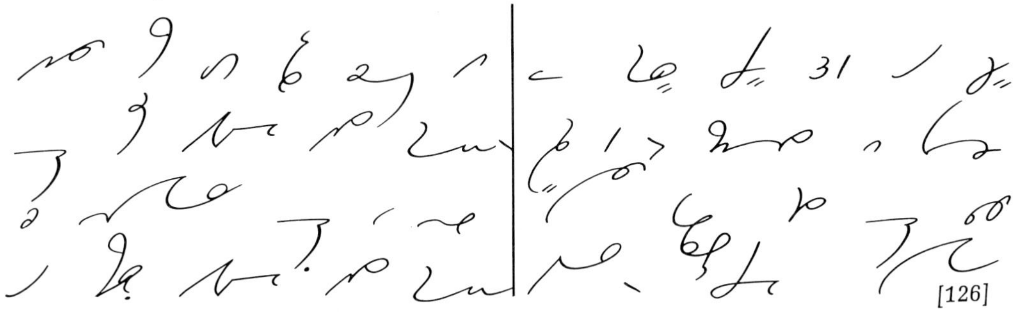

[126]

201

dan·ger

put·ting

like·ly

re·leas·es
stream

[137]

202

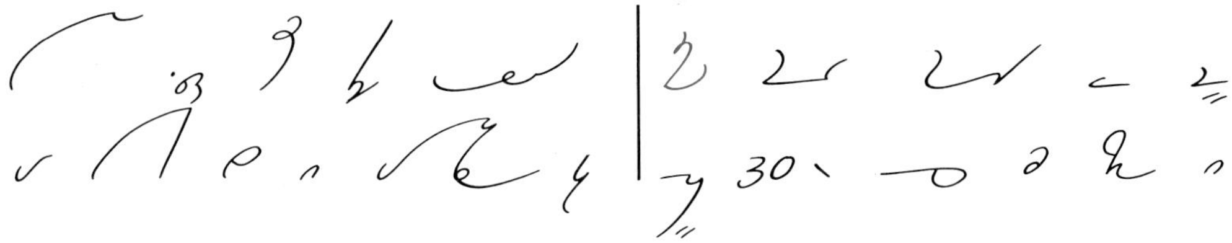

suf·fered

ours

spare

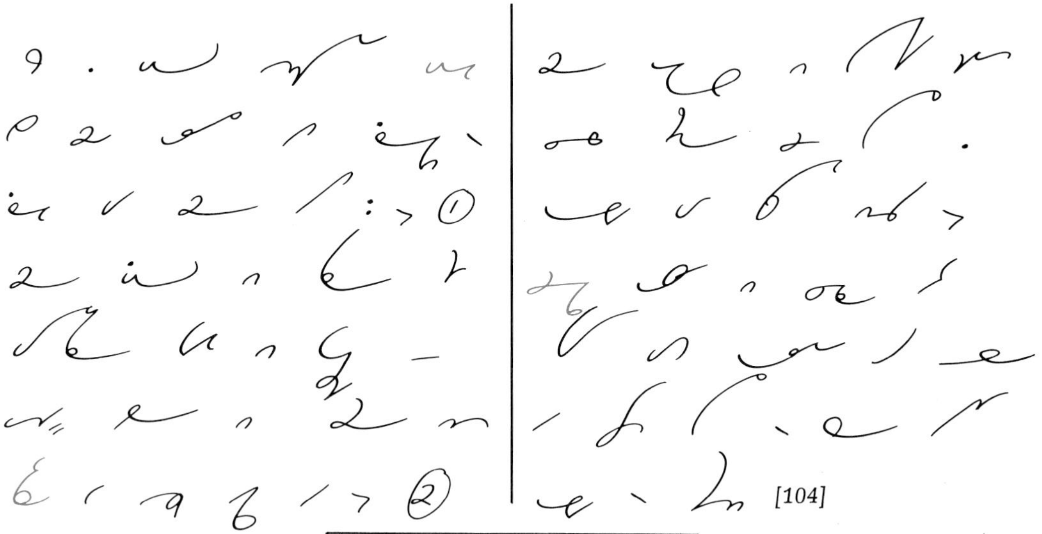

sim·ply

[104]

203

Feb·ru·ary

ans·wer

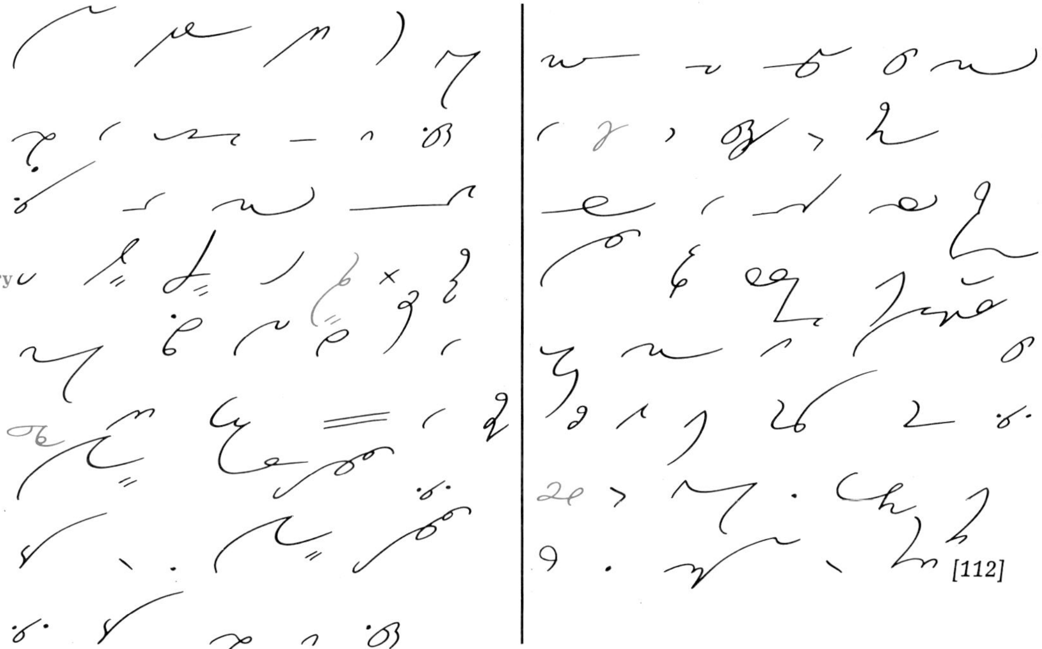

weath·er

wor·ries

[112]

204

bought

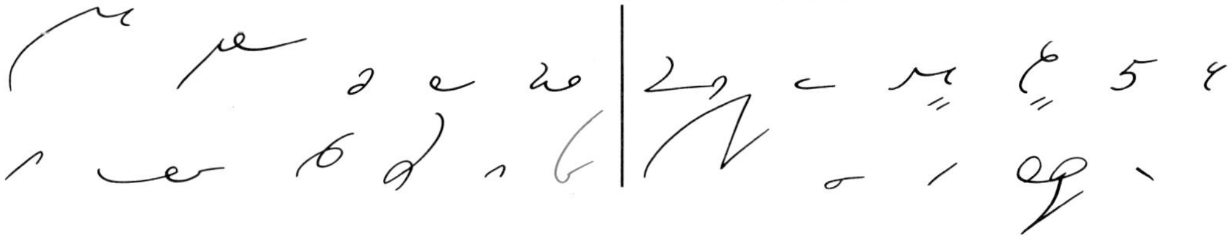

shelves

shipped

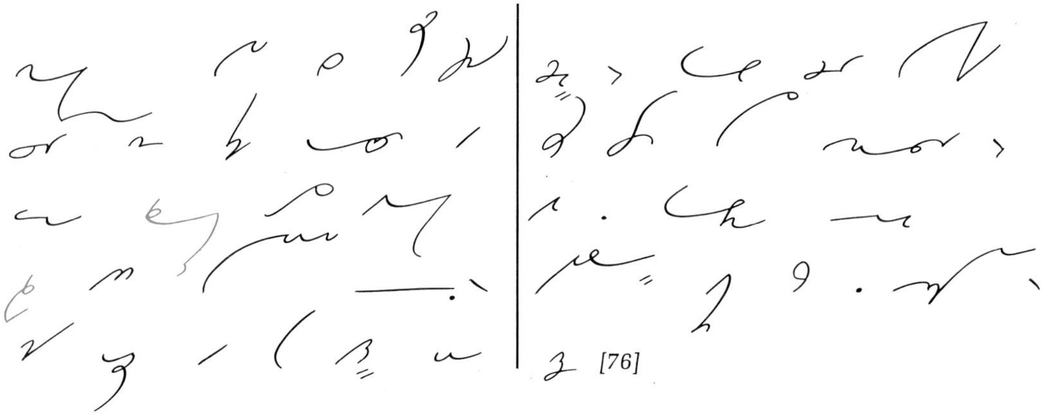
[76]

BRIEF-FORM CHECK LIST

Are you making good use of the brief-form chart that appears on the inside back cover of your textbook? Remember, the brief forms represent many of the commonest words in the language; and the better you know them, the more rapid progress you will make in developing your shorthand speed.

Are you—

☐ **1** Spending a few minutes reading from the chart each day?

☐ **2** Timing yourself and trying to cut a few seconds off your reading time with each reading?

☐ **3** Reading the brief forms in a different order each time—from left to right, from right to left, from top to bottom, from bottom to top?

LESSON 23

Principles

205 Brief Forms After this group, you have only five more groups to learn.

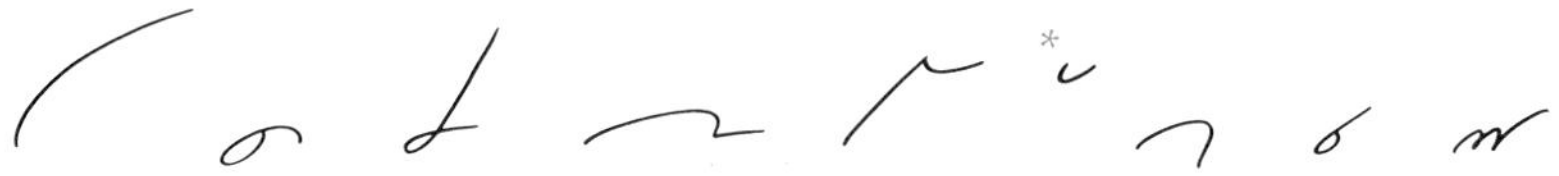

Time, acknowledge, general, gone, during, over, question, yet, worth.

*The outline for *over* is written above the following character. It is also used as a prefix form, as in:

Overdo, overcame, oversee, overdraw, overtake.

206 Def, Dif By rounding off the angle between *d-f*, we obtain the fluent *def, dif* blend.

Def, Dif 

Spell: *def-n-e-t, definite*

Definite, defied, defeat, defined, different, differences.

207 Div, Dev The stroke that represents *def, dif* also represents *div* and *dev.*

Spell: *div-ī-d, divide*

Divide, division, dividend, devoted, devised, developed.

208 **U represented by OO** The *oo* hook is often used to represent the sound of *u*, as in *new*.

Spell: *n-oo, new*

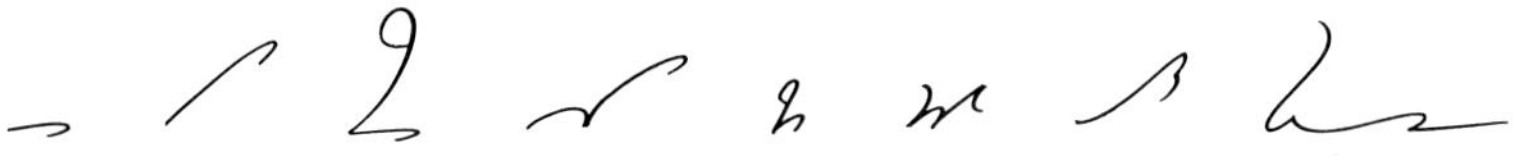

New, due, avenue, continue, issue, suits, induce, volume.

Building transcription skills

209 **SIMILAR-WORDS DRILL | to, too, two**

to (*preposition*) In the direction of. (*To* is also used as the sign of the infinitive.)

I should like to talk to you about this matter.

too Also; more than enough.

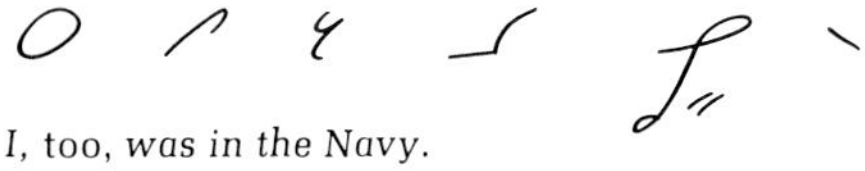

I, too, was in the Navy.

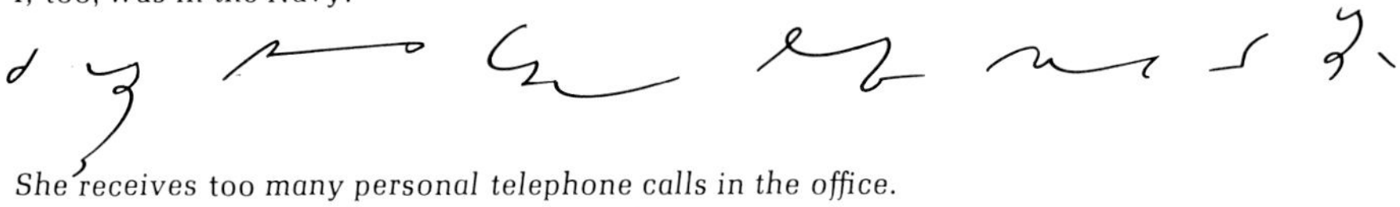

She receives too many personal telephone calls in the office.

two One plus one.

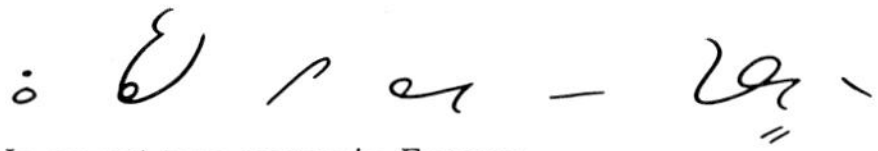

He spent two years in France.

The word in this group on which stenographers often stumble is *too*—they carelessly transcribe *to*. Don't you make that mistake.

210

Business vocabulary builder

overhead Business expenses such as rent, heat, and taxes.

tentative Not final.

defer Put off; delay.

sales volume The amount of sales made to customers.

Reading and writing practice

211 Brief-Form Letter

pol·i·cies

raised

over·head

cat·a·log

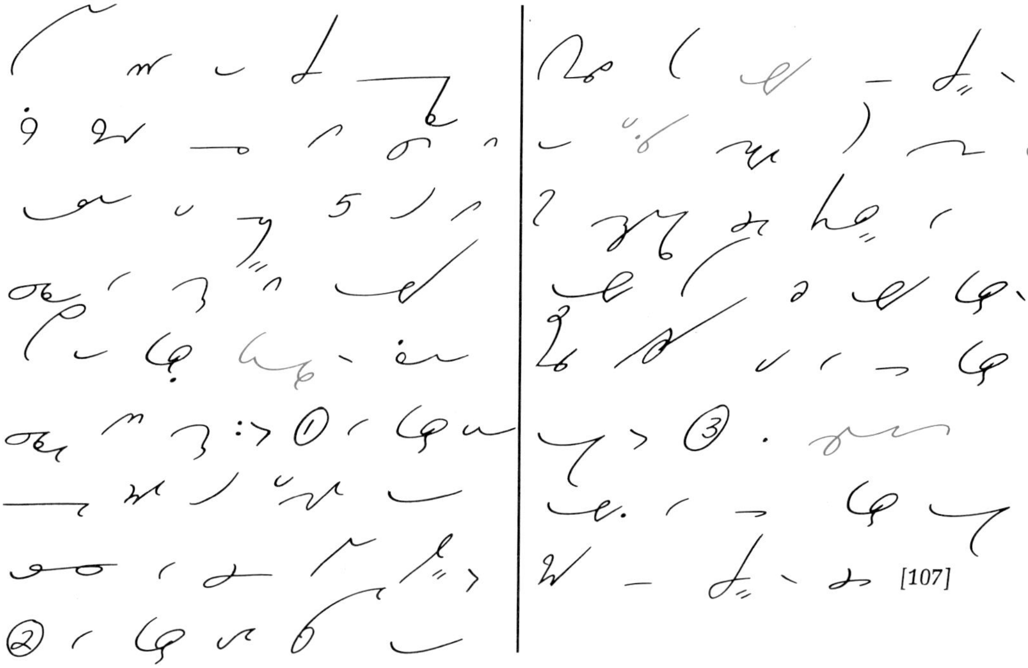

212

re·ceipt

vol·ume

de·vised

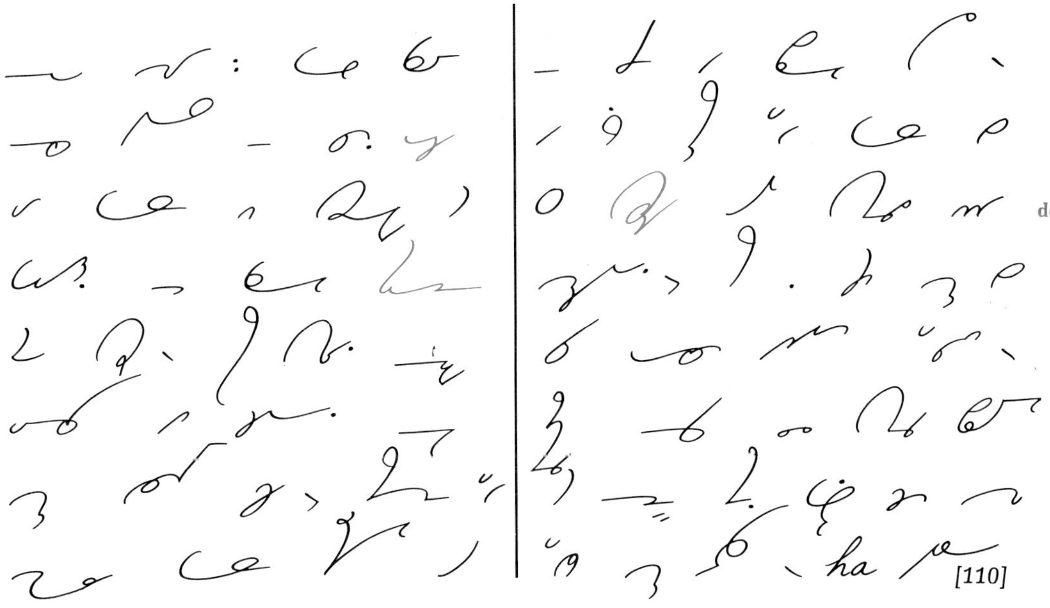

213

week

Re·duc·ing

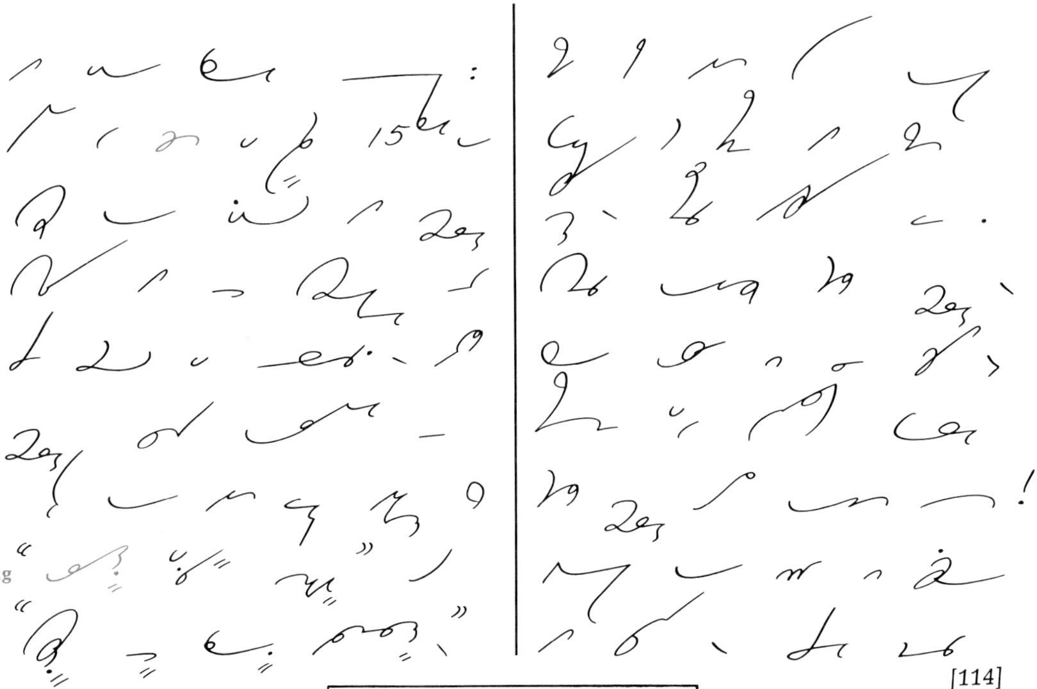

[114]

214

over·due

lose

de·fer

le·gal

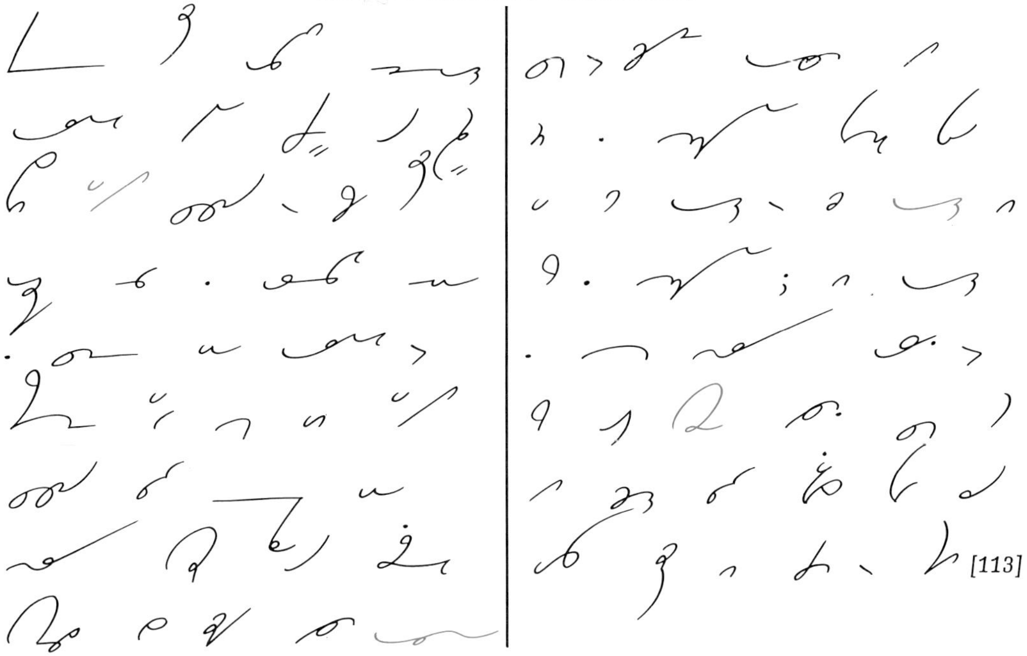

[113]

215

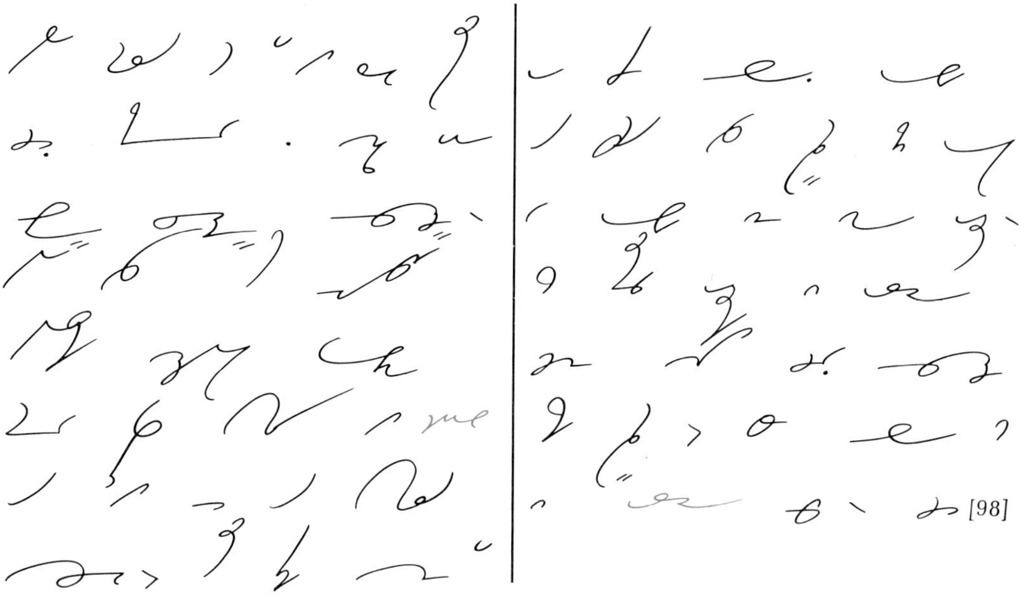

stor·ies

[98] re·new·al

216

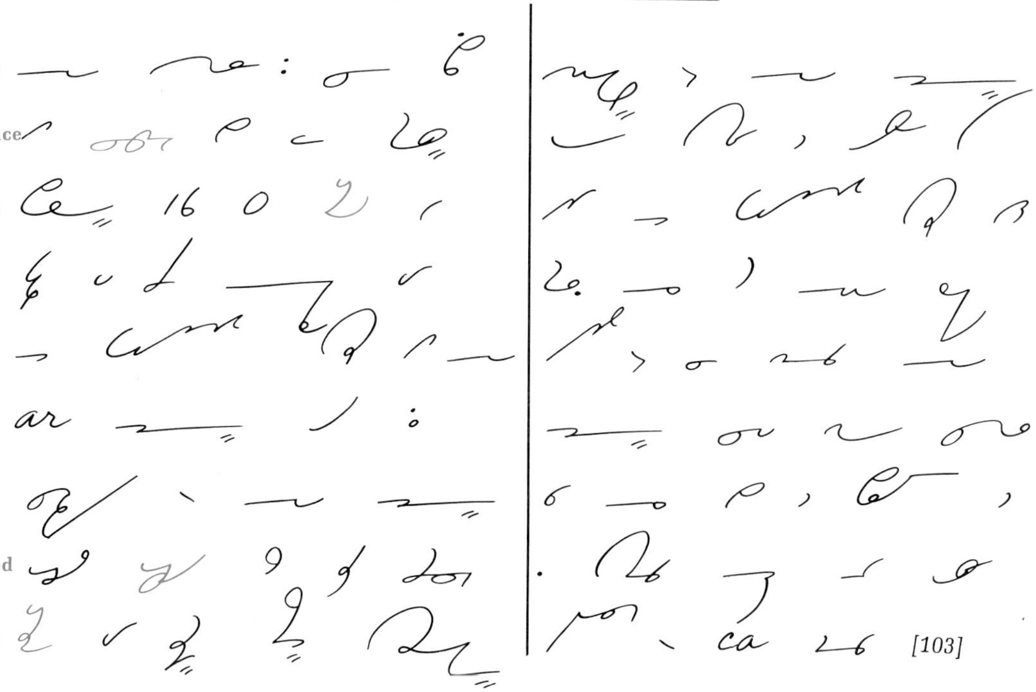

an·nounce

of·fered

re·signed

of·fi·cer

[103]

LESSON 24

Recall

In Lesson 24 you will have no new shorthand devices to learn; you will have a little time to "digest" the devices that you have studied in previous lessons.

217 Recall Chart This chart contains all the brief forms in Chapter 4 and one or more illustrations of all the shorthand devices you have studied in Chapters 1 through 4.

The chart contains 84 words. Can you read the entire chart in 7 minutes or less?

WORDS

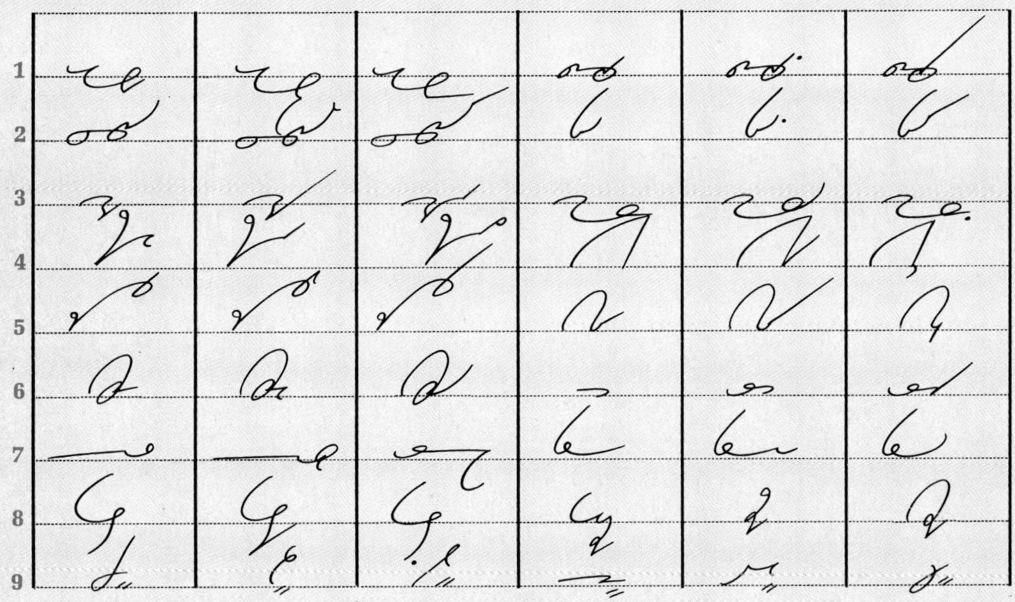

BRIEF FORMS AND PHRASES

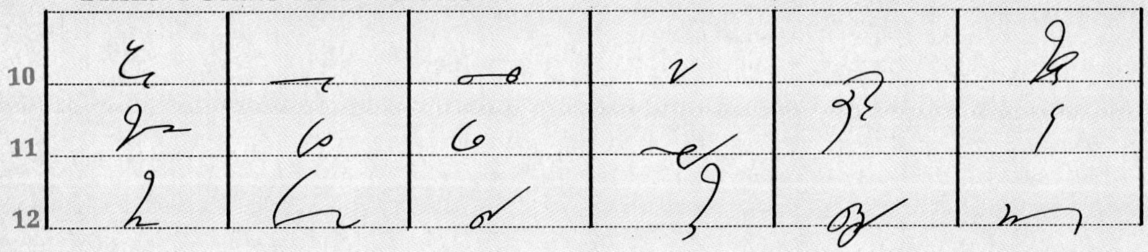

13
14

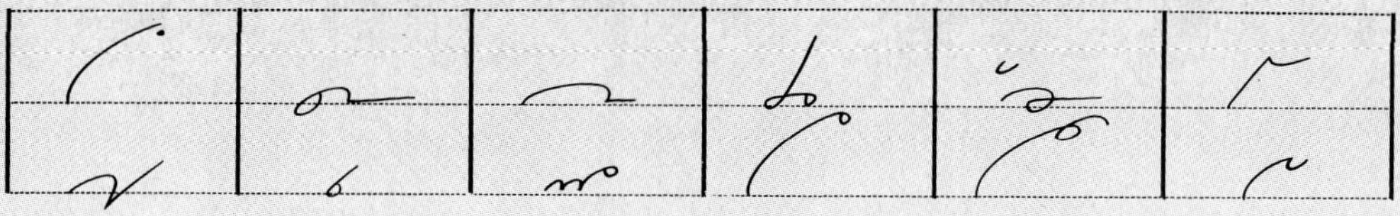

Building transcription skills

218

Business vocabulary builder	**prominent** Readily noticeable; important. **participation** Act of taking an active part in anything. **comprehend** Understand. **skim** Read quickly without concern for details.

Reading and writing practice

219 A Race With the Clock

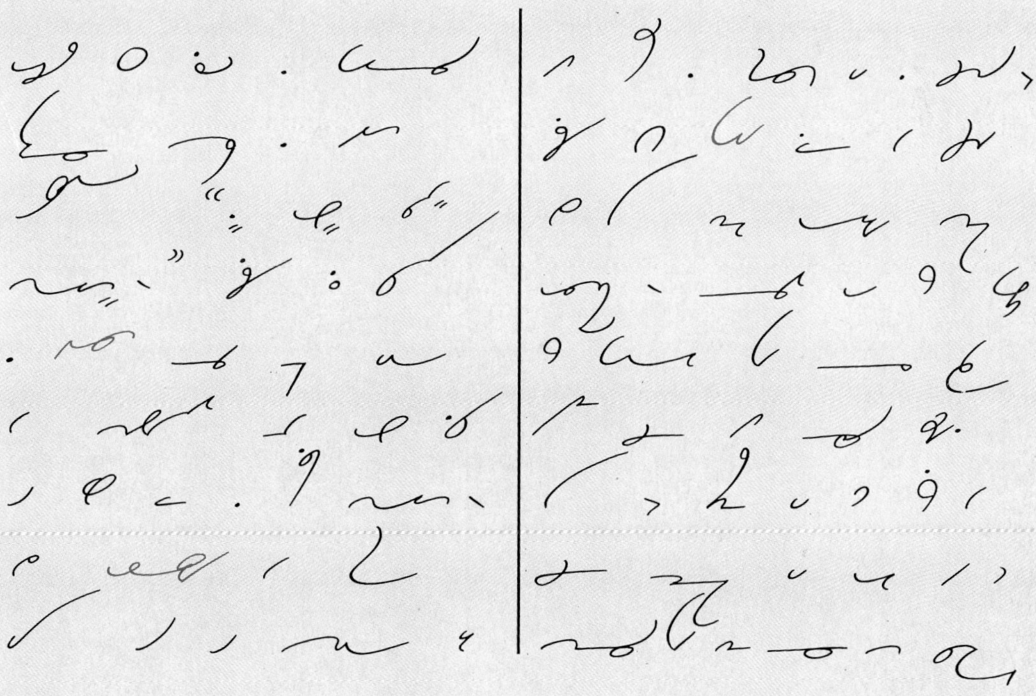

brought

track

re·al·ized

neigh·bor

los·er

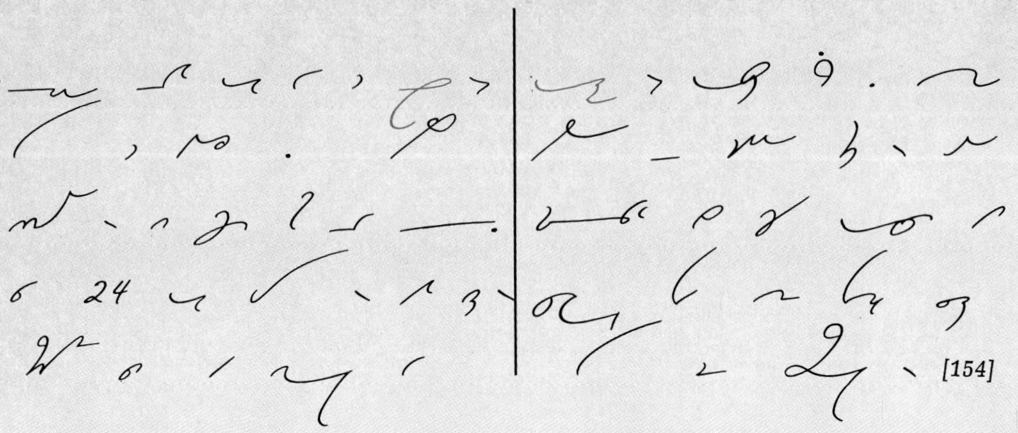

[154]

220 Check Your Study Habits

re·cite

study·ing

through

graphs

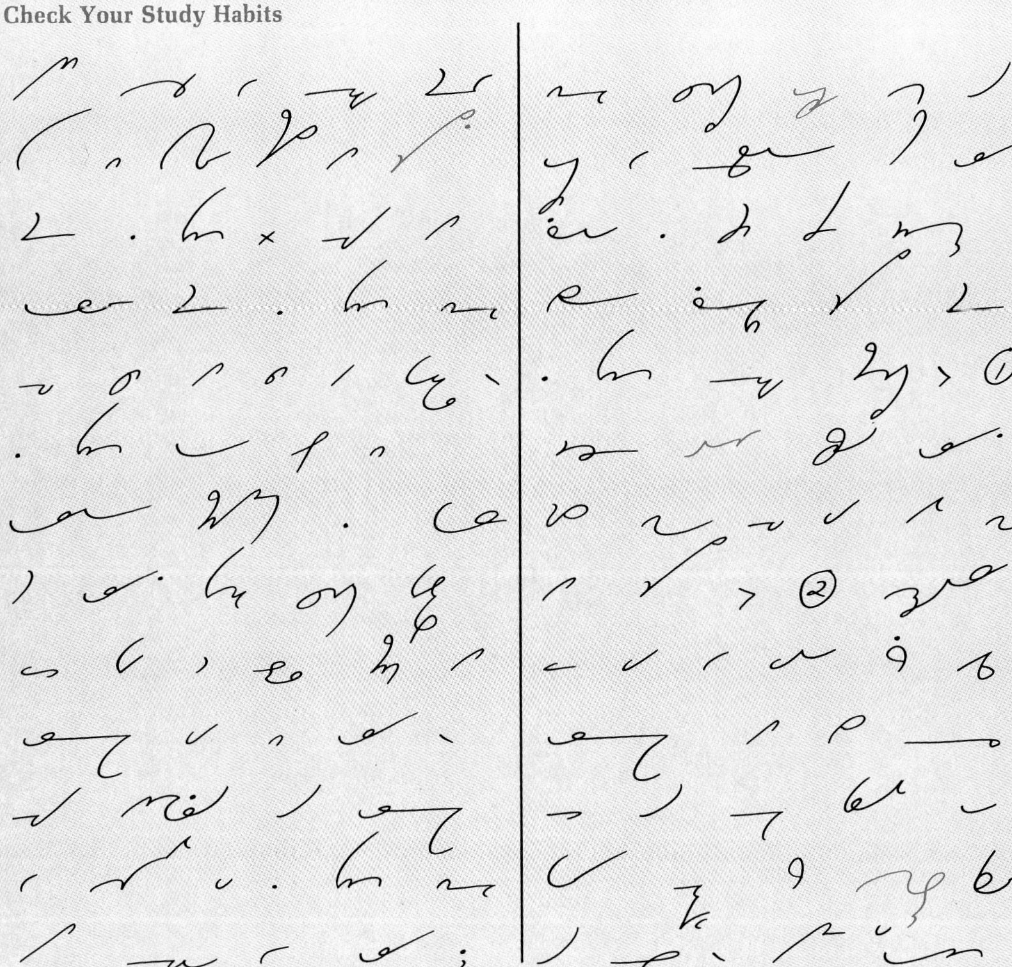

brief

ses·sions

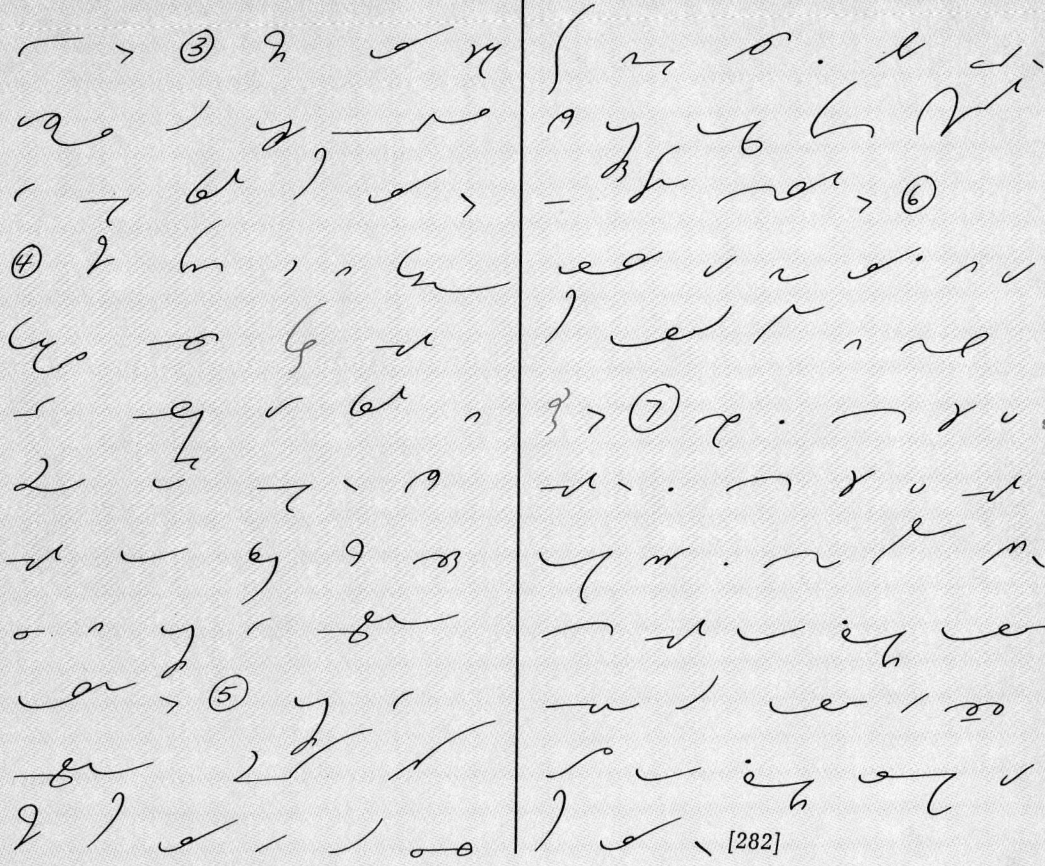

[282]

221 Life or Death

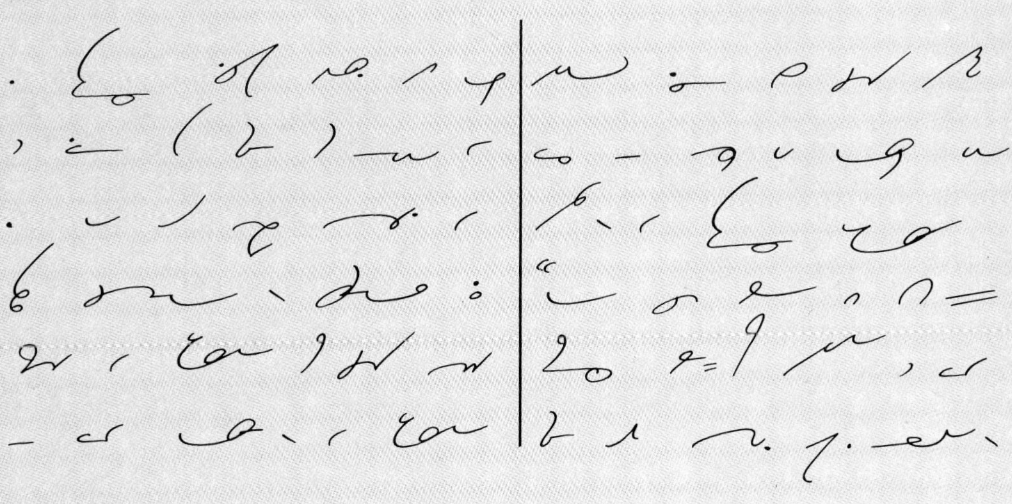

[69]

Chapter 5

The secretary takes dictation

A very important part of every executive's job is communications. Each day he must dictate letters to customers, memorandums to salesmen or other executives, and reports to the board of directors. The secretary who can take his dictation comfortably, without constantly interrupting him because he is dictating too fast, and who can transcribe rapidly and accurately is worth her weight in gold!

An efficient secretary quickly learns her boss's dictating habits so that executive and secretary can work together as a team. Some dictators know exactly what they want to say, and their secretaries must constantly use every ounce of skill to keep pace with them. Others think in spurts, that is,

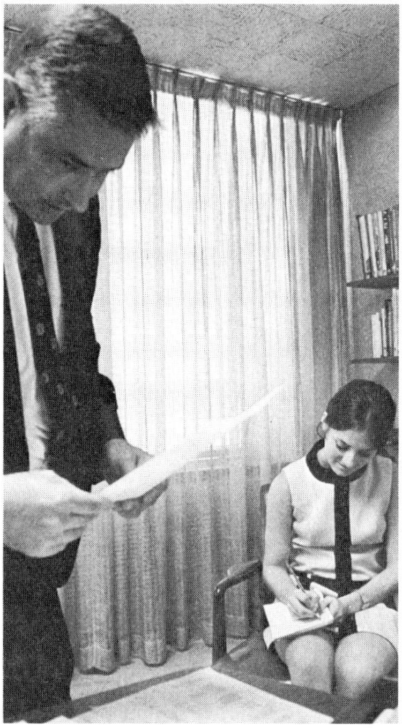

there will often be long pauses between thoughts. Then when an idea has been framed in their minds, they are off at a fast clip for a minute or more. Then for a moment or so—nothing. Still other dictators are more deliberate. They think slowly, especially on difficult letters, and may change their minds many times during the dictation of a letter. Even so, their secretaries must be prepared for sudden bursts of speed when the dictators' ideas jell and they know what they want to say. No two executives dictate alike, and the secretary must be prepared for all types.

The good secretary has a reserve speed for any emergency. This reserve speed enables her to write for long periods of time without fatigue. It enables her to write legible notes that are easy to transcribe. It enables her to cope with the occasional spurts in her employer's dictation.

The more rapidly you can write, the easier will be your task of taking and transcribing dictation. It will pay you, therefore, to build up your speed to the highest point possible.

LESSON 25

Principles

222 Brief Forms

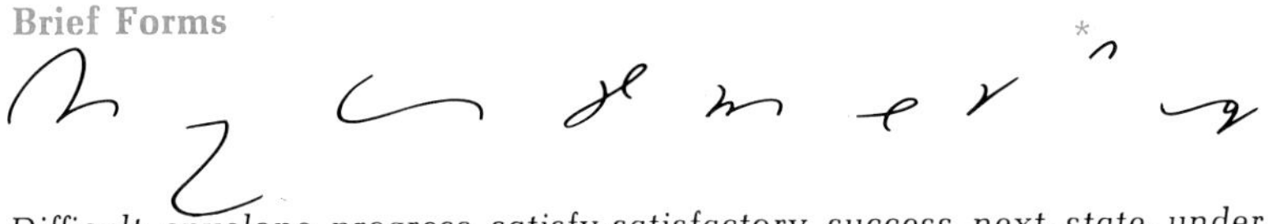

Difficult, envelope, progress, satisfy-satisfactory, success, next, state, under, request.

*The outline for *under* is written above the following shorthand character. It is also used as a prefix form, as in:

Underneath, undergo, understudy, underpay, undertake, underground.

223 Cities and States In your work as a stenographer and secretary, you will frequently have occasion to write geographical expressions. Here are a few important cities and states.

Cities

New York, Chicago, Boston, Philadelphia, Los Angeles, St. Louis.

States

Michigan, Illinois, Massachusetts, Pennsylvania, Missouri, California.

224 Useful Business Phrases The following phrases are used so frequently in business that special forms have been provided for them. Study these phrases as you would study brief forms.

Of course, as soon as, as soon as possible, to do, I hope, we hope, let us, to us, your order.

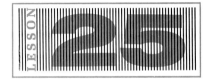

225

Business vocabulary builder

statement Summary of a financial account showing the balance due.

preserve Keep or save.

manila envelope Envelope made of a strong brown paper.

Reading and writing practice

226 **Brief-Form Letter**

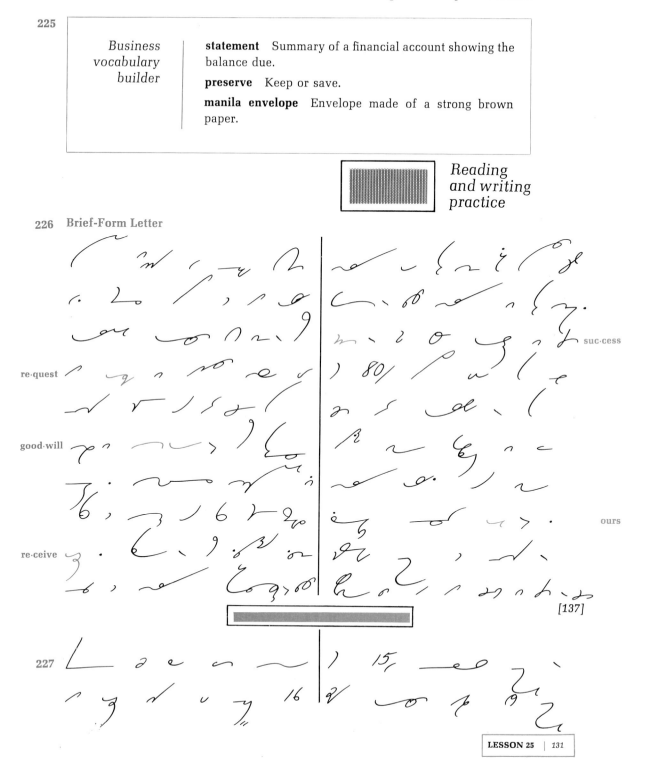

re·quest

good·will

re·ceive

suc·cess

ours

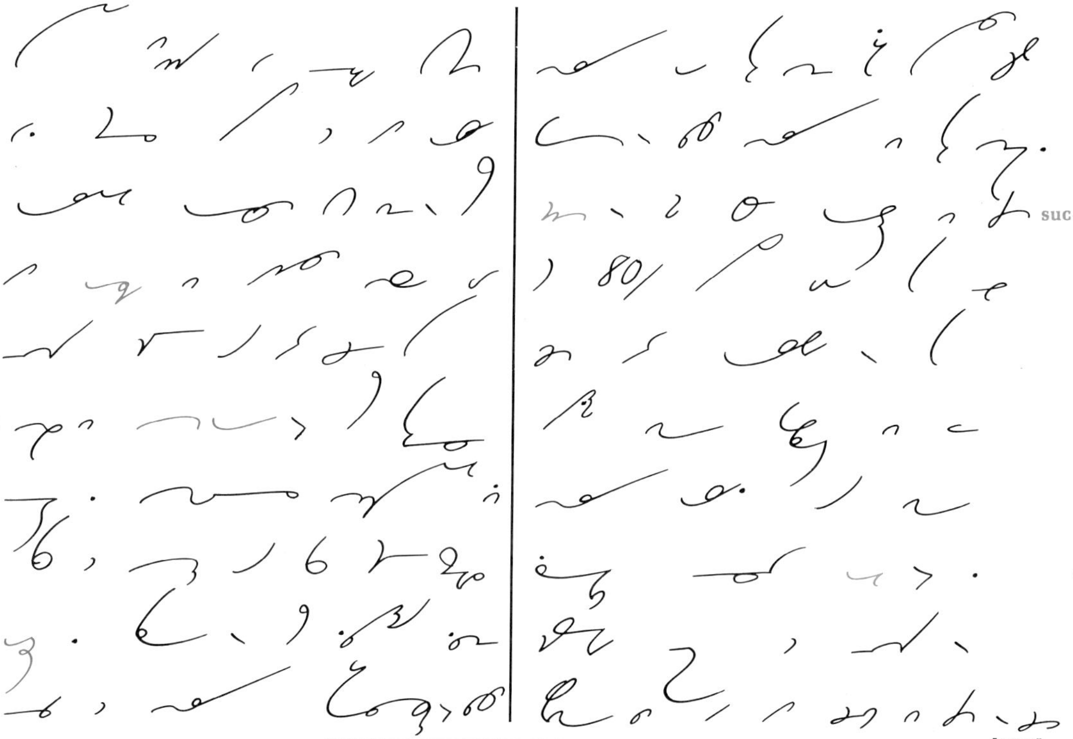

[137]

227

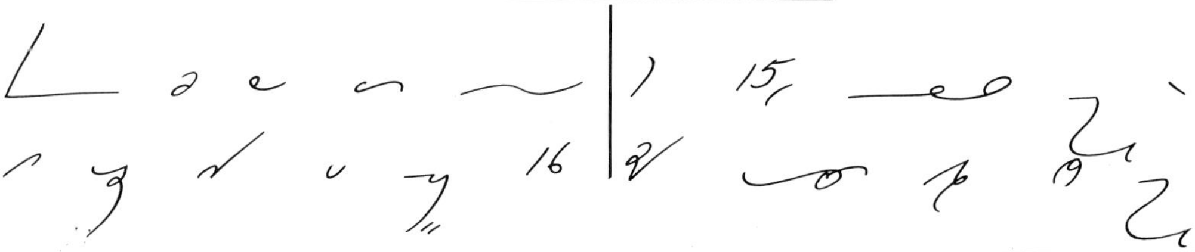

won't

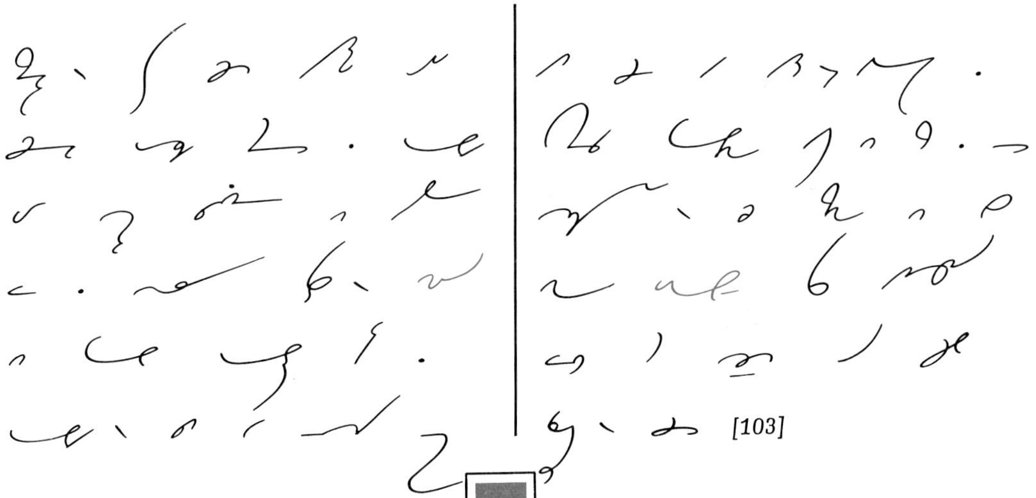

al·ways

[103]

228

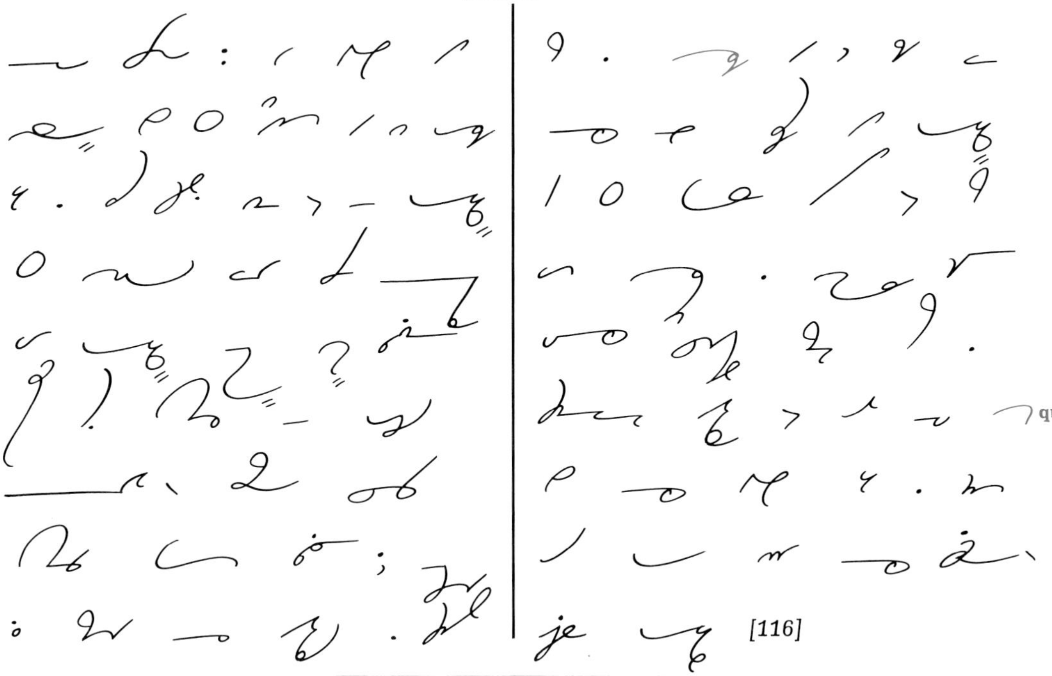

guest

ques·tion

[116]

229

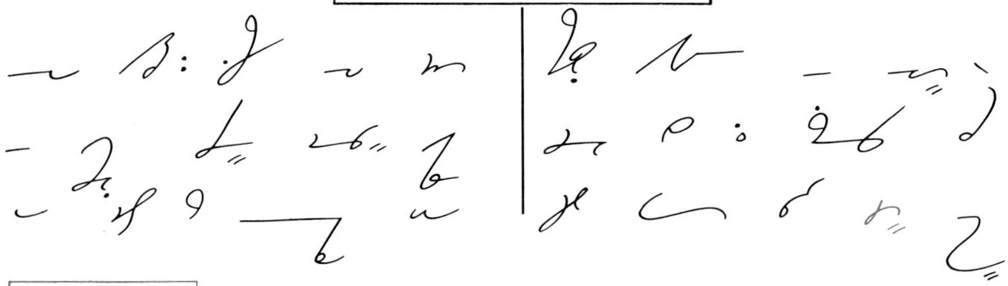

Chi·ca·go

source

[86]

230

con·fess

sug·gest

[114]

231

16

shipped

[80]

LESSON 26

Principles

232 Long I and a Following Vowel Any vowel following long *i* is represented by a small circle within a large circle.

Compare: *quite*  *quiet* 

Spell: *s-īah-n-s, science*

Science, trial, prior, drier, client, reliance, compliance.

233 Ia, Ea The sounds of *ia*, as in *piano*, and *ea*, as in *create*, are represented by a large circle with a dot placed within it.

Spell: *a-r-eah, area*

Area, created, appropriate, appreciate, piano, initiate, brilliantly.

234 Word Beginnings In-, Un-, En- The word beginnings *in-*, *un-*, *en-* are represented by *n* before a consonant.

Spell: *in-k-r-e-s, increase; un-f-a-r, unfair; en-j-oi, enjoy*

In-

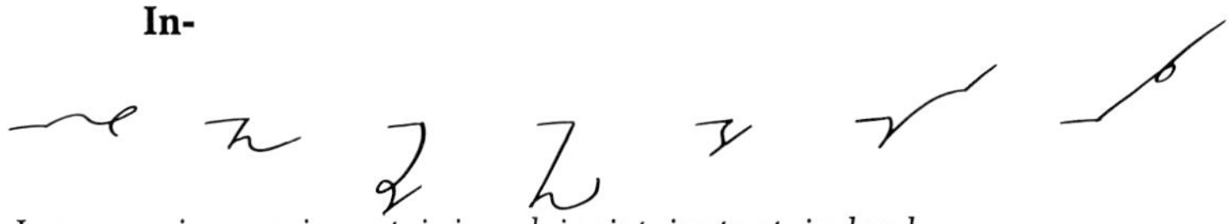

Increase, insure, invest, injured, insist, instant, indeed.

Un-

Unfair, unpaid, uncertain, unfilled, until, unless, undo.

En-

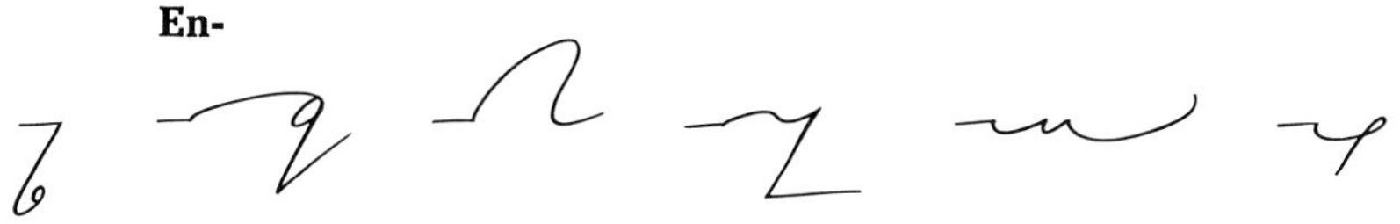

Enjoy, engaged, endeavor, encouragement, enrolled, enrich.

Building transcription skills

235

Business vocabulary builder	
	home appliances Items for the home, such as refrigerators, stoves, dryers, and washing machines.
	prior Earlier in time; coming ahead.
	associates (*noun*) Fellow workers; partners.
	appropriate (*adjective*) Proper; fitting.

Reading and writing practice

236 Brief-Form Review Letter

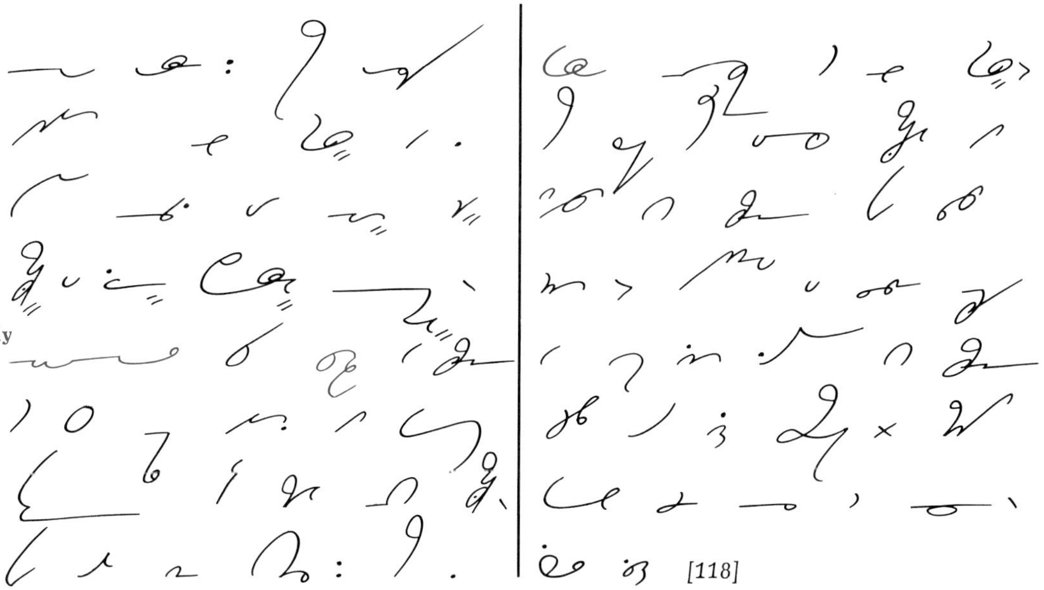

pri·or

nor·mal·ly
ac·cept

[118]

237

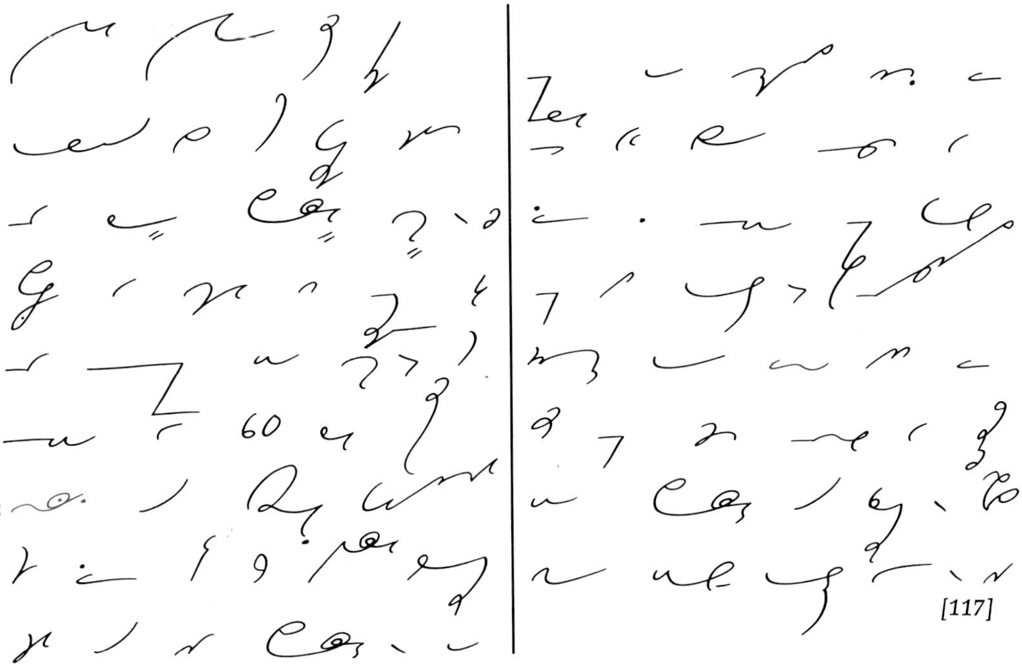

oc·cur

cre·at·ing

[117]

238

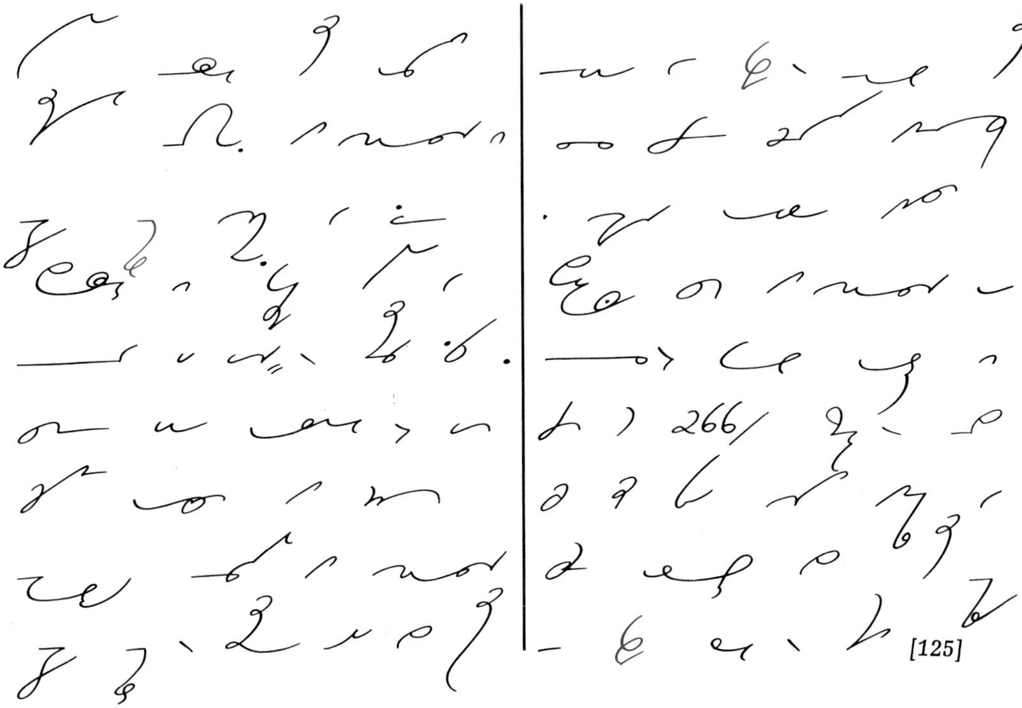

pa·tient

in·voice

past

[125]

239 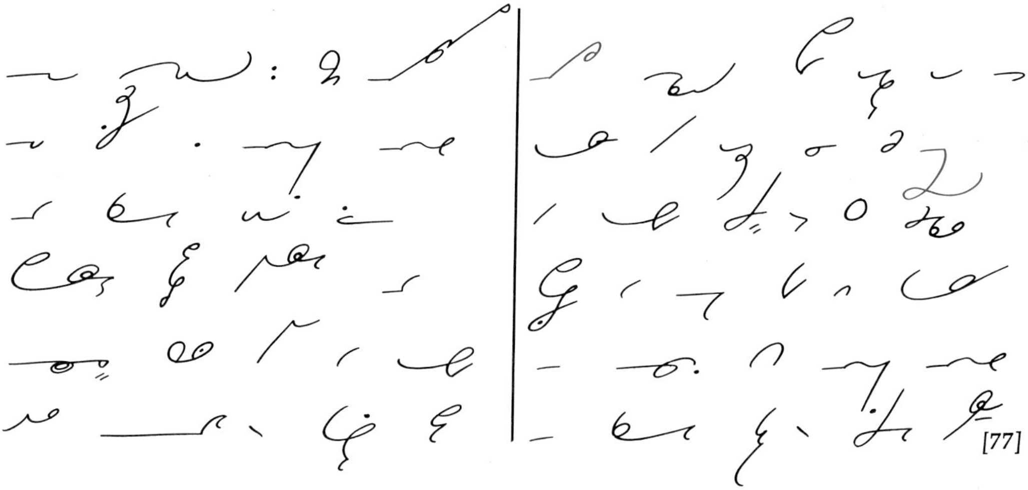

un·du·ly

un·veiled

[77]

240 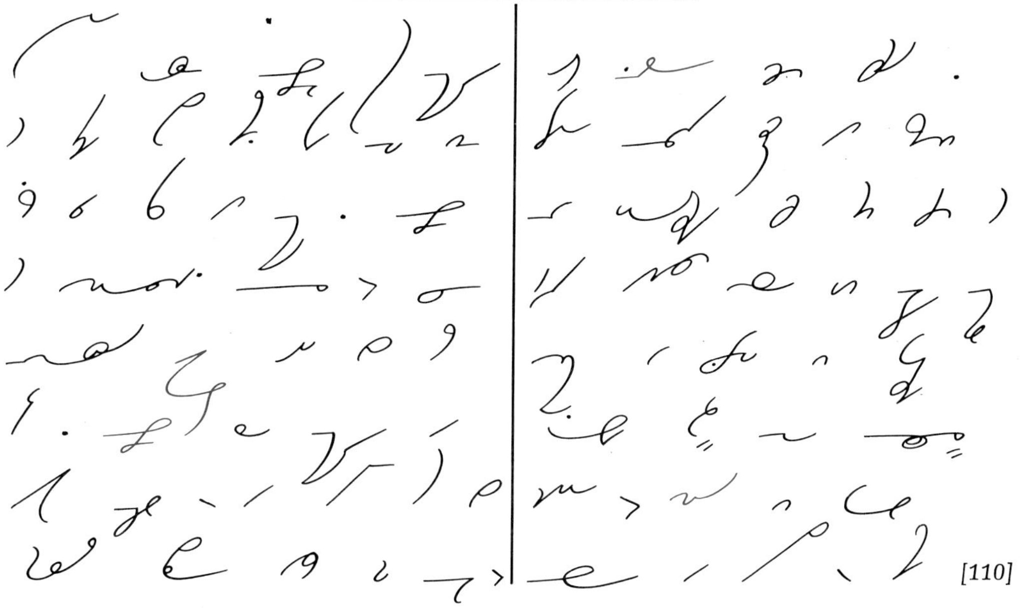

un·til

be·lieve

ma·chine

won't

[110]

241 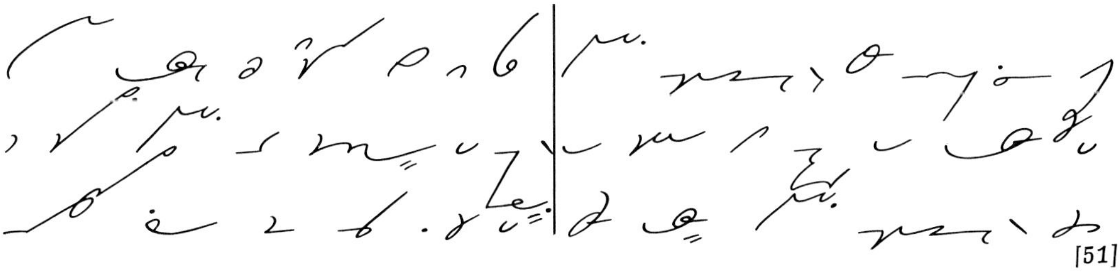

[51]

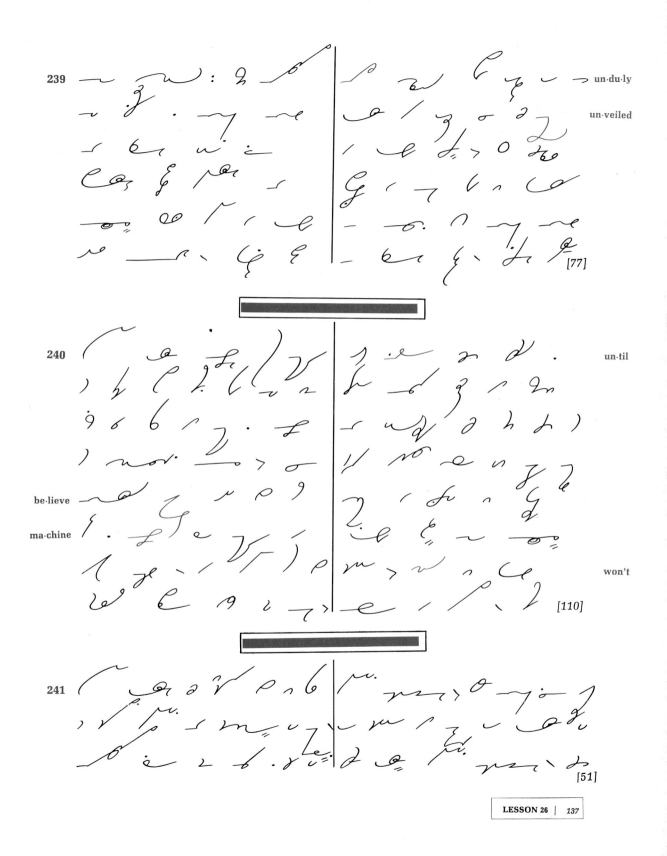

LESSON 27

Principles

242 Brief Forms After you have learned the following brief forms, you have only three more groups to go!

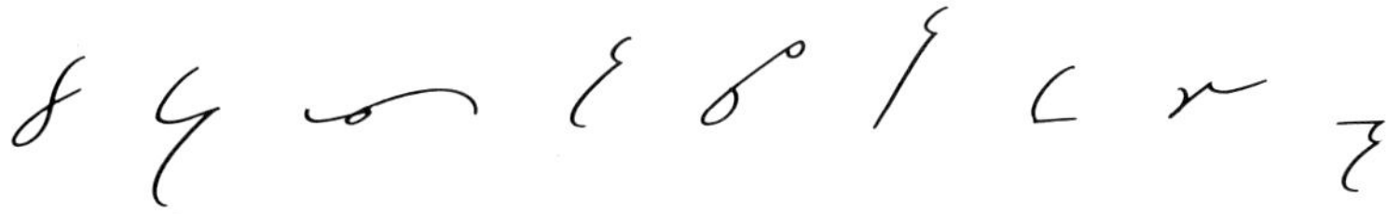

Particular, probable, regular, speak, idea, subject, upon, street, newspaper.

243 Ng The sound of *ng* is written .

Compare: *seen* *sing*

Spell: s-e-ing, sing; s-a-ing, sang

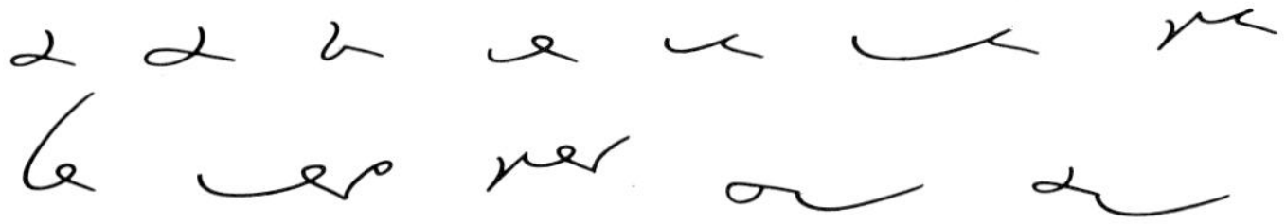

Sing, sang, song, ring, wrong, long, strong.
Bring, lengthy, strength, angle, single.

244 Ngk The sound of *ngk* (spelled *nk*) is written .

Compare: *seem* *sink*

Spell: r-a-ink, rank; oo-ink-l, uncle

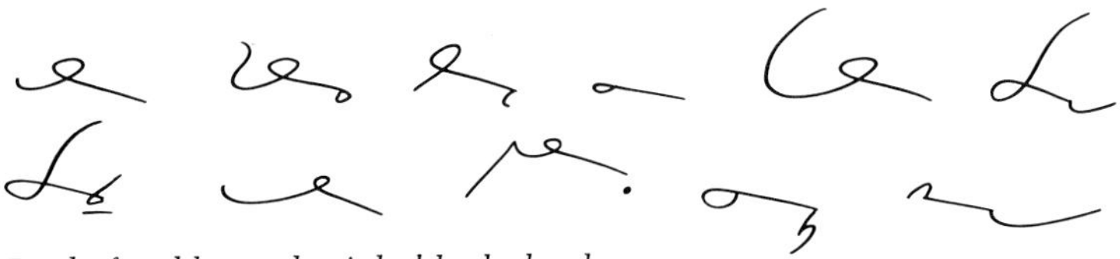

Rank, frankly, tanks, ink, blank, banker.
Banquet, link, drinking, anxious, uncle.

245 Omission of Vowel Preceding -tion When *t*, *d*, *n*, or *m* is followed by *-ition*, *-ation*, the circle is omitted.

Admission, conditions, reputation, commission, donation, addition, quotations, stationed.

Building transcription skills

246

Business vocabulary builder	**stationery** Such items as paper, pens, ink, clips. **estimation** Opinion; judgment. **major** Of great importance.

Reading and writing practice

247 Brief-Form Letter

suf·fered
se·vere
length
sta·tio·nery

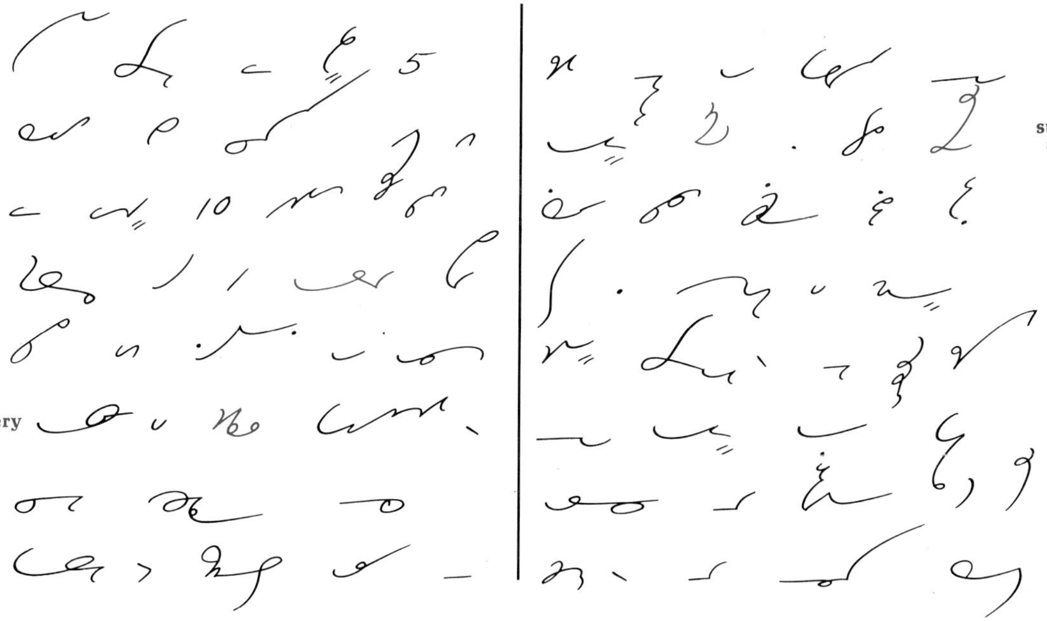

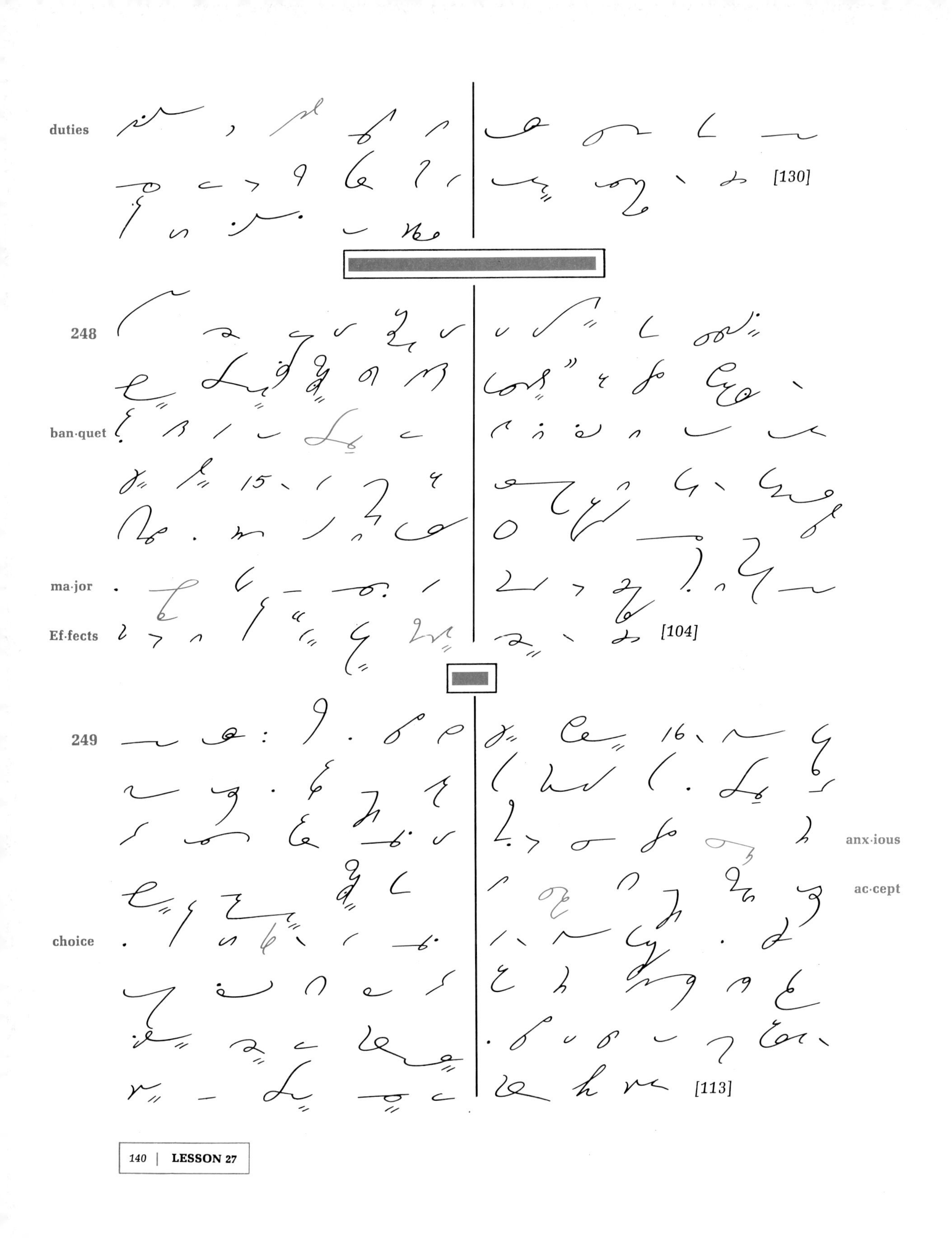

duties

[130]

248

ban·quet

ma·jor

Ef·fects

[104]

249

anx·ious

ac·cept

choice

[113]

250

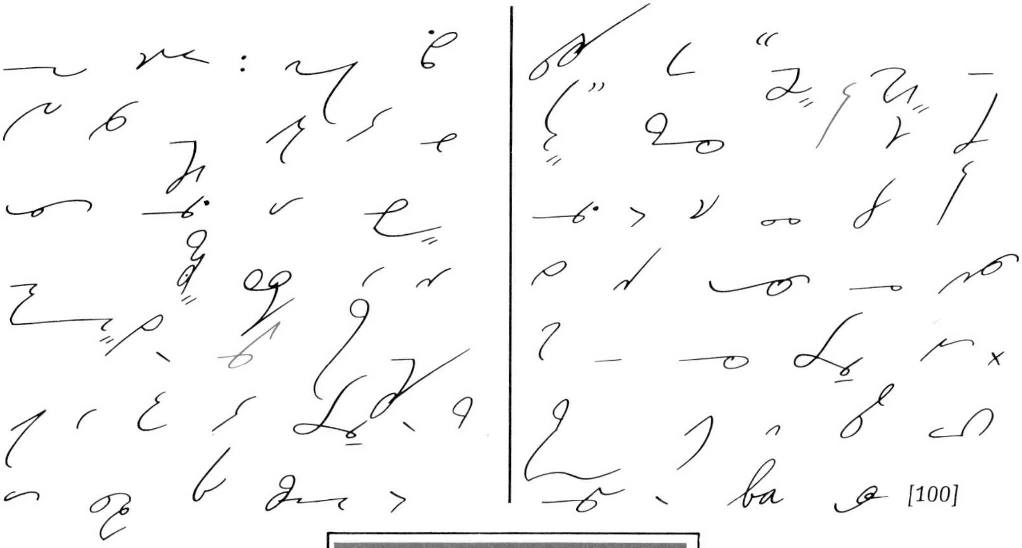

sub·ject

ad·di·tion

[100]

251

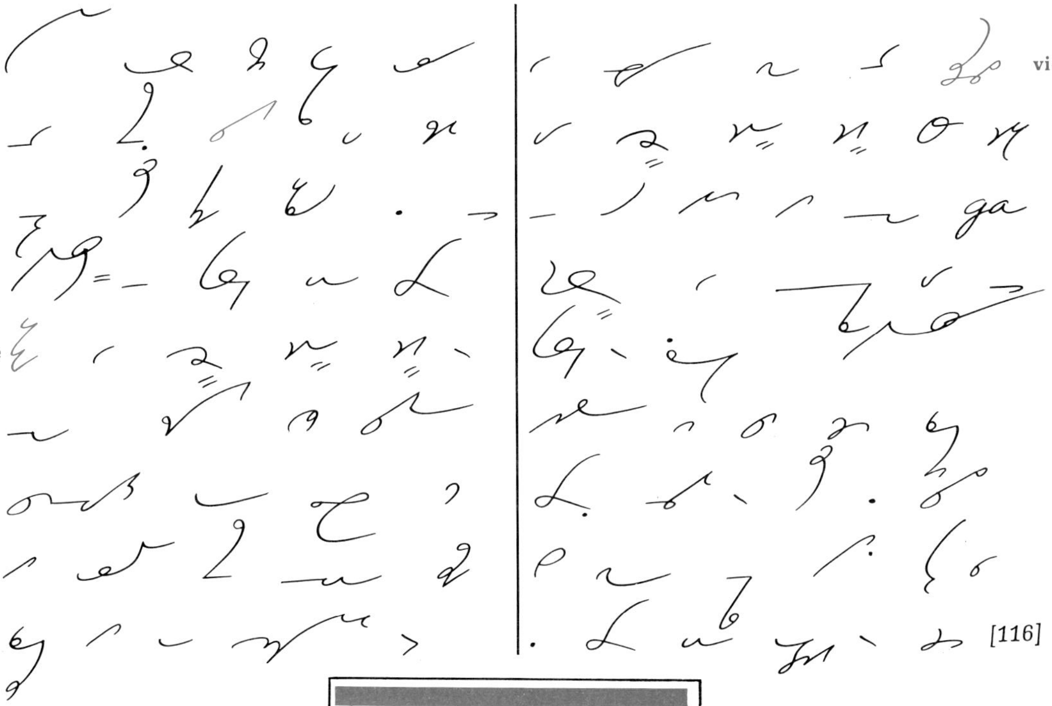

vi·cin·ity

edi·tion

op·po·site

[116]

252

proud

of·fi·cer

sur·prised

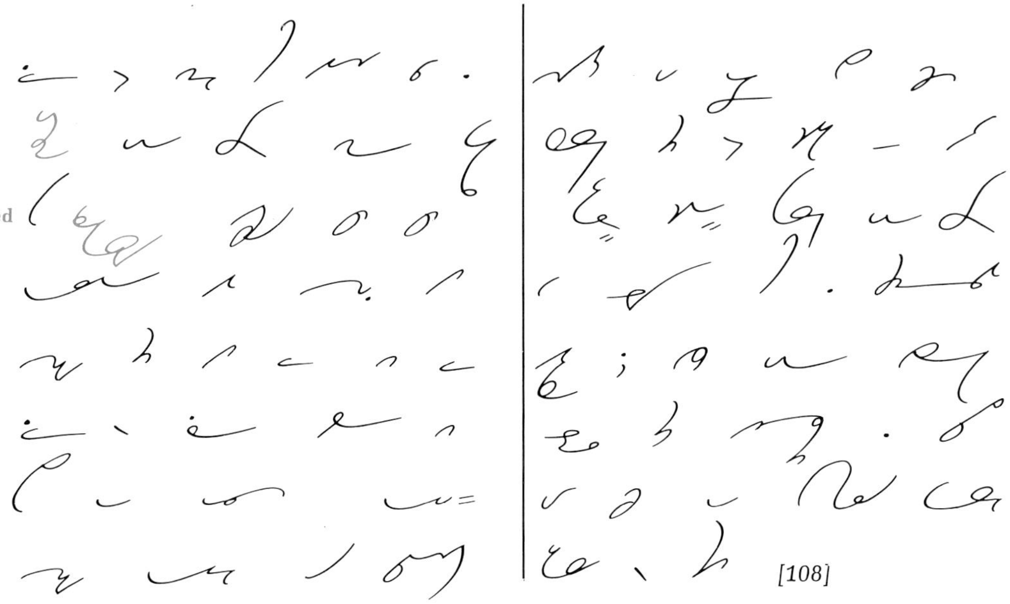

[108]

UP AND DOWN CHECK LIST

Do you always write the following strokes upward?

☐ **1** and their-there ☐ **2** it-at would

Do you always write the following strokes downward?

☐ **1** is-his for have ☐ **2** shall which

LESSON 28

Principles

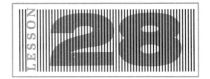

253 Ah, Aw A dot is used for *a* in words that begin with *ah* and *aw*.

Spell: *a-h-e-d, ahead; a-oo-a, away*

Ahead, away, await, awaited, awake, awoke, aware.

254 Y Before *o* and *oo*, *y* is represented by the small circle, as *y* is pronounced *e*. *Ye* is expressed by a small loop; *ya*, by a large loop.

Spell: *wīē-l-o, yellow; wīē-ard, yard*

Yawn, youth, yellow, yielded, yard, yarn.

255 X The letter x is usually represented by an *s* written with a slight backward slant.

Compare: miss  mix 

fees  fix 

Spell: *b-o-ex, box; b-o-exes, boxes*

Box, boxes, relax, relaxes, tax, taxes, mix, mixes.

256 Omission of Short U In the body of a word, short *u* is omitted before *n, m,* or a straight downstroke.

Before N

Son, fun, ton, done, gun, begun, run.

Before M

Some-sum, summer, come, become, lumber, column.

Before a Straight Downstroke

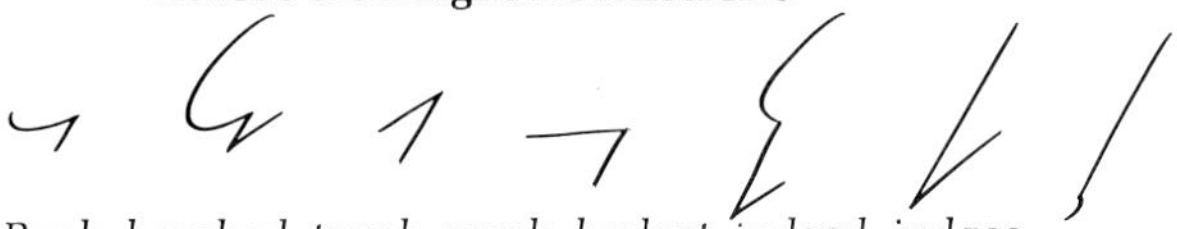

Rush, brushed, touch, much, budget, judged, judges.

Building transcription skills

257

Business vocabulary builder	**budget** The amount of money that is available for a particular purpose, as an advertising budget. **agenda** List of things to be done. **perplexing** Puzzling. **blunt** Having an edge that is not sharp.

Reading and writing practice

258 Brief-Form Review Letter

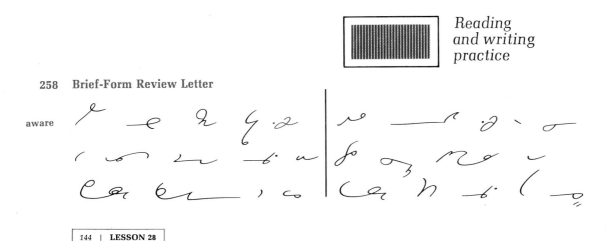

aware

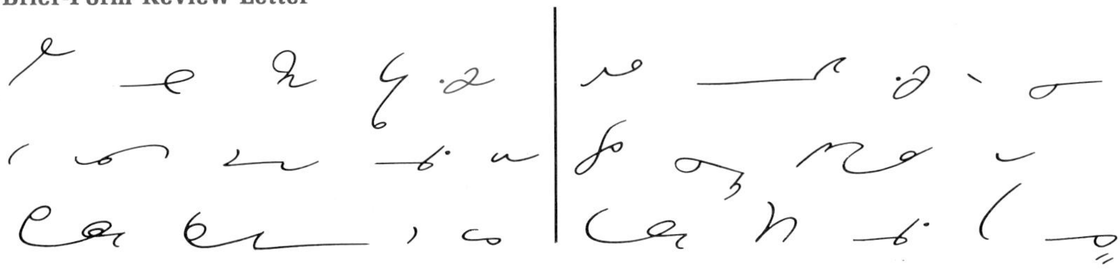

wel·come

bud·get

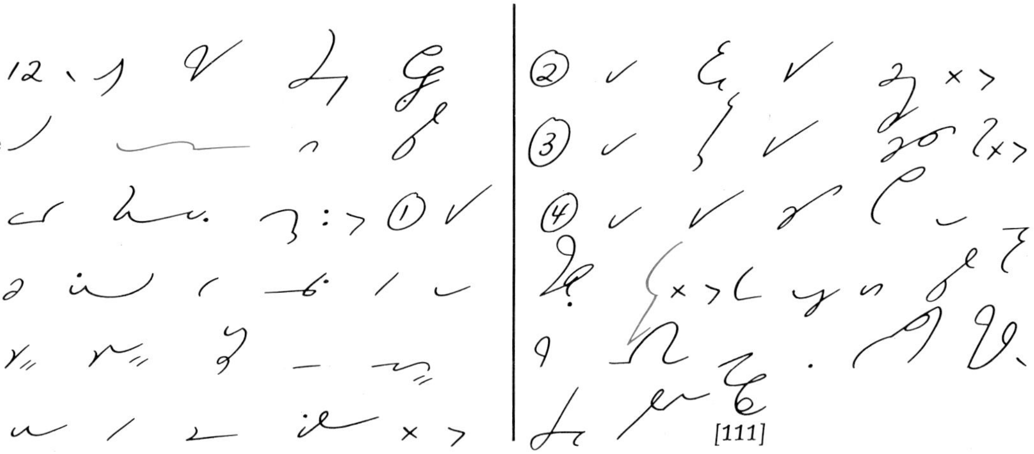

[111]

259

over·due

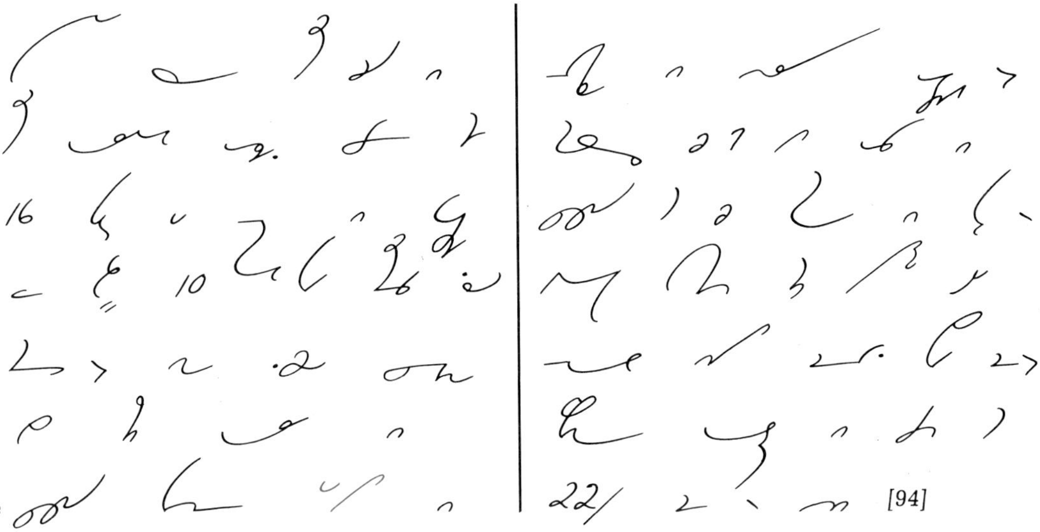

[94]

260

shipped

judg·ing

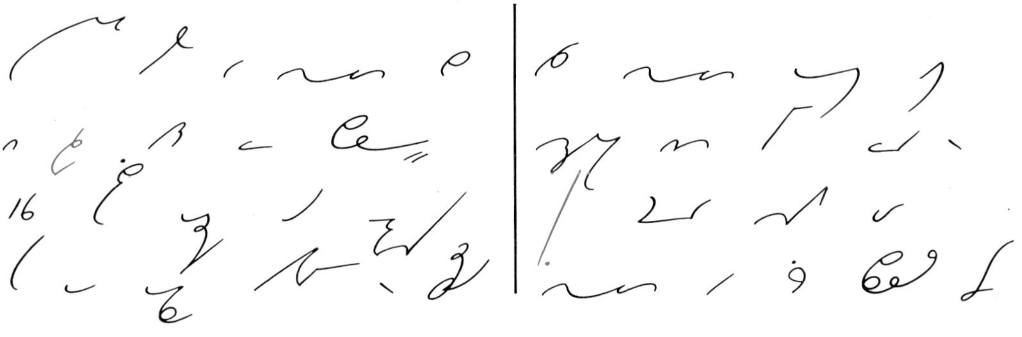

wheth·er

[107]

touch

261

nice·ly

plan·ning

fu·el

[103]

262

bal·ance

sum

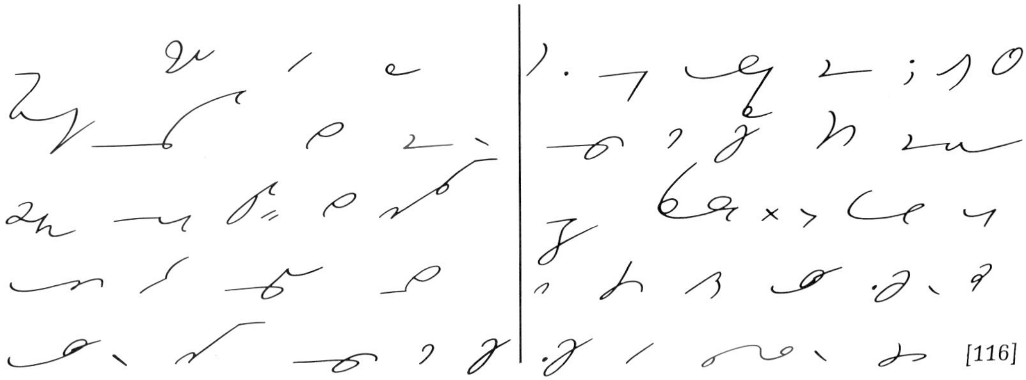

[116] ea·ger·ly

263 Confidential

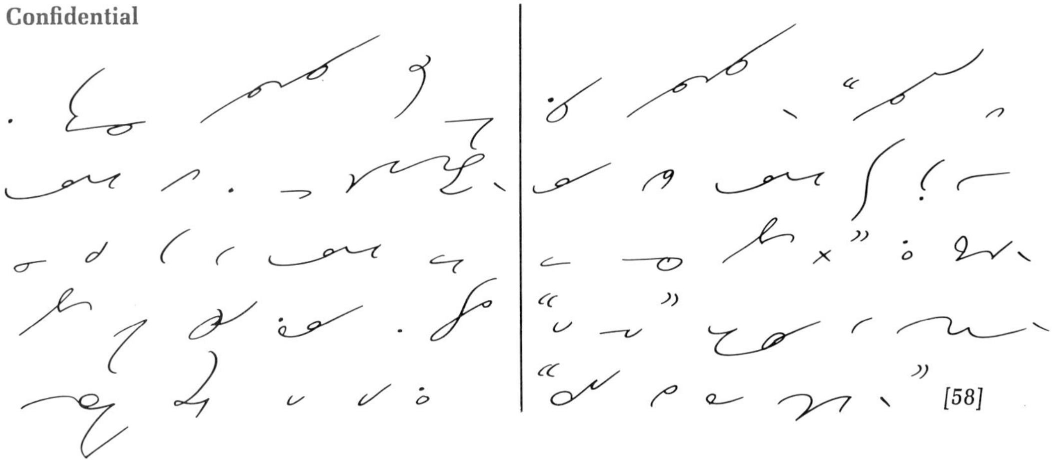

[58]

LESSON 29

Principles

264 Brief Forms

Purpose, regard, opinion, circular, responsible, organize, public, publish-publication, ordinary.

265 Word Beginning Ex- The word beginning *ex-* is represented by *e-s*.

Spell: ex-p-n-s, *expense*

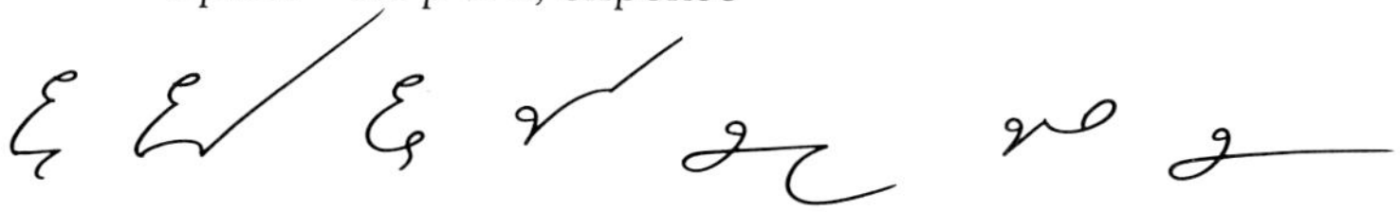

Expense, expected, expresses, extend, example, extra, examine.

266 Md, Mt By rounding off the angle between *m-d,* we obtain the fluent *md* blend. The same stroke also represents *mt.*

Md, Mt 

Compare: seem  seemed 

Spell: f-r-a-emd, *framed;* emt-e, *empty*

Framed, claimed, named, confirmed, trimmed, prompt, empty.

267 Word Ending -ful The word ending *-ful* is represented by *f*.

Spell: k-a-r-ful, *careful*

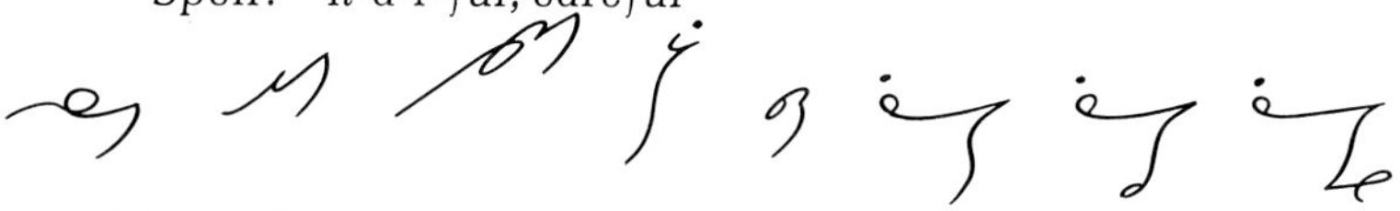

Careful, thoughtful, doubtful, hopeful, useful, helpful, helpfully, helpfulness.

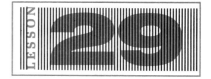

268 SIMILAR-WORDS DRILL ▎ addition, edition

addition Anything added.

She will be a fine addition *to your staff.*

edition All the copies of a book printed at one time.

The second edition *of the book is beautifully illustrated.*

269

Business vocabulary builder

public relations department The people in an organization whose purpose is to develop goodwill between the organization and the public.

commended Praised.

overwhelmed Overpowered; crushed.

ailing Sick.

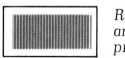

Reading and writing practice

270 Brief-Form Letter

cir·cu·lar

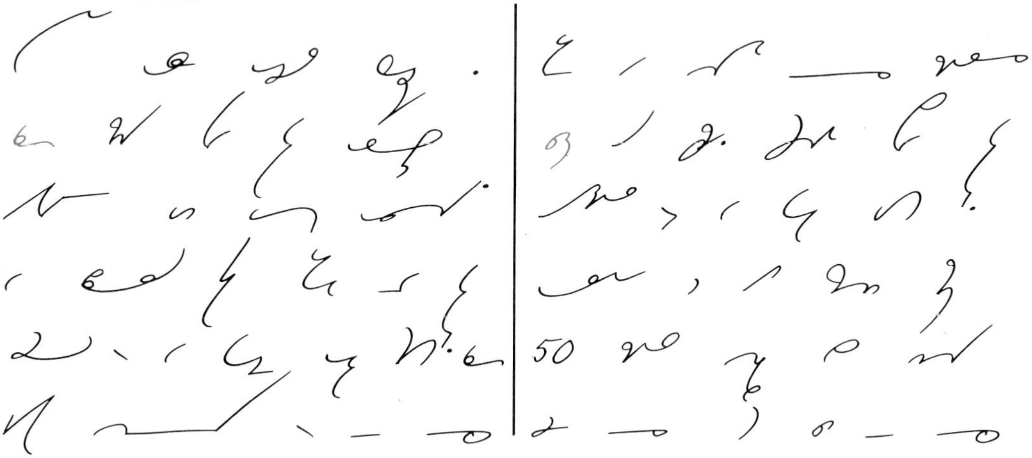

use·ful

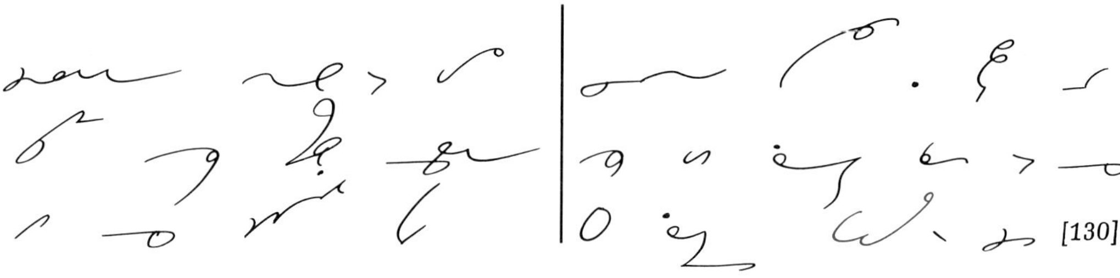

[130] prompt·ly

271 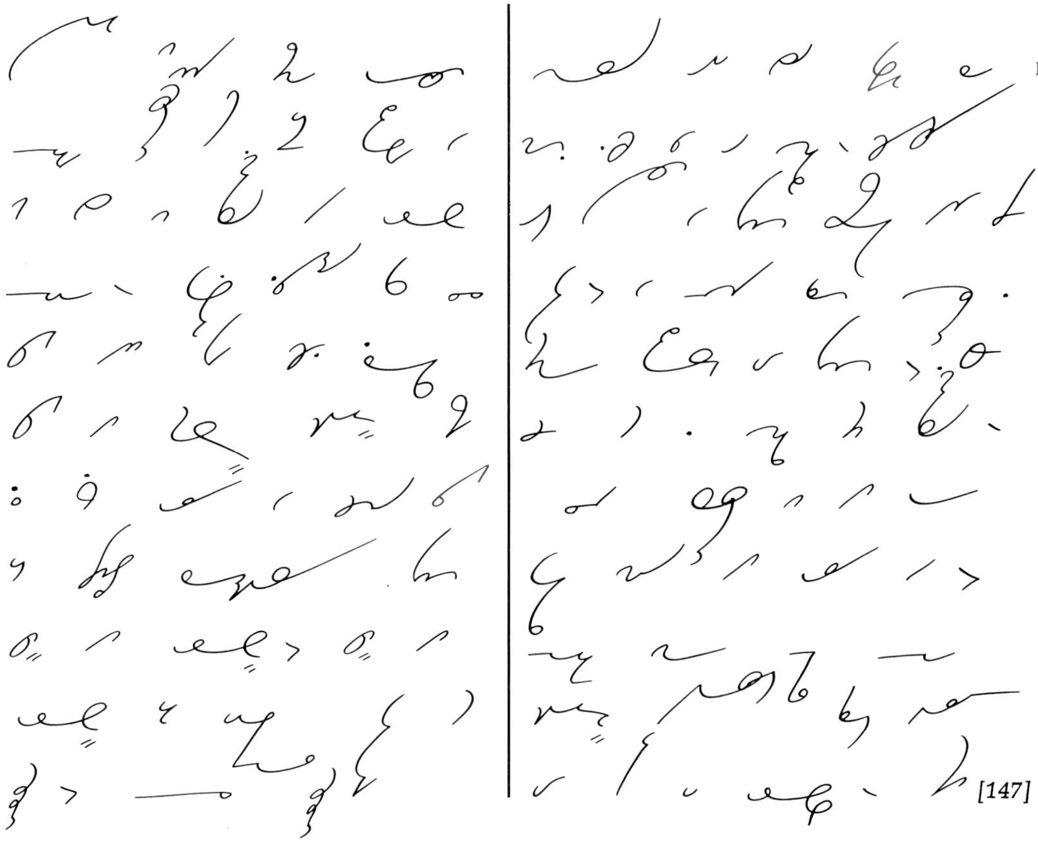

pa·tients

edi·tion

[147]

272 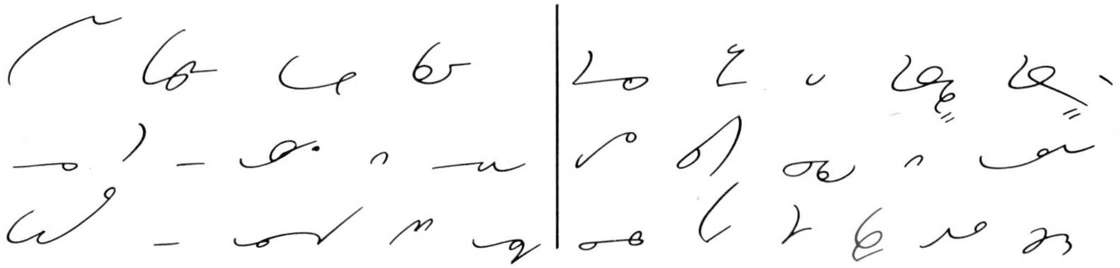

past

ail·ing

ad·di·tion

[118]

273 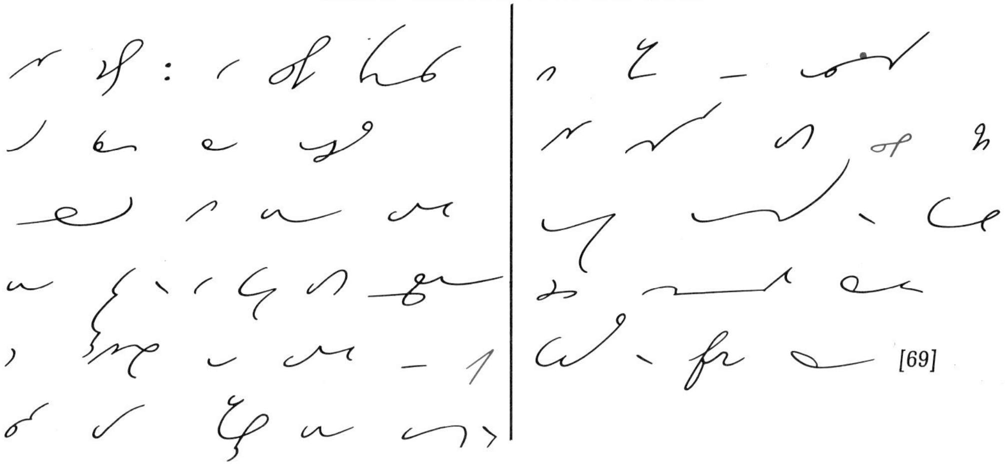

ini·tial

touch

[69]

274 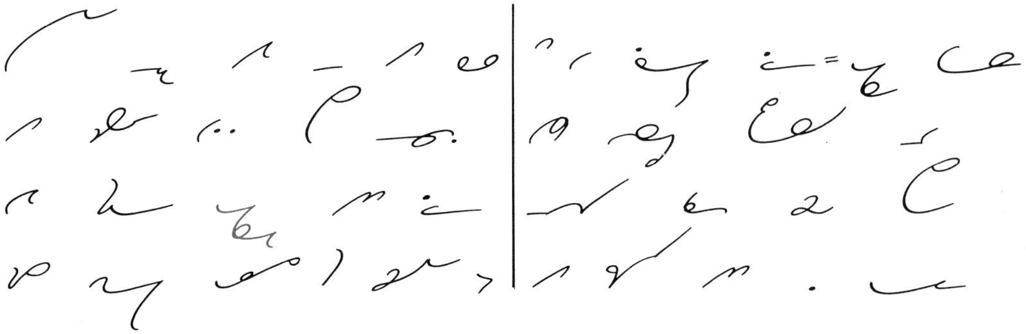

re·pairs

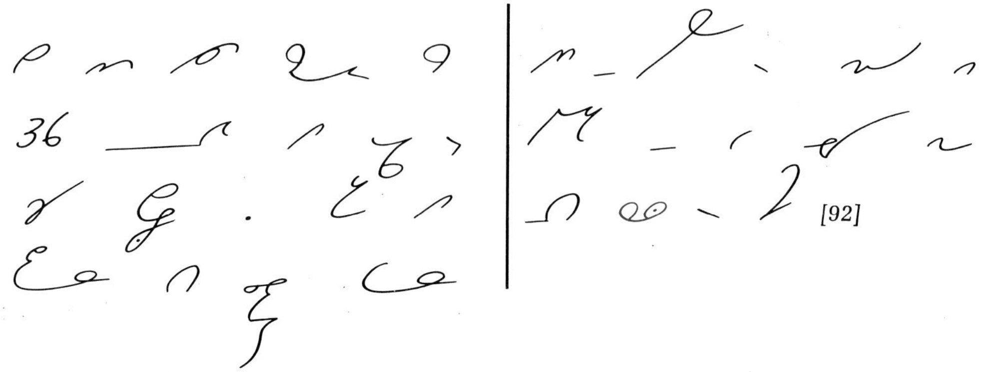
36
[92]

ar·ea

275

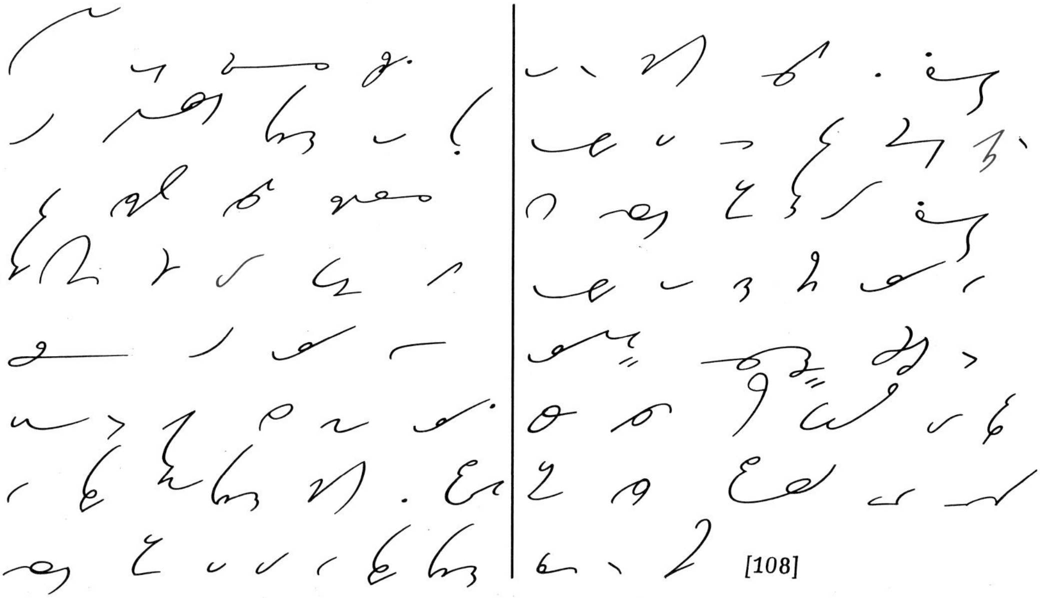
[108]

or·di·nary

choose

LESSON 30

Recall

After studying the new shorthand devices in Lessons 25 through 29, you have earned another breathing spell! Therefore, you will find no new shorthand strokes or principles in Lesson 30.

In this lesson you will find a Recall Chart and a Reading and Writing Practice that offers you some interesting suggestions on how to be a good conversationalist.

276 Recall Chart This chart contains all the brief forms in Chapter 5 and one or more illustrations of the word-building principles you studied in Chapters 1 through 5.

As you read through the words in this chart, be sure to spell each word that you cannot read immediately.

Can you read the 84 words in the chart in 6 minutes or less?

BRIEF FORMS AND DERIVATIVES

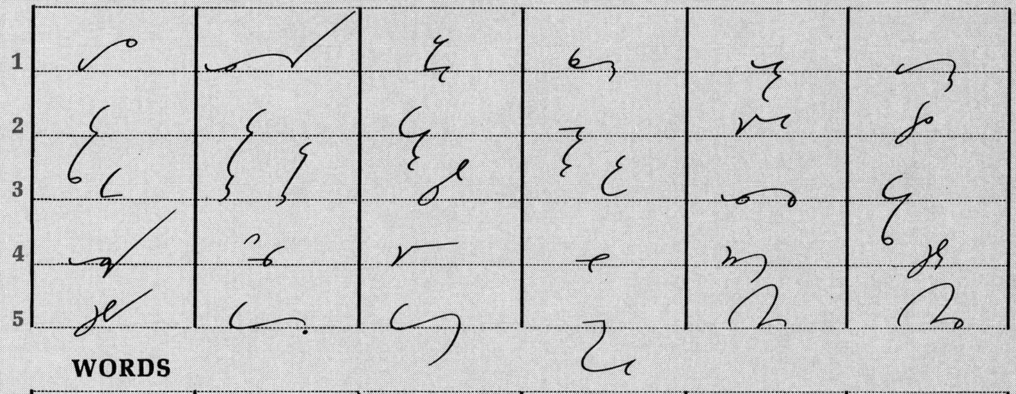

WORDS

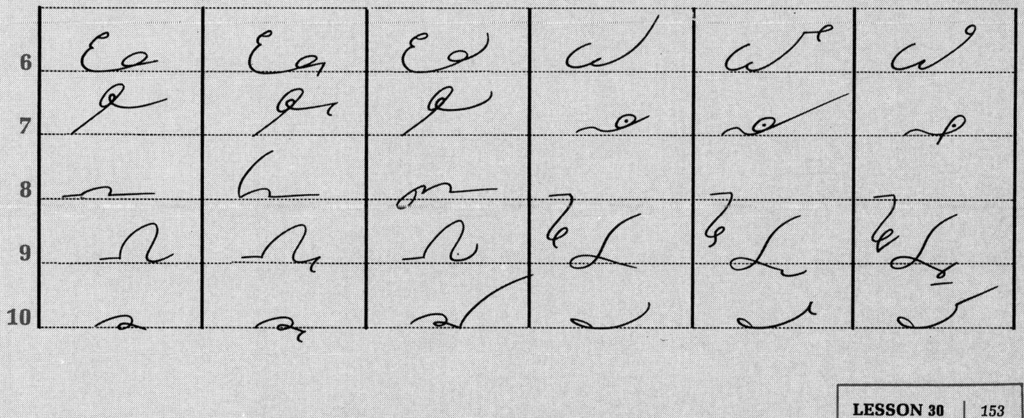

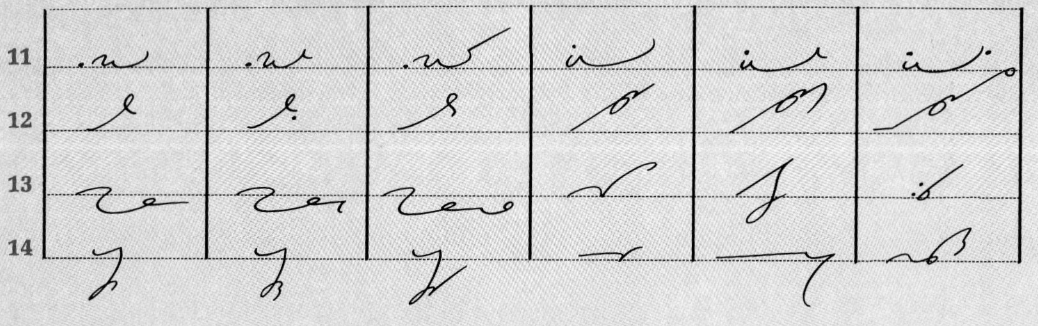

Building transcription skills

277

Business vocabulary builder	
	friction Disagreement between two persons having different views.
	digresses Gets off the main subject.
	minute Very small; of little importance.
	trite Worn out; old.

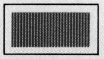

Reading and writing practice

Reading Scoreboard The previous Reading Scoreboard appeared in Lesson 18. If you have been studying each Reading and Writing Practice faithfully, no doubt there has been an increase in your reading speed. Let us measure that increase on the *first reading* of the material in Lesson 30. The following table will help you.

Lesson 30 contains 504 words.

If you read Lesson 30 in **14 minutes** *your reading rate is* **36 words a minute**
If you read Lesson 30 in **16 minutes** *your reading rate is* **31 words a minute**
If you read Lesson 30 in **18 minutes** *your reading rate is* **28 words a minute**
If you read Lesson 30 in **20 minutes** *your reading rate is* **25 words a minute**
If you read Lesson 30 in **22 minutes** *your reading rate is* **23 words a minute**
If you read Lesson 30 in **24 minutes** *your reading rate is* **21 words a minute**
If you read Lesson 30 in **26 minutes** *your reading rate is* **19 words a minute**

If you can read Lesson 30 in 14 minutes or less, you are doing well. If you take considerably longer than 26 minutes, perhaps you should review your homework procedures. For example, are you:

1 *Practicing in a quiet place at home?*

2 *Practicing without the radio or television set on?*

3 *Spelling aloud any words that you cannot read immediately?*

278 Nine Lessons in Living

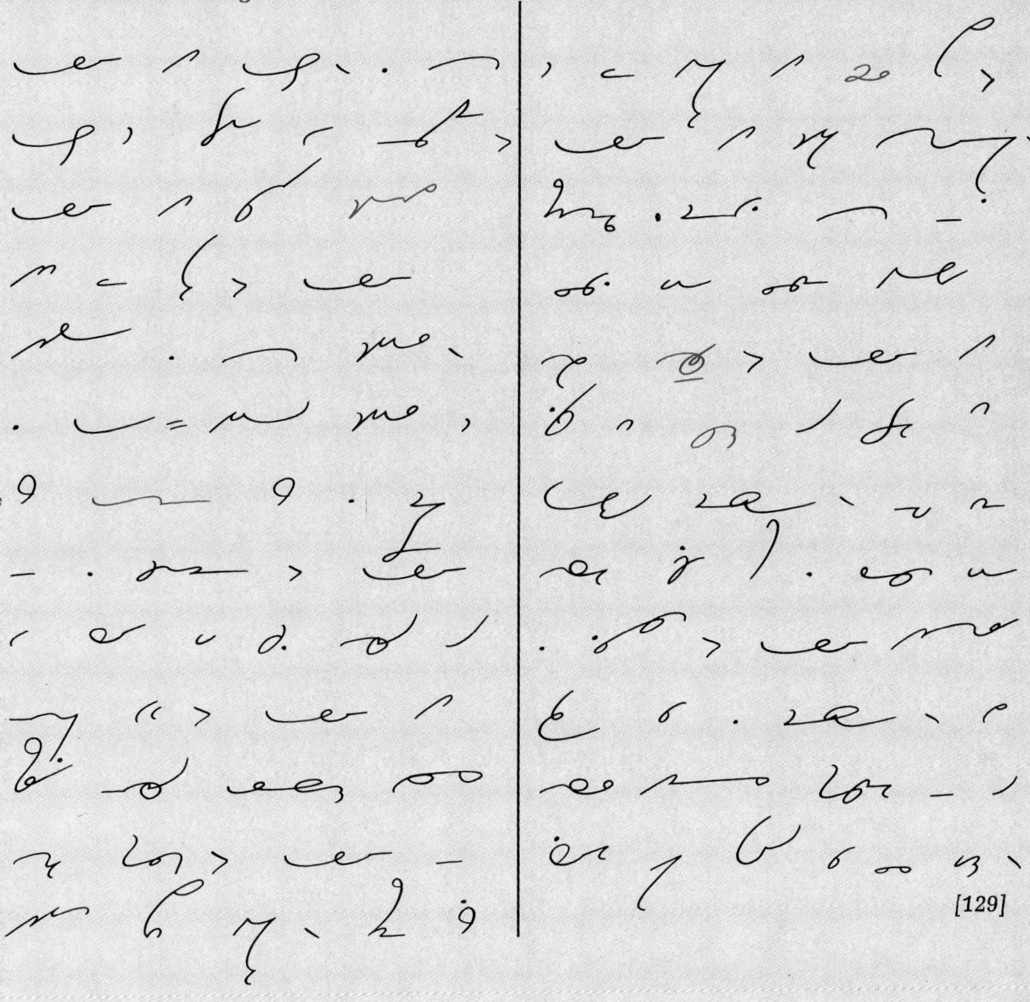

strict·ly wel·come wor·ry qui·et aches

[129]

279 Conversation Check List

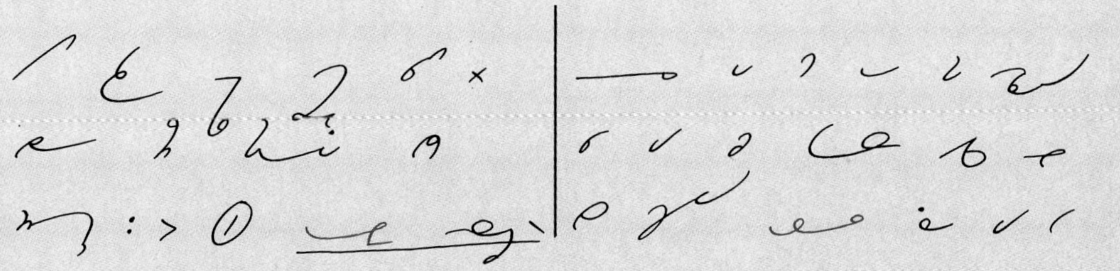

lis·ten re·al·ly

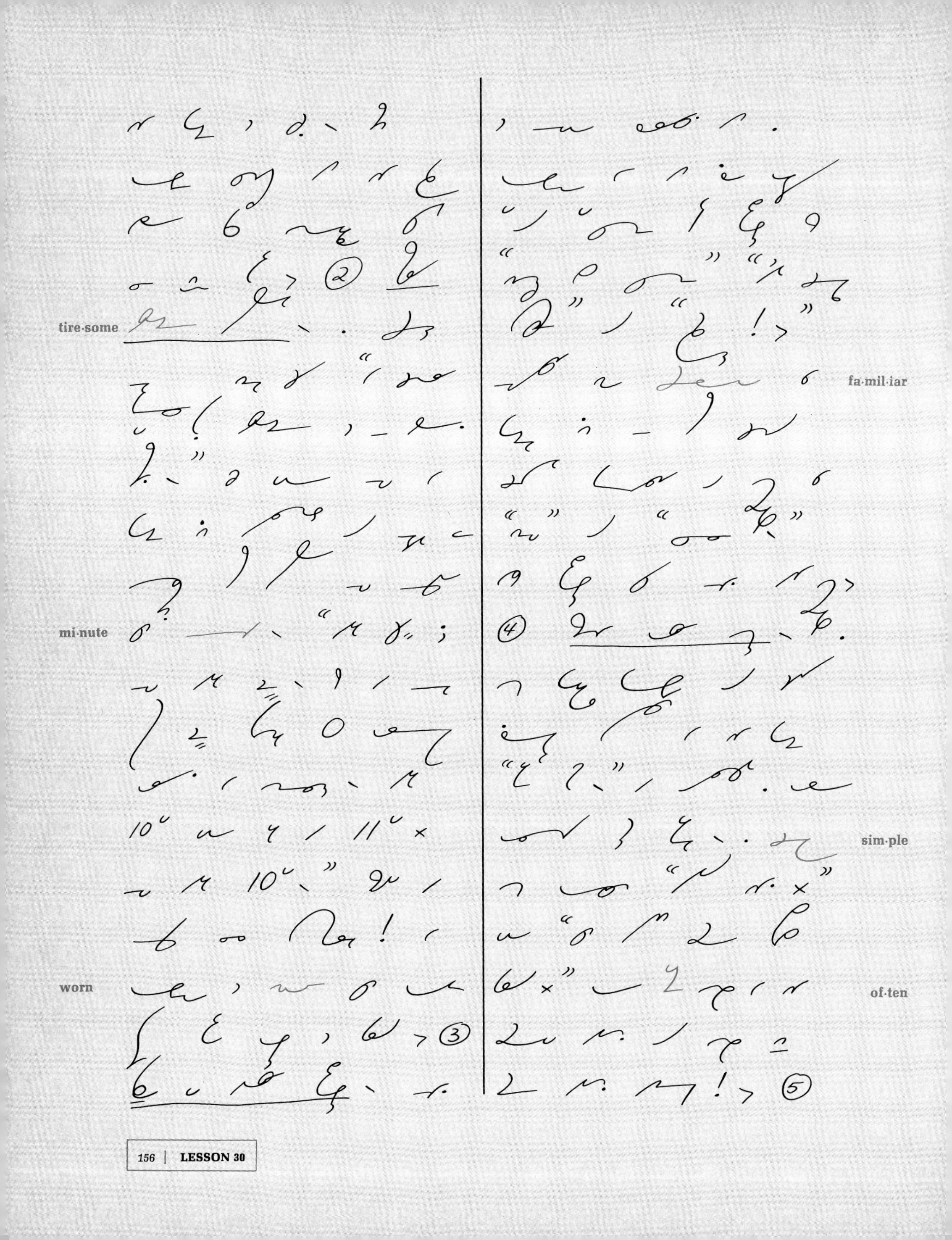

tire·some

mi·nute

worn

fa·mil·iar

sim·ple

of·ten

like·ly

giv·ing

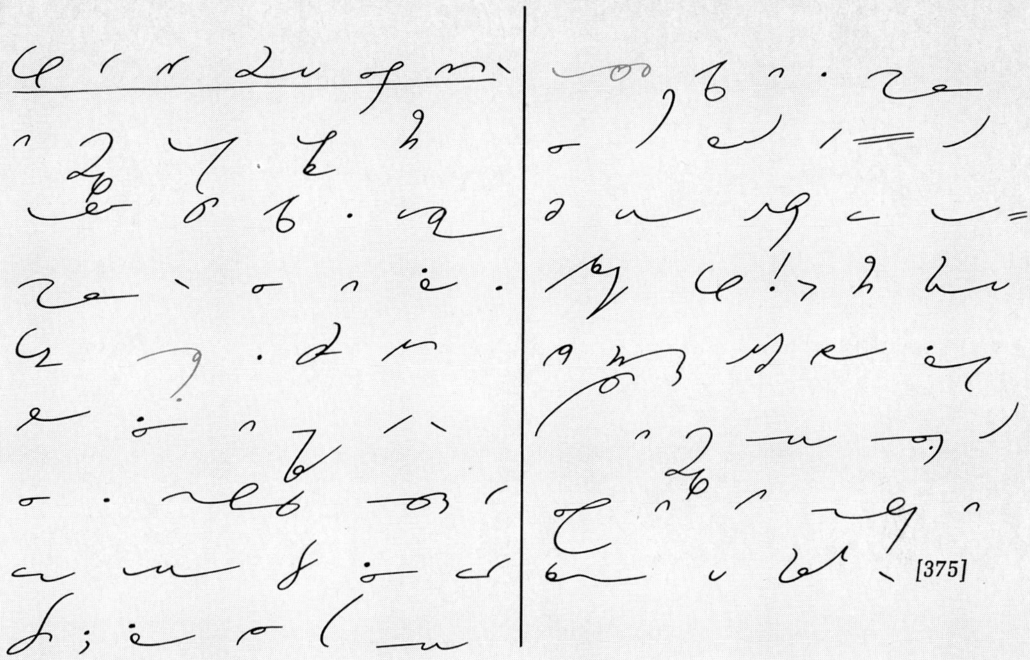

[375]

Chapter 6

The secretary—master of English

The successful secretary is a master of the English language. She has a large vocabulary to which she is constantly adding new words. She has a firm grasp of such mechanics of English as grammar, punctuation, and spelling. If you are to be a successful secretary, you, too, must become a master of the English language.

The executive for whom you will work will doubtless know what he wants to say, but he may not know the correct spelling, punctuation, and grammatical construction—that is, how to say it. He may have a college degree in engineering, accounting, history, or chemistry, but somewhere along the line he missed the opportunity to learn the finer points of grammar. This is where you come in. The executive's re-

quest of the secretary, "Fix the letter so that it 'reads' right," is not rare. And he really means it.

Many employers are highly expert in the English language. They may dictate every punctuation mark and spell every unusual word. If you get one of these for a boss, your job of transcribing will be greatly simplified.

Then there is the dictator who thinks he knows grammar, but doesn't, and will expect you to transcribe everything just as he dictated it, whether it is really right or not. Of course, in this case there is nothing for you to do but to follow his wishes—he takes the responsibility.

But if your boss says, "You know English and I don't, so you fix this letter," then you must know. It is your responsibility. Badly constructed letters can cost your company a sale or can result in the loss of goodwill.

No matter how rapidly you can type or can write shorthand, these skills are greatly weakened if you cannot produce a finished transcript that is grammatically perfect. The top-notch secretary must be a real expert in business English. The surer she is of the accepted rules of English, the more secure her job and the better her chances for advancement.

Any time you spend improving your mastery of the English language and building your vocabulary will be well spent!

LESSON 31

Principles

280 Brief Forms Only one more group to learn after this one!

Merchant, merchandise, recognize, never, experience, between, short, quantity, situation.

281 Word Ending -ure The word ending *-ure* is represented by *r*.

Spell: *f-a-l-r, failure*

Failure, figure, procedure, picture, nature, naturally.

282 Word Ending -ual The word ending *-ual* is represented by *l*.

Spell: *g-r-a-d-l, gradual*

Gradual, equal, actually, eventual, annual, annually.

Building transcription skills

283 PUNCTUATION PRACTICE

Another "must" for the successful stenographer or secretary is the ability to punctuate correctly. Most businessmen rely on their stenographers or secretaries to supply the proper punctuation when they transcribe. Because the inclusion or omission of a punctuation mark may completely alter the meaning of a sentence, it is important that you know when to use each punctuation mark.

To sharpen your punctuation skill, you will hereafter give special attention to punctuation in each Reading and Writing Practice.

In the lessons ahead you will review nine of the most common uses of the comma. Each time one of these uses of the comma occurs in the Reading and Writing Practice, it will be squared in the shorthand, thus calling it forcefully to your attention.

PRACTICE SUGGESTIONS

If you follow these simple suggestions in your homework practice hereafter, your ability to punctuate should improve noticeably.

1 Read carefully the explanation of each comma usage (for example, the explanation of the parenthetical comma given below) to be sure that you understand it. You will encounter many illustrations of each comma usage in the Reading and Writing Practice exercises, so that eventually you will acquire the knack of applying it correctly.

2 Continue to read and copy each Reading and Writing Practice, as you have done before. However, add these two important steps:

a *Each time you see a squared comma in the Reading and Writing Practice, note the reason for its use, which is indicated directly above the squared comma.*

b *As you copy the Reading and Writing Practice in your shorthand notebook, insert the commas in your shorthand notes, squaring them as in the textbook.*

PUNCTUATION PRACTICE ▌ , parenthetical

A word or a phrase or a clause that is used parenthetically (that is, one not necessary to the grammatical completeness of the sentence) should be set off by commas.

If the parenthetical expression occurs at the end of the sentence, only one comma is used.

There is, of course, no charge for this service.

Never hesitate to let us know, Mr. Strong, when our organization can help you.

We actually print your picture on the card, Mr. Short.

Each time a parenthetical expression occurs in the Reading and Writing Practice, it will be indicated thus in the shorthand: par [,]

284 *Business vocabulary builder*

reputable Favorably known; respected.

manual Handbook.

revealing Bringing to light something that was not evident before.

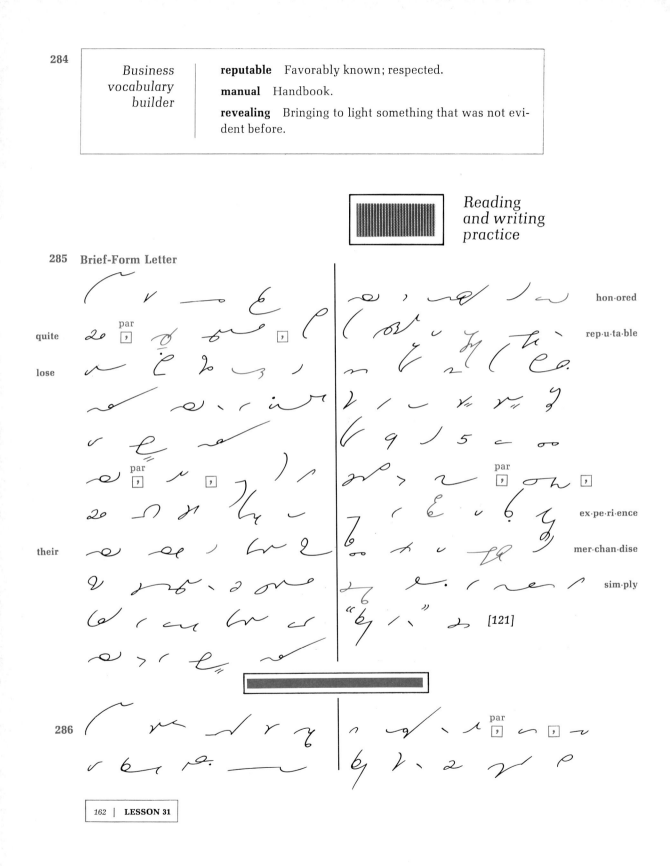

Reading and writing practice

285 Brief-Form Letter

quite · lose · their · hon·ored · rep·u·ta·ble · ex·pe·ri·ence · mer·chan·dise · sim·ply

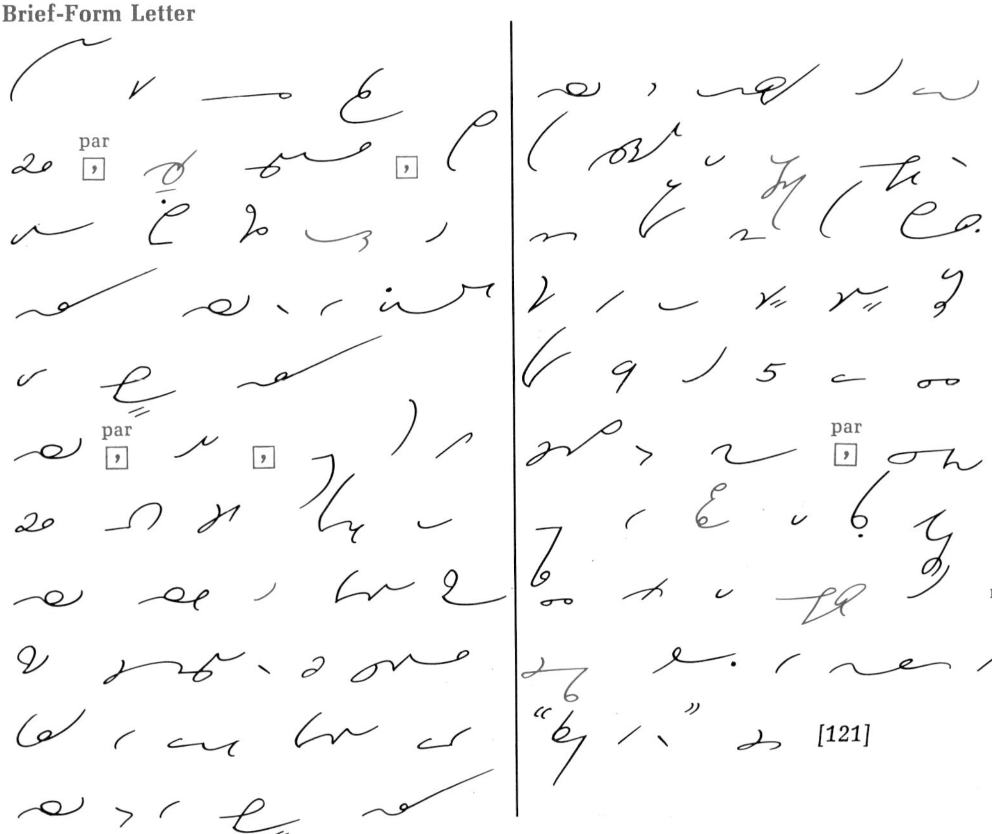

par
par
par
[121]

286

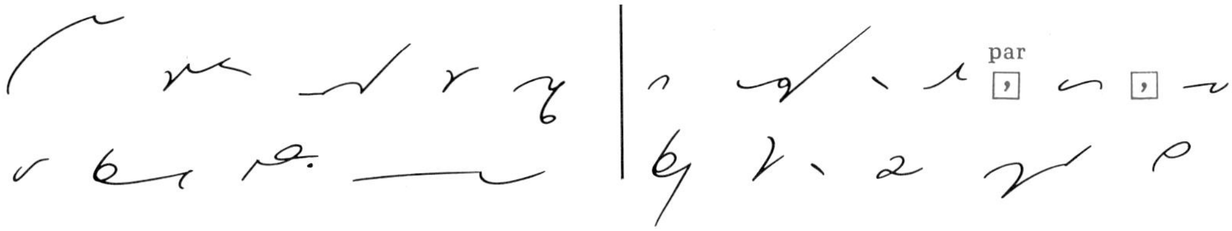

par

an·nu·al·ly

sched·uled

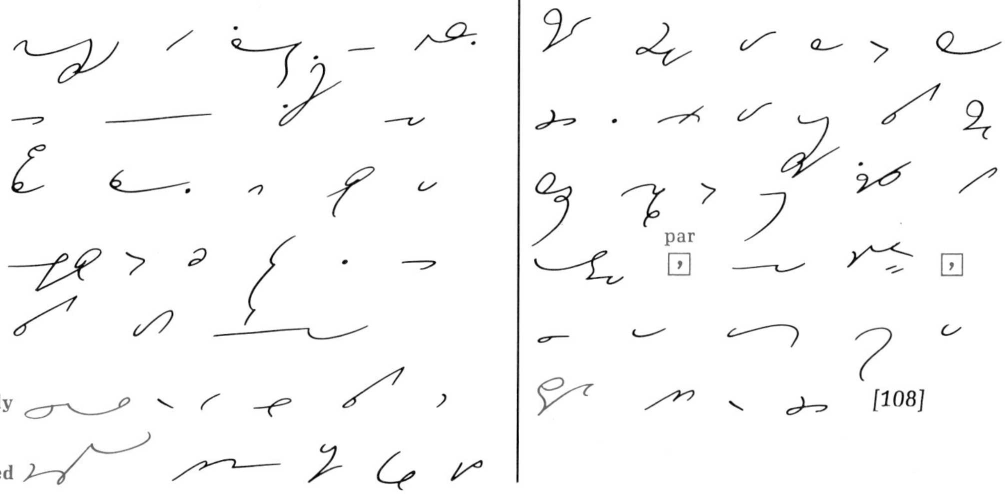

par
,
,
[108]

as·sis·tance

[redacted]

287

suc·cess·ful

rec·og·nize

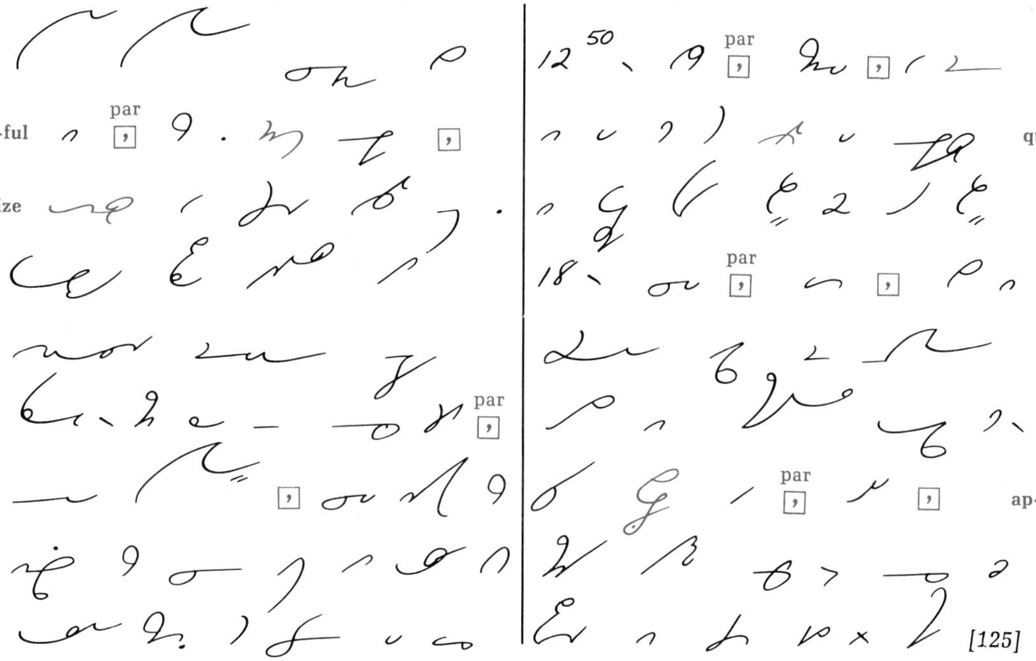

par
,
,
12:50
par
,
,
18
par
,
,
par
,
,
par
,
,
[125]

sum

quan·ti·ties

ap·pre·ci·ate

[redacted]

288

re·veal·ing

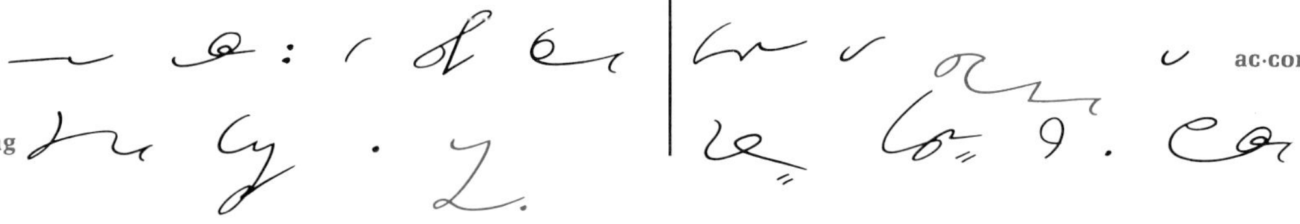

ac·com·plish·ments

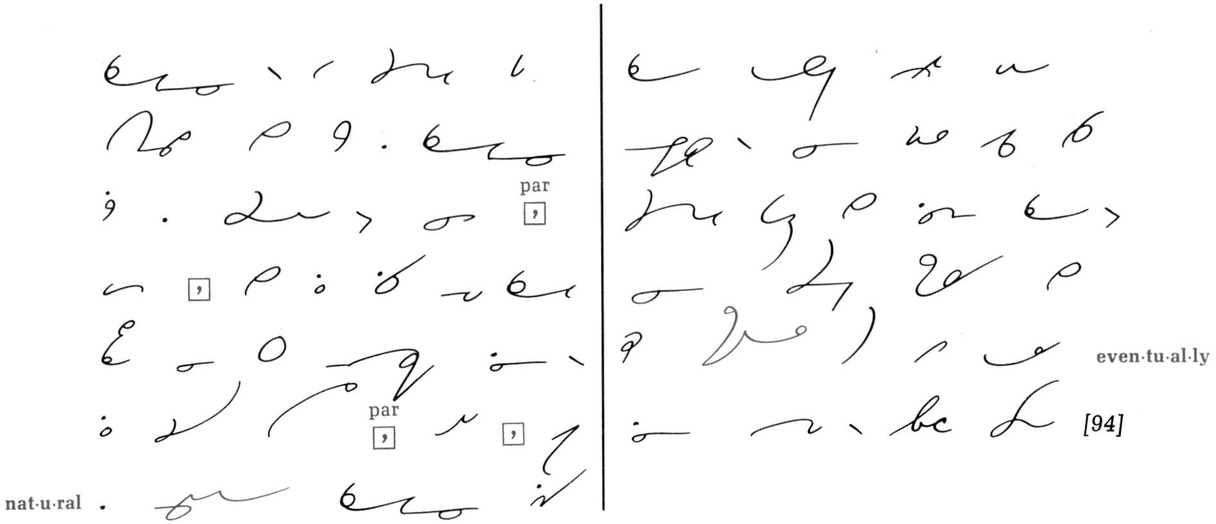
par
par
nat·u·ral
even·tu·al·ly
[94]

289

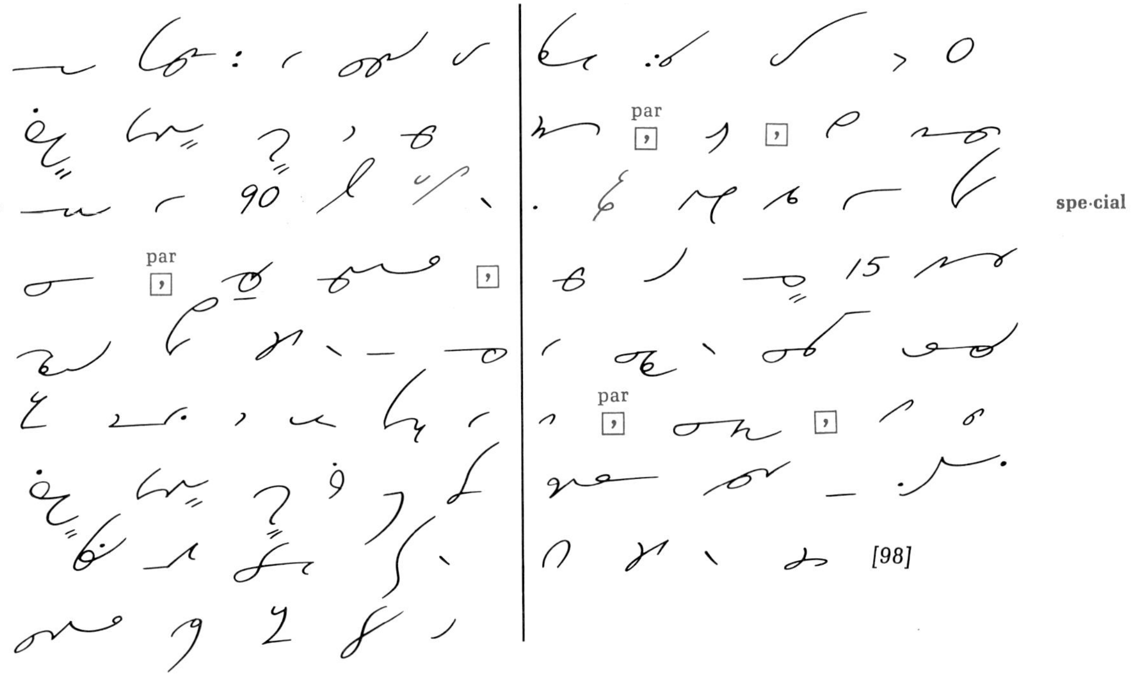
over·due
90
par
par
par
spe·cial
15
[98]

LESSON 32

Principles

290 Word Ending -ily The word ending *-ily* is expressed by a narrow loop.

Compare: *steady* 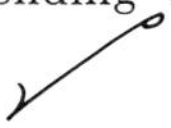 *steadily* 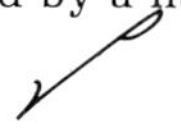

Spell: *e-s-ily, easily*

Easily, readily, heartily, temporarily, family, heavily, hastily, speedily.

291 Word Beginning Al- The word beginning *al-* is expressed by *o*.

Spell: *all-s-o, also*

Also, almost, altogether, already, although, alter, altered, alteration.

292 Word Beginning Mis- The word beginning *mis-* is represented by *m-s*.

Spell: *mis-t-a-k, mistake*

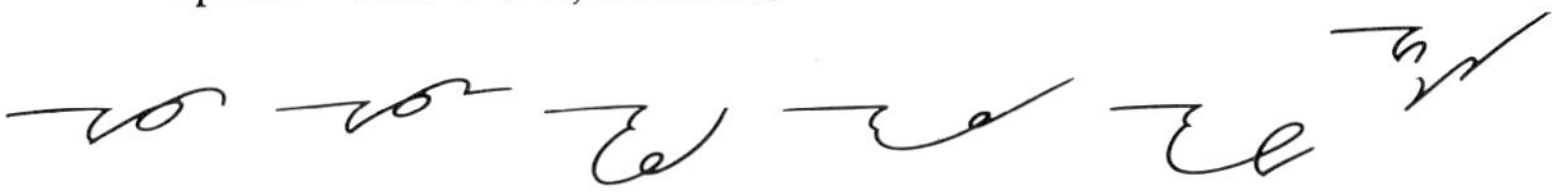

Mistake, mistaken, misprint, mislead, misplaced, misunderstood.

293 Word Beginnings Dis-, Des- The word beginnings *dis-, des-* are expressed by *d-s*.

Spell: *dis-k-oo-shun, discussion; dis-k-r-ī-b, describe*

Dis-

Discussion, disposed, discouragement, discount, distances, discover.

Des-

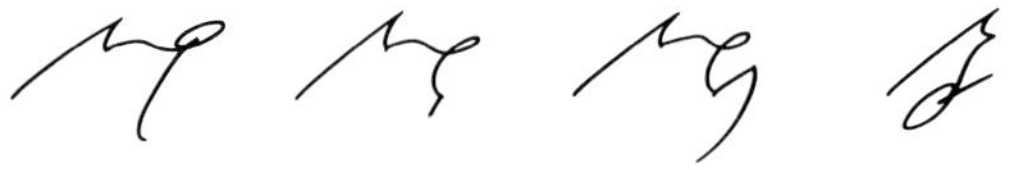

Describe, description, descriptive, despite.

Building transcription skills

294 PUNCTUATION PRACTICE | , apposition

Sometimes a writer mentions a person or thing, and in order to make his meaning perfectly clear to the reader, he says the same thing in different words. The clarifying word or phrase or clause is known as an "expression in apposition." Each expression in apposition should be set off by commas. When the expression occurs at the end of a sentence, only one comma is necessary.

Our latest booklet, Gracious Living, *is enclosed.*

The meeting will be held on Friday, June 16, at the Hotel Brown.

Please have him get in touch with Mr. Roy, our personnel manager.

He lives in Chicago, Illinois.

▶ Note: When the clarifying term is very closely connected with the principal noun so that the sense would not be complete without the added term, no commas are required.

My sister Jane will be home soon.

The word embarrass *is often misspelled.*

Each time an expression in apposition occurs in the Reading and Writing Practice, it will be indicated thus in the shorthand: ap [,]

295

Business vocabulary builder

merchandising Building sales by presenting goods to the public attractively.

disturbing Troubling.

in the red Losing money.

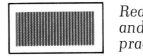

Reading and writing practice

296 Brief-Form Review Letter

rec·og·nized

leath·er

vol·ume

al·ready

mer·chan·dis·ing

quan·ti·ties

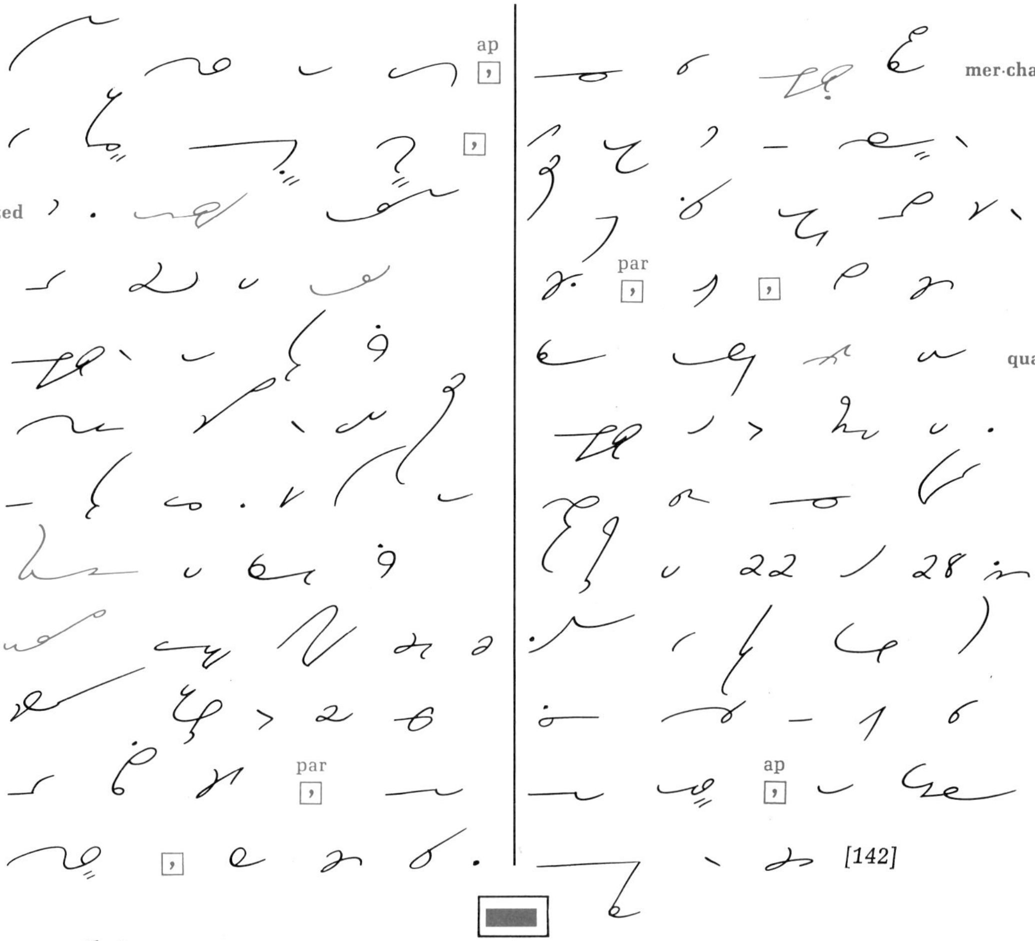

297

de·scrib·ing

mis·spelled

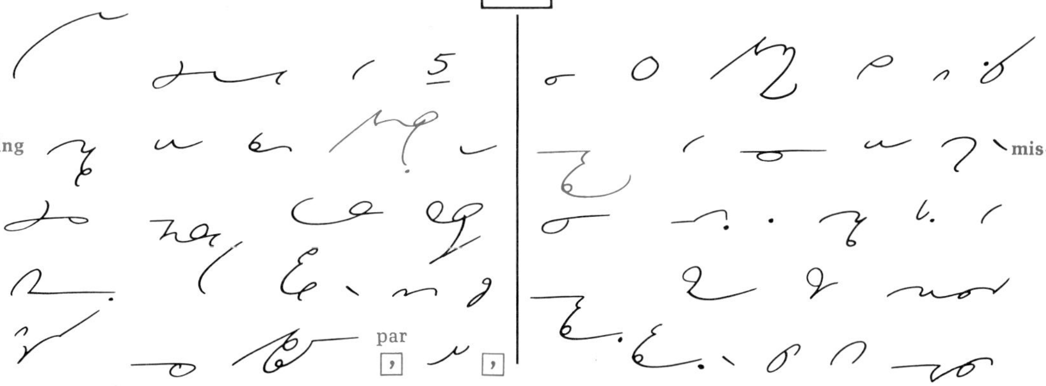

de·scrip·tive
con·ven·tion

par

ap

ap

[121]

298

ar·ea

dis·cuss

ap

ap

par

ap

Gra·cious

[118]

299

ap

dis·con·tin·ue

dis·ap·point·ing

ap

31

heav·i·ly
debt

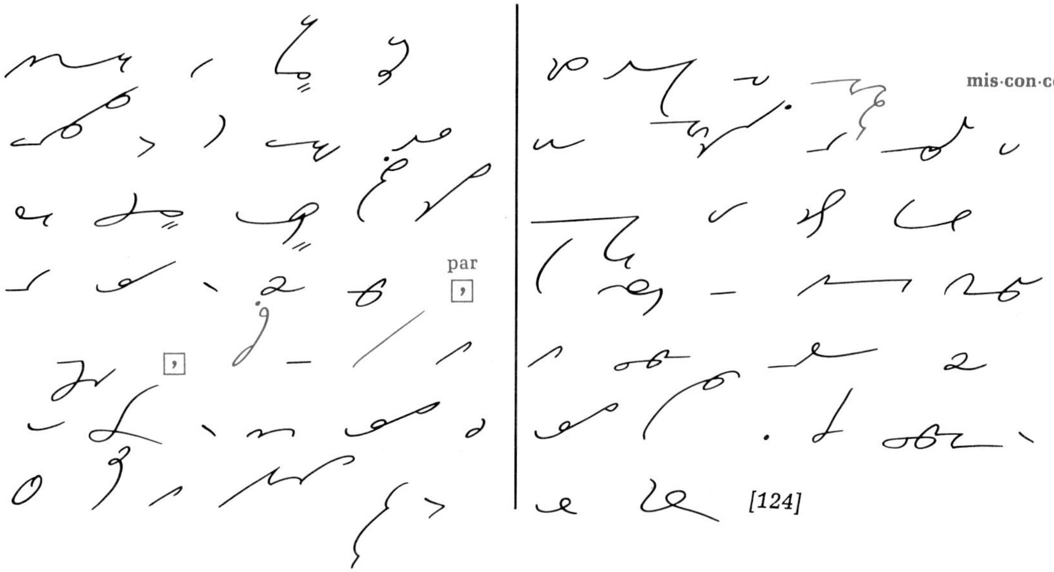
par
[124]

mis·con·cep·tion

300 Quick Service

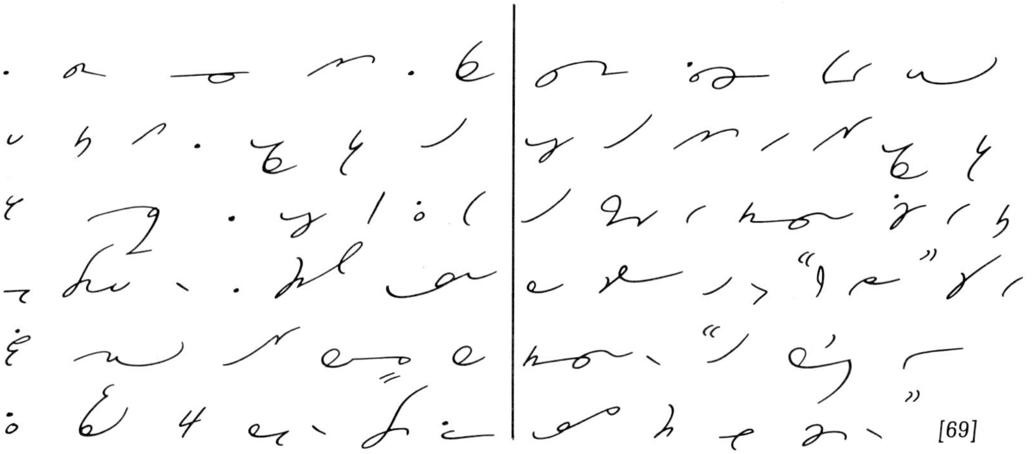
[69]

LESSON 33

Principles

301 Brief Forms This is the last set of brief forms you will have to learn.

Railroad, world, throughout, object, character, govern.

302 Word Beginnings For-, Fore- The word beginnings *for-*, *fore-* are represented by *f*.

Spell: *for-gay-e-v, forgive*

Forgive, forget, form, informed, force, effort, forth, forever.

303 Word Beginning Fur- The word beginning *fur-* is also represented by *f*.

Spell: *fur-n-a-s, furnace*

Furnace, further, furthermore, furnish, furnishes, furnished, furniture.

304 Ago in Phrases In expressions of time, *ago* is represented by g.

Days ago, years ago, weeks ago, long ago, months ago.

305 PUNCTUATION PRACTICE | , series

When the last member of a series of three or more items is preceded by *and, or,* or *nor*, place a comma before the conjunction as well as between the other items.

The railroads are recognized to be a major problem confronting the cities, towns, and villages throughout the country.

The meetings will be held on June 5, July 8, and July 16.

Her duties consisted of receiving calls, answering the telephone, and opening the mail.

▶ Note: Some authorities prefer to omit the comma before the conjunction. In your shorthand textbook, however, the comma will always be inserted before the conjunction.

Each time a series occurs in the Reading and Writing Practice, it will be indicated thus in the shorthand: ser [,]

306

Business vocabulary builder	
	confronting Facing.
	character reference One who vouches for the qualities, habits, and behavior of another.
	foreman The man in charge of a gang or crew of workers.
	succeeded Followed; took the place of.

Reading and writing practice

307 Brief-Form Letter

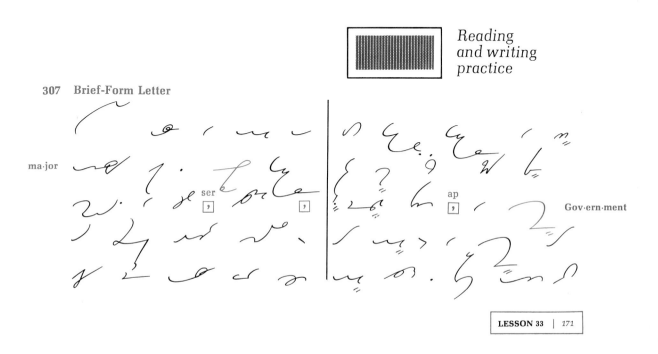

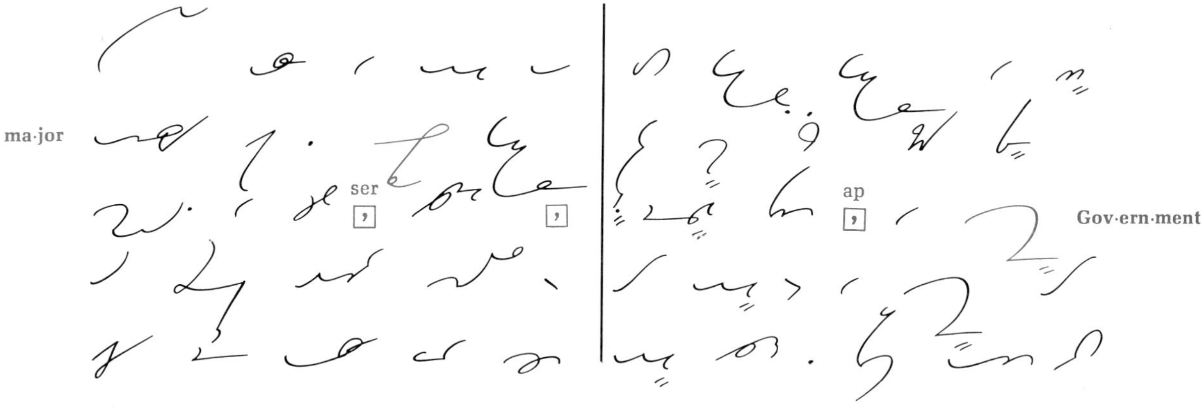
ma·jor
ser
ap
Gov·ern·ment

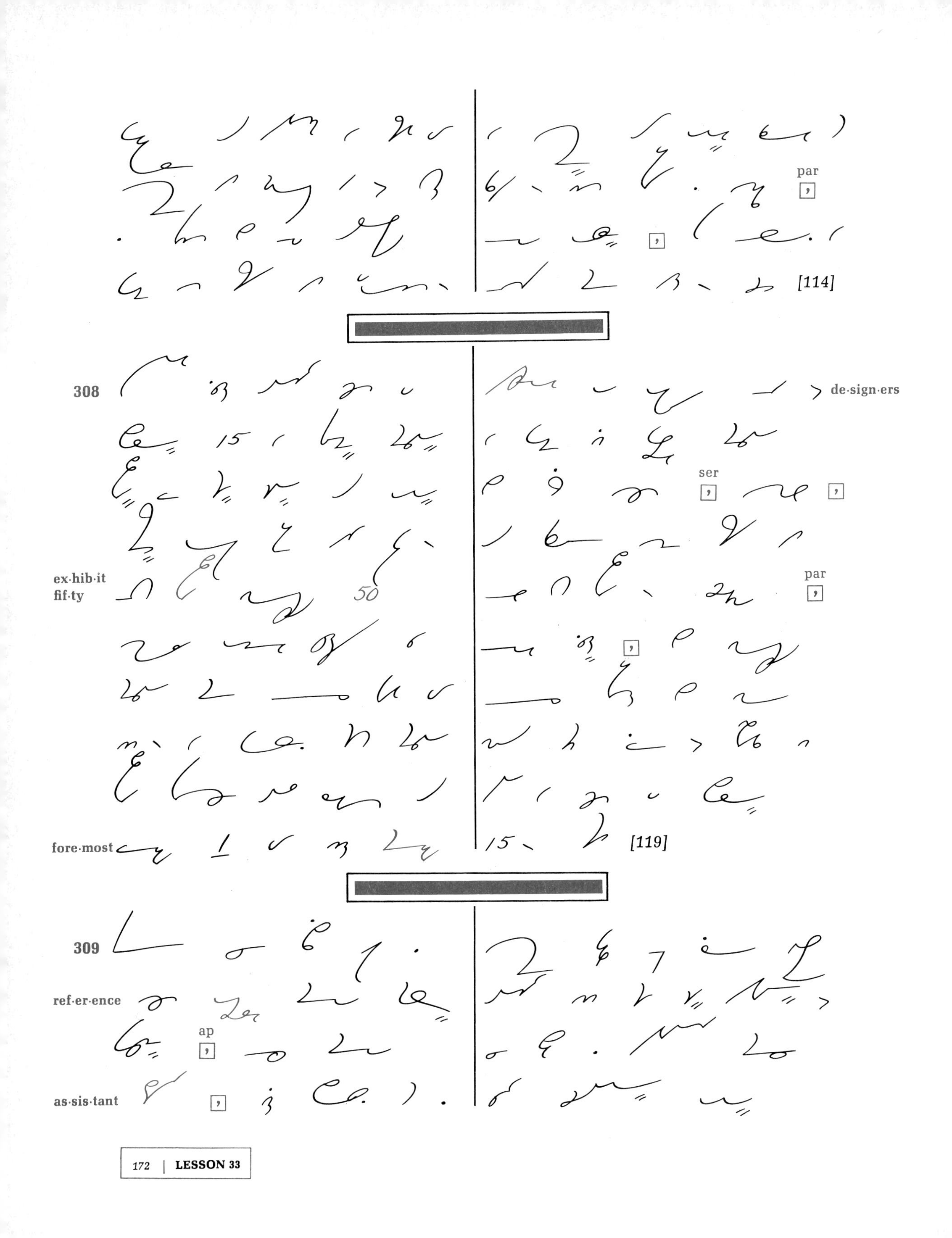

par

[114]

308

de·sign·ers

15

ser

ex·hib·it
fif·ty

50

par

fore·most

15

[119]

309

ref·er·ence

ap

as·sis·tant

re·spon·si·ble

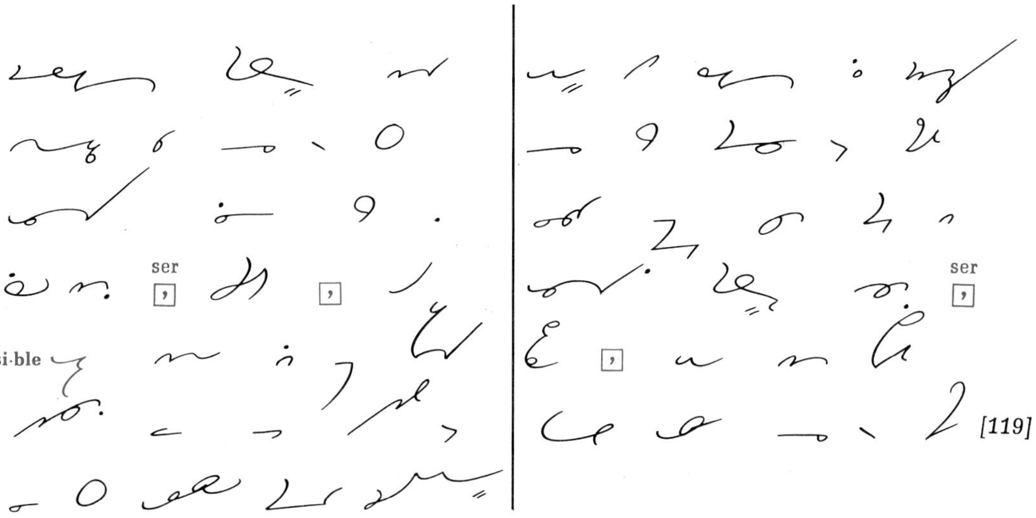

ser
ser
ser
[119]

310

al·ready
por·ing

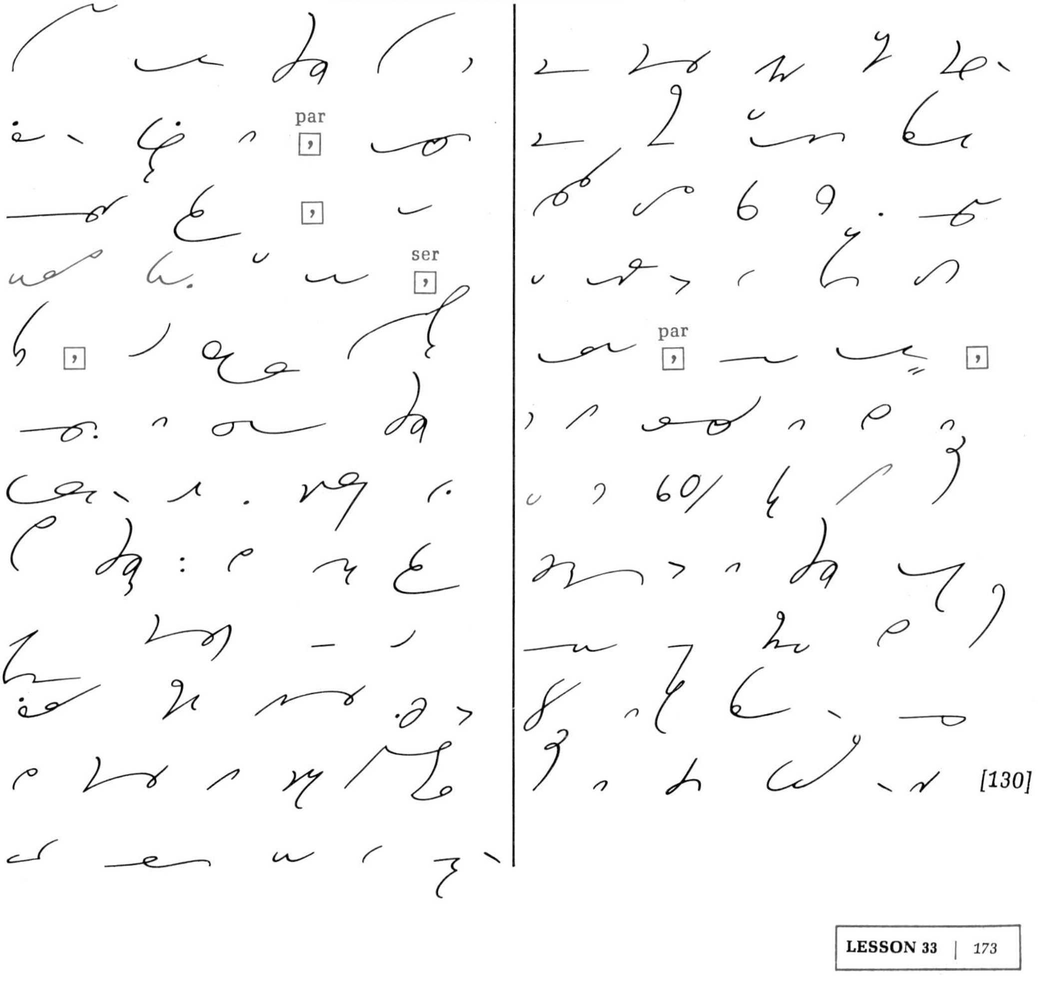

par
par
ser
par
60/
[130]

owe
due

311

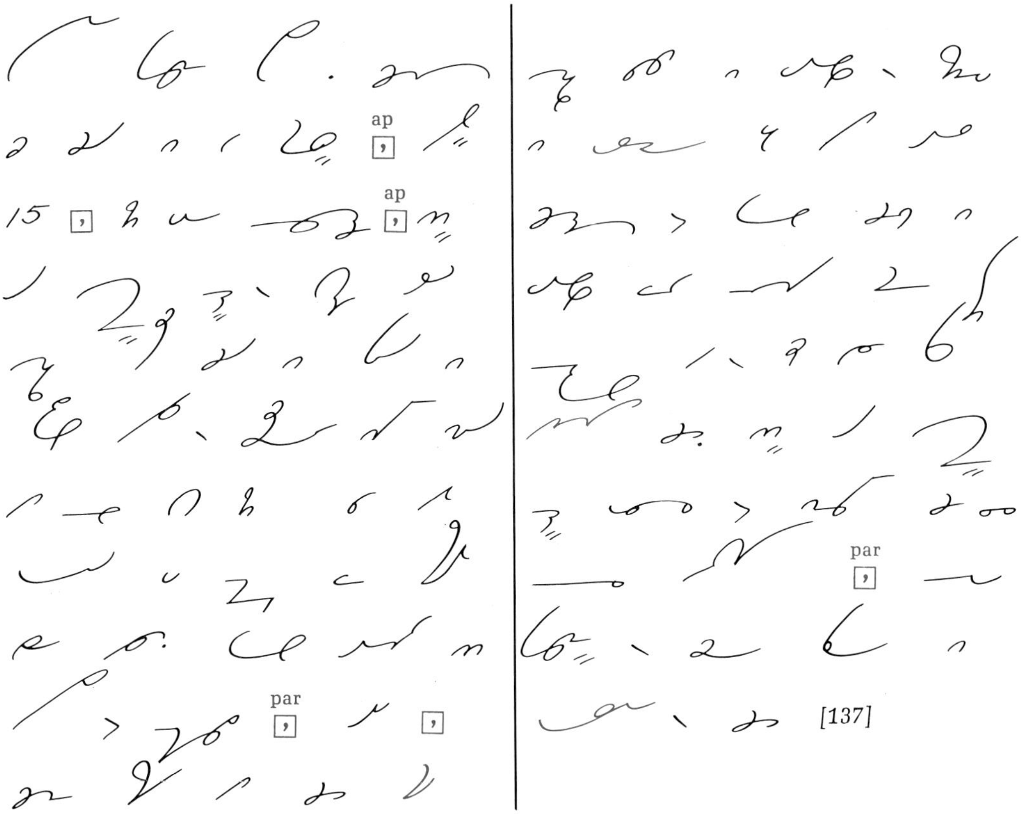
ap
ap
par
par
[137]

re·new·al
con·tin·ue
lat·er
fur·ther

PROPORTION CHECK LIST

As a result of the shorthand writing that you have already done, no doubt you have come to realize how important it is to—

☐ **1** Make the *a* circles huge; the *e* circles tiny.

☐ **2** Make the short strokes like *n* and *t* very short; the long strokes like *men* and *ted* very long.

☐ **3** Keep the straight lines straight; the curves deep.

☐ **4** Keep the *o* and *oo* hooks deep and narrow.

The readability of your shorthand will depend to a large extent on how you observe these pointers in your everyday writing.

LESSON 34

Principles

312 Want in Phrases In phrases, *want* is represented by *nt*.

I want, you want, he wants, I wanted, if you want, do you want, he wanted.

313 Ort The *r* is omitted in the combination *ort*.

Spell: re-p-o-t, report

Report, exported, quart, quarterly, sort, sorted, mortally.

314 R Omitted in -ern, -erm The *r* is omitted in the combinations *tern, term, thern, therm, dern, derm.*

Spell: t-e-n, turn

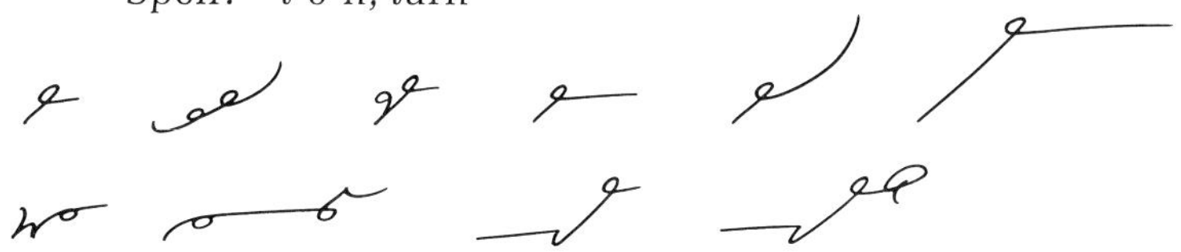

Turn, returned, eastern, term, termed, determine.
Southern, thermometer, modern, modernize.

315 Word Endings -cal, -cle The word endings *-cal, -cle* are represented by a disjoined *k*.

Spell: k-e-m-ical, chemical; a-r-t-ical, article

Chemical, critical, medical, technical, logical, article, physically.

316

Business vocabulary builder

decorators Those who design the inside of a home or office and select the furniture.

clerical help Stenographers, clerks, bookkeepers, typists, etc.

routine Commonplace; ordinary.

Reading and writing practice

317 Brief-Form Review Letter

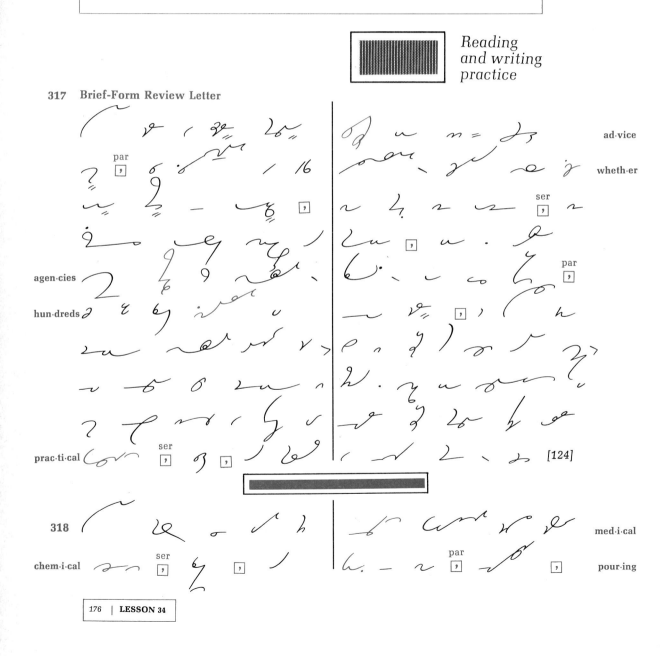

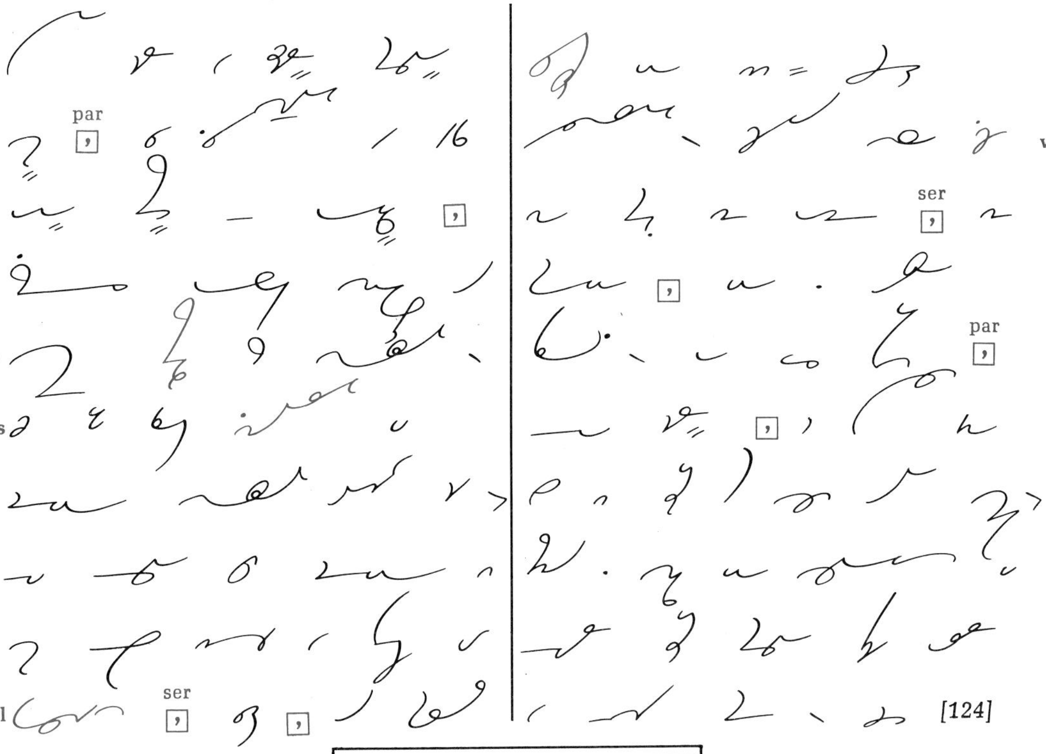
par
ser
par
ser
[124]

agen·cies
hun·dreds
prac·ti·cal
ad·vice
wheth·er

318

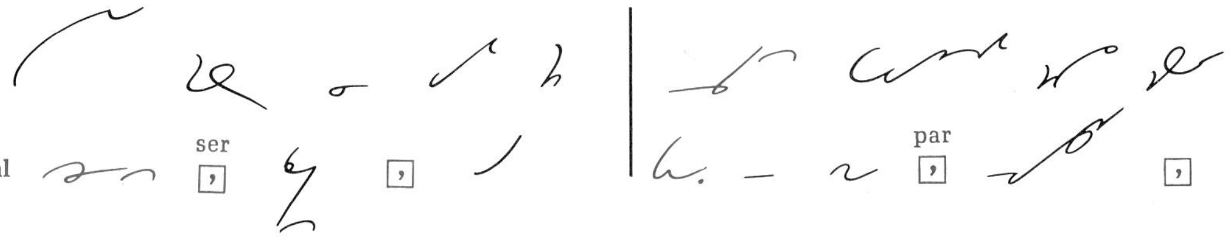
ser
par

chem·i·cal
med·i·cal
pour·ing

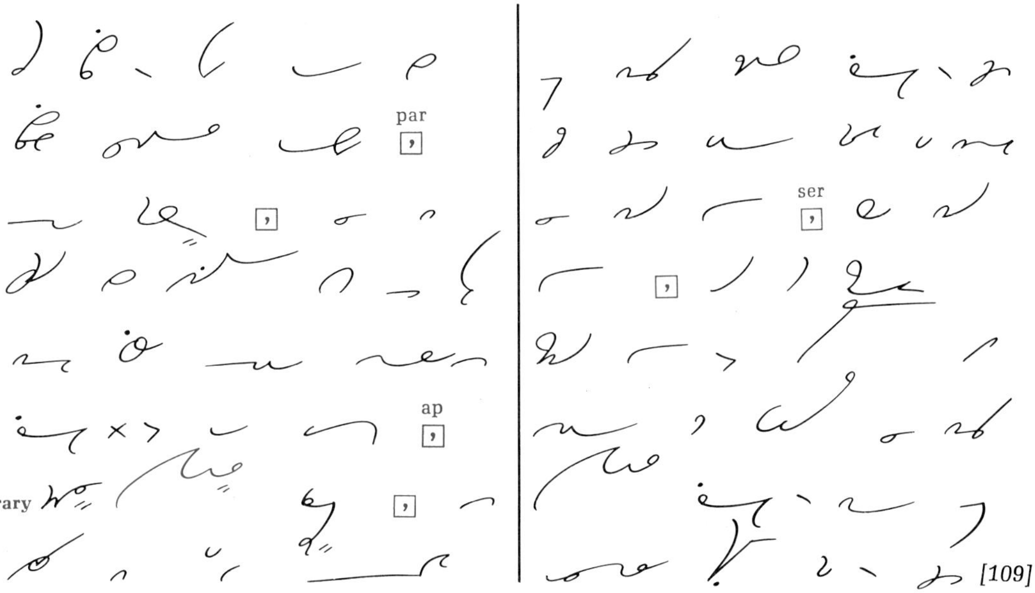

Tem·po·rary

[109]

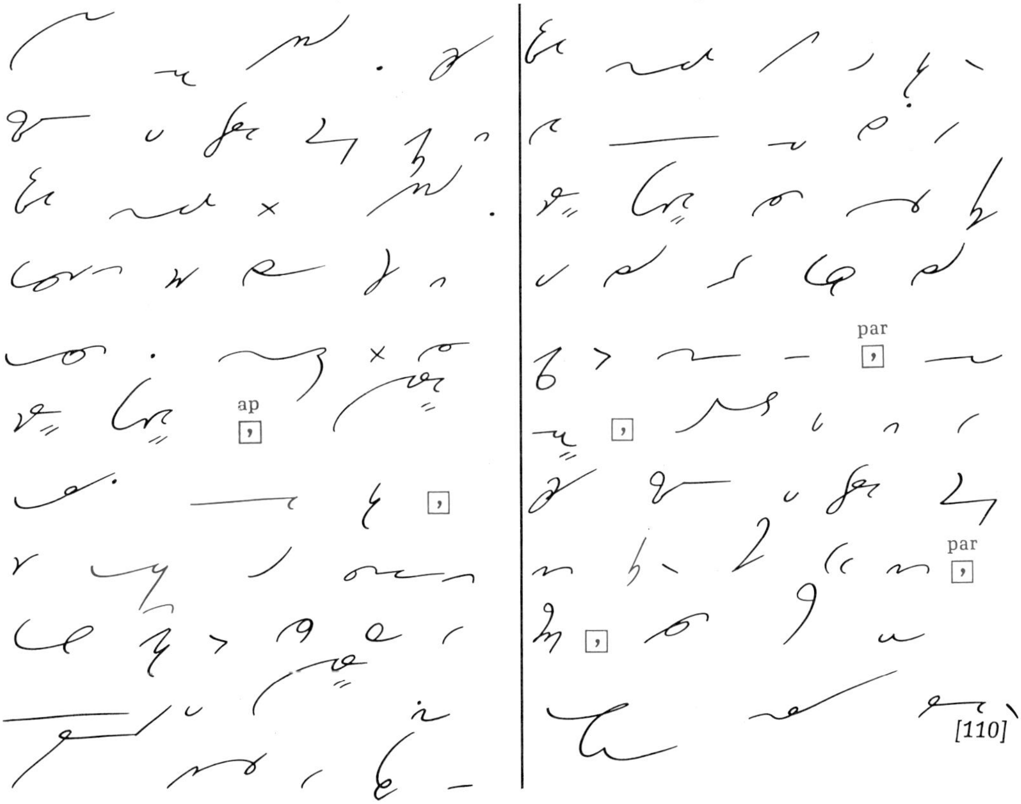

319

men's

log·i·cal

choose

[110]

320

ser
ser
par

sight

of·fi·cials

mod·ern

re·turn

[131]

321

de·vel·op·ment

safe·ty

[98]

LESSON 35

Principles

322 Word Beginnings Inter-, Intr-, Enter-, Entr- The word beginnings *inter-, intr-, enter-, entr-* are represented by a disjoined *n*. This disjoined word beginning, as well as other disjoined word beginnings that you will study in later lessons, is placed above the line of writing, close to the remainder of the word.

Inter-

Spell: *inter-s-t, interest*

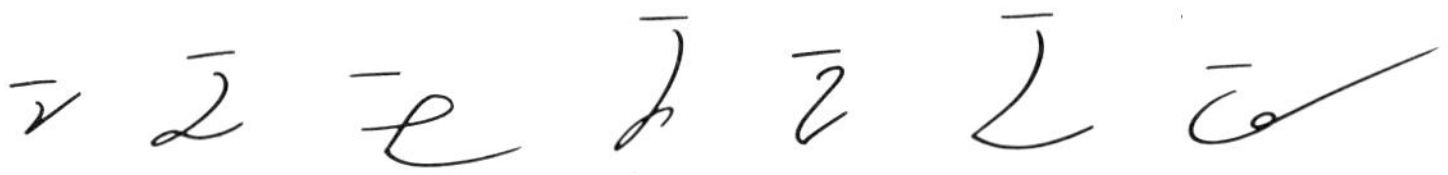

Interest, interfere, international, interview, interrupt, interval, interpreted.

Intr-

Spell: *intro-d-oo-s, introduce*

Introduce, introduces, introduction, intricate, intrude.

Enter-, Entr-

Spell: *enter-d, entered; enter-n-s, entrance*

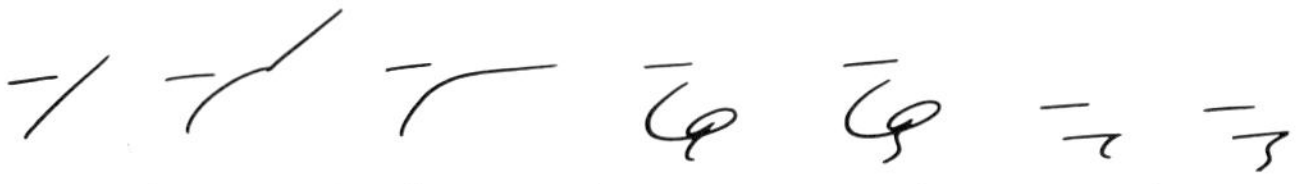

Entered, entertained, entertainment, enterprise, enterprises, entrance, entrances.

323 Word Ending -ings The word ending *-ings* is represented by a disjoined left *s*.

Spell: *o-p-n-ings, openings*

Openings, savings, earnings, meetings, evenings, proceedings, hearings, holdings.

324 Omission of Words in Phrases It is often possible to omit one or more unimportant words in a shorthand phrase. In the phrase *one of the*, for example, the word *of* is omitted; we write *one the*. When transcribing, the stenographer will insert *of*, as the phrase would make no sense without that word.

One of the, one of them, some of our, up to date, will you please, many of these, in the future.

Building transcription skills

325 SIMILAR-WORDS DRILL | quite, quiet

quite Completely; entirely.

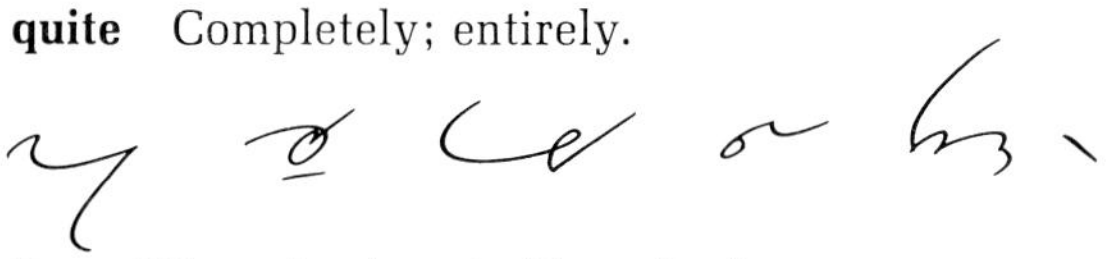

You will be quite pleased with our books.

quiet Free of noise; not excited.

Notice how quiet the room is.

He is a quiet person who seldom has anything to say.

326

Business vocabulary builder	
	absorb Soak up.
	interior Inside.
	instantly Without the least delay.
	expire Die; come to an end.

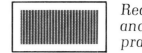

Reading and writing practice

327 Phrase Letter This letter contains several illustrations of the omission of words in phrases.

as·signed

ex·pe·ri·enced

con·fi·dence shown

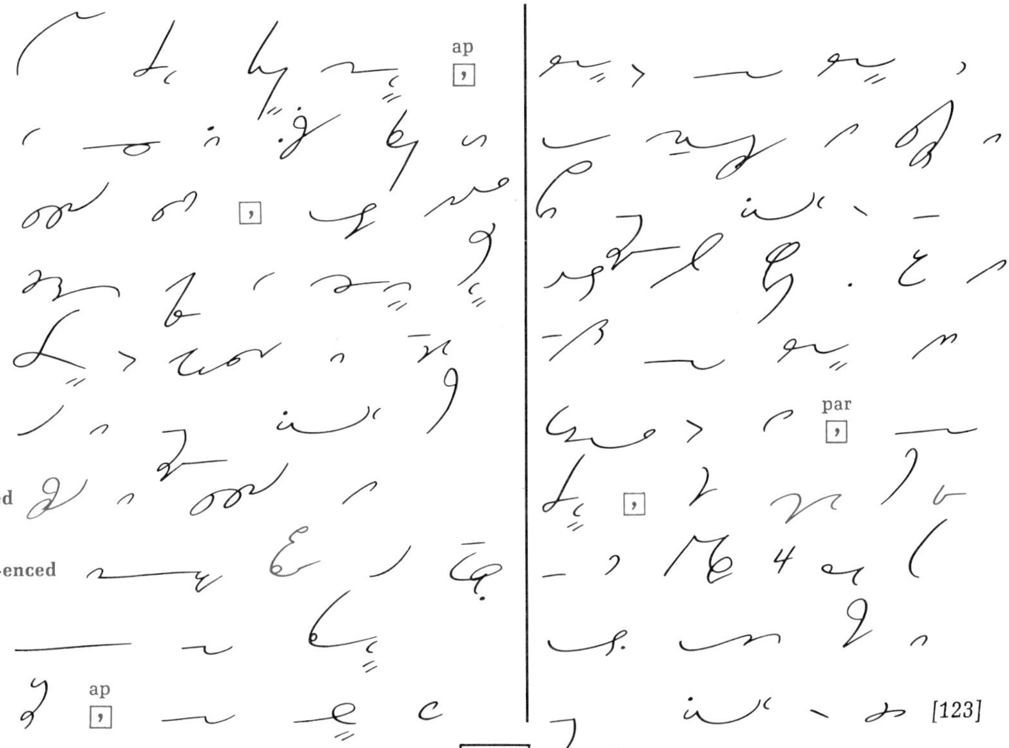

ap
ap
par
[123]

328

in·for·ma·tive

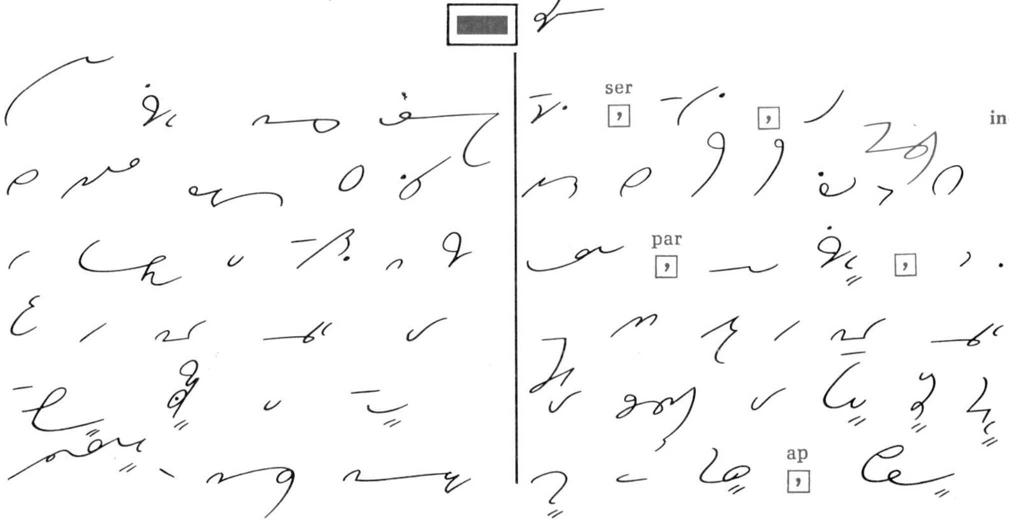

ser
par
ap

17 par par

ex·pens·es

po·si·tion

[130]

329

par

quiet

par

ceil·ings

par

ab·sorb

75,

[133]

330

ap

30

in·tro·duc·to·ry

40

[58]

331

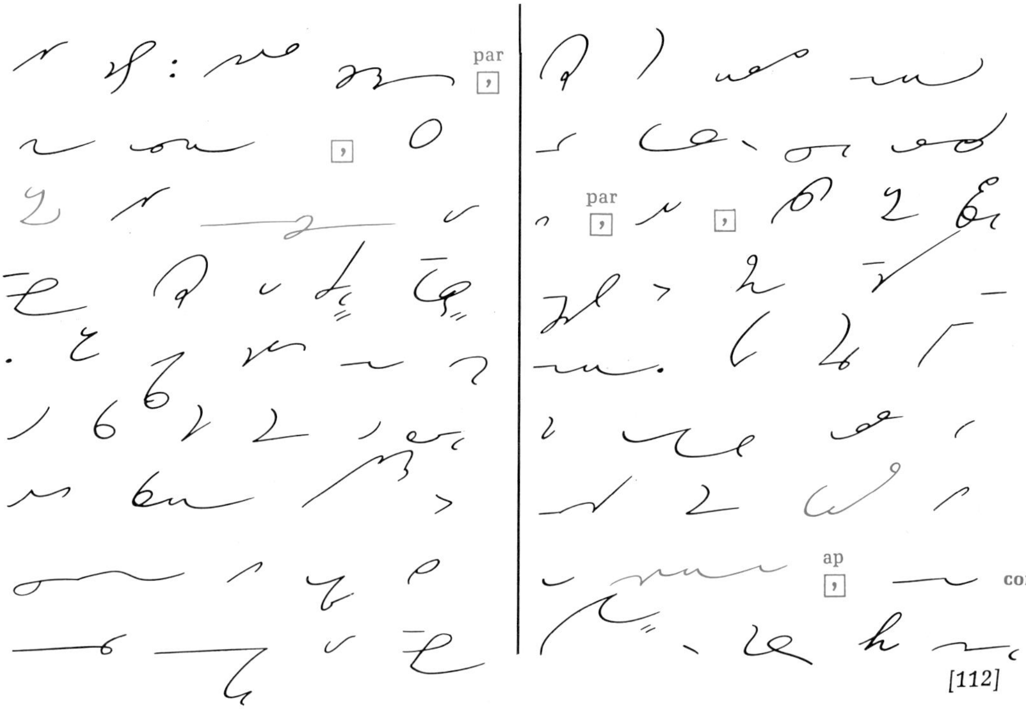
par
par
ap
[112]

of·fered
wom·en
prompt·ly
comp·trol·ler

332

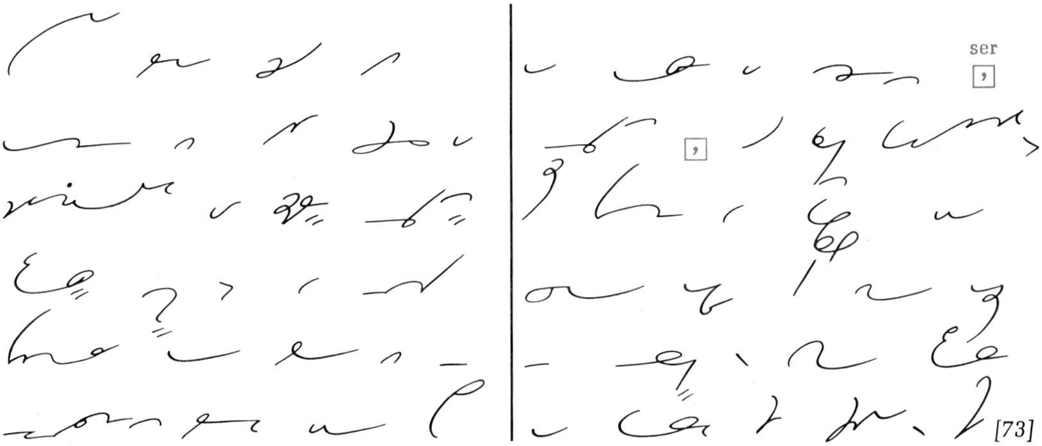
ser
[73]

LESSON 36

Recall

Lesson 36 is another breather. In Lesson 36 you will find a chart that contains a review of the shorthand devices you studied in Lessons 1 through 35 and a Reading and Writing Practice that tells what businessmen think about their secretaries. It should give you food for thought!

333 **Recall Chart** This chart contains a review of the shorthand devices you studied in previous lessons. It contains 78 brief forms, words, and phrases. Can you read the entire chart in 5 minutes?

BRIEF FORMS AND DERIVATIVES

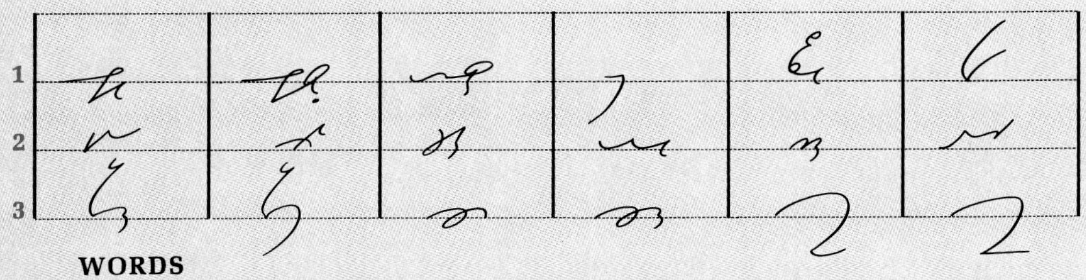

WORDS

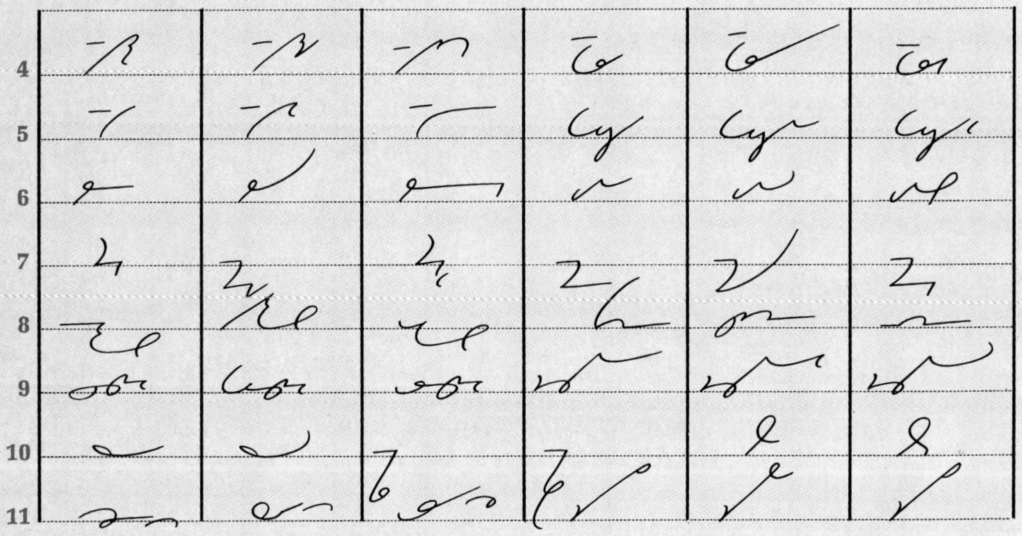

PHRASES

12
13

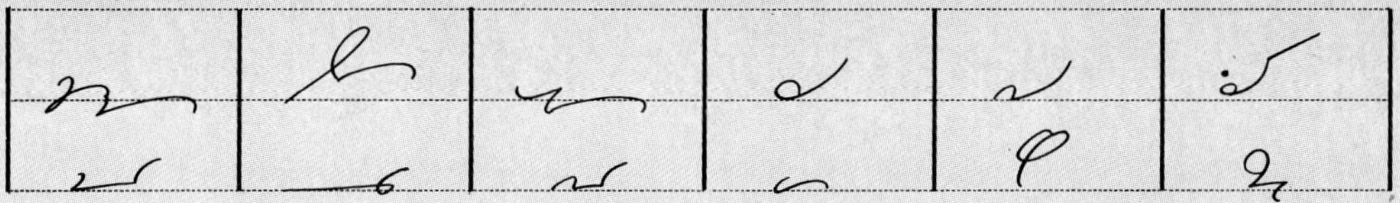

Building transportation skills

334

Business vocabulary builder	**utmost** Greatest. **conservative** Tending to maintain existing views or conditions. **comprehensive** Covering a wide range. **indispensable** Absolutely necessary; essential.

Reading and writing practice

335 Business Dress

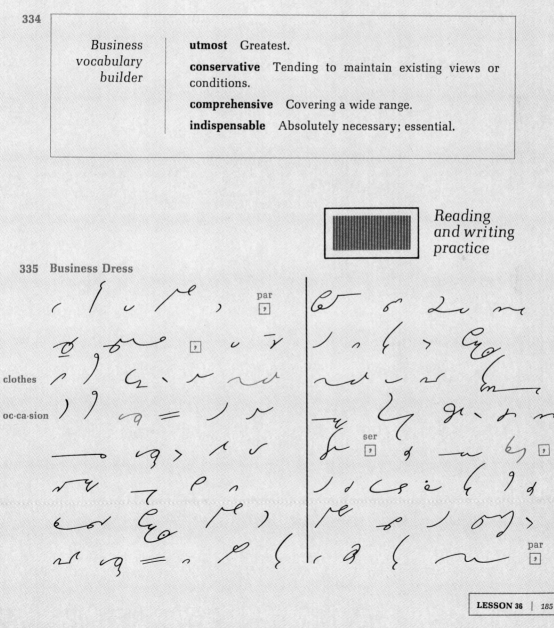

clothes
oc·ca·sion

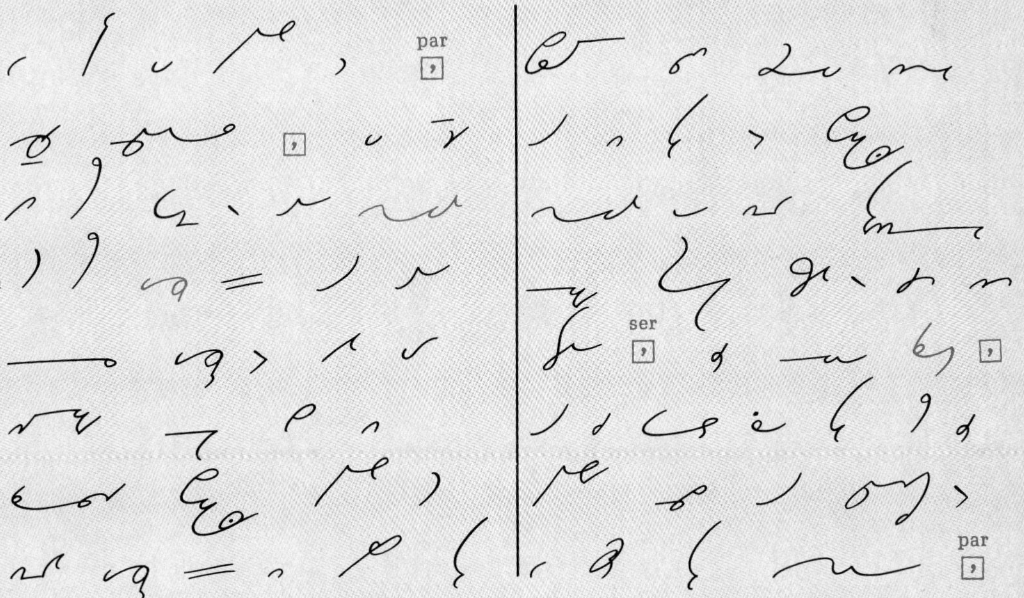
par
ser
par

cheer·ful

over·dressed

[159]

336 How Do You Look?

match col·ors

peeves

ap·pear·ance

(4)

(1)

(2)

jaws

ser

par

night

(3)

ap

glam·our

ser

cloth·ing

in·dis·pens·able

ser

[218]

337 Courtesy

par

ser

greet

cour·te·sy

pleas·ant

pres·ence

ab·sence

[157]

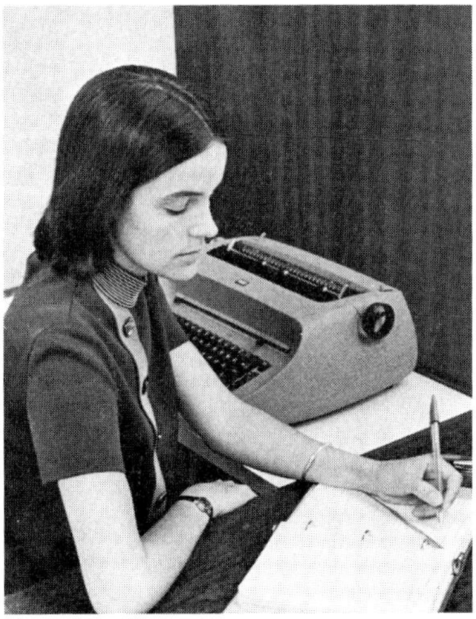

Chapter 7
What does a secretary do?

The answer to the question, "What does a secretary do?" will be different for almost every secretary. Most people think of a secretary as one who merely takes dictation and transcribes it. The fact is that taking dictation and transcribing it is a highly important— if not the most important—part of the secretary's job. But it is only one of many things that occupy her time.

The business executive thinks of the secretary as his "strong right arm." She frees him of the details of his job so that he will have time for managing people and procedures. Besides taking his dictation and transcribing it into good-looking letters, memoranda, and reports, she keeps his appointment calendar, answers his telephone, meets callers who wish to see him, files his important papers, writes letters and short reports, takes care of his mail, and arranges his business-travel accommodations. She may also do his banking and keep his income tax records—she may even shop for him and his family.

Each secretary has duties connected with her job that differ in some respects from those of another secretary, depending on the kind of work her boss is engaged in and his willingness to delegate details to her. The secretary to an accountant, to a retail store owner, or to a company treasurer is likely to need to know bookkeeping. The secretary to a lawyer must know legal forms and terminology. The secretary to a doctor may be required to know something about medical laboratory procedures and

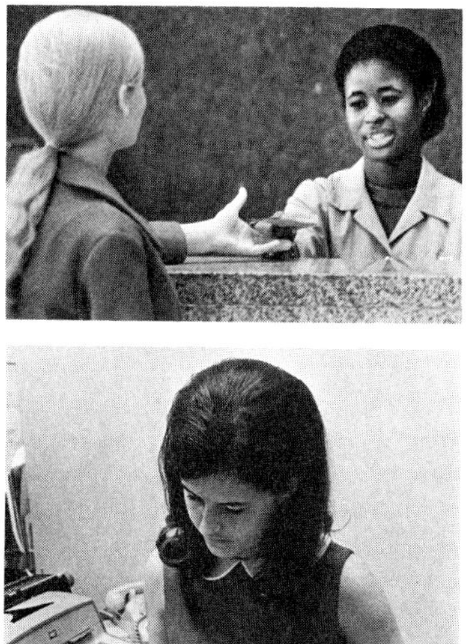

medical record keeping; she most certainly will have to know medical terminology. The secretary to a dentist may double as a technician—preparing the dental equipment for use, sterilizing instruments, assisting the dentist with X rays, keeping his records, and following up on appointments. No two secretarial jobs are alike. Each is different, and each has its interesting facets. But there is a common thread that runs through all of them—taking dictation and transcribing it quickly and accurately.

LESSON 37

Principles

338 **Word Ending -ingly** The word ending *-ingly* is represented by a disjoined *e* circle.

Spell: *a-k-o-ard-ingly, accordingly*

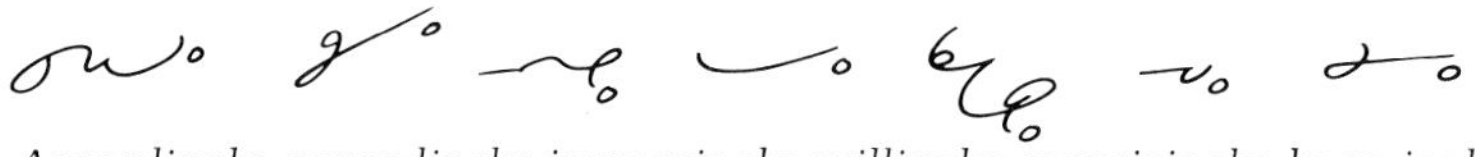

Accordingly, exceedingly, increasingly, willingly, surprisingly, knowingly, seemingly.

339 **Word Beginning Im-** The word beginning *im-* is represented by *m*.

Spell: *im-p-o-t, import*

Import, impressed, impose, impossible, improve, improperly, imply.

340 **Word Beginning Em-** The word beginning *em-* is also represented by *m*.

Spell: *em-p-l-oi, employ*

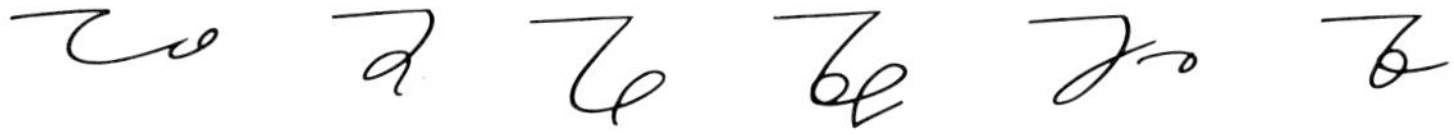

Employ, emphasis, embrace, embarrassed, emphatically, empire.

341 **Omission of Minor Vowel** When two vowel sounds come together, the minor vowel may be omitted.

Courteous, serious, previously, genuine, union, period, theory, ideal.

342 PUNCTUATION PRACTICE | , if clause

One of the most frequent errors made by the beginning transcriber is the failure to make a complete sentence. In most cases the incomplete sentence is a dependent or subordinate clause introduced by *if, as,* or *when.* The dependent or subordinate clause deceives the transcriber because it is a complete sentence except that it is introduced by a word such as *if;* therefore, it requires another clause to complete the thought.

The dependent or subordinate clause often signals the coming of the main clause by means of a subordinate conjunction. The commonest subordinating conjunctions are *if, as,* and *when.* Other subordinating conjunctions are *though, although, whether, unless, because, since, while, where, after, whenever, until, before,* and *now.* In this lesson you will consider clauses introduced by *if.*

A subordinate clause introduced by *if* and followed by the main clause is separated from the main clause by a comma.

If you can do this for us, we will be exceedingly grateful.

If I can help you obtain material for the bulletin, please let me know.

Each time a subordinate clause beginning with *if* occurs in the Reading and Writing Practice, it will be indicated thus in the shorthand: if [,]

343 Business vocabulary builder

exceedingly Very much.

previous Coming before.

imperative Not to be avoided; urgent.

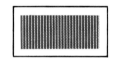

Reading and writing practice

344 Brief-Form Review Letter

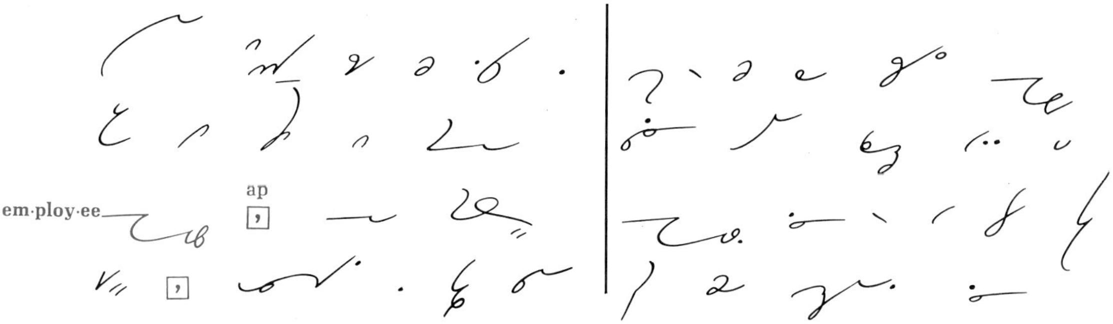
em·ploy·ee
ap

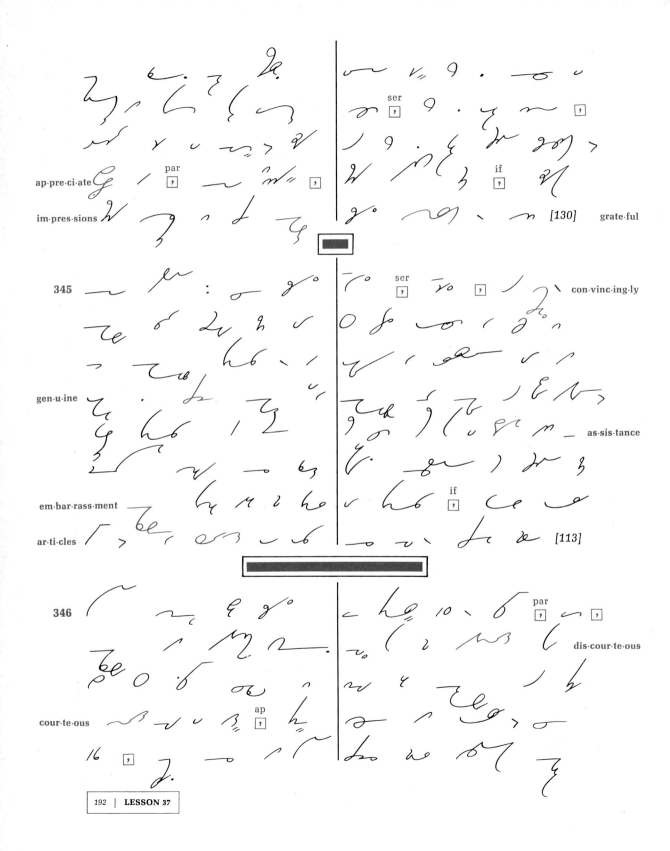

ap·pre·ci·ate

par

im·pres·sions

ser

if

[130] grate·ful

[redacted]

345

ser

con·vinc·ing·ly

gen·u·ine

as·sis·tance

if

em·bar·rass·ment

ar·ti·cles

[113]

[redacted]

346

par

dis·cour·te·ous

cour·te·ous

ap

16

accept

previous

if

[110]

347

par

ap

impressed

referring

if

further

[121]

348

if

par

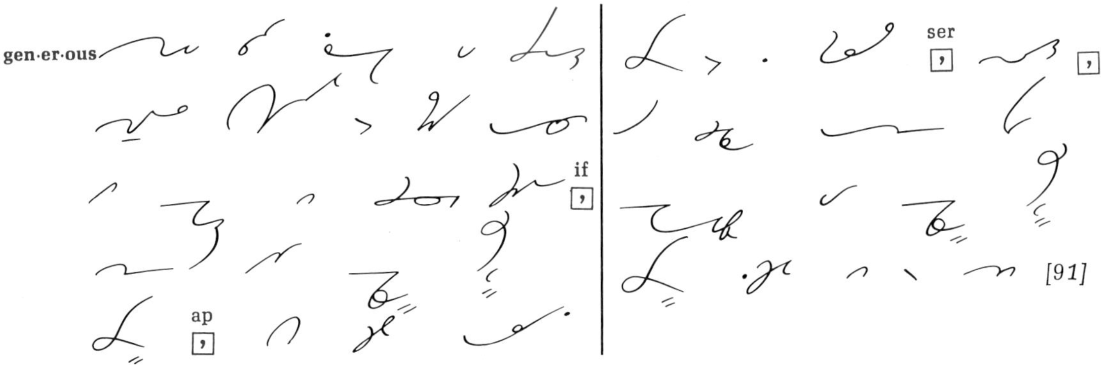
gen·er·ous
ser
if
ap
[91]

349 Good Sign

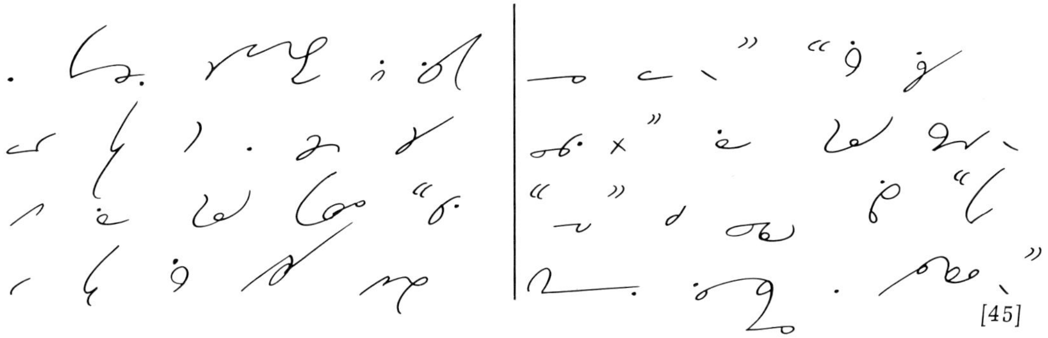
[45]

LESSON 38

Principles

350 Word Ending -ship The word ending *-ship* is represented by a disjoined *sh*.

Spell: s-t-e-m-ship, steamship

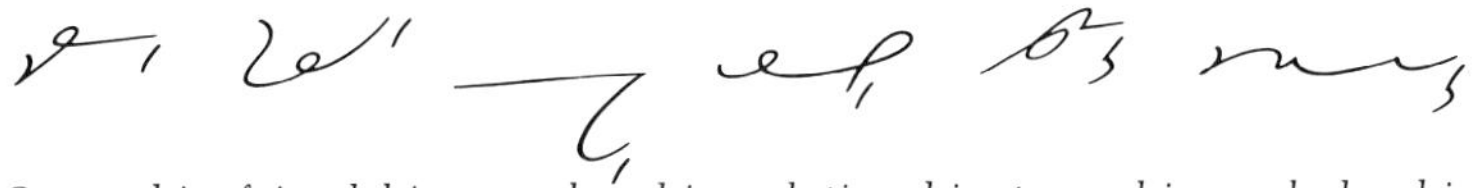

Steamship, friendship, membership, relationship, townships, scholarships.

351 Word Beginning Sub- The word beginning *sub-* is represented by *s*.

Spell: sub-m-e-t, submit

Submit, subscribed, substantial, subdivide, sublet, suburbs, subway.

352 Joining of Hook and Circle Vowels When a hook and a circle vowel come together, they are written in the order in which they are pronounced.

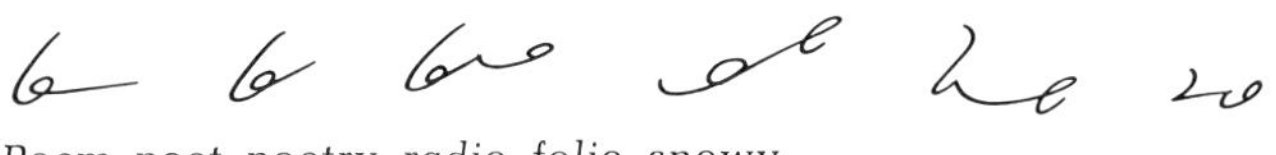

Poem, poet, poetry, radio, folio, snowy.

Building transcription skills

353 PUNCTUATION PRACTICE | , as clause

A subordinate clause introduced by *as* and followed by a main clause is separated from the main clause by a comma.

As you know, there is a substantial sum due on your account.

As you will see by the enclosed report, our plans for the convention are almost complete.

Each time a subordinate clause beginning with *as* occurs in the Reading and Writing Practice, it will be indicated thus in the shorthand: as [,]

354

Business vocabulary builder	
	colleagues Fellow workers.
	substantially To a large extent.
	jeopardizing Risking the loss of.

Reading and writing practice

355 Brief-Form Review Letter

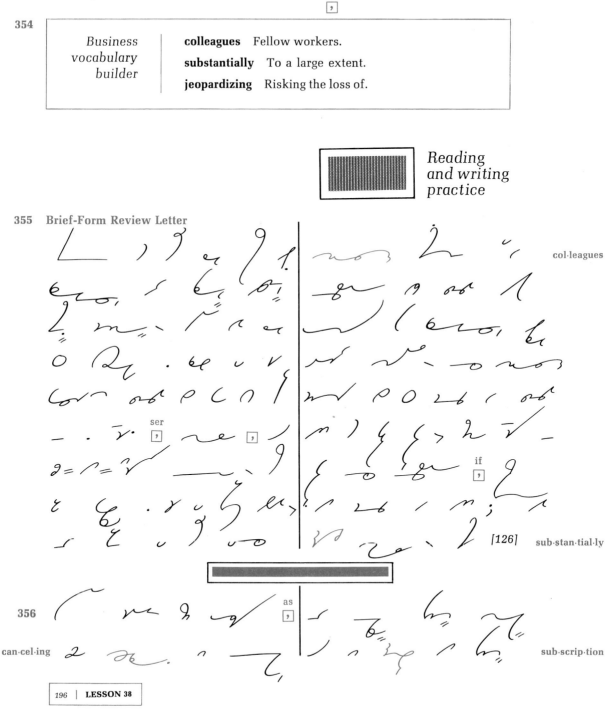

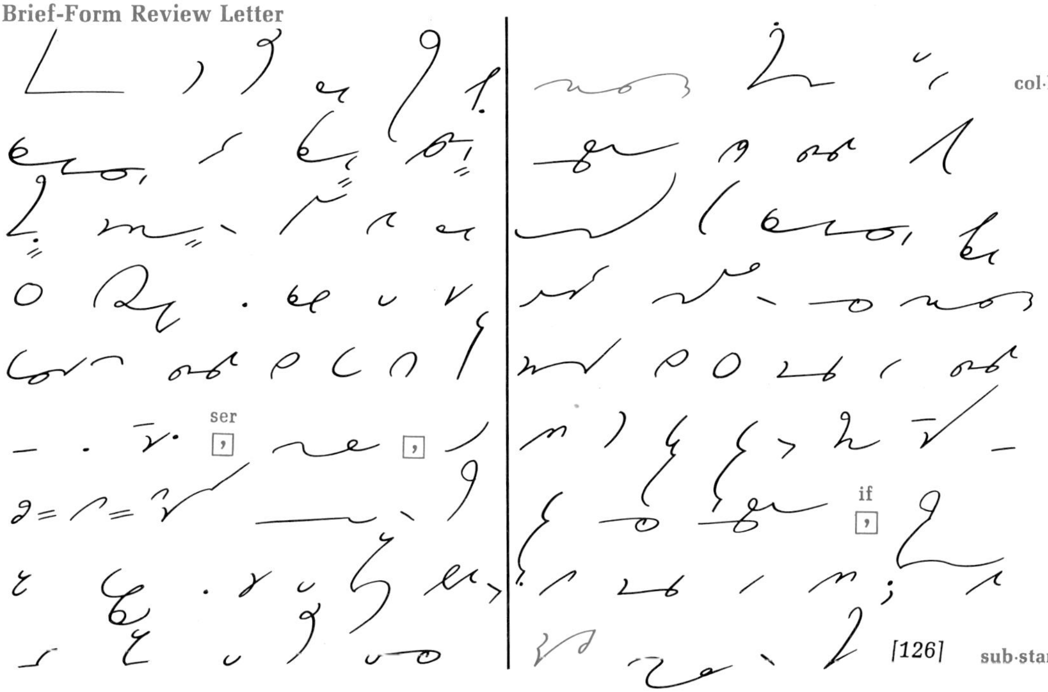

ser
if
[126]

col·leagues

sub·stan·tial·ly

356

as

can·cel·ing

sub·scrip·tion

sum

par

as

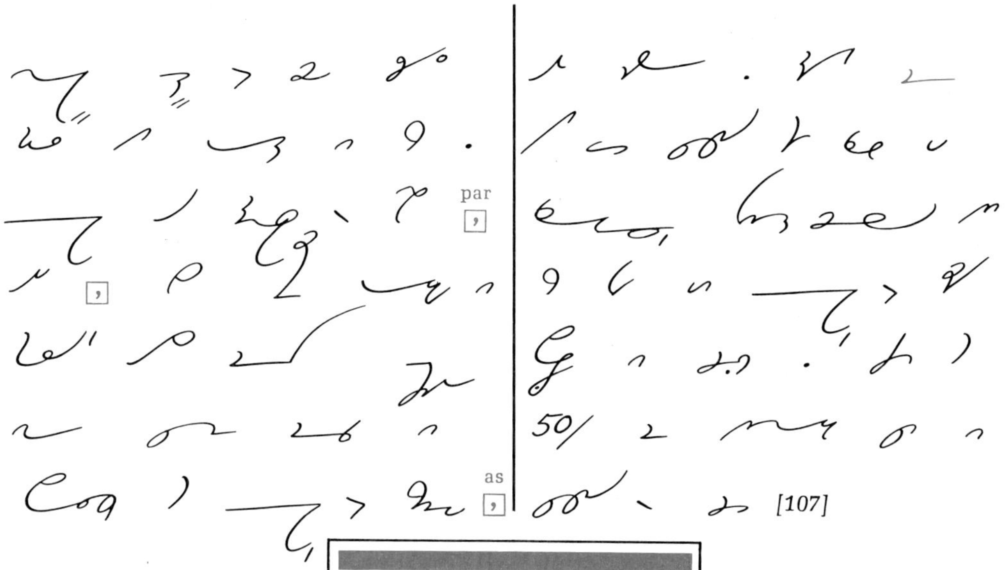

[107]

357

ser

if

par

au·to·mat·i·cal·ly

as

as·so·ci·a·tion

bul·le·tin

an·nu·al

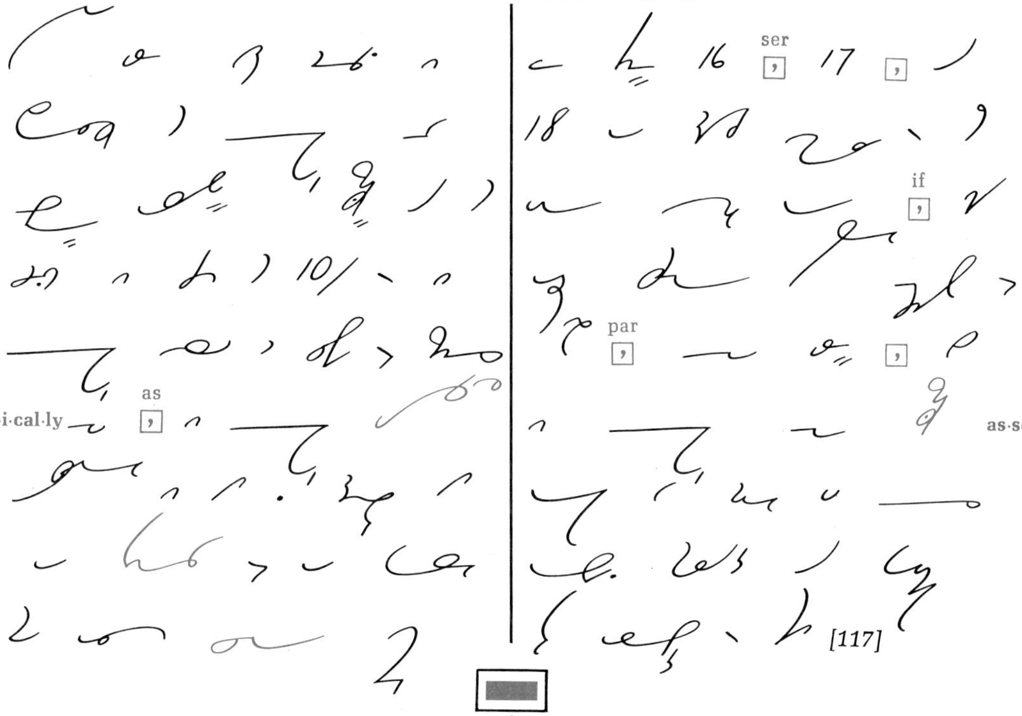

[117]

358

as

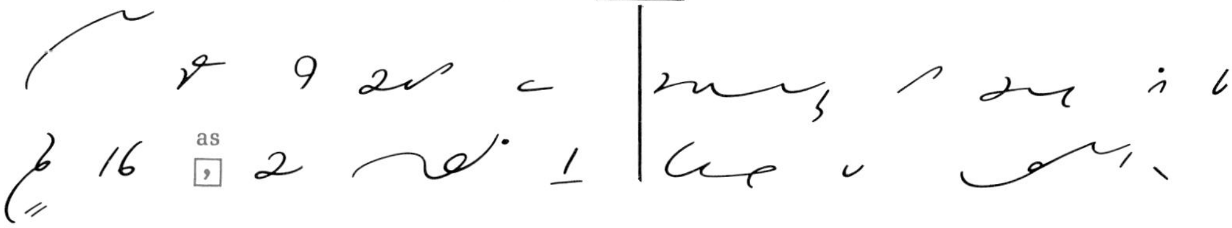

ap

as

com·pe·ti·tion if par

sub·mit·ted [113] prompt·ly

359 re·la·tion·ship

as

pre·serve

over·due

jeop·ar·diz·ing 550

par

dis·turb·ing [110]

360

ap 10

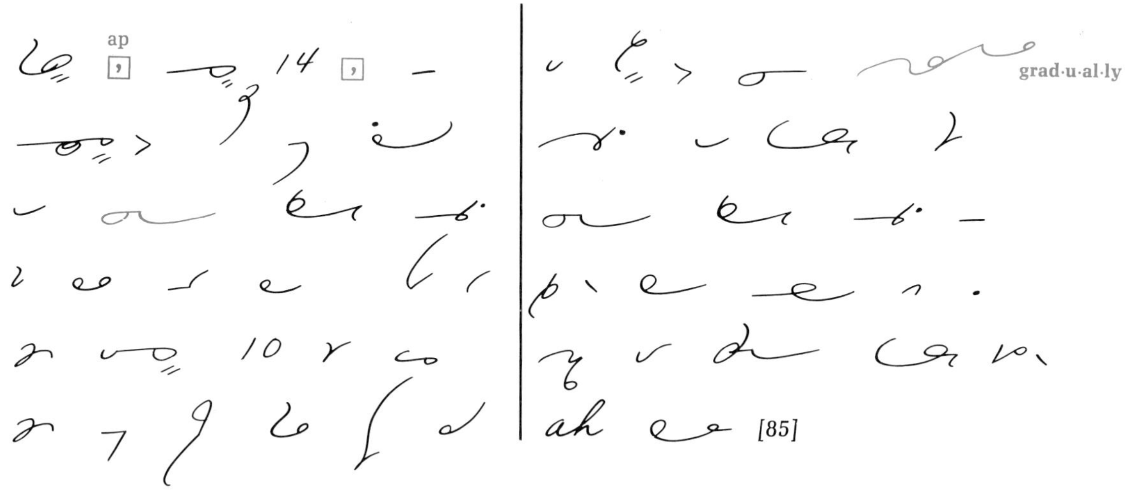
ap
an·nu·al
grad·u·al·ly
[85]

361

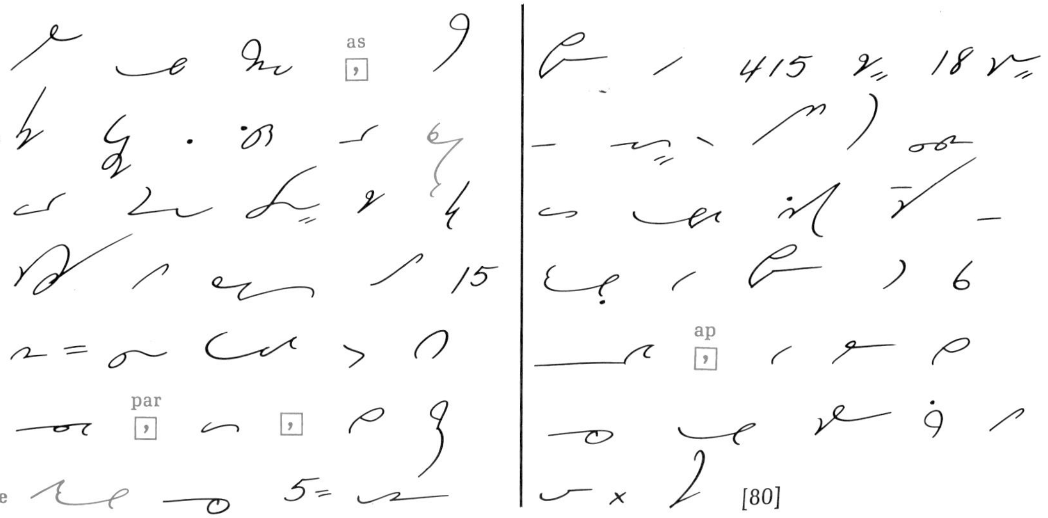
as
sub·urbs
par
sub·lease
ap
[80]

LESSON 39

Principles

362 Word Ending -rity The word ending *-rity* is represented by a disjoined *r.*

Spell: s-e-k-rity, security

Security, authorities, maturity, majority, popularity, sincerity, prosperity.

363 Word Ending -lity The word ending *-lity* is represented by a disjoined *l.*

Spell: a-b-lity, ability

Ability, facilities, personality, possibility, reliability, qualities.

364 Word Ending -lty The word ending *-lty* is also represented by a disjoined *l.*

Spell: f-a-k-ulty, faculty

Faculty, penalty, loyalty, royalty, casualty.

365 Word Endings -self, -selves The word ending *-self* is represented by *s; -selves,* by *ses.*

Spell: h-e-r-self, herself; your-selves, yourselves

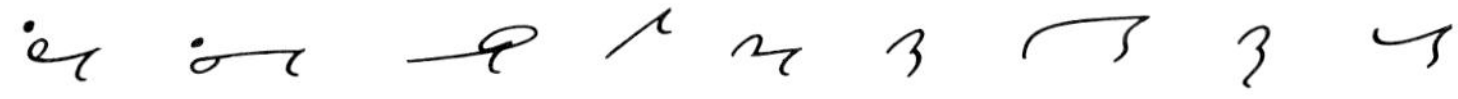

Herself, himself, myself, itself, oneself, yourself, themselves, yourselves, ourselves.

366 PUNCTUATION PRACTICE **|** **, when clause**

A subordinate clause introduced by *when* and followed by the main clause is separated from the main clause by a comma.

When I was in town last month, I discussed with you the possibility of holding our meetings in your hotel.

When you delay paying your bills, you are endangering your credit reputation.

Each time a subordinate clause beginning with *when* occurs in the Reading and Writing Practice, it will be indicated thus in the shorthand: when [,]

367

Business vocabulary builder	
	faculty Teachers in a school.
	reality Fact; a real event.
	security holdings Stocks and bonds that an investor owns.
	impressive Creating a feeling of admiration.

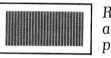

Reading and writing practice

368 Brief-Form Review Letter

aware

fa·cil·i·ties

anal·y·sis

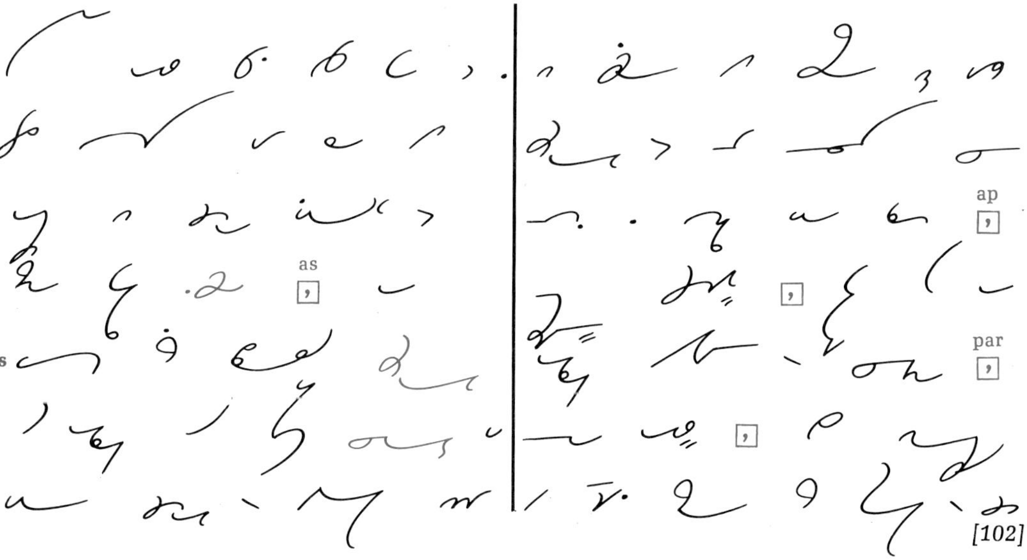

as
ap
par

[102]

369

dis·cussed

fac·ul·ty

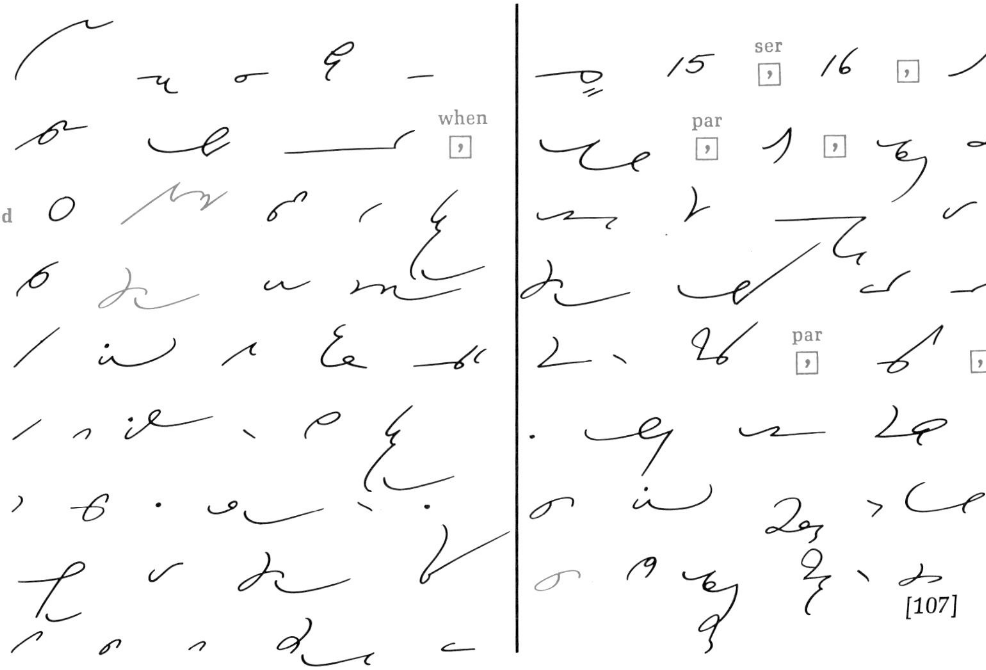
ser
when
par
par
[107]

ac·knowl·edge

370

be·lieve

fa·mil·iar·i·ty

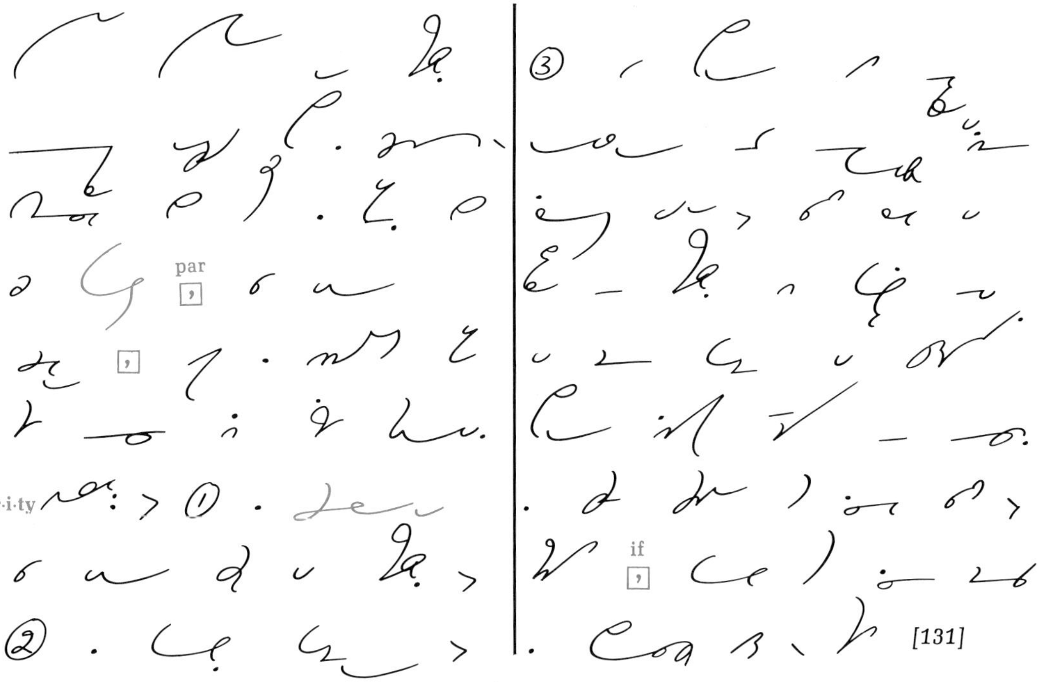
par
if
[131]

371

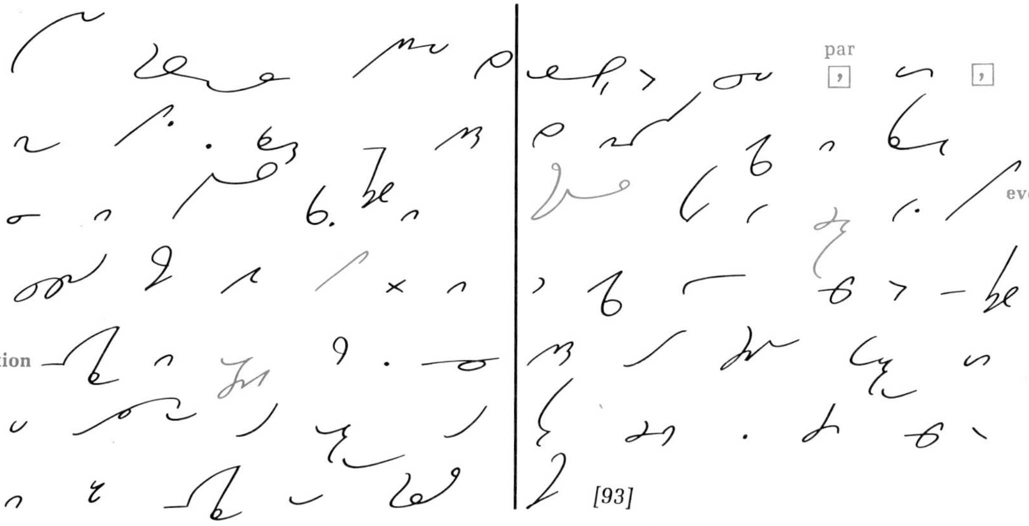

par
eventually
sensible
due
reputation

[93]

372

reasonably
choose
ser
when
individuality

[84]

373

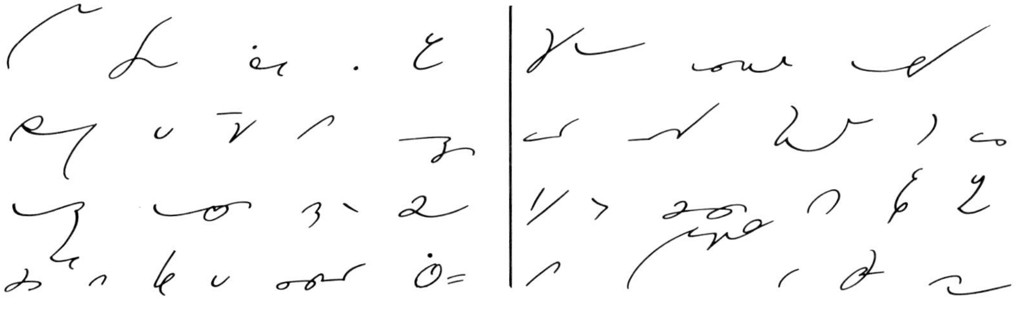

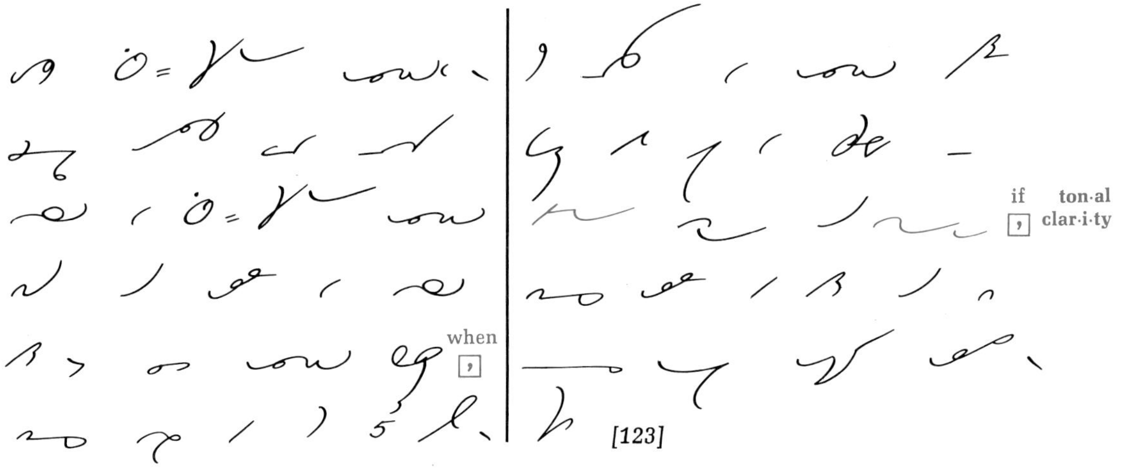
when
if
ton·al
clar·i·ty
[123]

HOMEWORK CHECK LIST

When you do your homework assignment each day—

☐ **1** Do you study the Business Vocabulary Builder and the other transcription helps in the lesson before you start your work on the Reading and Writing Practice?

☐ **2** Do you read aloud each Reading and Writing Practice before copying it?

☐ **3** Do you spell each shorthand outline that you cannot immediately read? Remember, nothing builds shorthand speed more rapidly than the regular reading and writing of shorthand.

☐ **4** Do you note carefully the reason for the use of each comma that is boxed in the Reading and Writing Practice?

☐ **5** Do you spell aloud all the words given in the margins of the shorthand in the Reading and Writing Practice?

LESSON 40

Principles

374 Abbreviated Words—in Families Many long words may be abbreviated in shorthand by dropping the endings. This device is also used in longhand, as *Jan.* for *January*. The extent to which you use this device will depend on your familiarity with the words and with the subject matter of the dictation. When in doubt, write it out! The ending of a word is not dropped when a special shorthand word-ending form has been provided, such as *-lity*.

Notice how many of the words written with this abbreviating device fall naturally into families of similar endings.

-tribute

Tribute, attribute, contribute, contributed, contribution, distribute, distributor.

-quent

Consequent-consequence, consequently, subsequent, subsequently, frequent, eloquent.

-quire

Require, requirement, inquire, inquires, inquired, inquiry, esquire.

-titute

Substitute, institute, constitute, constitution, substitution.

-titude

Aptitude, gratitude, latitude, altitude, attitude.

Building transcription skills

375 PUNCTUATION PRACTICE | , introductory

A comma is used to separate the subordinate clause from a following main clause. You have already studied the application of this rule to subordinate clauses introduced by *if, as,* and *when.* Here are additional examples:

While I understand the statement, I do not agree with it.

Although it was only 3 o'clock, he closed the office.

Before you award your next advertising contract, give us an opportunity to discuss it with you.

A comma is also used after introductory words or phrases such as *furthermore, on the contrary,* and *for instance.*

Furthermore, you made a mistake in grammar.

On the contrary, you are at fault.

For your convenience in sending me the information I need, I am enclosing a stamped envelope.

Each time a subordinate (or introductory) word, phrase, or clause other than one beginning with *if, as,* or *when* occurs in the Reading and Writing Practice, it will be indicated thus in the shorthand: intro [,]

▶ Note: If the subordinate clause or other introductory expression follows the main clause, the comma is usually not necessary.

I am enclosing a stamped envelope for your convenience in sending me the information I need.

376

Business vocabulary builder	
	counsel (*noun*) Advice.
	eloquent Marked by forceful expression.
	distributors Agents who market goods.
	attributes (*noun*) Characteristics; qualities.

Reading and writing practice

377 Brief-Form Review Letter

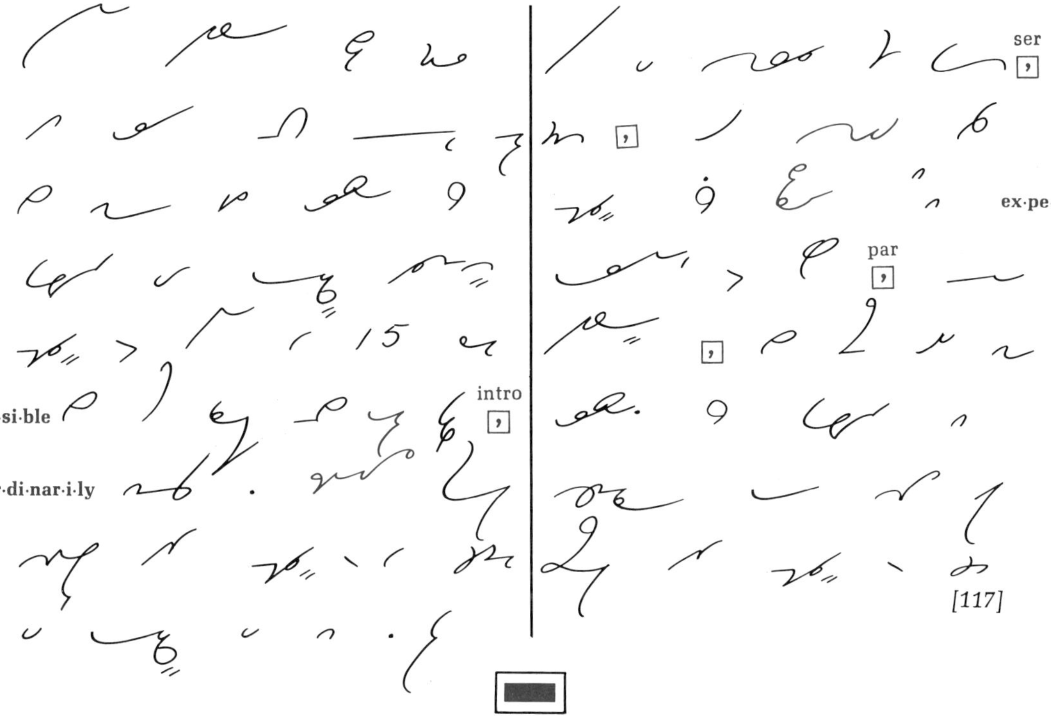

ser
growth
ex·pe·ri·enced
par
re·spon·si·ble
intro
ex·traor·di·nar·i·ly
[117]

378

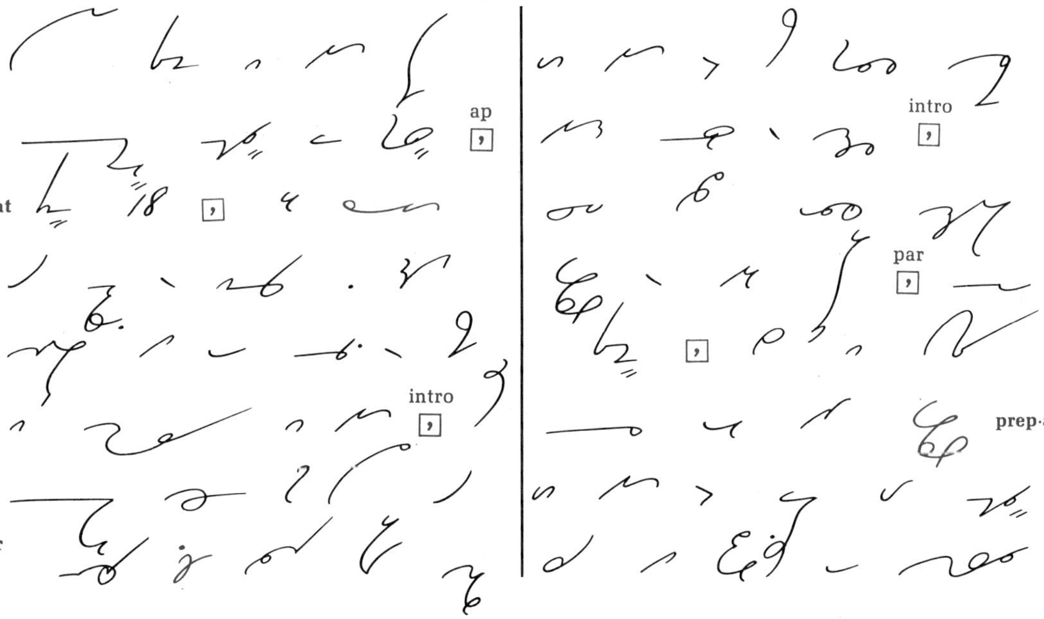

ap
intro
el·o·quent
par
intro
prep·a·ra·tion
wheth·er

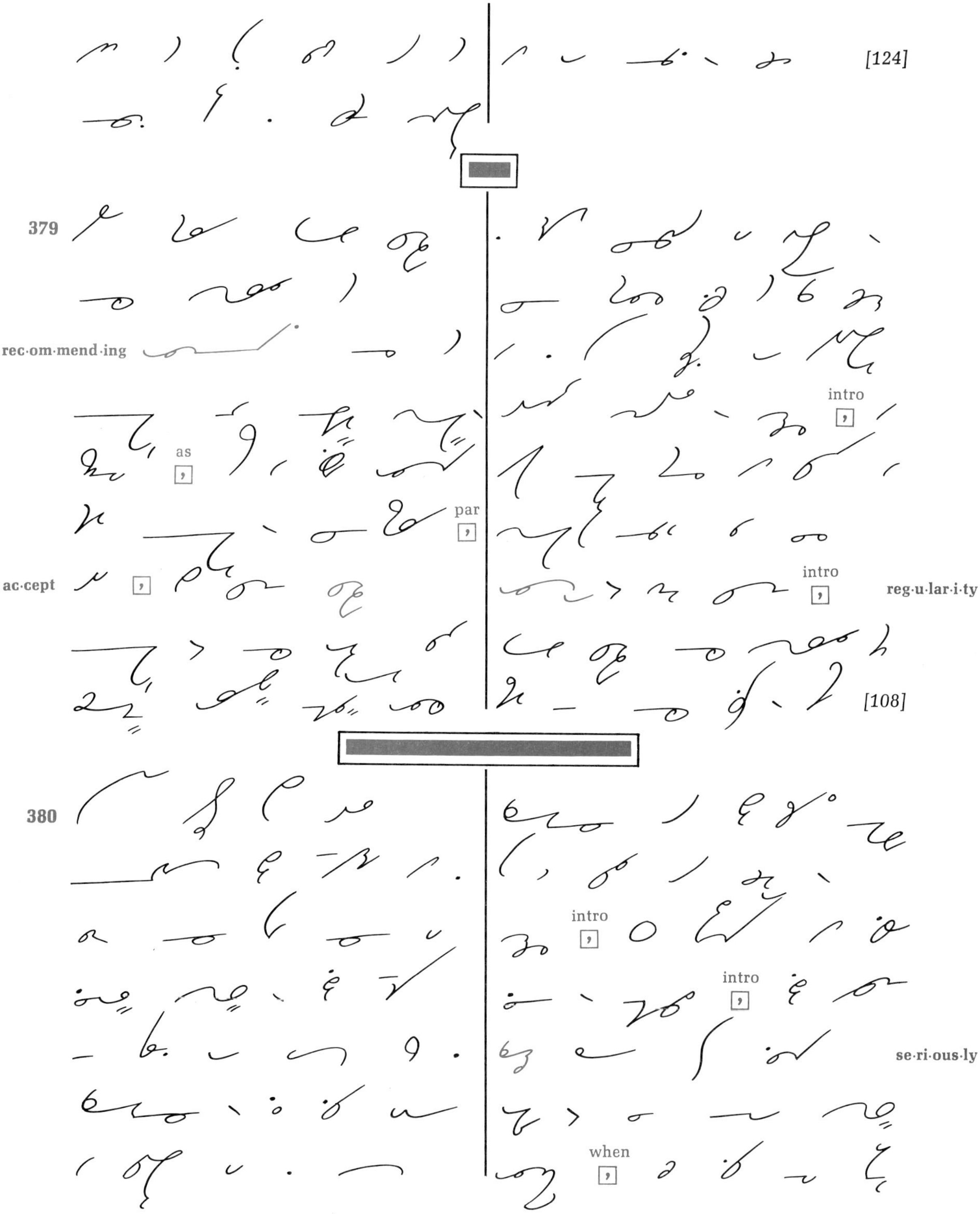
[124]
379
rec·om·mend·ing
as
par
intro
intro
ac·cept
reg·u·lar·i·ty
[108]
380
intro
intro
se·ri·ous·ly
when

avail·able

rec·om·mend

if

[113]

381

par

if par

intro

de·lin·quent

when

par

intro

co·op·er·ate

dis·trib·u·tor

[107]

382 Addition

[59]

LESSON 41

Principles

383 Abbreviated Words—Not in Families The ending may be omitted from some long words even though they do not fall into a family.

Anniversary, convenient-convenience, memorandum, equivalent, significant-significance, reluctant-reluctance, privilege, privileges, privileged.

384 Word Beginning Trans- The word beginning *trans-* is represented by a disjoined *t.*

Spell: trans-a-k-t, transact

Transact, translate, transported, transferred, transplant, transcriber, transit.

385 Word Ending -ification The word ending *-ification* is represented by a disjoined *f.*

Spell: k-l-a-s-ification, classification

Classification, justification, notification, modification, specifications, qualifications, verification.

386 SIMILAR-WORDS DRILL | their, there

their Belonging to them.

I cannot approve the plans in their present form.

there In or to that place.

I went there at his request.

(Also watch out for *they're,* the contraction of *they are.*)

387

Business vocabulary builder	
	significant Important.
	clarification Act of making something clear or understandable.
	gratification Satisfaction.
	reluctant Unwilling.

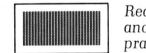

Reading and writing practice

388 Brief-Form Review Letter

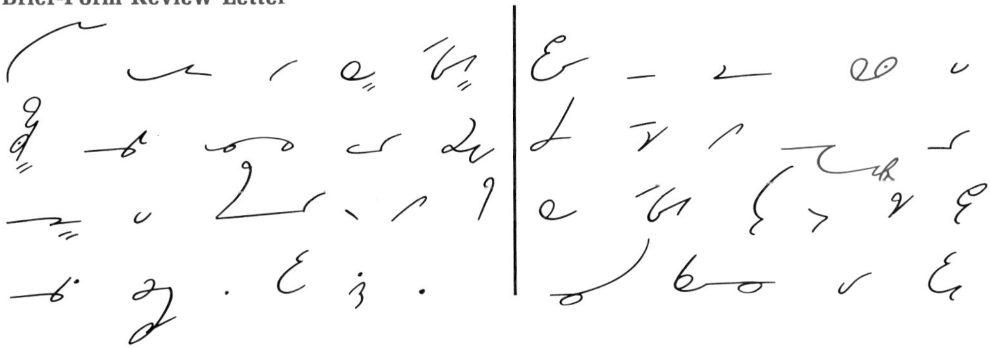

ar·ea

em·ploy·ees

con·ve·nient

par

ac·cept

priv·i·lege

Gov·ern·ment's

ap [124]

389 as

sig·nif·i·cant

en·gi·neers

par

par

proud

ser

re·vi·sion

[115]

390

ap

ap

an·ni·ver·sa·ry

ac·knowl·edge

suc·cess

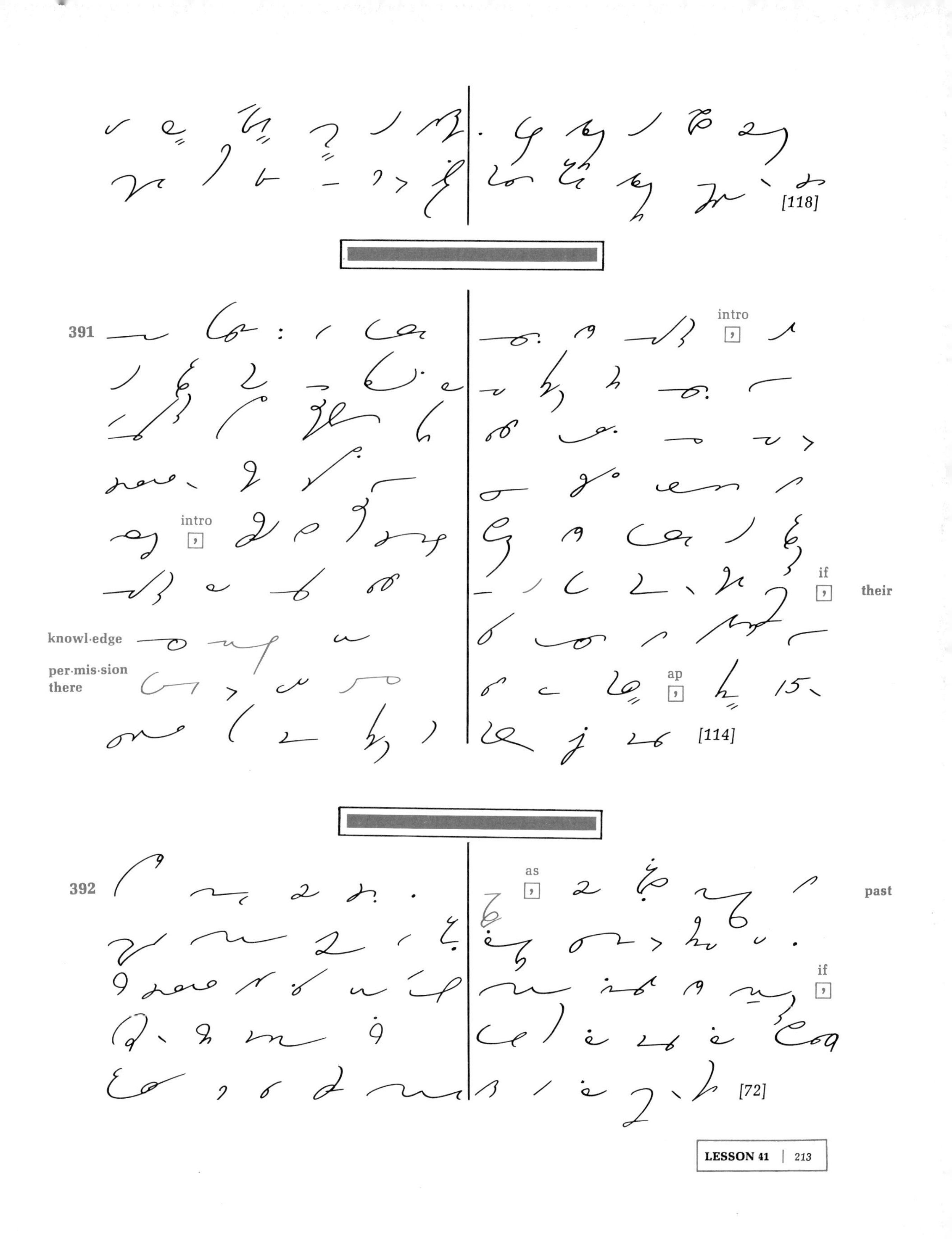

[118]

391

intro

intro

if

their

knowl·edge

per·mis·sion
there

ap

[114]

392

as

past

if

[72]

393

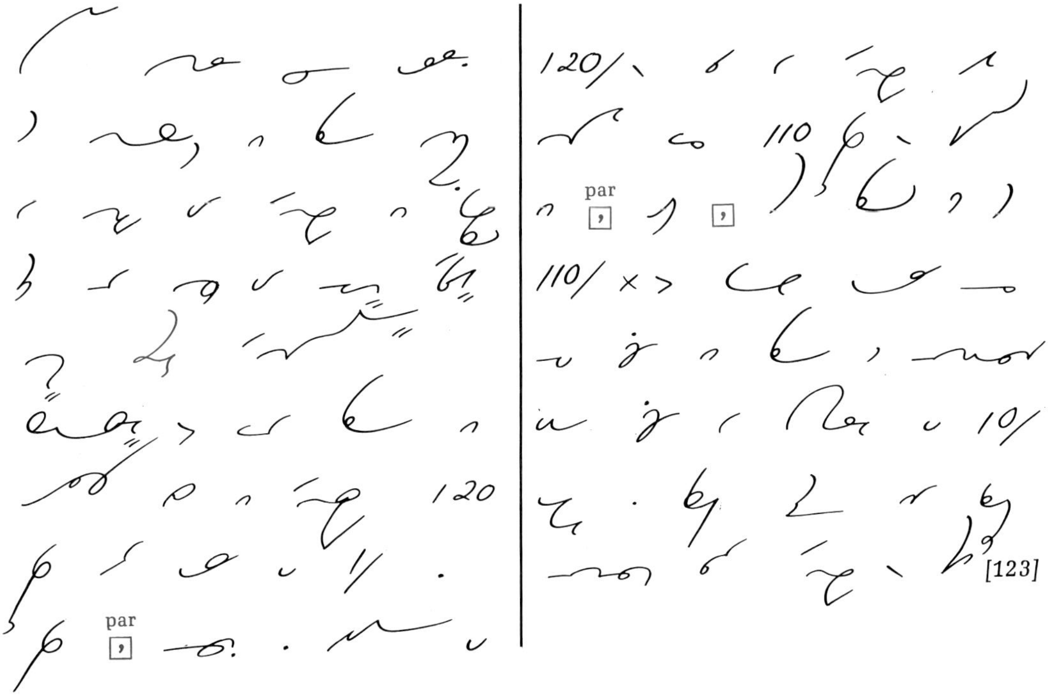
par
par
[123]

ver·sus

394

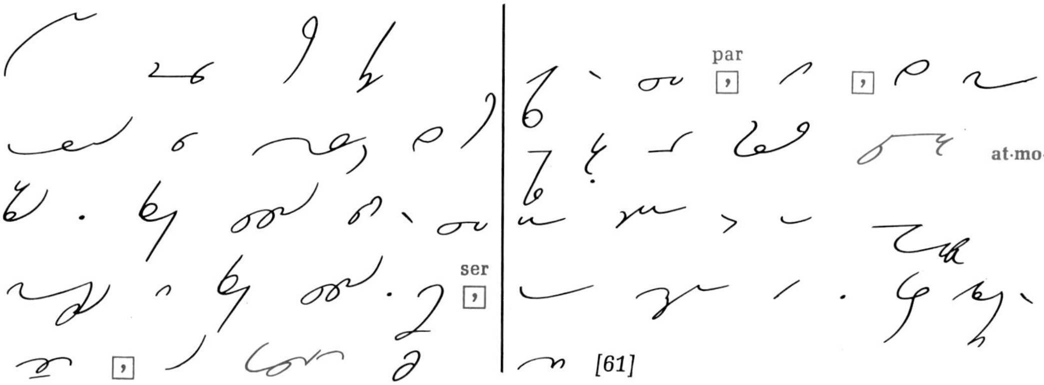
par
ser
[61]

prac·ti·cal

at·mo·sphere

LESSON 42

Recall

There are no new shorthand devices for you to learn in Lesson 42. However, it does contain a review of the word beginnings and endings you have studied thus far and an interesting Reading and Writing Practice.

395 Recall Chart There are 84 word beginnings and endings in the following chart. Can you read them in 5 minutes?

WORD BEGINNINGS AND ENDINGS

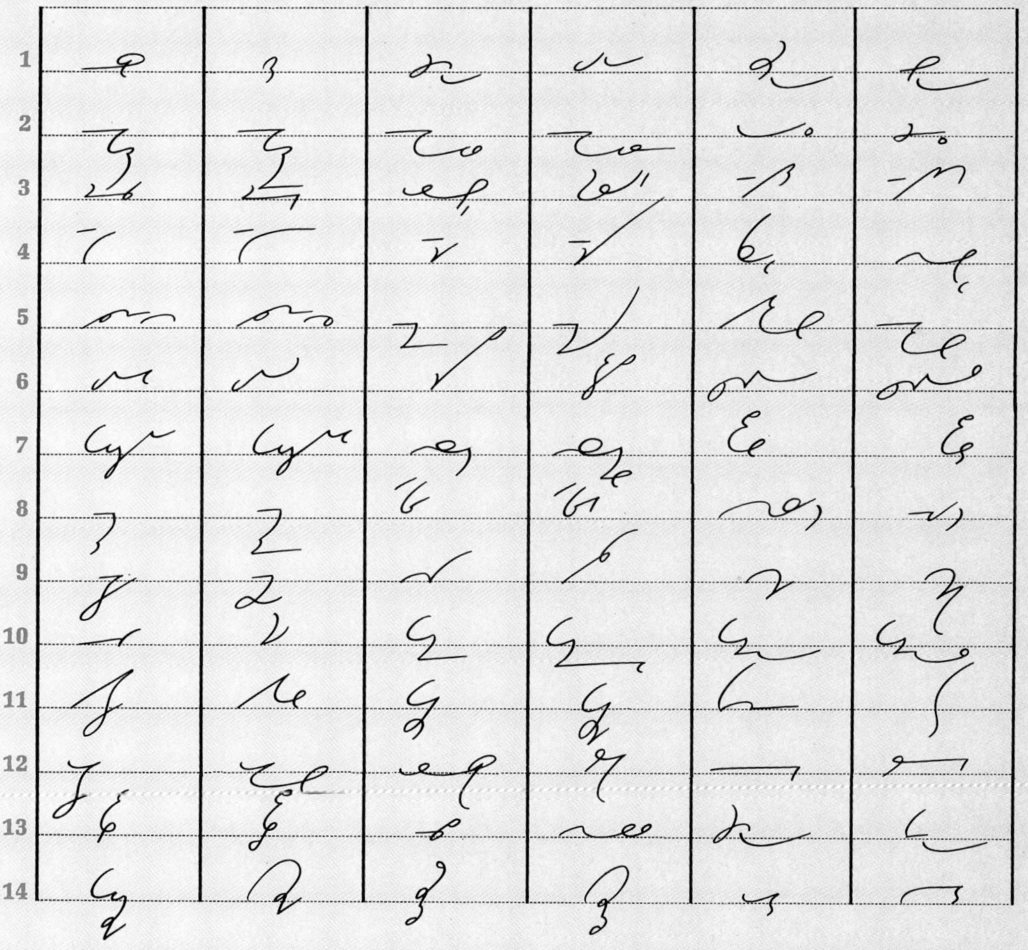

Building transcription skills

396

Business vocabulary builder	
	glance (*noun*) A quick look.
	vaguely In an unclear manner; uncertainly.
	compile Collect facts into a list or into a volume.

Reading and writing practice

Reading Scoreboard Twelve lessons have gone by since you last measured your reading speed. You have, of course, continued to do each Reading and Writing Practice faithfully, and, consequently, your reading speed will reflect this faithfulness! The following table will help you measure your reading speed on the *first reading* of Lesson 42.

Lesson 42 contains 529 words.

If you read Lesson 42 in **15 minutes** *your reading rate is* **35 words a minute**
If you read Lesson 42 in **17 minutes** *your reading rate is* **31 words a minute**
If you read Lesson 42 in **19 minutes** *your reading rate is* **28 words a minute**
If you read Lesson 42 in **21 minutes** *your reading rate is* **25 words a minute**
If you read Lesson 42 in **23 minutes** *your reading rate is* **23 words a minute**
If you read Lesson 42 in **25 minutes** *your reading rate is* **21 words a minute**

If you can read Lesson 42 through the first time in less than 15 minutes, you are doing well. If you take considerably longer than 25 minutes, perhaps you should:

1 *Pay closer attention in class while the shorthand devices are being presented to you.*
2 *Spend less time trying to decipher outlines that you cannot read.*
3 *Review, occasionally, all the brief forms you have studied through the chart on the inside back cover.*

397 **How Is Your Vocabulary?**

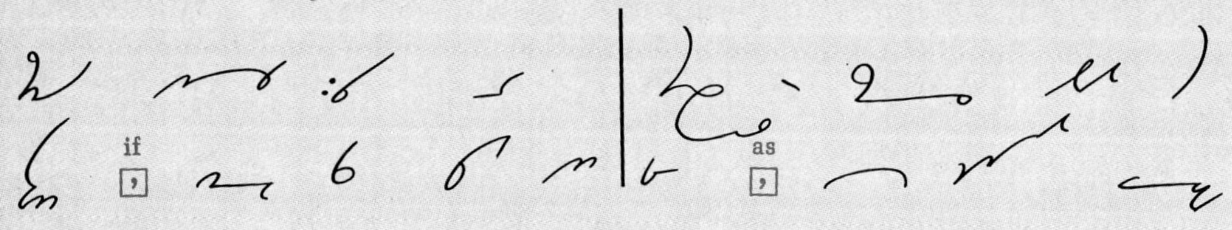
if
as

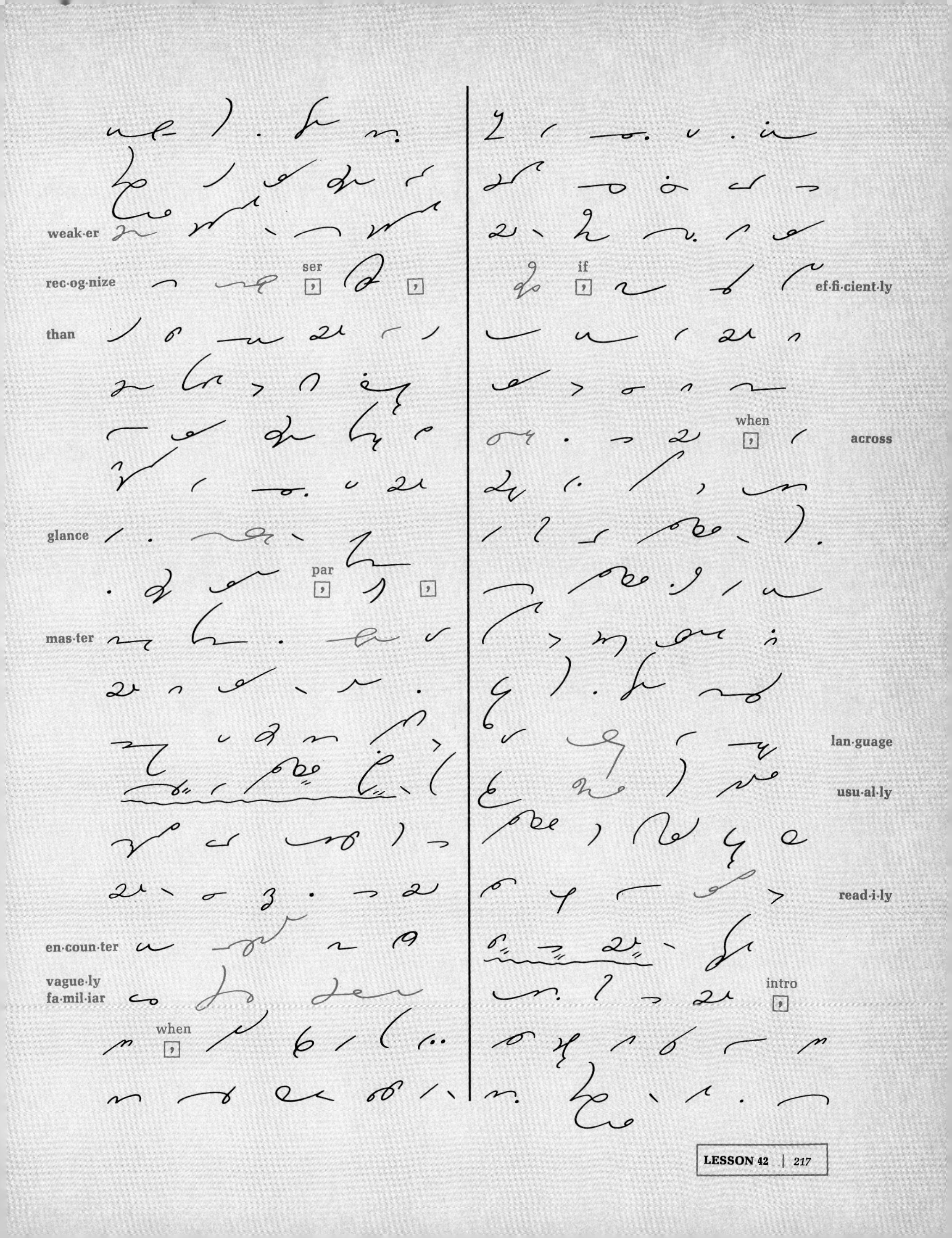

weak·er

rec·og·nize

ser

than

glance

par

mas·ter

en·coun·ter

vague·ly
fa·mil·iar

when

if

ef·fi·cient·ly

when

across

lan·guage

usu·al·ly

read·i·ly

intro

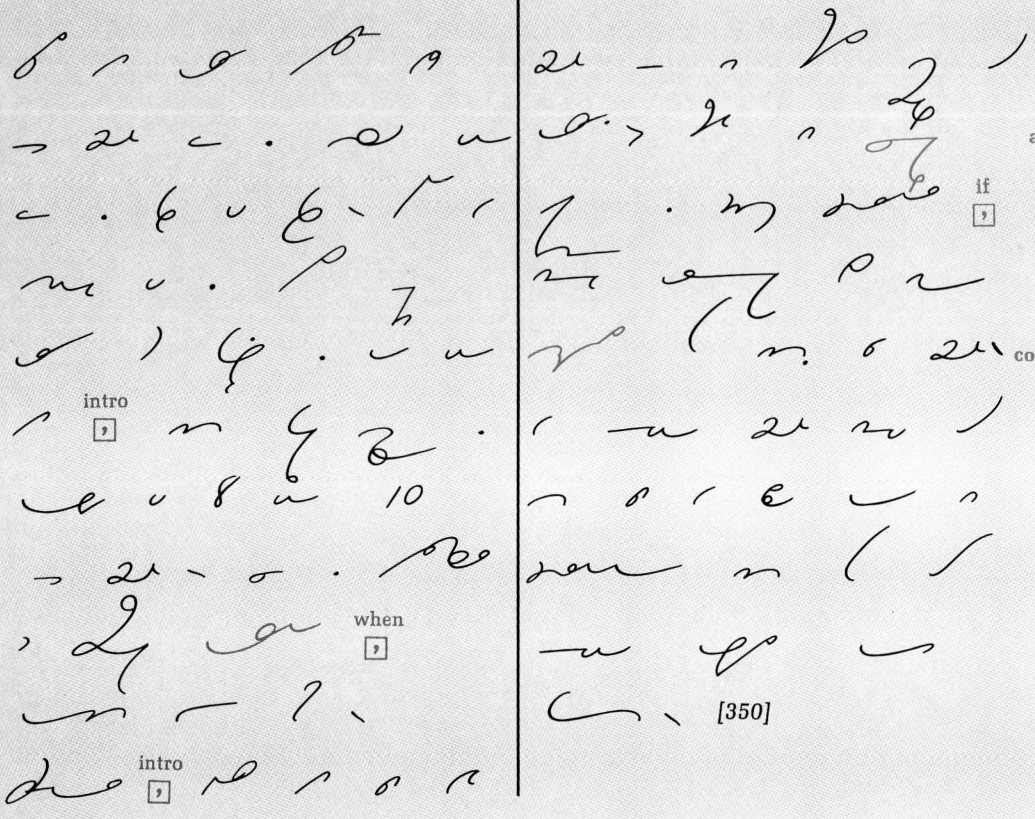
am·bi·tion
if
con·stant·ly
intro
lat·er
when
intro
[350]

398 Economy

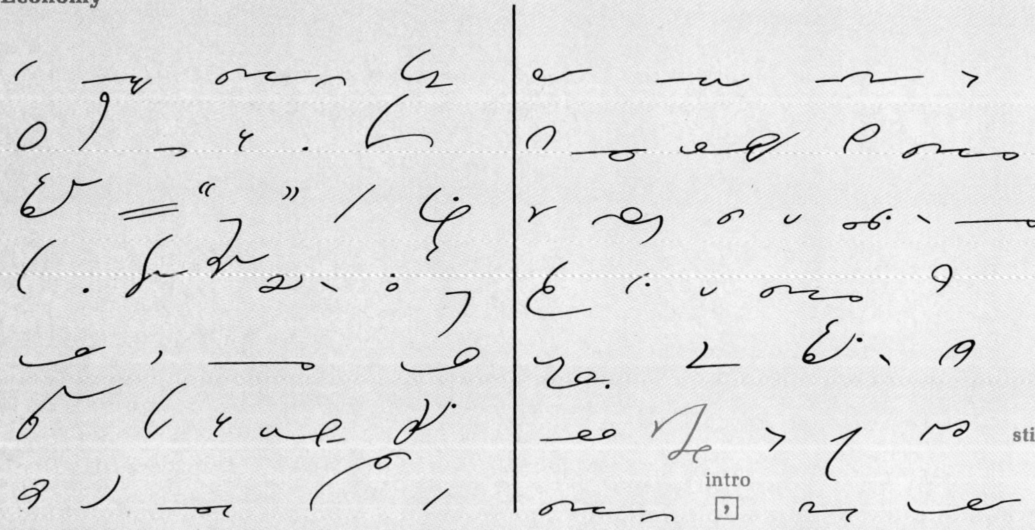
stin·gi·ness
intro

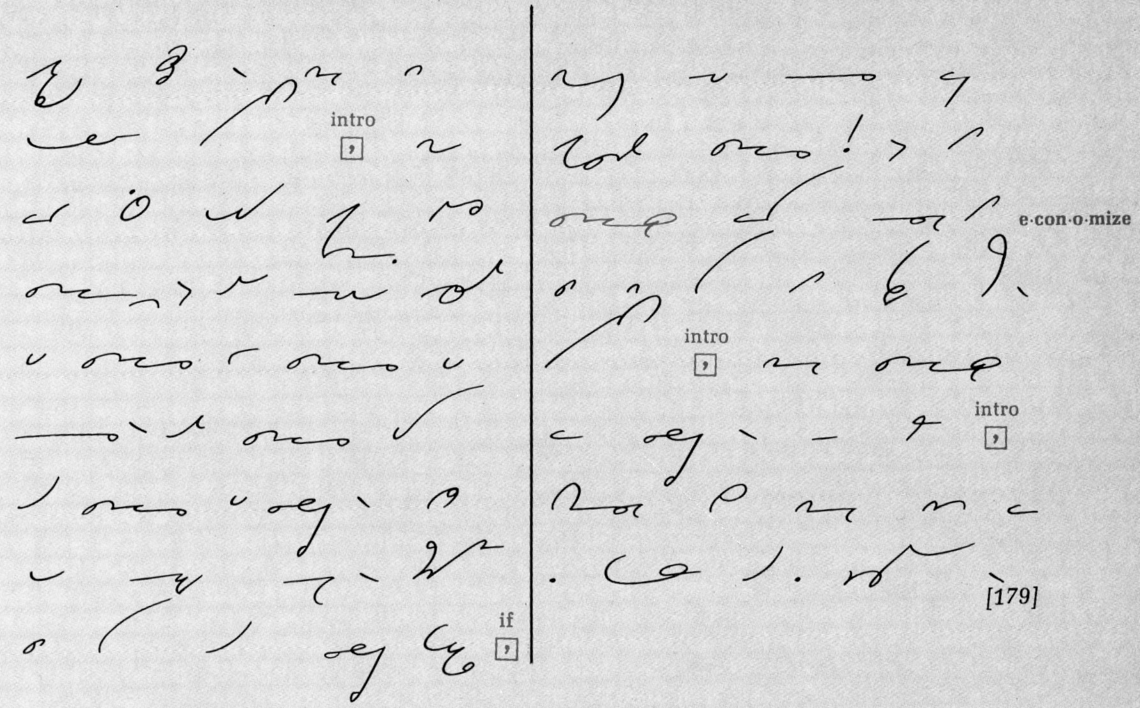
intro
if
e·con·o·mize
intro
intro
[179]

SPELLING AND PUNCTUATION CHECK LIST

Are you careful to punctuate and spell correctly when—

- ☐ **1** You write your compositions in English?
- ☐ **2** Prepare your reports for your social studies classes?
- ☐ **3** Correspond with friends to whom you must write in longhand?

In short, are you making correct spelling and punctuation a habit in all the longhand writing or typing that you do?

Chapter 8

The secretary communicates

What is communication? In the office, communication refers to anything having to do with the written or spoken word. Most of what the secretary does in the office is concerned with communications in one form or another.

In the first place, she talks in person or by phone to many people outside the company for which she works — friends of her boss, customers, business executives, sales representatives, messengers, and various visitors. She talks with many people inside the company — her boss, other executives, secretaries, department heads, accountants, repairmen, receptionists, and janitors. She talks informally in groups and more formally in meetings. Oral communication goes on con-

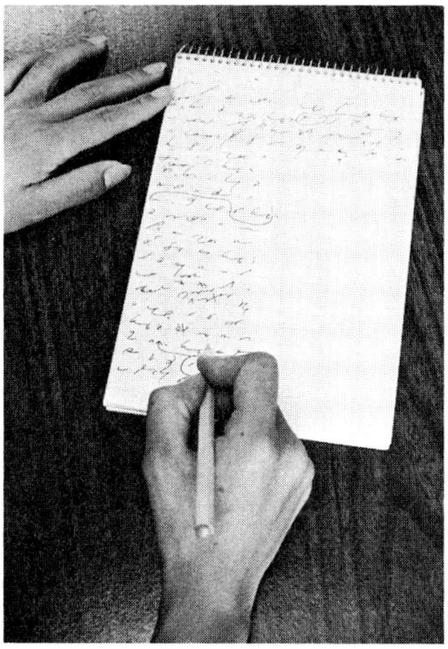

stantly — much of it highly important, some of it trivial. All of it, however, requires skill. Skill in "handling" people by means of the spoken word is vital to harmonious relations both inside and outside the company. The secretary's boss depends on her to say the right thing at the right time, because what she says and how she says it reflects on him.

The secretary needs skill in written communications, too. She must know how to write letters — letters asking for information, letters answering requests for information, and thank-you letters for favors received. She needs to know how to write interoffice memos — memos about meetings, about changes in procedures, or about routine matters of company business. She may write telegrams, minutes of meetings, and messages of various kinds.

The extent to which the secretary is given responsibility for written communications depends entirely on her own initiative and the willingness of her boss to delegate these details to her. In all cases, however, her shorthand comes in very handy. Shorthand is an ideal instrument for composing written communications of all kinds. It helps the writer to think through what he is going to say before he types it — he can revise to his heart's content without sacrificing too much time and energy. Form the habit now of using your shorthand for thinking through all your written work.

LESSON 43

Principles

399 Word Ending -ulate The word ending *-ulate* is represented by a disjoined *oo* hook.

Spell: *a-k-u-m-ulate, accumulate*

Accumulate, circulate, congratulate, tabulate.
Stipulate, stipulated, regulate, regulator, regulates.

400 Word Ending -ulation The word ending *-ulation* is represented by *oo-tion.*

Spell: *s-e-r-k-ulation, circulation*

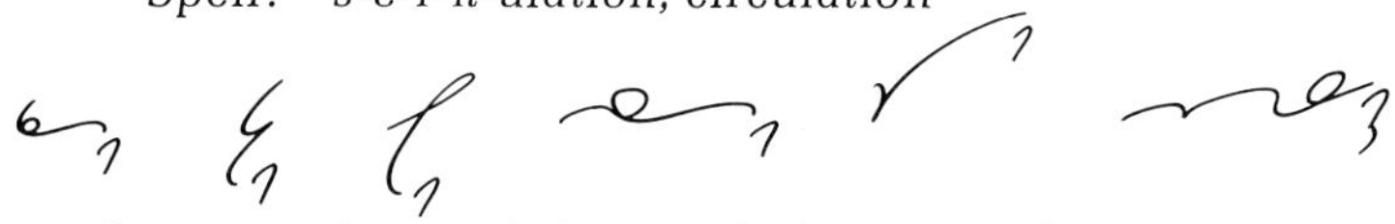

Circulation, population, tabulation, calculation, stimulation, congratulations.

401 Word Beginning Post- The word beginning *post-* is represented by a disjoined *p.*

Spell: *post-j, postage*

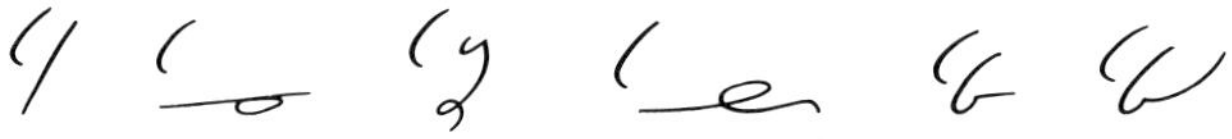

Postage, postman, post office, postmark, postpone, postponed.

402 Word Beginning Super- The word beginning *super-* is represented by a disjoined right s.

Spell: *super-v-ī-s, supervise*

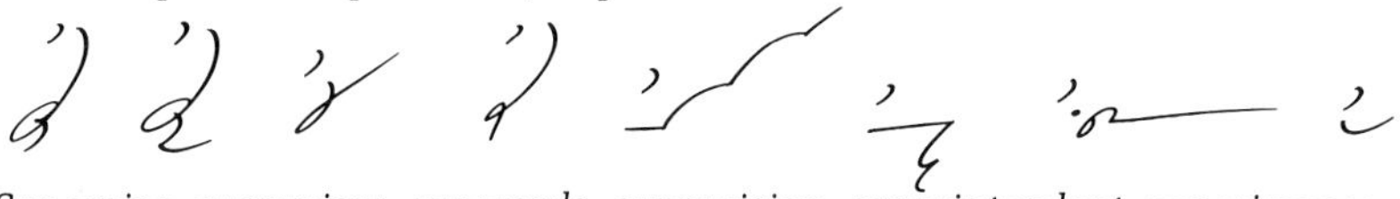

Supervise, supervisor, supersede, supervision, superintendent, superimpose, superhuman, superior.

403 PUNCTUATION PRACTICE ❙ , conjunction

A comma is used to separate two independent clauses that are joined by one of the following conjunctions: *and, but, or, for, nor.*

An independent clause (sometimes called a main or a principal clause) is one that has a subject and a predicate and that could stand alone as a complete sentence.

Your speech was taped by one of our people, and I have had my secretary transcribe it.

The first independent clause is:

Your speech was taped by one of our people

and the second independent clause is:

I have had my secretary transcribe it

Both clauses could stand as separate sentences, with a period after each. Because the thoughts of the two clauses are closely related, however, the clauses were joined to form one sentence. Because the two independent clauses are connected by the coordinating conjunction *and,* a comma is used between them, before the conjunction.

Each time this use of the comma occurs in the Reading and Writing Practice, it will be indicated thus in the shorthand: conj [,]

404

Business vocabulary builder	
	stimulating Exciting to greater activity.
	superb Of great excellence.
	circulation The total number of copies of a publication distributed per issue.

Reading and writing practice

405 Brief-Form Review Letter

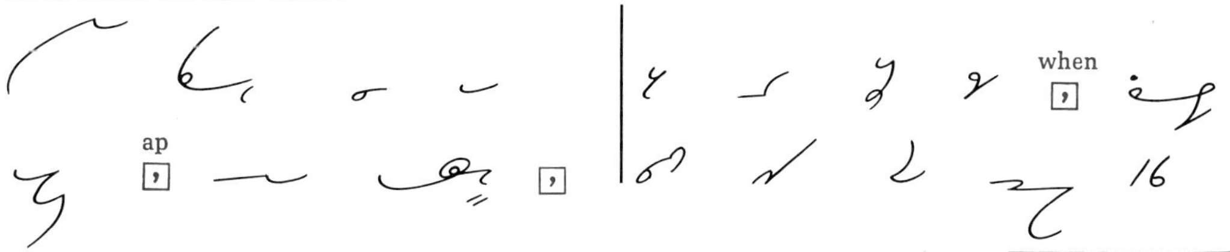

when
ap
16

par

cal·cu·la·tor

conj

par

par

be·gin·ning

[117]

406

tran·scribe

ap

ser

su·per·vi·sors

su·perb

ap

su·per·vi·so·ry

Ex·plo·sion

taped

conj

[111]

407

sup·plies

250

ser

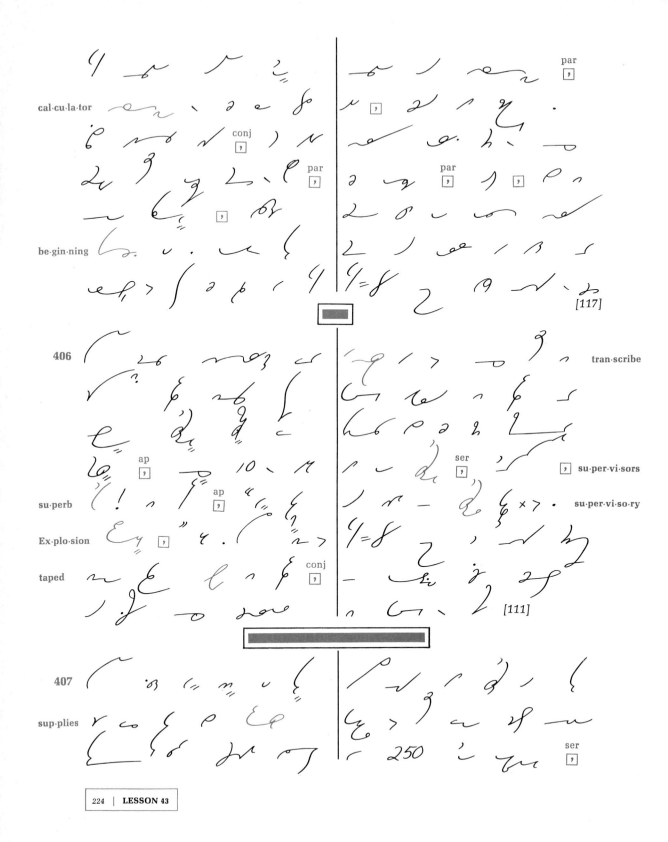

ed·i·tors

stead·i·ly

if

cir·cu·la·tion

conj

[119]

408

when

be·lieve

as

80

ap

re·al·ize

conj

[102]

409

par

sched·ule

intro

un·able

15

[50]

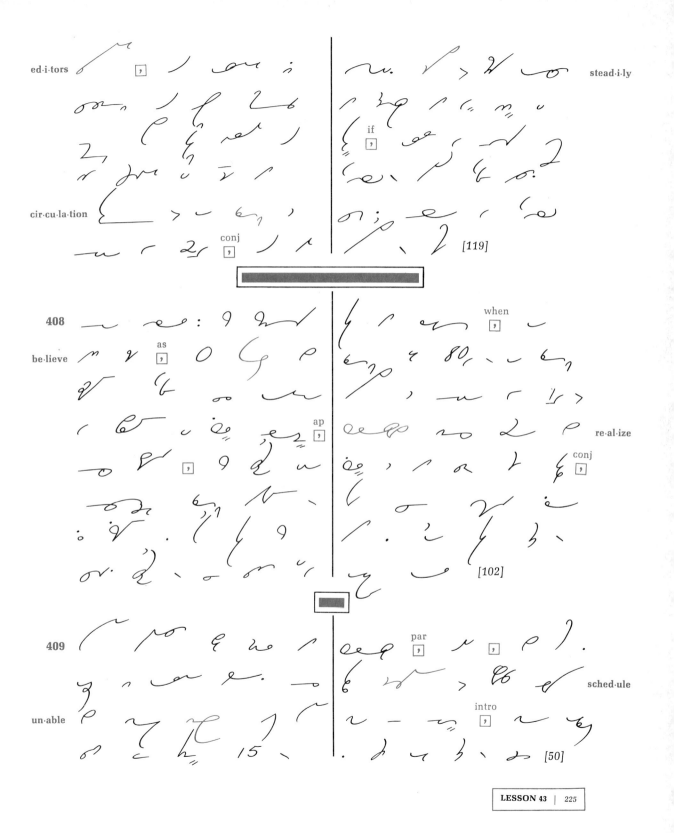

410

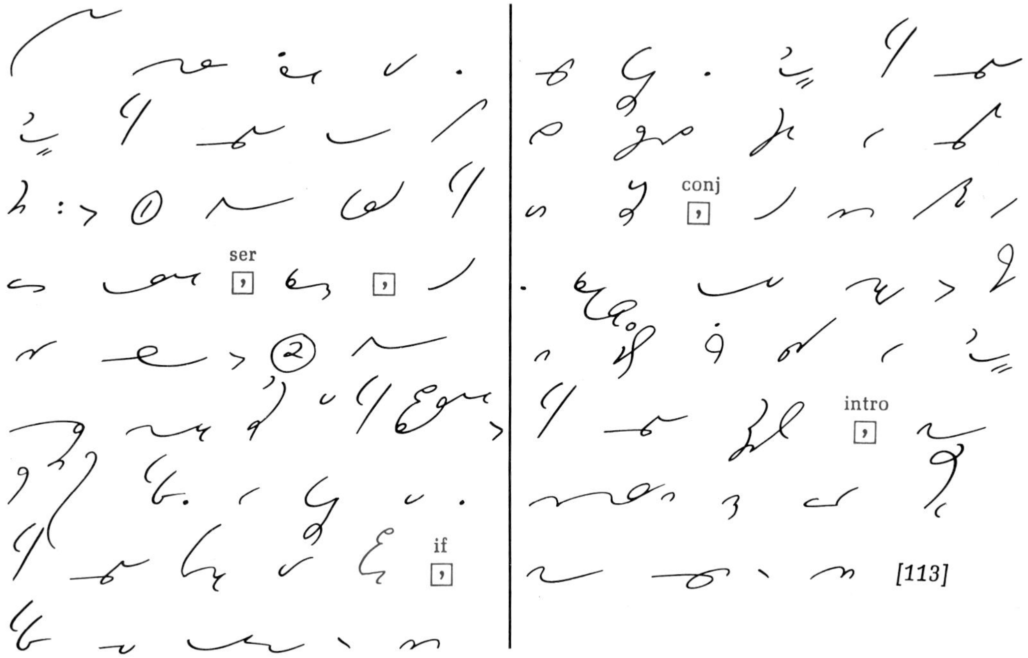
ser
if
conj
intro
[113]

ex·pense

411

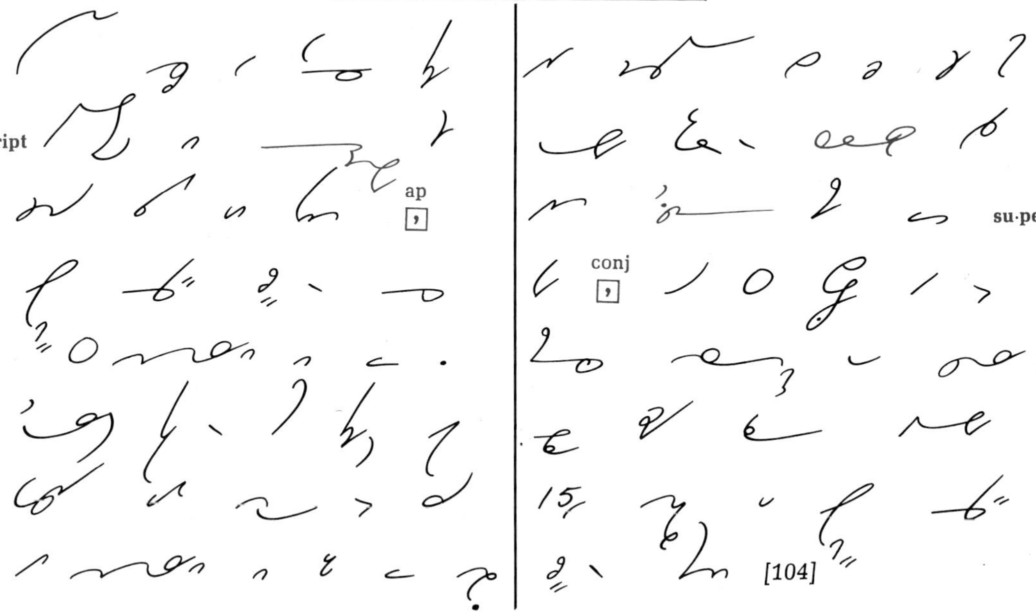
ap
conj
if
[104]

manu·script

re·al·ize

su·per·hu·man

LESSON 44

Principles

412 Word Ending -sume The word ending *-sume* is represented by *s-m*.

Spell: re-s-m, resume

Resume, consume, assume, presume, consumer, consumed.

413 Word Ending -sumption The word ending *-sumption* is represented by *s-m-tion*.

Spell: re-s-m-shun, resumption

Resumption, consumption, presumption, assumption.

414 Word Beginning Self- The word beginning *self-* is represented by a disjoined left s.

Spell: self-m-a-d, self-made

Self-made, self-confident, self-reliant, self-defense, selfishness, selfishly.

415 Word Beginning Circum- The word beginning *circum-* is also represented by a disjoined left s.

Spell: circum-s-ten-s, circumstance

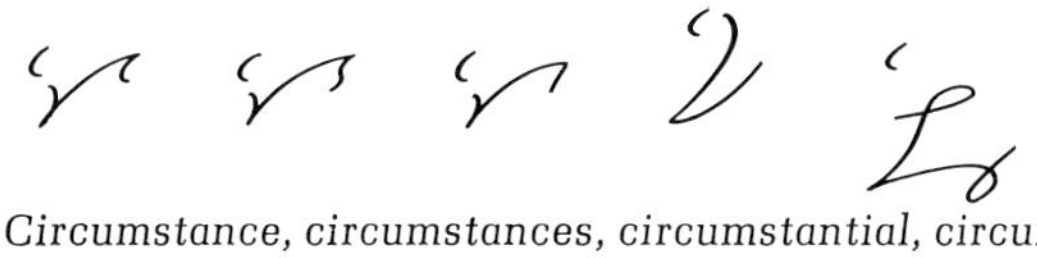

Circumstance, circumstances, circumstantial, circumvent, circumnavigate.

416 PUNCTUATION PRACTICE | , and omitted

When two or more adjectives modify the same noun, they are separated by commas.

He was a quiet, efficient worker.

However, the comma is not used if the first adjective modifies the combined idea of the second adjective plus the noun.

She wore a beautiful green dress.

▶ Note: You can quickly determine whether to insert a comma between two consecutive adjectives by mentally placing *and* between them. If the sentence makes good sense with *and* inserted between the adjectives, then the comma is used. For example, the first illustration would make good sense if it read:

He was a quiet and *efficient worker.*

Each time this use of the comma occurs in the Reading and Writing Practice, it will be indicated thus in the shorthand: and o ,

417

Business vocabulary builder	
	clarity Clearness.
	dynamic Having lots of force or energy.
	consumer One who buys or uses merchandise or services.
	manuscript The written or typewritten copy prepared for publication.

Reading and writing practice

418 Brief-Form Review Letter

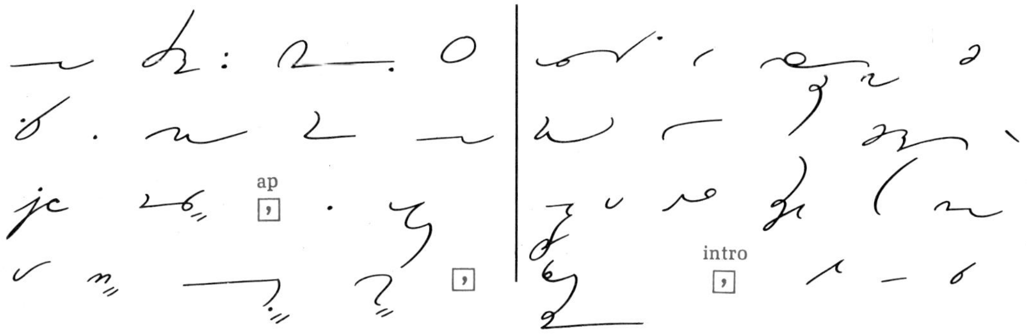
ap
,
,
intro
,

self-in·ter·est

per·son·al·ly

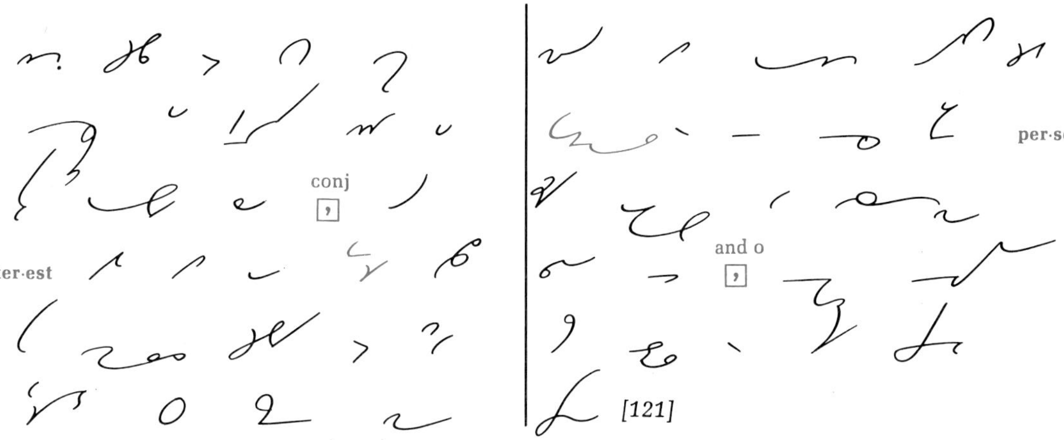
conj
and o
[121]

419

self-as·sur·ance

self-re·li·ance

qual·i·ties

clar·i·ty

dy·nam·ic

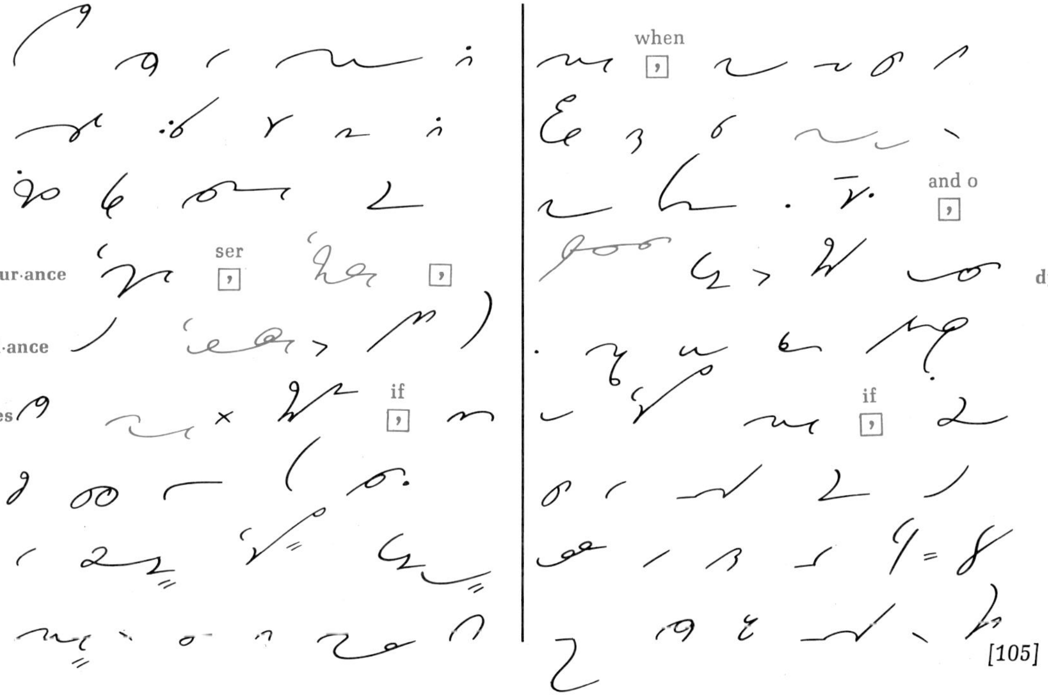
ser
if
when
and o
if
[105]

420

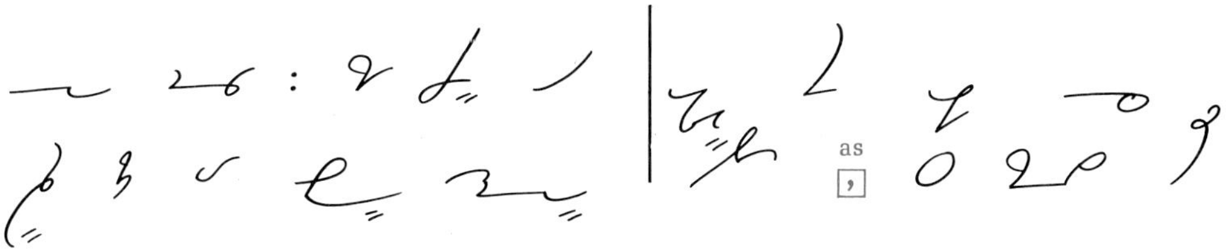
as

sub·scrip·tion

su·per·vi·sors

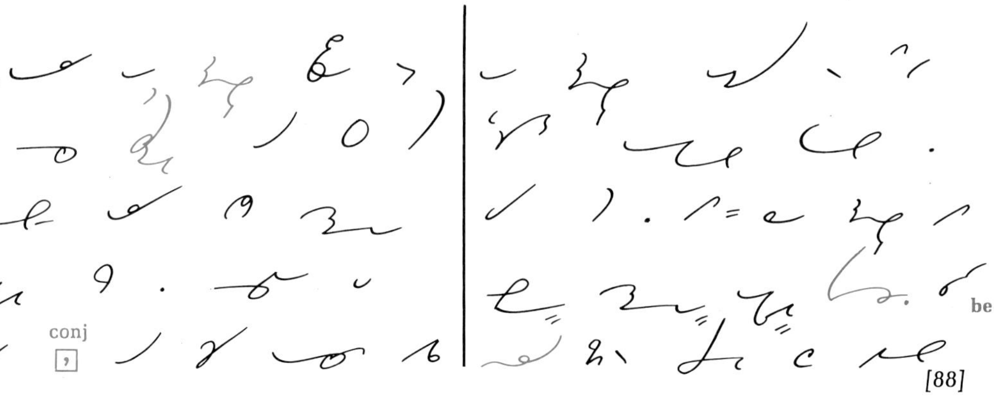
conj
[88]

be·gin·ning

cur·rent

421

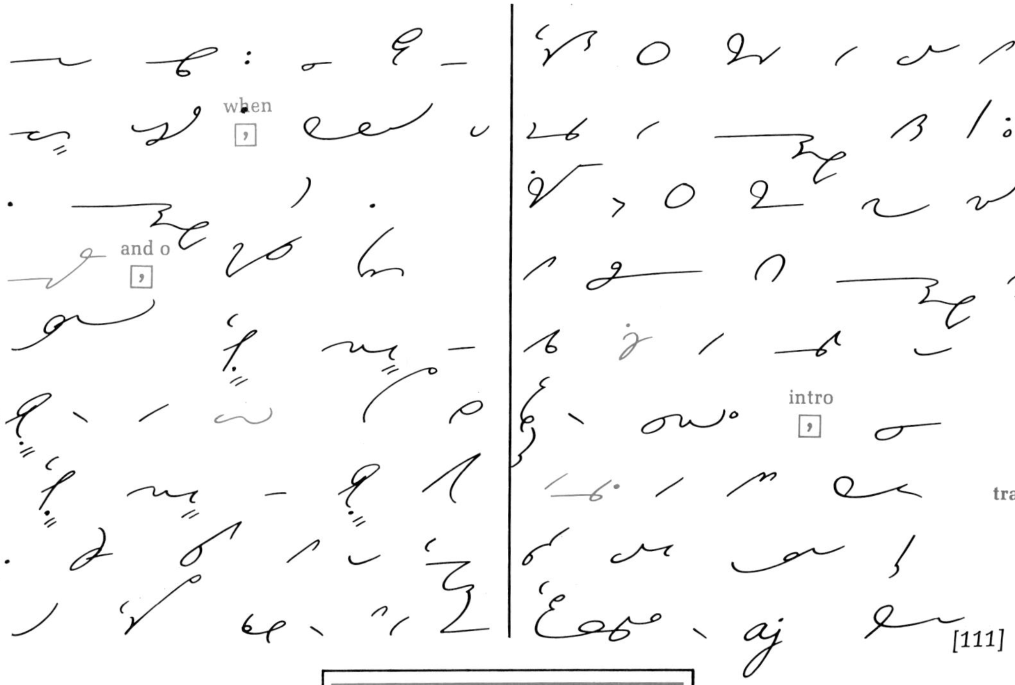
when
and o
intro
[111]

mod·ern

oc·curred

wheth·er

trans·mit·ting

422

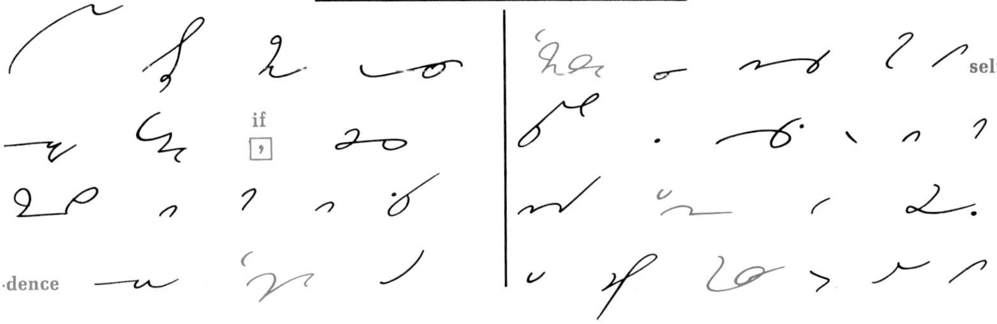
if

self-as·sur·ance

over·come

self-con·fi·dence

fright

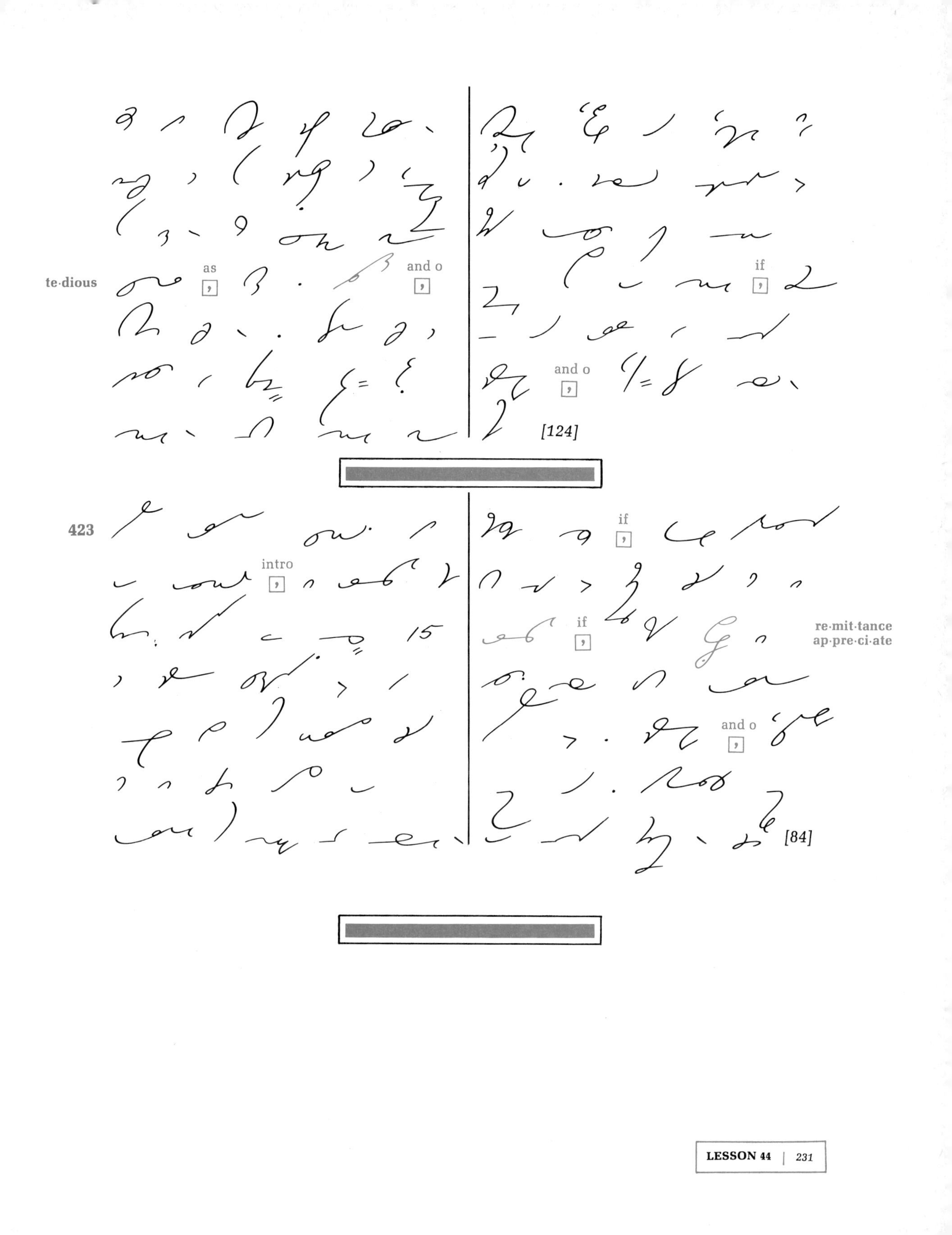

te·dious

as

and o

if

and o

[124]

423

intro

if

if

re·mit·tance
ap·pre·ci·ate

and o

[84]

LESSON 45

Principles

424 Word Ending -hood The word ending *-hood* is represented by a disjoined *d*.

Spell: *n-a-b-r-hood, neighborhood*

Neighborhood, manhood, childhood, brotherhood, motherhood, boyhood.

425 Word Ending -ward The word ending *-ward* is also represented by a disjoined *d*.

Spell: *o-n-ward, onward*

Onward, afterward, backward, awkwardly, forward, forwarded, reward.

426 Ul *Ul* is represented by *oo* when it precedes a forward or upward stroke.

Spell: *con-s-ul-t, consult*

Consult, result, ultimate, adults, multiply, culminate.

427 Quantities and Amounts Here are a few more helpful abbreviations for quantities and amounts.

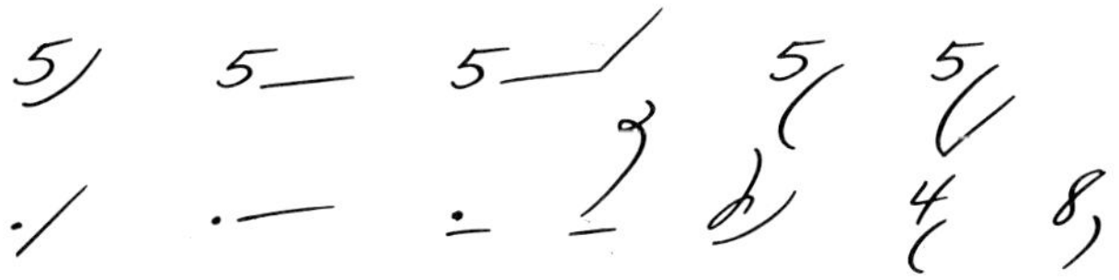

$500; 5,000,000; $5,000,000; 5,000,000,000; $5,000,000,000.
A dollar, a million, a hundred, several hundred, few hundred dollars, 4 pounds, 8 feet.

▶ Notice that the *m* for *million* is written beside the figure, as a positive distinction from *hundred,* in which the *n* is written underneath the figure.

Building transcription skills

428 SPELLING FAMILIES | silent e dropped before -ing

An effective device to improve your ability to spell is to study words in related groups, or spelling families, in which all the words contain the same spelling problem, for example, words in which silent *e* is dropped before *ing*.

To get the most benefit from these spelling families, practice them in this way:

1 *Spell each word aloud, pausing slightly after each syllable.*

2 *Write the word once in longhand, spelling it aloud as you write it.*

You will find several of the words in the following spelling family used in the Reading and Writing Practice.

Words In Which Silent E Is Dropped Before -ing

de·sir·ing	**guid·ing**	**pro·duc·ing**
en·clos·ing	**hous·ing**	**re·ceiv·ing**
ex·am·in·ing	**in·creas·ing**	**typ·ing**
forc·ing	**mer·chan·dis·ing**	**us·ing**

429

Business vocabulary builder

consultation Act of asking for advice or opinion.

ultimately Finally.

awkward Causing embarrassment.

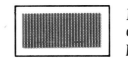

Reading and writing practice

430 Brief-Form Review Letter

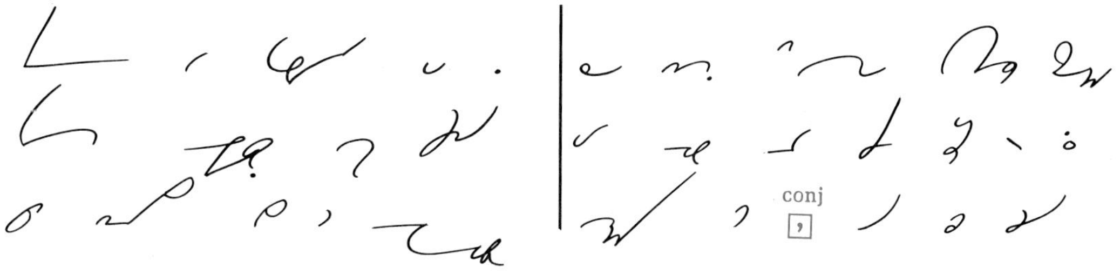
conj

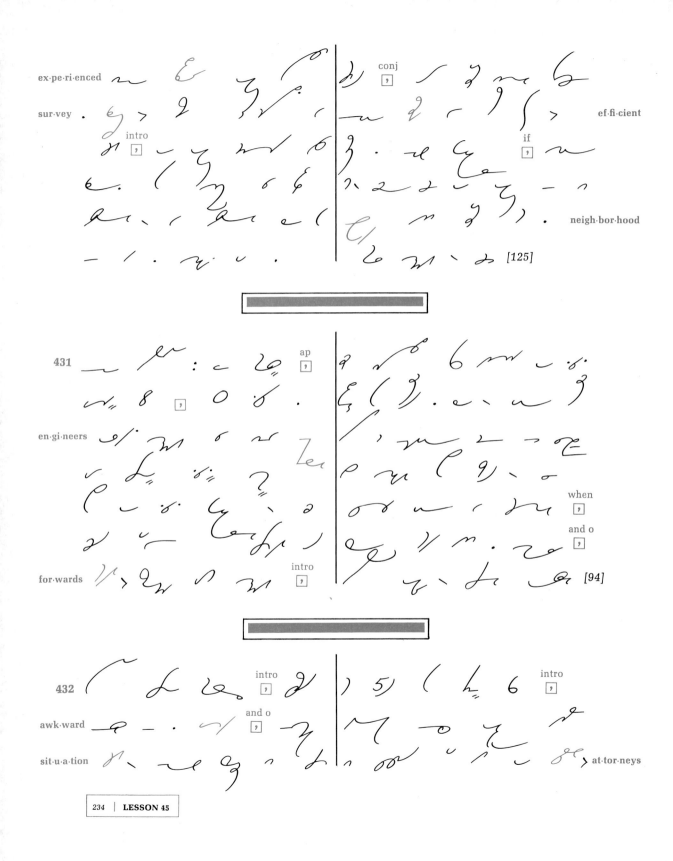

ex·pe·ri·enced

conj

sur·vey

ef·fi·cient

intro

if

neigh·bor·hood

[125]

431

ap

en·gi·neers

when

and o

for·wards

intro

[94]

432

intro

intro

awk·ward

and o

sit·u·a·tion

at·tor·neys

as

ser

par

won't

and o

[129]

con·ve·nience

433

ap

text·book

conj

par

ses·sion

al·ready

[98]

434

Mu·tu·al

intro

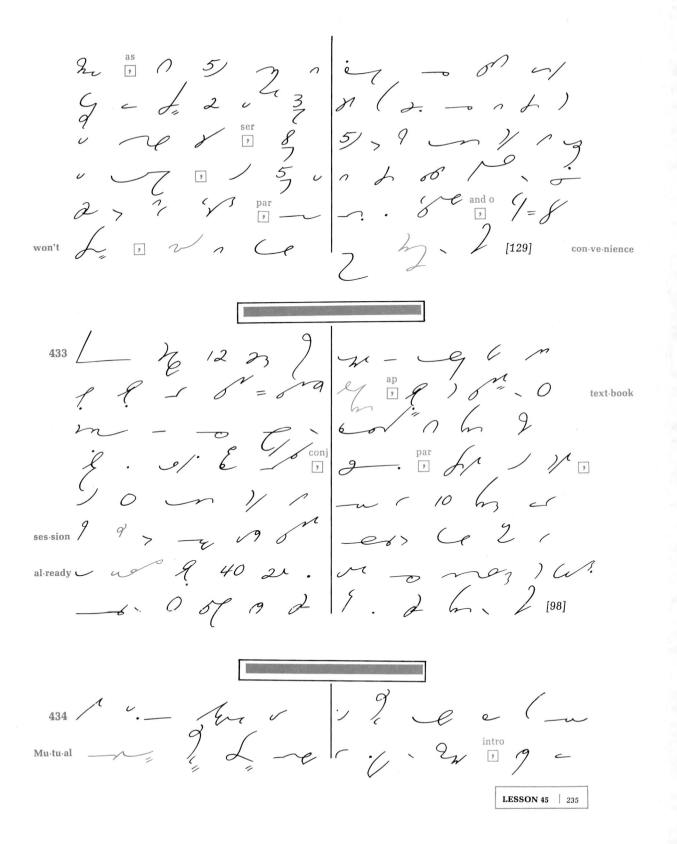

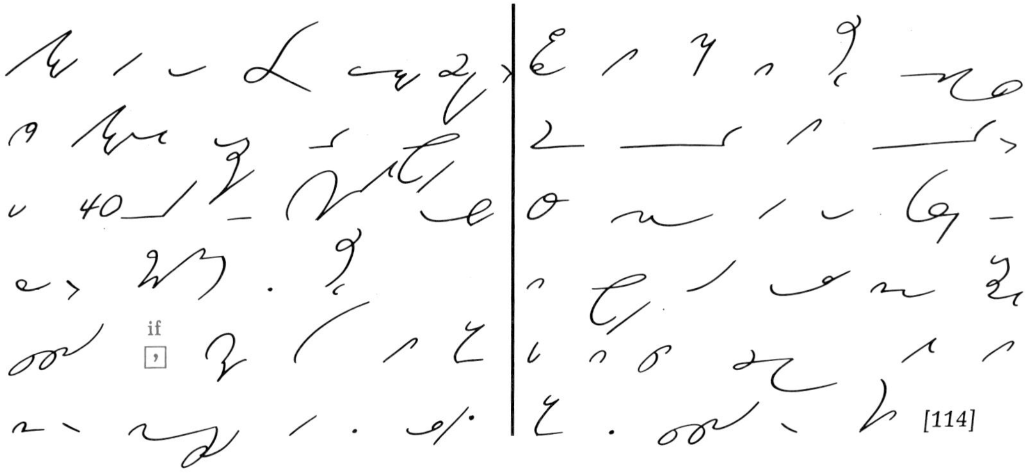
if
[114]

435 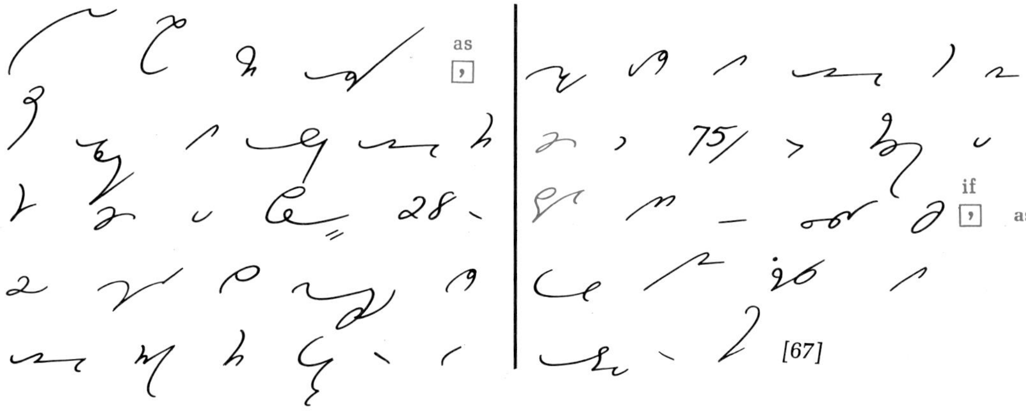
as
if
[67]

week

as·sis·tance

PERSONAL-USE CHECK LIST

Do you substitute shorthand for longhand wherever possible when you—

- ☐ **1** Take down your daily assignments?
- ☐ **2** Correspond with your friends who know shorthand?
- ☐ **3** Draft compositions and reports?
- ☐ **4** Make entries in your diary?
- ☐ **5** Make notes to yourself on things to do, people to see, appointments to keep, etc.?

LESSON 46

Principles

436 Word Ending -gram The word ending *-gram* is represented by a disjoined g.

Spell: t-e-l-gram, *telegram*

Telegram, diagram, programs, cablegram, radiogram.

437 Word Beginning Electric The word beginning *electric* is represented by a disjoined *el.*

Spell: electric-l, *electrical*

Electric, electrical, electrically, electric fan, electric wire, electric motor.

438 Word Beginning Electr- The word beginning *electr-* is also represented by a disjoined *el.*

Spell: electro-n-e-k, *electronic*

Electronic, electrotype, electroplate, electrician, electricity.

439 Compounds Most compound words are formed by simply joining the outlines for the words that make up the compound. In some words, however, it is desirable to modify the outline for one of the words in order to obtain a facile joining.

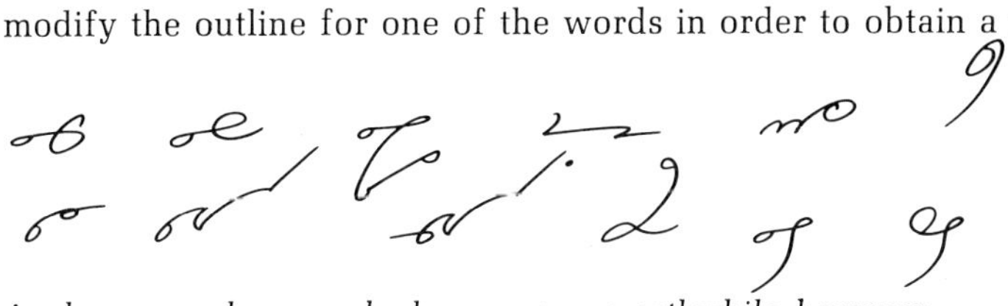

Anyhow, anywhere, anybody, someone, worthwhile, however.
Within, withstand, notwithstanding, everywhere, whenever, wherever.

440 **Intersection** Intersection, or the writing of one character through another, is sometimes useful for special phrases. You should not, however, attempt to memorize lists of such phrases; you should devise such phrases only when the constant repetition of certain phrases in your dictation makes it clearly worthwhile to form special outlines.

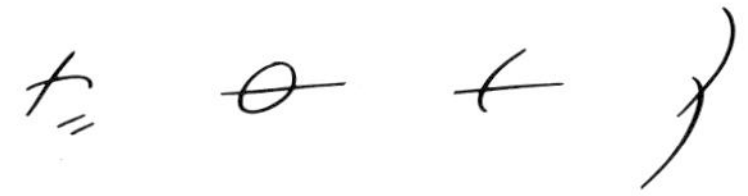

Chamber of Commerce, a.m., p.m., vice versa.

Building transcription skills

441 **SIMILAR-WORDS DRILL | brought, bought**

brought The past tense and past participle of *bring.*

John brought *the book back after having read it.*

bought Purchased.

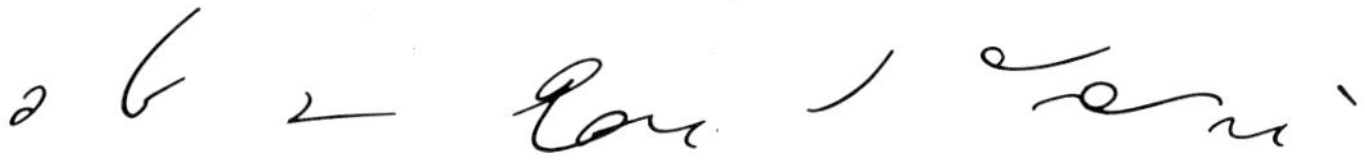

We bought *some typewriters and electric calculators.*

442

Business vocabulary builder	**proof** In printing, the copy of typeset material on which corrections and changes are indicated. **alerted** Warned of possible danger. **transmission wires** The wires through which electricity is conducted.

Reading and writing practice

443 **Brief-Form Review Letter**

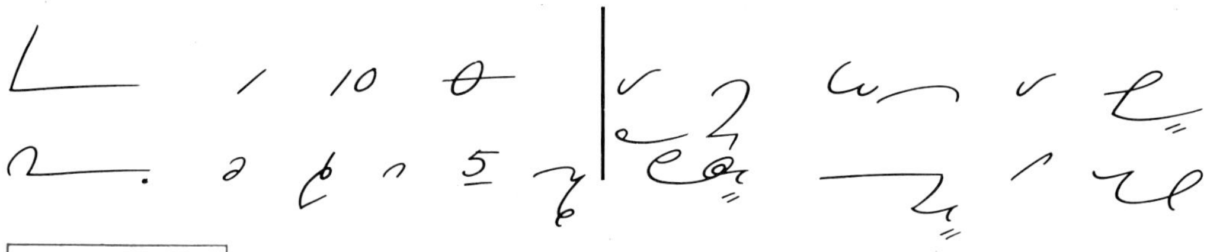

mis·spelled par

conj

or·di·nar·i·ly and o suc·cess·ful

cir·cu·lar ser [119] worth·while

444 dis·cuss

for·ward in·stal·la·tion

ap

intro [104]

445

mir·a·cle intro

pi·ano

tones

intro ,

brought

neigh·bor·hood

ap ,

wel·come

de·vel·ops

[116]

446

sac·ri·fice

breaks

trans·mis·sion

10

24

par ,

,

5

elec·tri·cal

3

when ,

ser ,

intro ,

su·per·vi·sors

not·with·stand·ing

,

and o ,

grate·ful

intro ,

[126]

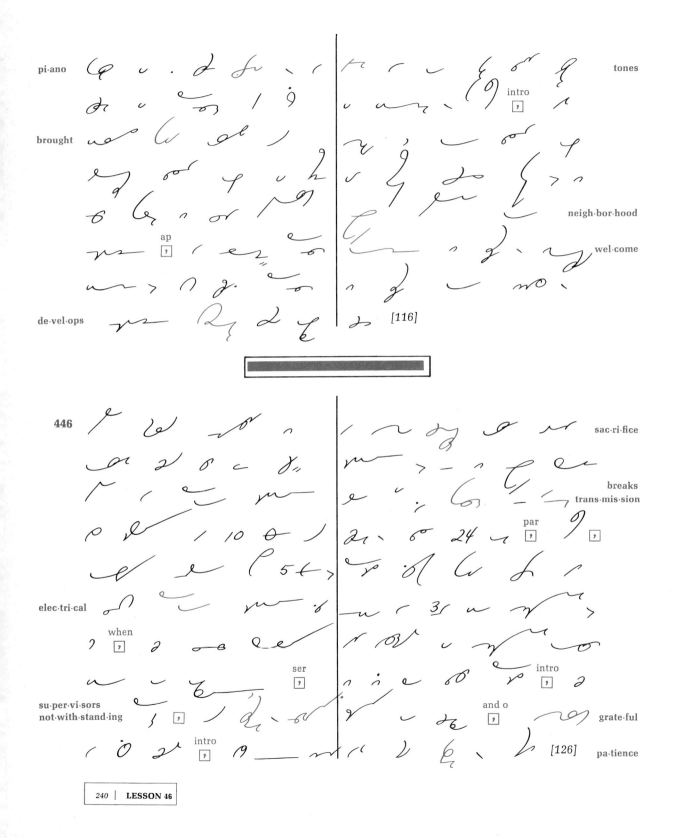

pa·tience

447 re·ceive es·caped Guide in·ter·rup·tion re·new·al

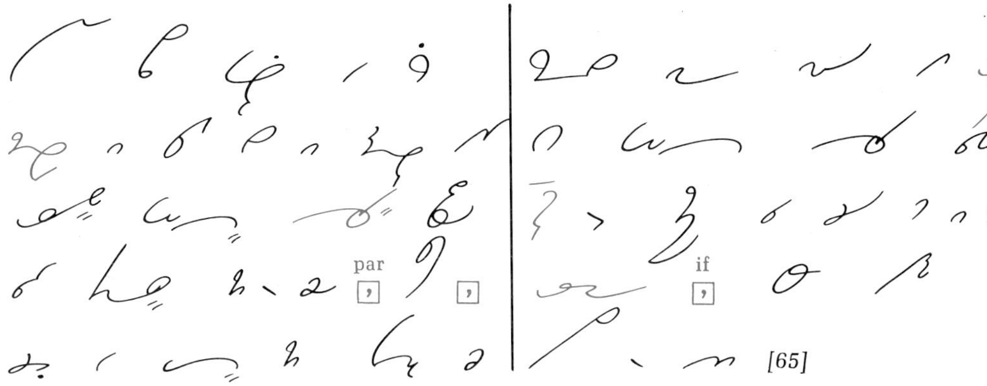

par
if
[65]

448 elec·tri·cians

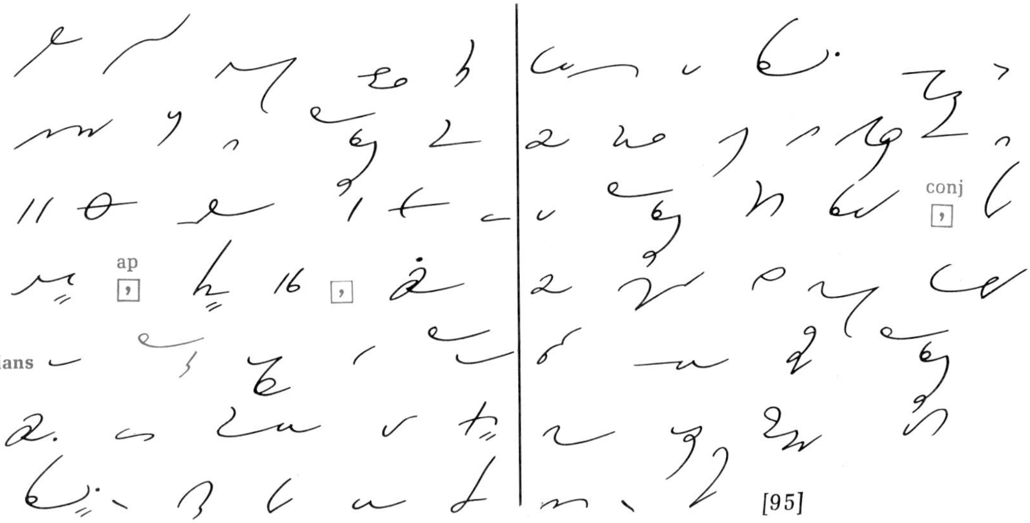

ap
conj
[95]

LESSON 47

Principles

449 Geographical Expressions In geographical expressions, *-burg* is represented by *b; -ingham,* by a disjoined *m; -ington,* by a disjoined *ten* blend; *-ville,* by *v.*

-burg

Spell: h-a-r-e-s-berg, Harrisburg

Harrisburg, Pittsburgh, Greensburg, Bloomsburg, Newburgh.

-ingham

Spell: b-oo-k-ingham, Buckingham

Buckingham, Cunningham, Framingham, Nottingham, Birmingham.

-ington

Spell: l-e-x-ington, Lexington

Lexington, Washington, Wilmington, Burlington, Huntington.

-ville

Spell: n-a-ish-ville, Nashville

Nashville, Jacksonville, Evansville, Brownsville, Louisville, Danville.

450 GRAMMAR CHECKUP | subject and verb

Most businessmen have a good command of the English language. Some rarely make an error in grammar. There are times, though, when even the best dictators will perhaps use a plural verb with a singular noun or use the objective case when they should have used the nominative. They usually know better. In concentrating intently on expressing a thought or idea, however, they occasionally suffer a grammatical lapse.

It will be your job as a stenographer or secretary to catch these occasional errors in grammar and to correct them when you transcribe.

From time to time in the lessons ahead you will be given an opportunity to brush up on some of the rules of grammar that are frequently violated.

subject and verb

A verb must agree with its subject in number.

Our representative is *looking forward to the pleasure of serving you.*
Your *canceled* checks are *mailed to you each month.*

The inclusion of a phrase such as *in addition to, as well as,* or *along with* after the subject does not affect the number of the verb. If the subject is singular, use a singular verb; if the subject is plural, use a plural verb.

Our representative, *as well as our managers,* is *looking forward to the pleasure of serving you.*
Your *canceled* checks, *along with your statement,* are *mailed to you each month.*

451

Business vocabulary builder

professional men Doctors, lawyers, engineers.

authorized (*verb*) Gave permission to.

duplicate (*verb*) Make copies of an original.

complicated Hard to solve.

Reading and writing practice

452 Brief-Form Review Letter

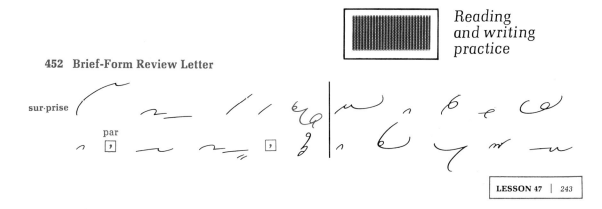

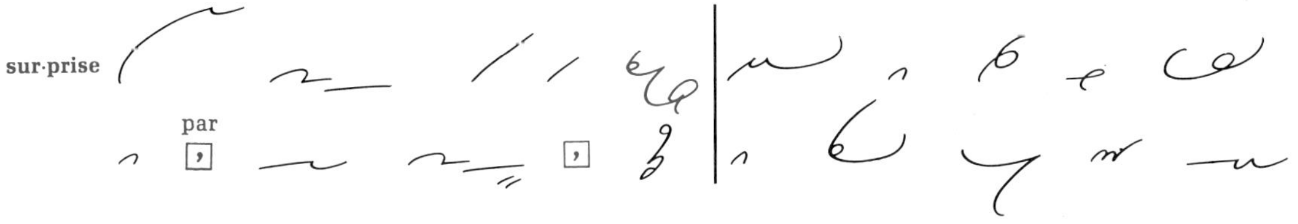
sur·prise
par

as
if
electricity
ser
professional
par
when
sites
[118]

453

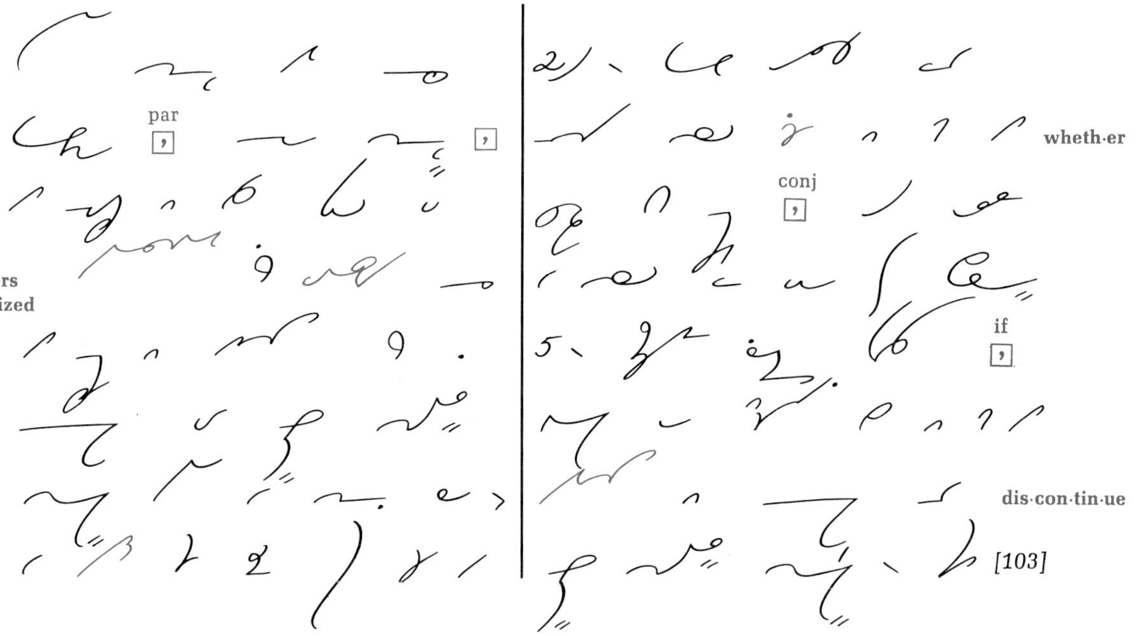
par
directors
authorized
dues
whether
conj
if
discontinue
[103]

454

ser

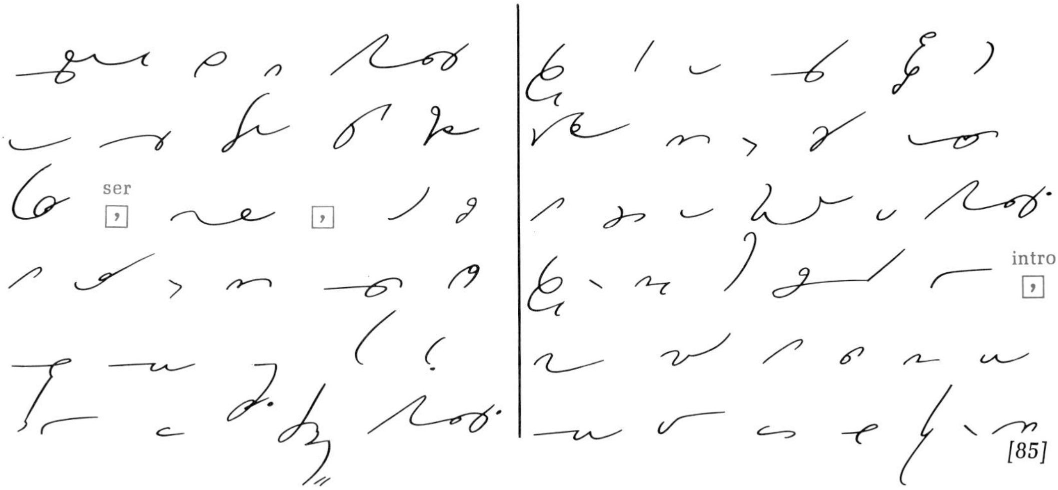

ser
intro

[85]

455

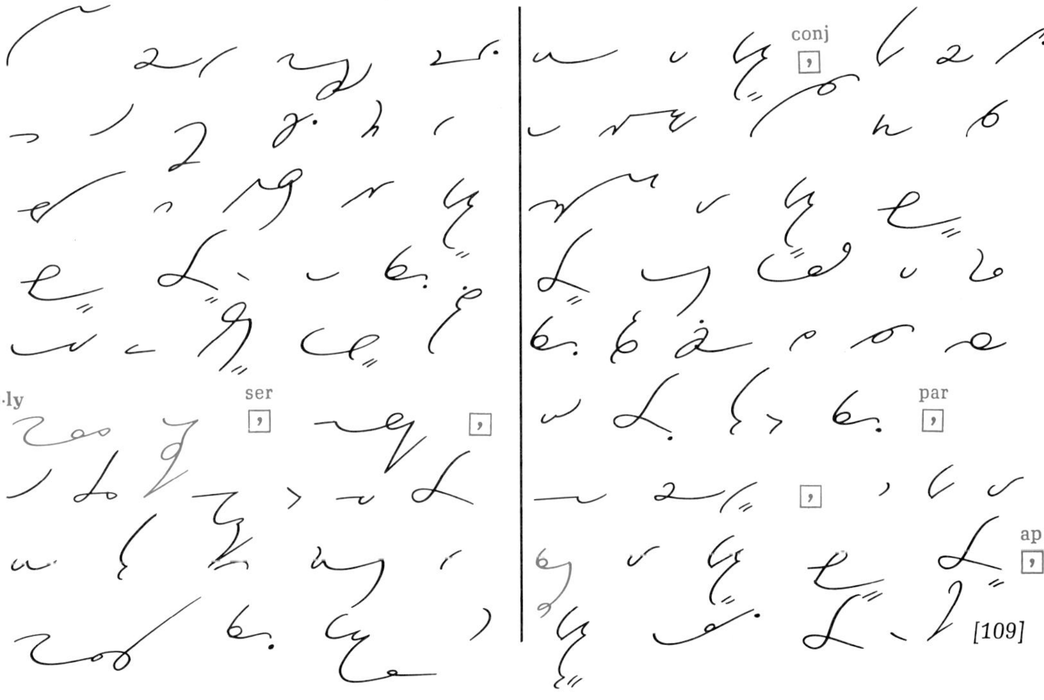

conj
ser
par
ap

com·plete·ly
re·paved

ser·vice

[109]

456

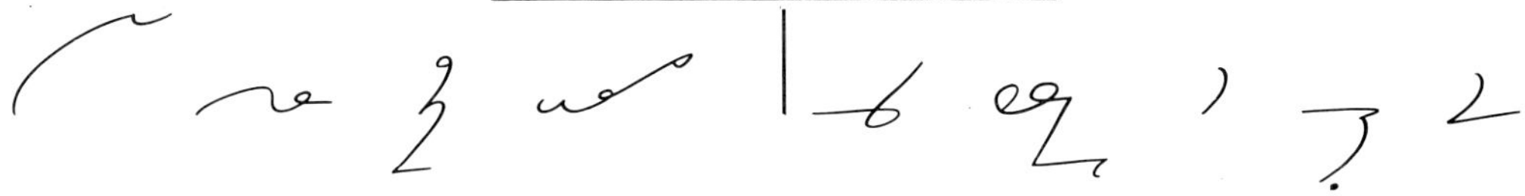

well-known

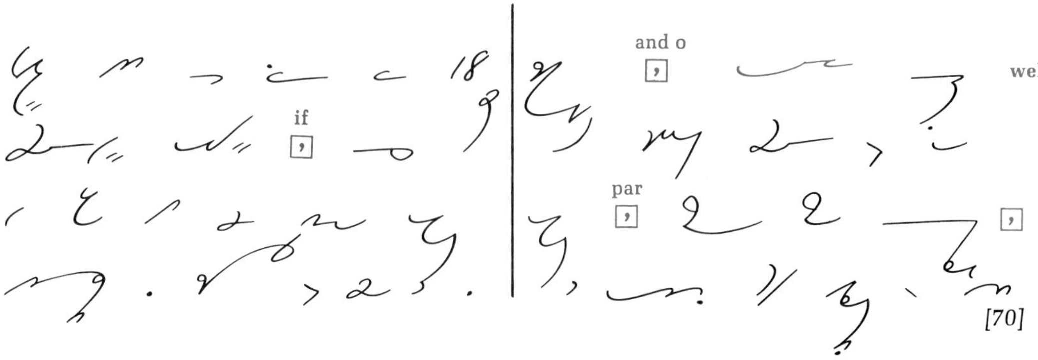
and o
if
par
[70]

457

loss

car·ry·ing

sums

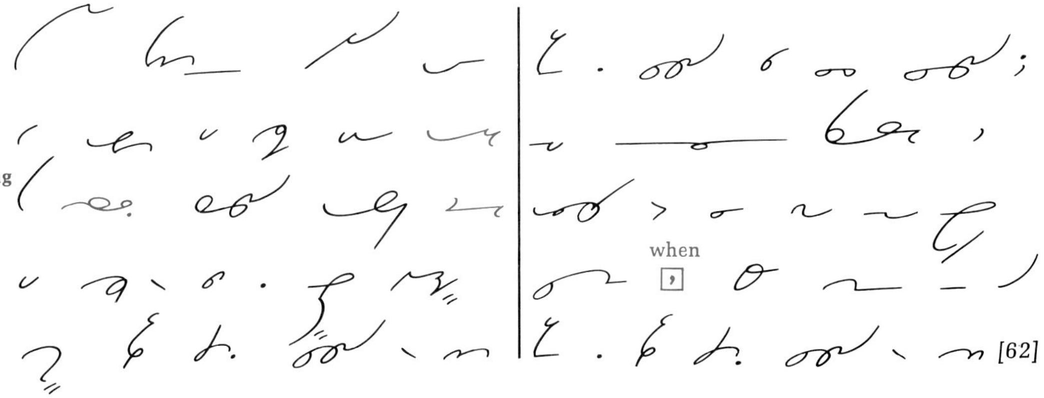
when
[62]

458

wel·come

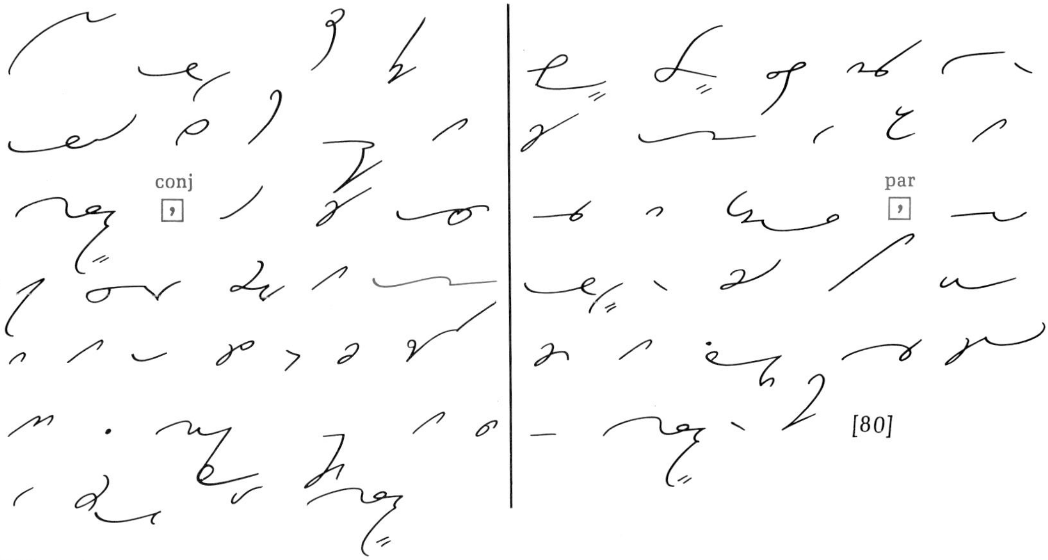
conj
par
[80]

LESSON 48

Recall

In Lesson 47 you studied the last of the new shorthand devices of Gregg Shorthand. In this lesson you will find a Recall Chart that reviews all the word-building principles of Gregg Shorthand and a Reading and Writing Practice that contains some "food for thought."

459 Recall Chart This chart contains one or more illustrations of every word-building and phrasing principle of Gregg Shorthand.

WORDS

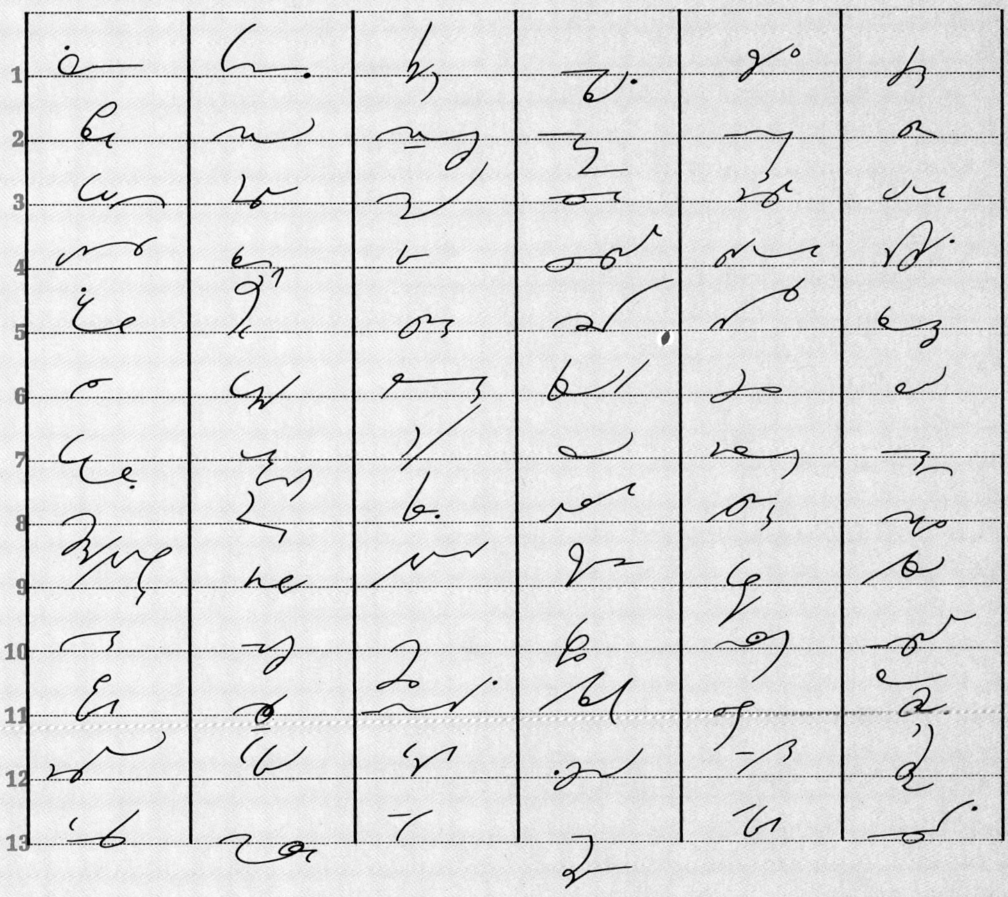

14
15

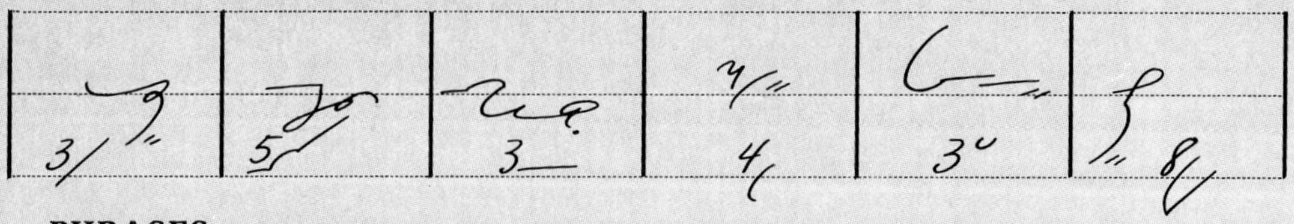

PHRASES

16
17

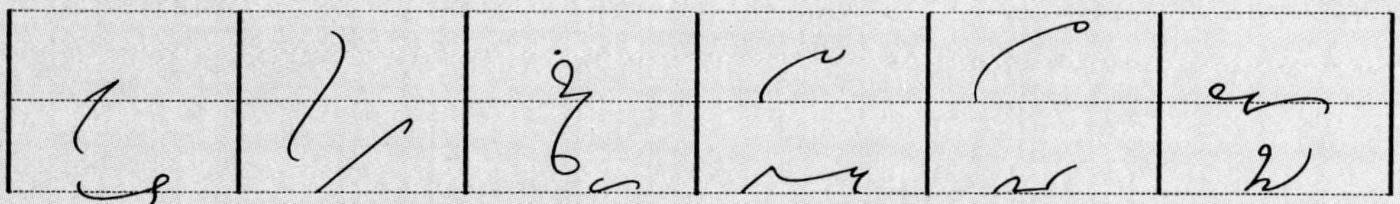

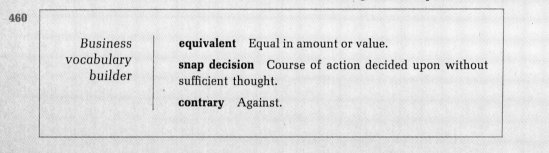

Building transcription skills

460

Business vocabulary builder	
	equivalent Equal in amount or value.
	snap decision Course of action decided upon without sufficient thought.
	contrary Against.

Reading and writing practice

461 Faithful Servant

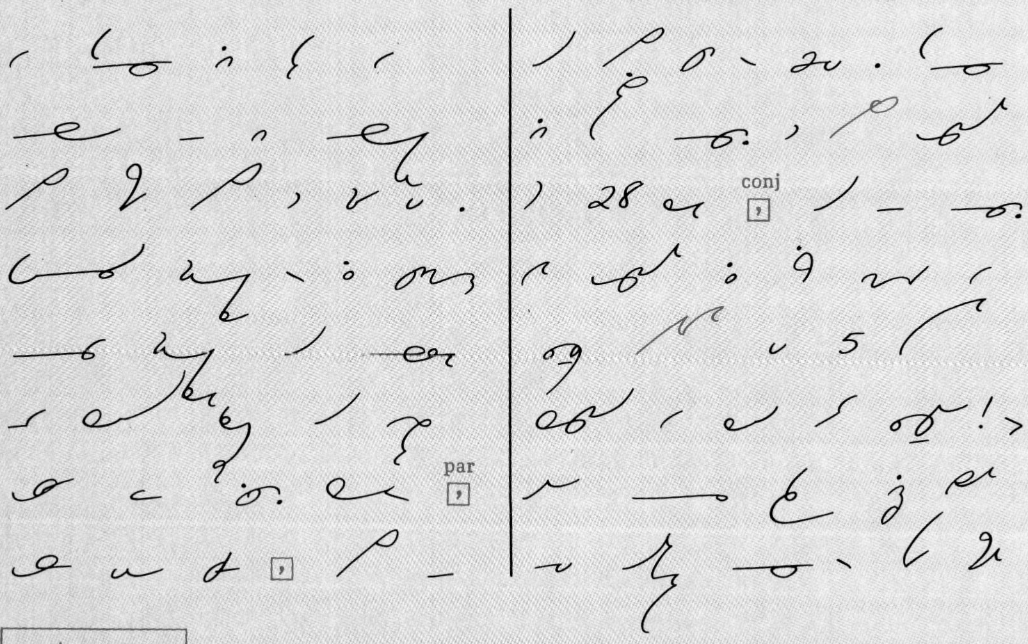
conj
par

dai·ly

dis·tance

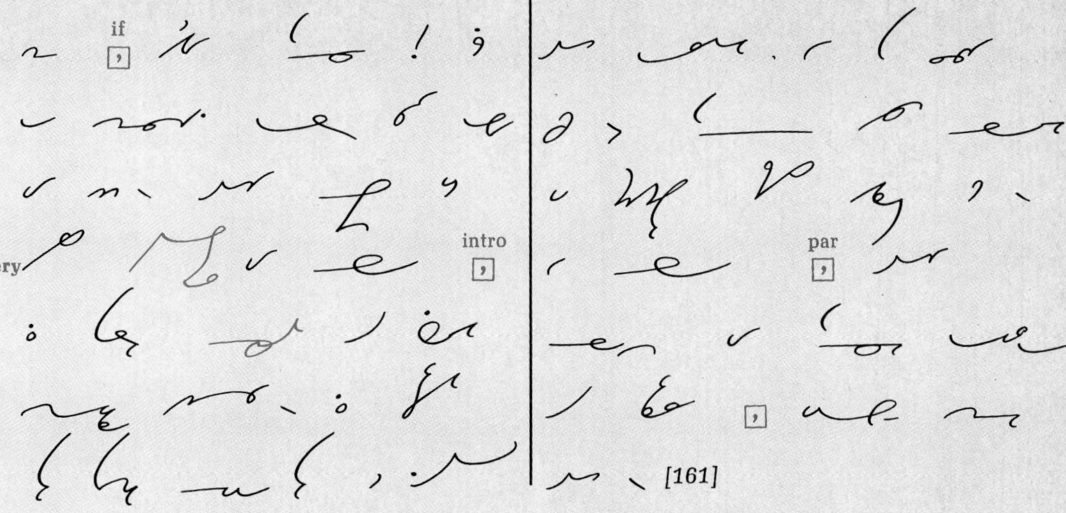
if
intro
par
[161]

de·liv·ery

minds

462 Self-Control

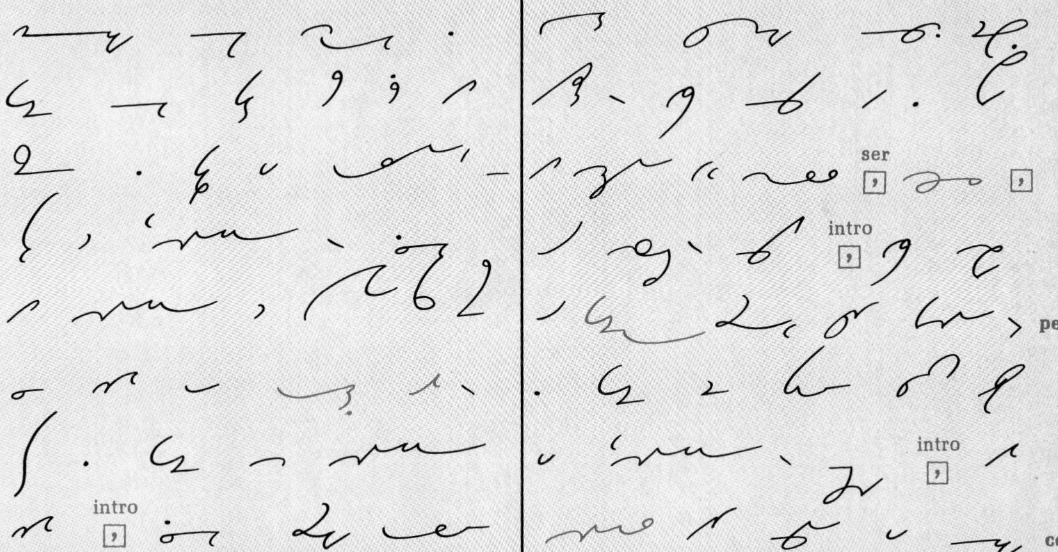
ser
intro
intro
intro
conj
if
[150]

calm·ly

per·son·al

los·ing
theirs

con·trary

ex·am·ine
traits

463 Pride

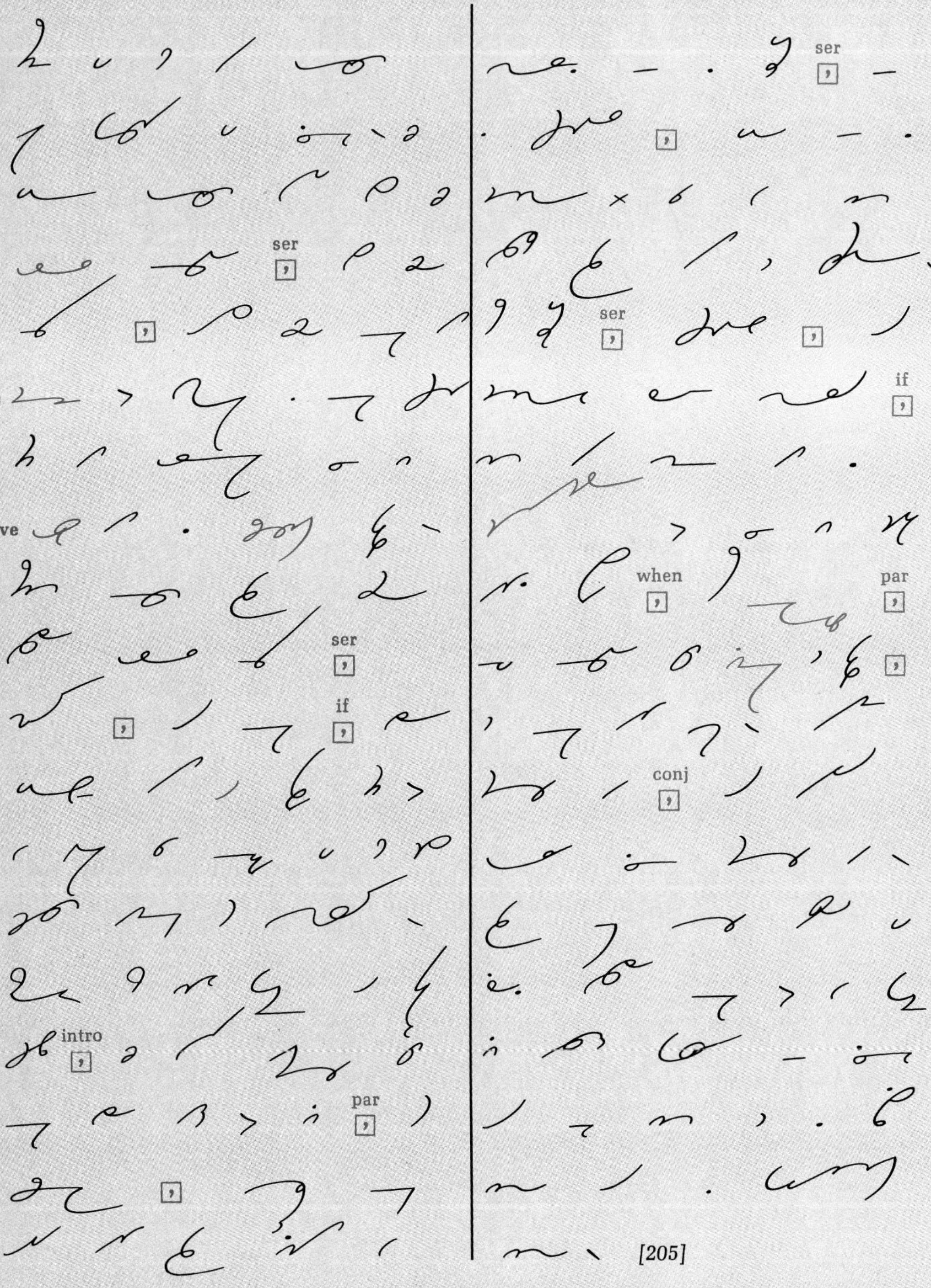
ser
ser
if
ser
if
intro
par
ser
ser
if
when
par
conj

re·al·ly
some·one
rise
ex·ec·u·tive
their
stand·still
em·ploy·ee
hum·ble

[205]

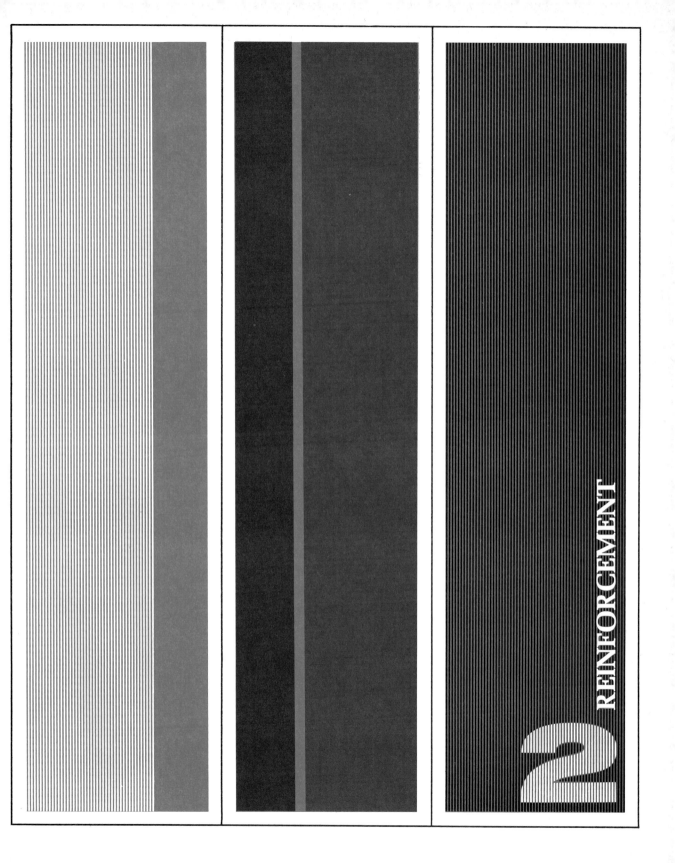

2 REINFORCEMENT

Chapter 9

The secretary "looks it up"

Suppose a strange word is given to you in dictation. It sounds like "ingenuous." Or was it "ingenious"? Both are perfectly good words. But which is correct? You read your notes carefully and you look up these two words in the dictionary; then you make your choice. You are right, because you make sure the word fits the meaning your notes show was intended. The smart secretary doesn't guess—she looks it up.

"I don't expect my secretary to be a 'walking encyclopedia,'" says the executive, "but I do expect her to know when she *doesn't know—and to know where to look things up."*

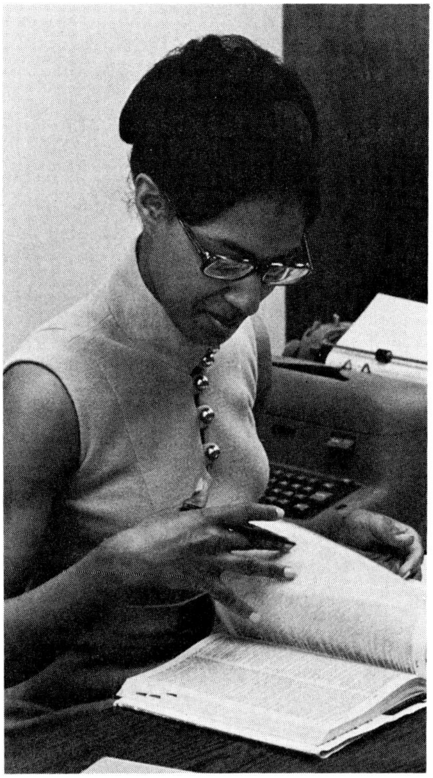

Do you know when and where to look things up? Now is the time to begin forming the habit of looking things up when you aren't sure. Even the experienced secretary turns to several reference sources during the course of a day to make absolutely sure she is right. She may use the dictionary, a grammar handbook, a company style manual for typists and stenographers, an encyclopedia, a book on filing, a letter-writing handbook, and a book on etiquette. Nothing is left to chance. To be right is important. It's the smart secretary who knows when she doesn't know.

Do you know how to address a member of the clergy? a senator? Do you know how to write an acceptance to a formal invitation? Do you know the correct salutation when writing to a company composed entirely of women? Which is correct: "Whom are you expecting?" or "Who are you expecting?" How do you address a package to someone in a foreign country? What is meant by the Latin expression sine qua non? *You may have to answer questions such as these every day. Of course, you aren't expected to know the answers to everything asked of you, but you are expected to know where to find the information you need.*

It's smart to be right.

LESSON 49

The practice material in this lesson concentrates on the shorthand principles you studied in Chapter 1.

464 BRIEF FORMS AND DERIVATIVES

In-not, it-at, am, a-an, will-well, wills, willing, of, are-hour-our, ours. With, have, that, can, cannot, you-your, yours, Mr., but, I.

Reading and writing practice

465

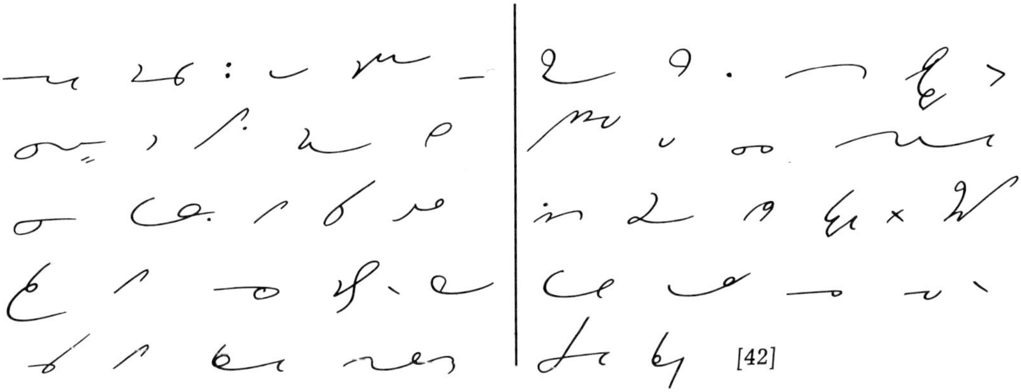

[42]

466

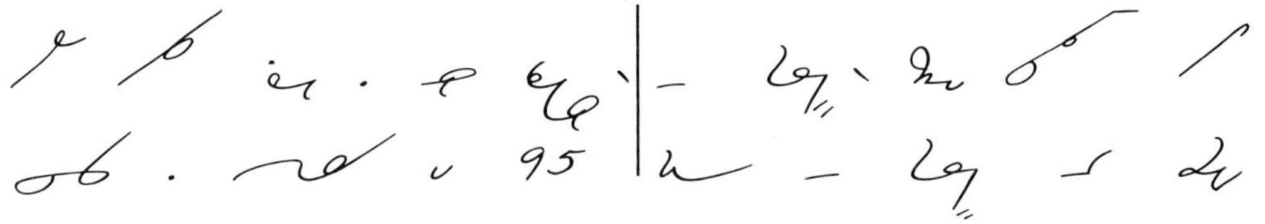

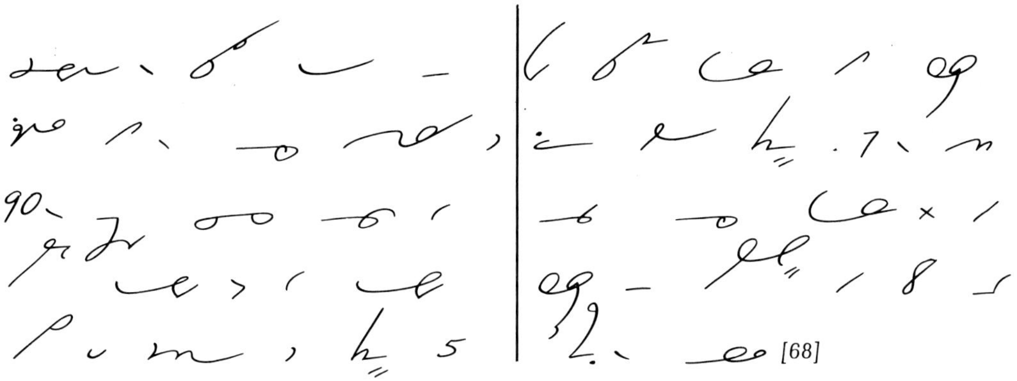
[68]

467 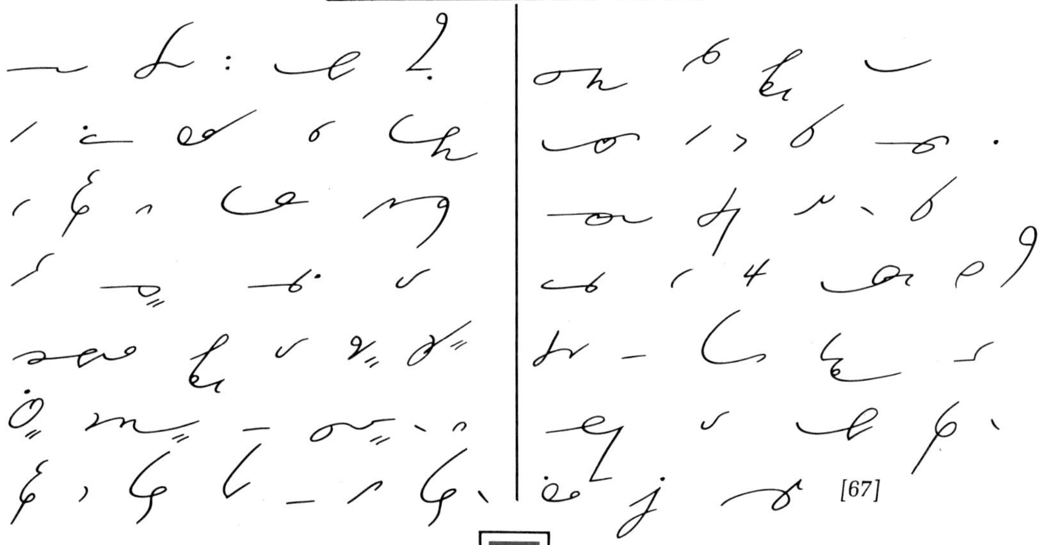
[67]

468 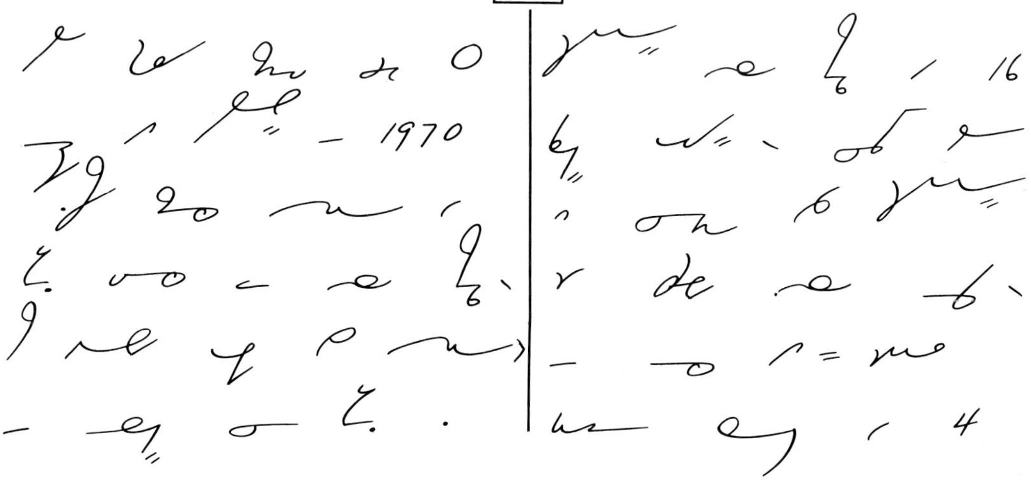

[94]

469

[46]

470

[65]

471

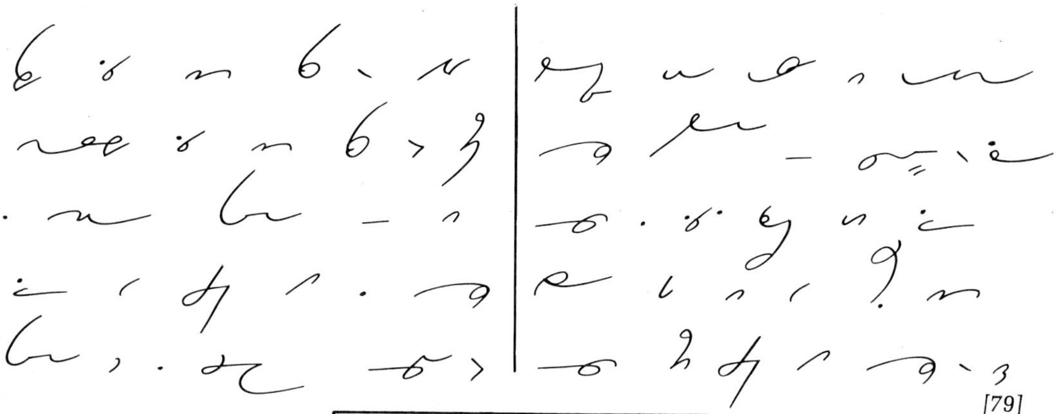

[79]

472 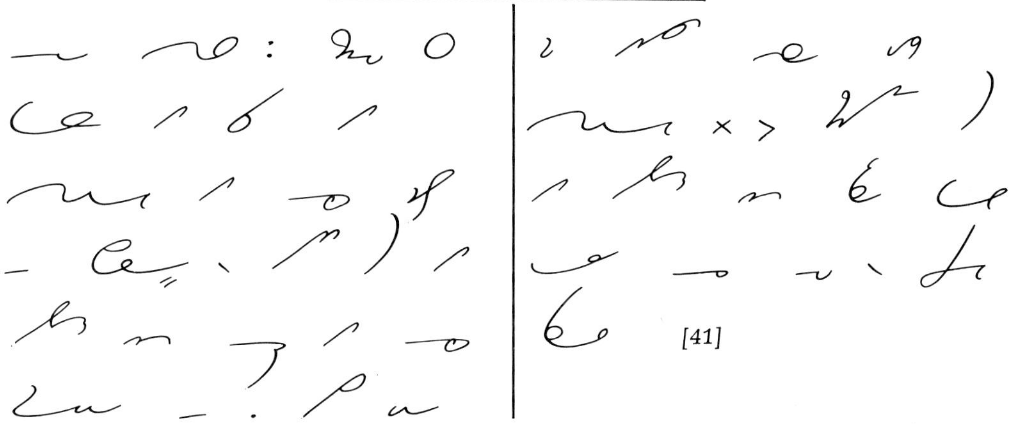

[41]

473 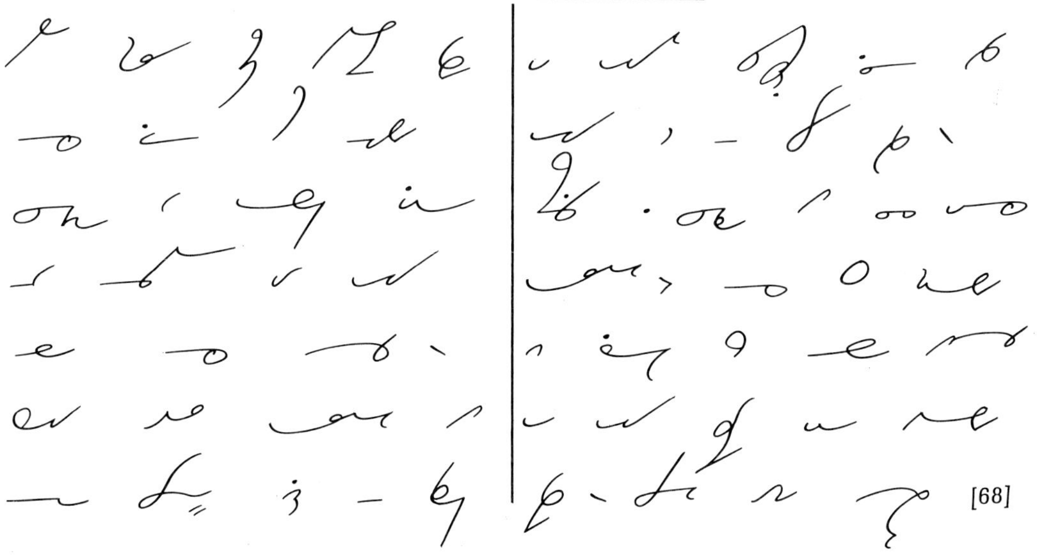

[68]

474

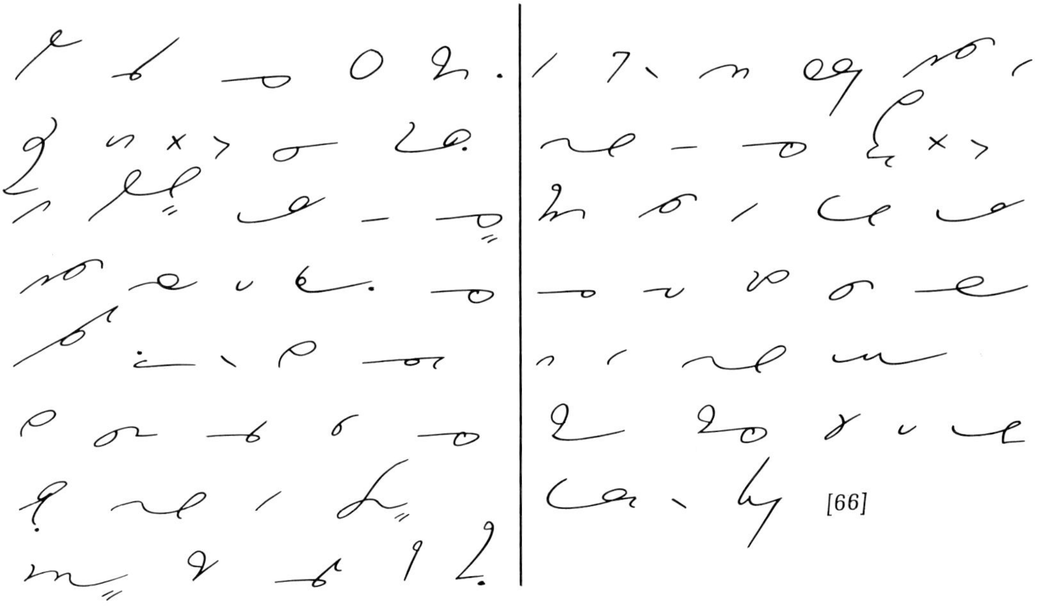
[66]

PHRASING AND SHORTHAND SPEED

Occasionally, students gain the impression that phrasing is the key to shorthand speed and that the more a writer phrases, the faster he will write. Consequently, they try to phrase as many combinations of words as possible and sometimes even devise phrases of their own.

This practice may seriously reduce a writer's speed rather than increase it. Why? A phrase is valuable only if it can be written without the slightest hesitation. If the writer must pause for even the smallest fraction of a second in composing or thinking of a phrase, that phrase becomes a speed handicap.

The phrase that can be written without hesitation is the one that has occurred again and again in the writer's practice work, so that it has impressed itself permanently on his mind. If you have been reading and copying each Reading and Writing Practice faithfully, you have encountered the common phrases of the English language many times. These phrases will come to you naturally when you take dictation.

If you have the feeling that you should be phrasing more, dismiss the matter from your mind. Simply continue to read and copy faithfully each Reading and Writing Practice, and your ability to phrase will take care of itself.

LESSON 50

The practice material in this lesson concentrates on the shorthand principles you studied in Chapter 2.

475 BRIEF FORMS AND DERIVATIVES

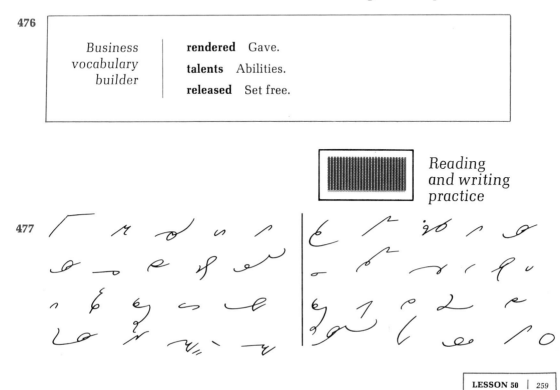

Good, goods, this, their-there, would, putting, being, which, shall, for.
Them, they, was, when, from, should, could, send, sender.

Building transcription skills

476

Business vocabulary builder	
	rendered Gave.
	talents Abilities.
	released Set free.

Reading and writing practice

477

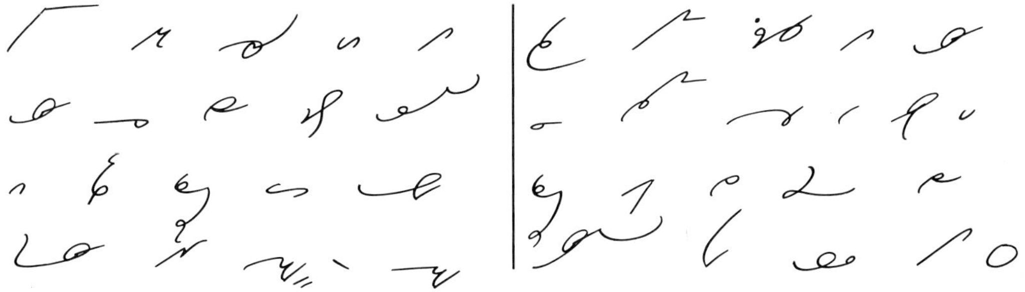

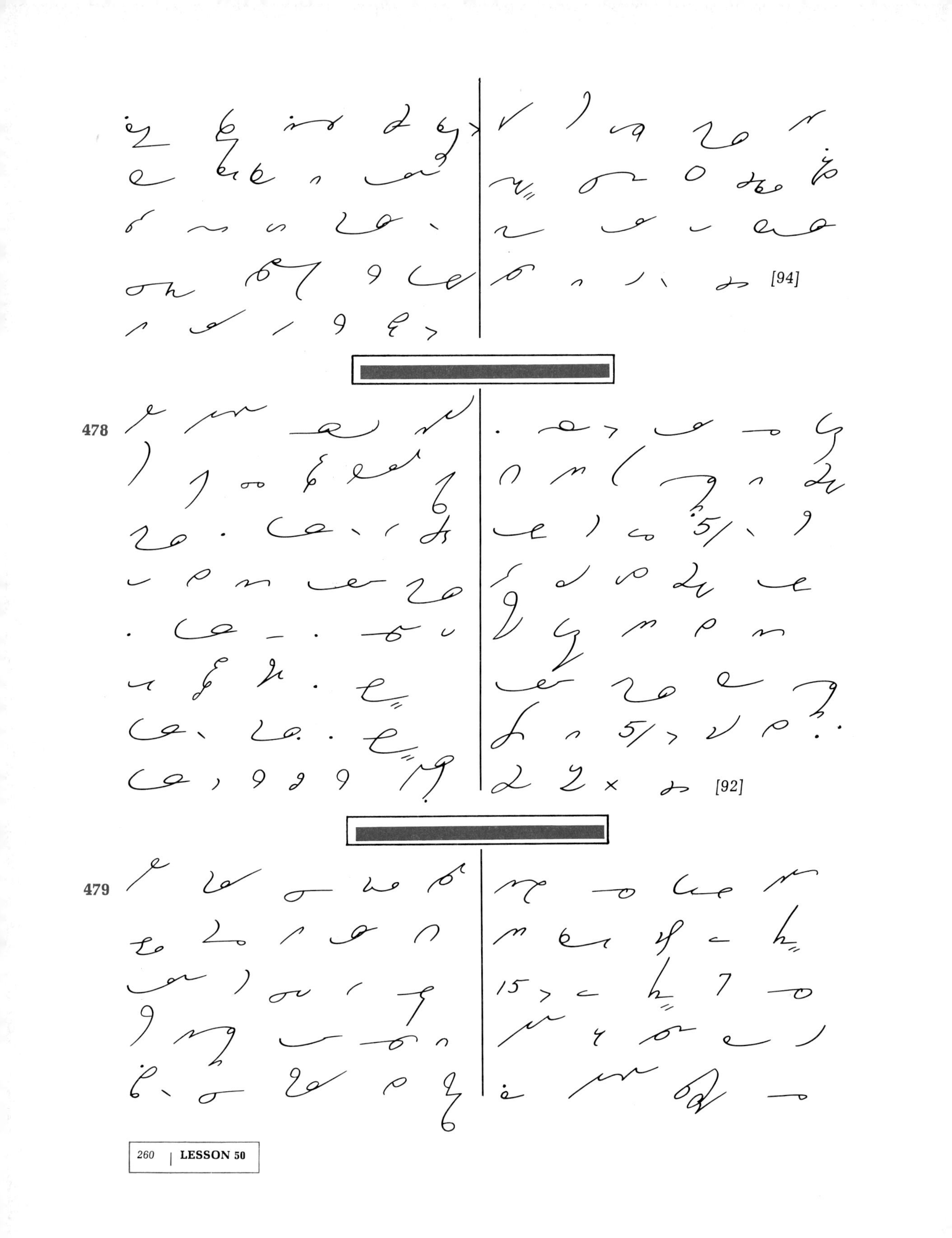

[94]

478

[92]

479

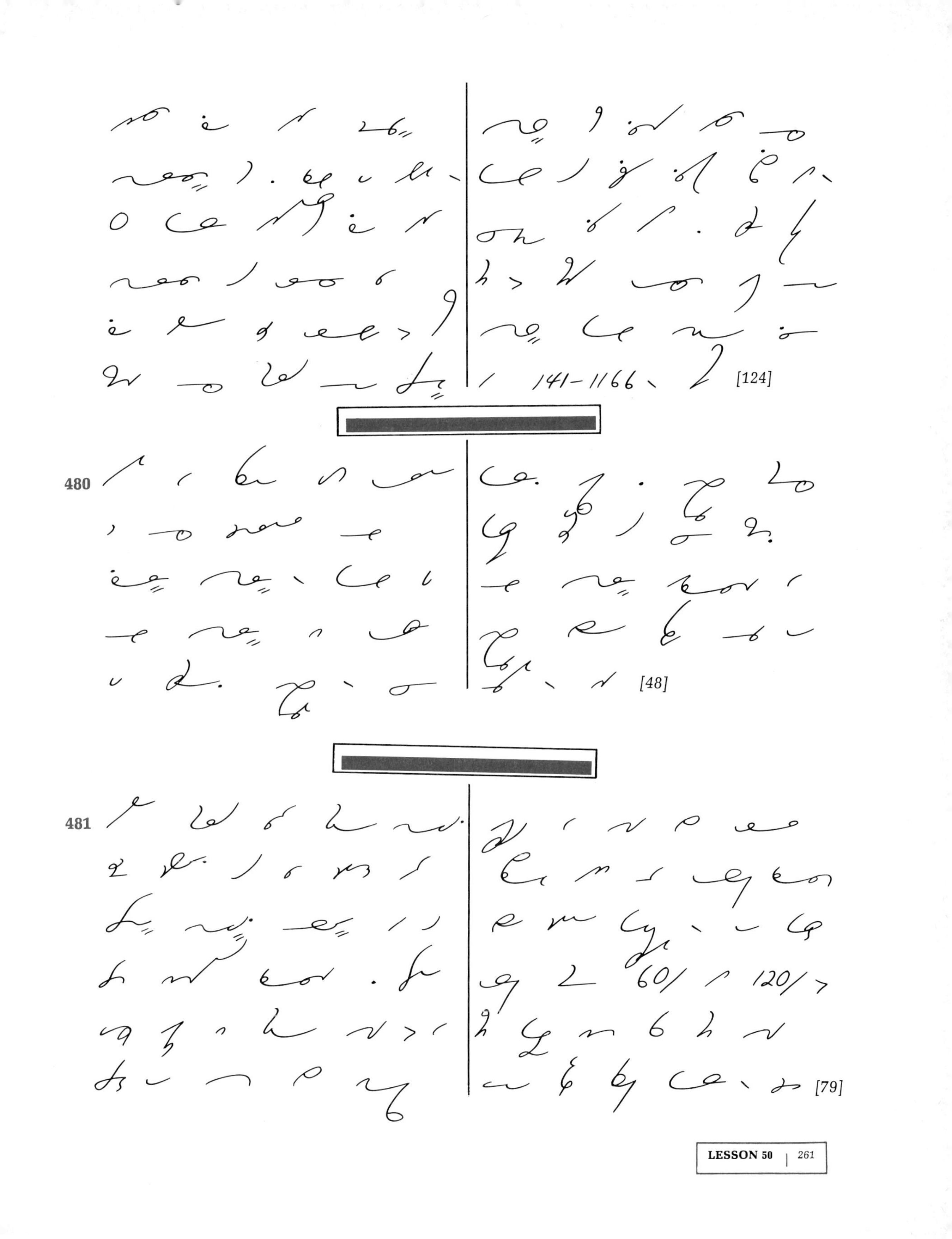

141-1166 [124]

[redacted]

480

[48]

[redacted]

481

60 120

[79]

482

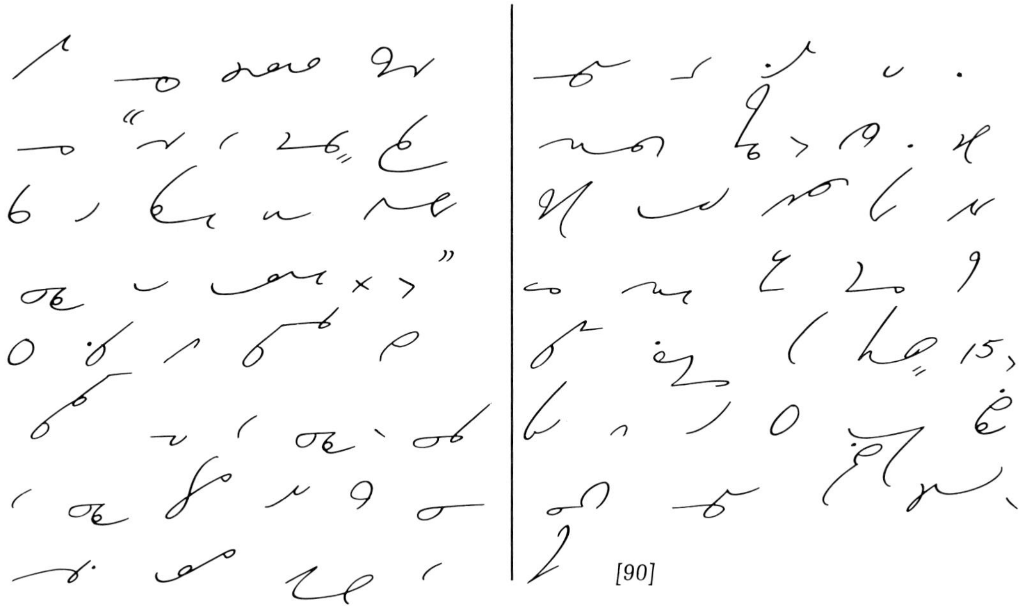

[90]

483

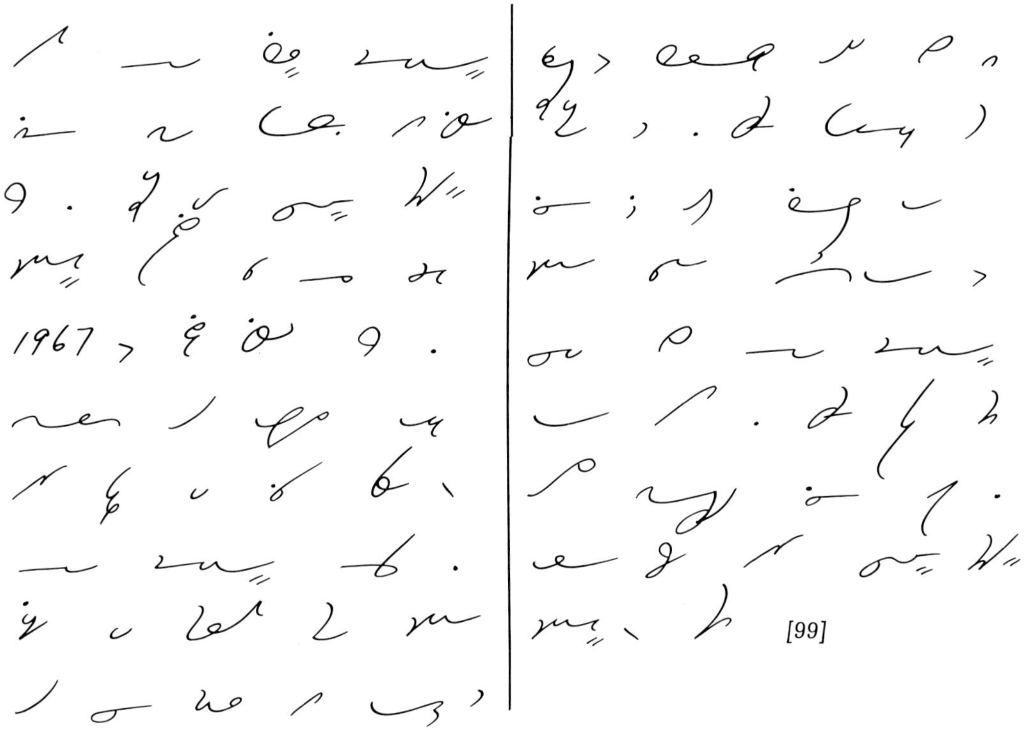

[99]

LESSON 51

The practice material in this lesson concentrates on the shorthand principles you studied in Chapter 3.

484 BRIEF FORMS AND DERIVATIVES

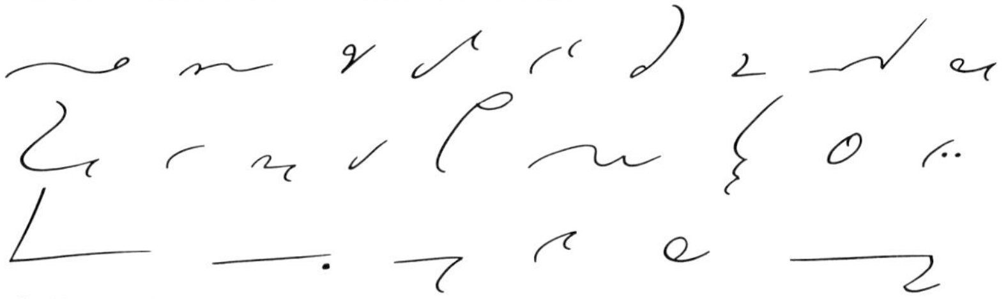

Gladly, worker, yesterday, orders, thanks, very, soon, enclosed, years.
Values, than, once, what, about, greater, businesses, why, thinking.
Gentlemen, morning, important-importance, those, where, manufacturer.

Building transcription skills

485

Business vocabulary builder	
	register (*verb*) Enroll.
	brochure Pamphlet or booklet.
	offended Displeased; angered.

Reading and writing practice

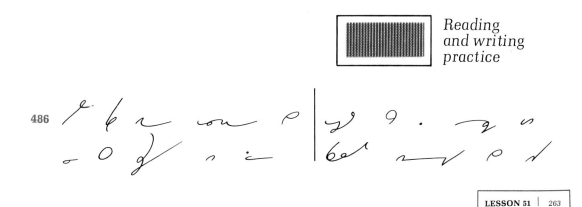

486 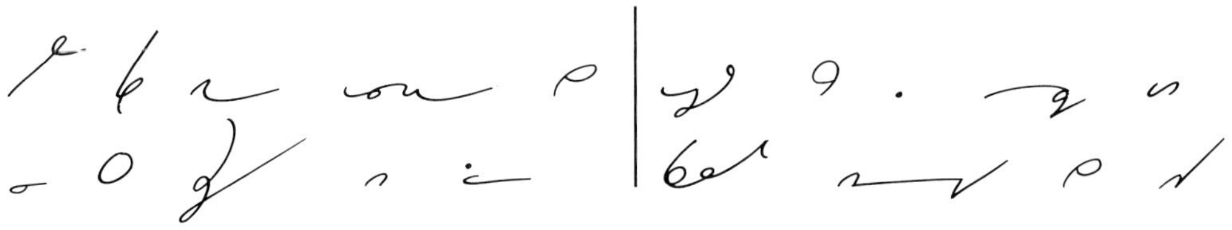

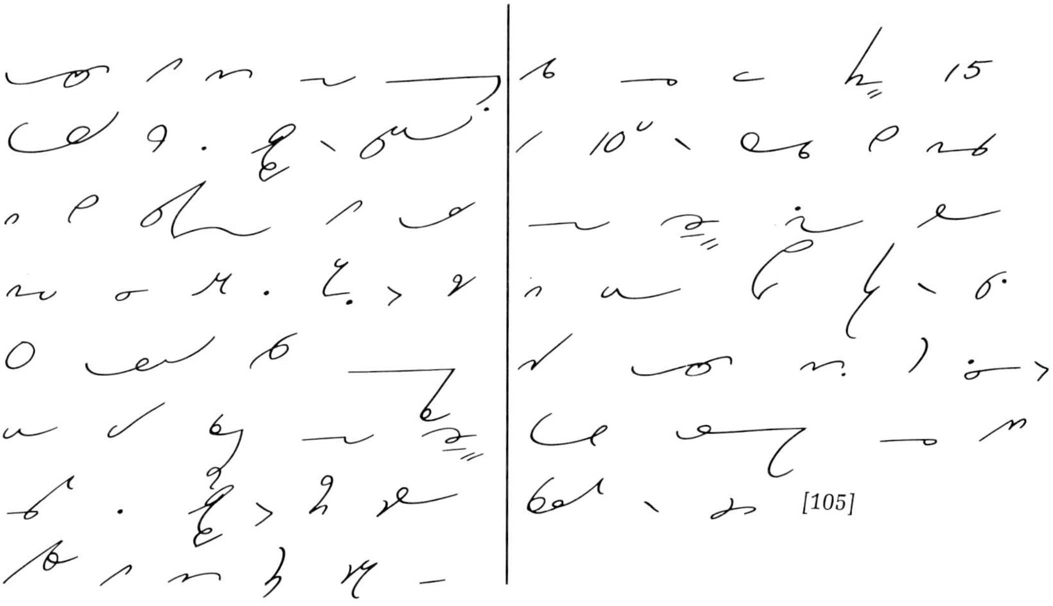
15
10
[105]

487

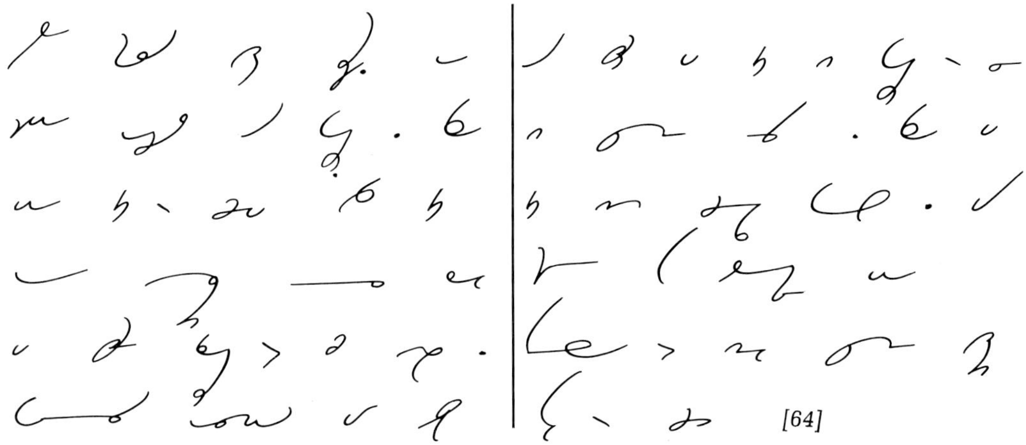
[64]

488

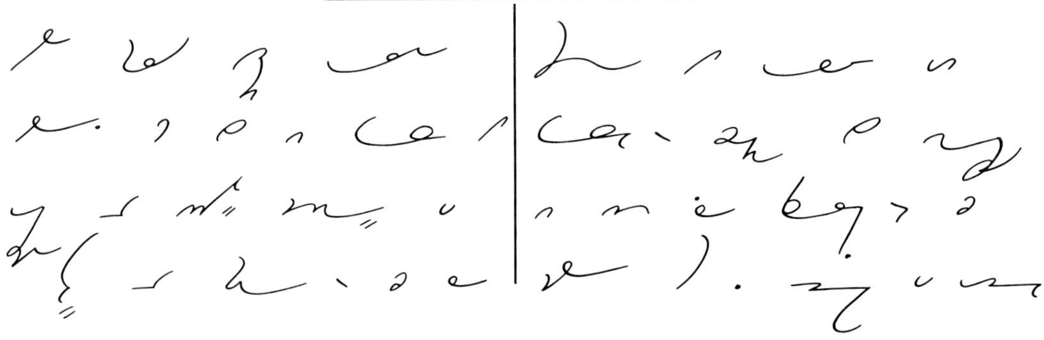

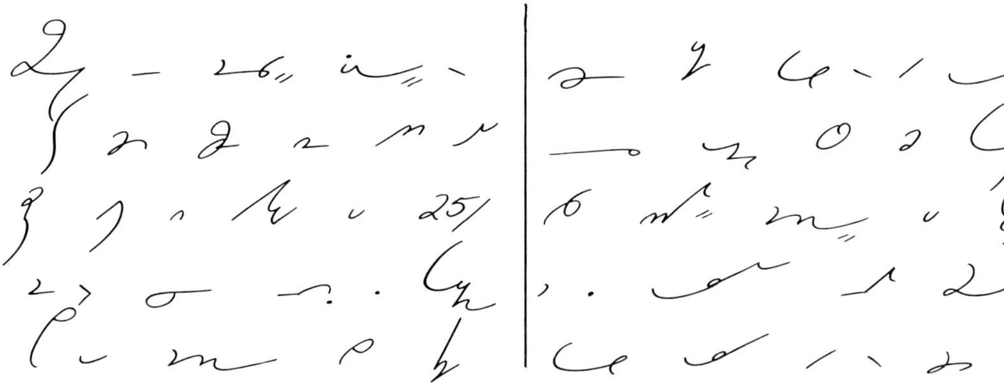

[101]

489

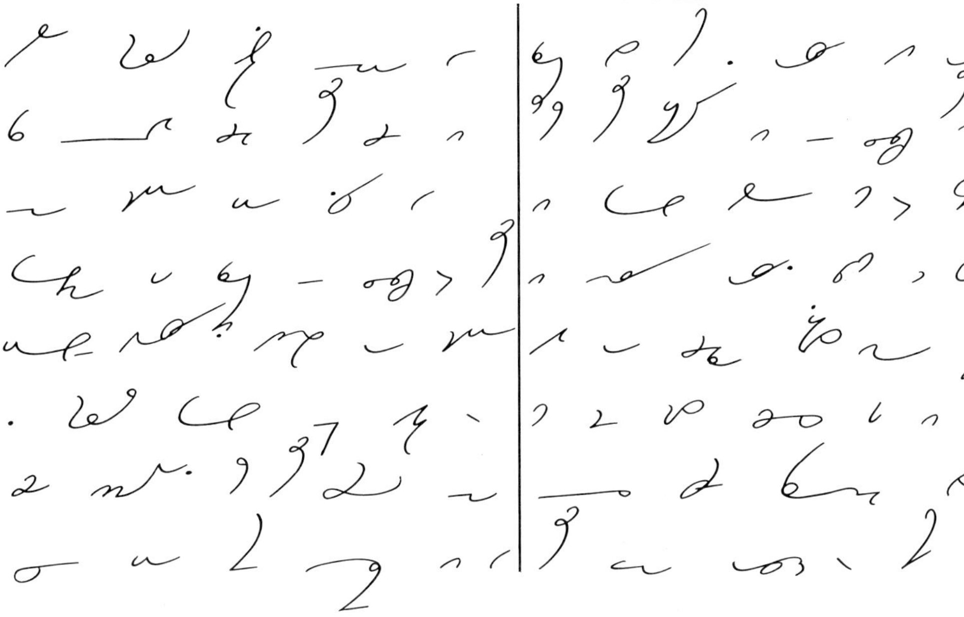

[100]

490

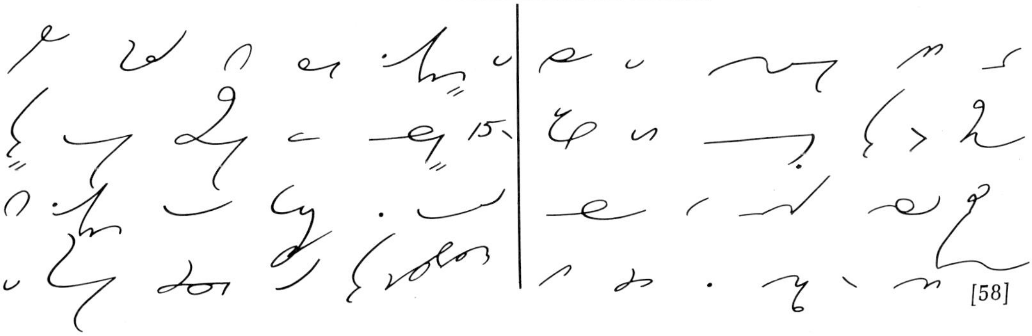

[58]

491

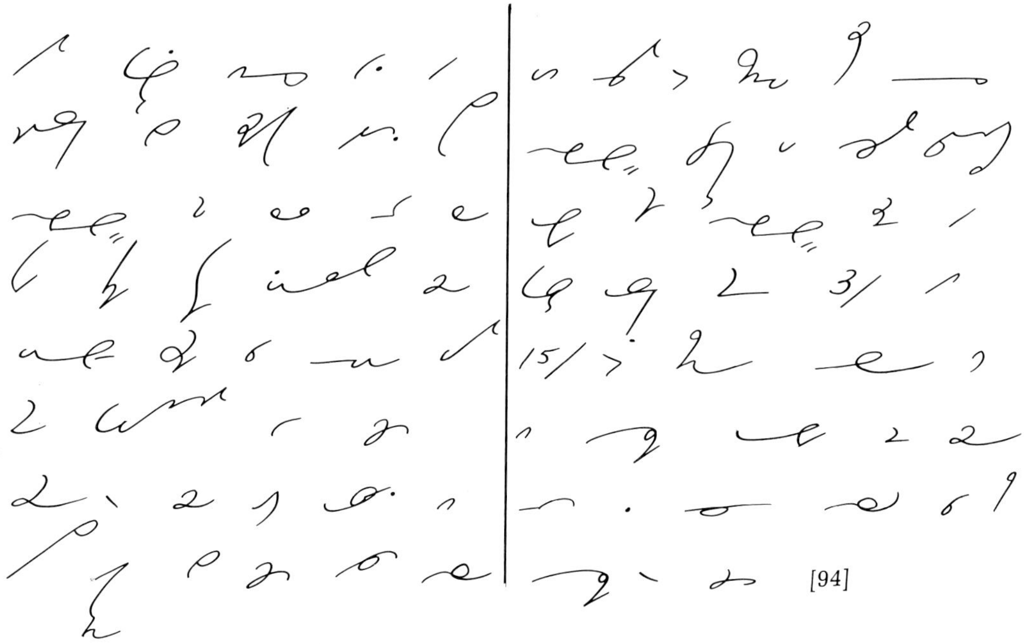

[94]

492

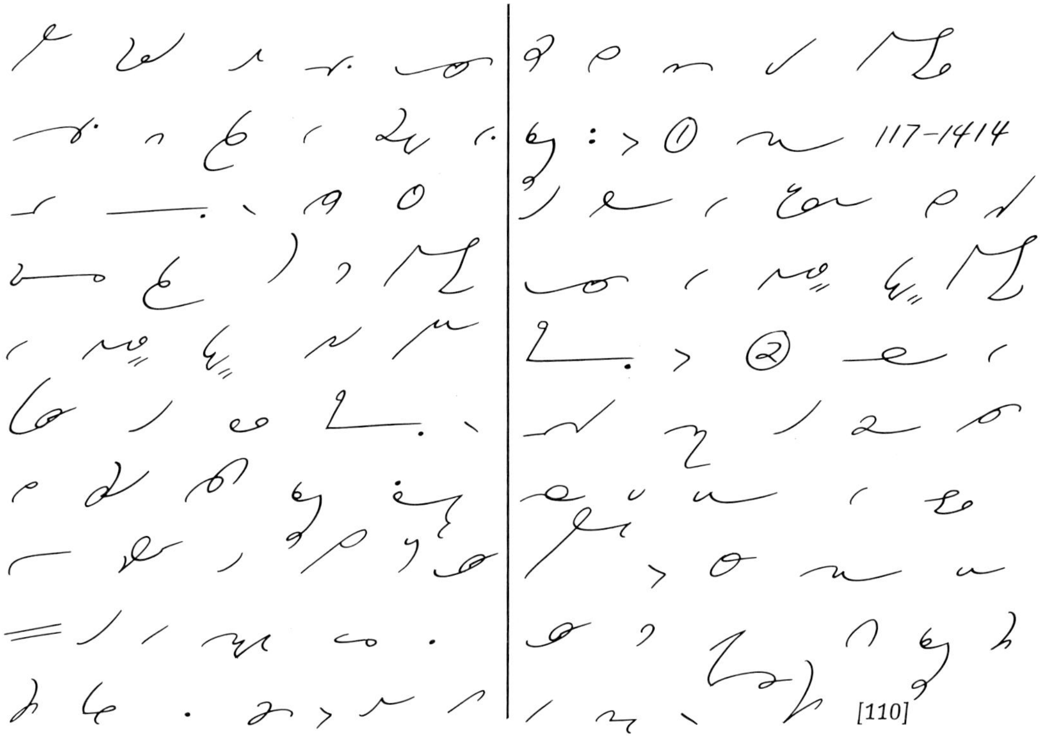

[110]

LESSON 52

The practice material in this lesson concentrates on the shorthand principles you studied in Chapter 4.

493 BRIEF FORMS AND DERIVATIVES

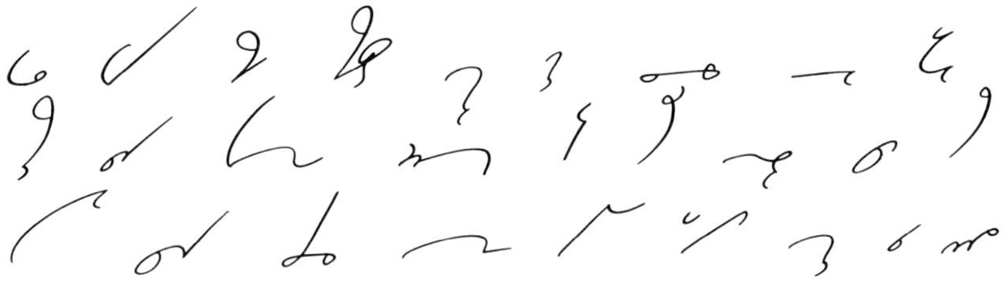

Presently, parted, after, advertises, companies, wishes, immediately, must, opportunities. Advantages, used, bigger, suggestion, such, several, corresponds, how-out, ever-every. Times, acknowledged, generally, gone, during, overdue, questions, yet, worthy.

Building transcription skills

494 SPELLING FAMILIES | -tion, -sion

Words Ending in -tion

ac·tion	**con·nec·tion**	**lo·ca·tion**
ap·pli·ca·tion	**cor·rec·tion**	**po·si·tion**
col·lec·tion	**dem·on·stra·tion**	**ques·tion**
com·ple·tion	**il·lus·tra·tion**	**re·la·tion**

Words Ending in -sion

con·clu·sion	**di·vi·sion**	**pro·vi·sion**
de·ci·sion	**pen·sion**	**tele·vi·sion**
de·pres·sion	**per·sua·sion**	**ten·sion**

495

Business vocabulary builder

depart Leave.

confidential Private; secret.

gratifying Pleasing; satisfying.

Reading and writing practice

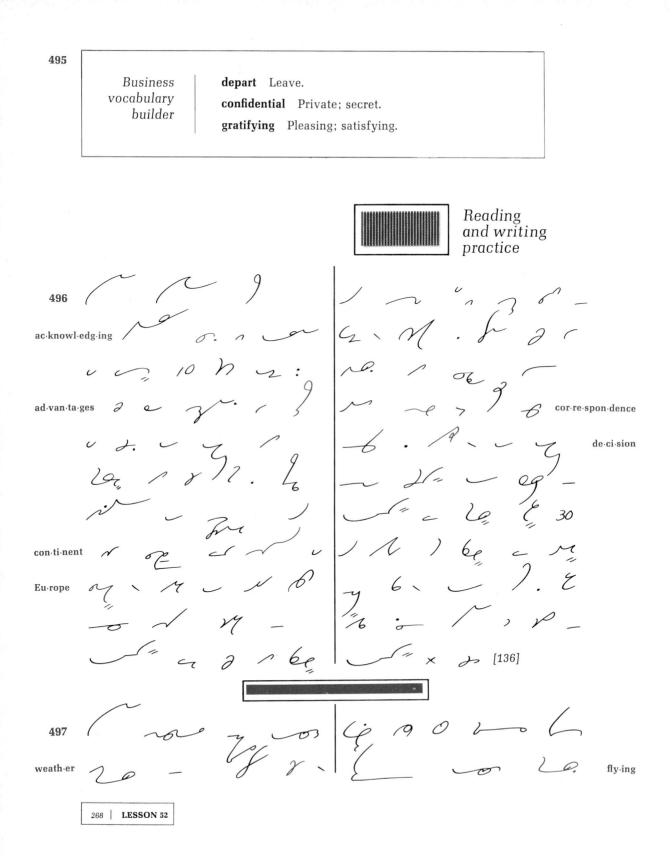

496

ac·knowl·edg·ing

ad·van·ta·ges

con·ti·nent

Eu·rope

cor·re·spon·dence

de·ci·sion

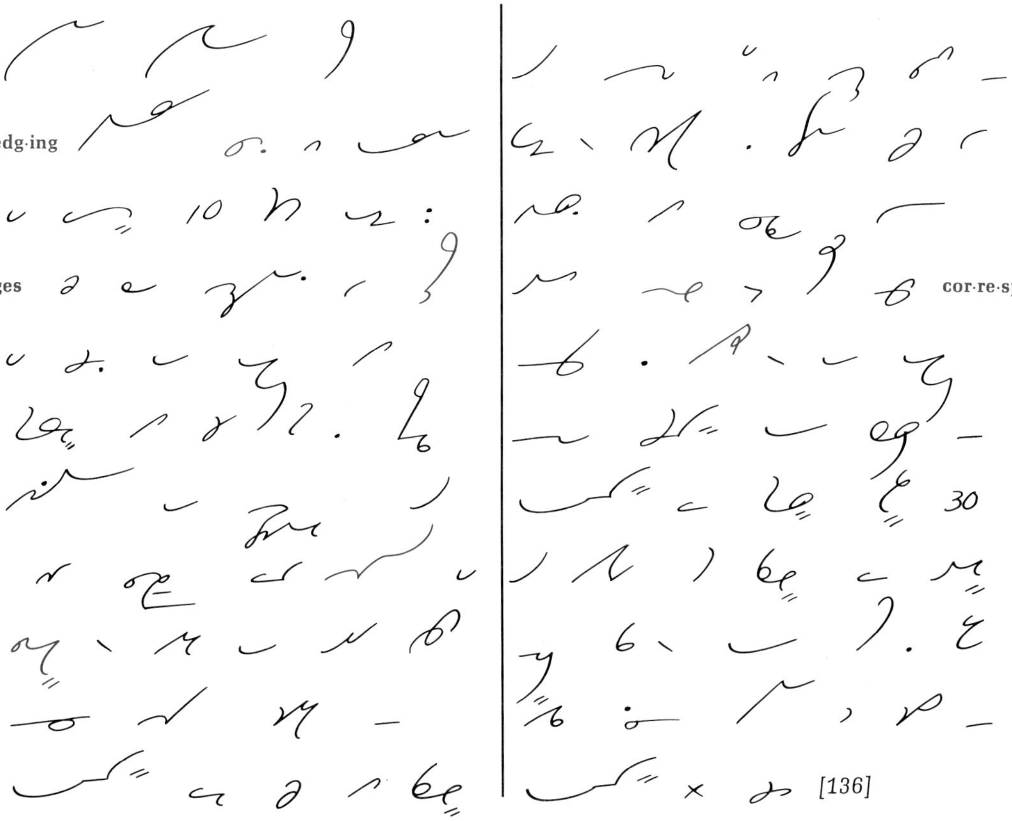

497

weath·er

fly·ing

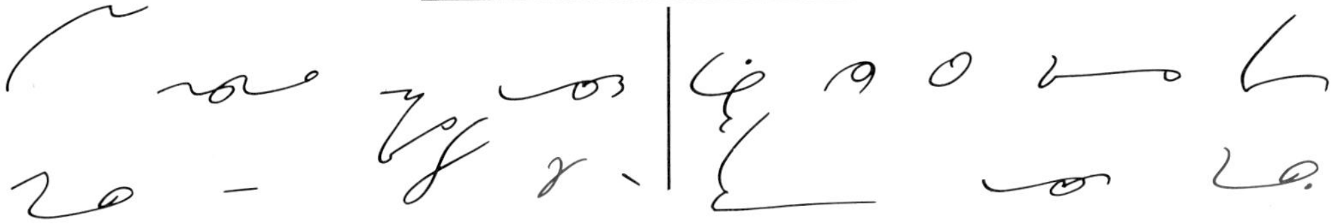

de·vel·ops

com·mer·cial

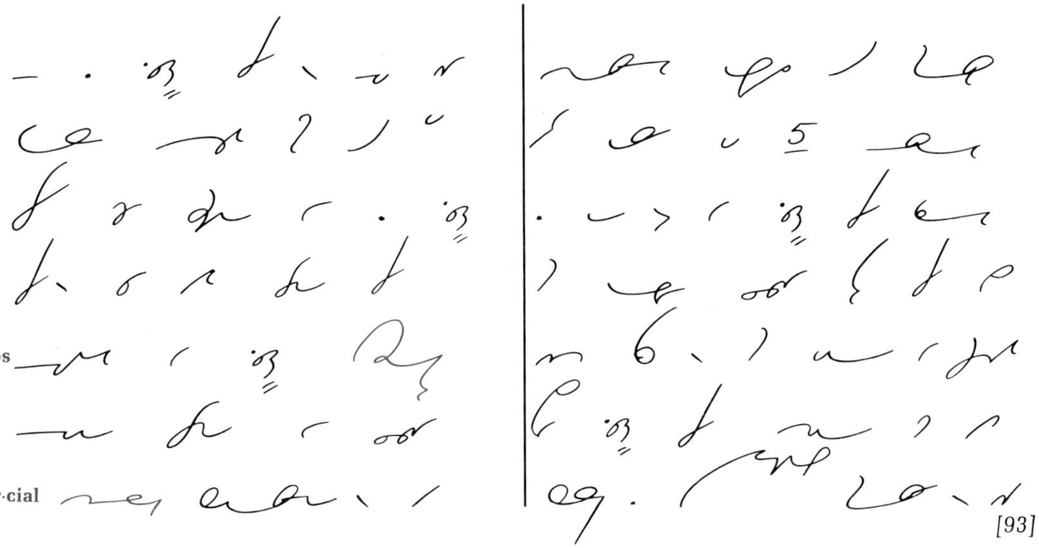

[93]

498

im·me·di·ate·ly

rea·son

bor·row

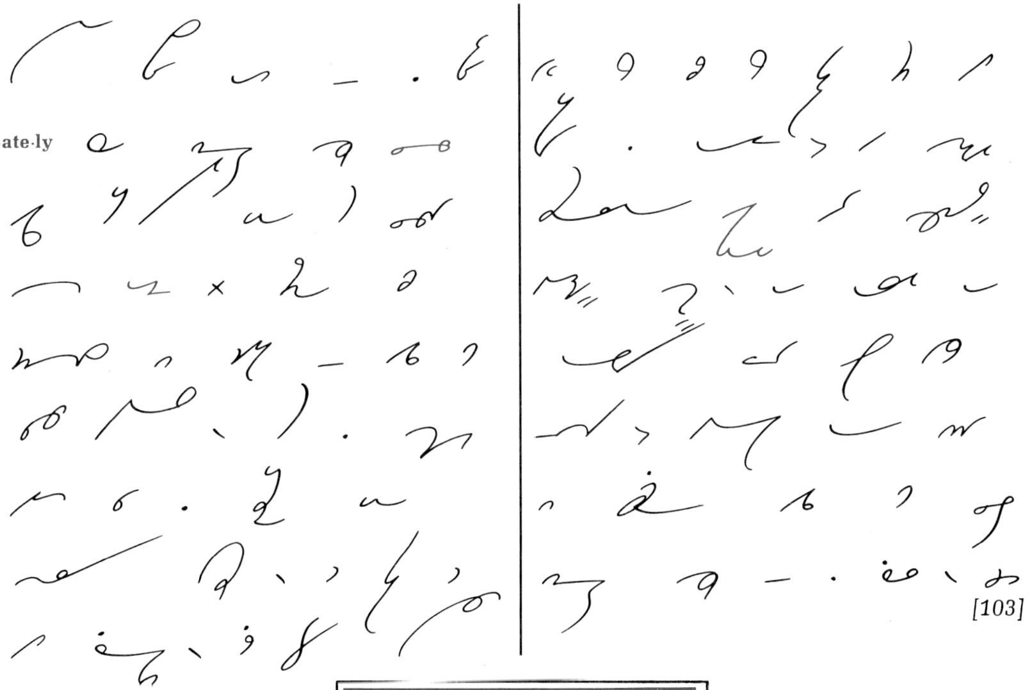

[103]

499

cor·re·spon·dent

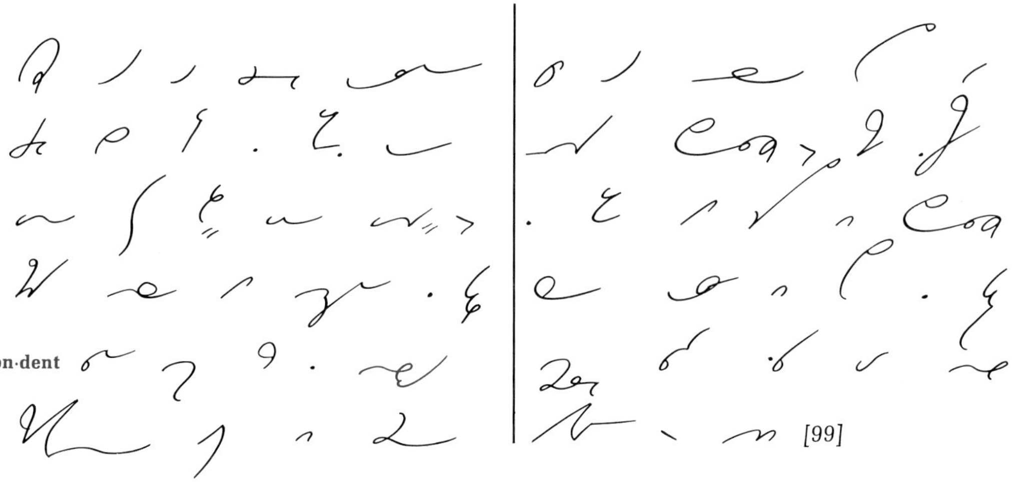

[99]

500

re·plies

grat·i·fy·ing

ad·ver·tis·ing

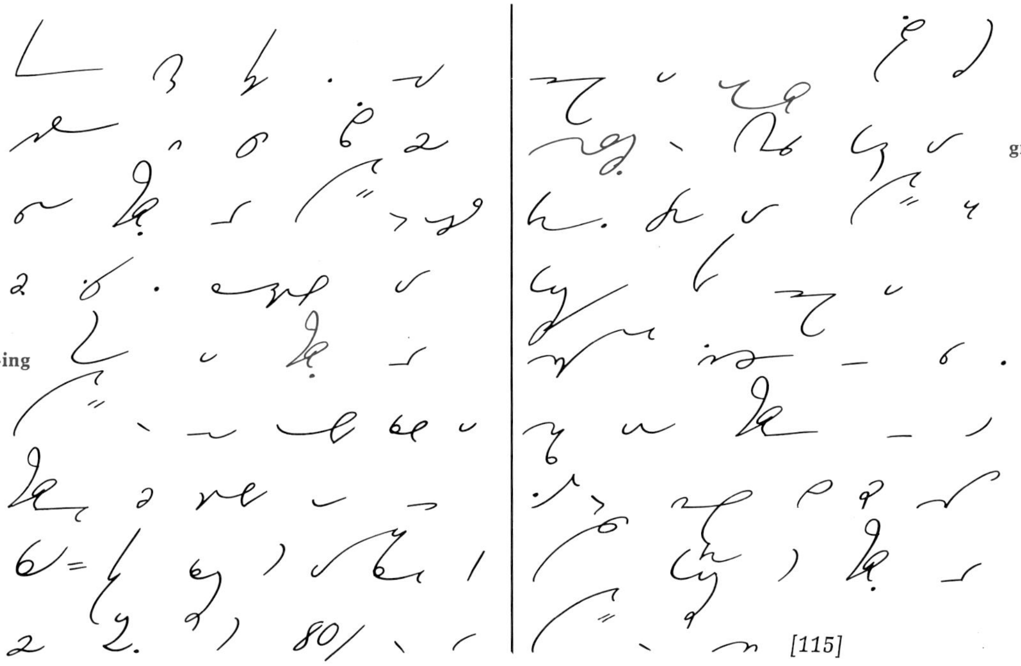

[115]

LESSON 53

The practice material in this lesson concentrates on the shorthand principles you studied in Chapter 5.

501 BRIEF FORMS AND DERIVATIVES

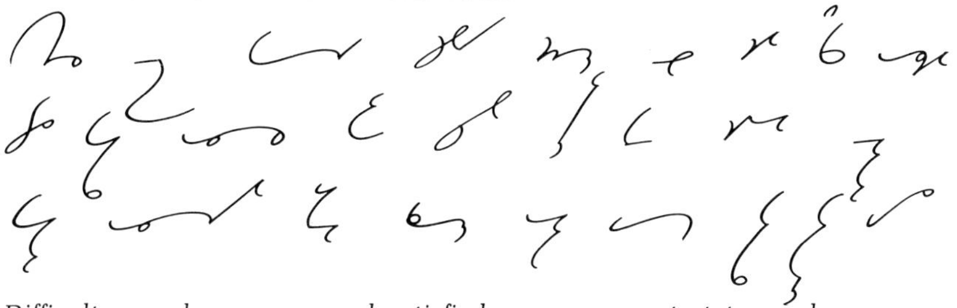

Difficulty, envelope, progressed, satisfied, successes, next, states, underpay, requests. Particularly, probably, regularly, speaker, ideas, subjects, upon, streets, newspapers. Purposes, regards, opinions, circulars, responsible, organization, publicly, publications, ordinarily.

Building transcription skills

502

Business vocabulary builder	
	creative Being able to produce something through imaginative skill.
	extended (*verb*) Made an offer to.
	summarized Presented briefly.

Reading and writing practice

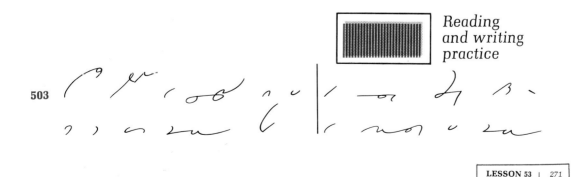

503

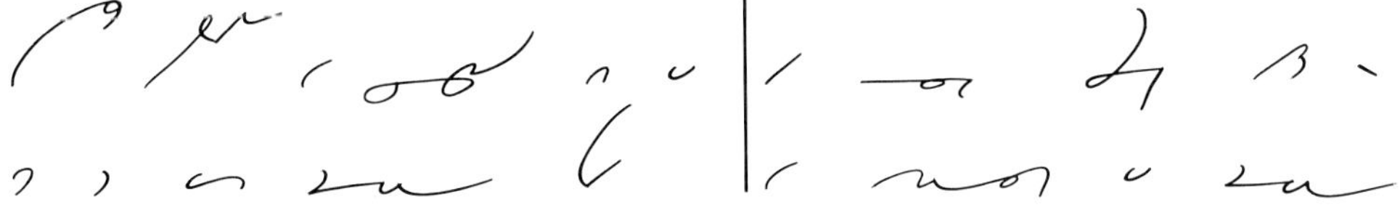

sums
or·ga·ni·za·tion
wealth
cre·ative

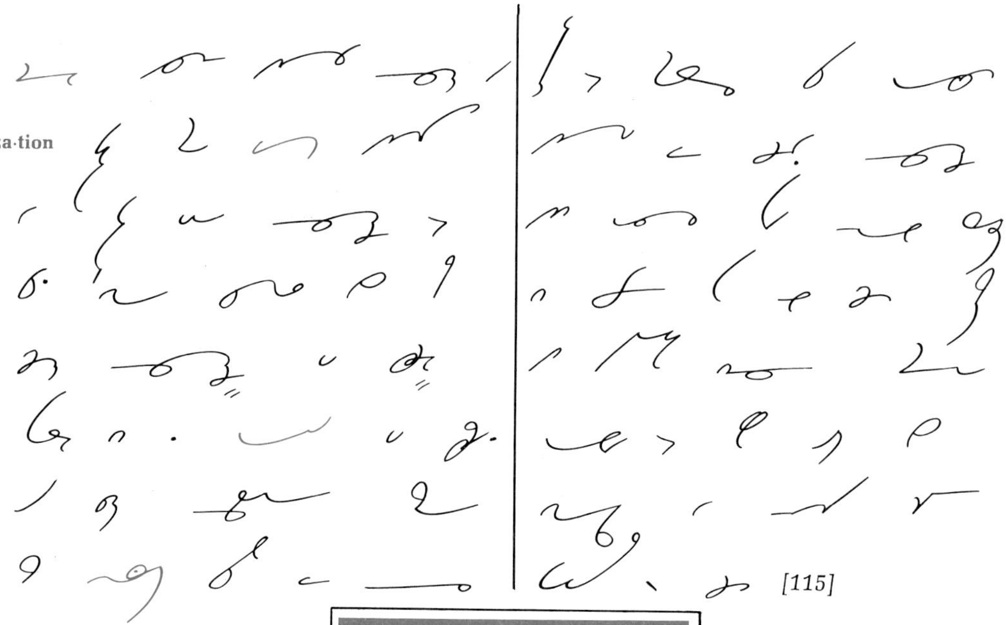

[115]

504

re·spon·si·ble
speak·er's
di·rec·tors

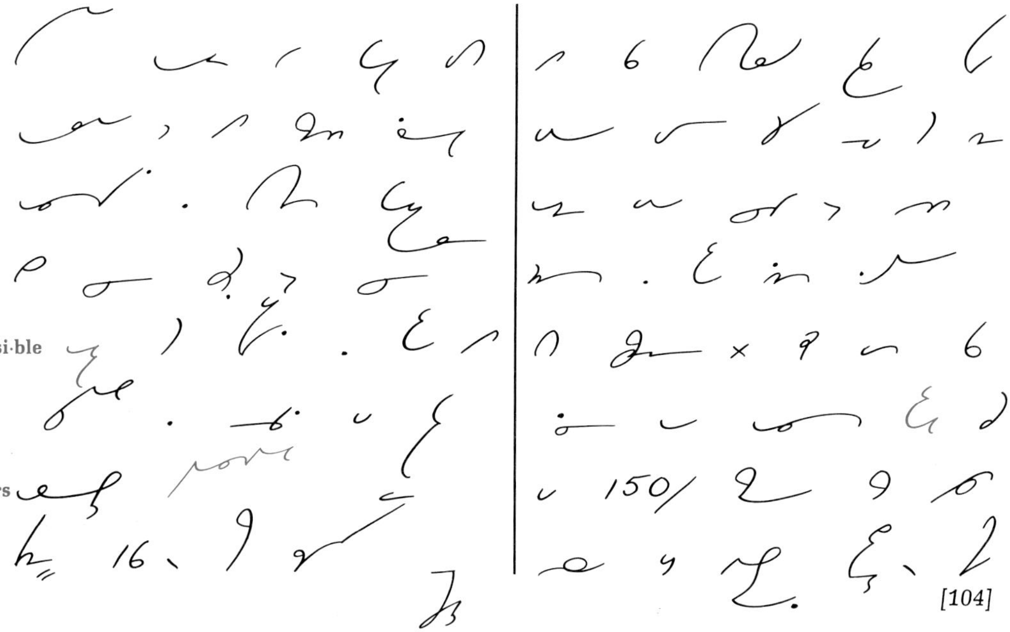

[104]

505

fac·tor

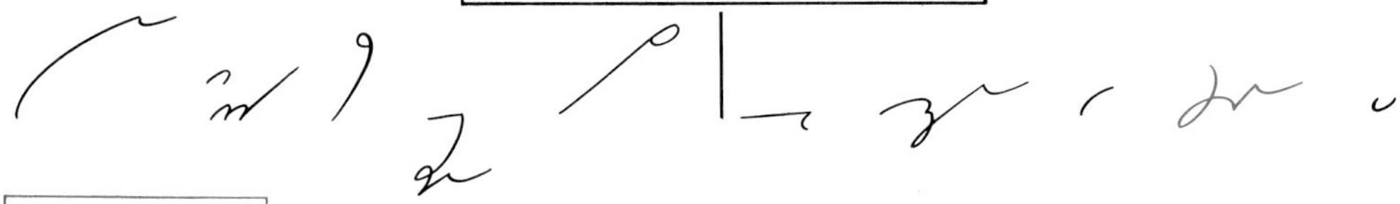

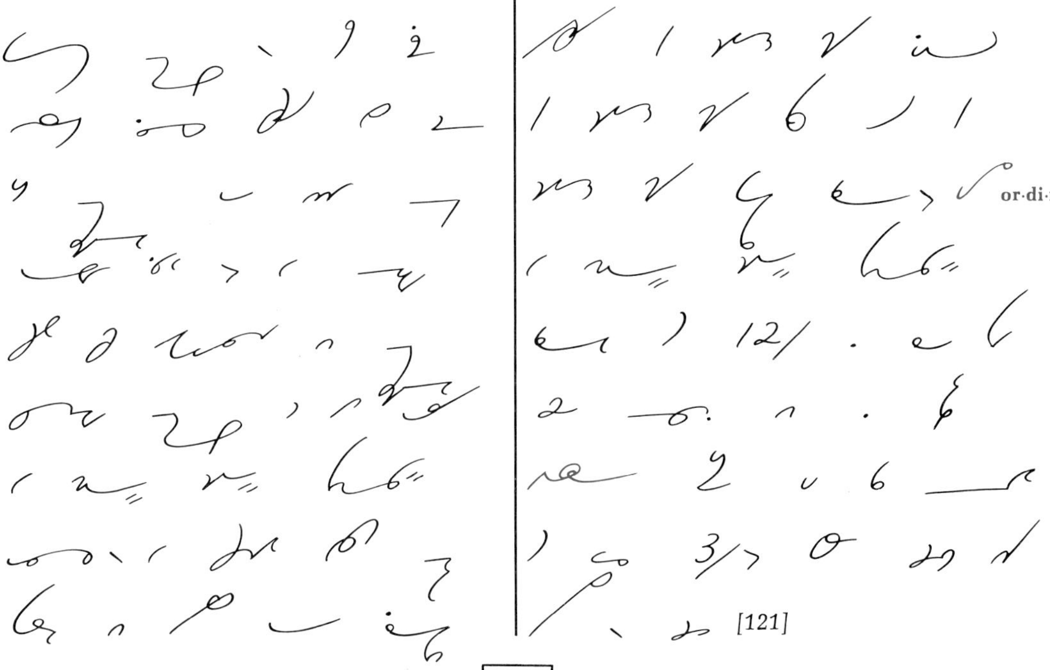

or·di·nar·i·ly

tri·al

[121]

506

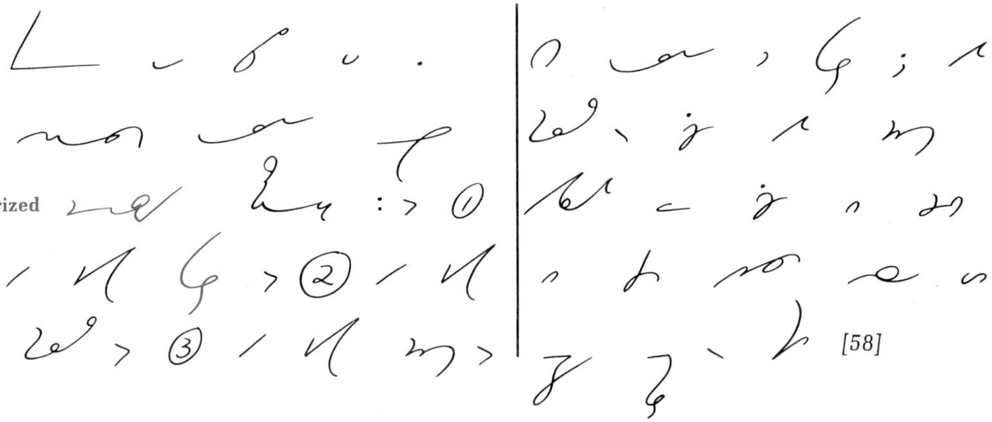

sum·ma·rized

brief

[58]

507

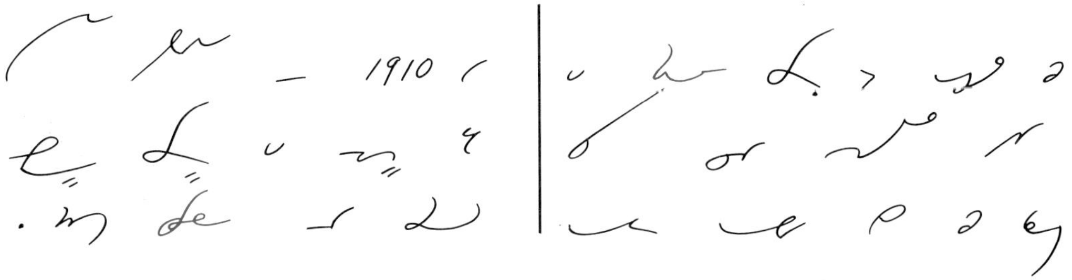

for·eign

pi·o·neer

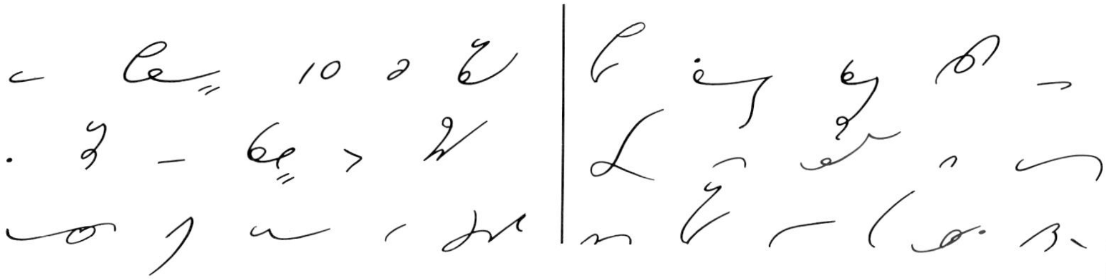

rend·er

writ·ing

[77]

508

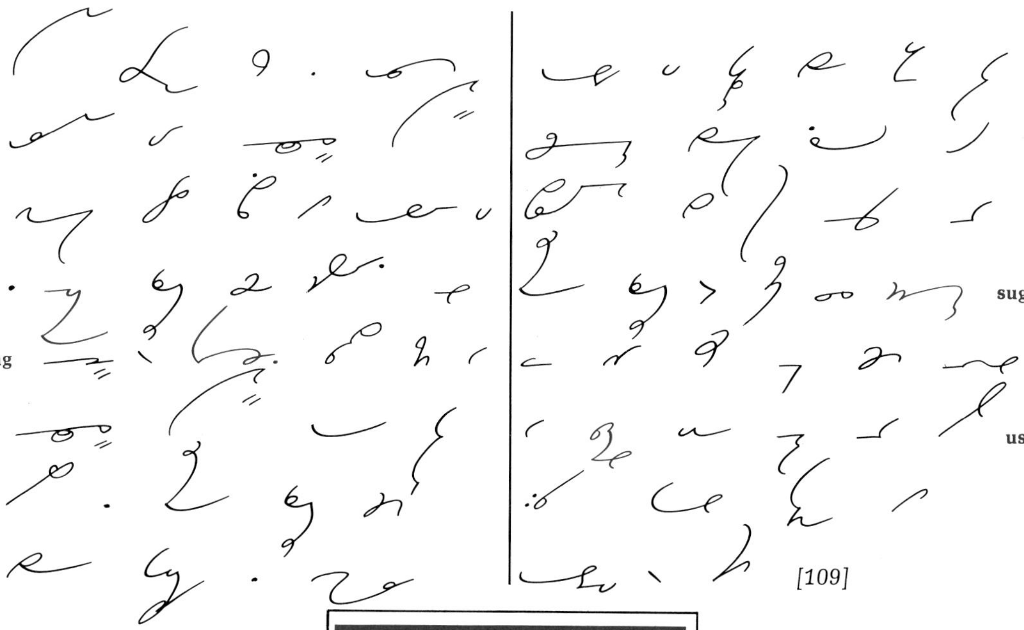

nov·el

be·gin·ning

sug·ges·tions

use·ful·ness

[109]

509

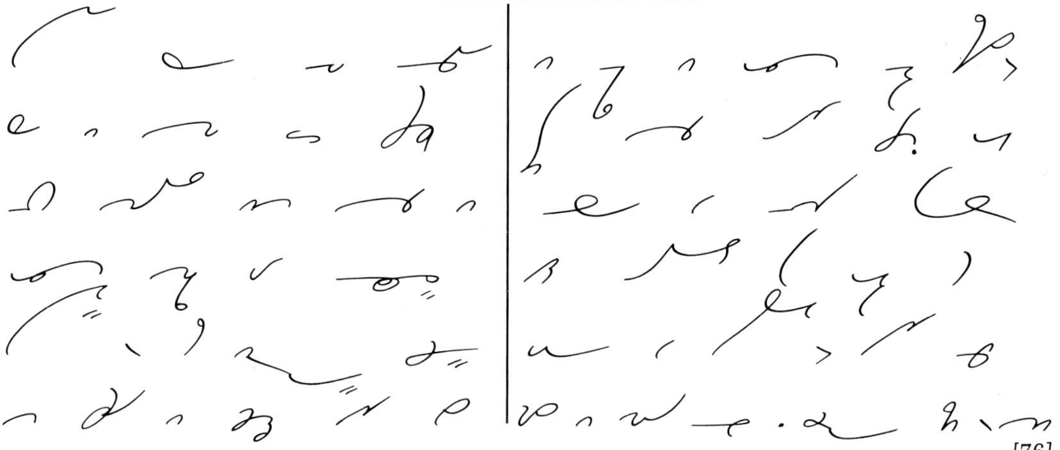

[76]

LESSON 54

The practice material in this lesson concentrates on the shorthand principles you studied in Chapter 6.

510 BRIEF FORMS AND DERIVATIVES

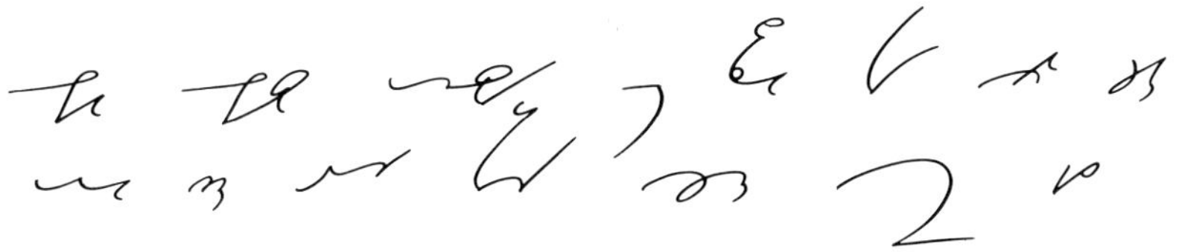

Merchants, merchandise, recognized, never, experiences, between, quantities, situations. Railroads, worlds, throughout, objected, characters, government, shortly.

Building transcription skills

511 SIMILAR-WORDS DRILL | weather, whether

weather State of the atmosphere with respect to wetness or dryness, cold or heat; climate.

You can take a good picture regardless of the weather.

The game was called because of the weather.

whether Indicating a choice (often followed by *or*). Also used to introduce an indirect question.

You can take a good picture whether *the sun is shining or* whether *it is raining.*

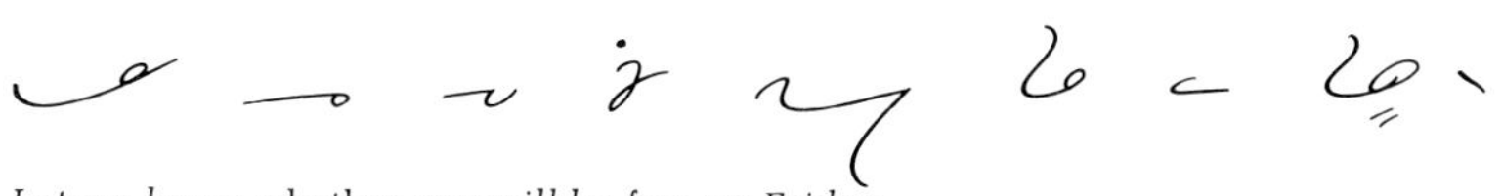

Let me know whether you will be free on Friday.

512

Business vocabulary builder	
	altered Changed.
	vouch for Give personal assurance; guarantee.
	settings Backgrounds.

Reading and writing practice

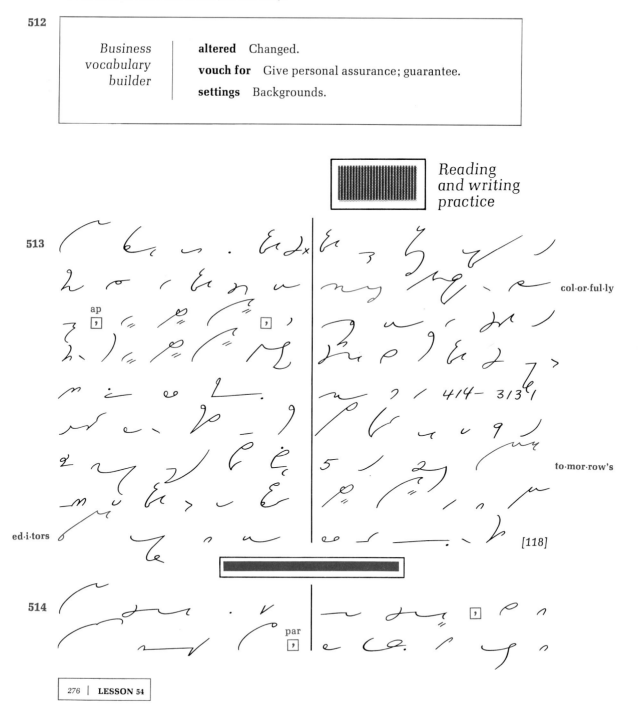

513

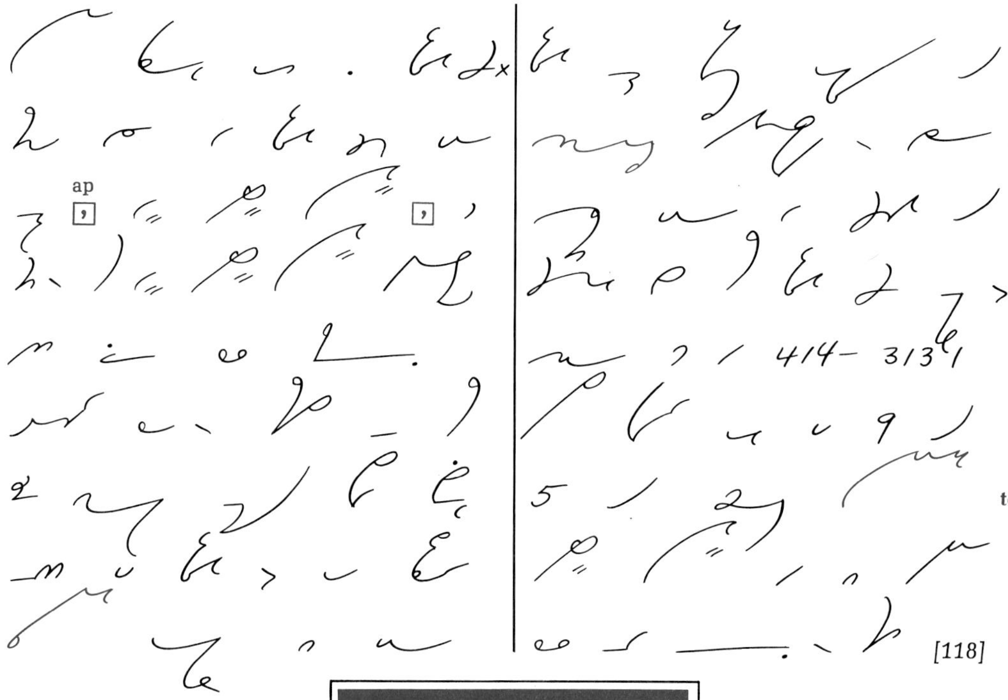

col·or·ful·ly

to·mor·row's

ed·i·tors

[118]

514

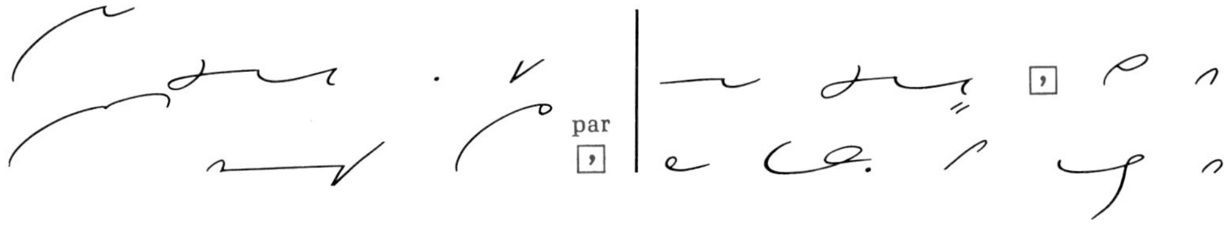

gov·ern·ment

phase

de·scribed

tech·ni·cal

vouch

char·ac·ter

ref·er·ence

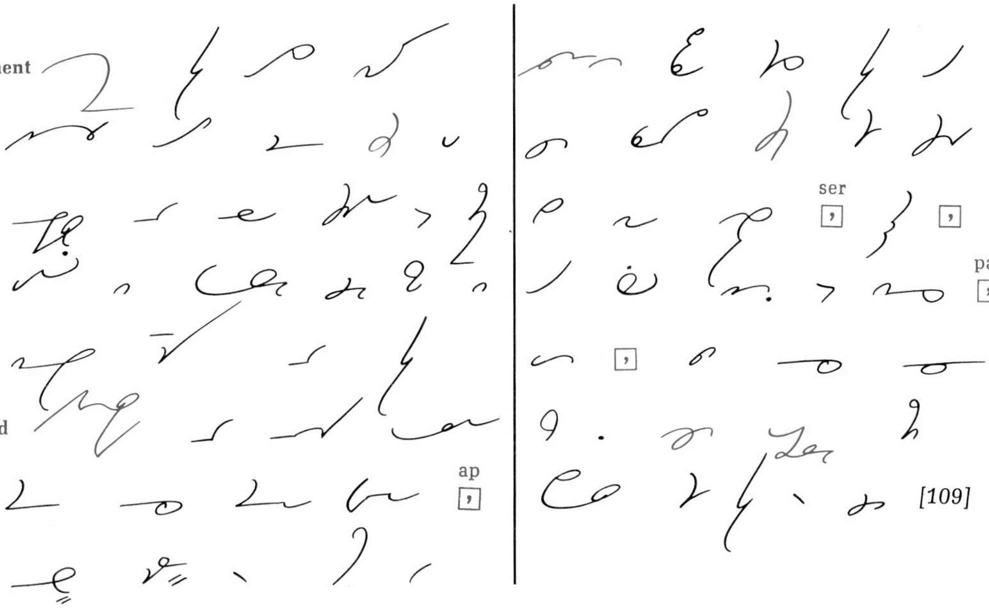

ser
par
ap
[109]

515

prac·ti·cal

weath·er

whether

cloudy

de·scrip·tive

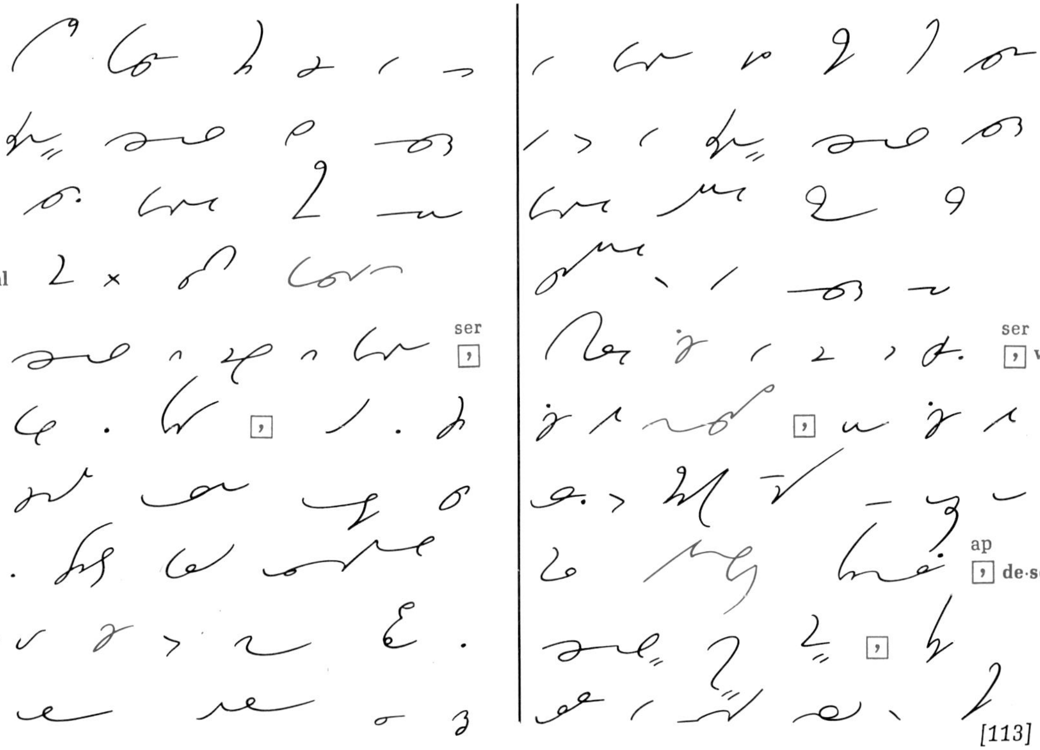

ser
ser
ap
[113]

516

mod·ern

show·rooms

ad·vi·sors

rec·og·nized

pleas·ant

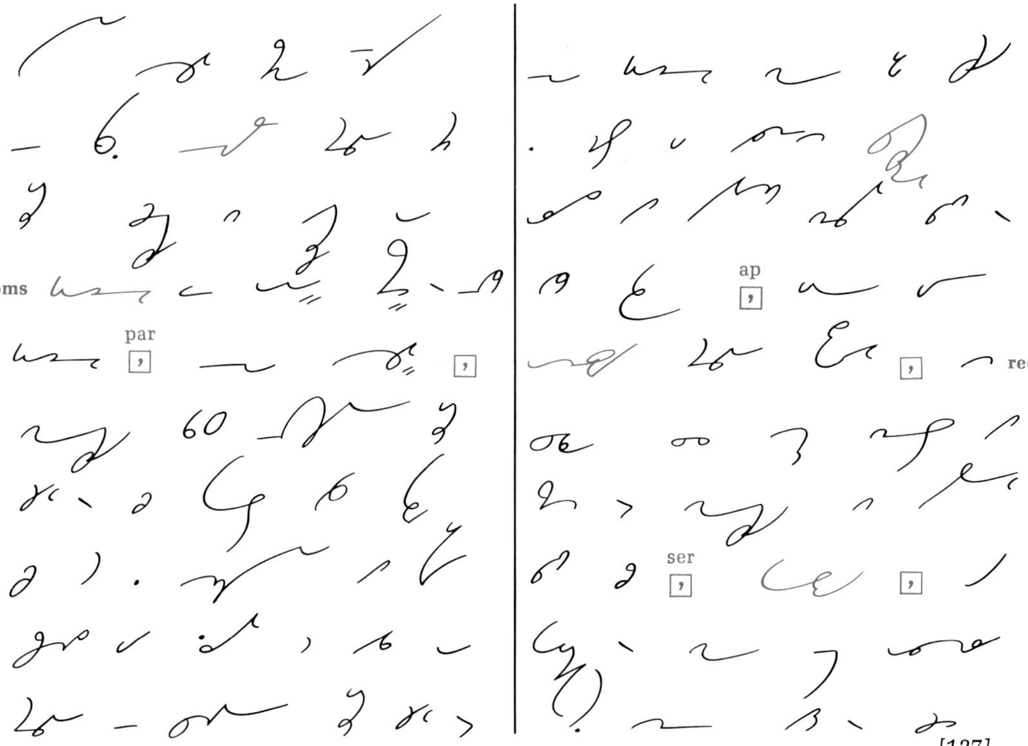

par
ap
ser
60

[127]

517

ad·vance

mer·chan·dise

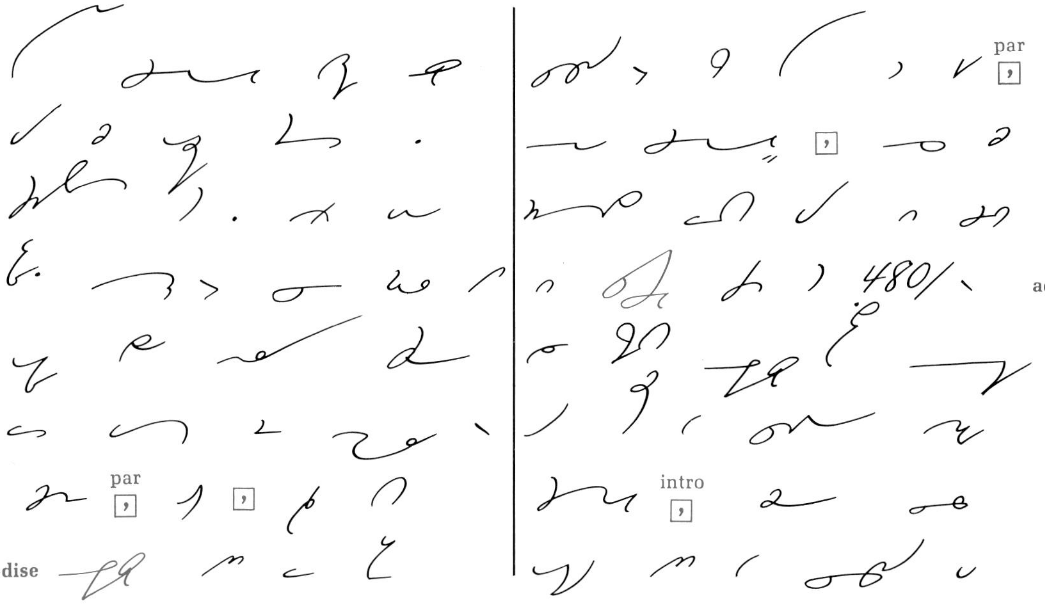

par
intro
480/

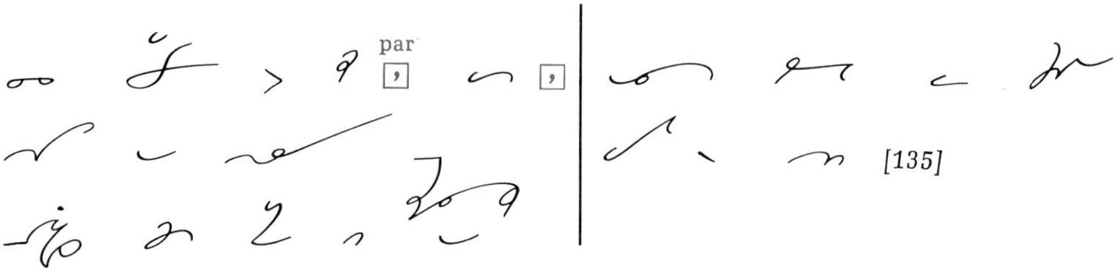
par
[135]

518 Car

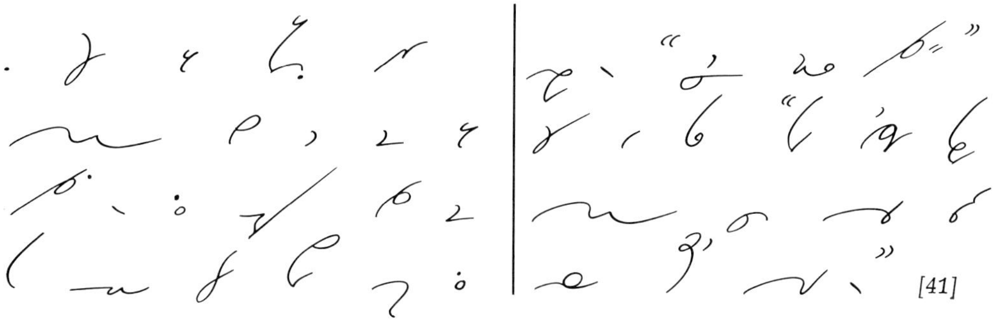
[41]

SHORTHAND NOTEBOOK CHECK LIST

So that you can use your notebook efficiently, do you—

☐ **1** Write your name on the cover of your notebook?

☐ **2** Indicate on the cover the first and last days on which you used the notebook?

☐ **3** Place the date *at the bottom* of the first page of each day's dictation?

☐ **4** Place a rubber band around the completed pages of your notebook so that you lose no time finding the first blank page on which to start the day's dictation?

☐ **5** Draw a line through the shorthand notes that you have transcribed or read back so that you will know you are through with them?

LESSON 55

The practice material in this lesson concentrates on the shorthand principles you studied in Chapter 7.

519 BRIEF-FORM DERIVATIVES

Greater, sooner, bigger, shorter, worker, sender, manufacturer.
Particularly, successfully, timely, immediately, partly, presently, gladly, purposely.
Suggested, corresponded, timed, progressed, organized, governed.

Building transcription skills

520 GRAMMAR CHECKUP | the infinitive

The infinitive is the form of the verb usually introduced by *to—to see, to be, to have, to do.*

Careful writers try to avoid "splitting" an infinitive, that is, inserting a word or phrase between *to* and the following word.

no

To properly do the job, you need better tools.

yes

To do the job properly, you need better tools.

no

He was told to carefully prepare the report.

yes

He was told to prepare the report carefully.

521

Business vocabulary builder	
	shabby Showing the effects of wear.
	gruff Deep and harsh.
	convey Get across.

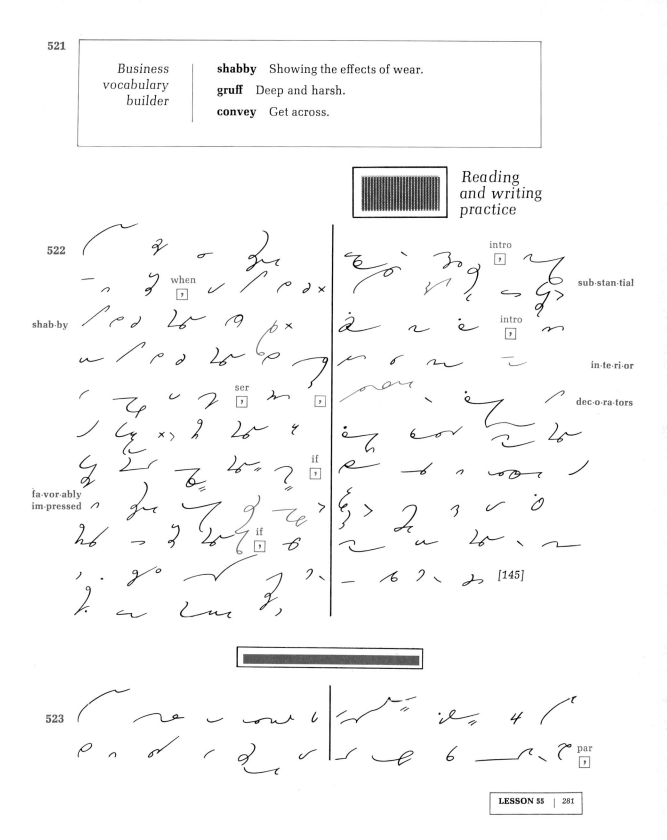

Reading and writing practice

522

shab·by

fa·vor·ably im·pressed

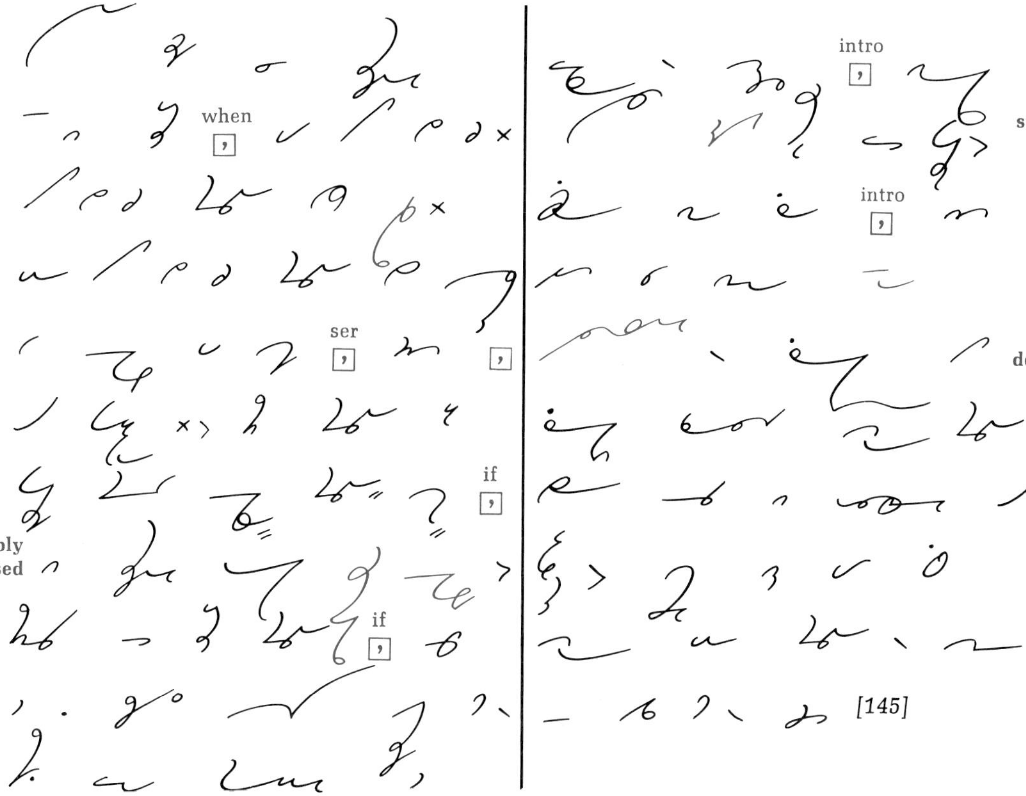

when
ser
if
if
intro
intro
[145]

sub·stan·tial

in·te·ri·or

dec·o·ra·tors

523

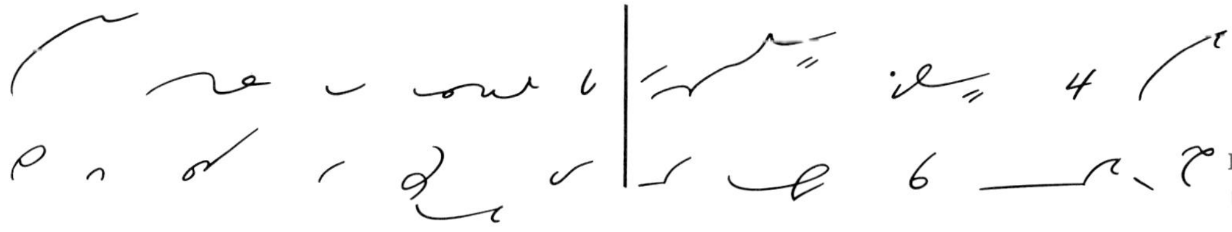

par

en·joyed

con·ve·nience

priv·i·lege

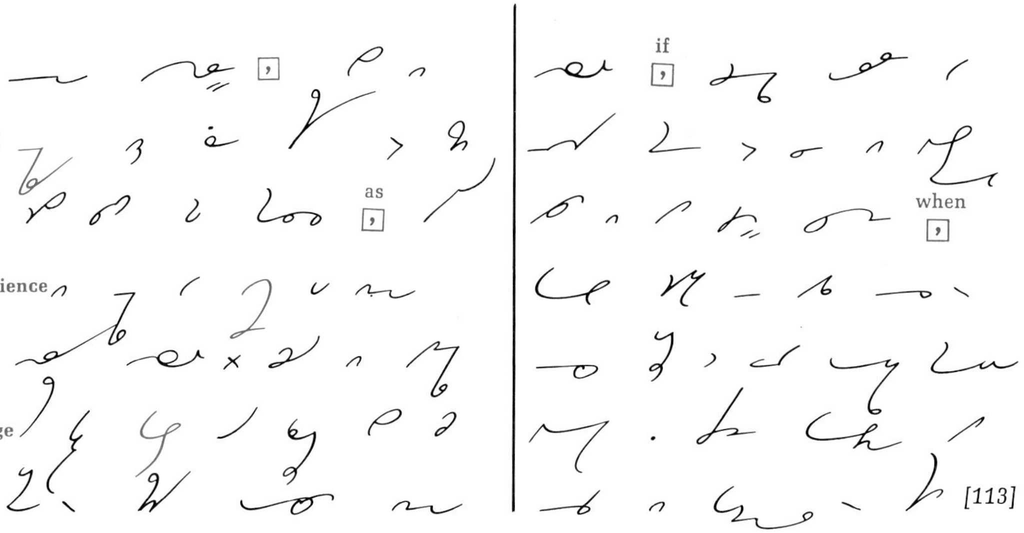
as
if
when
[113]

524 Your Telephone Voice

pleas·ant

im·pressed

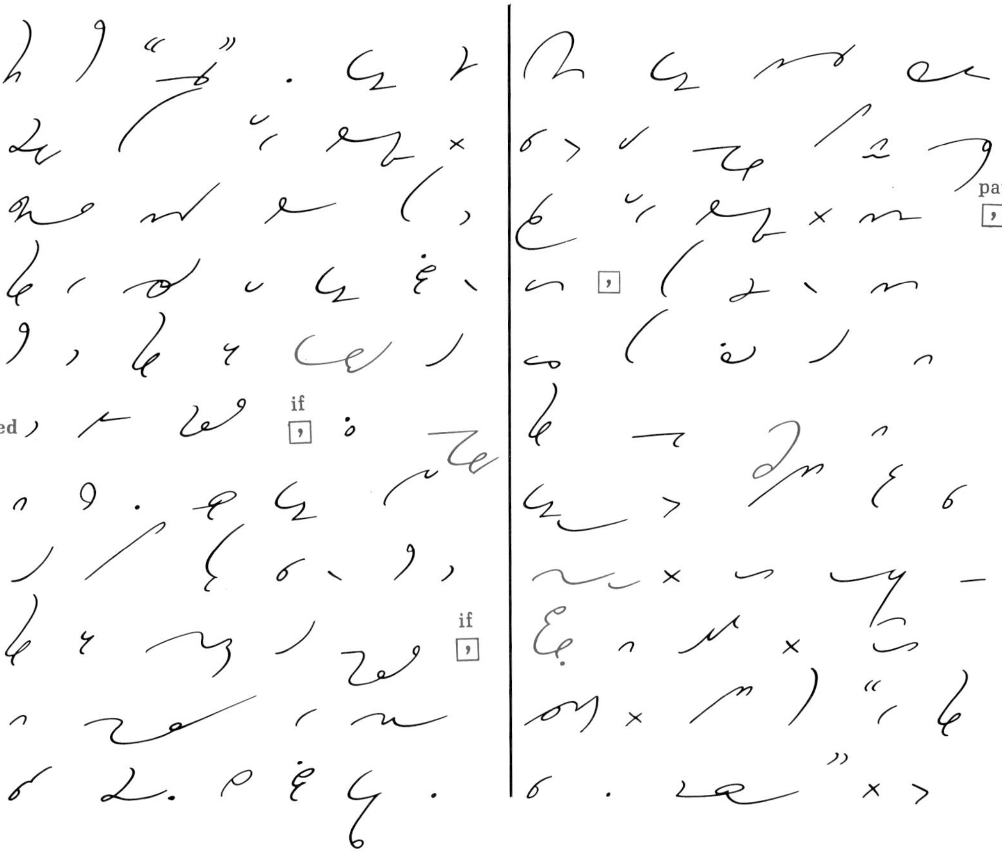
if
if
par

con·vey

clar·i·ty

ex·press·ing

soft·ly
choos·ing

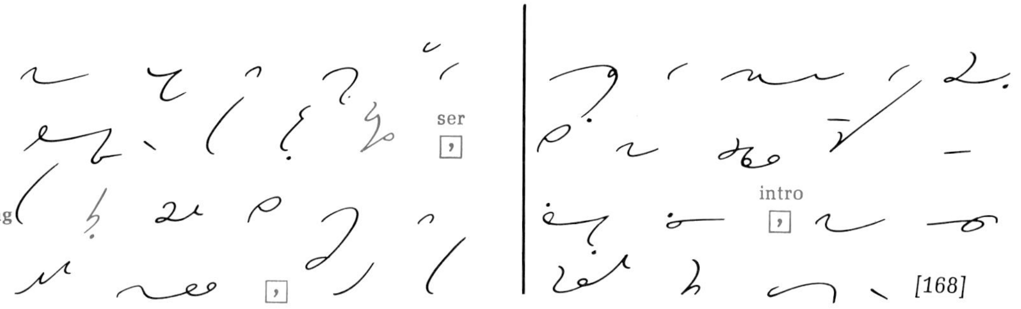

ser
intro
[168]

525

enough
slop·py

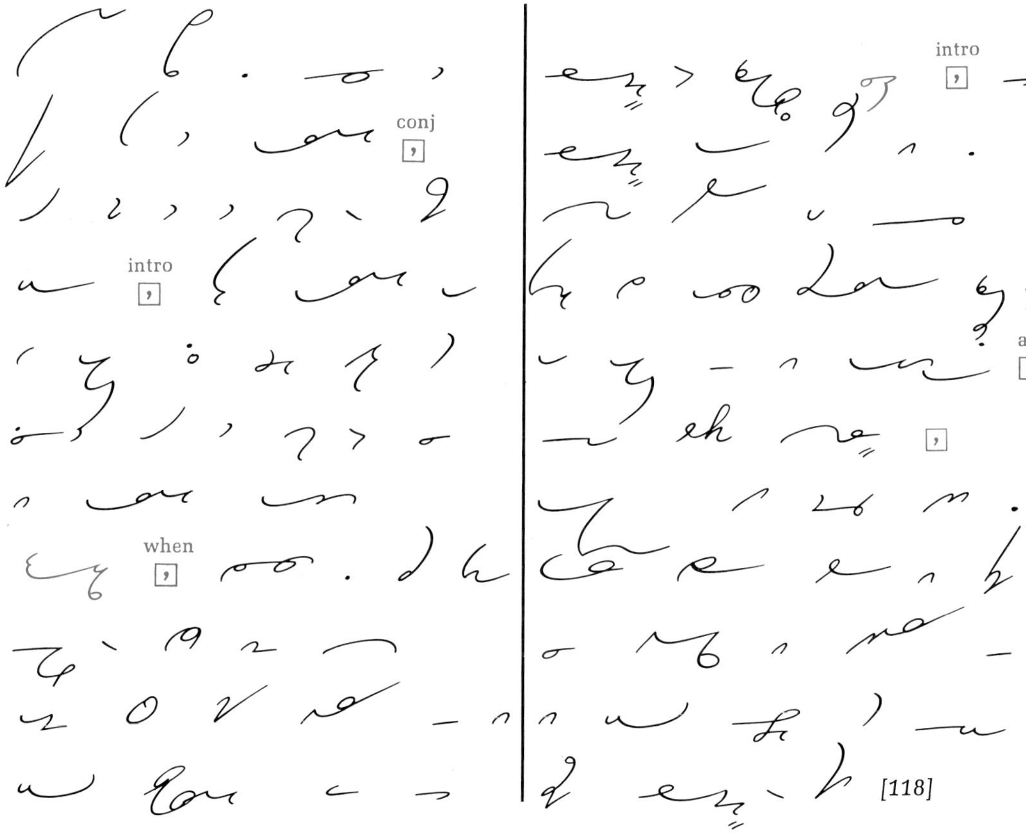

conj
intro
intro
ap
when
[118]

LESSON 56

The practice material in this lesson concentrates on the shorthand principles you studied in Chapter 8.

526 BRIEF FORMS AND DERIVATIVES

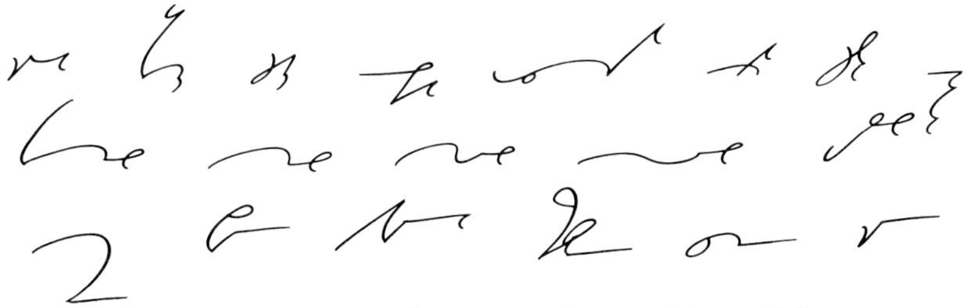

Streets, objects, situations, merchants, regards, quantities, satisfies, newspapers.
Bigness, goodness, greatness, gladness, orderliness.
Government, apartment, departments, advertisement, acknowledgment, statement.

Building transcription skills

527 COMMON PREFIXES | super-

Many words in the English language contain common prefixes. An understanding of the meanings of these prefixes will often give you a clue to the meaning of words with which you are unfamiliar.

Perhaps you never heard the word *posterity*. However, if you know that *post* means *after*, you may be able to figure out that *posterity* refers to those who come after, or descendants.

In each "Common Prefixes" exercise you will be given a common prefix, its meaning, and a list of words in which the prefix is used.

Read each definition carefully, and then study the illustrations that follow. A number of the illustrations are used in the Reading and Writing Practice of this lesson.

super- over, more than

supervise To oversee.

supervisor One who oversees.

superior Over in rank, higher.

supertax A tax over and above a normal tax.

528

Business vocabulary builder

self-service elevators Elevators on which there are no operators.

executive Person charged with running a company or department of a company.

simultaneously At the same time.

Reading and writing practice

529

em·ploy·ees

en·roll

for·ward

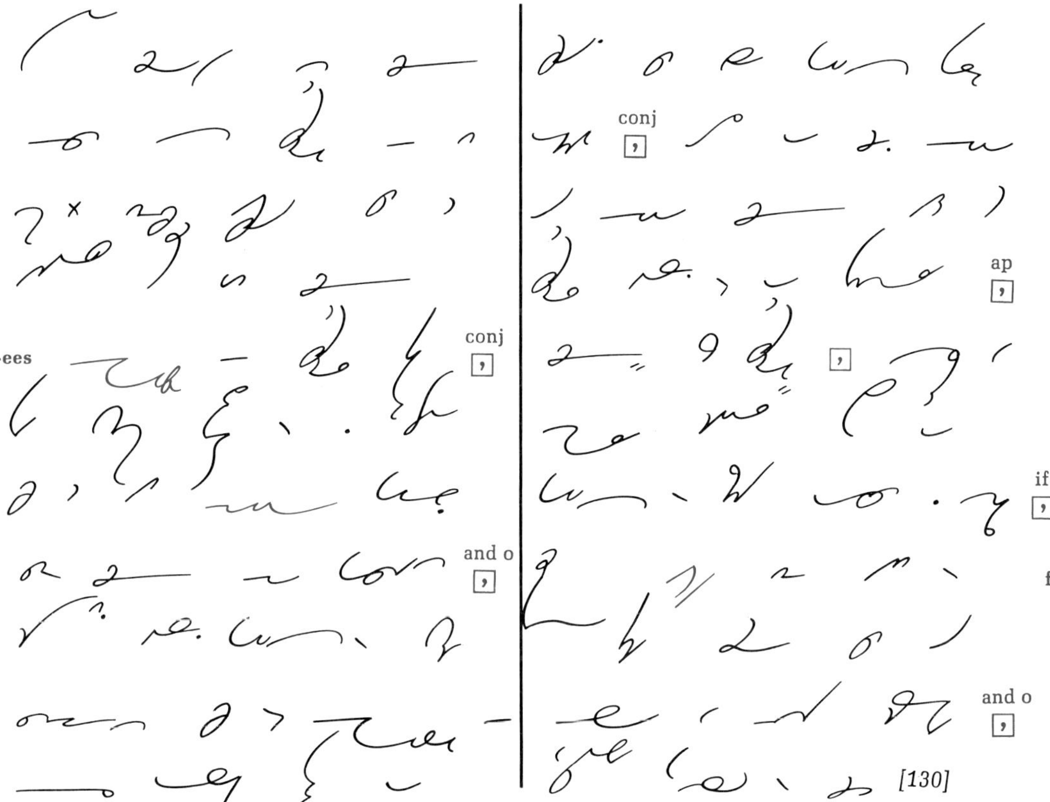

conj
conj
ap
if
and o
and o
[130]

530

el·e·va·tors
suc·cess·ful

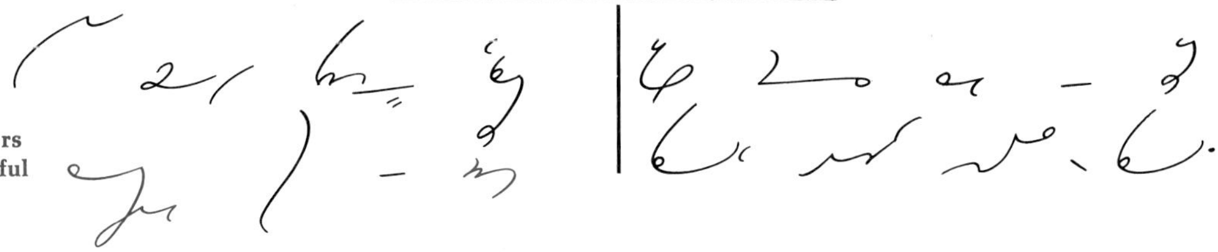

in·stal·la·tion
el·e·va·tors
worth·while
re·ceive
prompt·ly

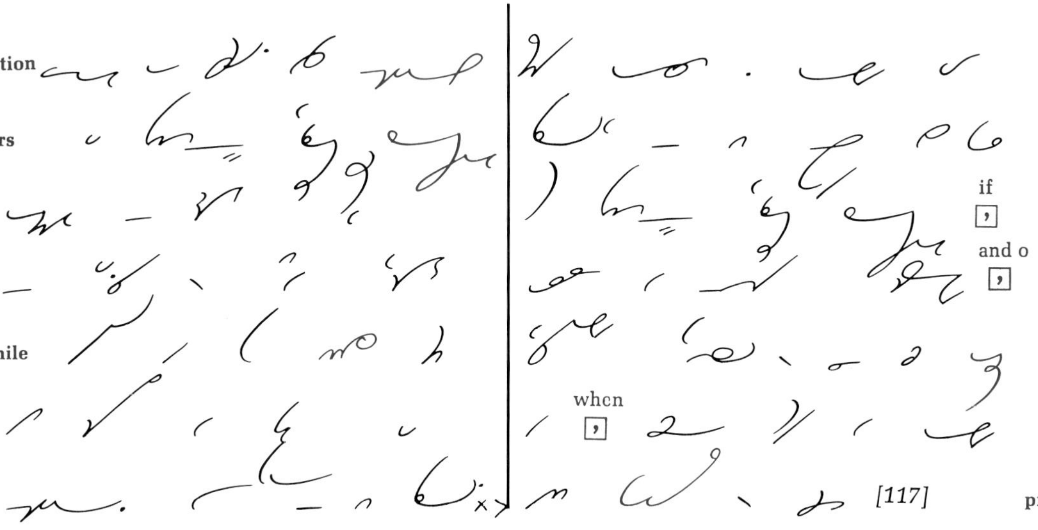

if
and o
when
[117]

531

su·per·vise
si·mul·ta·neous·ly
su·pe·ri·or
equip·ment
shirk

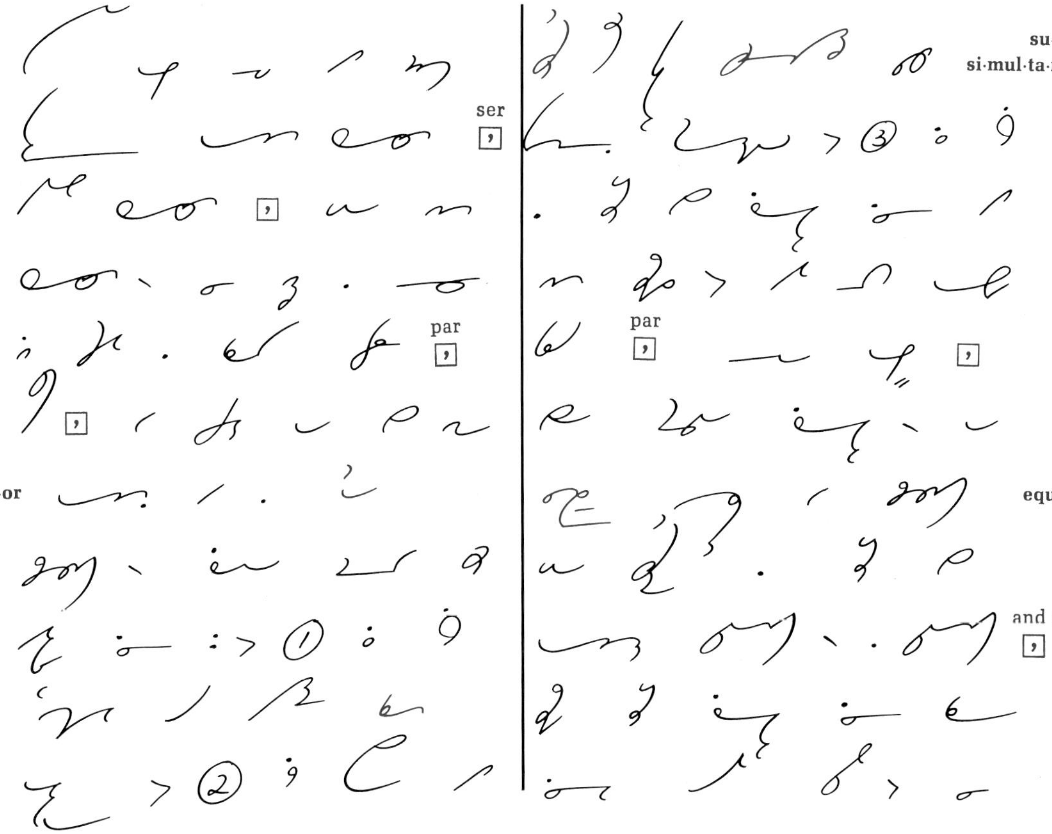

ser
par
par
and o

when
[144]

532

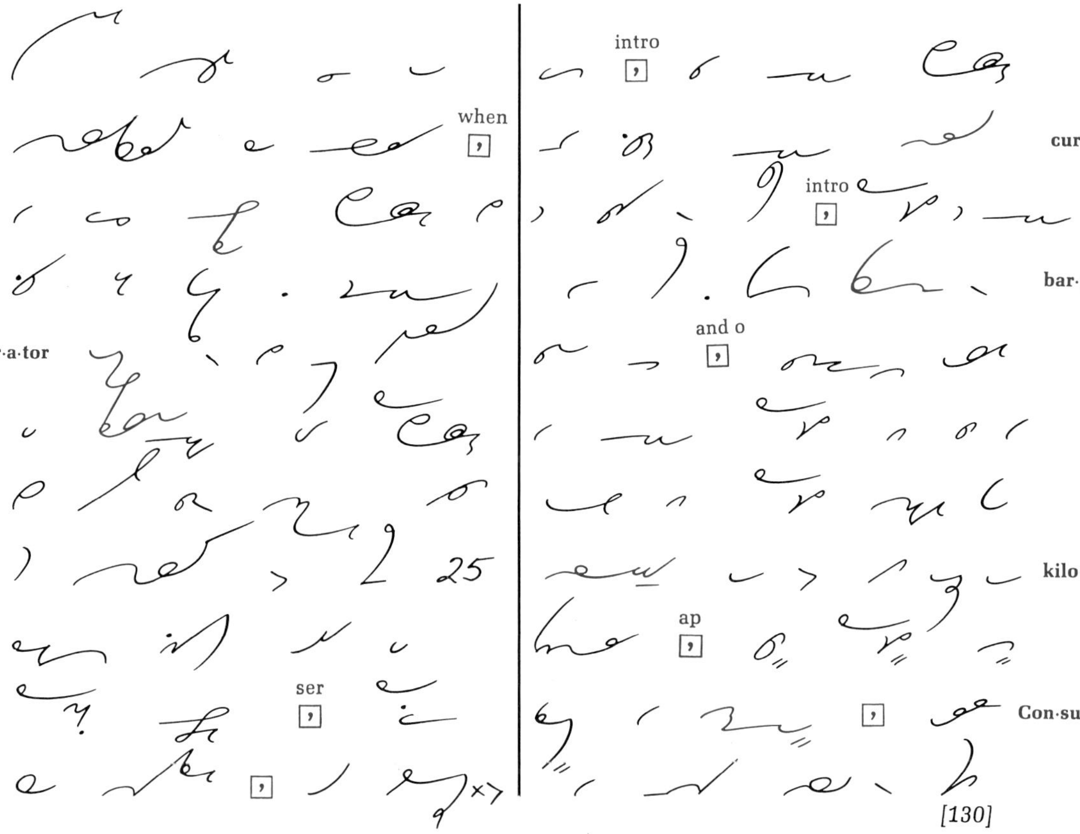
when
intro
intro
and o
ap
ser

ma·jor

re·frig·er·a·tor

cur·rent

bar·gain

kilo·watt

Con·sum·er

[130]

533

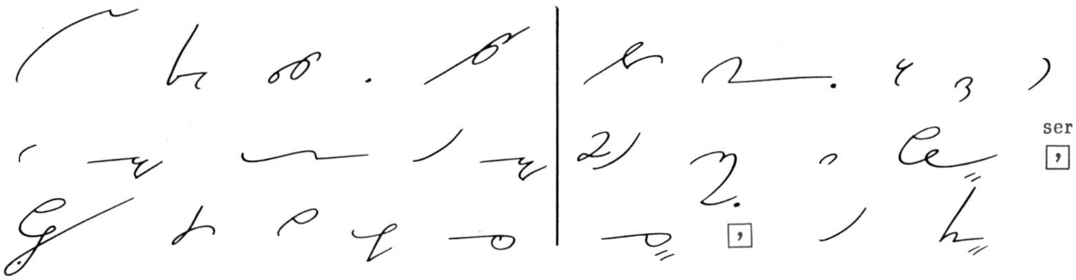
ser

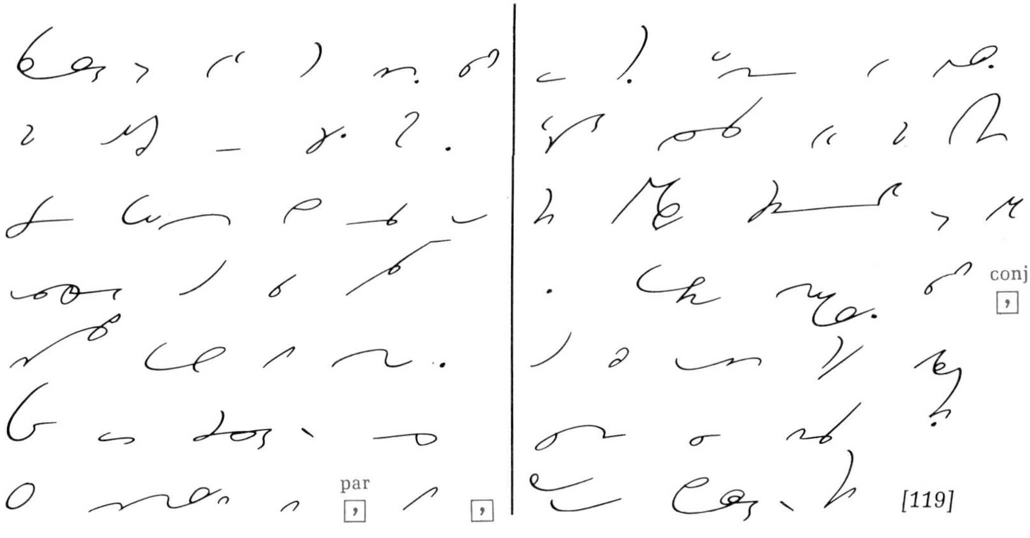
par
conj
[119]

534

for·ward·ed

Agree·ment

ac·crue

avail

min·i·mum

as
conj
[110]

3

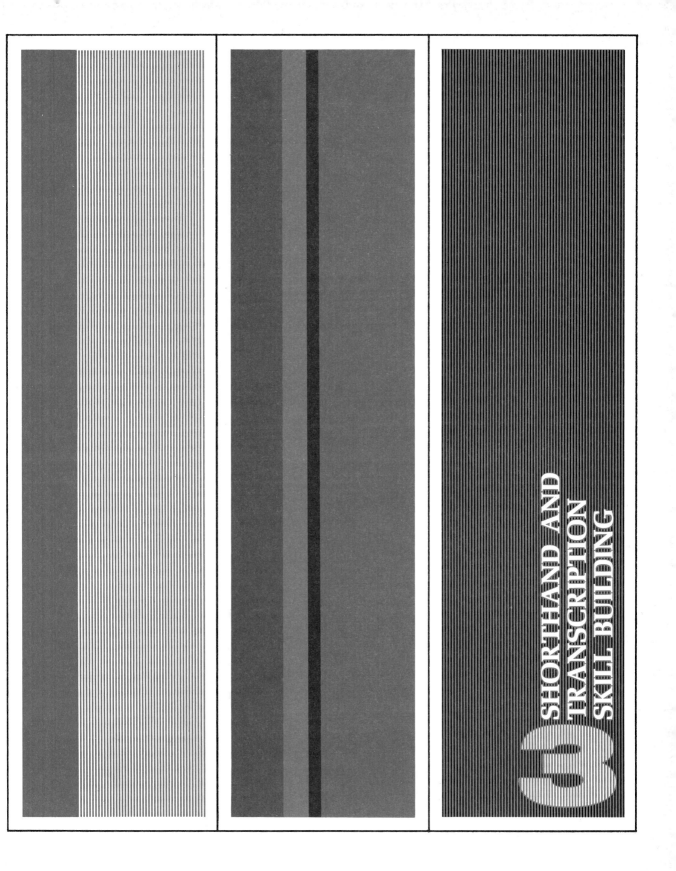

SHORTHAND AND TRANSCRIPTION SKILL BUILDING

Chapter 10

The secretary moves up

The kind of job you will get and the progress you will make in it will depend almost entirely on you. Does this sound old-fashioned? Well, it is still true. Good looks and a sparkling personality are wonderful assets to anyone; if you are blessed with these gifts, make the most of them. But they are by no means everything. They are merely "frosting on the cake." If you manage to use your head and make the most of the talents, looks, and abilities you do have, your opportunities for promotion are great.

The business executive wants his secretary to have interest *and* ability. *With those two qualities she can lick the world. Of course, he expects her to look smart, neat, and clean. Note that we did not say he insists that she be a raving beauty. While he is not averse to a sparkling personality and good looks, he can't afford to let these qualities influence his*

Vice Pres

decision in hiring and promoting.

In a secretarial position the opportunity to learn is unlimited. You will have an orchestra seat to all the important goings-on in your executive's domain. It has happened many times that the secretary moved into the boss's shoes when he was promoted.

Even if you don't aspire to the boss's job, your future will depend on how well he does his job. Are you skeptical? Let's examine this statement. In a typical company there are many executive promotions every year. Those promotions go to the people who have proved to be outstanding in their jobs and who "have a future." An executive can hardly be outstanding if he is saddled with inefficient secretarial help. Usually when he receives a promotion, his secretary gets one, too. Suppose he is a department head and is promoted to the position of vice-president. Automatically his salary is increased. And the secretary to a vice-president is a more important person than the secretary to a department manager; so she generally gets a salary increase, too. If the secretary is really good, she moves right up the ladder with her boss.

You and your boss will be a team. Your success will depend on his success. It's that simple.

LESSON 57

The practice material in this lesson is "loaded" with brief forms and derivatives. Counting repetitions, it contains 360 brief forms and derivatives. If you gave proper attention to the brief forms as they were introduced, you should be able to complete this lesson in record time!

Building transcription skills

535 **SPELLING FAMILIES | silent e before -ment**

Words in Which Silent E Is Retained Before -ment

ad·vance·ment	**en·gage·ment**	**re·tire·ment**
ad·ver·tise·ment	**man·age·ment**	**re·quire·ment**
amuse·ment	**move·ment**	**state·ment**
en·cour·age·ment	**re·place·ment**	

Words in Which Silent E Is Omitted Before -ment

ac·knowl·edg·ment	**ar·gu·ment**	**judg·ment**

536 *Business vocabulary builder*

variety Collection of many different things.

speculates Wonders; thinks.

browse Examine casually merchandise offered for sale.

Reading and writing practice

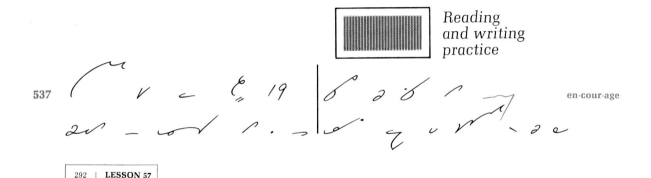

537 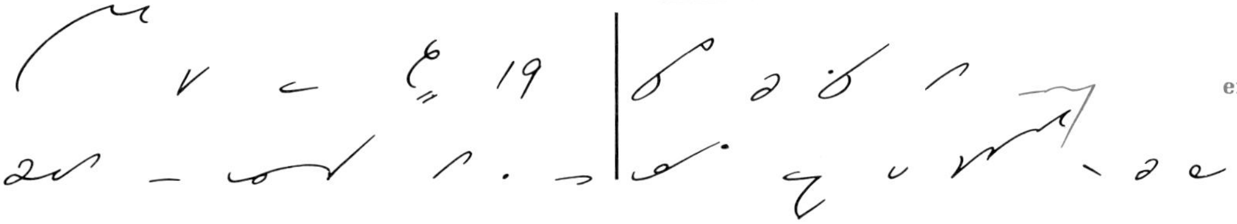 en·cour·age

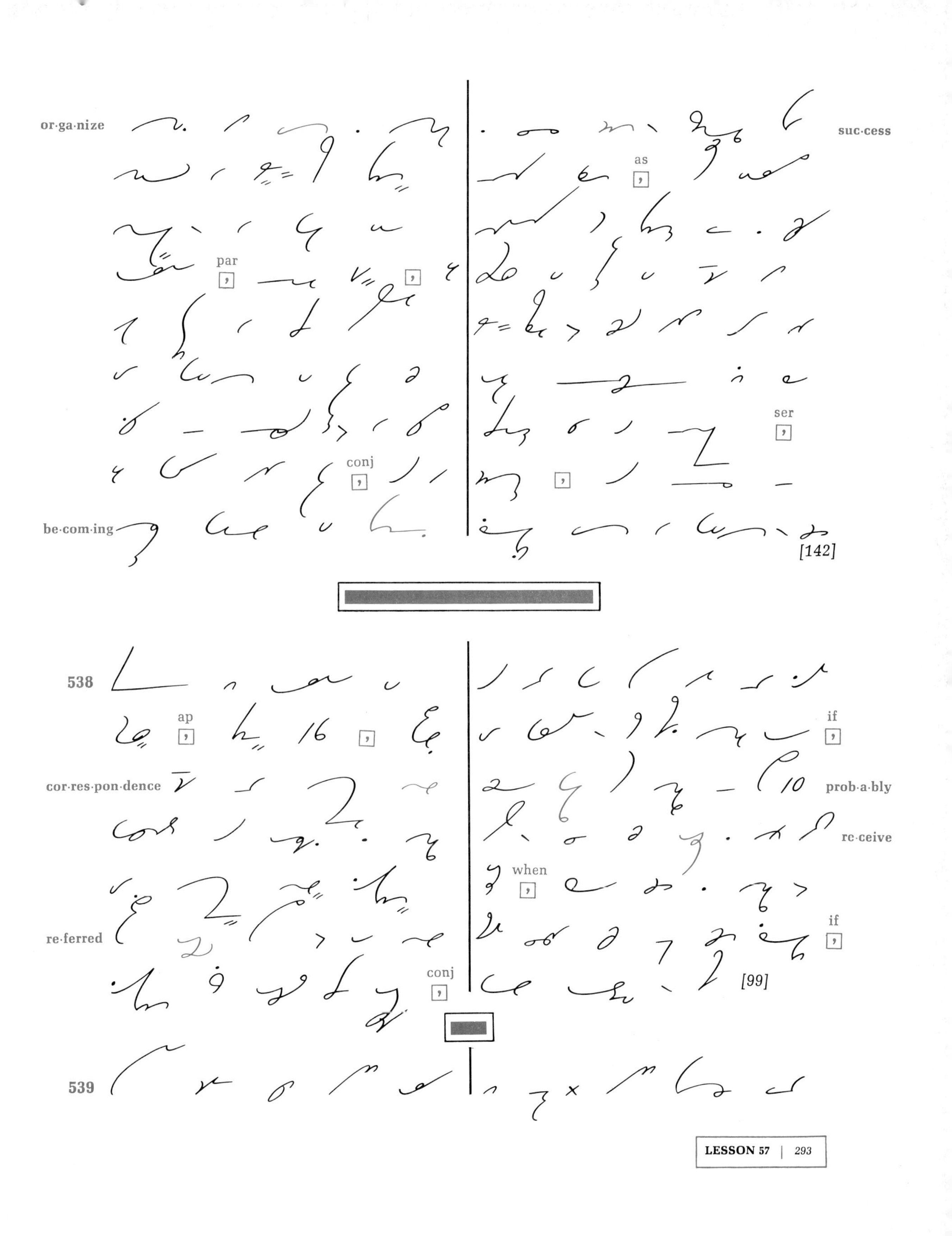

or·ga·nize

par

conj

be·com·ing

suc·cess

as

ser

[142]

538

ap

cor·res·pon·dence

re·ferred

conj

if

prob·a·bly

re·ceive

when

if

[99]

539

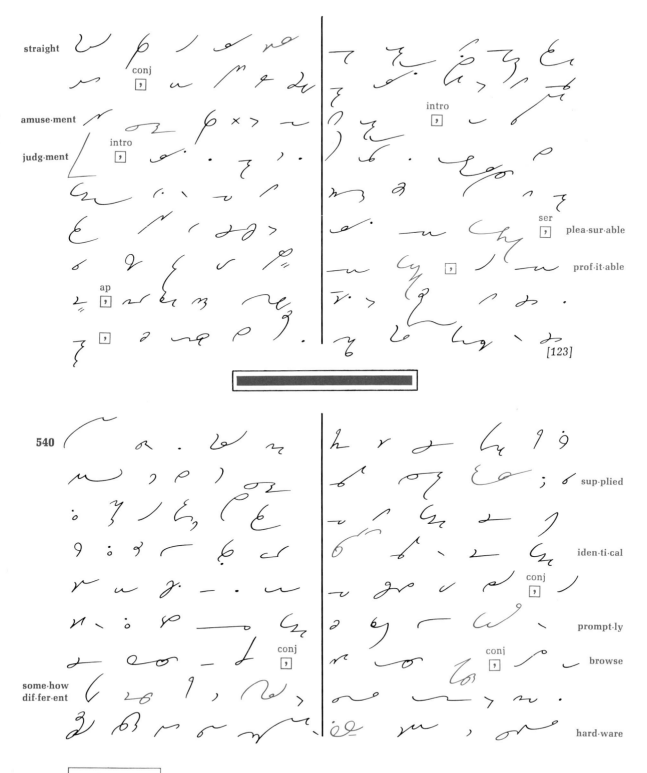

straight

conj

amuse·ment

judg·ment

intro

ap

intro

ser

plea·sur·able

prof·it·able

[123]

540

sup·plied

iden·ti·cal

conj

prompt·ly

conj

conj

browse

some·how

dif·fer·ent

hard·ware

fas·ci·nat·ing

[125]

541

be·com·ing

for·eign

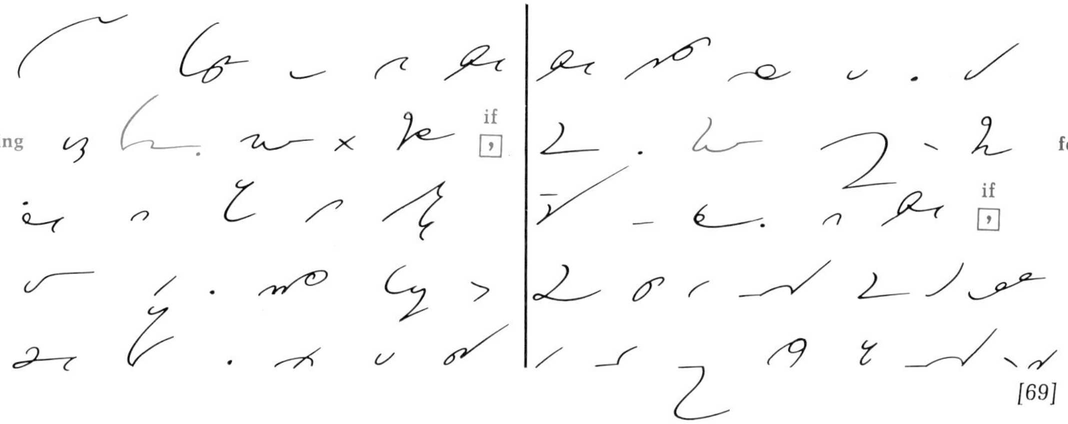

[69]

542 Transcription Quiz Beginning with Lesson 57, you will have an opportunity to see how well you have mastered the nine uses of the comma that were introduced in Chapters 6, 7, and 8. Lessons 57-69 contain one letter each that is called a "Transcription Quiz." It contains several illustrations of the uses of the comma that you have studied. The commas, however, are not indicated in the printed shorthand. It will be your job, as you copy the letter in shorthand in your notebook, to insert the commas in the proper places and to give the reasons why the commas are used. The shorthand in your notebook should resemble the following example:

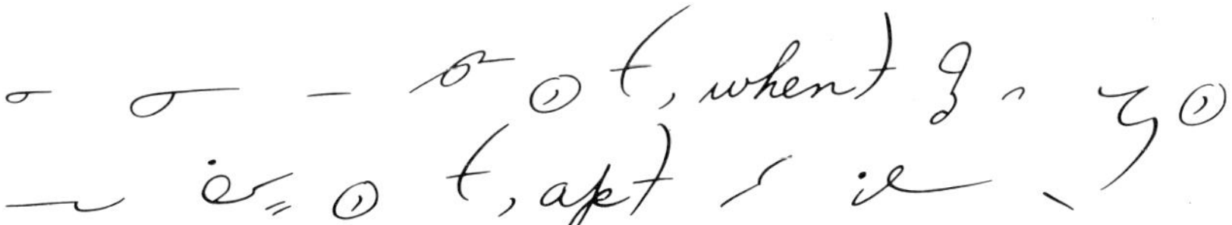
when
ap

▶ Caution: Please do not make any marks in your shorthand textbook. If you do, you will destroy the value of these quizzes to anyone else who may use the book.

The correct punctuation of the following letter calls for 4 commas—1 comma *as* clause, 2 commas parenthetical, 1 comma introductory.

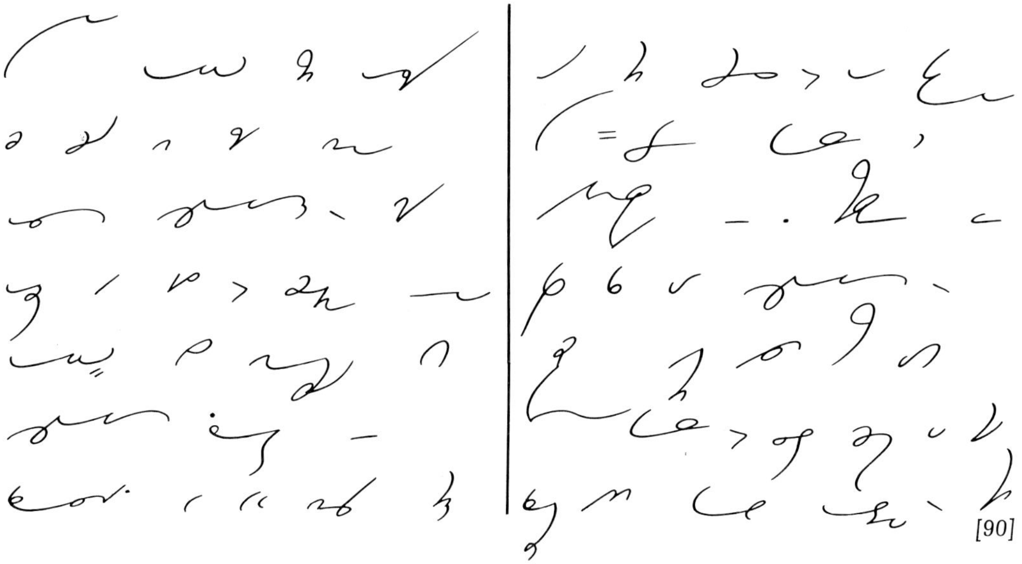
[90]

543

wheth·er

Man·u·al

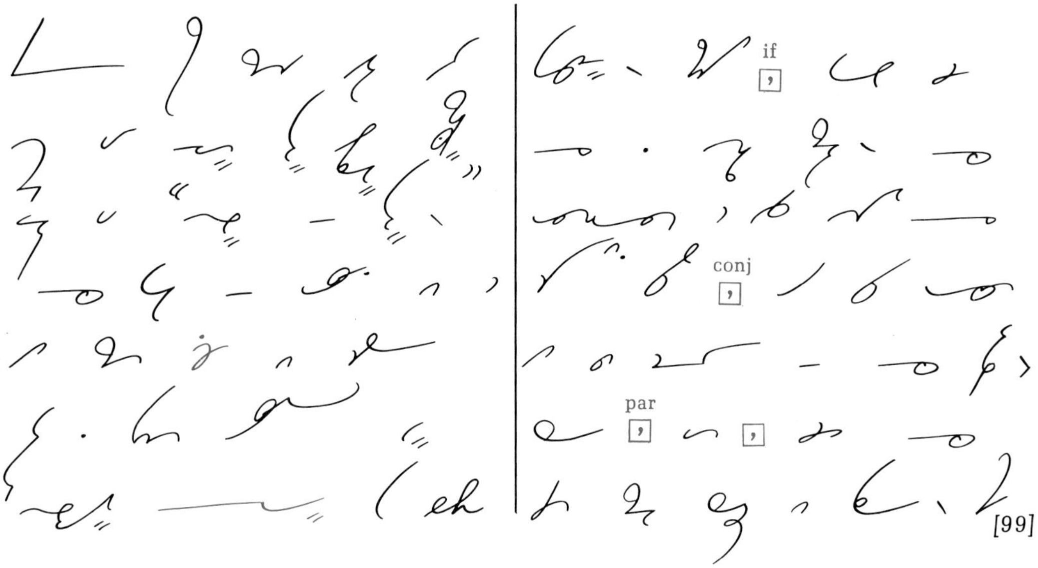
if
conj
par
[99]

LESSON 58

This lesson is designed to increase further your ability to use the frequent phrases of Gregg Shorthand. It contains several illustrations of all the phrasing principles. Altogether, there are 107 phrases, counting repetitions.

Building transcription skills

544 **GRAMMAR CHECKUP | sentence structure**

Parallel ideas should be expressed in parallel form.

no

I hope our relationship will be long, pleasant, and of profit *to both of us.*

yes

I hope our relationship will be long, pleasant, and profitable *to both of us.*

no

As soon as we receive the necessary information, your account will be opened and we will ship your order.

yes

As soon as we receive the necessary information, your account will be opened and your order will be shipped.

It is especially important to keep parallel all ideas in a tabulation.

no

Her main duties were:

1. *Taking dictation and transcribing*
2. *Answering the telephone*
3. To take care *of the files*

yes

Her main duties were:

1. *Taking dictation and transcribing*
2. *Answering the telephone*
3. Taking care *of the files*

545

Business vocabulary builder	
	adequate Sufficient.
	expanding Getting larger.
	solution Answer.

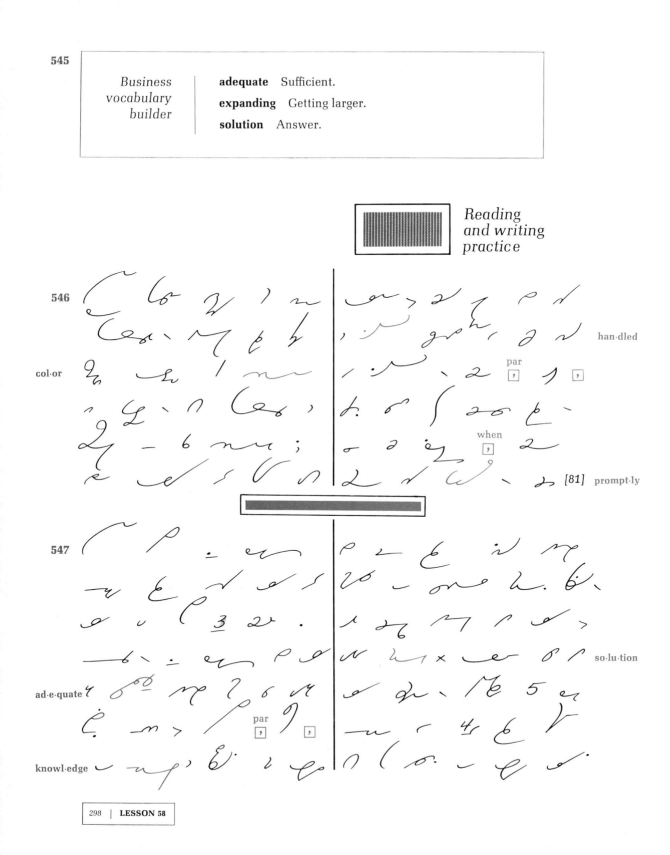

Reading and writing practice

546

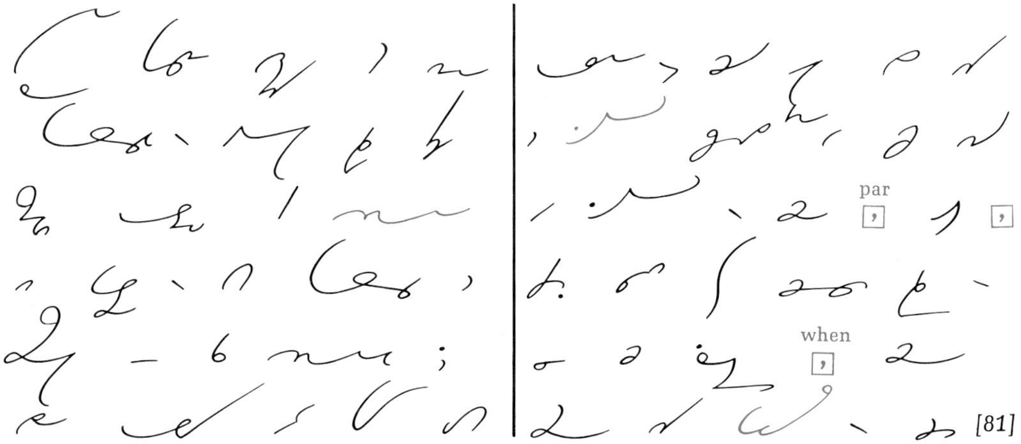

par
when
[81]

col·or

han·dled

prompt·ly

547

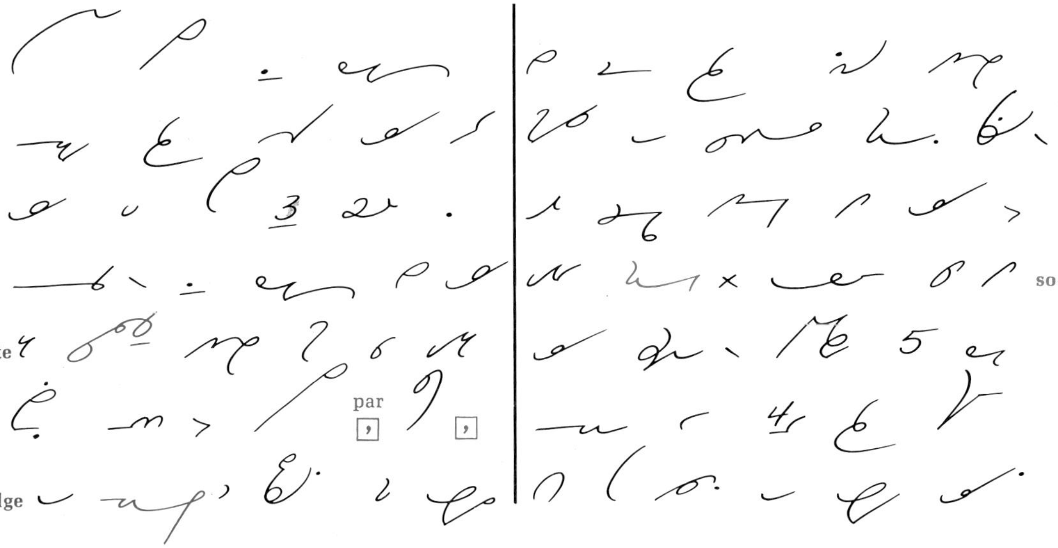

par

ad·e·quate

knowl·edge

so·lu·tion

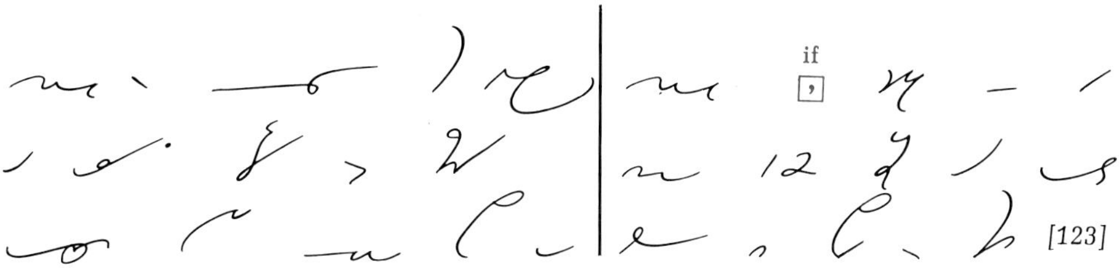
if
[123]

548

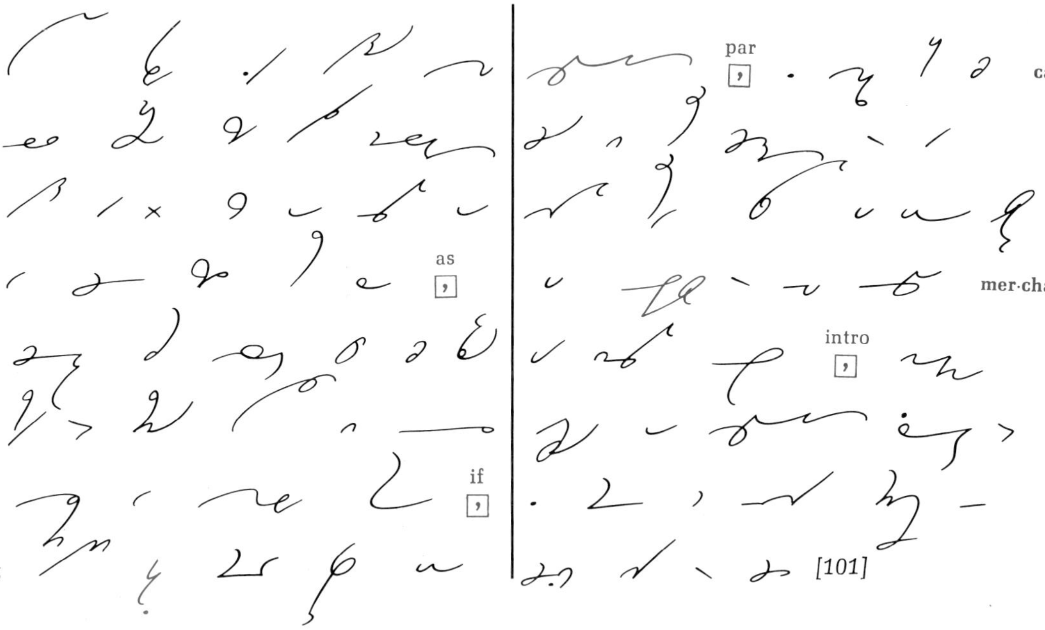
par
as
intro
if
[101]

cat·a·log

mer·chan·dise

shop·ping

549 Transcription Quiz To punctuate the following letter correctly, you must supply 5 commas—1 comma conjunction, 2 commas series, 2 commas parenthetical.

No marks in the textbook, please!

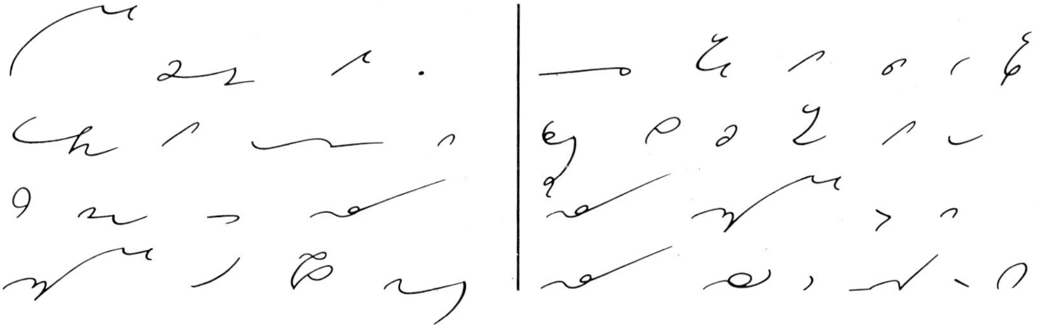

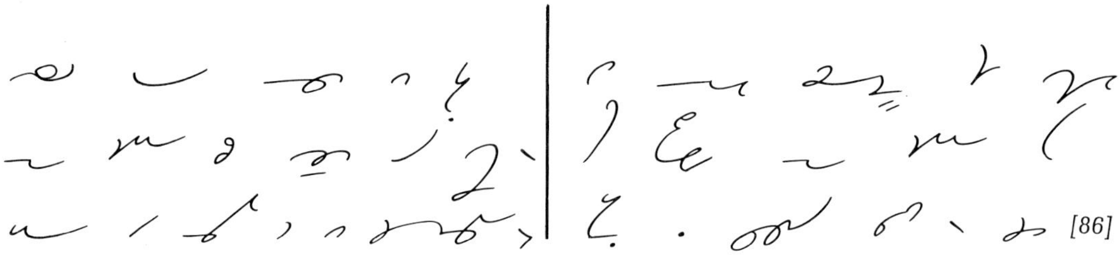
[86]

550 re·quest·ed

bro·chures

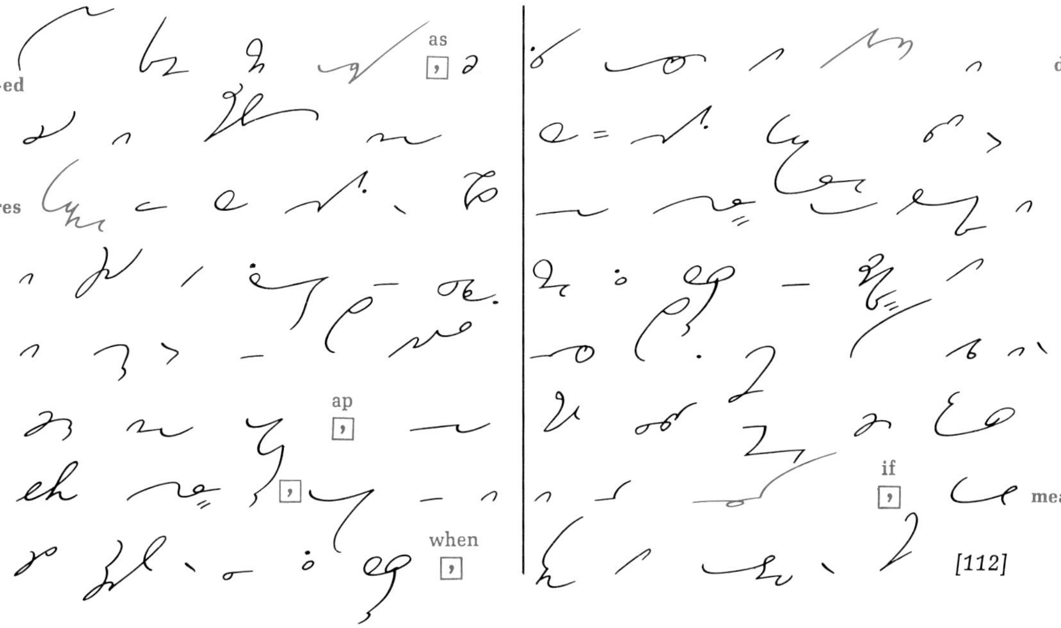
as
ap
when
if
[112]

dis·cuss

mean·time

551

sta·tio·nery

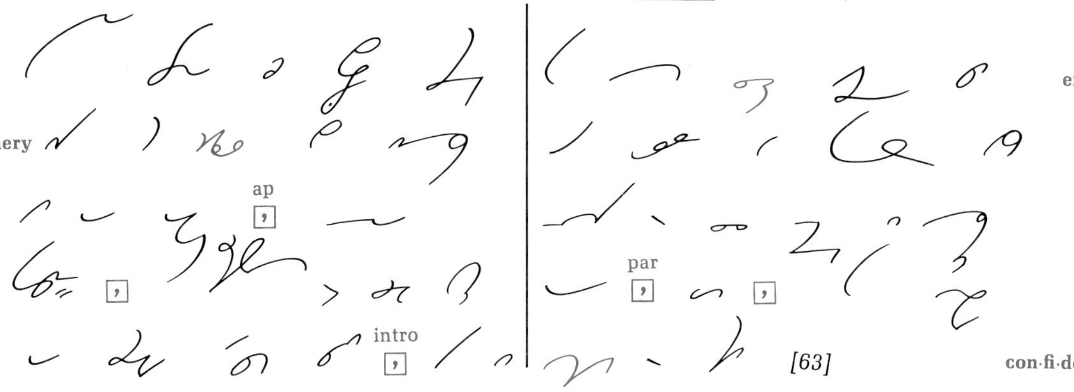
ap
intro
par
[63]

enough

con·fi·den·tial

LESSON 59

Are some of the joined word beginnings still a little hazy in your mind? The practice material in this lesson will help fix all the joined word beginnings more firmly in your mind. In this lesson you will find 88 joined word beginnings.

Building transcription skills

552 **SPELLING FAMILIES | -ence, -ance**

Words Ending in -ence

com·mence	**ev·i·dence**	**neg·li·gence**
con·fer·ence	**ex·is·tence**	**obe·di·ence**
con·fi·dence	**ex·cel·lence**	**oc·cur·rence**
con·va·les·cence	**ex·pe·ri·ence**	**ref·er·ence**
con·ve·nience	**in·de·pen·dence**	**vi·o·lence**

Words Ending in -ance

abun·dance	**bal·ance**	**in·sur·ance**
ac·cep·tance	**cir·cum·stance**	**is·su·ance**
al·low·ance	**en·dur·ance**	**per·for·mance**
as·sis·tance	**ig·no·rance**	**re·li·ance**
as·sur·ance	**in·stance**	**sub·stance**

553 *Business vocabulary builder*

formerly In the past.

encounter Meet.

incurred Brought upon oneself.

minor Of little importance.

Reading and writing practice

554

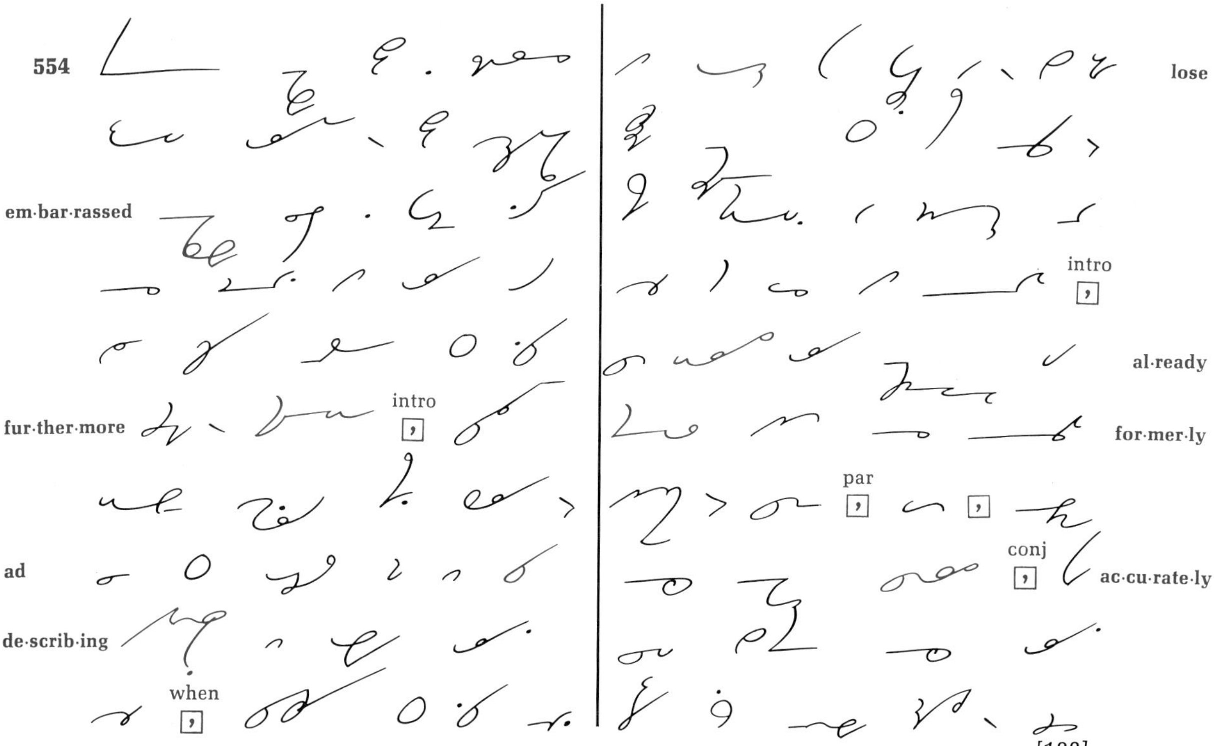

lose
em·bar·rassed
intro
al·ready
fur·ther·more
intro
for·mer·ly
par
conj
ad
ac·cu·rate·ly
de·scrib·ing
when

[128]

555

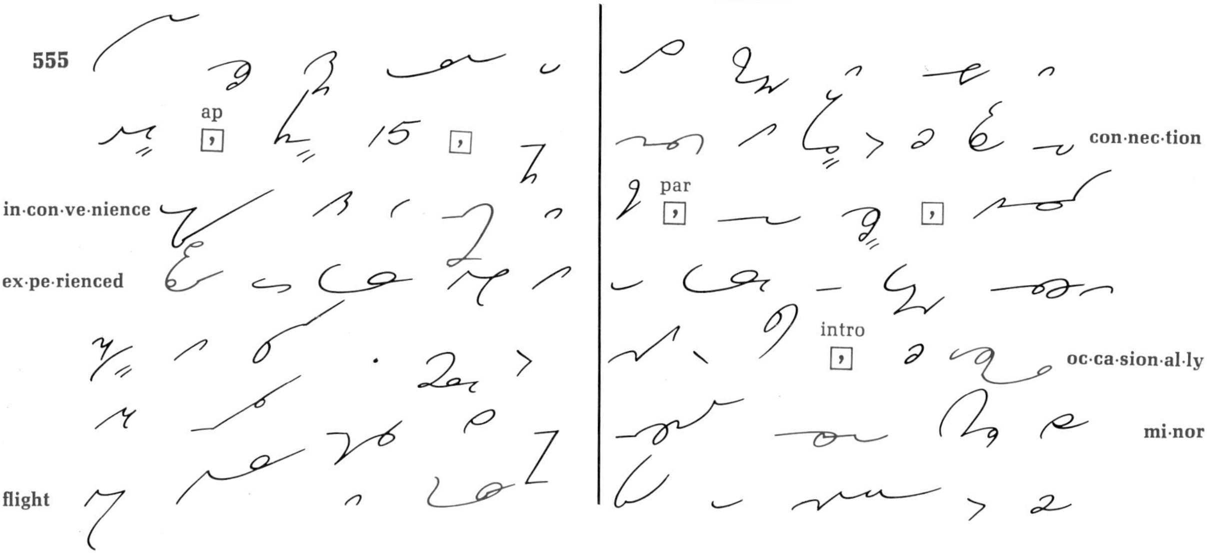

ap
15
con·nec·tion
in·con·ve·nience
par
ex·pe·ri·enced
intro
oc·ca·sion·al·ly
mi·nor
flight

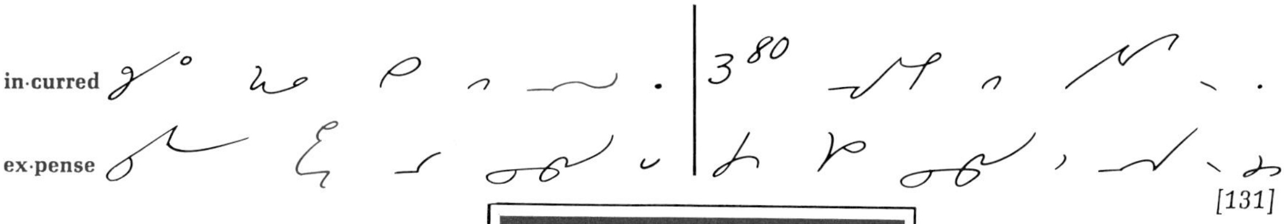
in·curred
ex·pense
[131]

[redacted]

556

and o
intro
conj
priv·i·le·ges
routes
de·pos·it
[99]

557 Transcription Quiz The correct punctuation of the following letter calls for 8 commas—1 comma conjunction, 2 commas series, 4 commas parenthetical, 1 comma *and* omitted.

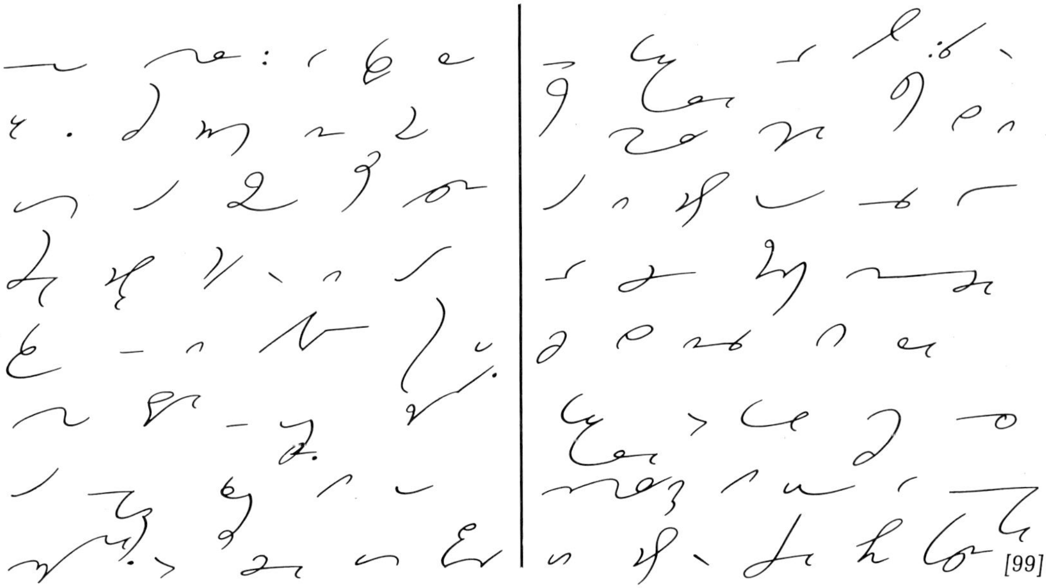
[99]

558

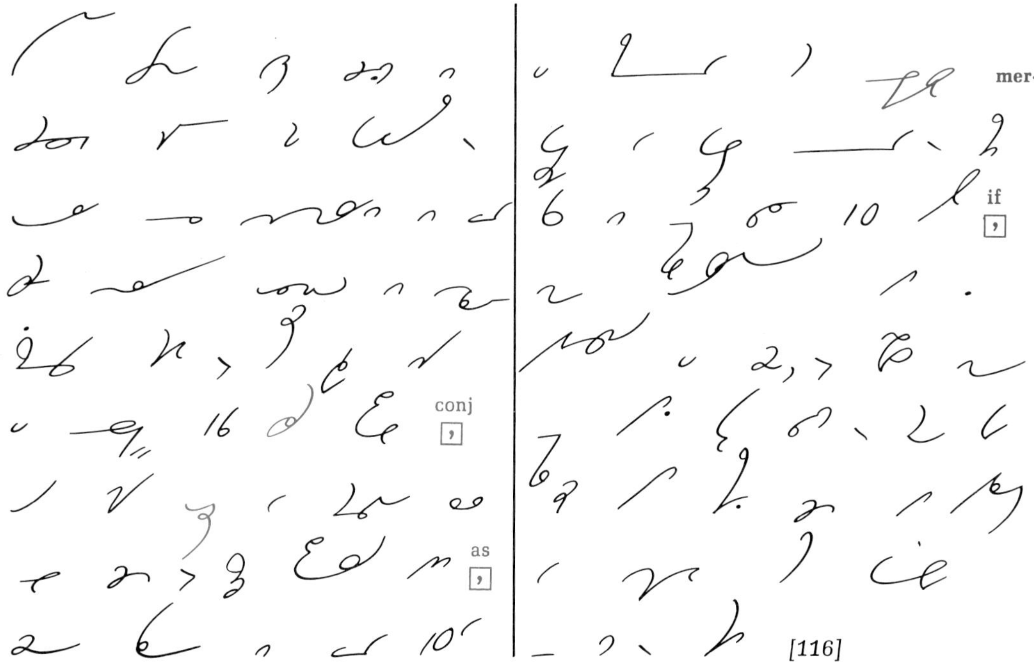
conj
as
if
[116]

via
re·ceive
mer·chan·dise

559

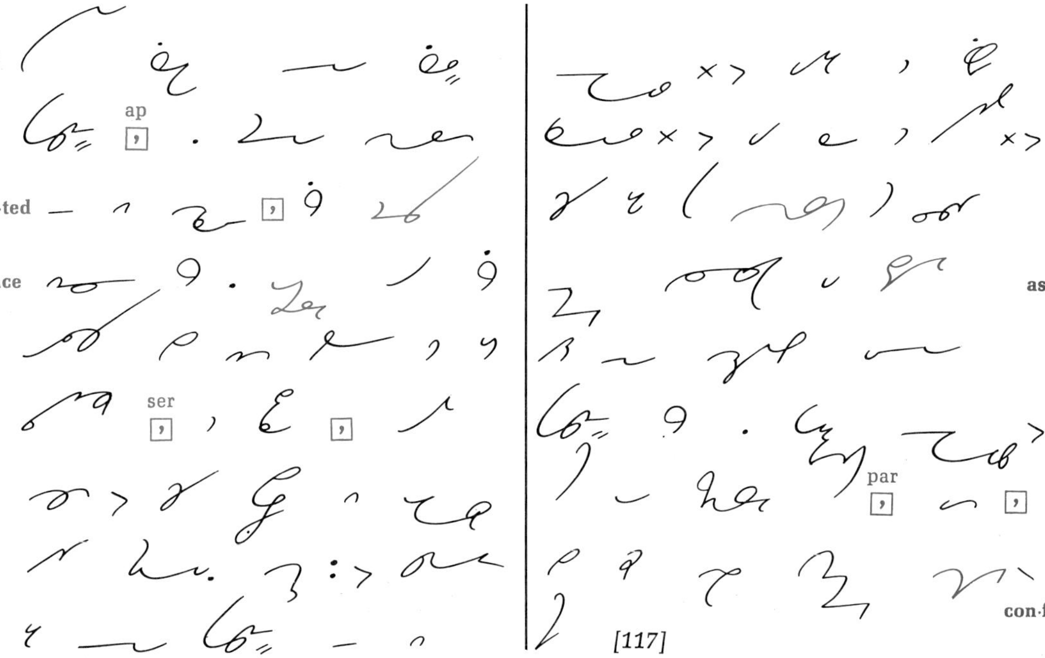
ap
ser
par
[117]

sub·mit·ted
ref·er·ence
grate·ful
as·sis·tance
con·fi·den·tial

LESSON 60

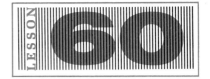

In this lesson you will "brush up" on joined word endings—there are 93 of them!

Building transcription skills

560 COMMON PREFIXES | re-

re- again

repack To pack again.

repeat To say again.

reconsider To take up again.

replenish To fill or supply again.

561 *Business vocabulary builder*

impartial Not favoring one side or the other; fair.

humid Moist.

annual Once a year.

Reading and writing practice

Reading Scoreboard How much has your reading speed increased over your first score in Lesson 18? The table on the next page will help you determine your reading speed on Lesson 60.

Lesson 60 contains 749 words.

If you read Lesson 60 in **19 minutes** *your reading rate is* **40 words a minute**
If you read Lesson 60 in **21 minutes** *your reading rate is* **36 words a minute**
If you read Lesson 60 in **23 minutes** *your reading rate is* **33 words a minute**
If you read Lesson 60 in **25 minutes** *your reading rate is* **30 words a minute**
If you read Lesson 60 in **27 minutes** *your reading rate is* **28 words a minute**
If you read Lesson 60 in **29 minutes** *your reading rate is* **26 words a minute**

562

sched·uled **im·par·tial** **com·mer·cial** **ques·tion·naire** **won't** **con·ve·nience**

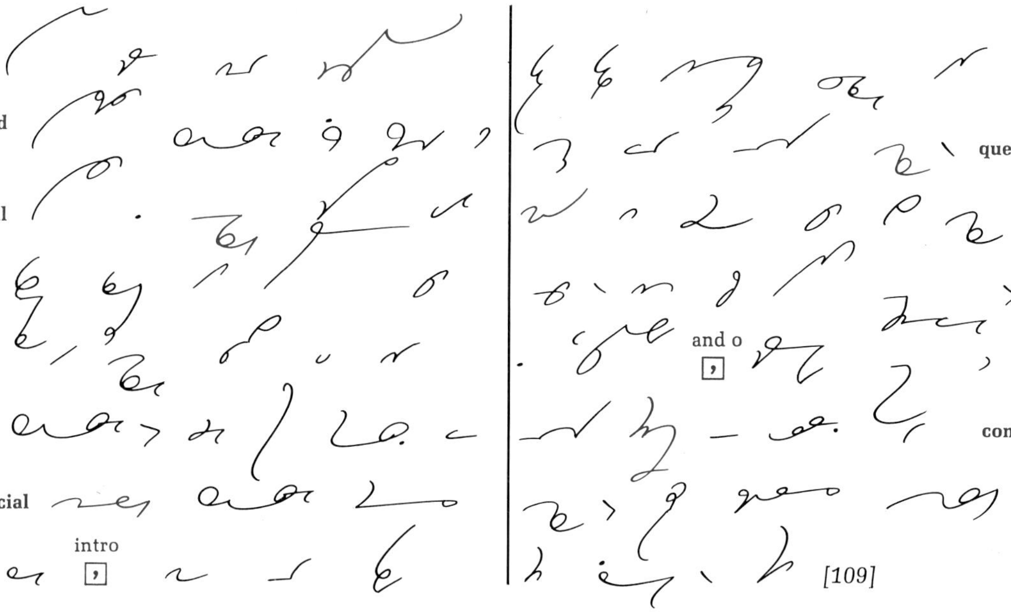
intro
and o
[109]

563

un·doubt·ed·ly **ef·fi·cient** **de·pend·able**

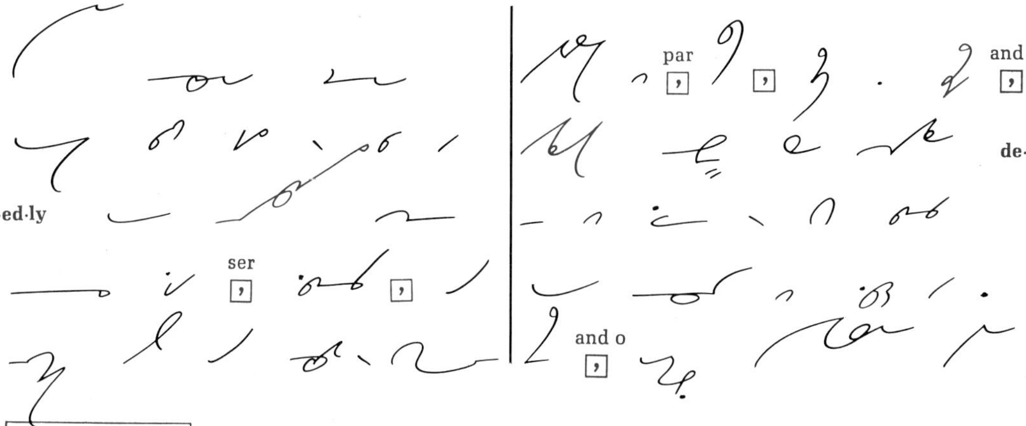
ser
par
and o
and o

intro

conj

weath·er

[123]

564 ca·pa·ble

if

ap

and o

if

pro·fit·ably

if

[113]

565

de·sir·able

econ·o·my

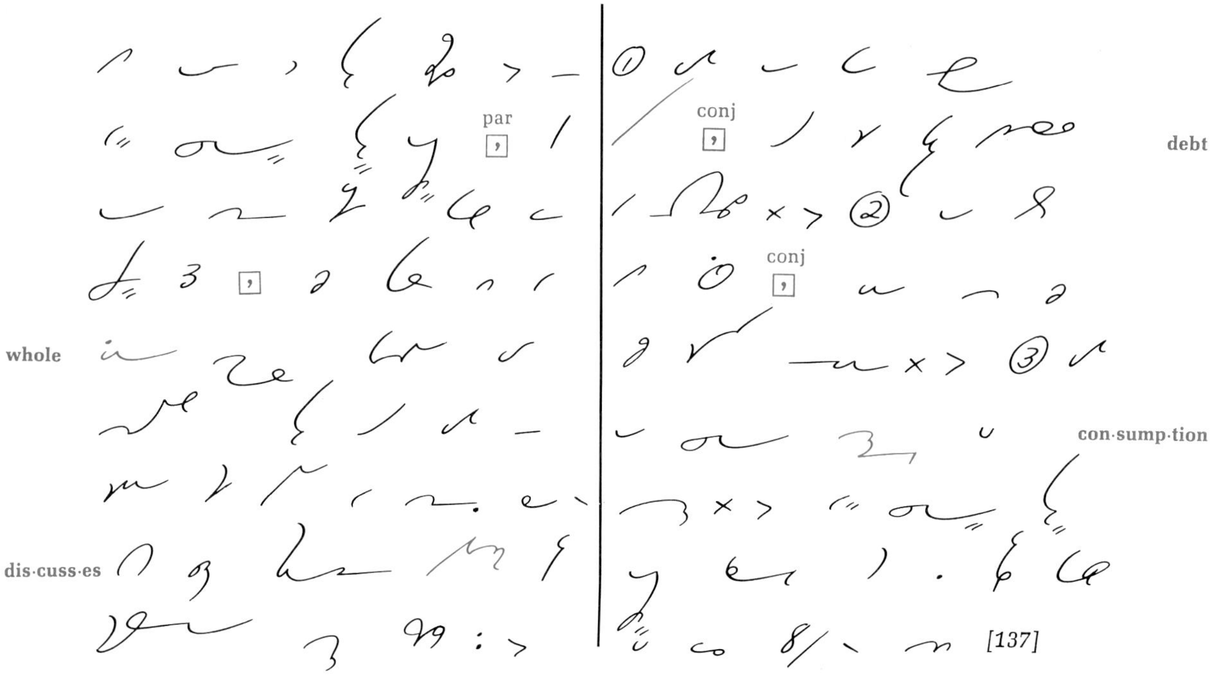
par
conj
conj
debt
whole
con·sump·tion
dis·cuss·es
[137]

566 Transcription Quiz The correct punctuation of the following letter calls for 4 commas—1 comma apposition, 1 comma *and* omitted, 2 commas series.

As you copy the letter in your notebook, be sure to insert the necessary commas at the proper points and to indicate the reason for the punctuation.

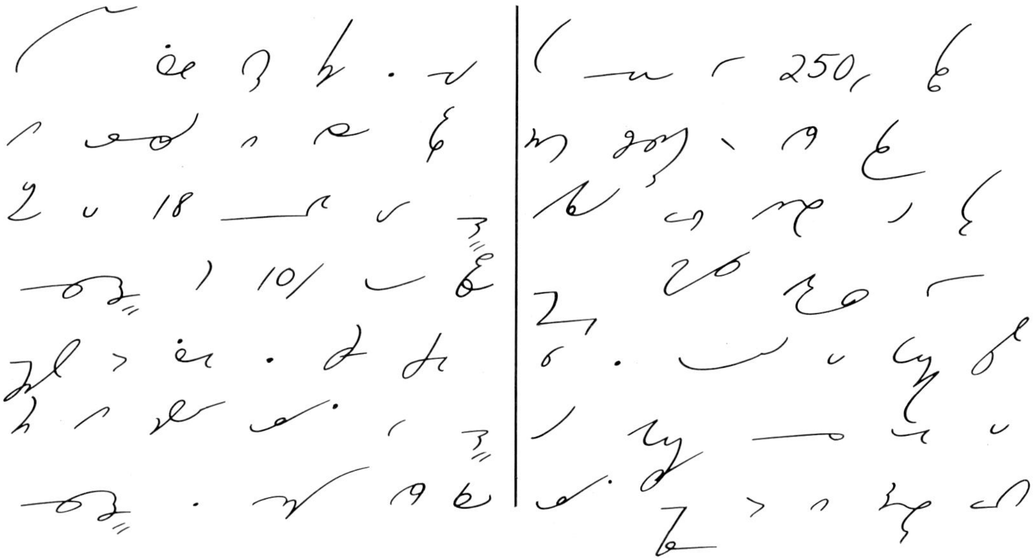

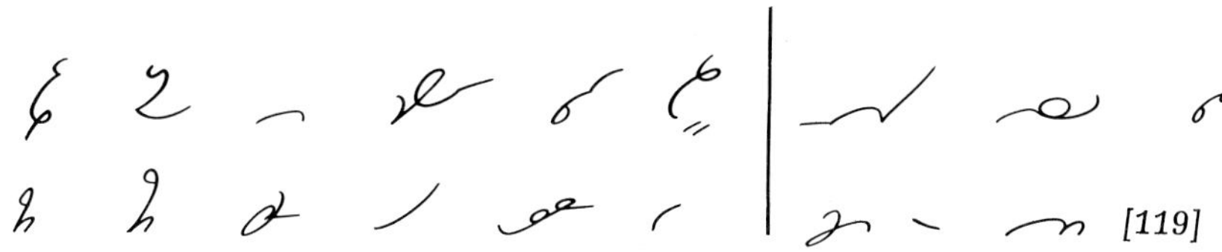
[119]

567

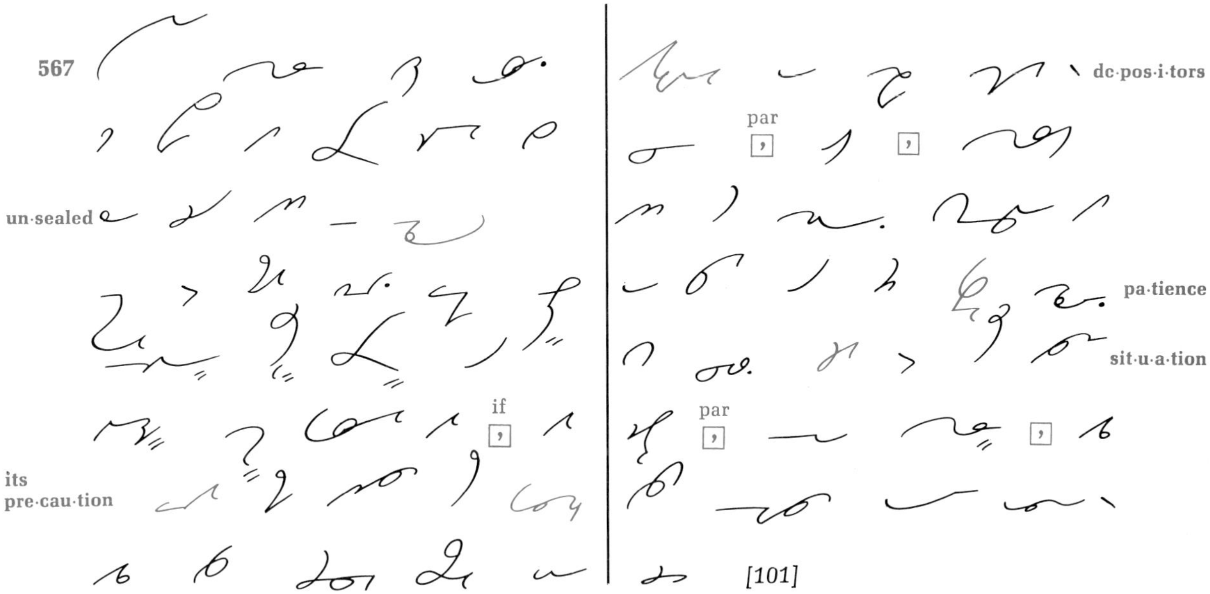
dc·pos·i·tors
par
un·sealed
pa·tience
sit·u·a·tion
if
par
its
pre·cau·tion
[101]

568 Doctor

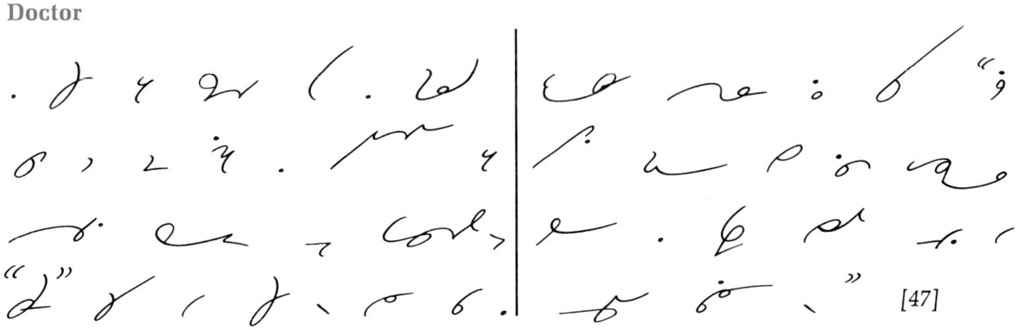
[47]

LESSON 61

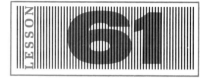

Disjoined word beginnings are given intensive treatment in this lesson. You will find 57 of them.

Building transcription skills

569 **GRAMMAR CHECKUP** | **comparisons**

The comparative degree of an adjective or adverb is used when reference is made to two objects; the superlative degree is used when reference is made to more than two objects.

comparative

Of the two boys, Jim is the taller.
Which boy is more efficient, Jim or Harry?
Is Mr. Smith or Mr. Green better qualified to do the job?

superlative

Of the three boys, Jim is the tallest.
Which of the boys is the most efficient, Jim, Harry, or John?
Is Mr. Smith, Mr. Green, or Mr. Brown the best qualified to do the job?

570

Business vocabulary builder	
	transmit Hand over to.
	necessitated Made necessary.
	overall Including everything.

Reading and writing practice

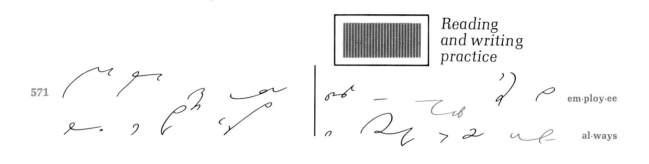

571

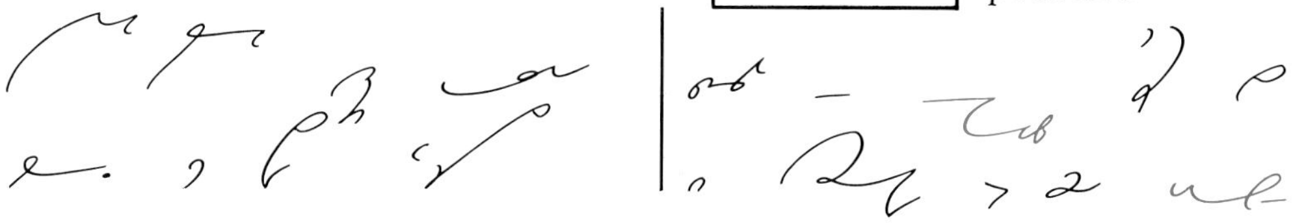

em·ploy·ee

al·ways

intro

ar·eas wheth·er

par

thought·ful·ness

if

ed·i·tor

[106]

572 ap

trans·ferred 15 intro sud·den·ness

ne·ces·si·tat·ed

16 over·all

[124]

573

par

mod·el

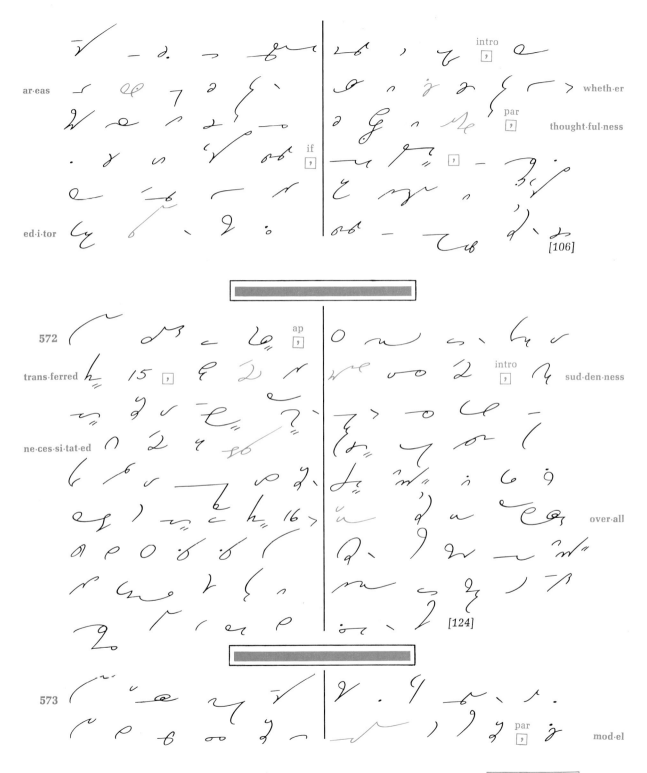

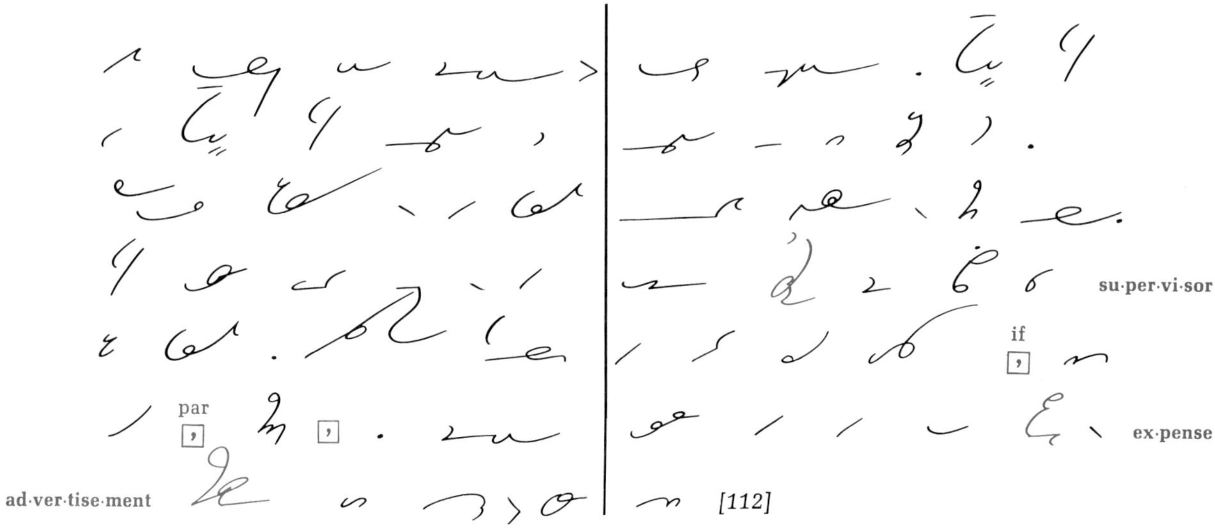
su·per·vi·sor
if
par
ex·pense
ad·ver·tise·ment
[112]

574 Transcription Quiz In the following letter you must supply 3 commas to punctuate it correctly—1 comma *when* clause, 2 commas series.

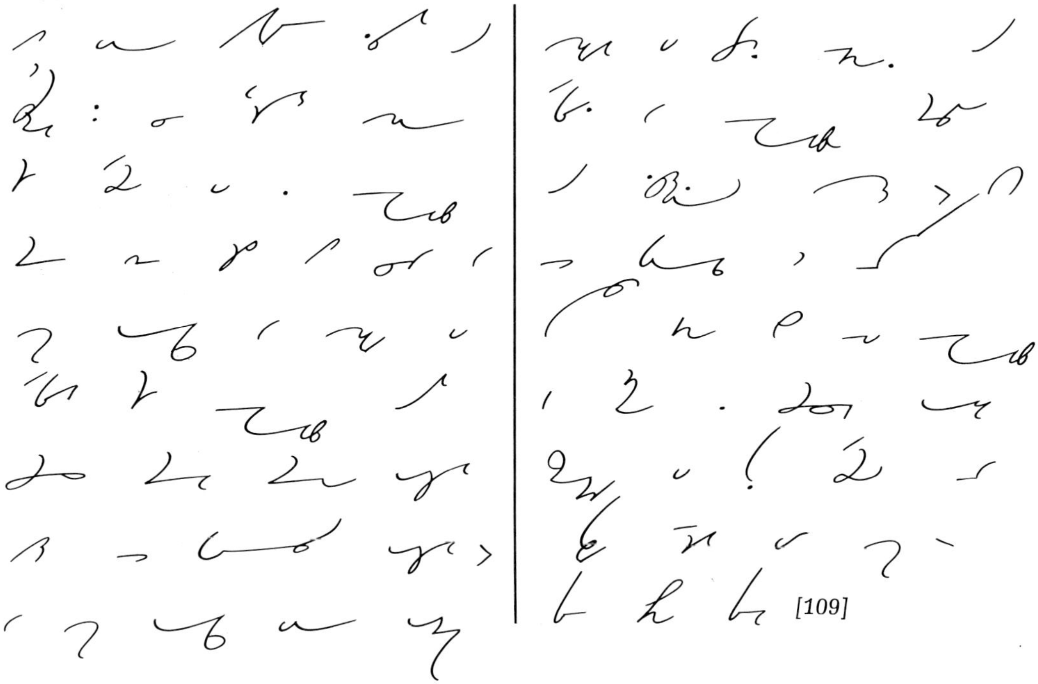
[109]

575 site, ex·pan·sion, ad·van·ta·ges, en·ter·prise, ours, re·cruit·ed, ar·ea

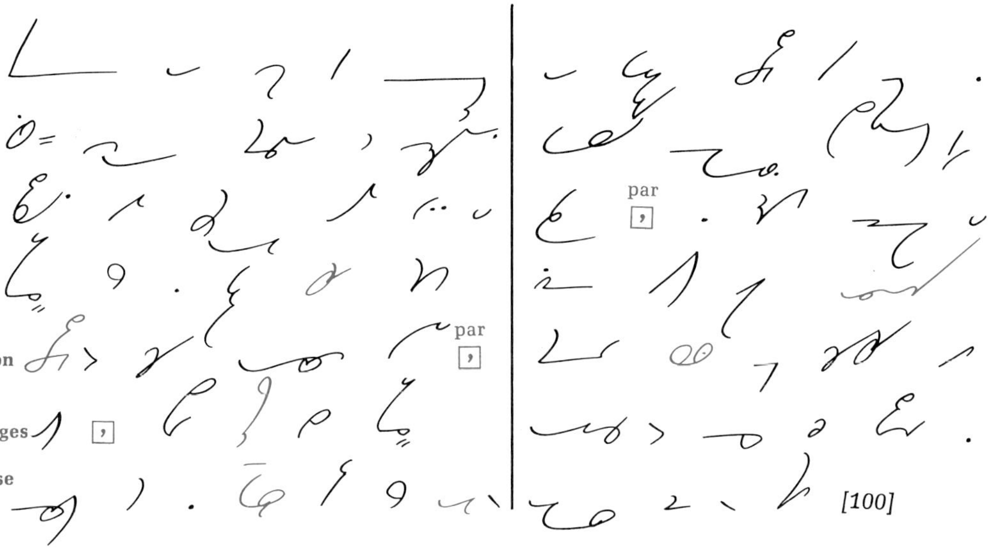
par
par
[100]

576 al·ter·na·tive, com·pelled

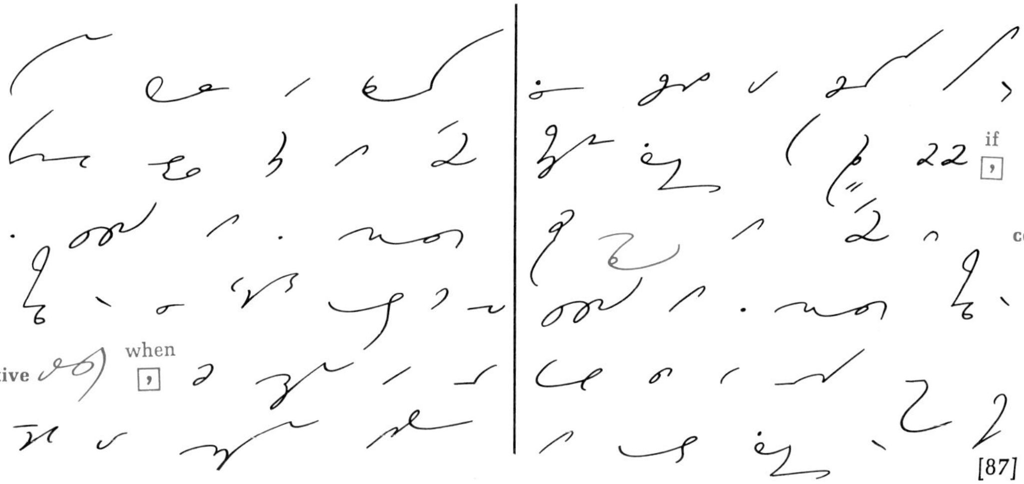
when
if
[87]

577 re·cent

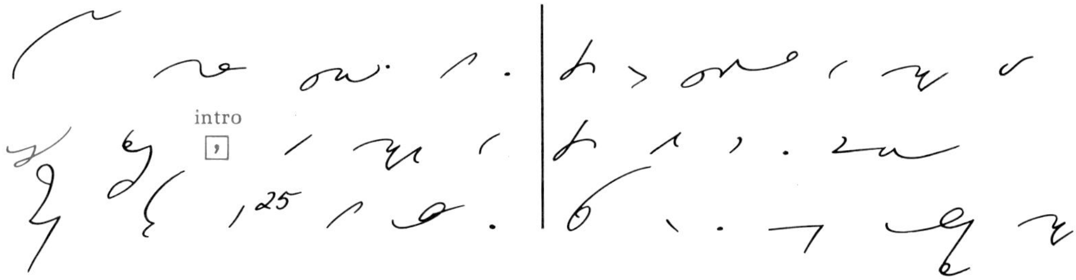
intro

over·head

sim·i·lar

ser

sub·stan·tial·ly

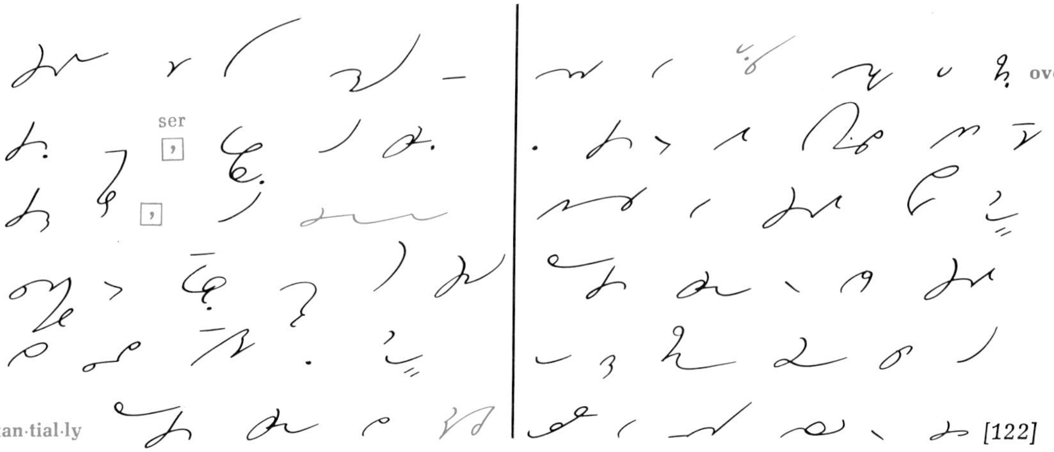

[122]

578

de·scribe

ed·u·ca·tors

man·u·fac·tur·ers

as

de·vel·op·ments

[107]

LESSON 62

Do you find that you don't know the disjoined word endings as well as you would like? Then practice this lesson carefully. There are 67 disjoined word endings in it.

Building transcription skills

579 SIMILAR-WORDS DRILL | past, passed

past (*noun*) A former time. (*Past* is also used as an adjective.)

The program has been very successful in the past.

Please take care of your past-due *account.*

passed Went by; moved along; transferred.

I passed *him on the street.*

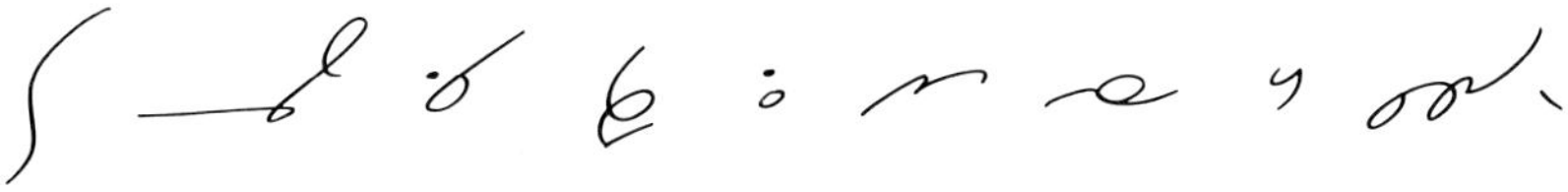

Before many days had passed, *he took care of his account.*

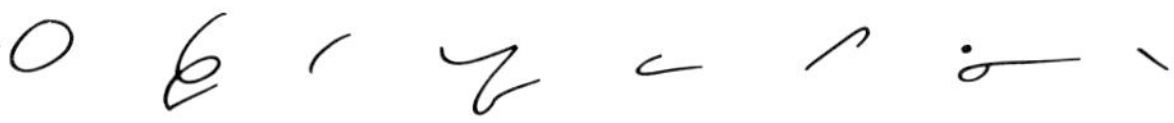

I passed *the report on to him.*

580

Business vocabulary builder	**formulate** Prepare; make. **potential** In the making; possible. **with mixed feelings** Be both happy and unhappy about the same situation.

Reading and writing practice

581

tech·ni·cal

lose ben·e·fit

conj
conj
par
intro
[129]

neigh·bor·hood oc·ca·sion·al·ly

582

se·cu·ri·ties

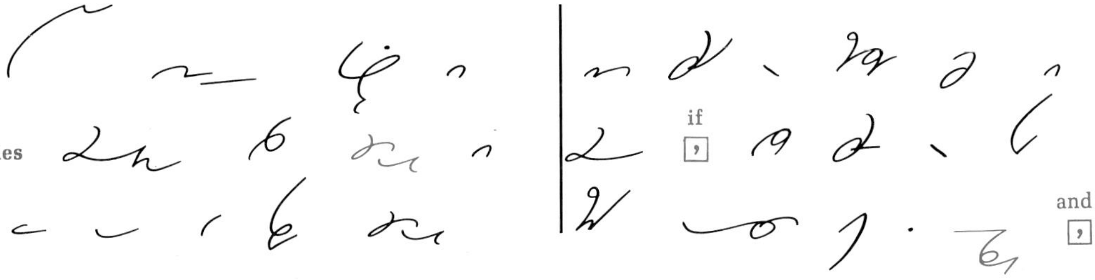
if

and o

im·par·tial

tech·ni·cal·ly

if

if

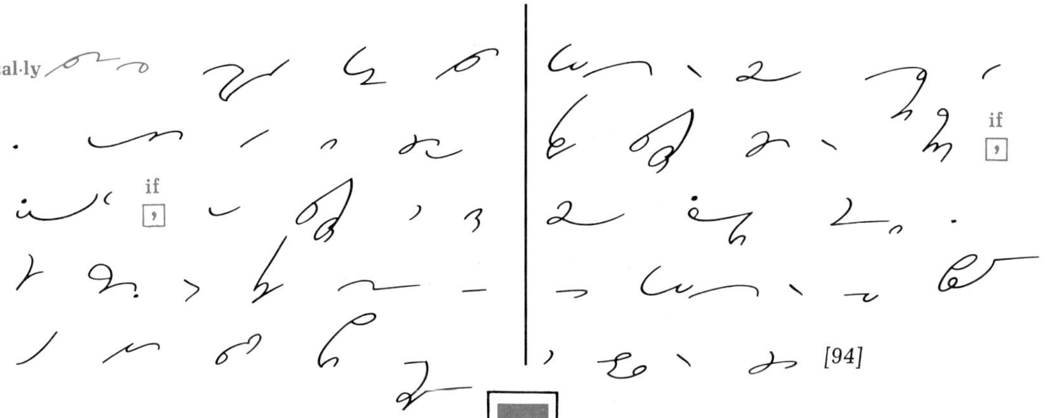

[94]

583

de·vel·op

passed

com·pre·hen·sive

and o

ser

if

as·sis·tance

po·ten·tial

be·lieve

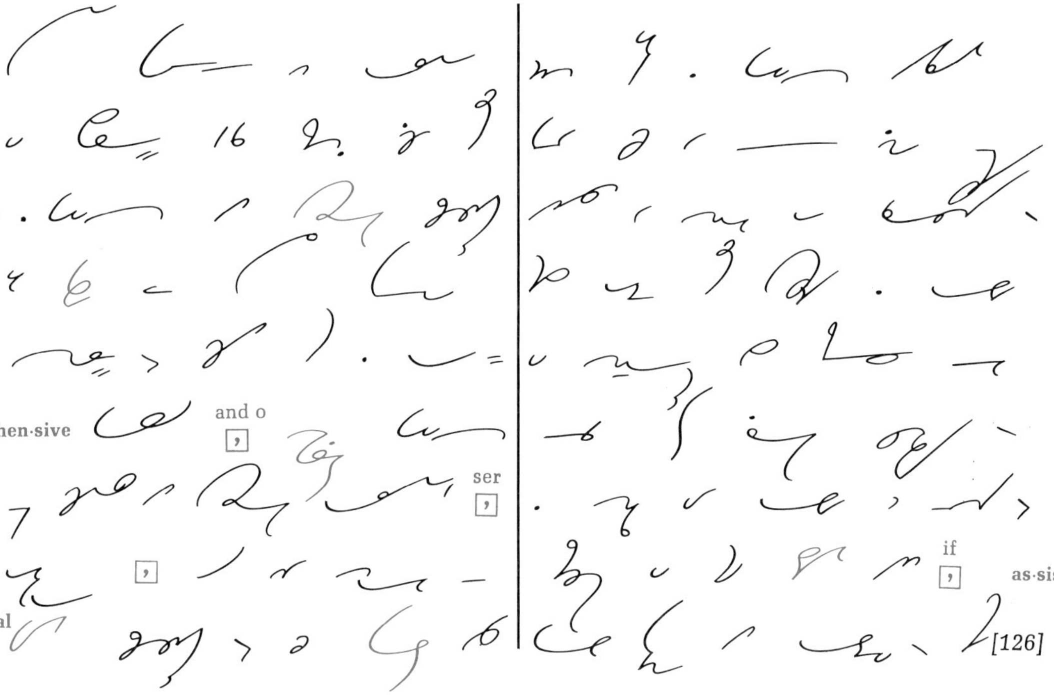

[126]

584 **Transcription Quiz** The following letter calls for 4 commas—1 comma introductory, 1 comma *when* clause, 2 commas parenthetical. Can you supply them?

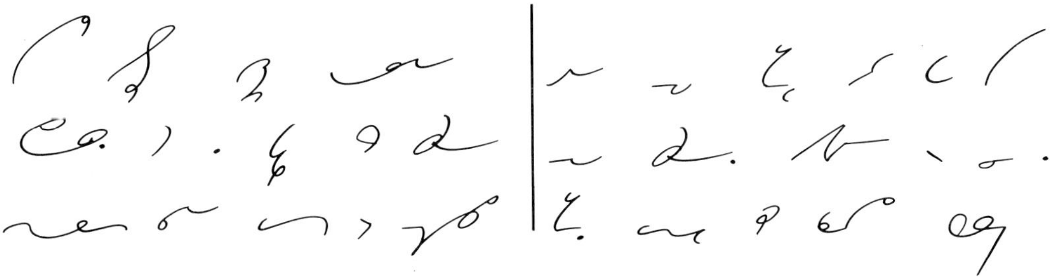

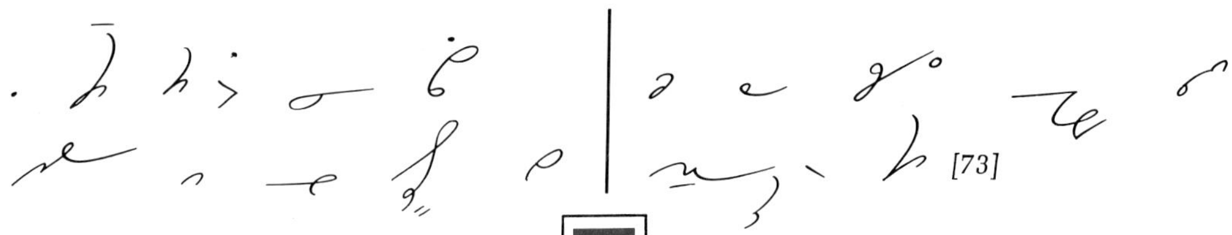

[73]

585

typ·i·cal
pro·vid·ing
worst
if
as
par

[117]

586

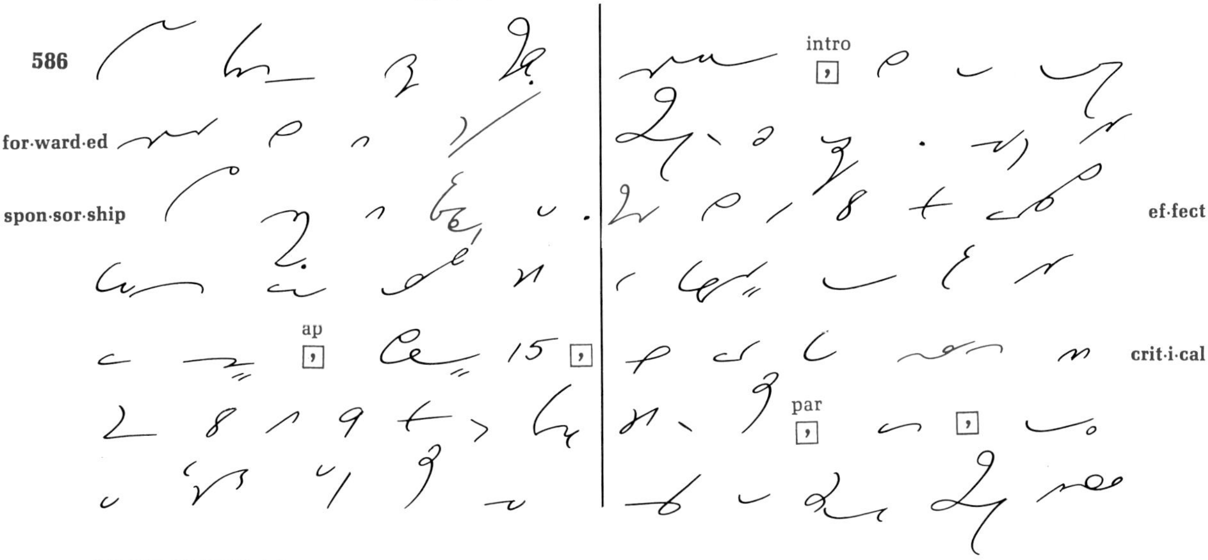

intro
for·ward·ed
spon·sor·ship
ef·fect
ap
15
crit·i·cal
par

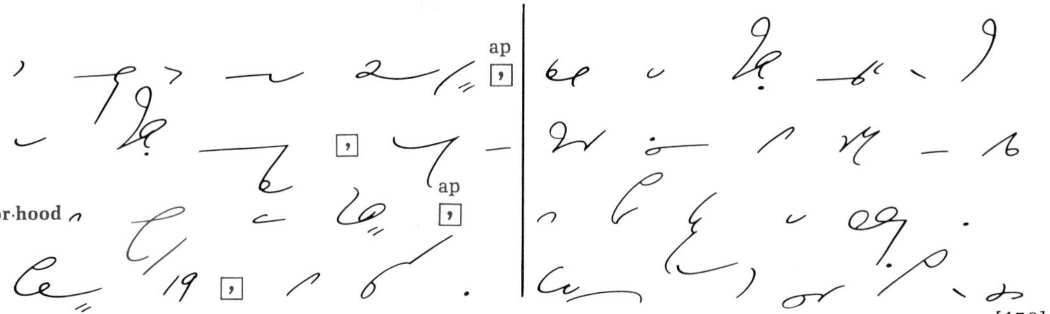

ap

neigh·bor·hood

[156]

587

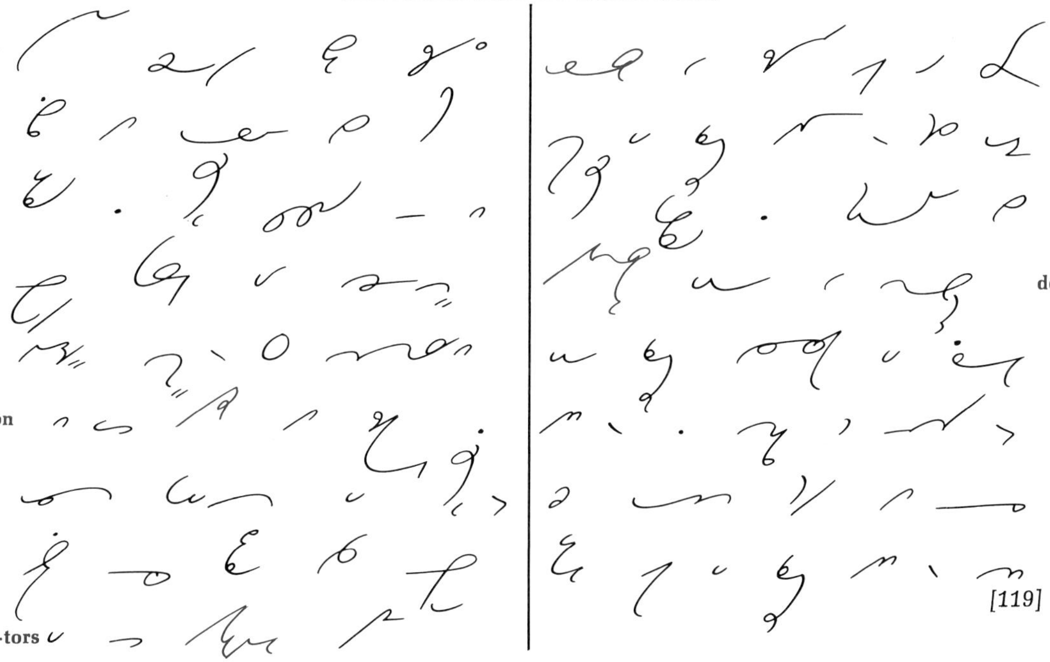

re·al·ize

de·scribes

de·ci·sion

de·pos·i·tors

[119]

LESSON 63

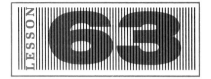

Blends form a very important part of Gregg Shorthand. The material in this lesson reviews all the blends many times. In all, there are 131 words and phrases containing one or more blends.

Building transcription skills

588 COMMON PREFIXES | co-

co- with, together, jointly

cooperation Act of working together.

coeducation Joint education; especially the education of boys and girls at the same school.

coordinate Bring together.

coherence A sticking together.

589

Business vocabulary builder

testimonial letter Letter expressing appreciation.

remedy (*verb*) Cure or correct.

exceeded Gone beyond.

net worth Difference between the total assets owned by a company and its total debts and obligations.

Reading and writing practice

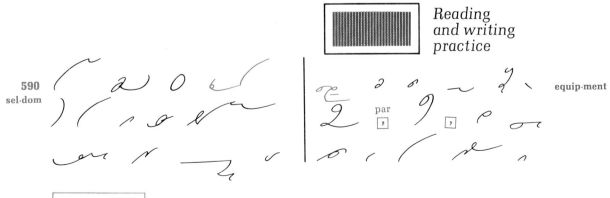

590 sel·dom

par

equip·ment

ex·ceed·ed

in·stalled

intro ,

over·head

intro ,

sub·stan·tial

when ,

ex·cel·lent

[113]

591

re·quest·ing

straight·en·ing

sub·scrip·tion

intro ,

conj ,

for·ward

[124]

ar·riv·al

can·celed

592

conj ,

wheth·er

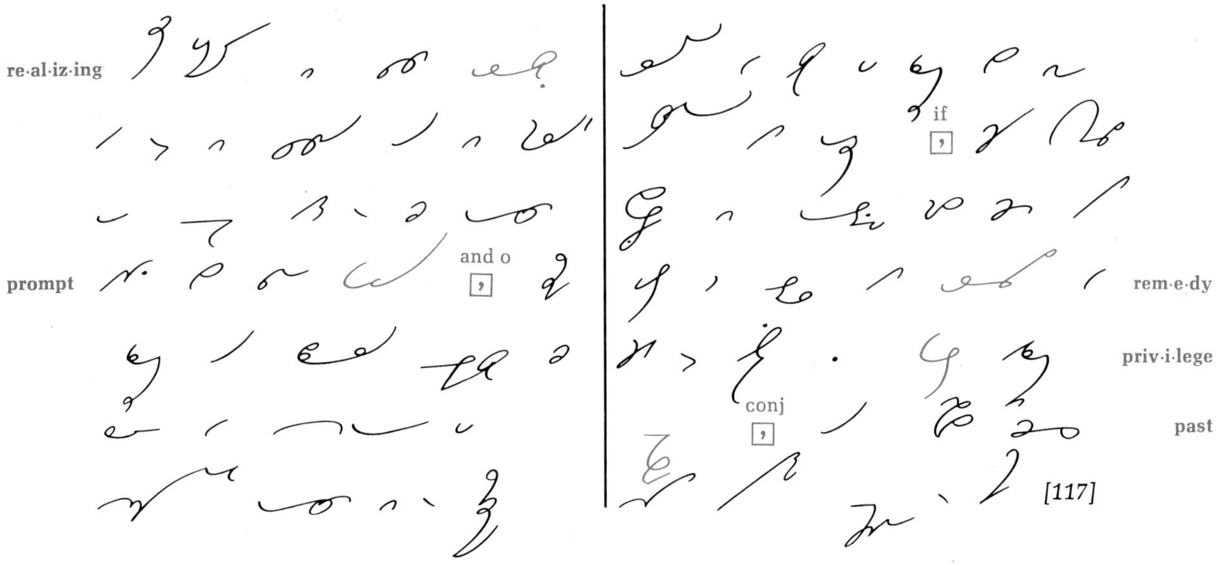
re·al·iz·ing
prompt
and o
if
rem·e·dy
priv·i·lege
conj
past
[117]

593 Transcription Quiz The following letter requires 6 commas to be punctuated correctly—2 commas conjunction, 2 commas parenthetical, 2 commas series. Remember to indicate these commas in your shorthand notes and to give the reason for their use.

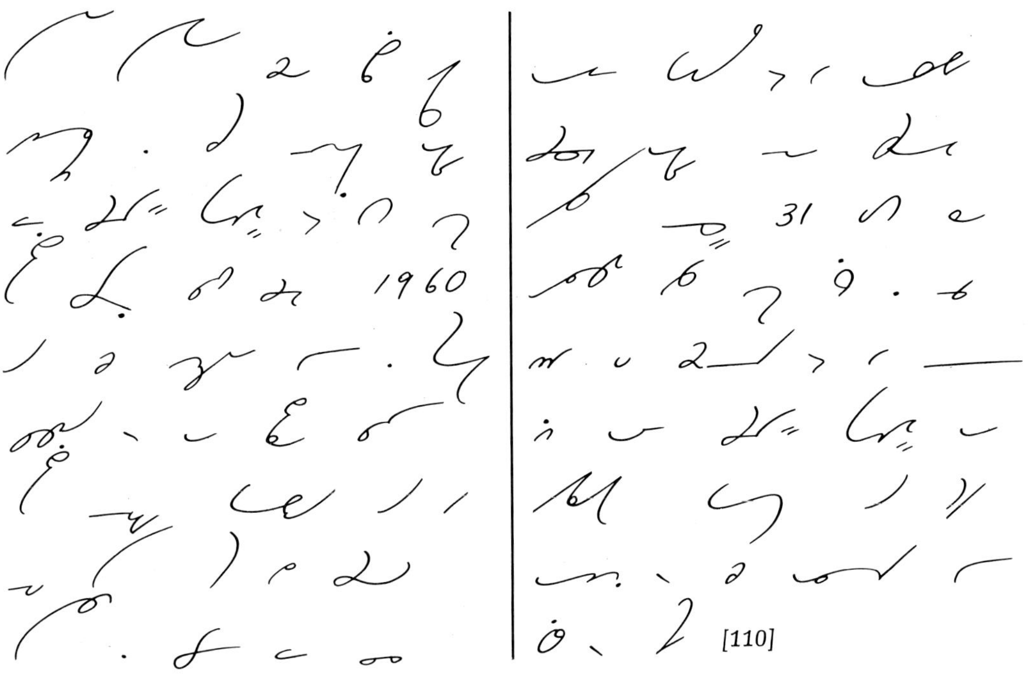
[110]

594

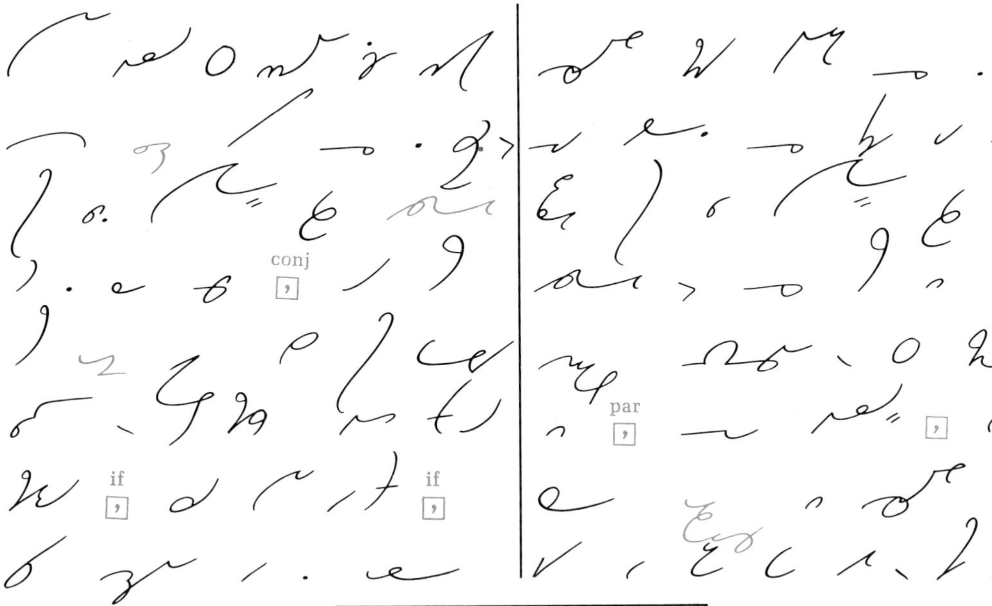

conj
par
if
if

enough
tow·els
rea·son
re·cip·ro·cate
[107]

595

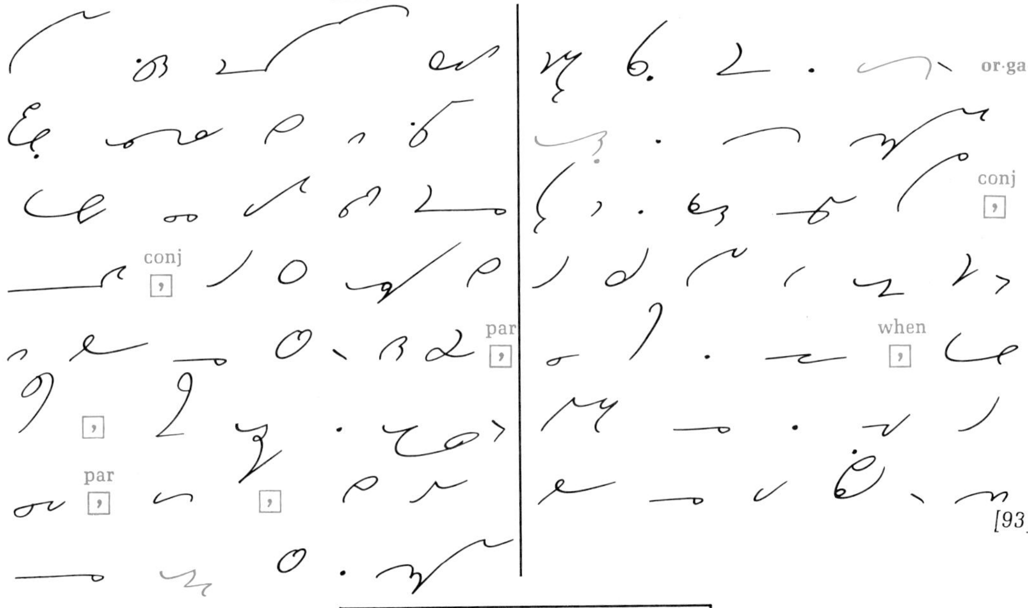

conj
conj
par
when
par

or·ga·ni·za·tion
los·ing
rea·sons
[93]

596

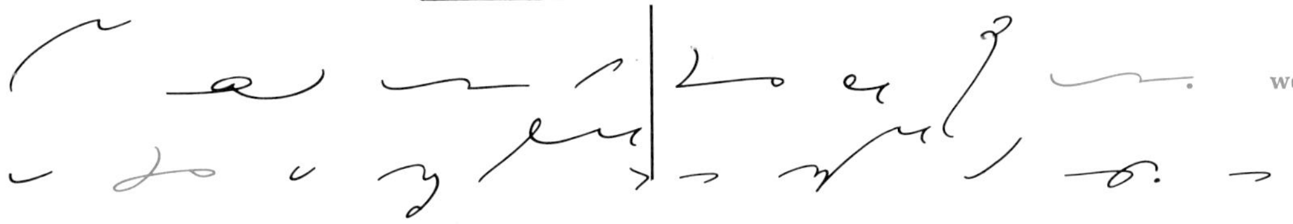

wel·com·ing
fam·i·ly

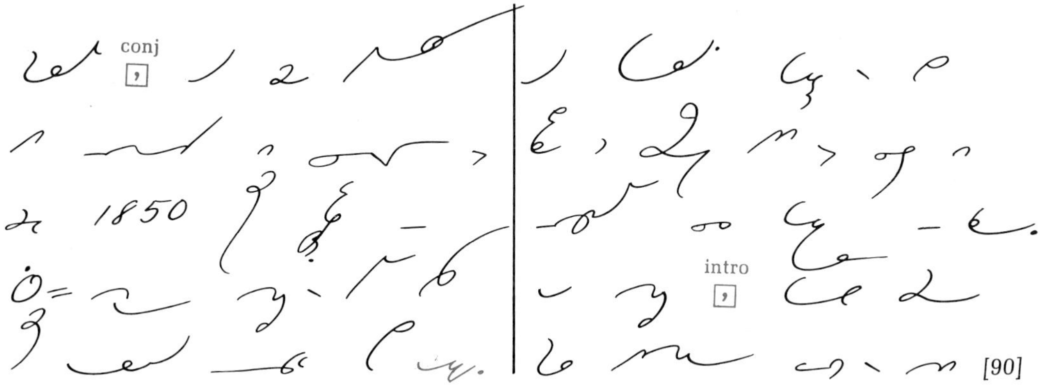
conj
intro
roast·ing
[90]

597

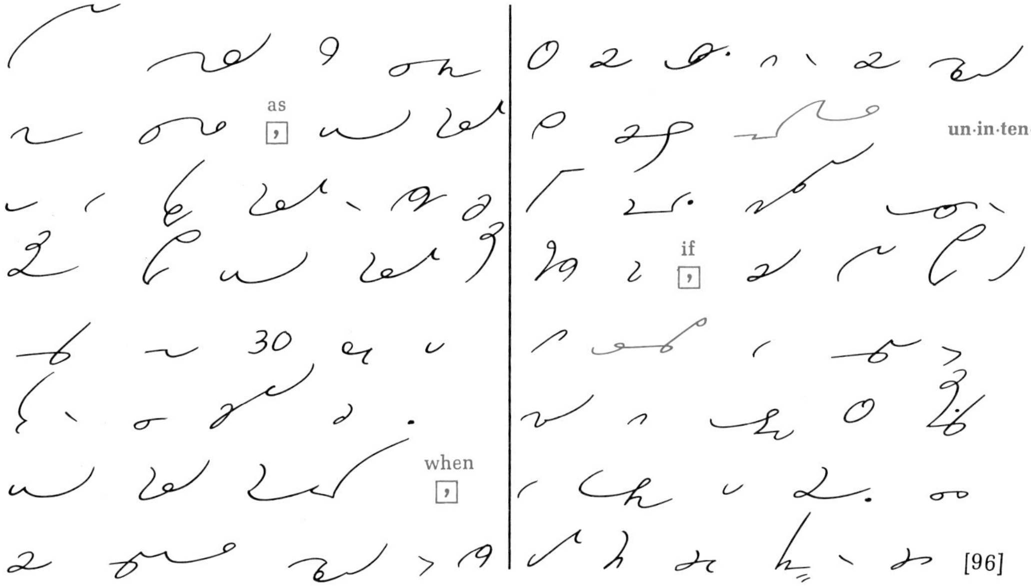
as
when
if
un·in·ten·tion·al·ly
rem·e·dy
[96]

LESSON 64

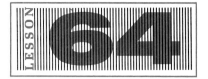

As you learned during the early stages of your study of Gregg Shorthand, vowels are omitted in some words to help gain fluency of writing. In this lesson you will find many illustrations of words from which vowels are omitted.

Building transcription skills

598 **SPELLING FAMILIES | -ary, -ery, -ory**

Words Ending in -ary

an·ni·ver·sa·ry	**el·e·men·ta·ry**	**sec·re·tary**
com·pli·men·ta·ry	**li·brary**	**sum·ma·ry**
cus·tom·ary	**nec·es·sary**	**tem·po·rary**
dic·tio·nary	**sec·on·dary**	**vo·cab·u·lary**

Words Ending in -ery

bind·ery	**mas·tery**	**re·fin·ery**
dis·cov·ery	**re·cov·ery**	**sce·nery**

Words Ending in -ory

di·rec·to·ry	**his·to·ry**	**ter·ri·to·ry**
fac·to·ry	**in·ven·to·ry**	**vic·to·ry**

599 *Business vocabulary builder*

situated Located.

complimentary Expressing approval or admiration; favorable.

customary Usual.

Reading and writing practice

600

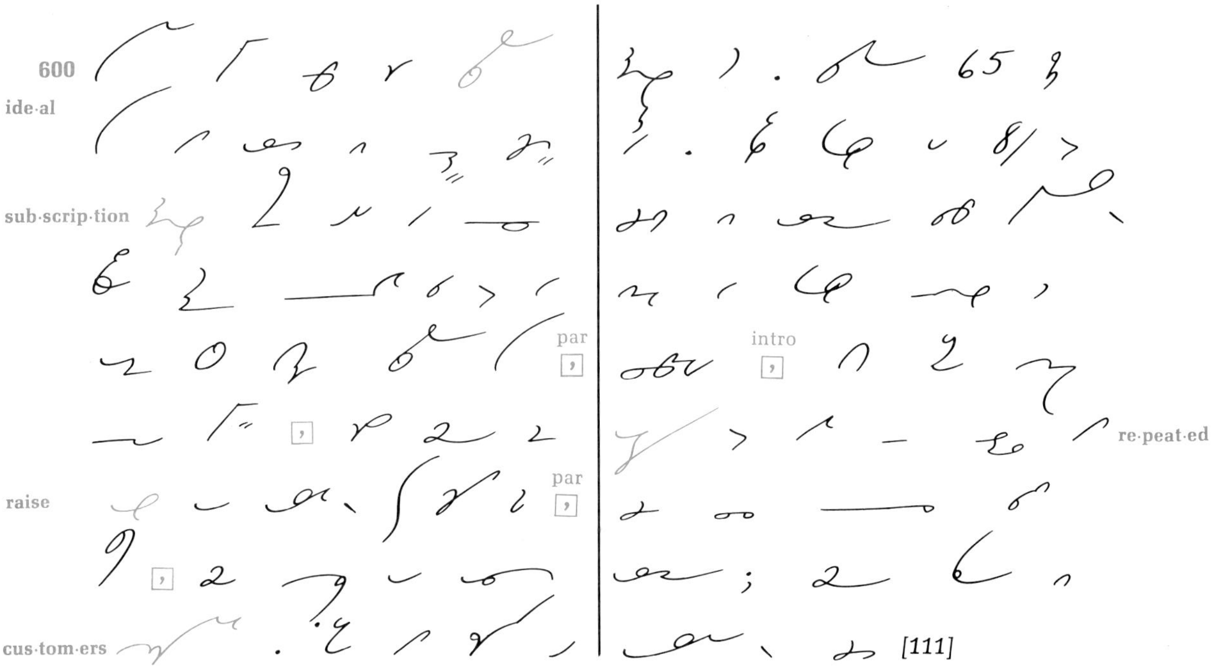
ide·al
sub·scrip·tion
raise
cus·tom·ers
par
par
intro
re·peat·ed
[111]

601

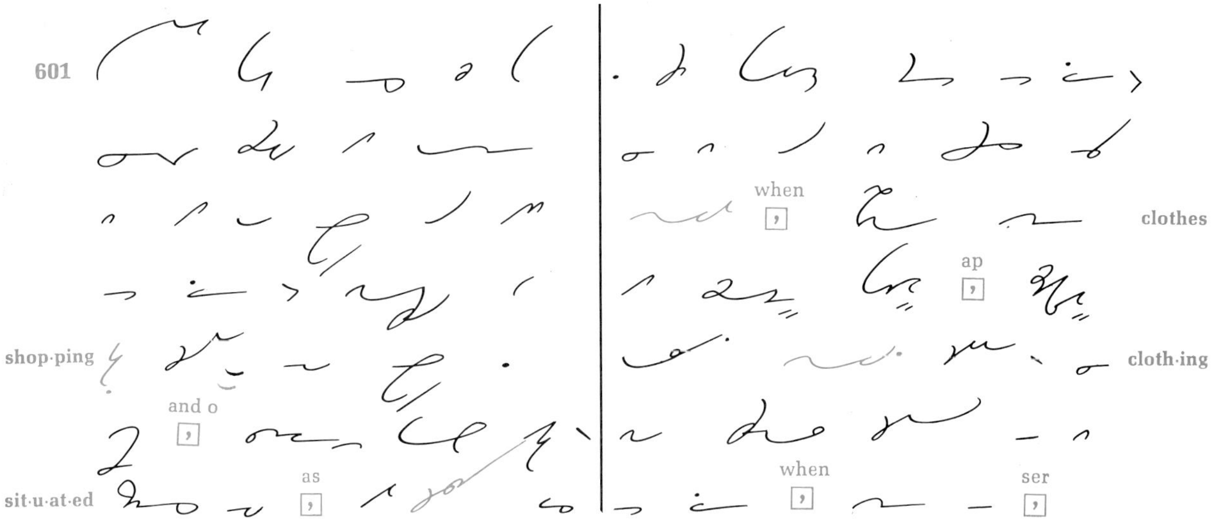
shop·ping
and o
sit·u·at·ed
as
when
clothes
ap
cloth·ing
when
ser

cour·te·ous

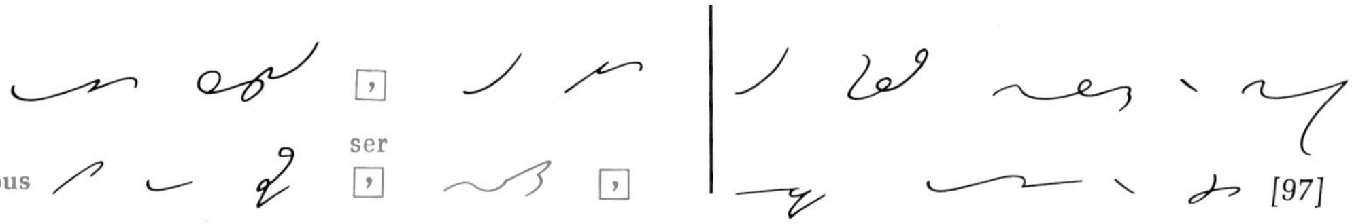
ser
[97]

[redacted]

602

sum·ma·ry

ca·reer

uti·lize
ex·cel·lent

va·can·cy

com·pli·men·ta·ry

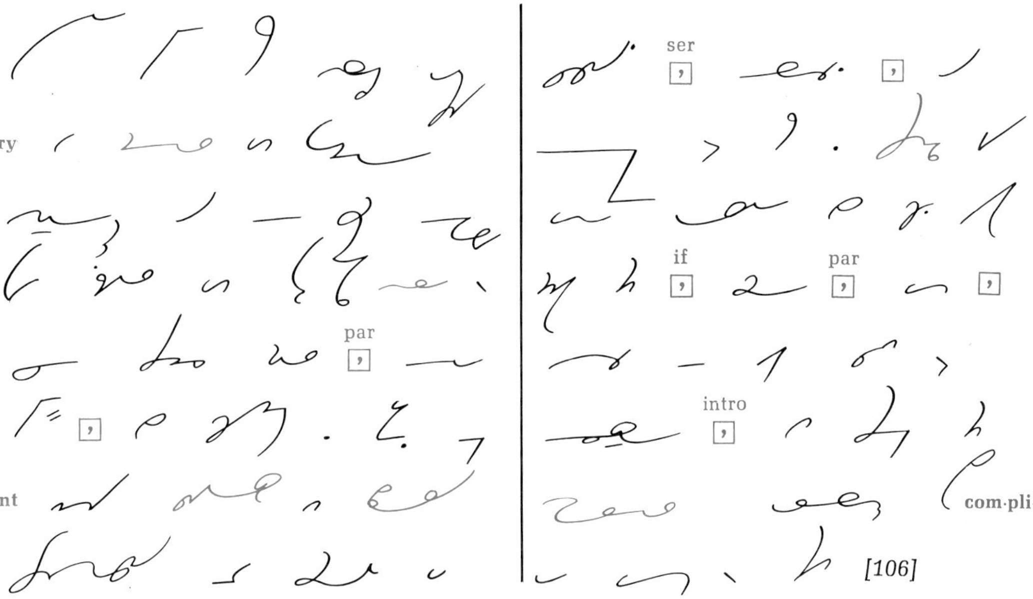
ser
par
if
par
intro
[106]

603 Transcription Quiz For you to supply: 3 commas—2 commas introductory, 1 comma parenthetical.

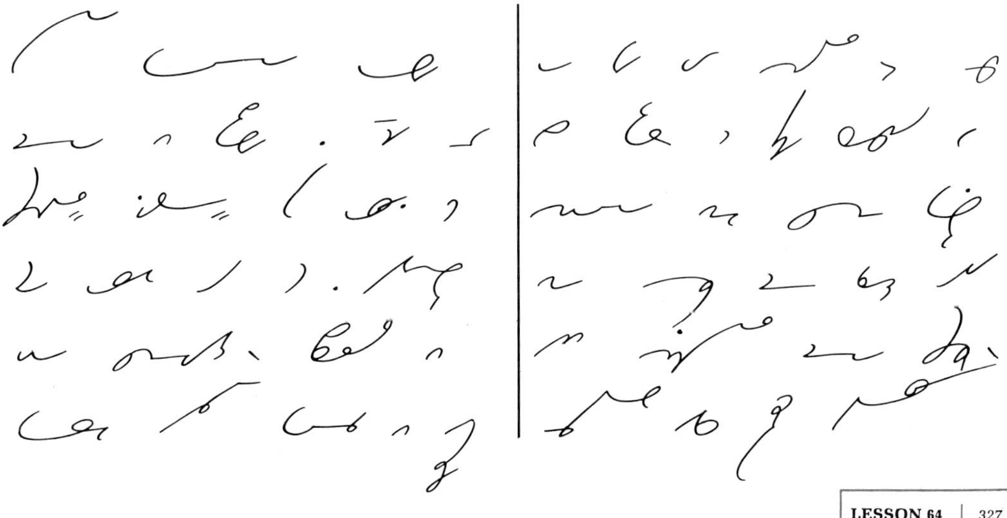

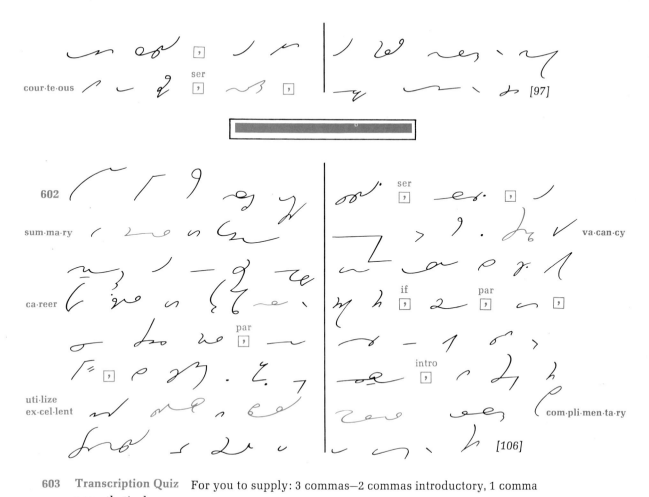

[113]

604

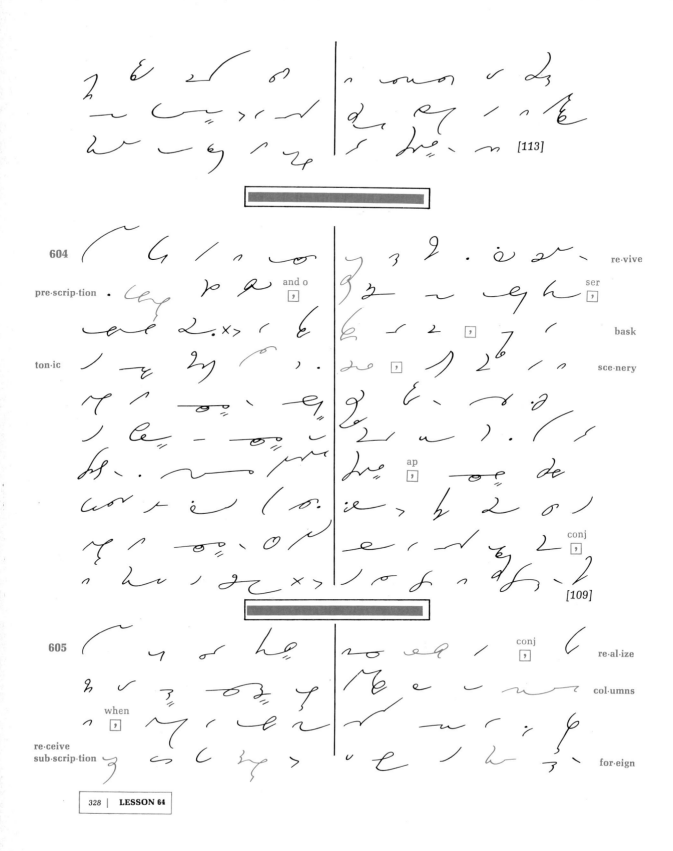

pre·scrip·tion

and o

ton·ic

re·vive

ser

bask

sce·nery

ap

conj

[109]

605

re·al·ize

conj

col·umns

when

re·ceive
sub·scrip·tion

for·eign

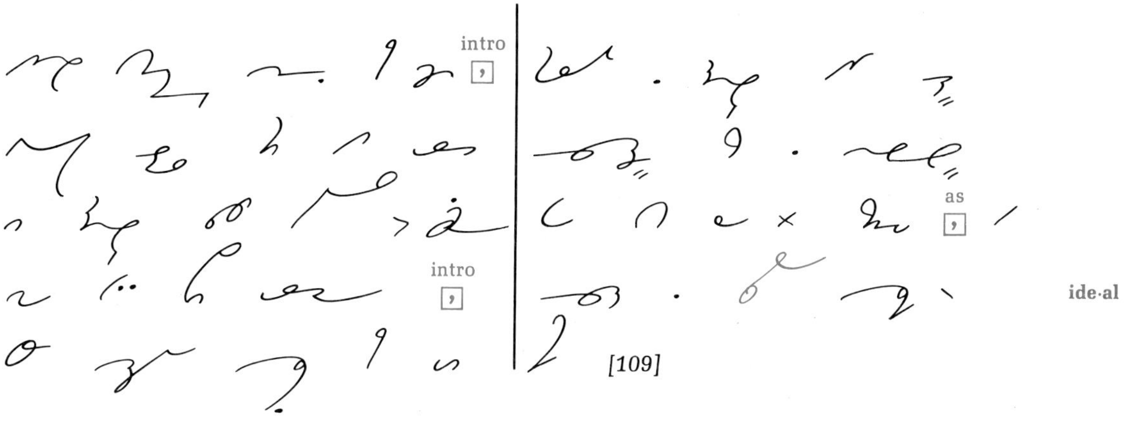
intro
as
ide·al
intro
[109]

606

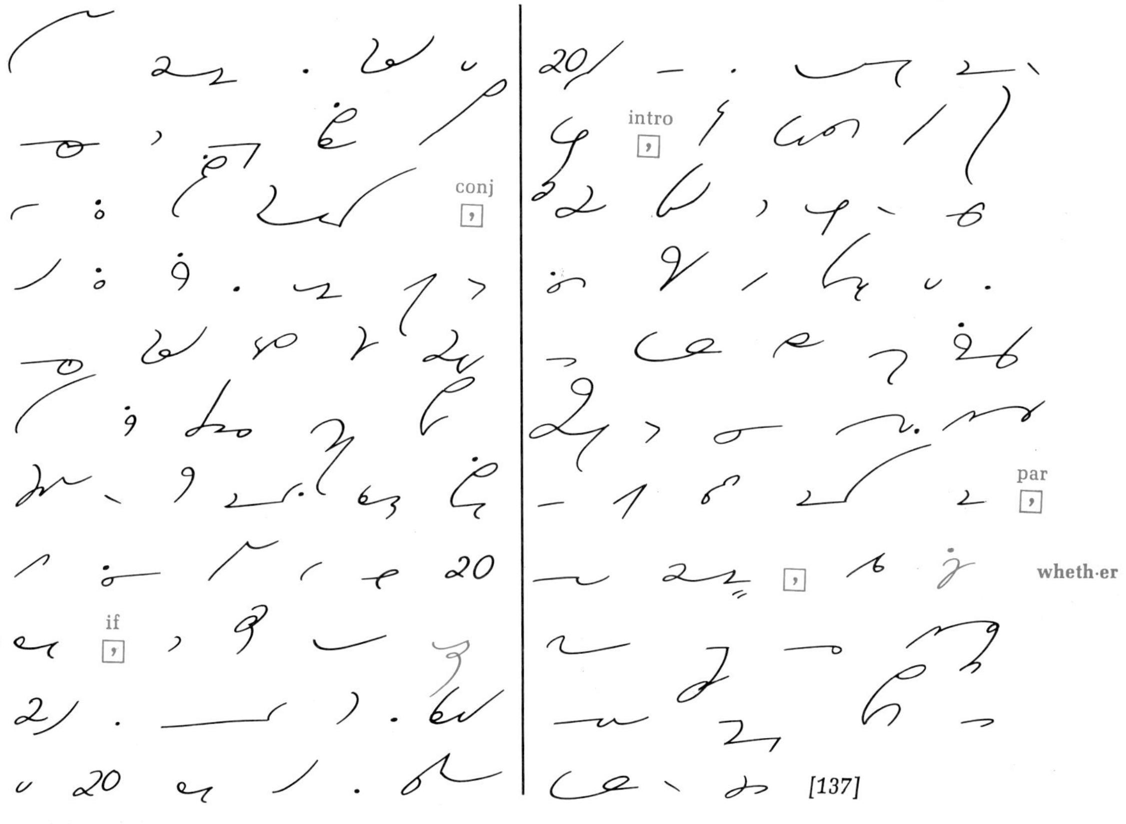
intro
conj
par
wheth·er
re·ceive
if
[137]

LESSON 65

You will frequently have to write numbers in business dictation. Because of the tremendous importance of accuracy in transcribing numbers, you must take special care to write numbers legibly in your notes. The material in this lesson will help you fix more firmly in your mind the various devices for expressing amounts and quantities in Gregg Shorthand.

Building transcription skills

607 **SIMILAR-WORDS DRILL** | **country, county**

country A nation.

He joined the armed forces of our country.

county A political division of a state.

Miami is in Dade County, *Florida.*

608

Business vocabulary builder	
	exceeded Went beyond.
	pledges Promises.
	juvenile Relating to children.

Reading and writing practice

609

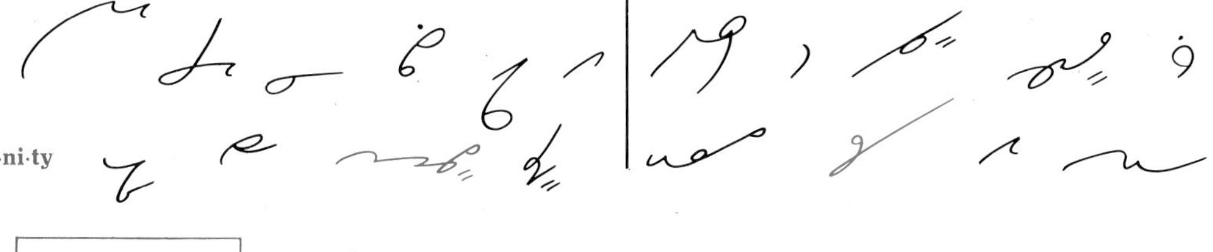

Com·mu·ni·ty

ex·ceed·ed

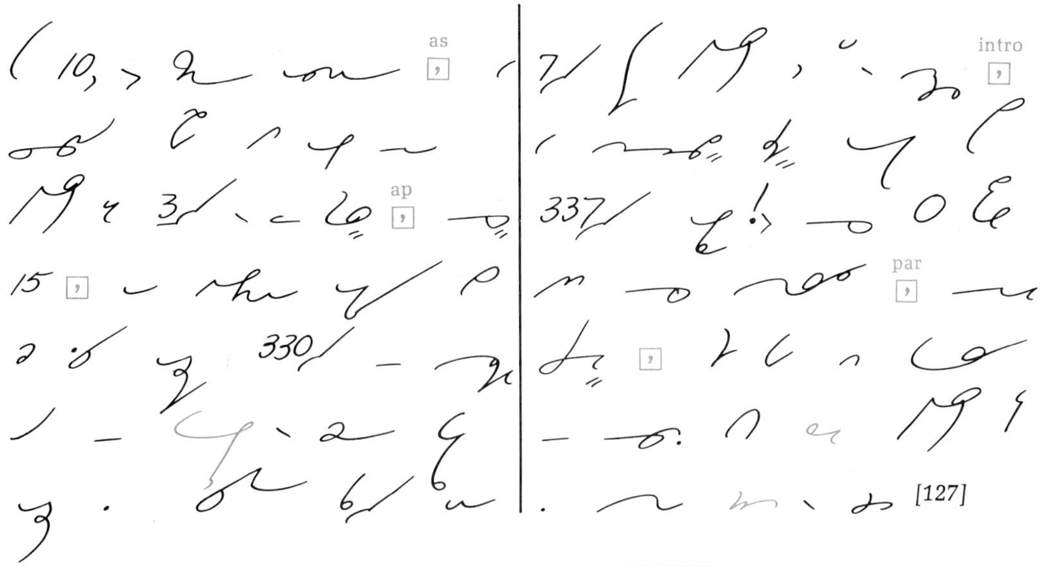
as
intro
ap
par
pledg·es
year's
suc·cess
[127]

610

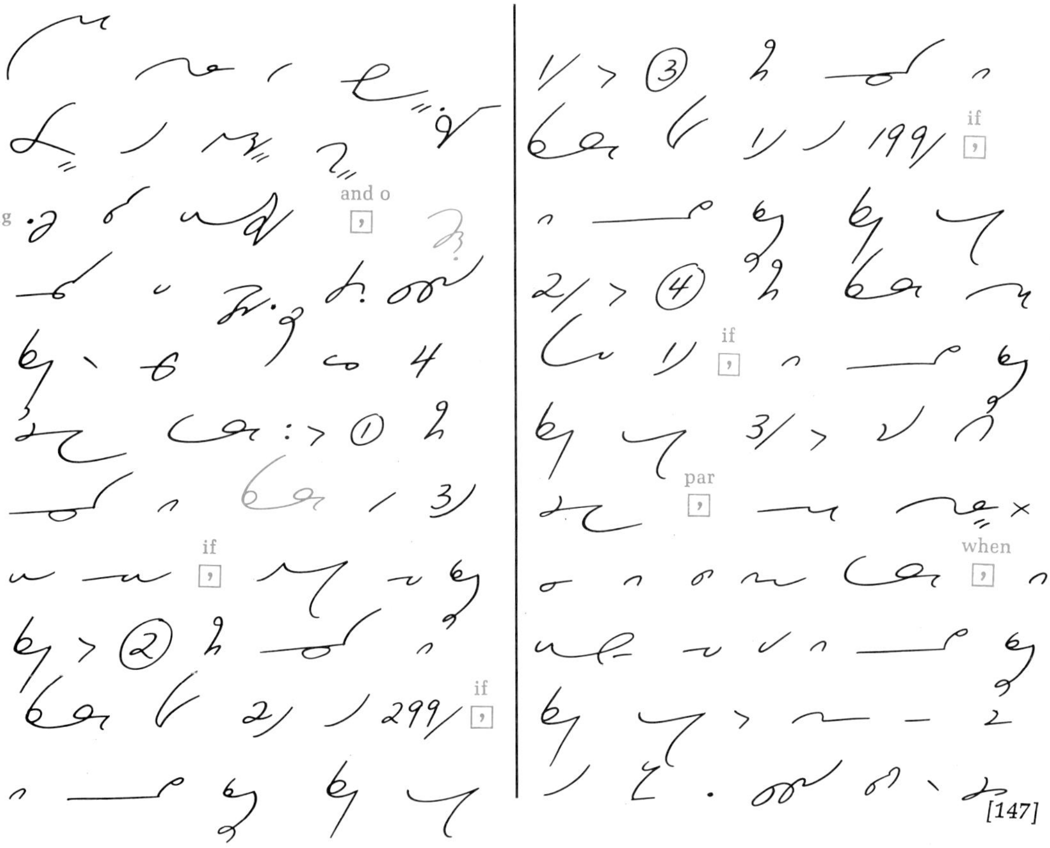
con·fus·ing
and o
if
bal·ance
par
when
[147]

611 America's Cultural Growth

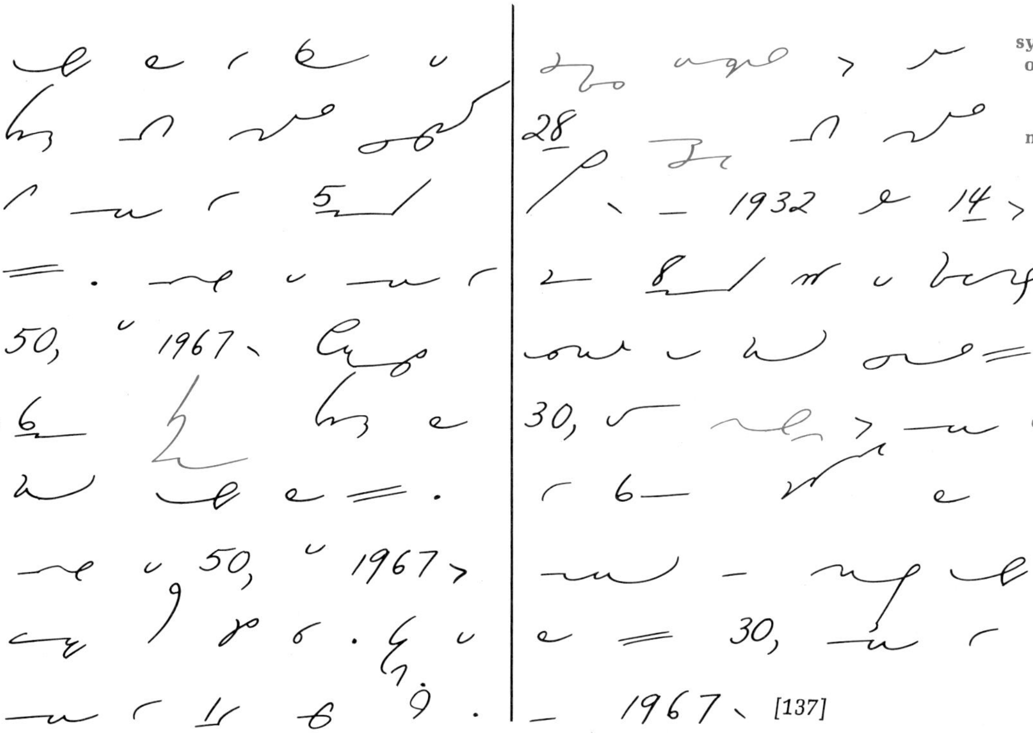

sym·pho·ny
or·ches·tra
mu·se·ums
ju·ve·nile
clas·si·cal

612

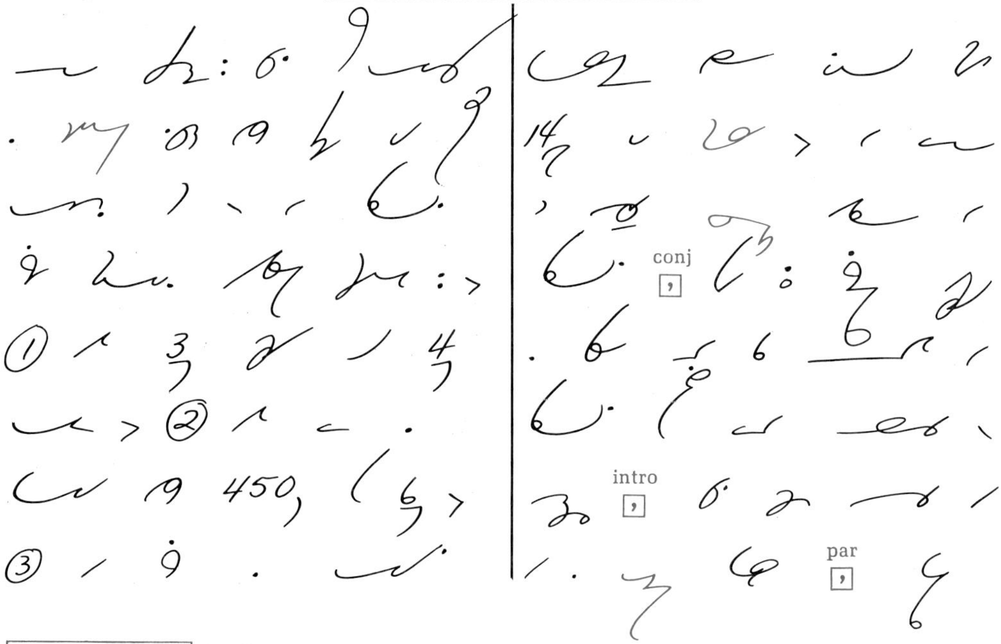

stor·age
freight
anx·ious
rea·son·able

if

ar·range·ments

[133]

613

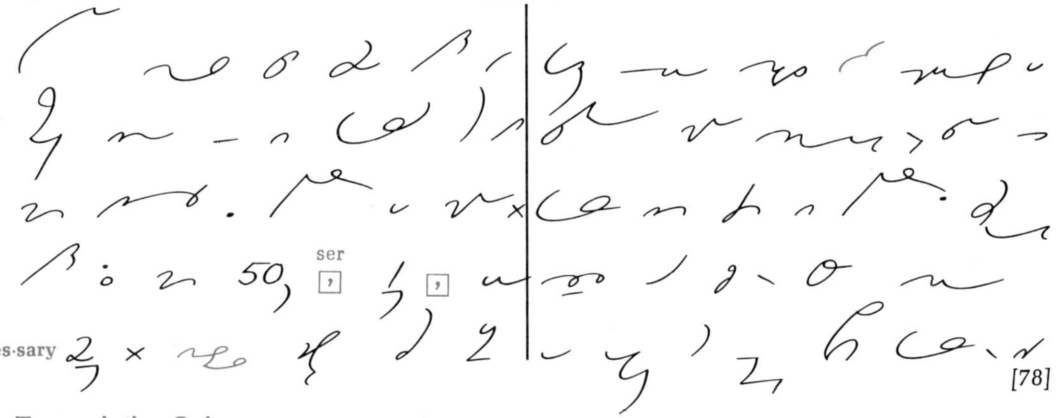

than

ser

un·nec·es·sary

[78]

614 Transcription Quiz For you to supply: 8 commas—4 commas parenthetical, 1 comma introductory, 1 comma *and* omitted, 1 comma *if* clause, 1 comma apposition.

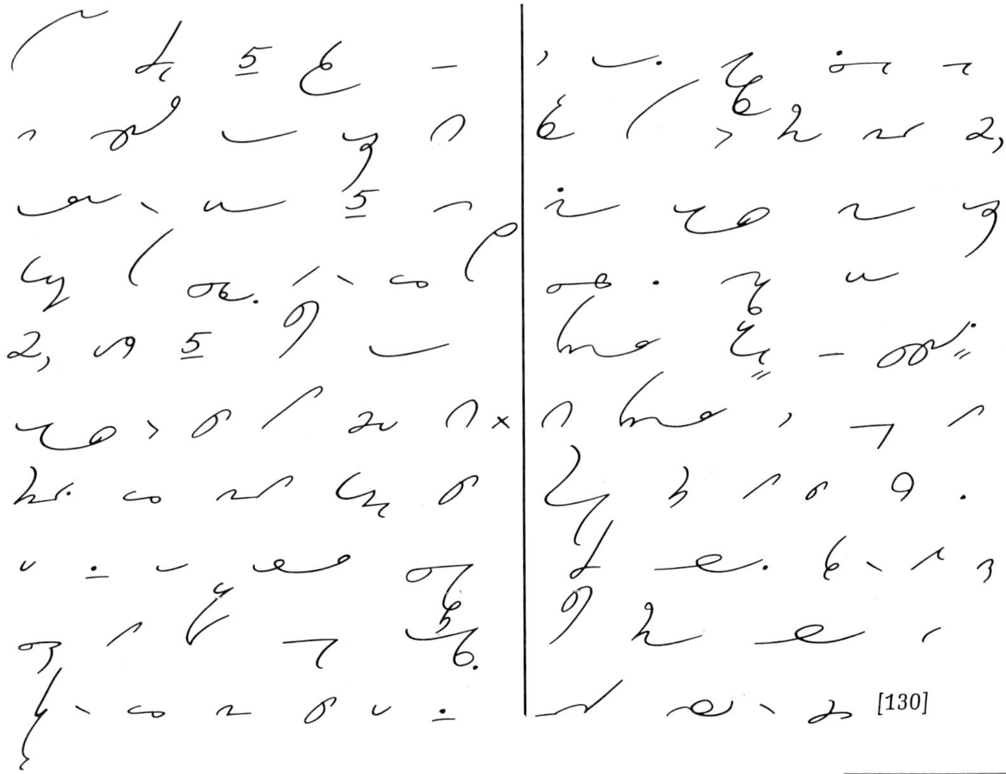

[130]

LESSON 66

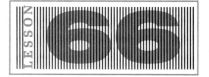

This is another lesson that concentrates on brief forms. Counting repetitions, it contains 405 brief forms and derivatives.

Building transcription skills

615 COMMON PREFIXES | un-

un- not

unusual Not usual; rare.

unnecessary Not needed.

unhappy Not happy; sad.

unsatisfactory Not satisfactory; bad.

616

Business vocabulary builder

fallout shelter A room, usually underground, that provides protection from the particles resulting from a nuclear explosion.

remiss Careless; negligent.

airfreight A method of shipping merchandise, usually heavy and bulky, by airplane.

Reading and writing practice

617

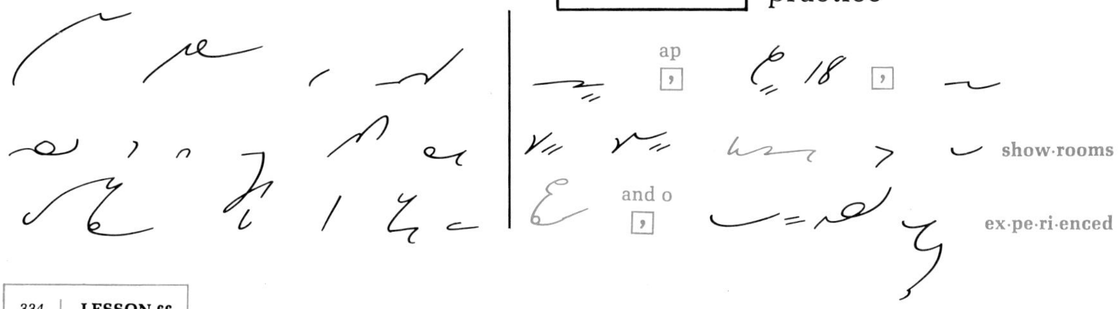
ap
and o
show·rooms
ex·pe·ri·enced

dough·nuts

per·son·al·ly

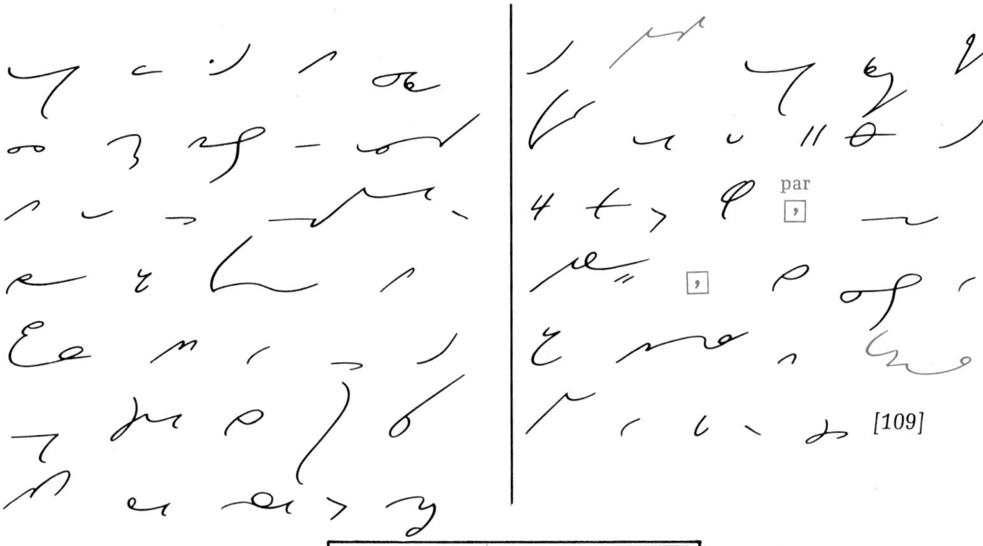
par
[109]

618

de·fense

shel·ter

conj
intro
ap
[117]

619

ad·van·tage

won't

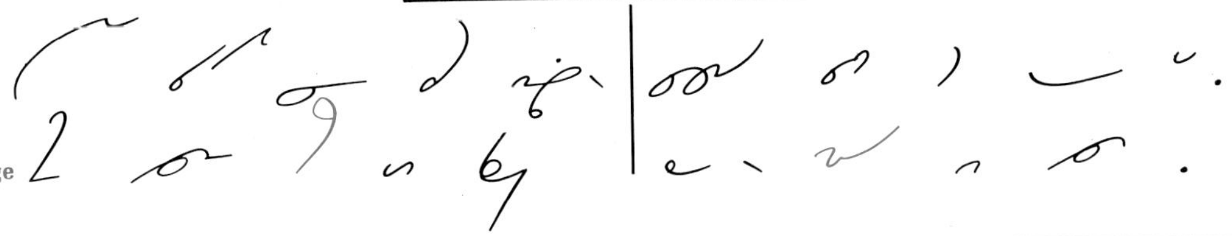

ab·sence

mind

wheth·er

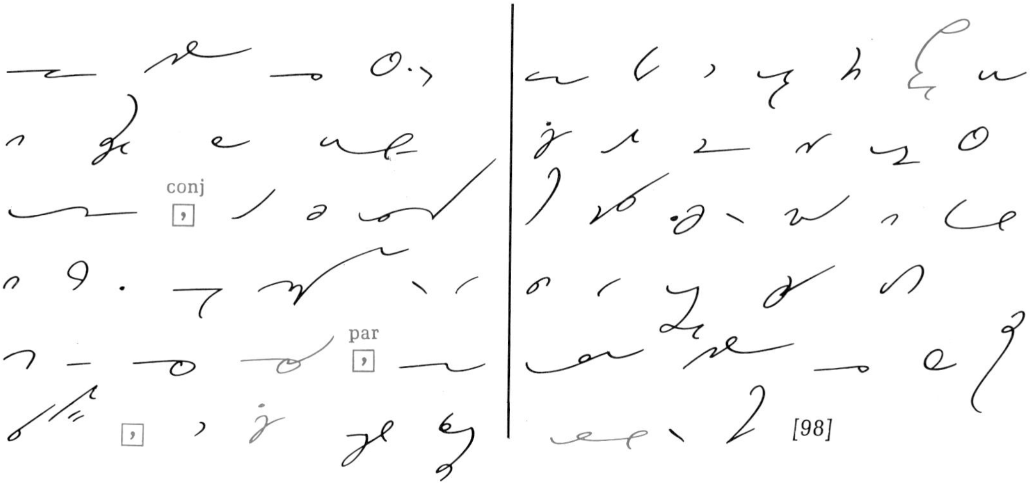
conj
par
[98]

re·miss

620 **Transcription Quiz** For you to supply: 4 commas—1 comma *when* clause, 2 commas series, 1 comma introductory.

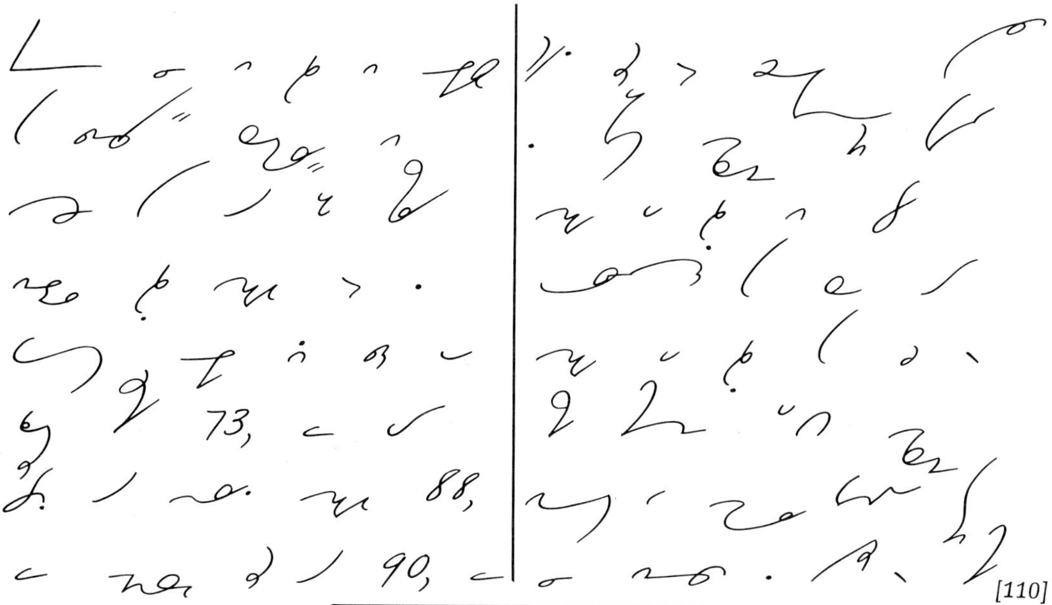
73,
88,
90,
[110]

621

man·age·ment

com·pa·ny's

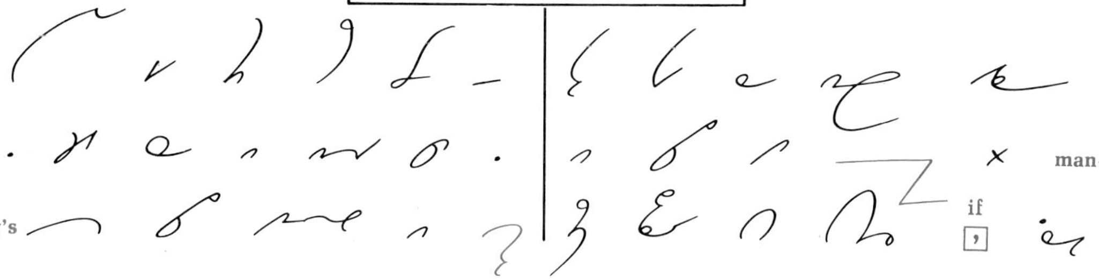
if

mod·ern

ad·ver·tis·ing

Per·sua·sion

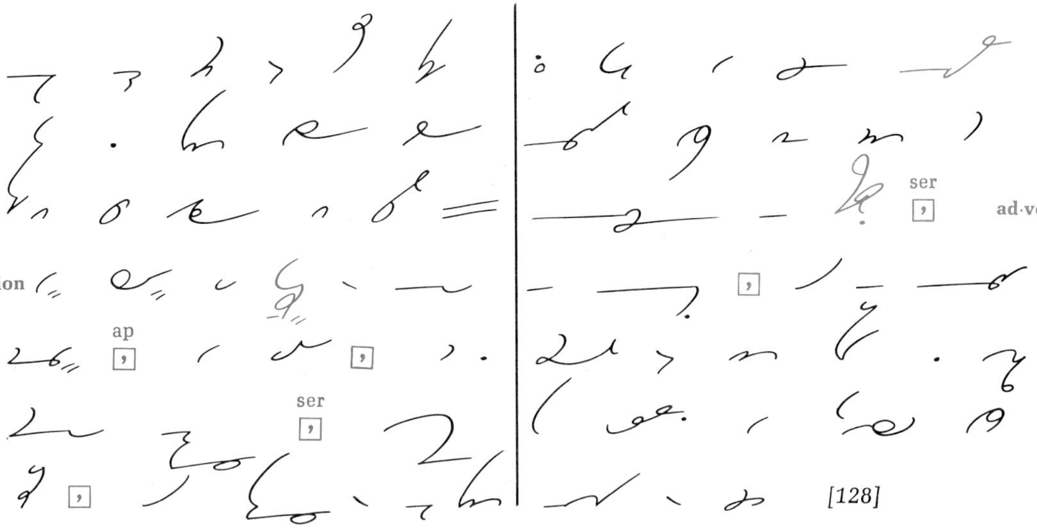

[128]

622

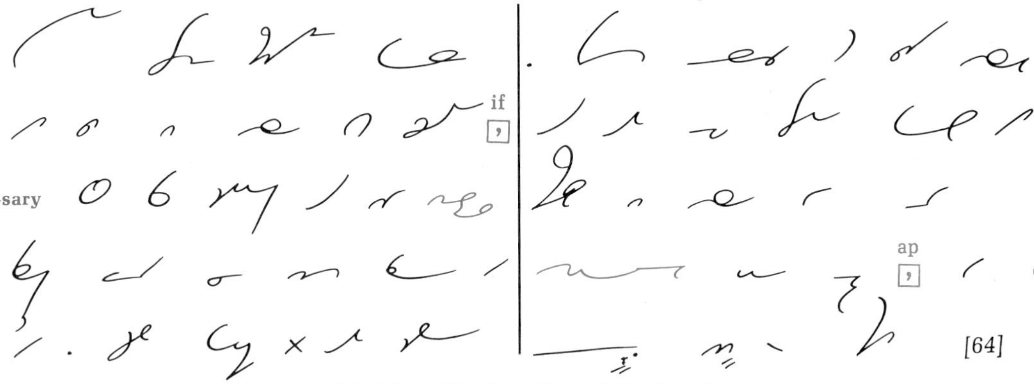

un·nec·es·sary

col·umns

[64]

623

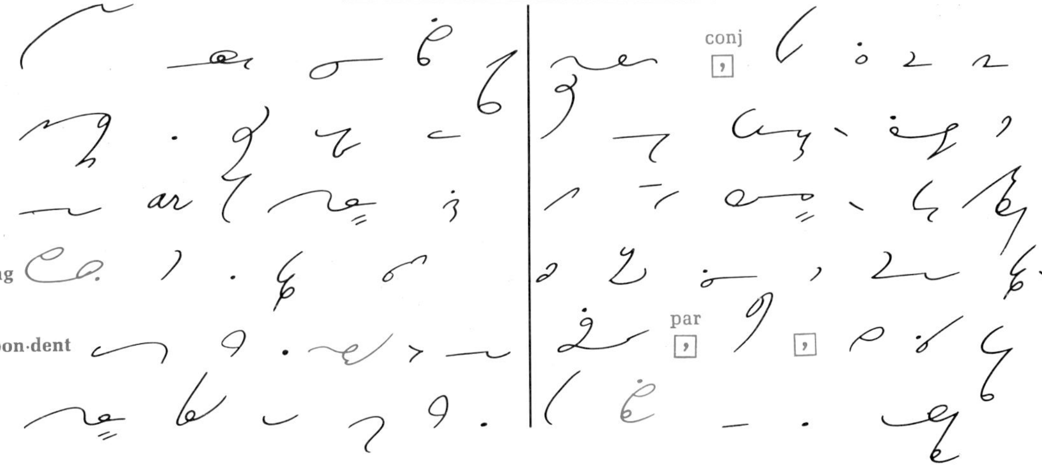

ap·ply·ing

cor·re·spon·dent

hap·pier

ca·pac·i·ty

[114]

624

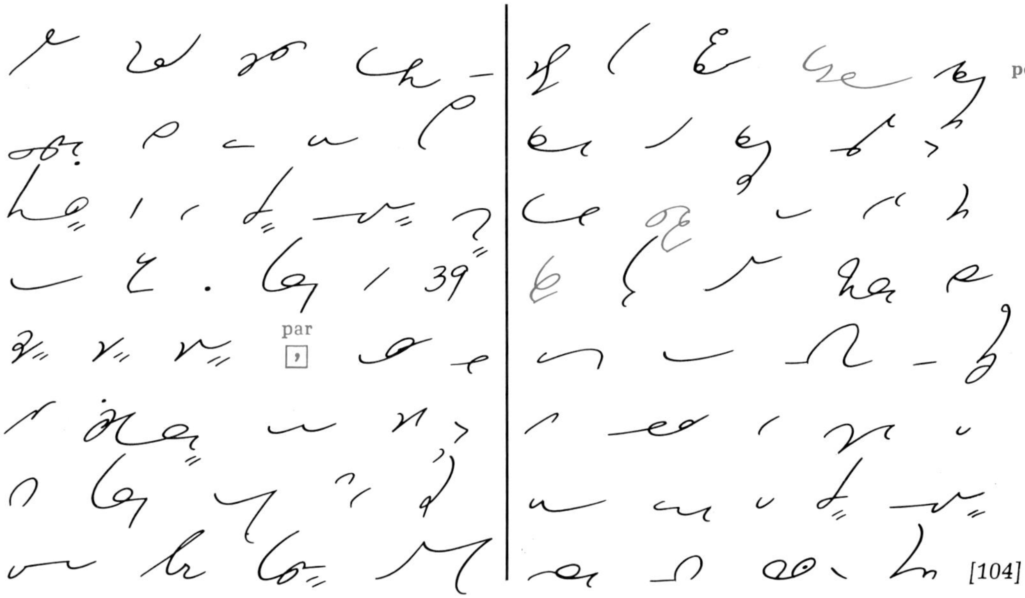

per·son·nel

par

ac·cept

past

[104]

LESSON 67

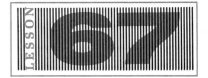

Here is another opportunity to check up on your phrasing skill. This lesson contains 165 phrases.

Building transcription skills

625 **GRAMMAR CHECKUP** | **verbs—with "one of"**

1 In most cases, the expression *one of* takes a singular verb, which agrees with the subject *one*.

One *of the men on the staff* is *ill.*
One *of our typewriters* does not *work.*

2 When *one of* is part of an expression such as *one of those who* or *one of the things that,* a plural verb is used to agree with its antecedent in number.

He solved one of the problems *that* have been (*not* has been) *annoying businessmen for years.*
He is one of the men *who* drive (*not* drives) *to work.*

626

Business vocabulary builder	
	comptroller (pronounced *kon-tro-ler*) The officer of a company who has the responsibility for accounting and financial operations.
	modernize Bring up to date.
	harassing Worrying.

Reading and writing practice

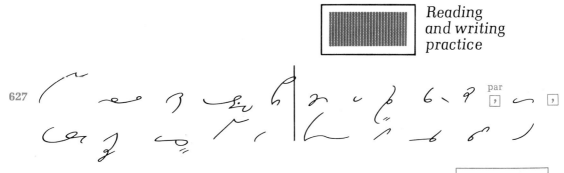

627 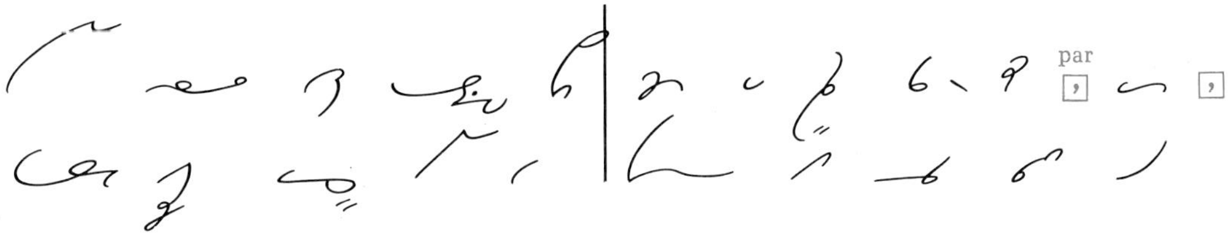

dis·cuss

intro

intro

comp·trol·ler

ap

em·ploy·ees

par

[102]

628

if

wom·en

if

mod·ern·ize

proud

equal·ly

kitch·en

sur·vey

intro

ap

intro

[113]

629

ser

intro

sten·cils

ha·rass·ing

im·me·di·ate·ly

if
if
par
[112]

ob·li·ga·tion

630

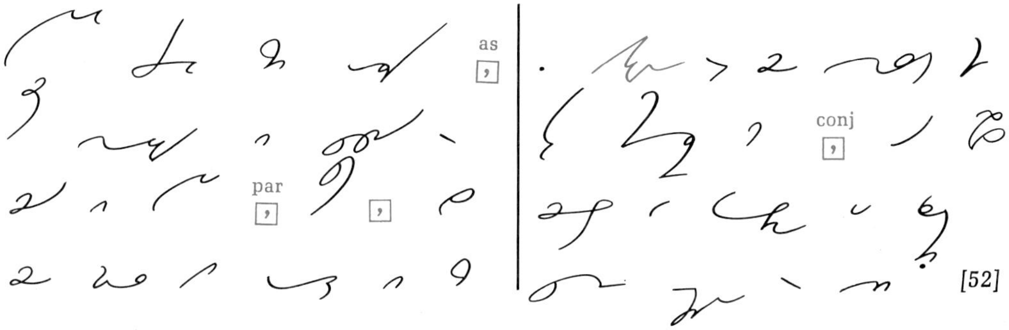
as
par
conj
[52]

de·pos·i·tor

631 Transcription Quiz For you to supply: 5 commas—2 commas introductory, 1 comma *as* clause, 2 commas parenthetical.

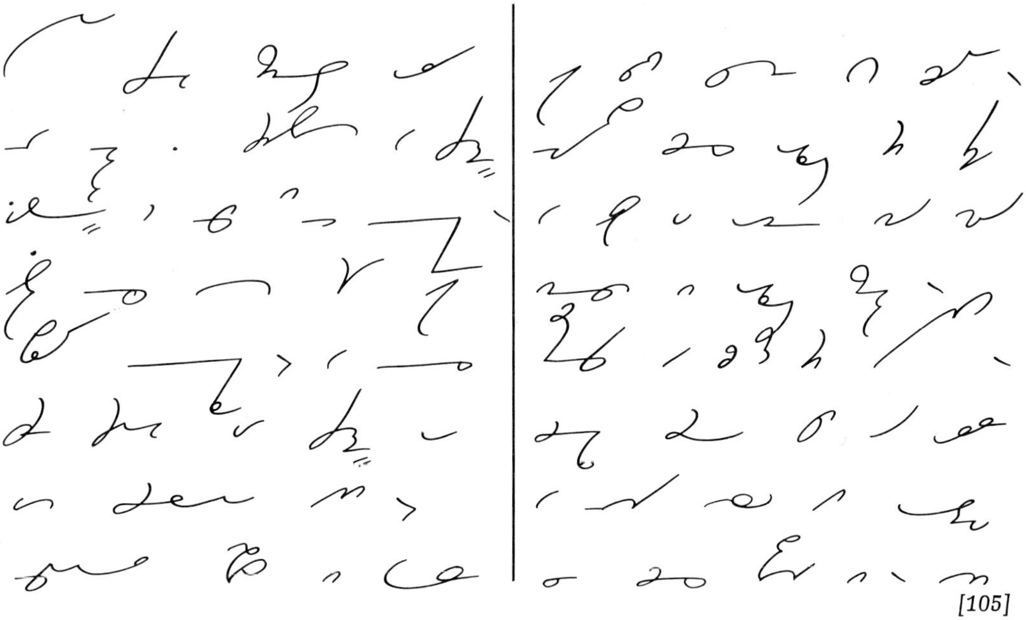
[105]

632

ap·proach·es

past

ris·ing

pros·per·ous

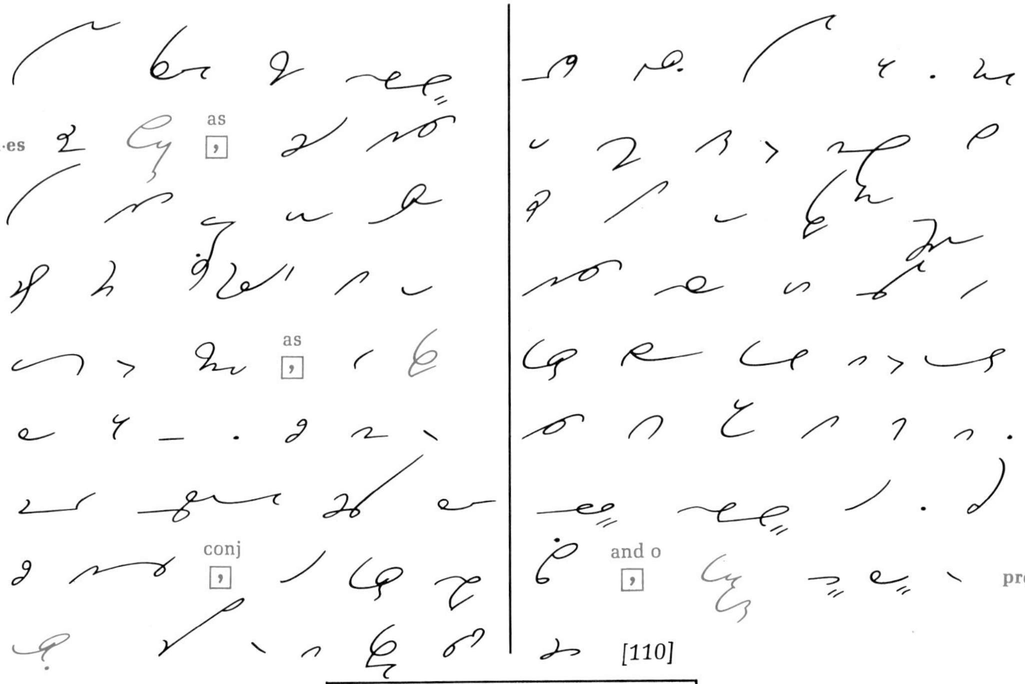
as
as
conj
and o
[110]

633

pur·chase

sal·a·ry

suc·cess·ful

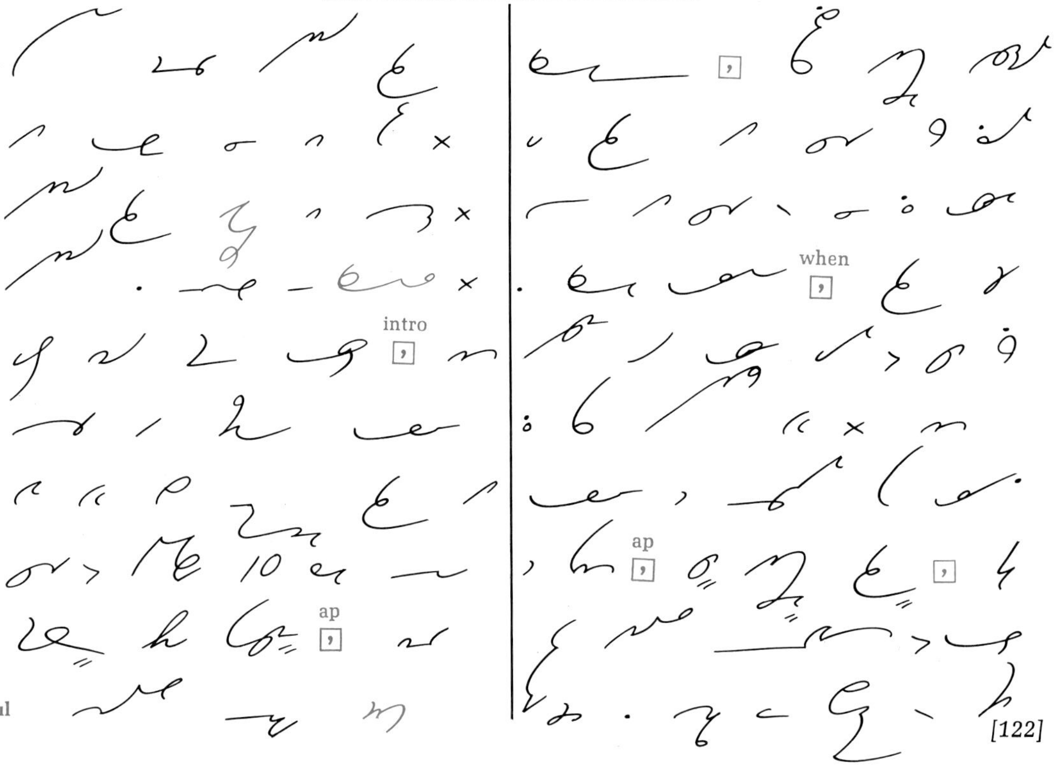
when
intro
ap
ap
[122]

LESSON 68

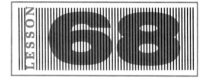

This lesson contains a general review of the major principles of Gregg Shorthand.

Building transcription skills

634 **SIMILAR-WORDS DRILL** | **assistance, assistants**

assistance Help.

You will find many suggestions that will be of assistance *to you.*

assistants Helpers.

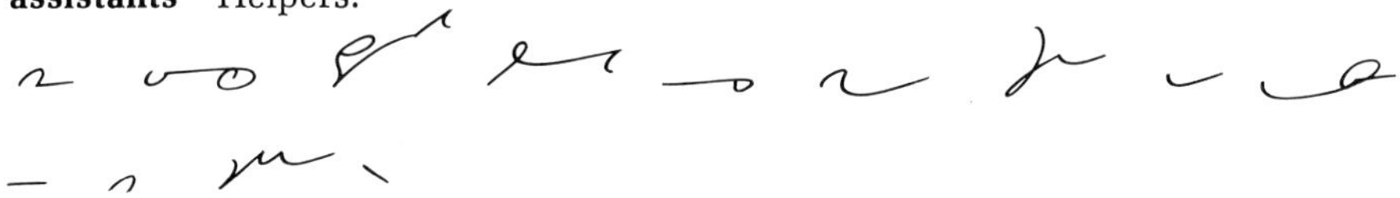

One of my assistants *tells me you will feature our line in your store.*

635

Business vocabulary builder	
	shortcomings Deficiencies; defects.
	fascinating Extremely interesting; charming.
	compensate Pay.

Reading and writing practice

636

sub·scrip·tion

Week·ly

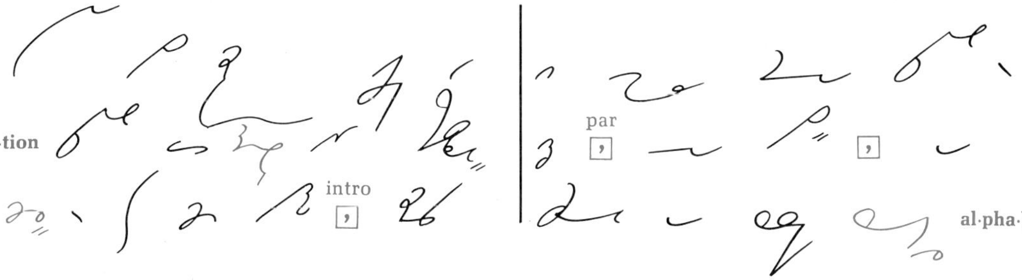
par
intro

al·pha·bet·i·cal·ly

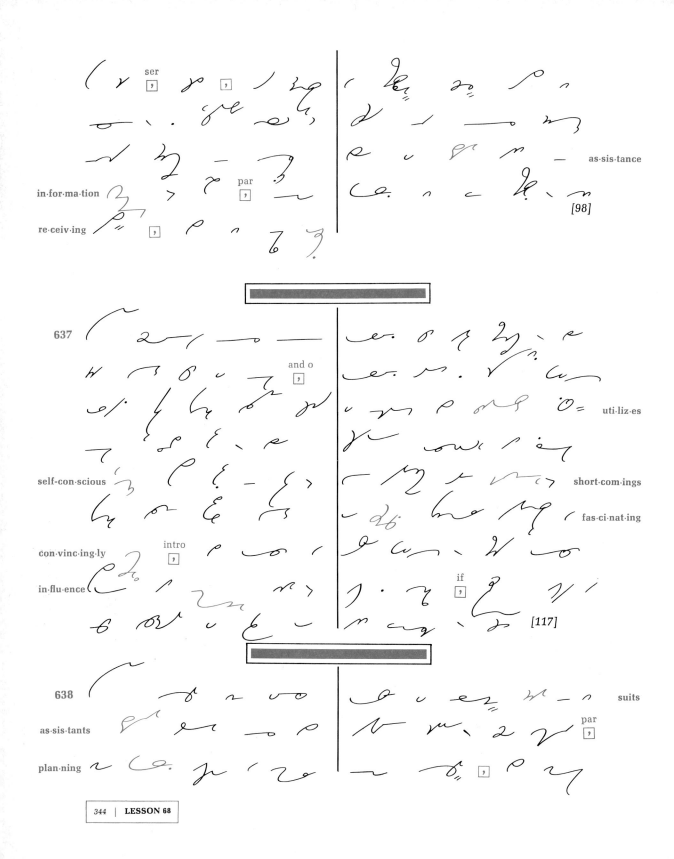

ser

par

in·for·ma·tion

re·ceiv·ing

as·sis·tance

[98]

637

and o

self-con·scious

con·vinc·ing·ly

intro

in·flu·ence

uti·liz·es

short·com·ings

fas·ci·nat·ing

if

[117]

638

as·sis·tants

plan·ning

suits

par

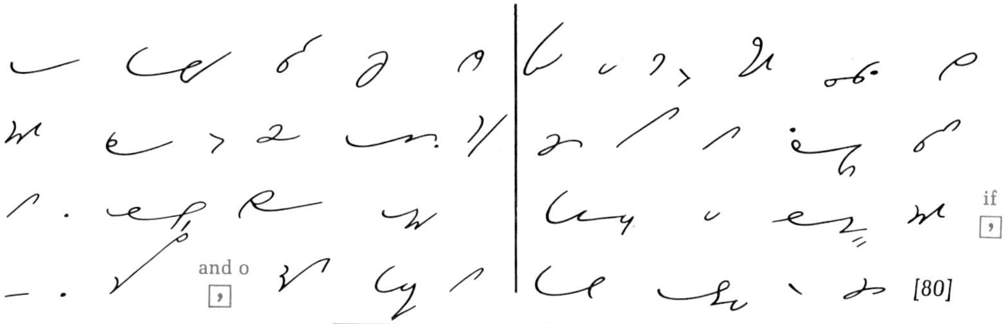
and o
if
[80]

639

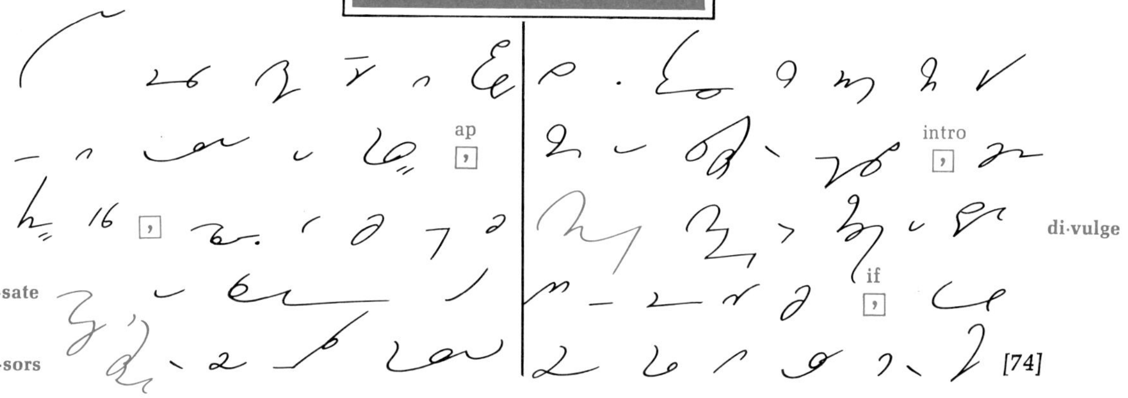
ap
intro
di·vulge
com·pen·sate
if
su·per·vi·sors
[74]

640 Transcription Quiz For you to supply: 5 commas—1 comma conjunction, 2 commas series, 1 comma introductory, 1 comma *when* clause.

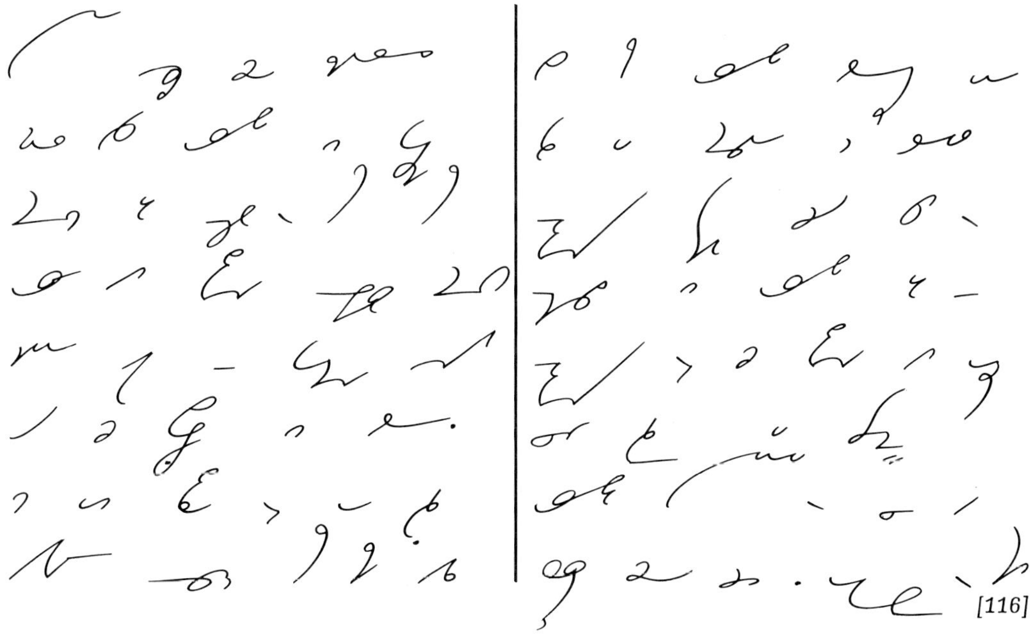
[116]

641
al·ways
su·pe·ri·or
switch·ing
op·er·a·tor
pro·fi·cient

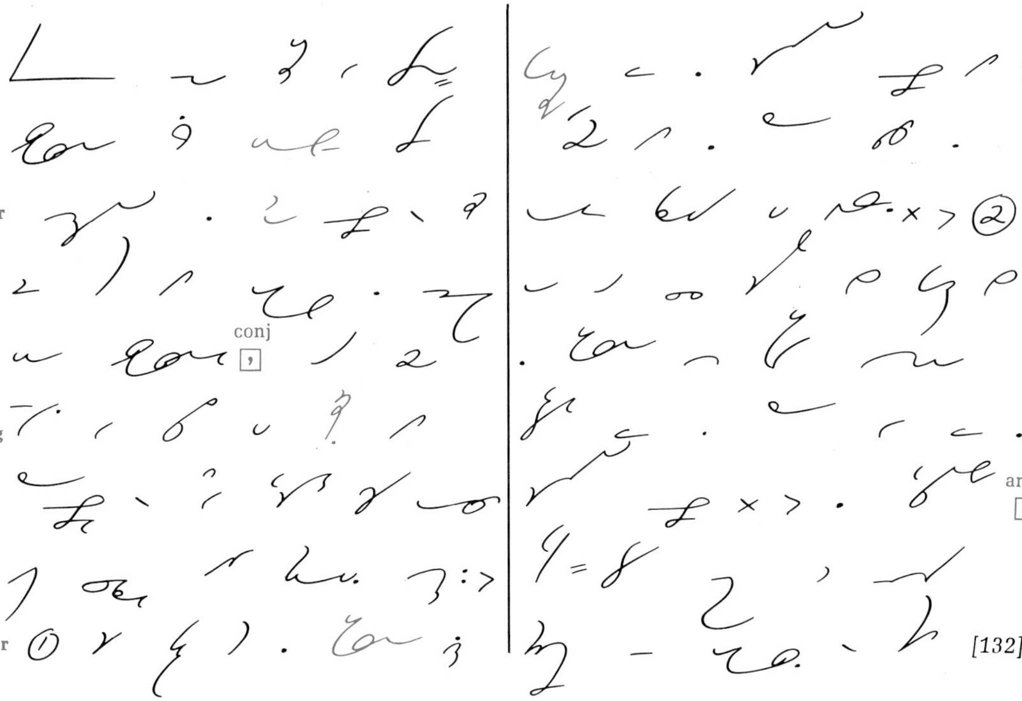
conj
and o
[132]

642
fran·chise
dif·fi·cult
pa·tient

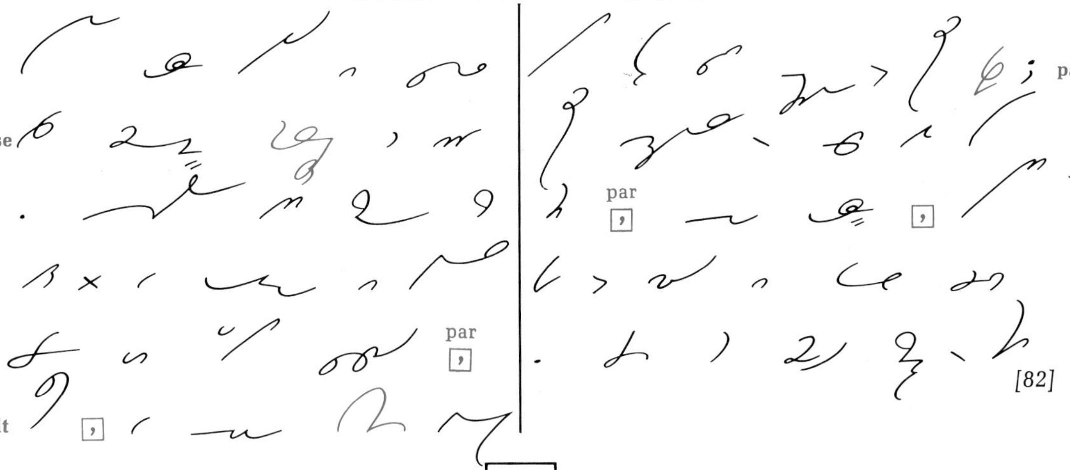
par
par
[82]

643

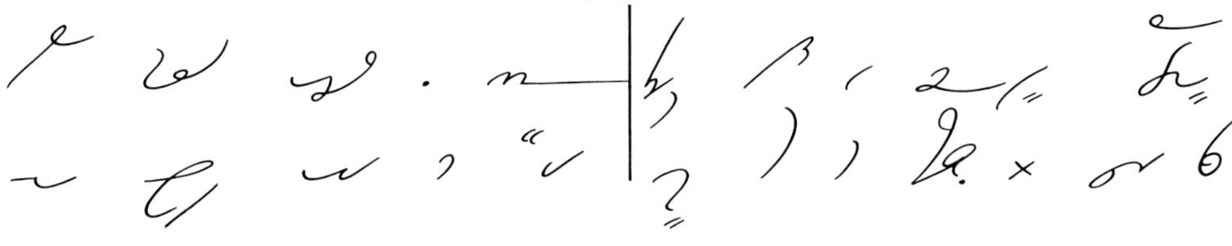

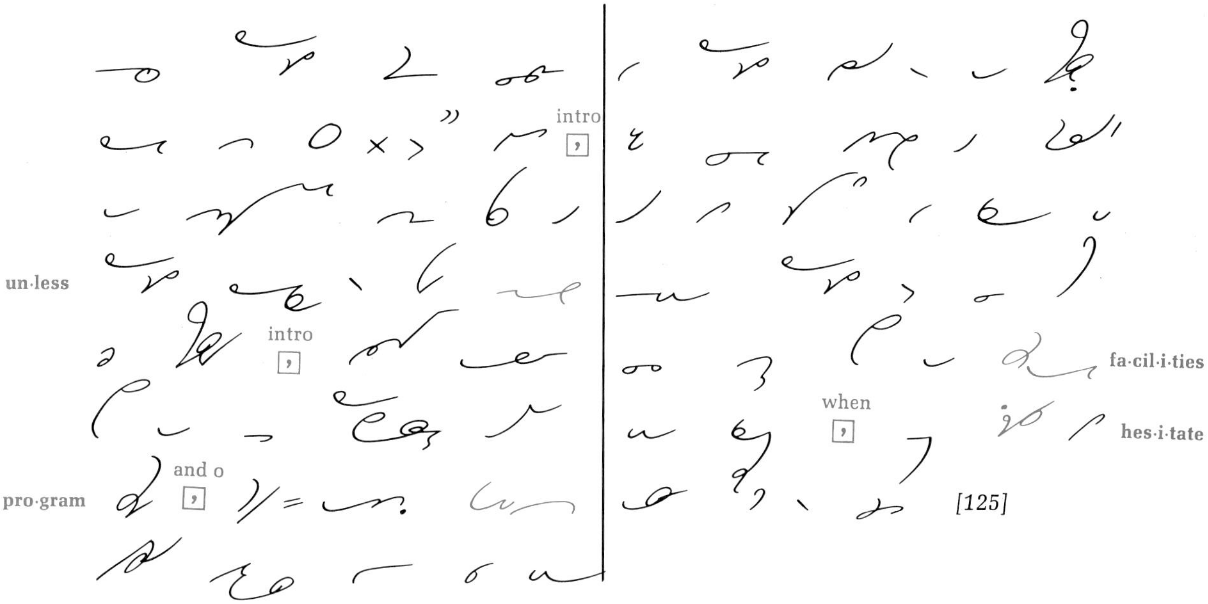
un·less
intro
intro
and o
pro·gram
fa·cil·i·ties
when
hes·i·tate
[125]

DICTATION CHECK LIST

When you take dictation, do you—

☐ **1** Make every effort to keep up with the dictator?

☐ **2** Refer to your textbook whenever you are in doubt about the outline for a word or phrase?

☐ **3** Insert periods and question marks in your shorthand notes?

☐ **4** Make a real effort to observe good proportion as you write—making large circles large, small circles small, etc.?

☐ **5** Write down the first column of your notebook and then down the second column?

LESSON 69

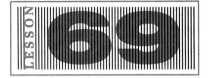

You won't be able to refrain from chuckling as you read the "hotel" letters in the Reading and Writing Practice of this lesson. They are an exchange of letters between a hotel manager and a guest.

Building transcription skills

644 COMMON PREFIXES | **pre-**

pre- before, beforehand

predict To tell beforehand; to prophesy.

preliminary Coming before the main business.

premature Happening before the proper time.

prearrange To arrange beforehand.

645

Business vocabulary builder	
	desolated Sad; unhappy; disappointed.
	conceivably Possibly.
	establishment Place of business.

Reading and writing practice

646

cus·tom·ary

wool·en

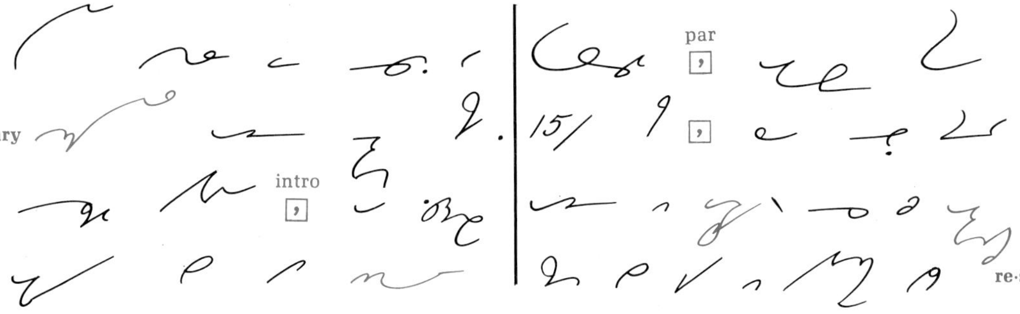

intro
par

oc·cu·pied

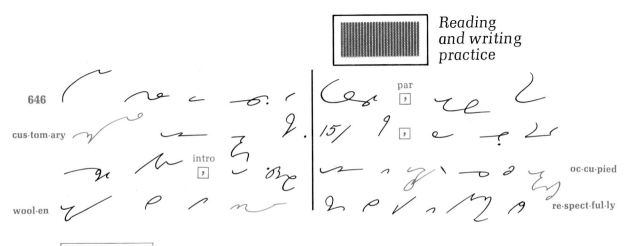

re·spect·ful·ly

catch

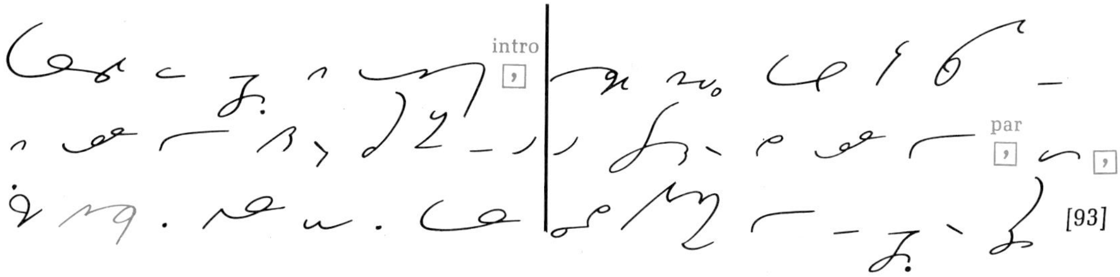

intro
par
[93]

647

des·o·lat·ed

slight
sou·ve·nirs

vis·i·tor

con·ceiv·ably

oc·cu·pied

ap
par
par
intro
intro

lan·guage

maid

gen·tle·man·ly

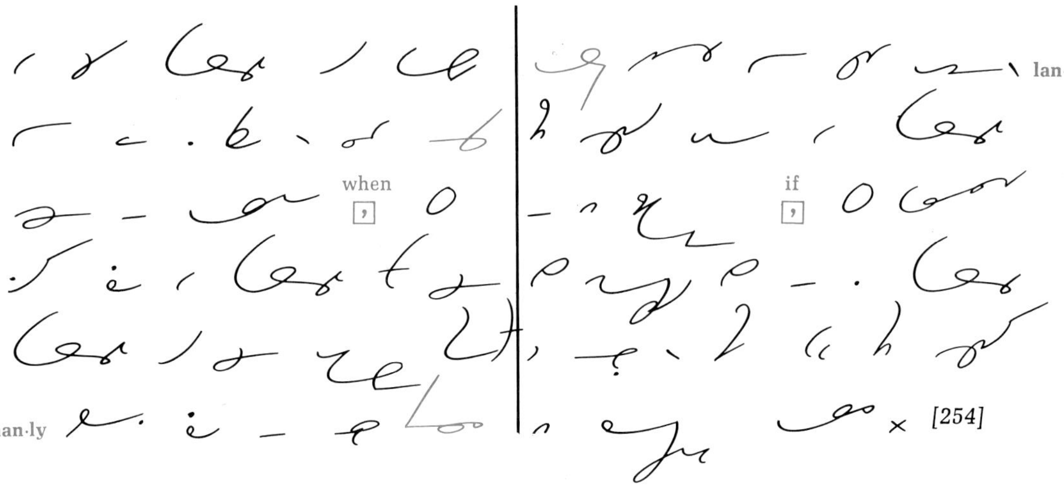

when
if
[254]

648 Transcription Quiz For you to supply: 6 commas—2 commas series, 1 comma introductory, 1 comma conjunction, 2 commas parenthetical.

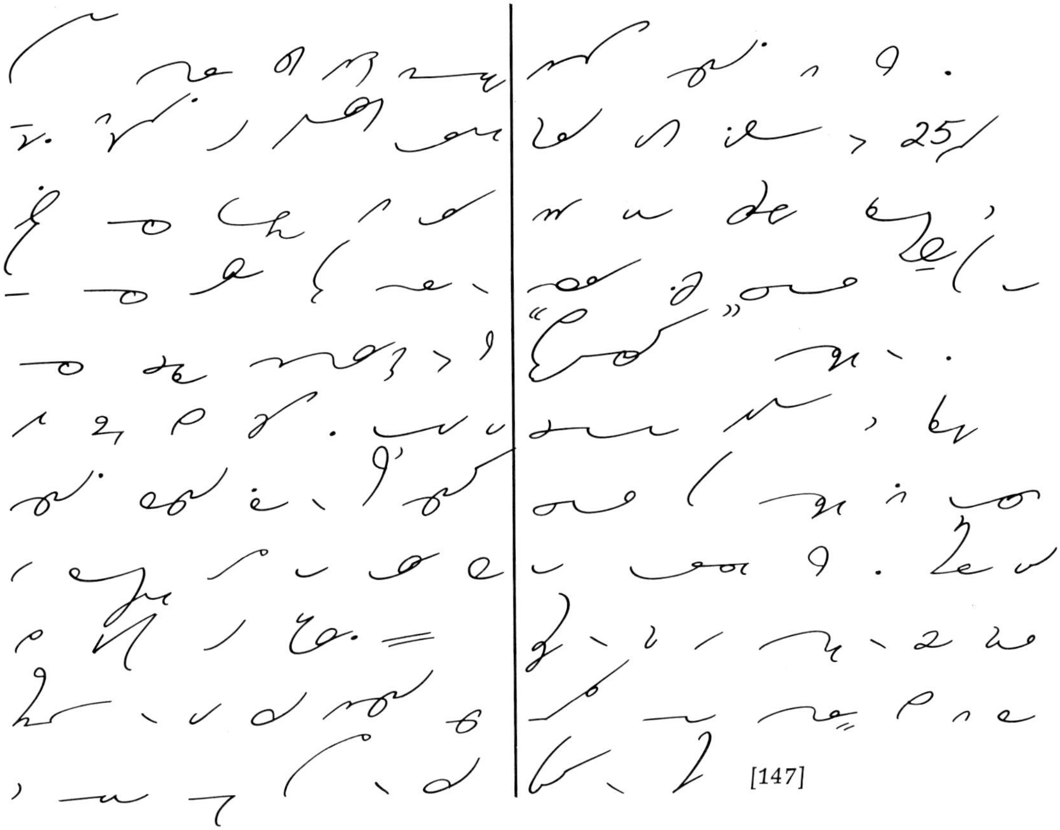

[147]

649

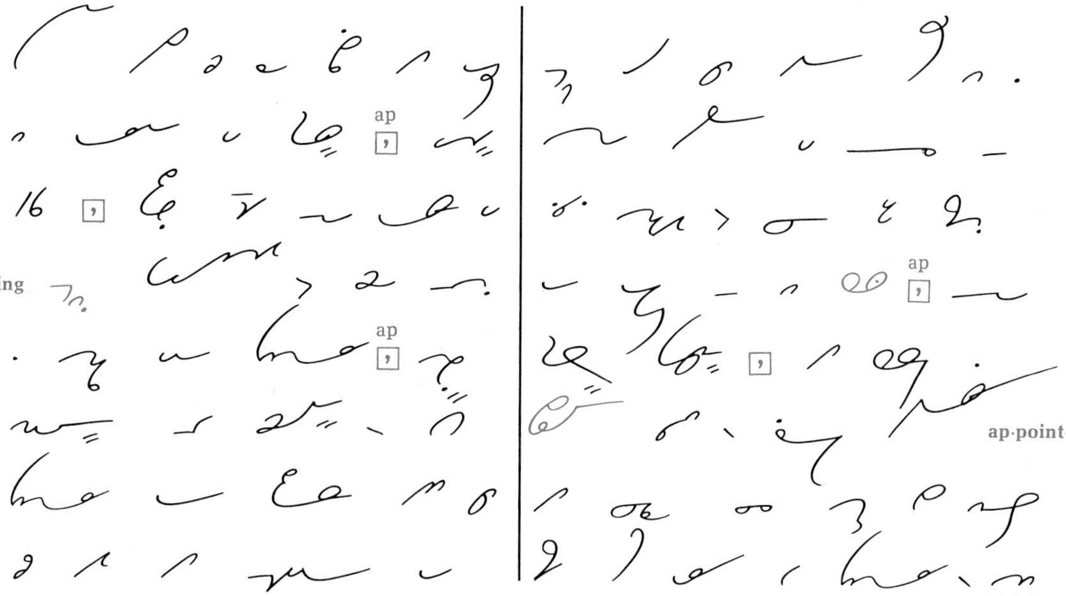
ap
ap
ap

in·su·lat·ing

ar·ea

ap·point·ment

[110]

650

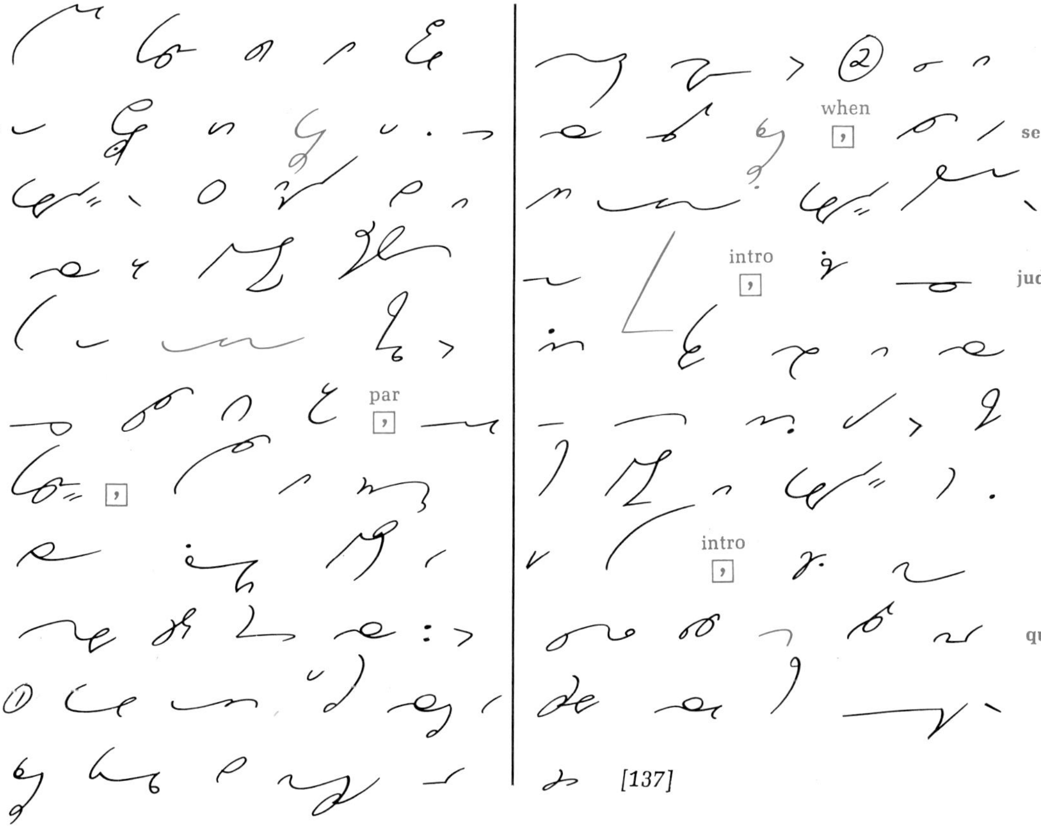
when
intro
par
intro

pur·chase

serv·ic·ing

judg·ment

lo·cal

ques·tion

[137]

LESSON 70

The articles in this lesson contain information that will be of great help to you when you enter the business world. Read and study the articles carefully.

Building transcription skills

651 **SPELLING FAMILIES** | **past tense with r**

Past Tenses in Which R Is Doubled

blurred	**de·ferred**	**pre·ferred**
con·curred	**in·ferred**	**re·ferred**
con·ferred	**oc·curred**	**trans·ferred**

Past Tenses in Which R Is Not Doubled

cov·ered	**ma·jored**	**hon·ored**
dif·fered	**of·fered**	**suf·fered**

652 *Business vocabulary builder*

exerting Putting forth.

habitually Usually; by force of habit.

clue Hint.

dedication Devotion.

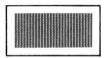

Reading and writing practice

Reading Scoreboard Now that you are on the last lesson, you are no doubt very much interested in your final shorthand reading rate. If you have followed the practice suggestions you received early in the course, your shorthand reading rate at this time should be a source of pride to you.

To get a real picture of how much your shorthand reading rate has increased with practice, compare it with your reading rate in Lesson 18, the first time you measured it.

Lesson 70 contains 702 words.

If you read Lesson 70 in **14 minutes** *your reading rate is* **50 words a minute**
If you read Lesson 70 in **16 minutes** *your reading rate is* **44 words a minute**
If you read Lesson 70 in **18 minutes** *your reading rate is* **39 words a minute**
If you read Lesson 70 in **20 minutes** *your reading rate is* **35 words a minute**
If you read Lesson 70 in **22 minutes** *your reading rate is* **32 words a minute**
If you read Lesson 70 in **24 minutes** *your reading rate is* **29 words a minute**

653 Names

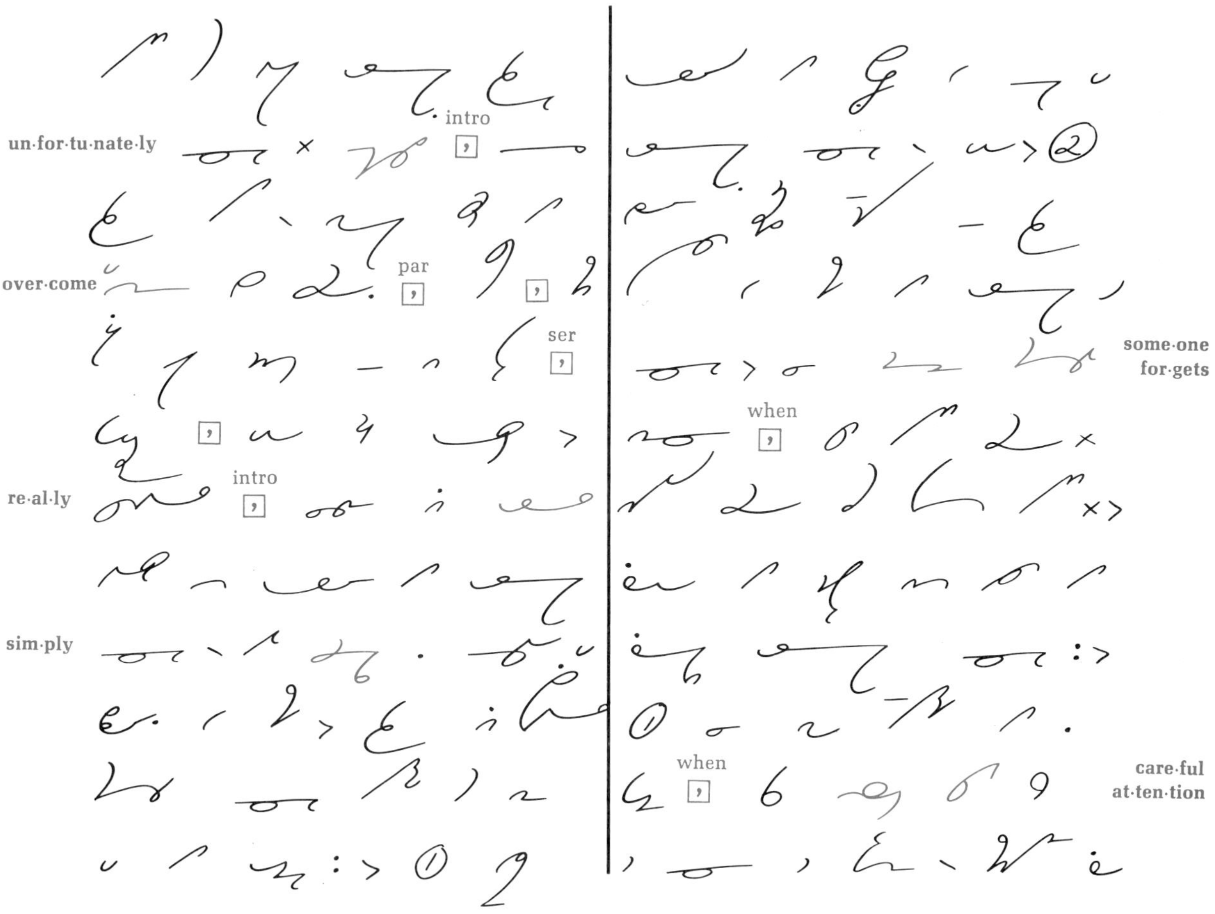
un·for·tu·nate·ly
intro
over·come
par
ser
re·al·ly
intro
sim·ply
when
some·one
for·gets
when
care·ful
at·ten·tion

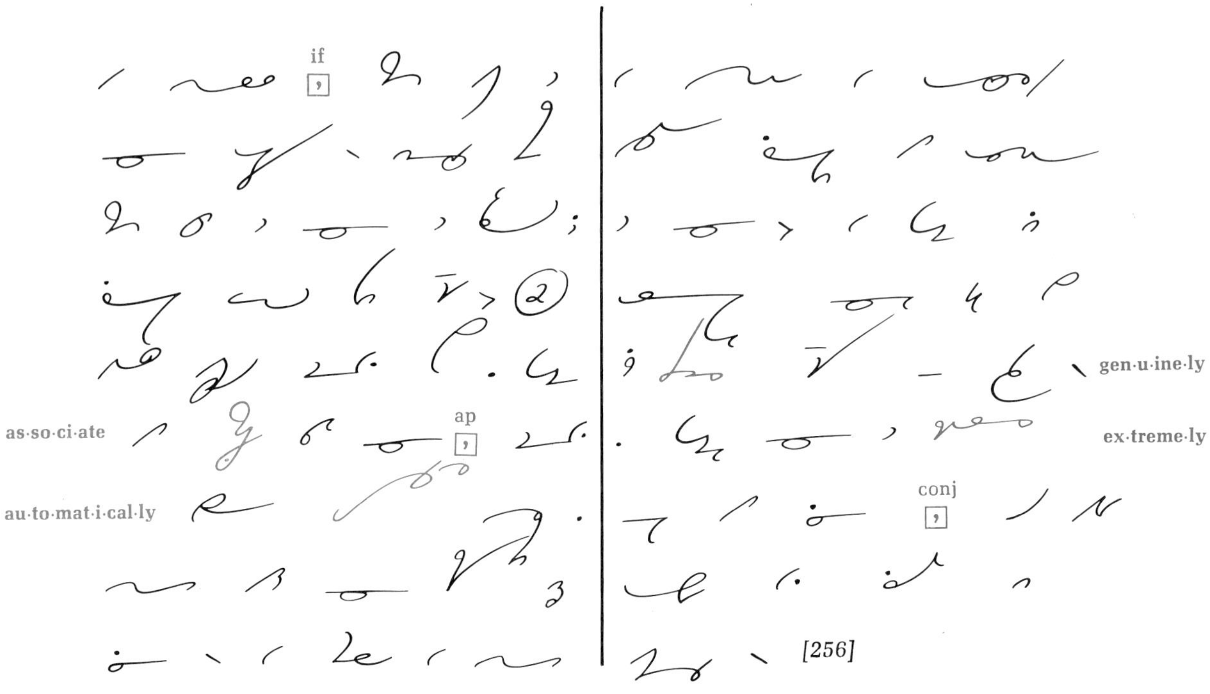
if
gen·u·ine·ly
as·so·ci·ate
ap
ex·treme·ly
au·to·mat·i·cal·ly
conj
[256]

654 Loyalty

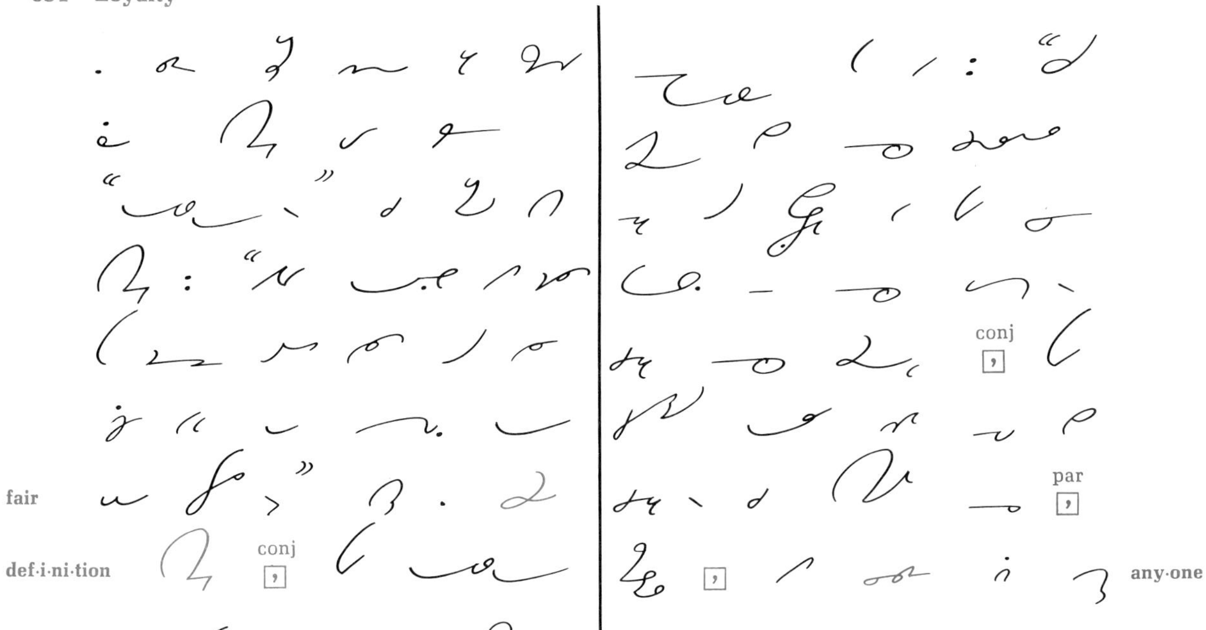
conj
par
fair
def·i·ni·tion
conj
any·one

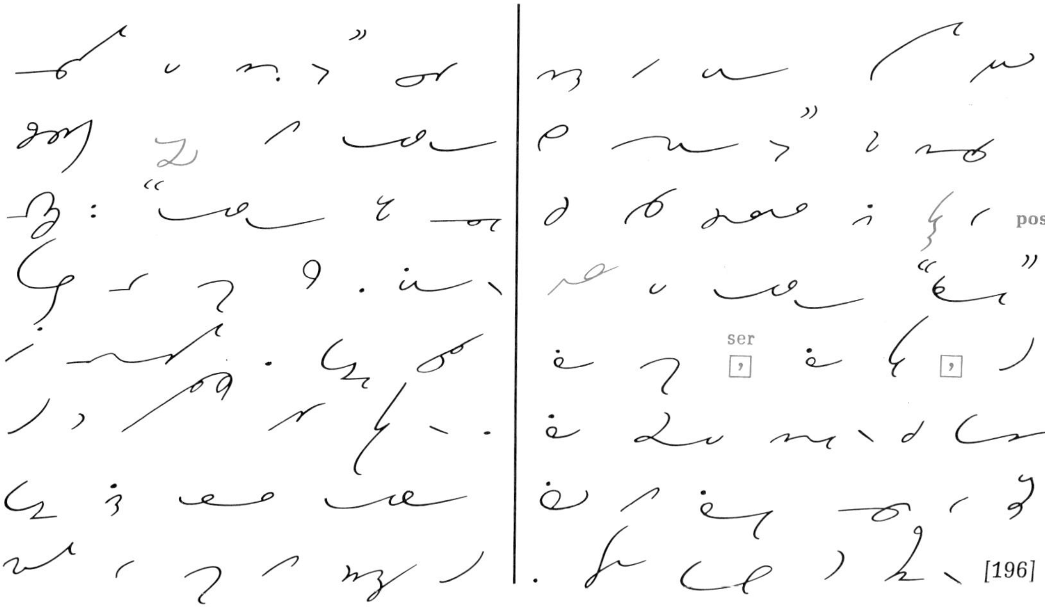
ser
[196]

re·ferred

pos·ses·ses

trait

655 Judgment

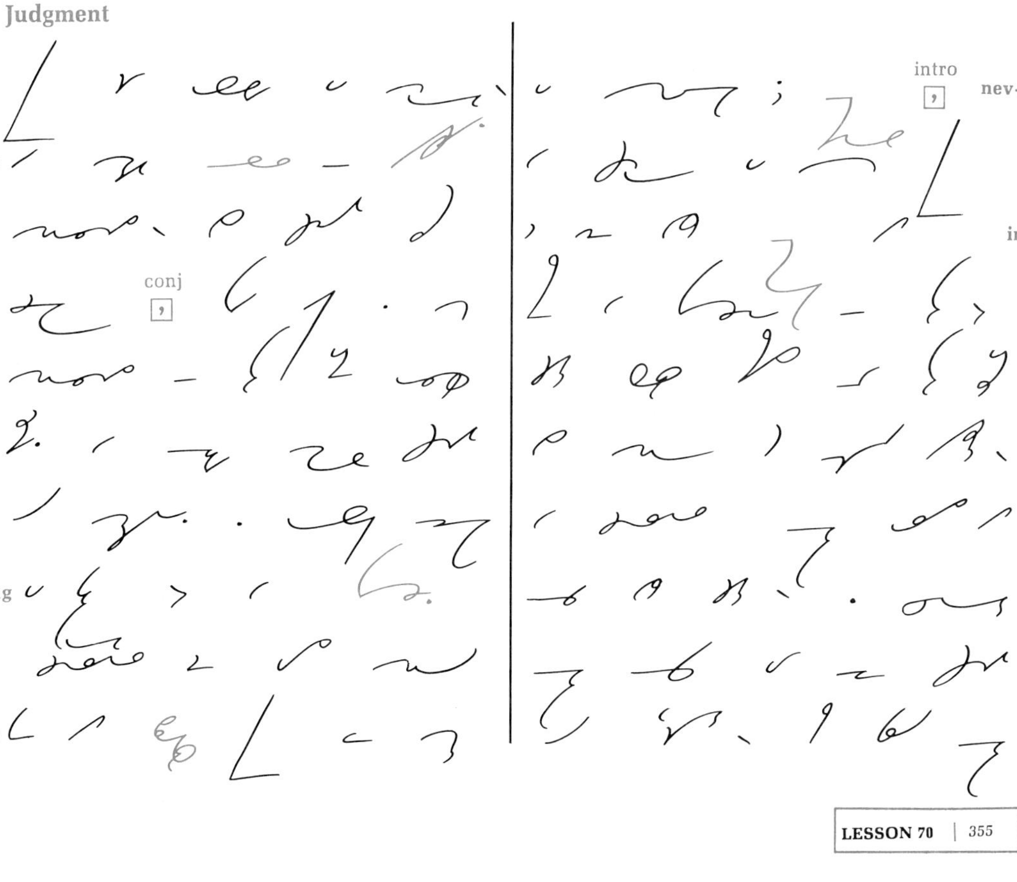
conj
intro

mere·ly

de·cid·ing

nev·er·the·less

in·valu·able

be·gin·ning

ex·er·cise

weighed

rea·son·ing

im·pulse

ax·i·om

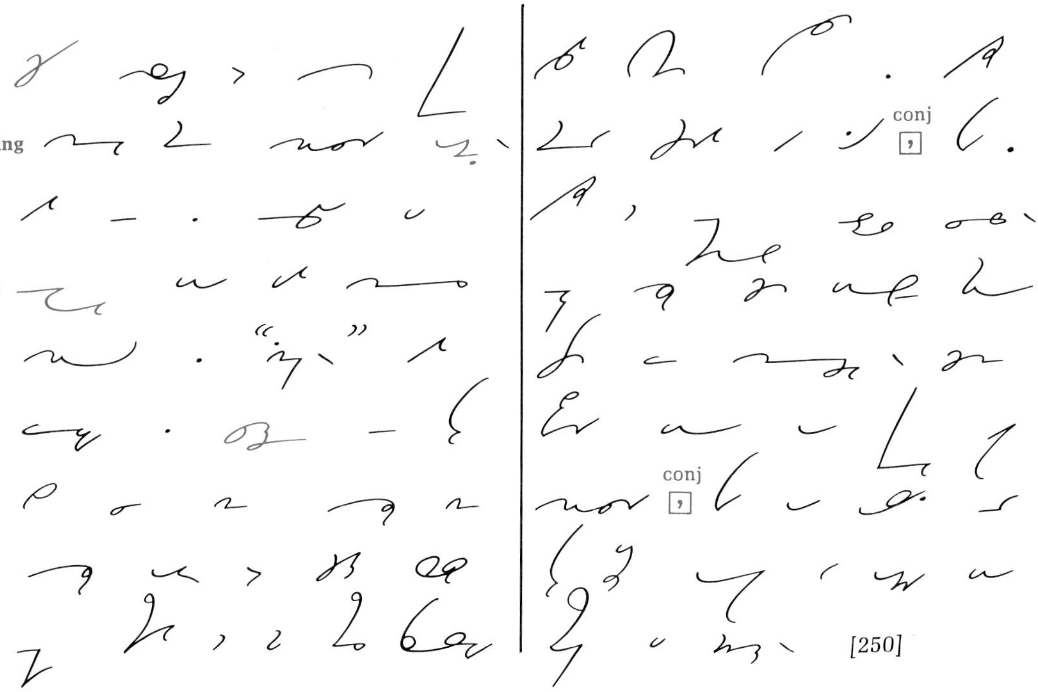
conj
conj
[250]

APPENDIX

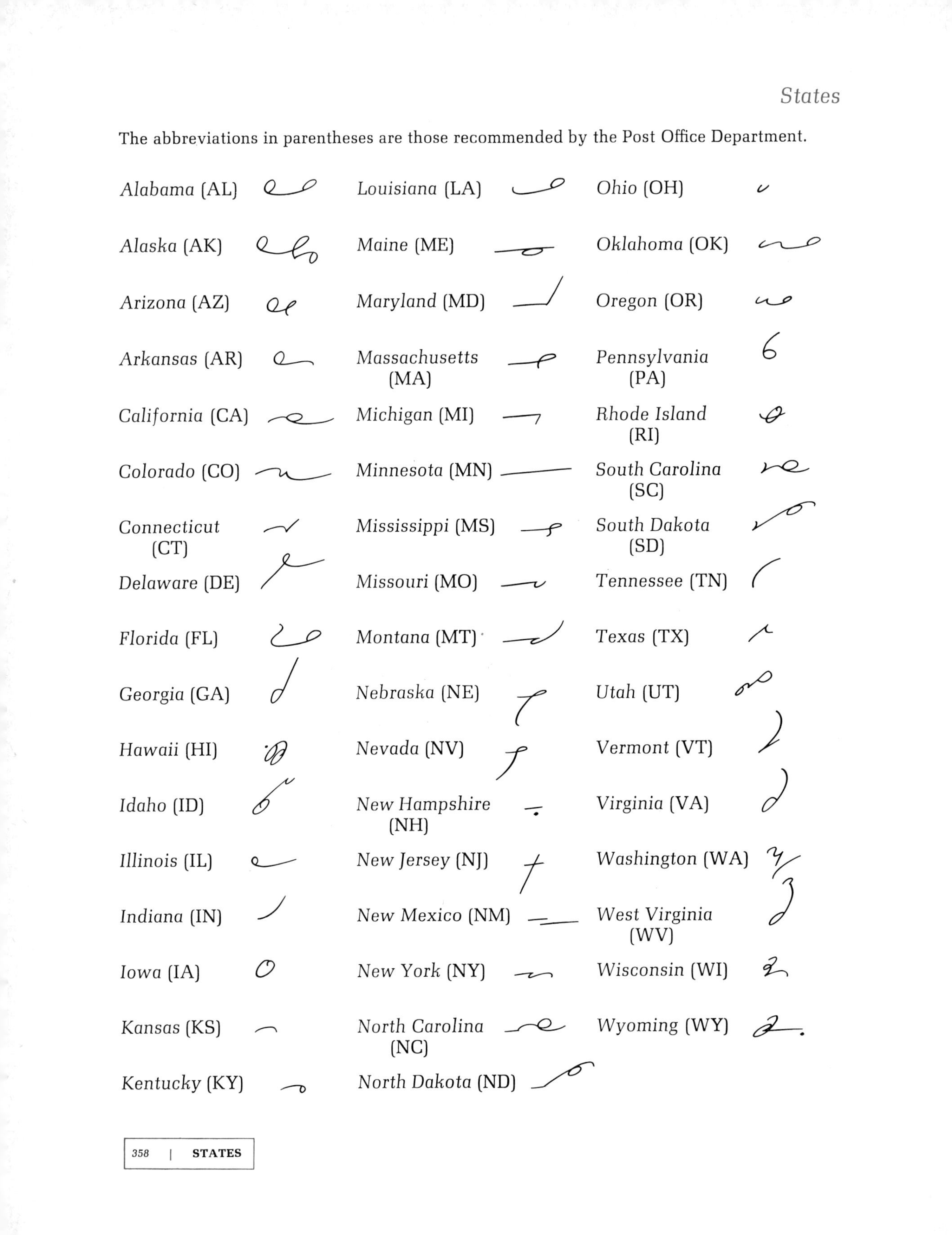

The abbreviations in parentheses are those recommended by the Post Office Department.

Alabama (AL)
Alaska (AK)
Arizona (AZ)
Arkansas (AR)
California (CA)
Colorado (CO)
Connecticut (CT)
Delaware (DE)
Florida (FL)
Georgia (GA)
Hawaii (HI)
Idaho (ID)
Illinois (IL)
Indiana (IN)
Iowa (IA)
Kansas (KS)
Kentucky (KY)
Louisiana (LA)
Maine (ME)
Maryland (MD)
Massachusetts (MA)
Michigan (MI)
Minnesota (MN)
Mississippi (MS)
Missouri (MO)
Montana (MT)
Nebraska (NE)
Nevada (NV)
New Hampshire (NH)
New Jersey (NJ)
New Mexico (NM)
New York (NY)
North Carolina (NC)
North Dakota (ND)
Ohio (OH)
Oklahoma (OK)
Oregon (OR)
Pennsylvania (PA)
Rhode Island (RI)
South Carolina (SC)
South Dakota (SD)
Tennessee (TN)
Texas (TX)
Utah (UT)
Vermont (VT)
Virginia (VA)
Washington (WA)
West Virginia (WV)
Wisconsin (WI)
Wyoming (WY)

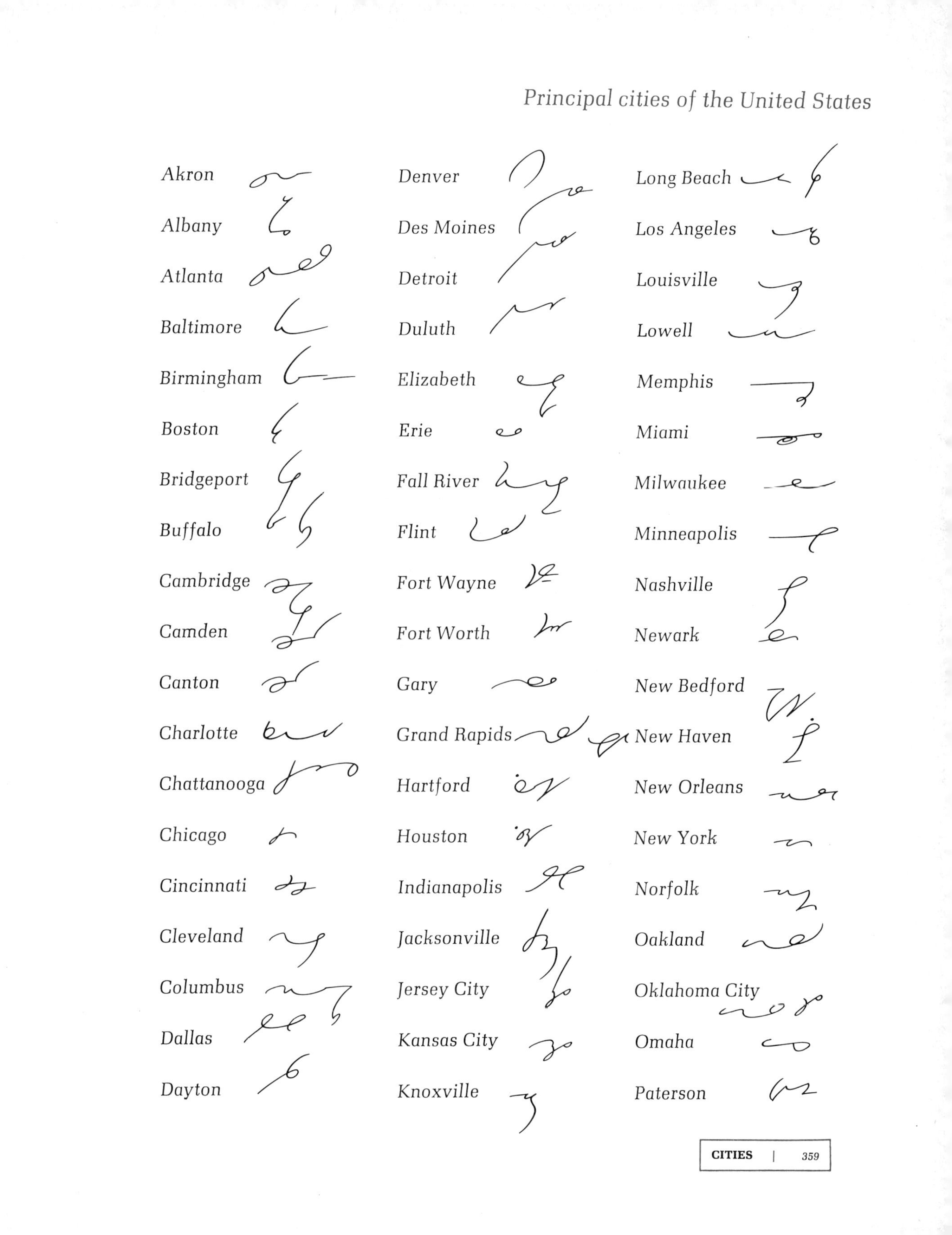

Akron
Albany
Atlanta
Baltimore
Birmingham
Boston
Bridgeport
Buffalo
Cambridge
Camden
Canton
Charlotte
Chattanooga
Chicago
Cincinnati
Cleveland
Columbus
Dallas
Dayton

Denver
Des Moines
Detroit
Duluth
Elizabeth
Erie
Fall River
Flint
Fort Wayne
Fort Worth
Gary
Grand Rapids
Hartford
Houston
Indianapolis
Jacksonville
Jersey City
Kansas City
Knoxville

Long Beach
Los Angeles
Louisville
Lowell
Memphis
Miami
Milwaukee
Minneapolis
Nashville
Newark
New Bedford
New Haven
New Orleans
New York
Norfolk
Oakland
Oklahoma City
Omaha
Paterson

Peoria
Philadelphia
Pittsburgh
Portland
Providence
Reading
Richmond
Rochester
Sacramento
St. Louis
St. Paul

Salt Lake City
San Antonio
San Diego
San Francisco
Scranton
Seattle
Somerville
South Bend
Spokane
Springfield
Syracuse

Tacoma
Tampa
Toledo
Trenton
Tulsa
Utica
Washington
Wichita
Wilmington
Worcester
Yonkers

Common geographical abbreviations

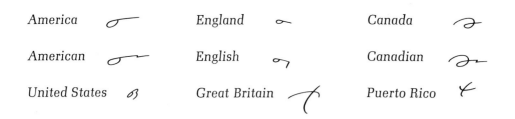

America
American
United States

England
English
Great Britain

Canada
Canadian
Puerto Rico

JOINED WORD ENDINGS

1 -ment

2 -tion

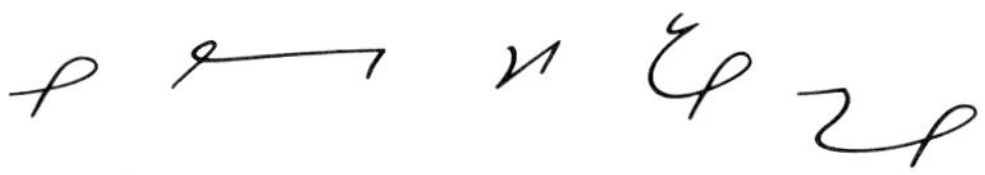

3 -tial

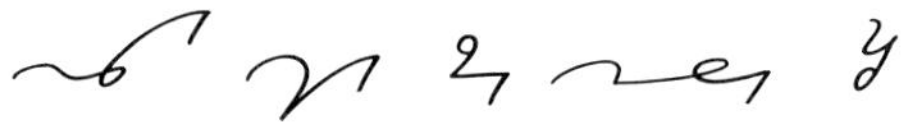

4 -ly

5 -ily

6 -ful

7 -sume, -sumption

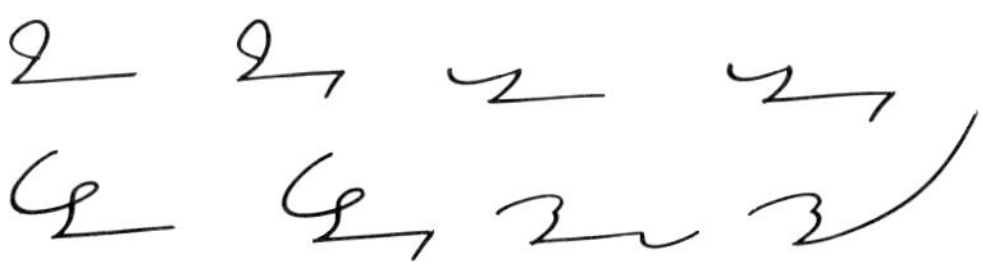

8 -ble

9 -ther

10 -ual

11 -ure

12 -self, -selves

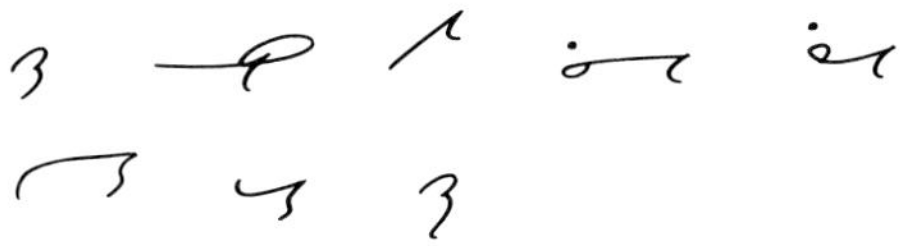

13 -ort

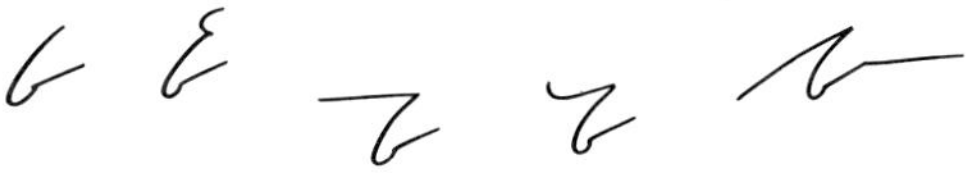

14 -tain

15 -cient, -ciency

DISJOINED WORD ENDINGS

16 -hood

17 -ward

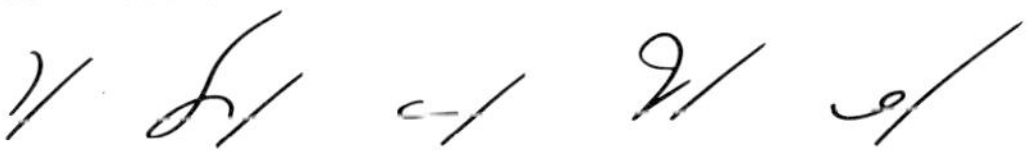

18 -ship

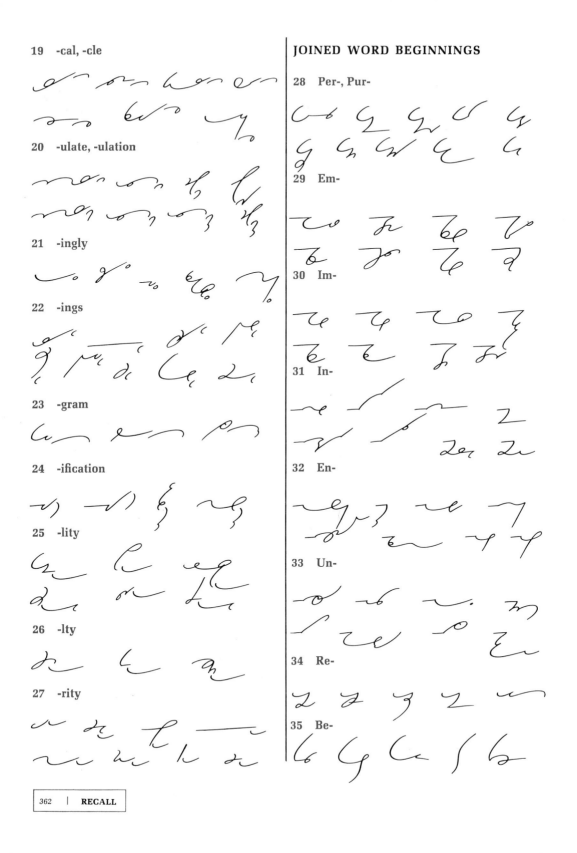

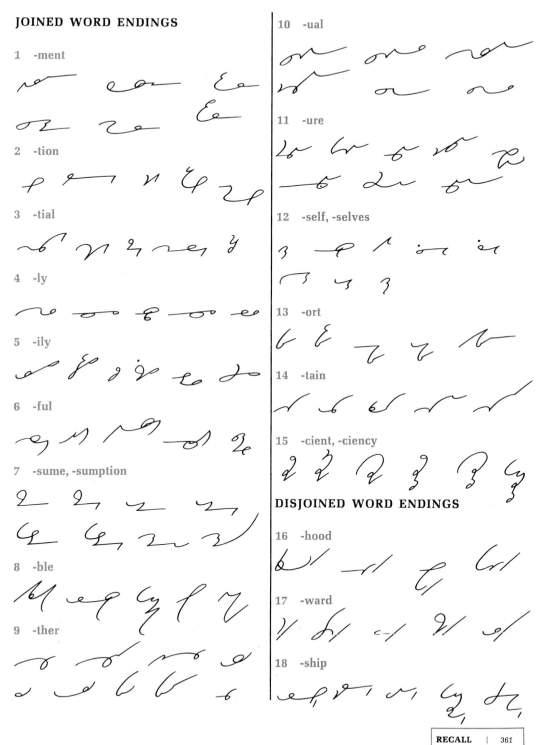

19 -cal, -cle

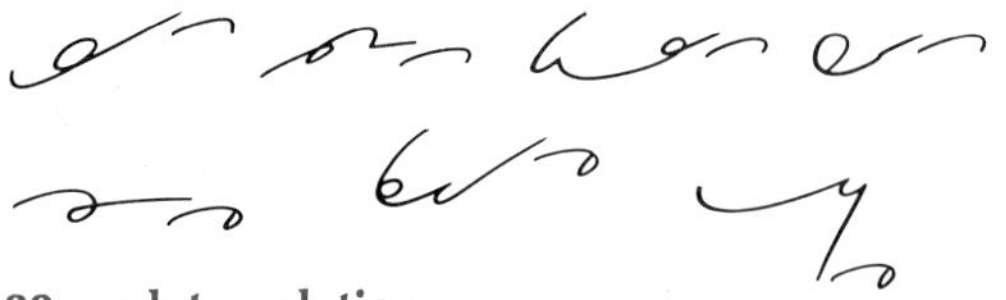

20 -ulate, -ulation

21 -ingly

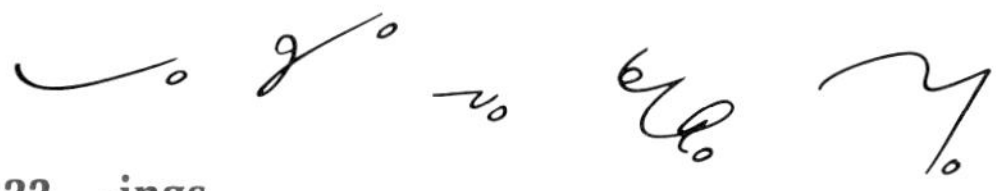

22 -ings

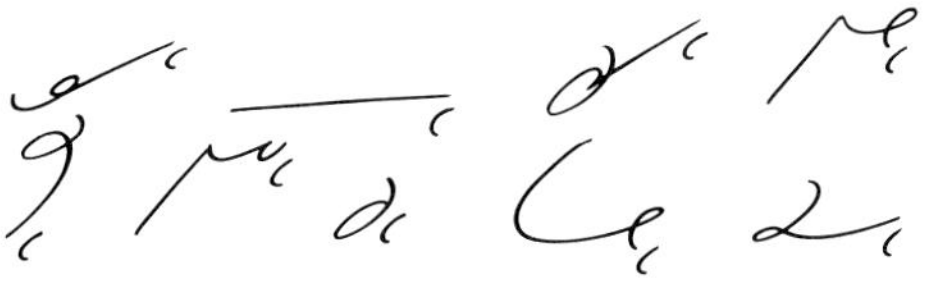

23 -gram

24 -ification

25 -lity

26 -lty

27 -rity

JOINED WORD BEGINNINGS

28 Per-, Pur-

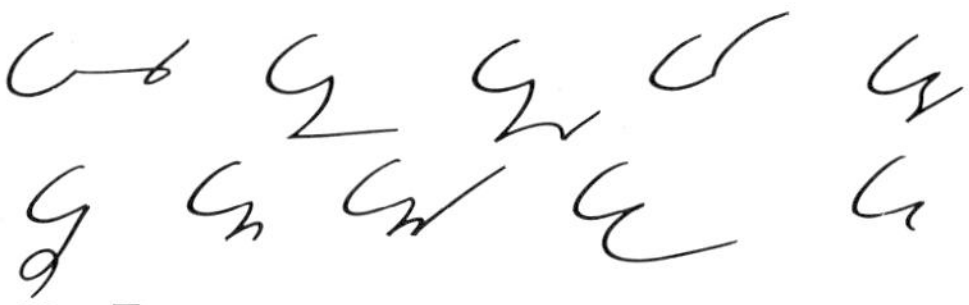

29 Em-

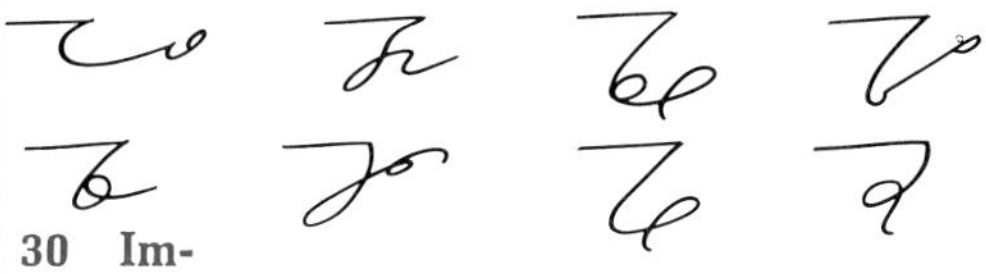

30 Im-

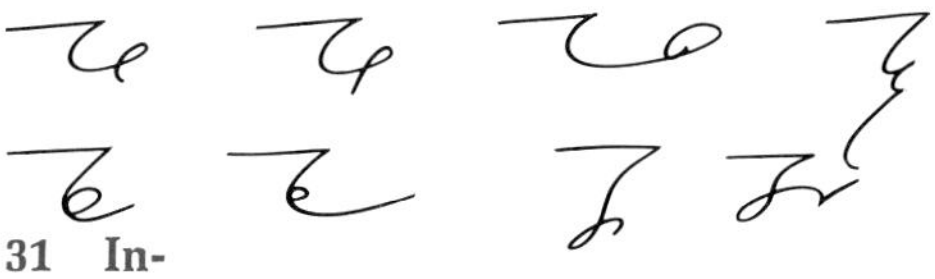

31 In-

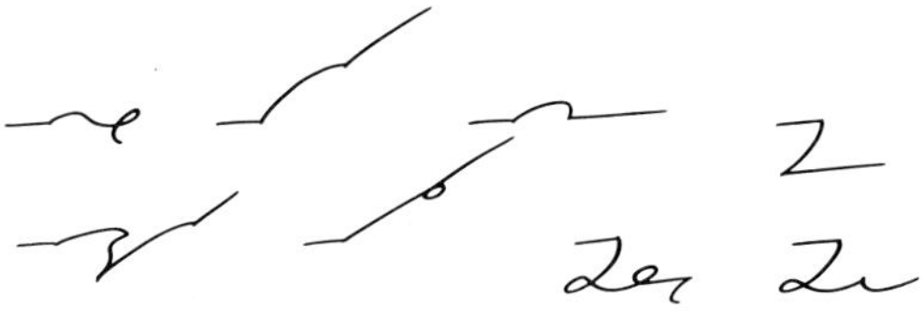

32 En-

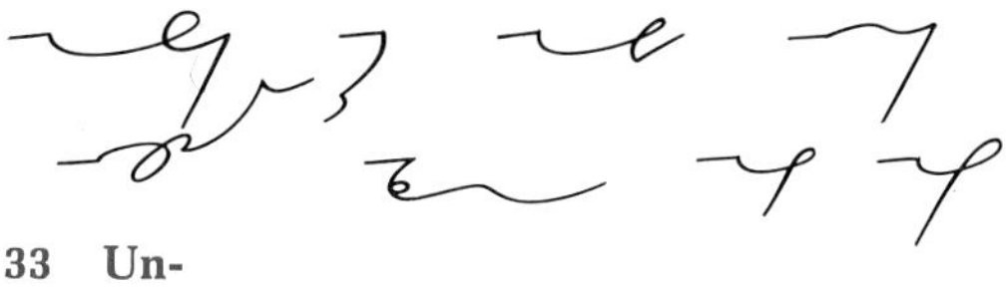

33 Un-

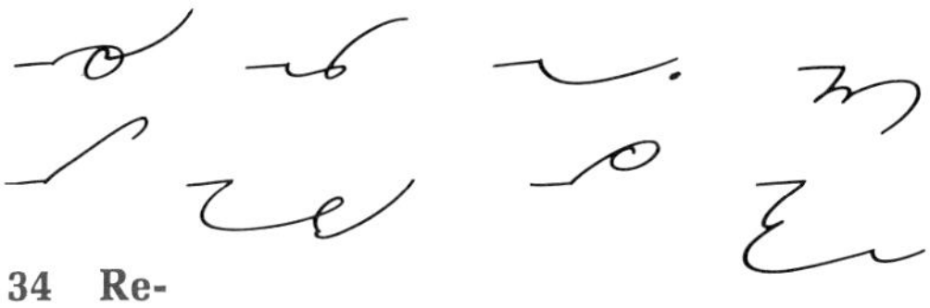

34 Re-

35 Be-

36 De-, Di-

37 Dis-, Des-

38 Mis-

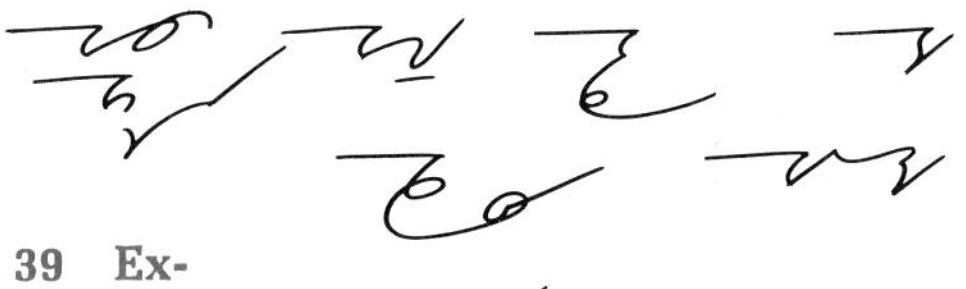

39 Ex-

40 Com-

41 Con-

42 Sub-

43 Al-

44 For-, Fore-

45 Fur-

46 Tern-, Etc.

47 Ul-

DISJOINED WORD BEGINNINGS

48 Post-

49 Inter-, Etc.

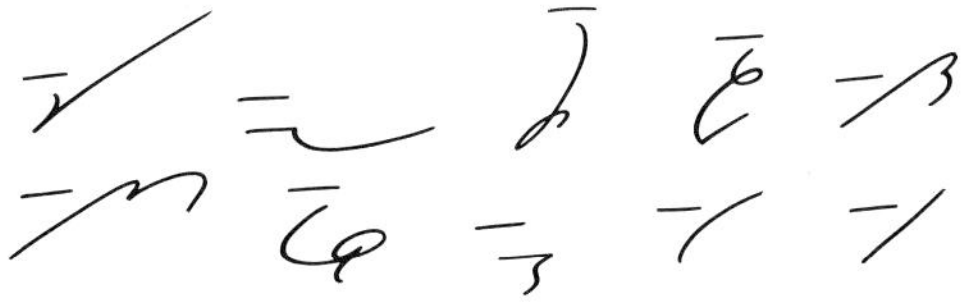

50 Electr-, Electric

51 Super-

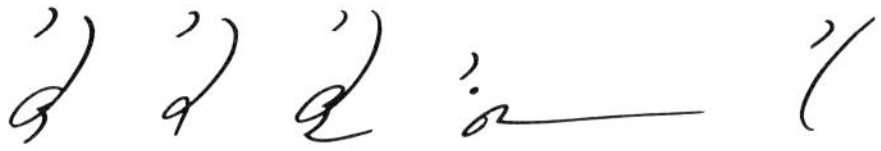

52 Circum-

53 Self-

54 Trans-

55 Under-

56 Over-

Transcript of shorthand

(The material is counted in groups of 20 standard words or 28 syllables for convenience in timing the reading or dictation.)

Chapter 1

LESSON 2

10 *Alphabet Review*

E, a, s, f, v, n, m, t, d.

LESSON 3

15 *Alphabet Review*

R, n, t, m, d, s, v, a, f, e; l, o, h, i.

Group A

1 Mr. Stevens will not release me.

2 Please leave my paper in our library. I will read it later.

3 I have placed[1] my will in my private file.

4 I will see my neighbor, Mr. Bates, in an hour or so. I know Mr. Bates well.

5 Most[2] people read at a slow rate.

6 I have not seen Mr. Deering, nor have I seen Dale.

7 Our sales are high; I am well pleased.[3] [60]

Group B

8 I will buy a spare tire in Mr. Day's store.

9 Please buy more typing paper. I am failing in typing.

10 Dale reads at[1] least an hour a day.

11 Mr. Stone will not buy our stove at our price.

12 My neighbor, Mr. Bates, knows Mary well.

13 I will[2] read my evening paper at home at night.

14 I have not made my will. [52]

Group C

15 I will not drive late at night; I have no spare tire.

16 I am writing a story in my spare hours.

17 I hear Mr. Bates[1] will open a retail store in Erie.

18 Please see me at my home at eight.

19 Our sales in our Erie store are high; our[2] sales in our Reno store are low.

20 I have a pain in my ear; I may stay home.

21 Our plane will not leave at nine; it will[3] leave at ten. [62]

Group D

22 My niece will meet our plane in Mobile.

23 He drove at least sixty miles an hour.

24 I need more filing[1] space; I need at least four more files. [28]

LESSON 4

20 *Alphabet Review*

S, o, a, e, h, r, t, p, m; d, l, s, b, v, n, f, i.

Group A

1 I am going to take my niece to grade

school at noon. She likes to go to grade school.

2 Our peach trees are not doing well.[1]

3 Here are my keys. Please do not lose my keys.

4 My neighbor, Mr. Page, will make a brief speech in Rome. He will take a plane[2] to Rome in an hour or so.

5 I try to keep my room at school clean.

6 Who will shine my gray shoes?

7 Each girl will have to write[3] at least two papers. [64]

Group B

8 James gave me a blue shade.

9 I changed my course in June.

10 It will take me at least an hour to read my paper.

11 I feel Mary's[1] grades are too low; Mr. James shares my feeling.

12 Jane Drew will reach age 65 in June. She will have to retire[2] in June.

13 Jane showed me a speech she wrote. I liked Jane's speech.

14 At my age I am not able to eat fried foods. [58]

Group C

15 I am teaching typing to my niece. She likes to type. She types four pages in an hour.

16 I am not able to locate[1] my keys.

17 Kate Gray will fly home. She will change planes in Reno.

18 Whose keys are in my safe?

19 I am flying to Rome in[2] May. My plane will reach Rome in eight hours.

20 Mr. James will teach in Rome.

21 I do not know who will drive to Erie. Mr. James[3] wrote me a note saying he will not drive.

22 I like to go sailing in my sailboat.

23 Please shine my riding boots.

24 I[4] do not like to drive at night. [85]

LESSON 5

23 *Alphabet Review*

S, sh, o, h, r, t, ch, a, p, n, j, e, f; i, m, oo, d, s, b, k, l, v, g.

28 Mrs. Smith: I am afraid that I cannot go with you to the May 15 showing of your line of ladies' clothes[1] at the Keith Hotel.

As you know, I did plan to go to your showing, but I have had to cancel my plans.

My chief,[2] Mr. Parks, is having an emergency meeting of his whole staff. I cannot miss that meeting.

Please accept my[3] sincere regrets. Earl Harvey [65]

29 Mrs. Day: In July Mr. Harry Smith will take charge of the clothing factory that our firm is opening[1] in Akron. His plans are to move to Akron in June with his bride Katherine.

May I ask you as a favor to[2] help the Smiths locate a place to live in or near Akron. Please phone me at 114-1156 if you know[3] of a home that the Smiths can buy or lease.

I know that you will like the Smiths. James Gray [74]

30 Mrs. Keith: I am happy to write you that your niece Ethel passed her history test; in fact, she passed the test with[1] a grade of 85. Her teacher, Mr. Drew, is pleased with her, too. He said that she made the best mark in his class.[2]

I cannot give you Ethel's French grade, but her French teacher feels that she passed that test, too. Dean Harry S. Smith [58]

31 Mrs. Stone: I have your letter asking me to act as chairman of your meeting in March. I am afraid, though, that[1] I cannot do so. In March I have arranged to give a series of five speeches in Dallas. I can cancel three[2] of these speeches, but two I cannot cancel.

Mrs. Church is not busy in March. You might arrange with her to act[3] as your chairman. A. H. Smith [65]

LESSON 6

32 *Alphabet Review*

D, p, s, sh, n, th, o, j, b, s; h, e, k, r, f, l, t, i; v, ch, m, g, a, oo, th.

33 *Recall Chart*

1 Act, acts, acting; late, later, latest.

2 Change, changes, changed; keep, keeps, kept.

3 Ship, shipping, shipped; notify, notifies, notified.

4 Throw, throws, thrown; approach, approached, approaches.

5 Move, moves, moved; rule, ruling, ruler.

6 Face, faced; brace, braced; grow, grows.

7 I, are-our-hour, am, is-his, can, with.

8 Mrs., will-well, it-at, the, have, but.

9 You-your, a-an, in-not, that, of, Mr.

10 I will, I can, I am; he will, he can, he may.

11 You will, you can, you are; of the, of our, of your.

12 In the, in that, in these; at the, at that, at least.

13 It will, it will not; he is, he is not; it is, here is.

14 With the, with our, with him; to the, to that, to get.

34 Mr. Gray: Attached is the first draft of our latest price list. I am well pleased with the plan of the price list, but I[1] am not happy with its size. It is too large.

Please go through the draft of the price list; then let me know if you agree[2] with me. James Green [43]

35 Mrs. Church: Last night I read with pleasure your story, *The Late Mr. Page.* You have a smooth, pleasing writing style.

I[1] am afraid, though, that I cannot accept your story. You see, Mrs. Church, our magazine is a trade magazine;[2] it serves the people who are retail-store owners.

You might take your story to a magazine like *The Readers Journal.*[3] I am sure your story will appeal to the readers of a magazine of that type. James Jones [76]

36 Mr. Farmer: My chief billing clerk, Mr. Gray, is leaving my staff; his health is failing. He hopes to leave in the[1] middle of July, but he will stay till he can train a man to take his place.

Can you supply me with a man who[2] can take Mr. Gray's place? If you can, please phone me at 116-1151. Fred Harper [56]

37 Mr. Mead: I notice that the sales in Harry's territory have slipped again in March.

Harry is a fine chap,[1] but I am afraid he is not a salesman. I have to admit that I made an error in hiring him in the[2] first place. I will write him to notify him of his release effective May 15.

Do you have a man who can[3] take Harry's territory starting the middle of

May? Allen G. Bates [73]

38 Mrs. Stone: Last evening I read the series of sales letters that Mr. Smith is planning to mail to your list of[1] food dealers in the East. I am well pleased with the letters. I like Mr. Smith's style of writing. I did not realize[2] that he wrote so well.

I feel, though, that he can omit the two letters I have checked with blue pencil. These letters[3] are not clear. Bill Green [64]

Chapter 2

LESSON 7

42 Mrs. Paul: As you know, our fall catalog lists a two-hour course in marketing. Professor John Sharp promised to[1] teach the course in the fall semester, but I am sorry to tell you that he is leaving on July 18 to[2] take a job as dean of a small college in Maine.

As I cannot get a teacher to take his place, I plan, with regret,[3] to cancel the course.

Please notify the people on your office staff of my plans. George Locke [76]

43 Dear Keith: I am afraid I will have to call off our June 15 golf date. My boss has asked me to go abroad to[1] take care of a problem that has arisen in our Paris office.

I will call you the day I get back. Very[2] truly yours, [42]

44 Dear Sir: The Model 16 office desk I bought at your store on March 20 arrived last evening. I am sorry[1] to write you, though, that it arrived with two deep scratches on the top. I cannot accept the desk as it is.

Please[2] have your man call to take the desk back to your factory. Yours very truly, [54]

45 Dear Tom: I am mailing to your daughter Ethel a copy of the Red River College catalog.

I realize[1] that Ethel has her heart set on our school, but I have a feeling that Red River College will not admit her[2] in the fall semester; her grades are too low.

As bursar of the college I will do all I can to help Ethel.[3] As you know, she is a favorite of mine. Sincerely yours, [71]

46 Dear Paul: On July 15 my private secretary, Mrs. Small, is leaving to take a promising job with[1] a travel agency abroad.

Is your daughter ready to take a job as a private secretary? If she[2] is, ask her to call at my office on June 30 or July 1. My office is in Room 16 on the first[3] floor. Sincerely yours, [63]

47 Mr. Shelley: I am attaching a draft of a letter I plan to mail to all the typing teachers on our[1] college mailing list. You will note that I am offering to mail each typing teacher a set of our typing charts[2] at cost price. I plan to mail with the letter a copy of our latest catalog of supplies.

Please read the draft[3] with care. Make all your changes in red or blue pencil. James J. Sharp [72]

LESSON 8

52 Dear James: As you surely know, the sales of our goods on the East Coast are dropping rapidly. The sales of our goods for[1] June dropped to only $300,-000, which is a decrease of nearly 10

percent since April. I shall[2] not be too surprised if our sales drop to $250,000 or less in July.

I honestly feel[3] that a good deal of the blame for this drop can be put on the poor packaging of our goods.

Would you please check on[4] the matter of packaging with your sales people. Let me know their thoughts on packaging by 3 o'clock on July[5] 10. Sincerely, [103]

53 Mrs. Grace: I am well pleased with your two plans for remodeling our library. I am not sure which plan I like[1] better; both plans are good. I have a feeling that I shall finally vote for the plan that is less costly. Charles Green[2] [40]

54 Dear Salesman: Suppose you are caught in a snow or ice storm. Will you have to "call it a day"? You will not have to if[1] you carry a set of Thomas tire chains in your car.

Thomas tire chains will enable you to drive your car in safety[2] on icy roads. Yours very truly, [47]

55 Dear Jack: There is a fairly good chance that I shall be in Dallas early in July for a sales meeting which will[1] take place in the Hotel Smith. This meeting will last three days.

If I can arrange the trip, I earnestly hope that you[2] can spare an hour or so to take me through your main office. I am most eager to observe the billing machines you[3] have put in.

Would you please let me know by June 15 if you can do this for me. Yours very truly, [78]

56 Mr. Deems: There is a bad error in our price list. On page 18 the price of our Model 45 clock is[1] given as $50. As you know, at our last meeting I set the price at $65. C. J. Casey[2] [41]

57 To All Dealers: As you may know, the cost of paper has risen nearly 15 percent since last April, but the[1] price of our notepads has risen only 5 percent.

To take care of these rising costs, I shall have to raise the price[2] of our whole line of pads; therefore, the following price changes will be put in effect on July 5:

Style 16[3] pads will sell for $110 a gross.

Style 17 pads will sell for $115 a[4] gross.

Style 18 pads will sell for $120.50 a gross.

I sincerely hope that this price[5] change will be the last. Harry S. James [107]

58 Mr. Bates: At 6 o'clock last night I talked briefly with Harry Smith, whom you picked for the job as head of our shipping[1] room.

I am as highly pleased with Harry as you are. I sincerely feel this man will do a good job as[2] head of our shipping room. I am highly pleased, too, with the fact that he will take $8,000 as a starting[3] salary.

Please put his name on the payroll as of May 15. James R. Baker [74]

LESSON 9

64 Dear Sir: There is a position open on my staff for a girl who is a good typist. In this position the girl[1] would have charge of our national mailing list of physicians, on which there are 10,000 names. The pay is good.

Would[2] you by any chance know of a proficient typist who might like this position? If you do, please let me know; I shall[3] be happy to put her on my staff. Sincerely yours, [70]

65 Dear Sir: I sincerely regret to have to write you that I cannot accept your offer to be a special[1] advisor to the financial section of Coastal Airlines. My physician advised me not to take any position[2] in which I would have to travel a good deal.

I am sorry that I cannot accept your fine offer. Sincerely yours, [61]

66 Mr. Rich: Please make a special trip to see Mr. Smith, of the National Paper Corporation in Mobile.[1] Mr. Smith has not paid his July bills in spite of the four collection letters that I wrote him.

May I caution[2] you to be patient but firm with him. It is essential that you get his check for $950 but[3] keep his goodwill.

I sincerely hope that I shall not have to take legal action against him. A. B. Teller [79]

67 Dear Sir: On my last visit to Ocean City, I saw an efficient ranch-type home that I know you will like. It[1] is on a half-acre plot in a fine section of Ocean City.

The owners are asking $12,000[2] for it, but there is a chance that you can get it for $10,000 or less. Even at $12,000,[3] though, it would still be a good bargain.

If you would care to see the place, I shall be happy to show it to you. Yours[4] very truly, [83]

68 To the Staff: It is official that the financial section will move to the first floor. The day set for the move is June[1] 5. It is essential, therefore, that all preparations for moving be made on or before June 4, as the[2] movers will arrive at 9 o'clock on June 5.

If no problems arise, the office will be operating with[3] normal efficiency by June 6 or 7. James Harper [71]

69 Dear Keith: As our factory is finally operating with a high degree of efficiency, I am going[1] to fly to Dallas to see my daughter. This will be my first vacation since 1966.

Will you be[2] free to play a little golf with me on July 15 or 16? If you will not be free to play golf, I[3] sincerely hope that you will save an evening to visit with me. It will be good to see you again. Sincerely[4] yours, [81]

70 Mrs. Smith: An official of the National Clothing Corporation has applied for a special loan of[1] $3,000. Before I can take efficient action on this loan, I shall have to have more data on the[2] financial position of the National Clothing Corporation.

Can you collect the data for me on or before[3] March 16? Harry J. Barnes [66]

71 Mr. Hall: My physician tells me that I shall have to have an operation to remove the bone chips in my[1] right elbow. I shall, therefore, have the operation at 10 o'clock on June 15 at the National Hospital.[2]

I know that I can rely on you to see that the office operates with efficiency in my absence.[3] James Green [62]

LESSON 10

76 Mr. Moses: On May 15 Mr. James Sands applied for a position as paint salesman with our firm. He seems[1] to be a pleasant, efficient chap, but before I can offer him this position, I shall have to have more facts.[2] Would you assist

me in getting these facts by answering the following:

1. Did Mr. Sands do any selling for[3] you? If so, did you find him to be a good salesman?

2. Can he meet people well?

3. Would you put him back on[4] the payroll if you had a vacancy?

May I have your answers by July 3? James Green [95]

77 Mr. Grant: Samples of the special mailing pieces you asked me to have printed for you are attached. Five hundred[1] copies of these mailing pieces will be sent to your Flint plant this evening; six hundred copies will be sent to your[2] offices in Atlanta on June 6.

The cost of printing these mailing pieces is $80. I will mail[3] you a bill for $80 on July 1.

I sincerely hope that you will be pleased with these mailing pieces.[4] Charles Gray [81]

78 Mr. Crandall: I am sorry to say that I am not entirely pleased with the sale of our mattresses in our[1] Atlanta store. In April, the Atlanta store had a decrease of 10 percent; in May, the decrease is even[2] larger—12 percent.

These decreases are causing me to lose a good deal of sleep!

Can you arrange to take a trip[3] to Atlanta to see if you can find an answer to these losses in sales? A. H. Davis [77]

79 To the Staff: This evening I learned with regret that Mr. Trent will be leaving our firm on April 10 to take the[1] position of financial secretary of the National Paint Corporation in Flint. I know that all of you[2] will be as sorry to have Mr. Trent leave as I am.

A tea is being planned in Mr. Trent's honor on April[3] 6 at 3 o'clock in the Hotel Francis. I sincerely hope that you can arrange to be there. James R. Baker[4] [80]

80 Mr. Baker: I find on checking through our central file of current magazines that the copy of the June *Printer's*[1] *Guide* is missing. Did you borrow it or do you know who did?

The June *Printer's Guide* has a list of the printing firms[2] in the East to whom I am planning to mail our latest catalog. Bob Smith [54]

81 Mr. Strand: On March 15 our binder, Mr. Bond, phoned me to say that our stock of the initial printing of[1] *The Nurse's Guide* is low; in fact, he says that there are only 5,000 copies in the bindery. At the[2] current rate of sale, the chances are that these 5,000 copies will not last through July. Who would have imagined[3] last fall that *The Nurse's Guide* would sell half so well?

Please start the ball rolling for a second printing of 50,000[4] copies. James R. Smith [81]

82 Dear Sir: My sister said that she left her reading glasses in the center drawer of the desk in Room 25 on[1] the second floor of your premises.

Would you please check to see if the glasses are there. If the glasses are there, please[2] phone me at 156-1166. I shall then arrange to call for the glasses before your office closes [3] at 5 o'clock. Sincerely yours, [68]

LESSON 11

89 Mr. Gordon: I have finally been able to arrange my travel plans as they relate to your sales meeting[1] in Akron on May

4 and 5. I was not sure till April 10 that I could be with you.

I will arrive in Akron[2] from Dallas on the night of May 3 and stay at the Garden Hotel. I will be ready for action bright and[3] early on May 4. If you could have breakfast with me on May 4, I should be honored. I will call you when I arrive.[4]

I prepared six charts especially for this sales meeting, and I am sending them to you by parcel post. Please hold them[5] for me. J. C. Mild [104]

90 Dear Sir: It is my pleasant task to write you that our agent has been able to collect from the Harold Children's Shop the[1] $475 that they have owed you since June 12.

Our fee for this collection is $50.[2] I am sending you our check for $425.

It has been a pleasure to serve you. Sincerely[3] yours, [61]

91 Dear Fred: When I was in Toledo, I heard Mrs. Helen Fields make two speeches on hobbies for children that I[1] feel should be printed in our magazine, *Child Care*. When I asked Mrs. Fields for copies of her speeches, she was flattered[2] and said she would send me the originals.

You should be able to print the first speech in June and the second in[3] July. Sincerely yours, [64]

92 Mr. Fields: When I was in Ocean City on May 10, I called on the owners of the Ocean City Children's[1] Shop. They told me that they have not been pleased with the service they have been getting from our local salesman, Mr. Shields.[2] In fact, he has not been in to see them since March.

I told them that I was sorry they felt they had been ignored and[3] that I would be happy to check into the matter.

Could you check the facts for me so that I can take the necessary[4] steps to see that they get the service to which they are entitled. James R. Mild [94]

93 Dear Sir: On April 12 I bought an airplane ticket from Dallas to Mobile at your ticket office in Dallas.[1] I bought the ticket with my air travel card. Since then, I have not been able to find my card.

Could I have left the card[2] on the desk in your office? If you find the card, please send it to my home at 4 Orchard Lane in Dallas. Sincerely[3] yours, [61]

LESSON 12

94 *Recall Chart*

1 Send, could, should, from, when, was.

2 They, them, and, good, this, their-there.

3 Would, put, be-by, which, shall, for.

4 Hard, harder, hardly; fold, folder, folded.

5 Patient, patients, patiently; proficient, proficiently, proficiency.

6 Initial, initially, initialed; brand, brands, branded.

7 Rent, rented, rental; arise, arising, arises.

8 Neat, neatly, neatness; cause, caused, causes.

9 Change, changes, changed; cool, cools, cooled.

10 Throw, throwing, thrown; thick, thicker, thickness.

11 Go, goes, going; share, shares, shared.

12 To put, to be, to have, to pay, to see, to blame.

13 Had been, have been, has been; I should be able, I have not been able, he will be able.

14 Sincerely yours, Yours very truly, Very truly yours, Yours truly; Dear Sir, Dear Madam.

15 $4; 400; 400,000; $400,000; 5 percent; 6 o'clock.

96 Mr. Macy: A course entitled "Building Reading Efficiency" will be offered to our staff starting March 10[1] at 5 o'clock. This will be a 12-hour course and will be taught by Dr. David Jones, of Harper College. Classes will be[2] held in Room 16 on the third floor of the main building.

Please send me by March 2 a list of the people in your[3] section who would like to take the course. I will then provide you with cards that will admit these people to the initial[4] session. James Nathan [84]

97 Dear Sir: Your records will show that I was a passenger on the "Lone Star," which arrived in Savannah on March 18.[1] As I was leaving the ship, I noticed that my handbag was missing. In this handbag I had $150[2] in cash and $50 in traveler's checks.

I told the first officer of my loss. He made a search[3] for it but could not locate it. He said he would send a special notice of the loss to your office. Have you been able[4] to locate the handbag? Sincerely yours, [88]

98 Dear Sir: You will find attached the July gas bill for my cottage on Garden Lake. You will notice that the bill is[1] for $15.

I was in Mobile most of July visiting friends, and my cottage was vacant for all but[2] five or six days. Therefore, my bill for $15 cannot be correct. Yours very truly, [57]

99 Dear Sir: On your bill for July there is a charge of $10 for file folders that I bought in your store on June[1] 5. I paid for these folders by check on July 1; in fact, I have the canceled check in my possession. Apparently[2] you made an error in billing.

Please correct your records so that I will not be billed for these folders again.[3] Yours very truly, [64]

100 Mr. Smith: I have been asked by our salesman in Charlotte to send to Mr. E. H. Moses, who teaches in Charlotte[1] High School, 100 copies of our pamphlet on child care. He asks that I send them free of charge.

As you know, our[2] offices have been charging 10 cents apiece for these pamphlets. Should I send these copies free of charge as a token of[3] goodwill, or should I write our salesman that I shall have to bill Mr. Moses for this service? Harry Fields [78]

101 Dear Fred: I am sending you by parcel post a package of special records that I bought as Christmas gifts for your[1] children. Please let me know when the records arrive. I sincerely hope that the children will like them.

I had planned to[2] be with you and your children this Christmas, but I am afraid that I shall have to change my plans. I was asked by an[3] official of our firm to sail for Paris five or six days before Christmas to check on our foreign operations.[4]

May you have the merriest and happiest of Christmases. Sincerely yours, [94]

102 Dear Arnold: When I was in the city last night, I bought the two tickets you asked me to get for you for the game[1] on July 15. The seats are in the third row of Section 16. They are good seats, and you should be able to[2] see well from them.

Shall I put the tickets in the mail, or would you prefer to have me hold them till I see you on[3] July 10? Sincerely yours, [65]

Chapter 3

LESSON 13

107 Dear Dr. Cook: Thank you for the order for a Bud television set that you mailed to our Westfield office. It reached[1] us yesterday, and we were very glad to get it. You have chosen to buy a set that is the work of the finest[2] minds in the industry.

Since we sell only through dealers, we are unable to fill the order from our[3] factory. We are, though, sending the order to the Westfield Television Shop, which has been our dealer in this[4] city for a number of years. You should hear from them soon. Sincerely yours, [93]

108 Mr. Sweet: Yesterday I had a note from our production chief in which he tells me that you were chosen to print[1] our book, *The Hunter's Guide,* by Warren Wood, and that you will soon be given an order to print 5,000 copies.[2]

I was very glad to learn that you will do the printing, as I have been very pleased through the years with the efficient work[3] your plant does.

I am enclosing the copy for the first five chapters of the book. If all goes well, I should be able[4] to send you the remaining chapters soon. James Harris [90]

109 Dear Madam: Thank you for the order that you gave to Mrs. Woods of our West Side store for a dozen of our No.[1] 16 wool sweaters. The sweaters were shipped yesterday; they should reach you soon.

I am enclosing a copy of[2] our catalog, which lists our full line of ladies' wearing apparel. You will be very glad to learn that this year's[3] prices are the lowest in our history. We have worked hard to keep them in line.

We earnestly hope that you will[4] visit us again soon. Yours very truly, [88]

110 Dear Bud: Thank you for the help you gave Mrs. Cook and me yesterday in planning our vacation for this year. We[1] were very happy that we stopped in to see you.

My wife and I have finally made up our minds to take a two-week[2] cruise to the Virgin Islands—the last week in June and the first week in July. We can hardly wait, as this will be[3] our first vacation in eight years. I shall stop at your office soon to plan the entire trip.

Again, thank you for your help.[4] Sincerely yours, [83]

111 Dear Sir: We were very sorry to learn from your letter that we made an error in shipping your April 10 order[1] for 100 copies of Mrs. Sweet's *Cooking Is Not Work.*

The order was properly marked so that the books should[2] be sent to the Wood School and the bill mailed to your home address. Apparently our billing clerk did not see this note[3] on the order and sent both books and bill to your home address.

Let me assure you that we shall take steps to see that[4] this error does not occur again.

Thank you for your patience with us. Sincerely yours, [95]

LESSON 14

117 Dear Sir: Six dozen of our No. 18 frosted glasses were shipped to you yesterday; they should reach you soon. Thank[1] you for this fine order; we were very glad to get it.

These frosted glasses have sold quite well this year. I am sure[2] you will sell the six dozen quickly and will want to order more.

I am enclosing a copy of our catalog[3] in which all our glass products are listed. Our buyers have worked hard to provide our dealers with the finest in[4] glass goods. Sincerely yours, [84]

118 Dear Dr. White: On June 10 you asked us to quote on the cost of painting your office building on Park Square and[1] Broadway. We were very glad to send our man to study your building. On the basis of his detailed survey, we quoted[2] you a price of $2,000, provided the work could be started on or before June 30. Today[3] is June 25 and we have not heard from you.

On July 1 the cost of paint and labor will rise nearly 10[4] percent. Therefore, the price we quoted you will not apply if we are not authorized to proceed with the work by[5] June 30.

Please act quickly. Call us today and save 10 percent on your painting costs. Yours very truly, [118]

119 Mr. White: I have just finished a detailed study of our sales records for the past three years. This study indicates[1] that our sales of hardware always drop sharply in June and July. This fact is both surprising and alarming.[2] Please study the whole matter, and let me know the steps we should take to build up our sales of hardware in June and July[3] this year.

We should take positive action quickly. Harry P. Macy [73]

120 Dear Mary: It is a pleasure to write you that you have been accepted into the freshman class of Baldwin College.[1]

You have been assigned to Dwight Hall, in which you will share a room with Helen Green, whom you met when you visited[2] us last April.

It is our sincere hope that you will be happy with your studies and your social life at Baldwin.[3] Sincerely yours, [63]

121 Mr. Baldwin: Today I visited the Broadway Office Machines Shop on Broadway and Russell Square and selected[1] a mail meter that should meet our special needs very nicely. The salesman quoted me a price of $250[2] on the model that I selected.

Would you like to see the meter in operation before[3] I place an order for it? James B. Green [67]

122 Dear Dr. White: Buying tickets for our flights is quick and simple when you have our air-service credit card. All you need[1] do is phone our office at 415-1166, tell the clerk your needs, and give him your credit card number.[2] Your tickets will be sent to you by mail the same day. Hundreds of firms have adopted this quick and easy way to[3] buy tickets.

To get your air-service credit card, just fill in and mail the enclosed card.

We will take care of all the[4] details. Very truly yours, [85]

LESSON 15

128 Dear Dr. White: People occasionally wonder about our business methods. They wonder why we search the market[1] for the greatest clothing values, carry them in large selections, provide a capable, reliable staff[2] to sell them, and then offer these great values at the lowest possible prices.

Well, we have a motive in doing[3] these things: we strive to please the people who buy from us so well that they will tell their friends about us. This method of doing[4] business has been a profitable one for us; it has won us hundreds of friends.

Today we think our values[5] are even greater than they were last year. Why not stop in one day very soon and see what we have on our racks. Sincerely[6] yours, [121]

129 Dear Sir: If your firm is seeking a location on the East Coast on which to build a plant, why not look into the[1] valuable business services that we offer. Our research staff is equipped to give you reliable data on sites[2] that are available in all sections of Maine.

Our research staff will ask you what your needs are and then refer you to[3] one or more available locations that will meet your needs.

There is no charge for this service. We are glad to be able[4] to serve business in this way. Sincerely yours, [88]

130 Dear Sir: Recently we hired two reliable, capable mechanics for our night staff; therefore, we can make all types[1] of repairs at all hours of the day or night.

Think of what this means for your business. If one of your trucks has motor[2] trouble in the daylight hours, we shall be able to take care of all the necessary repair work that night. Your truck will[3] then be available for service the following day.

This repair service costs no more than our day service.

It is[4] our hope that you will give us a chance to take care of your repair needs. Yours very truly, [95]

131 Dear James: Will it be possible for you to replace me as a referee at the basketball game at the high school[1] on April 15? I think the game starts about 8 o'clock in the evening.

Yesterday I received a cable from[2] my sister telling me that she will arrive from France on April 15 and asking me to meet her at the pier.[3]

If you can do this for me, you will be doing me a great favor. Sincerely yours, [75]

132 Dear Sir: If you were to ask a businessman what the most valuable asset of his business was, I think he[1] would reply, "A good credit rating." Your fine bill-paying habits through the years have won you a very favorable[2] credit rating, but you are about to lose that rating—and for only $150, which you[3] have owed us for more than 90 days.

If it is not possible for you to pay the entire $150,[4] at least tell us the reason why. Of one thing you can always be sure: you will find us patient and reasonable.[5] Sincerely yours, [104]

133 Dear Sir: Thank you for writing me about the error we made on your July bill. A corrected bill is enclosed.

We[1] value your business and will take steps to see that errors of this type do not happen again. Yours truly, [38]

LESSON 16

139 Dear Sir: Haven't you often felt annoyed because you met a man whose face was familiar but whose name you could not[1] remember?

There is no greater or more valuable asset in business or social life than a good memory.[2] Many men would rise rapidly in business if they could remember more of what they see or hear or read.

There is no[3] reason why you cannot have a good memory. You can have one if you join our memory class. In this class you[4] will quickly learn to remember anything you choose to remember.

Read the enclosed booklet which tells all about our[5] memory course. I don't think it will take you more than ten minutes to read it. Sincerely yours, [117]

140 Dear Dr. Doyle: I believe your boy's birthday falls on March 10 and that he will be seven years old. I am sending[1] him a number of toys that I ordered yesterday at the Royal Toy Shop. As you know, I am immensely fond[2] of the boy.

Please remember me to him. Sincerely yours, [50]

141 Dear Sir: For one minute make believe that you are the credit manager of the Detroit Oil Corporation. The[1] Doyle Shop has owed you $25 for oil for many months. What would you do? I believe you would take all possible[2] measures to collect the money because that was your job.

That is why, as credit manager of our firm, I[3] am writing you this letter—to collect our money.

Do not let this small bill spoil our friendly and profitable business[4] relations. Yours very truly, [86]

142 Mr. Boyle: Because of the affection all of us held for John Francis, we are planning to have a special[1] thirty-minute memorial service for him. This memorial service will take place on May 10 in the main[2] assembly room beginning at 10 o'clock.

I believe that many members of the office staff, as well as the salesmen,[3] will want to be there.

Please make it a point to see that all your people receive word of this memorial service[4] soon. Keith Smith [83]

143 To the Members of the Staff: As I believe you all know, last month John H. Royal became the treasurer of the[1] *Women's Magazine*, succeeding Mr. Harry Joyce, who resigned. This left vacant Mr. Royal's old position[2] as sales manager.

It is a pleasure for me to be able to write you that we have just appointed Mr.[3] A. H. Quill as sales manager. I think you will agree that we have made a wise choice. James White [76]

LESSON 17

150 Gentlemen: This morning our board of directors made an important decision: We will purchase a plant on the[1] West Coast, where we will manufacture a four-color printing press that our research staff has designed and perfected.[2] The plant we desire should:

1. Be on a main road.

2. Be near a large city on which we can draw for skilled labor.

3.[3] Have a minimum of 20 acres of land.

It's a matter of great importance that we purchase a plant quickly.[4]

If you know of any available plants that meet those needs, please call me personally at 213-116-1185.[5] Sincerely yours, [107]

151 Gentlemen: Your financial and personnel records are of great importance to you. If you came to work one morning[1] and learned that those important records had been burned in a fire, you would have cause to worry, because you might not[2] be able to reopen your plant.

One way to be sure that those important records are well guarded is to place them in[3] a Troy safe, where they will be well protected. Why delay? Decide to take action today to guard those valuable records[4] properly.

If you will mail the enclosed card, we shall be delighted to send you the full story about our safes.[5] Yours very truly, [103]

152 Gentlemen: Please accept my personal thanks for the loan you granted us this morning. This loan will enable us to[1] purchase three delivery trucks. Those trucks will help us give more dependable delivery service to our dealers. Quick[2] delivery is an important factor in our business.

As you know, the Harper Manufacturing Corporation[3] is small, but we see many ways in which we can grow. When we again need financial help, we will know where to go. Sincerely[4] yours, [81]

153 Dear Sir: Perhaps one day soon you will make the important decision to purchase a car. When you do decide to[1] buy, proceed with caution. Before you make any decision, visit your local Baker dealer and ask him to take[2] you for a drive in our latest model.

In a matter of minutes you will decide that the Baker is the finest[3] car manufactured today and that its operating efficiency leaves nothing to be desired.

We assure[4] you that your visit to your Baker dealer will be a profitable and memorable one. Yours very truly, [98]

154 To the Staff: On April 10 I sent each of you a letter offering you a chance to buy stock in the White[1] Manufacturing Corporation. In that letter I listed the provisions of the offer.

This letter is to[2] remind you that if you desire to purchase stock in accordance with those provisions, it is important that you[3] do not delay filing the necessary papers.

We have to have your decision no later than 10 o'clock on[4] the morning of June 10.

It is my personal hope that no member of the staff will be deprived of this chance merely[5] because he did not act soon enough. John R. Parker [110]

155 Mr. Fields: This morning I received the cover design for our book, *Great Debates in History*, by H. R. Francis.[1] It's a very fine piece of work for which the designer, Mr. Hart, deserves a great deal of credit.

I am[2] delighted that you have persuaded Mr. Hart to join our staff permanently. I think you made a wise decision[3] by putting him on the staff. A. B. Smith [68]

156 *Coffee Break*

The secretary to a busy businessman was often absent from her desk, causing the businessman great[1] annoyance. One day he said to her, "Miss Green, when you hear the little bell on your typewriter, it doesn't mean a coffee[2] break." [41]

LESSON 18

157 *Recall Chart*

1 Were-year, enclosed, orders, sooner, thanking, worker.

2 Gladly, very, businesses, why, things-thinks, greater.

3 About, what, than, values, once, yesterday.

4 Gentlemen, morning, those, important-importance, where, manufacturer.

5 Color, colors, colored; want, wants, wanted.

6 Quote, quoting, quoted; deduct, deducts, deductions.

7 Boil, boiler, boiled; memorize, memorizing, memorized.

8 Salesmen, freshmen, women; begin, begins, beginner.

9 Person, personal, personally; persist, persists, persisted.

10 Desire, desired, desirable; repeat, repeated, repeatedly.

11 Proficient, proficiently, proficiency; hard, harder, hardly.

12 Special, specially, specialist; age, agent, agency.

13 Throw, throws, throwing; land, landing, landed.

14 To beat, to break, to plan; have been, I have been, I have not been.

15 500; $3; 6 o'clock; $8,000; $150,000; 800,000.

159 *The Power of a Smile*

All of us like the person who always has a smile on his face. It is so easy to smile. A smile costs us nothing,[1] but it is our most valuable asset.

We are all glad to meet a person who greets us with a smile. We[2] feel better at once for having met him. This feeling remains with us, and we pass it on to our friends and fellow[3] workers.

There are people who rarely let a smile reach their lips. Life seems to have little in the way of pleasure[4] for them. If these people would learn to smile, many of their troubles would not be so hard to bear.

No matter where you work[5] when you finish school, you will find that a pleasant smile will be a very great and important asset. [118]

160 *Desirable Traits*

A businessman whose secretary has been with him for many years was asked what traits he especially admired[1] about her. Here is his reply:

1. She likes her work. She approaches her job each morning as a fresh challenge.

2.[2] She likes people. She finds it easy to talk with people. Even more important, she is a good listener.

3.[3] She is loyal. She takes pride in the fact that she is a trusted member of the firm. She does not gossip with[4] anyone about its affairs, not even with her personal friends.

4. She is poised. She does not let anything rattle[5] her. She believes in keeping cool, even when nothing seems to be going right.

5. She knows that office production[6] calls for teamwork. She is glad to cooperate with all the members of the office

team for the good of the[7] firm. She does not look for personal glory.

When you are hired for your first job, will your boss find these desirable[8] traits in you? [163]

161 *Good Health*

Do you realize that good health is your greatest and most valuable asset? Good health can help you earn promotions,[1] or it can cause you to fail in business. You should, therefore, do all you can to protect your health.

Health is a personal[2] thing. Learn what is necessary for you to keep in good health. If you can honestly say that you do the[3] following things, your chances of keeping your health are very good:

1. Do you get sufficient sleep each day?
2. Do you[4] eat what is good for you and not just what you like to eat?
3. Do you see a physician about once a year for[5] a checkup?
4. Do you have a hobby from which you derive pleasure?

If your answer to any of the queries[6] listed here is "no," it is of great importance that you give earnest thought to the following:

1. Make it a point[7] to get a minimum of eight hours of sleep each day.
2. Learn what foods are essential for good health and learn to like[8] them.
3. Decide to try a number of hobbies and select the one that appeals to you most.

Remember, no person[9] can do his best work who does not possess reasonably good health. [192]

Chapter 4

LESSON 19

167 Dear Sir: I read in yesterday's *Tribune* that you have been placed in charge of the advertising department of the[1] United Manufacturing Company and that you will be located in Utica. This is a fine[2] opportunity for you; we wish you the best of luck.

An immediate problem that must be facing you is making[3] arrangements for moving to Utica. The Hughes Moving Company can look after those arrangements for you.

All[4] you need do is tell us the date on which you wish to move. The Hughes staff will pack your things for shipment and move them to[5] your home. You simply move in.

May we make an appointment to have a Hughes representative call on you to review[6] our services with you? Sincerely yours, [128]

168 Dear Dr. Hughes: Thank you for your flattering note about the presentation, "Making Company Advertising Pay,"[1] that I made before the United Management Bureau. I was delighted to have the opportunity to[2] talk to the members, and I am glad that the facts I presented were valuable.

I wish I could send you a copy[3] of my presentation, but I do not have one. I was told, though, immediately after my presentation that[4] it was taped. If that is the case, please feel free to print all or any part of my presentation in your magazine,[5] *The Management Review*. Sincerely yours, [107]

169 Dear Madam: This is just a note to

tell you that we were happy to have the opportunity to serve you in[1] our jewelry department recently. We are sure that the watch you purchased for your nephew as a Christmas present[2] will give him many years of fine service.

It is our hope that you will visit us again when you need anything in the[3] jewelry line.

Our catalog is enclosed. Yours very truly, [71]

170 Dear Sir: I was sorry to learn from your letter of March 30 that our March 2 shipment of watches has not arrived.[1] Our receipt shows that the shipment was placed in the hands of the United Trucking Company on the afternoon[2] of March 2, which means that you should have had the shipment by perhaps March 8.

We are putting a tracer on the[3] shipment immediately.

It is our sincere hope that the shipment will soon be located, as a few of the[4] units cannot be replaced. Yours very truly, [88]

171 Gentlemen: I must take this opportunity to write you about the effectiveness of our advertisment in[1] the *Tribune* in helping the sales department of our company locate capable office-equipment salesmen.[2]

Early in June our sales department needed two salesmen to represent us in Utica. We placed a small[3] advertisement in the June 18 *Tribune* and the following morning I had six applicants. We hired two[4] of them immediately.

Hereafter when we need salesmen quickly, you may be sure that we shall advertise for them[5] in the *Tribune*. Yours very truly, [107]

172 Dear Sir: I wish you could change places with me for the present.

If you had my job as credit manager of the[1] United Advertising Company, you would want to be paid for the advertisement that you ran in the *Tribune* for[2] the Hughes Fuel Company.

If I were in your place, I believe I would say: "It is too bad we kept the United[3] Advertising Company waiting. After all, we owe them the money. I must see what I can do for them[4] immediately."

Then I would send a check for $102 if it were humanly possible or make[5] at least a partial payment.

Finally, I would take the opportunity to write them a letter making[6] arrangements for the settlement of the balance.

Won't you let me hear from you soon. Yours very truly, [138]

LESSON 20

177 Dear Dr. Brown: I was very sorry to receive your letter telling me that you wish to cancel your contract for[1] the preparation of ten scripts for the advertising department of our company.

I realize that you[2] are the one who must decide whether or not you will be able to proceed with the work, and I respect the decision[3] that you made. I am, therefore, canceling your present contract immediately.

I am enclosing our check for[4] $250 for the script you completed.

When you have an opportunity, please send me the source[5] material I left with you after our last meeting. Sincerely yours, [113]

178 Gentlemen: We have always tried to provide our dealers with the best type of service at the lowest possible[1] cost. The fact that we have not received your payment leads us to wonder whether we have succeeded in our aim so[2] far as your account is concerned.

As you no doubt realize, leather goods are sold on a rather narrow margin of[3] profit. If we are to show any profit on the leather goods you purchased, we must receive payment for them according[4] to the provisions of your contract with us.

I know we can count on you either to pay your account now or[5] to write us why you cannot do so. Yours very truly, [110]

179 Dear Sir: We note with considerable regret that for many months we have not had an opportunity to serve you[1] in the leather goods department of our Troy store. This is a matter of great concern to all of us here. Because[2] we have always been proud to have you as a special friend, we wonder whether our service has failed you in any way.[3]

Won't you take a moment now to comment on the back of this letter whether we have failed you or whether there are[4] other reasons why we have not heard from you. If we have failed you, I have no doubt that we can make an adjustment[5] that will please you completely. Sincerely yours, [108]

180 Gentlemen: The building committee, which has been considering bids for the construction of the Girl Scout house, reached[1] its decision this morning. The committee has decided to give the contract to the Powers Construction Company[2] of South Orange. While your bid was a fair one, it was considerably higher than that of the Powers Construction[3] Company. Yours very truly, [65]

181 Miss Smith: I have finally been able to convince my mother and father to take a trip to South Bend to see the[1] flower show. My father will combine business and pleasure by visiting a few leather dealers while he is in[2] South Bend.

Would you be good enough to reserve a double room for my mother and father at the Hotel South Bend[3] for the week of July 18. If the South Bend cannot accommodate them, perhaps the Hotel Brown can. Please ask[4] the hotel to confirm the reservation.

As this will be the first vacation my mother and father will have[5] together in more than a decade, I sincerely hope that the weather will be good. A. H. Doyle [117]

182 Mr. Hughes: As you know, you and a number of other salesmen have sent us complaints from dealers in connection[1] with our ball-point pens. You will be glad to learn that our production committee has decided to change our pen so[2] that it will compare favorably with our competitor's product. I know that you will be proud to sell this pen.[3] A. H. White [62]

LESSON 21

188 Dear Dr. Benton: As president of the National Correspondence Schools I wish to tell you how happy I[1] am that you will be able to attend our meeting on May 10. My biggest worry now is to find a room large enough[2] to accommodate everyone who will want to take advantage of the opportunity to hear you.[3]

Whatever topic you choose for your presentation will certainly be fine with us, but may I suggest a topic such[4] as the following: "How to Train Outstanding Correspondents." If this topic meets with your approval, I will use[5] it in our announcement of the meeting in our bulletin.

Please plan to join several of us for dinner after[6] your presentation. Sincerely yours, [127]

189 Dear Captain Brandon: Mr. James Trenton has written our personnel department applying for a position[1] as assistant correspondent and used your name as a reference.

Because the job of assistant correspondent[2] is such a big and important one, we wish to find out everything we can about Mr. Trenton before[3] we offer him the position.

Could you tell us in confidence:

1. Does he have the competence for this[4] type of work?
2. How does he meet people?
3. Can you recommend him without hesitancy?

If we can ever help[5] you in a similar way, we certainly want you to call on us. Sincerely yours, [115]

190 Dear Captain Hughes: On July 18 our correspondent, Mr. Fenton, had a bad auto accident and will[1] be out for several months. It is the president's suggestion that I take charge of the correspondence department[2] till Mr. Fenton recovers.

This is a big job, and it means that I must work nights for at least ten days. Therefore,[3] my wife and I shall have to abandon our plans to have dinner with you at your cabin on July 22.[4]

It is our sincere hope that you will ask us again. Sincerely yours, [93]

191 Dear Sir: Every month we send out a unique correspondence bulletin to help correspondents write effective,[1] friendly letters. Each bulletin contains several samples of good letters as well as valuable suggestions[2] on how to write letters. These suggestions can be used to advantage whenever you have to compose letters of your[3] own.

If you would like to obtain complimentary copies of this correspondence bulletin every month,[4] I suggest that you fill out and mail the enclosed card. Yours very truly, [93]

192 Dear Madam: We have written you several letters asking for payment for the six cotton dresses you purchased[1] at our Detroit store on July 15. Evidently, these letters have escaped your attention, because we have[2] not heard from you.

If you are not happy with these dresses or cannot use them for any reason, I suggest that you[3] write us immediately. Whatever the trouble is, we are certain we can straighten out the matter quickly.

It[4] will be to your advantage to write us without delay. Sincerely yours, [93]

LESSON 22

200 To the Staff: The growth of our company has been such that we have had to add 100 persons to the staff since[1] August. The staff is so big that we are faced with a problem—how to provide working space for everybody.[2] We are now using every bit of available working space. To obtain at least temporary relief, we have[3] rented the third floor of our building. To take advantage of this space, we will have to move several departments[4] to that floor. We contemplate moving the correspondence and advertising departments to that floor on Friday,[5] January 31, and Saturday, February 1.

I suggest that you begin to make preparations for that[6] move without delay. James Temple [126]

201 Dear Mr. Fenton: In every plant there are danger spots where fire is likely to strike. You can guard those danger spots[1] with a Dayton automatic fire system.

At the first sign of fire, the system releases a stream of foam that[2] snuffs out the flames before they can take hold. The foam does not damage your equipment.

Give us an opportunity[3] to demonstrate our system and provide you with an itemized estimate of the cost of putting one in your[4] plant. Why not stop in to see us tomorrow. Or if you prefer, call or write us for our booklet, *Facts You Should Know[5] About the Dayton Automatic Fire System,* which contains full details. It will be a pleasure to send it to[6] you. You will find our telephone number listed at the top of this letterhead. Cordially yours, [137]

202 Dear Mr. Hughes: We have just learned of the damage that your automobile shop suffered from the flood on Sunday,[1] November 30. May we assure you, as an old customer of ours, that we are ready to help you. Here is what[2] we will do:

1. We will hold your bill for the automobile parts you purchased in October till you feel you can[3] spare the cash to pay it.

2. We will replace your damaged stock immediately if you will send to me a list of the[4] items you need.

Simply write your answer at the bottom of this letter and mail it back to me. I will do the[5] rest. Very cordially yours, [104]

203 Dear Mr. Doyle: Do you have trouble keeping the rooms in your house heated in the cold months of December, January,[1] and February? If so, you will be happy to know that we have the answer to your problem—the efficient[2] Temple automatic heating system. A Temple automatic heating system keeps your house warm no matter[3] how cold the weather is outside.

If you will mail the enclosed card, I shall be glad to make special arrangements to[4] have our representative call to demonstrate how easy it is to have freedom from heating worries.

It will be[5] a pleasure to have you as a customer. Very cordially yours, [112]

204 Dear Mrs. Doyle: We were sorry to learn that the vase you bought from us on Thursday, September 5, was damaged when[1] it arrived. You will be glad to know that we have found another one just like it on our shelves and that it will be[2] shipped to you tomorrow morning. You should receive it by Tuesday or Wednesday.

Please send the damaged vase back to me[3] collect.

It is a pleasure, Mrs. Doyle, to have you as a customer. Yours sincerely, [76]

LESSON 23

211 Dear Mr. Worth: Our general manager has asked me to acknowledge your letter of November 5 and to[1] answer the questions you listed about our pricing policies. Here are answers to your questions:

1. The prices of[2] our men's suits and overcoats will remain the same during December.

2. The prices of those items will definitely[3] be raised in January. Our over-

head costs have gone up considerably since July, the last time we raised prices.[4] We have not yet decided what the new prices will be.

3. A catalog listing the new prices will be issued[5] in January. Sincerely yours, [107]

212 Mr. Cotton: Please pardon my delay in acknowledging receipt of the plan you developed for producing[1] new sales volume for our division. I have been devoting most of my time to settling important questions that[2] could not wait.

I have gone over the complete plan several times, and in general, it appeals to me. It has[3] advantages over the plan that I devised and is definitely worth considering.

I have a few questions that[4] I would like to talk over with you. If you have not yet made any definite appointments for Monday evening, perhaps[5] we can go over these questions at that time. H. A. Doyle [110]

213 To All Sales Managers: During the week of February 15 our division will hold two conferences[1] devoted to new developments in the general field of marketing. At these conferences, acknowledged leaders[2] in business will talk on such topics as "Reducing Overhead Costs" and "Devising New Selling Techniques." After[3] each talk, time will be provided for everyone to ask questions. We have not yet decided on a definite[4] location for these conferences. I will write you when we do.

I have gone over the tentative plans for these[5] conferences and they look good! It will be well worth your while to attend. James Smith [114]

214 Gentlemen: We have written you numerous letters during January and February about your overdue[1] account. As yet we have received neither a remittance nor an acknowledgment of our letters.

I have gone[2] over the question of your overdue account with the manager of our credit division, and he feels definitely[3] that we should take legal action.

We do not like to sue a customer because both of us lose. We lose you[4] as a customer; you lose a good credit rating.

I shall, therefore, defer taking action for two weeks, with the[5] hope that by the end of that time we shall have your check. Very truly yours, [113]

215 Dear Friend: For over two years we have been sending you each month a copy of our *National Amusement Magazine*.[1] During that time you have no doubt derived considerable pleasure from the pages devoted to stories[2] and to new and different games.

We have just gone over our general mailing list and find that the February[3] issue will be the last one you will receive. As we have not yet received your renewal, we cannot continue[4] sending the magazine after February.

Why not mail us your renewal now. Sincerely yours, [98]

216 Mr. Green: I am happy to announce that on Friday, April 16, I offered the position of general[1] manager of the new products division to Mr. A. R. Newman and he accepted. Mr. Newman[2] recently resigned as chief financial officer of the Fifth Avenue Development Corporation.

Mr.[3] Newman will devote his entire time to the new products division, thus freeing me for more urgent duties.

When you[4] meet Mr. Newman, I know you will agree with me that his appointment is a definite move in the right direction.[5] C. A. Smith [103]

LESSON 24

217 *Recall Chart*

1 Replaced, replaceable, replacement; unite, uniting, united.

2 Amount, amounts, amounted; bother, bothering, bothered.

3 Consist, consisted, consistent; complain, complained-complaint, complaining.

4 Evidence, evident, evidently; damage, damaged, damages.

5 Estimate, estimates, estimated; devote, devoted, devotion.

6 Define, defines, defined; new, renew, renewed.

7 Memory, memorize, remember; boil, boiler, boiled.

8 Believe, believed, believing; proficient, efficient, deficient.

9 January, September, December; Monday, Thursday, Saturday.

10 Opportunities, must, immediately, wished, companies, advertises.

11 Afternoon, party, presently, corresponded, several, such.

12 Everyone, bigger, used, advantages, outside, suggestion.

13 Timing, acknowledgment, gone, generally, overcame, during.

14 Questioned, yet, worthy; to me, to make, to know.

219 *A Race With the Clock*

Recently I heard a prominent businessman give a talk entitled "A Race With the Clock." He said he attended[1] a track meet in which all the contestants in the race had their eyes on a huge clock. They realized the value[2] of time, and their goal was to save a fraction of a second.

He said this brought home the fact that time once lost cannot[3] be recovered. Minutes are as precious as pearls, but many people do not seem to mind wasting time.

Every one[4] of us has the same number of hours at his command, but one man can accomplish more in those hours than his neighbor.[5]

Time is truly a daily wonder. You wake up in the morning with 24 hours of time. It is yours. If you[6] do not use it, you will be the loser.

Life has a great deal in store for us. There are so many things that we would[7] like to accomplish but cannot because enough time is not available. [154]

220 *Check Your Study Habits*

Do you get the most from the time you devote every day to studying from a book? In order to learn from[1] a book, you must know how to use it properly. A book will teach you little if you do not have a plan for reading,[2] because active participation on your part is necessary if you wish to remember what you read.[3] In order to comprehend and remember the contents of a book, you must do more than read; you must actively[4] recite, question, and review the material you have read.

Here are a few general suggestions that will help[5] you study from a book most effectively.

1. Skim through the assigned reading so that you will know what it is you[6] are to study.

2. Concentrate on what the author has to say. Remember, too, that many

new and important[7] points are presented in such things as graphs, charts, and maps. Do not overlook them.

3. As you read, stop occasionally[8] and recite mentally the important points you have read.

4. If the book is your personal property, make[9] brief notes in the margins of the points you feel are important. These notes will serve as cues when you review the material[10] later.

5. Review the material from time to time after you have read it and immediately[11] before you must take a test on it. These reviews will pay big dividends in better grades.

6. Relate what you are[12] reading to what you have learned during your class sessions.

7. Keep a good set of notes. A good set of notes will[13] be worth a great deal to you. Good notes will help you learn more and learn it quickly, and they will help you remember what[14] you have read. [282]

221 *Life or Death*

A businessman had been trying to reach his home by phone for more than an hour and kept getting the busy signal.[1] Finally, he asked the operator if she could cut in on the line. The operator told him that she could[2] do so only in case of life or death. The businessman replied, "Well, I can tell you this—if my teen-age daughter[3] is on the phone, there is going to be a murder." [69]

Chapter 5

LESSON 25

226 Dear Mr. Underwood: The most difficult thing for me to do is to write letters like this one. I have to request[1] you to take care of the enclosed statement and at the same time keep your goodwill.

Every businessman must have a[2] great many customers who buy his goods and pay for them as soon as they receive a bill. If he doesn't, he cannot[3] meet his credit obligations.

Without credit, our business cannot hope to make satisfactory progress. Without[4] credit, your business cannot be a success. So why not let us have your check for $80 today or[5] by next week at the latest. By doing so, you will preserve your own credit rating and you will help us maintain[6] ours.

A stamped envelope is enclosed. I hope you will use it to send us your check. Sincerely yours, [137]

227 Gentlemen: We were, of course, glad to receive your order of November 16 for 15,000 manila[1] envelopes. We should like to ship these envelopes as soon as possible. Before we can do so, though, we must request[2] from you a list of the companies with whom you deal on a credit basis. Won't you please let us have such a[3] list. Use the enclosed envelope to send it to us.

It will be a definite pleasure to have you as a new[4] customer. We assure you that you will always be able to count on us for quick and satisfactory service.[5] Sincerely yours, [103]

228 Mr. Baker: The trip to California that I undertook at your request was a very satisfying one.[1]

In Los Angeles I called on the general manager of the Los Angeles Envelope Company, with[2] whom we have been having difficulty in recent months. I feel I made definite progress with him; in fact, he[3] asked me to spend a few days as a guest at his estate on my next visit to Los Angeles, which I plan to[4] do.

I shall, of course, give you a complete statement of my activities as soon as I have a few moments to[5] spare.

There is no question that my trip was a success and well worth my while. J. E. Lopez [116]

229 Mr. Duffy: I have had no success in convincing Jim Smith to join our staff as manager of our advertising[1] department in New York. It seems that he has made very satisfactory progress with the Chicago[2] Envelope Company, and I understand that he is in line for a fine promotion next year.

I should like to[3] fill this position as soon as possible; it is a source of concern to me. Do you have anyone to suggest[4] for the position? B. A. Brown [86]

230 Mr. Hughes: I have just looked over the sales record of Mr. E. H. Underwood, who represents us in the[1] cities of New York, Boston, and Philadelphia. I must confess that I am not completely satisfied with the[2] progress he is making. His lack of success in selling our goods is difficult for me to understand.

I have[3] written Mr. Underwood requesting him to meet me next week in Boston, at which time I hope to be able[4] to get a satisfactory answer to the problem.

If I should find it necessary to replace Mr.[5] Underwood, can you suggest a dependable man for his position? A. R. Green [114]

231 Dear Mr. Powell: Thank you for your order for 100 gross of our No. 16 manila envelopes[1] that you gave to our representative, Mr. Smith. As this was your first order for our envelopes, it was a[2] source of special satisfaction to Mr. Smith and to us.

The envelopes were shipped to your St. Louis, Missouri,[3] office, but as you requested, our statement will be sent to your Chicago office. Yours very truly,[4] [80]

LESSON 26

236 Mr. Ryan: I have been requested to talk next Friday at a dinner meeting of the New York State[1] Association of Home Appliance Manufacturers. Normally I would accept the assignment, for I[2] enjoy talking to progressive businessmen such as those in this association. But there is one difficulty:[3] I have a prior engagement for next Friday.

I have urged several of my associates to undertake[4] this assignment but without success.

Do you know of anyone inside the company who can handle this[5] assignment satisfactorily and who is available? If you do, please send me his name. Harry Hughes [118]

237 Dear Mrs. Temple: We have just learned that you have purchased stock in the Illinois Appliance Company. We[1] appreciate the confidence your investment shows in the management of our company.

For more than sixty years[2] we have been creating and developing products for the home, such as dryers, television sets, and other[3] appliances. Our engineers are constantly working on new things that will make the home a more enjoyable place[4] in which to live.

Undoubtedly, suggestions will occur to you on ways in which we can increase the efficiency[5] of our appliances and services. We hope that you will always let us have them. Yours truly, [117]

238 Dear Mr. Myers: We have written you several times endeavoring to collect your unpaid invoice covering[1] the home appliances you purchased during the month of October. We have not yet had an acknowledgment of[2] our letters.

Of course, we do not like to suggest unpleasant methods to collect unpaid invoices. We feel, though,[3] that we have been more than patient. Unless we have immediate payment, we intend to engage a competent[4] lawyer to take appropriate action to collect our money.

Please let us have your check for $266[5] as soon as possible. In that way we shall both continue to enjoy the fine relations that we have enjoyed[6] in past years. Very truly yours, [125]

239 Mr. Gold: As you undoubtedly know, we have had an encouraging increase in the sales of our home appliances,[1] especially dryers, in the Miami area during the last three months. Perhaps I was unduly concerned about the[2] reception our new line would receive when we unveiled it last January.

I sincerely appreciate the[3] important part you played in making this encouraging increase in sales possible. James Dwyer [77]

240 Dear Mr. Ryan: Machines have been invented for just about everything, but no one has yet been able to invent[1] a machine for collecting money.

I am inclined to believe, though, that if such a machine were invented,[2] it would be unsatisfactory. It would not have that friendly appeal that is so important.

Therefore, until[3] we can find a better method, we shall have to ask you in the old-fashioned way for your check for $1,000[4] to take care of your unpaid invoice covering the piano you purchased last September in our Miami[5] store.

Won't you please mail it today. Yours very truly, [110]

241 Dear Mr. Lyons: We understand that your boy is studying drawing in the School of Engineering. Undoubtedly,[1] he will soon need a set of drawing instruments.

Why not encourage him to visit our store to inspect[2] our line of fine Ryan drawing instruments. Sincerely yours, [51]

LESSON 27

247 Dear Mr. Banks: On September 5 I wrote you that I intended to visit you on October 10 to talk[1] with you frankly and at length about the idea of your handling our regular line of stationery products. I must[2] cancel my plans.

As you may have read in yesterday's newspapers, our president, Mr. Long, suffered a[3] particularly severe heart attack while he was speaking before a group of Wall Street bankers. In his physician's[4] estimation, Mr. Long will probably remain in the hospital for several weeks. In the meantime I will[5] have to handle his duties in addition to my own.

I shall bring up the subject of your handling our stationery[6] line again upon Mr. Long's recovery. Sincerely yours, [130]

248 Dear Mr. King: On behalf of the officers of the National Bankers Association, I wish to thank[1] you for speaking to us at our banquet on Saturday, De-

cember 15. The convention was definitely[2] a success, and you played a major part in making it so.

Your subject, "The Probable Effects of Automation[3] upon Accounting Practices," was particularly appropriate. Those who heard you will long remember[4] your presentation. Personally, I obtained many invaluable ideas from it.

We enjoyed having you, Mr.[5] King. Sincerely yours, [104]

249 Mr. Ryan: I have an idea that you will receive a special invitation to speak at the regular[1] spring meeting of the National Newspapermen's Association upon a subject of your choice. The meeting[2] will be held this year at the Hotel King on Franklin Street in Bangor, Maine, on Saturday, April 16. It will[3] probably be followed by a banquet in the evening.

I am particularly anxious for you to accept[4] this invitation as soon as you receive it. It will provide a fine opportunity for you to give these[5] people an idea of how our company operates. Frank H. Strong [113]

250 Mr. Strong: You will be happy to know that the invitation to speak at the next regular meeting of the[1] National Newspapermen's Association arrived the other day. In addition, I have been invited[2] to be the speaker at the banquet. I shall, of course, accept both assignments.

I decided upon "Unfair[3] Competition in Business" as my subject for the general meeting.

Is there any particular subject that you[4] would like me to take up in my banquet talk? I shall be glad to have your ideas on this matter. B. A. Ryan[5] [100]

251 Dear Mr. Lang: As you probably read in the evening edition of yesterday's newspaper, we have just opened[1] a new drive-in branch of our bank opposite the King Street Station. In our estimation, these additional[2] accommodations will enable us to render even more efficient service to our customers.

The next time[3] you are in the vicinity of the King Street Station, why not stop in and talk to Mr. G. A. Frank, the[4] manager of the new branch. He will be delighted to tell you how we can serve your banking needs. We have an idea[5] that you will enjoy doing business with a bank of our reputation. Sincerely yours, [116]

252 Dear Mr. Temple: A man is proud of his home because he owns it. Perhaps you would like to own your own home.

Once you[1] have talked with an officer of our bank, you will probably be surprised to find out how little it is going to[2] cost for you to own your own home. He will tell you about our regular low-cost loans and attractive conditions[3] of repayment that we can arrange for you.

Stop in at the Spring Street branch of our bank the next time you have a few[4] minutes to spare; that is all that will be necessary for us to give you an idea of the way our[5] different plans operate. Very truly yours, [108]

LESSON 28

258 Dear Max: As you are probably aware, the regular summer meeting of our appliance salesmen is only[1] three months away. I am particularly anxious to complete our plans for this meeting by May 12. Therefore, I[2] should very much appreciate and welcome your ideas on the following questions:

1. Should we hold the meeting at[3] our State Street office in New York or at some hotel?

2. What speakers should we invite?

3. What subjects should we take[4] up?

4. What should we do about our newspaper advertising budget?

Upon receipt of your ideas I shall[5] endeavor to prepare a tentative agenda. James Dexter [111]

259 Dear Mr. Yale: We have sent you several letters requesting payment for the 16 boxes of envelopes[1] you purchased on September 10, but we have not yet heard from you.

You are aware, I am sure, that if you let your[2] account become overdue, you endanger your credit reputation.

Frankly, we wish to retain your account, for[3] we value your business. It will be difficult for us to do so, though, unless you do something about it soon.[4]

I hope you will let us have your check for $22 soon. Cordially yours, [94]

260 Dear Mrs. Dix: The clock that you shipped to us on April 16 has been received and inspected by our repair[1] department. We find that the clock will have to have considerable work done on it. Judging from the condition of[2] the clock, it has apparently been hit with a blunt instrument.

We estimate that the cost of repairs will be[3] approximately $15. Because you requested that we get in touch with you before going ahead[4] if the cost was more than $10, we shall await your instructions as to whether we should make the repairs or[5] send the clock back to you. Very truly yours, [107]

261 Dear Mr. Yale: Is your home much too cold in the winter and much too hot in the summer? If it is, you need a[1] Johnson air conditioner, which both heats and cools.

A Johnson air conditioner will save you as much as 40[2] percent of your fuel budget. It will help to keep your house warm in the winter and nicely cool in the summer.[3]

For a welcome solution to a perplexing weather problem, put in a Johnson air conditioner without[4] delay. By planning ahead, we can arrange to have it installed while you are away on your vacation this spring.[5] Yours very truly, [103]

262 Dear Mrs. Yates: If you owed us $2,000, we know you would arrange some way to pay it without delay.[1] Of course, we are aware that you do not owe us that much. The balance is only $8.60, the price of[2] the mixer you purchased from us on October 18. Yes, this is a very small balance, but there is just as[3] much work involved as though it were many times that sum. We are sure, Mrs. Yates, that you did not look at the matter[4] in that light. You would not make us wait for a much larger sum; therefore, why make us wait for this small unpaid balance?[5]

Please rush your check to us right away. We shall await it eagerly. Sincerely yours, [116]

263 *Confidential*

A businessman dictated several important letters to a new stenographer. When she put the letters[1] on his desk to be signed, he read a badly garbled version of what he had dictated. "Didn't you read these letters[2] before putting them on my desk?" he asked. "Oh, no," replied the girl. "I thought they were confidential." [58]

LESSON 29

270 Dear Mr. Ryan: Recently I received a circular issued by the public relations department of[1] your organization regarding the excellent job opportunities in the publishing field. The person[2] responsible for this circular should be commended. In my opinion, it contains many extremely useful[3] and exciting facts about the publishing industry.

The purpose of this letter is to ask you if you have 50[4] extra copies that you could send me for use in my secretarial class.

Ordinarily I do not give[5] advertising material to my students, but I am glad to make an exception in the case of your helpful[6] circular.

May I hear from you promptly. Sincerely yours, [130]

271 Dear Mrs. Underwood: If you are like most wives, you have often expressed the wish that your husband would relax more.[1] Perhaps he doesn't pay any attention to you, but we think he will pay attention to Frank Strong after he has[2] read the second edition of his beautifully illustrated book, *How to Relax*.

How to Relax was[3] originally published for physicians. Many physicians claimed, though, that their patients were walking away with their copies.[4] We decided, therefore, to make the book available to the general public.

The enclosed circular gives[5] a full explanation of the book.

Why not send for a copy for your husband. When it arrives, you, too, will probably[6] want to read it.

In our opinion, you will enjoy Mr. Strong's delightful, cheerful treatment of the subject[7] of relaxation. Very truly yours, [147]

272 Dear Mr. Brown: Please pardon me for not writing you more promptly in regard to your request for my opinion[1] of Frances Frank. Ordinarily I would have answered your letter immediately, but for the past three weeks[2] I have been overwhelmed with work.

I regarded Miss Frank as a cheerful, thoughtful, and responsible person who[3] organized her work carefully. My opinion of Miss Frank is confirmed by several other executives in the[4] publications division.

Miss Frank seemed to enjoy working with us but decided to leave for the purpose of[5] taking care of her ailing mother. Miss Frank will be a fine addition to your staff. Yours very truly, [118]

273 To the Staff: The attached bulletin and circular were recently mailed to all authors of our publications.[1] The purpose of this material is to keep our authors in touch with the ordinary operations of[2] our organization.

Your opinion in regard to the content of this initial issue will be welcomed.[3] Please send your comments along promptly. F. R. Yale [69]

274 Dear Mr. Knox: It is not too early to start thinking about making those fall repairs to your home so that you[1] will be ready for winter.

Under the helpful home-repair plan that is carefully explained in the enclosed[2] circular, we are able to extend to you a loan that you can take as long as 36 months to repay.

We[3] would appreciate an opportunity to explain this inexpensive plan to you in detail. Won't you drop[4] in the next time you are in this area. Yours very truly, [92]

275 Dear Mr. Rush: So many exciting

and delightful books are being published these days that it is extremely[1] difficult for the ordinary person to examine and read them all.

To be sure that you are reading the[2] best books, you should have an expert's careful opinion of what the best books are. You should have, in addition, a helpful[3] list of new publications from which to choose. This careful opinion and the helpful list are yours if you read[4] the *Reader's Magazine* faithfully.

Why not take advantage promptly of the special offer that is explained on[5] the enclosed circular. Yours very truly, [108]

LESSON 30

276 *Recall Chart*

1 Ordinarily, regarded, opinions, circulars, responsible, organizations.

2 Publicly, publishes-publications, purposes, newspapers, streets, particularly.

3 Upon, subjects, ideas, speaker, regularly, probably.

4 Requested, underneath, statement, next, successful, satisfaction.

5 Satisfied, progressing, progressive, envelopes, difficult, difficulty.

6 Explain, explanation, explained; prompt, promptness, promptly.

7 Dial, dials, dialed; create, created, creation.

8 Income, become, outcome; invoice, invoices, invoiced.

9 Endeavor, endeavors, endeavored; bank, banker, banquet.

10 King, kings, kingdom; yield, yields, yielded.

11 Award, awards, awarded; hold, holds, holding.

12 Index, indexing, indexes; doubt, doubtful, undoubtedly.

13 Compliment, compliments, complimentary; continue, debate, ahead.

14 Review, reviews, reviewed; mother, memorable, credentials.

278 *Nine Lessons in Living*

Learn to laugh. A good laugh is better than medicine.

Learn to attend strictly to your own business.

Learn to tell a[1] good story. A well-told story is as welcome as a sunbeam in a sickroom.

Learn the art of saying kind and[2] encouraging things.

Learn to avoid unkind remarks that may cause friction.

Learn not to talk about your troubles.[3] Everyone has his own troubles to worry about.

Learn to stop grumbling. If you cannot see something good in anything[4] or anyone, at least keep quiet.

Learn to hide your aches and pains under a pleasant smile. No one cares whether[5] you have an earache or a headache.

Learn to greet people with a smile. They carry too many frowns in their hearts[6] to be burdened with any of yours. [129]

279 *Conversation Check List*

Do people enjoy conversing with you? They will if you follow these suggestions:

1. *Listen carefully*. Many[1] of us are so concerned with what we plan to say next that we don't really hear what the other person is saying.[2] If you listen actively to other people, they will pay closer attention when *you* speak.

2. *Avoid tiresome*[3] *details*. A famous newspaperman once said, "The secret

of being tiresome is in telling everything."[4] We all know the person who digresses and insists on giving you every detail no matter how minute.[5] "It was Saturday; no, it was Sunday. Yes, it must have been Sunday because I remember reading the comics.[6] It was ten o'clock, or was it eleven o'clock? No, it was ten o'clock." As though it made any difference![7] The listener is worn out long before the speaker reaches his point.

3. *Beware of trite expressions.* Nothing[8] is more irritating to a listener than to hear repeated over and over again such expressions[9] as "You can say that again," "It's simply divine," and "Fabulous!"

No doubt you are familiar with persons[10] who in every second sentence punctuate their conversation with "You know" and "I mean." These expressions add[11] nothing to the conversation.

4. *Ask the right questions.* A question properly placed and stated helps to make the[12] other person "open up." It indicates a real regard for his opinions. A simple question like "Don't you[13] think?" or "How do you feel about that point?" will often keep the other fellow talking and keep *you* from talking too[14] much!

5. *Praise the other fellow whenever you can.* Your conversation will be richer if you learn how to pay[15] an occasional compliment. When you hear a person giving a fine talk, tell him you enjoyed it. When a[16] classmate makes the honor roll, pat him on the back; he will then be more likely to pay you a compliment when you have[17] earned it —and we all thrive on well-deserved praise!

If you follow these suggestions thoughtfully, they will help to make your[18] conversation more meaningful and enable you to enlarge your circle of friends. [375]

Chapter 6

LESSON 31

285 Dear Mr. Short: Many people worry, quite naturally, about what will happen if they lose their credit card. The holders[1] of the National credit card, though, never have to worry in this situation because our card carries[2] their picture as well as their signature. We actually print the owner's picture on the card.

The National credit[3] card is recognized and honored by thousands of reputable merchants. You can obtain one by applying for[4] it at our State Street office between nine and five on any weekday.

You will, I am sure, enjoy the experience[5] of being able to purchase any quantity of merchandise and simply telling the clerk to "Charge it." Sincerely[6] yours, [121]

286 Dear Mr. Strong: Enclosed is the copy of the sales training manual you requested. There is, of course, no charge for[1] it. We are confident that you will find it helpful in training new men who have had no experience selling[2] your type of merchandise.

We publish a new edition of this manual annually. The next edition is scheduled[3] to come off the press shortly after the first of the year. I will send you a quantity of the revised edition[4] as soon as I receive copies.

Never hesitate to let us know, Mr. Strong, when our organization can[5] be of assistance to you. Sincerely yours, [108]

287 Dear Mr. Temple: I am sure that you, as a successful merchant, recognize the fact that it is never a[1] pleasant experience to try to collect small unpaid bills. If you were in my situation, Mr. Temple,[2] I know you would be as unhappy as I am to have to write this letter asking for payment of only[3] $12.50. That is, as you know, the sum you owe us for quantities of merchandise you purchased between[4] September 2 and September 18. I know, of course, that your failure to pay is not intentional and[5] that you eventually will pay us. I would appreciate it, though, if you would do so now.

May we expect your[6] check shortly? Yours very truly, [125]

288 Mr. Ryan: The attached sales figures provide a revealing picture of the accomplishments of Frank Brown as[1] an appliance salesman. The figures show definitely that as a salesman he is a failure.

I knew, of course,[2] that he had no sales experience when I engaged him. He seemed to me, though, to be a natural salesman who[3] would sell large quantities of our merchandise. I am sorry to say that the figures prove that he cannot sell.

I[4] am very much afraid that we shall eventually have to let him go. B. C. Baker [94]

289 Mr. Brown: The account of the Harper Picture Company is now more than ninety days overdue. I am, quite[1] naturally, concerned about the situation. In my opinion something is wrong, because the Harper Picture[2] Company has never been behind in its payments before. Actually, they have often paid their bills ahead of[3] time.

I suggest, therefore, that you make a special trip to see them between now and May 15 to get the answer.[4] I need not remind you, I am sure, to use extreme tact in handling this situation. Sincerely yours, [98]

LESSON 32

296 Dear Mr. Gray: Our organization, the Albany Manufacturing Company, is a recognized leader[1] in the field of leather merchandise. Our business has grown steadily. Although we have been in business only[2] a short time, our volume of sales has already almost doubled since we started operations.

We are now in the[3] happy situation, Mr. Gray, where we can add a man with merchandising experience to represent[4] us in California. We have never had representation in that state. We think, therefore, that we can sell large[5] quantities of our merchandise there.

If you know of a capable young man between the ages of 22[6] and 28 who can handle the job, please have him get in touch with Mr. Roy, our personnel manager.[7] Sincerely yours, [142]

297 Dear Mr. Samuels: The 500 copies of our circular describing our family insurance plan[1] arrived this morning by express. You can easily understand my disappointment, though, when I discovered that[2] you had misspelled the name of our company. I am enclosing a copy showing the misspelling as well as the[3] correct spelling. How this mistake could happen is a mystery to me.

We planned to use this descriptive

circular[4] at a convention on Monday, June 19, and here it is already Tuesday, June 13. Will it be possible,[5] Mr. Samuels, to reprint the circular promptly and get it to us in time for the convention? Yours very[6] truly, [121]

298 Dear Mr. Morris: Thank you for the opportunity to tell you about our latest product, the Worth fireplace. The[1] models we can manufacture are described in our booklet, *Gracious Living,* a copy of which is enclosed.

Why not[2] look through the booklet and select the fireplace you would like. Then permit our representative in the Albany[3] area, Mr. Green, to visit your home and discuss with you the cost of installation. You will, of course, be under[4] no obligation.

After you and your family have enjoyed a Worth fireplace for a week or so, you will[5] speedily discover why people consider it an investment in happy living. Yours very truly, [118]

299 Mr. Dwyer: I have some disappointing and disturbing news for you. We have definitely decided to[1] discontinue publication of our magazine, *Family Life,* on Friday, December 31. We also[2] intend to close the Albany office on that date.

For almost three years *Family Life* has been steadily in[3] the red. We are now, in fact, heavily in debt to our bank. You can readily see why we have to discontinue[4] publication.

So that there will be no misconception or misunderstanding in the minds of members of[5] the staff, please be careful not to mention this matter to anyone until we are ready to make a general[6] announcement. Rex Frank [124]

300 *Quick Service*

A young man took a pair of shoes to a repair shop and was given a receipt, which he put in his bureau. A[1] few days later he was called into the Army, where he spent four years. Back home again, he came upon the old[2] receipt and took it to the repair shop and asked the shoemaker whether the shoes were still there.

"Yes, they are," said the[3] shoemaker. "And I'll have them ready for you next week." [69]

LESSON 33

307 Dear Mr. Ryan: The railroads are recognized to be a major problem confronting the cities, towns, and[1] villages throughout the country. To shed some light on the character of this perplexing problem, the World Publishing[2] Company has issued John Smith's book, *The Government and the Railroads.*

The Government and the Railroads takes an[3] objective look at this problem and discusses the efforts of the government to solve it.

This is a book that no[4] intelligent person can afford to overlook. *The Government and the Railroads* sells for $6. You can obtain[5] a copy, Mr. Ryan, by mailing the enclosed form to us. Sincerely yours, [114]

308 Dear Mrs. Hughes: Throughout the week of April 15, the Johnson Furniture Exhibit on Fourth Street and Railroad[1] Avenue will be open to the public. In this exhibit you will find 50 complete rooms outfitted with[2] furniture from many parts of the world. The planning for this furniture exhibit began three years ago, and almost[3] 100 of the world's foremost designers are represented in it.

The person who prefers furniture that[4] has character, grace, and charm cannot afford to miss this exhibit. We are sure, Mrs. Hughes, that you will find many[5] objects that you will want for your home.

We hope to see you during the week of April 15. Very truly yours, [119]

309 Gentlemen: I am happy to be a character reference for Mr. Frank Brown, my former assistant, who[1] is applying for a government position in which he will travel throughout the world for the State Department.[2]

When I was a district foreman with the Central Railroad some years ago, Frank worked closely with me. I regarded him[3] as a hardworking, faithful, and responsible worker who never objected to taking on new duties.

When I retired[4] from the Central Railroad two years ago, he succeeded me as foreman.

If there is any other information[5] I can furnish you regarding Frank's character, experience, or work habits, please write me. Yours very truly, [119]

310 Dear Mr. Long: Vacation time is here. Perhaps you, like many other people, are already poring over railroad,[1] bus, and airplane timetables making your annual vacation plans. There is a strange thing about vacations: they cause[2] people to become forgetful in their hurried efforts to get away.

They forget to stop delivery on the milk[3] or the newspaper. Some forget to shut off the furnace. Some even overlook bills that they would ordinarily pay[4] as a matter of routine.

The object of this letter, Mr. Long, is to remind you that you owe us[5] $60, which was due several weeks ago.

Your vacation will be more enjoyable if you know that you have[6] paid your bill. May we have your check promptly. Yours truly, [130]

311 Dear Mr. Brown: About a week ago we sent you the Friday, December 15, issue of our magazine,[1] *World and Government News*. This is the third copy we have sent you beyond your expiration date. We felt you would[2] not want to miss this issue, with its wealth of information on events that are taking place throughout the world today.[3]

Unfortunately, though, we cannot afford to send you further copies without your authorization. As[4] you know, your renewal was due three weeks ago.

Please send us your authorization on the enclosed form before[5] you misplace it. We shall then be able to continue sending you *World and Government News* regularly.

You[6] need not send any money at this time, Mr. Brown. We will bill you later. Sincerely yours, [137]

LESSON 34

317 Dear Mr. Stern: The Western Furniture Company, with headquarters at 16 Railroad Avenue in Los[1] Angeles, has many large corporations and government agencies as clients. We also serve hundreds of small clients[2] throughout the state.

No matter how small your company may be, you get the benefit of the practical, useful,[3] and friendly advice of our world-famous decorators. We don't care whether you are furnishing one room, one[4] floor, or an entire building. Our only object, Mr. Stern, is to make sure that your offices have character[5] and are comfortable.

If you want a copy of our catalog of modern office furniture, just return the enclosed[6] form. Sincerely yours, [124]

318 Dear Mr. Frank: When orders for your chemical, surgical, and medical products suddenly start pouring in,[1] you are, no doubt, very happy. But will that happiness actually last, Mr. Frank, when you find that to handle[2] this new business you must hire more clerical help?

Our organization, Southern Temporary Services, can tide[3] you over the months in which you need extra help. We can easily send you all sorts of workers when you want them, where[4] you want them, and for as long as you want them.

Determine to call us promptly when you need temporary help. You will[5] never regret having done so. Sincerely yours, [109]

319 Dear Mr. Knox: Do you want a wide assortment of patterns from which to choose your sports clothes? Do you want a practical[1] suit that will fit you like a glove? Then Stern Brothers, Des Moines' leading men's shop, is the logical and economical[2] place to shop.

That is where the men of Des Moines who are determined to get the best in sports clothes do their shopping.[3] Those men know that at Stern Brothers they can get just what they want at the price they want to pay.

Come in, Mr. Knox,[4] and let us show you the wide assortment of patterns from which you can choose. Yours very truly,

P.S. You can, if you[5] wish, take advantage of our liberal credit terms. [110]

320 Dear Mr. Turner: Today it is a common sight to see a company-owned plane land at an airport and discharge[1] several of the company's officials. A few years ago that sight caused a definite stir around an airport.[2] That was before company-owned planes proved to be so practical and economical.

Today many companies[3] maintain a plane for the routine use of their technical, sales, and executive staffs. These companies have determined[4] that it pays off in terms of higher efficiency, in time saved, and in travel costs.

Would you like[5] a report on how little it costs to own a modern plane, Mr. Turner? We will be glad to send you a report[6] if you will return the enclosed card. Yours very truly. [131]

321 Dear Mr. Farmer: Safety comes first with the gas industry. Year after year national fire protection records[1] show that gas causes fewer fires than any other fuel.

Safety is a vital part of your gas service. The gas[2] industry has taken the lead over the years in the development of safety standards.

Our gas ranges are[3] tested and retested to comply with the highest standards of safe operation.

You will be making a smart[4] move if you visit our showrooms when you are thinking of replacing your present range. Very truly yours, [98]

LESSON 35

327 Dear Mr. Jennings: George Cummings, the man who has had charge of your account with us, left two or three weeks ago to join[1] the Chemical Savings Bank.

To protect your interests and your investment holdings, I have assigned your account[2] to one of the most experienced and enterprising men in our Billings office, Mr. Max C. Turner.

Mr.[3] Turner is well qualified to advise you about your investment holdings. In three or four days I hope to have[4] an opportunity to introduce Mr. Turner to you personally.

Thank you, Mr. Jennings, for the[5] confidence you have shown in us during the past four years by letting us look after your investment holdings.[6] Sincerely yours, [123]

328 Dear Mr. Hastings: You may remember that two or three years ago I had the pleasure of introducing you as[1] the speaker at one of the meetings of the International Association of Interior[2] Decorators. You gave one of the most interesting, entertaining, and informative talks that I have ever heard.

This[3] letter, Mr. Hastings, is an invitation to you to speak at one of the meetings of the executives[4] of the Interboro Office Furnishings Company on Friday, April 17. We will, of course, pay your[5] regular fee and also take care of your expenses.

I hope, Mr. Hastings, that you are in a position[6] to say yes to our invitation. Sincerely yours, [130]

329 Dear Mr. Jennings: Will you take a few moments to make an interesting experiment with us? Put your fingers[1] in your ears for two or three seconds. Notice how quiet things instantly become.

That is the kind of difference[2] Interboro ceilings will make in your home, Mr. Jennings. The tiny openings in Interboro ceilings[3] actually absorb up to 75 percent of the room noise.

Interboro ceilings have a nice[4] pattern that introduces new beauty into the interior of your home.

You can, of course, easily install[5] these ceilings without help. If you want the work done for you, though, call one of the dealers listed on the enclosed[6] folder. Some of these dealers are open evenings until nine. Yours very truly, [133]

330 Dear Mr. Temple: We are happy at this time to be able to offer you two years of the *Home Magazine* at[1] the special introductory price of $6.40. This offer will expire on Friday, August 30.[2]

To get the first issue of the *Home Magazine,* fill out and return the enclosed card. Yours very truly, [58]

331 To the Staff: Two or three weeks ago, you will recall, I offered to the men and women of the international[1] division of Jennings Enterprises an opportunity to buy stock in our company and pay for[2] it from their earnings through payroll deductions.

I am glad to report that many of the members of the international[3] division have already enrolled in the plan. I must remind you, though, that this offer expires in[4] a few days.

If you are interested in enrolling but have not yet done so, will you please return the enclosed[5] form promptly to our comptroller, Mr. Temple. Frank H. Cummings [112]

332 Dear Mr. Turner: We want to welcome you to the family of stockholders of the Western Medical Supply[1] Company.

The enclosed booklet will tell you in nontechnical terms all about our line of chemical, medical,[2] and surgical products.

We have begun the preparation of our annual report, which you will receive[3] in March. This will explain our plans for the future. Yours very truly, [73]

LESSON 36

333 *Recall Chart*

1 Merchants, merchandising, recognizes, never, experiences, between.

2 Shorter, quantities, situations, railroads, worlds, throughout.

3 Objects, objective, character, characters, governor, government.

4 Introduces, introduced, introduction; interpret, interpreted, interpretation.

5 Entertain, entertains, entertainment; proceed, procedure, proceedings.

6 Term, termed, termination; alter, altered, alteration.

7 Furnish, unfurnished, furnishings; inform, informed, information.

8 Misplace, displace, replace; become, outcome, income.

9 Announce, pronounce, renounce; schedule, schedules, scheduled.

10 Yell, yelled; enjoy, enjoyable; tax, taxes.

11 Chemical, article, radically; steady, steadier, steadily.

12 Weeks ago, days ago, hours ago; I want, you want, he wanted.

13 Some of the, many of the, one of the; of course, I hope, as soon as.

335 *Business Dress*

The subject of dress is, quite naturally, of interest to every person. There are clothes for every[1] occasion—and there are many occasions.

It is of the utmost importance that you select appropriate[2] dress for one of those occasions—your daily business appointment with your fellow workers and your boss.

Appropriate[3] clothes are one of the businesswoman's most valuable assets. She can work better, she is more cheerful, and[4] she pleases her boss if she is dressed neatly and attractively.

The wise business girl, though, guards against being[5] overdressed. It is far better for her to be conservative in dress than to be carried away by the extremes[6] of fashion. A business girl who goes to work as though she were ready to give a performance on[7] the stage is not only violating the rules of business dress but is endangering her position with the firm as well. [159]

336 *How Do You Look?*

A short time ago the staff of one of the Chicago newspapers undertook a comprehensive study in[1] which they asked businessmen to state the particular pet peeves they had about the appearance of their secretaries.[2] Here are some of the frank answers that were reported:

1. "My secretary wears altogether too much makeup."[3]

2. "My secretary chews gum. Her jaws are never still. They seem to be moving morning, noon, and night."

3. "My[4] secretary, a young man, doesn't know how to match colors. He is likely to wear a yellow tie with a blue[5] suit—and red socks!"

4. "I can always tell the evenings on which my secretary has a date. She comes to work[6] with her hair in big rollers."

Don't get the mistaken idea from these

statements, though, that a businessman[7] is interested only in glamour. Far from it. He values his secretary for her excellent grooming, her tasteful[8] choice of clothing, and her cheerful manner.

To achieve a smart appearance, you will find that attention to every[9] detail must become a natural daily routine. Any successful secretary will tell you that[10] personal details are indispensable factors in job getting, in job holding, and in job promotion. [218]

337 *Courtesy*

Whenever people work together, there is certain to be occasional friction. All it takes, though, to keep this[1] friction to a minimum is common courtesy.

Courtesy is a queer thing. We give it freely to strangers;[2] yet the better we know people, the less we think about using it. This is too bad, because showing courtesy—the[3] same kind we gladly accord to strangers—is a fine way to win cooperation and goodwill from the[4] people with whom we work.

Our courtesy shows up every day in many ways. It shows up in the way we greet people[5] in the morning, in the pleasant tone we use over the telephone, and in the considerate way we answer[6] questions.

People are conscious of courtesy. They are quick to notice its presence or its absence. Courtesy costs[7] us nothing; yet it can be an important factor in helping us succeed or fail in business. [157]

Chapter 7

LESSON 37

344 Dear Mr. Underwood: Yesterday we had an opportunity to interview your former employee, Mr.[1] Frank Short, regarding a position with our company. We were exceedingly impressed with him and are[2] seriously thinking of employing him. The particular job for which we are considering him involves selling[3] newspaper advertising to big business organizations throughout the state of New York.

We should appreciate[4] it, Mr. Underwood, if you would give us your general impressions of Mr. Short as a man of[5] character, as a responsible worker, and as a possible future executive.

If you would do this for[6] us, we should be exceedingly grateful. Cordially yours, [130]

345 Mr. Dexter: I am exceedingly impressed with the first issue of the new employee bulletin. It[1] represents a genuine improvement over the previous bulletin, which sometimes caused me serious embarrassment[2] because it was so poorly done.

The articles are written entertainingly, interestingly, and[3] convincingly. I particularly like the way you reported the retirement of the two employees in[4] the import and export department.

If I can ever be of assistance to you in obtaining material[5] for future issues of the bulletin, please let me know. James Sawyer [113]

346 Dear Mr. Cummings: I was exceedingly embarrassed to discover this morning that I had not answered your[1] courteous note of Tuesday, June 16, inviting me to dinner on July 10. I would not, of course, knowingly[2] be so discourteous, but your note was misplaced and just came to light.

I am genuinely sorry that it[3] will be impossible for me to accept your invitation because of a previous engagement that it[4] is imperative for me to keep.

If you are free upon my return to New York on July 20, may I[5] invite you to be my guest for dinner. Sincerely yours, [110]

347 Dear Mr. Long: I was exceedingly happy to receive your letter of Friday, August 15, telling us[1] how impressed you were with the courteous service you received from some of the employees in our import and export[2] division. It is not often that customers willingly write us when our service is good.

I want to share[3] your letter, Mr. Long, with the employees of the import and export division. Accordingly, I am[4] referring it to the head of that division with the suggestion that he put it on the bulletin board.

If you[5] ever have any suggestions that will help us further improve our services, please be sure to let us know. Yours very truly,[6] [121]

348 Dear Mr. Ryan: If you are to improve your net worth, you must save regularly. It is surprisingly easy[1] to save at the Empire Savings Bank. You will be exceedingly impressed, Mr. Ryan, as you watch your account[2] grow with the help of generous quarterly dividends.

If you would like to improve your financial future, come[3] to the Empire Savings Bank, this city's leading bank.

A friendly, courteous, and sincere welcome by the employees[4] of the Empire Savings Bank awaits you. Cordially yours, [91]

349 *Good Sign*

A beginning stenographer who had been on the job for a week said to her friend brightly, "I think the boss has[1] decided to keep me on." "Has he said anything?" her friend asked. "No," she answered happily, "but this morning he[2] gave me a dictionary." [45]

LESSON 38

355 Gentlemen: For several years I have been teaching salesmanship at the Billings Township Evening School. During those[1] years I developed a series of short, practical units that present this subject in an interesting, clear,[2] and easy-to-understand manner. I have also prepared a set of objective tests.

In the opinion of several[3] of my colleagues who have gone over the material, these units would be welcomed by salesmanship teachers throughout[4] the country. My colleagues suggested that I submit the units to you for possible publication.

If you[5] are interested in publishing my material, I shall be glad to submit it to you; it is substantially[6] complete. Yours very truly, [126]

356 Dear Mr. Strong: As you requested, we are canceling your membership in the Empire Book Club and your subscription[1] to *Book Club News*.

We are exceedingly sorry to lose you as a member and subscriber. We hope, though, that[2] we have not lost your friendship and that sometime in the future you will again submit your application for membership.[3]

As you know, there is still a substantial sum due on your account for the series of salesmanship books we mailed[4] to you as part of your membership.

We should appreciate your sending us a check for $50 soon to[5] close out your account. Sincerely yours, [107]

357 Dear Mr. Owen: Thank you for

submitting your application for membership in the National Radio[1] Association and for sending us your check for $10. Your membership card is attached.

As you may know, your[2] membership automatically entitles you to a subscription to our bulletin.

Our plans for our regular[3] annual convention on June 16, 17, and 18 are substantially complete. If all goes well, you[4] should receive final details in a few days.

We hope, Mr. Owen, that your membership in our association[5] will be the source of many lasting friendships and profitable business relationships. Very truly yours, [117]

358 Dear Mr. Stern: As we wrote you on February 16, we are granting 100 scholarships to seniors who[1] show promise of leadership. At that time we suggested that you fill out and submit to us the report form that[2] we enclosed. We have not yet heard from you.

If you plan to have your students enter the competition, may I impress[3] on you that all applications must be submitted by Friday, May 10.

As we also wrote you, we feel that[4] the seniors of Baker Township High School would profit substantially by competing for these scholarships. We hope,[5] therefore, that you will submit your applications promptly. Cordially yours, [113]

359 Dear Mr. Leon: As you can well imagine, this letter is a difficult one for me to write because I[1] must collect the overdue balance that you owe us without jeopardizing your friendship. I know, of course, that by writing[2] this letter I run the risk of disturbing our pleasant relationship, on which the success of our partnership[3] depends.

I hope that this letter will not only persuade you to pay your account but will also preserve that[4] pleasant relationship.

Your check for $550 or a substantial part of it will bring your account[5] up to date. May we hear from you soon. Very truly yours, [110]

360 Mr. Ferris: I have decided to schedule our annual sales meeting for sometime between Monday, May 10,[1] and Friday, May 14, in Miami.

We have never held our annual sales meeting so early in the year,[2] but the week of May 10 is the only week in which I shall be free before the end of September.

I am[3] gradually getting our plans for the annual sales meeting in shape. I will mail you a copy of the final[4] plans shortly. A. H. Allen [85]

361 Dear Leo: As you know, I have just purchased a house in the suburbs on the former Baker estate, which was subdivided[1] two years ago into 15 one-acre plots.

This means, of course, that I shall have to sublease my five-room[2] apartment at 415 East 18 Street in New York. Do you have anyone on your lists who would be interested[3] in subleasing the apartment for six months, the term that my lease still has to run? Yours very truly,[4] [80]

LESSON 39

368 Dear Mr. Roy: I think that the present is a particularly good time of the year to review your security[1] holdings.

As you are probably aware, our organization has excellent facilities for research[2] and objective analysis of all securities. It will be worth your while to avail yourself of these[3] facilities.

In the meantime I am enclosing a copy of our circular, *Investment Facts,* published by[4] our research department. I am sure, Mr. Roy, that you will find it interesting as well as valuable.[5] Sincerely yours, [102]

369 Dear Mr. Knox: When I was in town last month, I discussed with you the possibility that the faculty of[1] our school would hold its spring meetings at your hotel. That possibility is now a reality. A majority[2] of the faculty voted to use your facilities on May 15, 16, and 17.

Will you[3] please, therefore, reserve single rooms for the members of the faculty listed on the enclosed form. I shall need, in[4] addition, a large room for myself in which I can hold conferences.

Please acknowledge these reservations as[5] soon as possible. Sincerely yours, [107]

370 Dear Mr. Temple: Our advertising manager resigned about a week ago. This means that we have an opening[1] that we believe, with all sincerity, to be a wonderful opportunity for the man who[2] has the following traits:

1. A familiarity with all phases of advertising.
2. A pleasing[3] personality.
3. The ability to inspire loyalty in the employees over whom he will have[4] authority.

With your years of experience in advertising, you perhaps know of some person of outstanding[5] ability who would be interested in making a fine future for himself with us.

If you do, please have[6] him submit an application to us. Very truly yours, [131]

371 Dear Mr. Franklin: Do you know that you are doing a serious injustice to yourself when you delay paying[1] your account after it is due? You endanger your reputation as a man of integrity and[2] responsibility, and you also endanger our friendly relationship.

I know, of course, that you intend to pay[3] your bills eventually, but the sensible thing to do is to pay them now.

In justice to yourself and the future[4] prosperity of your business, send us a check now. Yours very truly, [93]

372 Dear Mrs. Dwyer: When you are looking for some reasonably priced article to give your husband or other member[1] of your family, you are sure to find it in our store.

Our store is crammed with all kinds of impressive gifts. The[2] wide selection enables you to choose gifts that reflect your personality, originality, and[3] individuality.

You will enjoy the quiet surroundings of our store. Why not come in and see for yourself. Yours[4] very truly, [84]

373 Dear Mr. Baker: Here is an opportunity that will be of interest to music lovers like yourself.[1] We will send you your choice of any one of the high-fidelity records listed on the enclosed folder for only[2] $1.

We make this special offer to demonstrate the fine quality of these high-fidelity recordings.[3] Simply indicate on the enclosed card the high-fidelity record you want and return the card to us.

When your[4] record arrives, you may keep it for five days. If in that time the record does not prove itself to be the finest[5] in tonal quality and clarity, you may return it to us and your money will be refunded readily.[6] Very truly yours, [123]

LESSON 40

377 Dear Mr. Doyle: I was sorry to read in this morning's newspaper that you will shortly retire as president[1] of the Los Angeles Technical Institute.

During the fifteen years that you have served in that responsible[2] position, you made an extraordinarily valuable contribution to the Institute. The citizens of[3] Los Angeles owe you a public debt of gratitude for the progress, success, and growth that the Institute has[4] experienced under your leadership.

I hope, Mr. Doyle, that even though you are retiring as[5] president, your counsel will continue to be available to the Institute. Sincerely yours, [117]

378 Dear Mr. Johnson: Your talk before the Manufacturers Institute on Friday, June 18, was eloquent[1] and inspiring. You made a substantial contribution to our meeting. After you completed your talk, several[2] members came up to me and inquired whether they could obtain copies of your talk.

I have frequently given[3] talks myself. Consequently, I know that they require considerable preparation. It was obvious, Mr.[4] Johnson, that you devoted many hours to the preparation of your talk.

On behalf of the Institute I want[5] to express our gratitude to you for being with us and for making such a fine contribution to our meeting.[6] Sincerely yours, [124]

379 Dear Fred: Please accept my gratitude for recommending me for membership in the Merchants Club. As you know, I[1] have the highest regard for its members. I am afraid, though, that I cannot accept membership.

My responsibilities[2] with the Wilson Radio Institute require a substantial amount of travel. I am frequently away[3] for six weeks at a time visiting our distributors throughout the country. Consequently, it would be impossible[4] for me to attend the club meetings with any regularity.

Once again, please accept my gratitude for[5] your efforts in my behalf. Yours very truly, [108]

380 Dear Mr. Davis: About three months ago I was introduced to a young man by the name of Henry Gray. He[1] was interested in joining our organization as a salesman. He had all the attributes of a good salesman,[2] and I was exceedingly impressed by his attitude and sincerity. Consequently, I expected to[3] hire him. Unfortunately, he was taken seriously ill before he could report.

When Mr. Gray[4] recovered, we had no openings available.

If you require a competent salesman for your staff, I[5] can recommend Mr. Gray without hesitation. Very truly yours, [113]

381 Dear Mr. Blair: If part of your sales are made on credit, you, like the rest of us, have no doubt had your share of[1] delinquent customers. When accounts are delinquent, they require a great deal of extra attention. Consequently,[2] you can appreciate the satisfaction that a distributor like yourself, who pays his bills promptly, gives to[3] the credit department.

Unfortunately, we frequently take

friends like you for granted and fail to express our[4] gratitude. The only purpose of this letter, therefore, is to express our gratitude for the way in which you[5] co-operate with us. Sincerely yours, [107]

382 *Addition*

"Miss Smith," a businessman said to his secretary, "I want you to add a column of figures at least three times[1] before you show me the total."

A few days later she came to him with a big grin. "Mr. Brown," she said, "I added[2] these figures ten times." "Fine. I like a secretary to be thorough." "And here," she said, "are my ten answers." [59]

LESSON 41

388 Dear Mr. Long: The Air Transportation Association meets regularly on the first Monday of every[1] month. To each meeting we invite a speaker who is an expert in some area of general interest to[2] employees in the air transportation business.

Yesterday I was named chairman of the speaker's committee, and[3] it is my responsibility to obtain speakers for next year's meetings.

Could you speak to us on the subject[4] "The Government's Part in Air Transportation" on Monday, January 3?

I hope you will find it convenient[5] to accept this invitation, Mr. Long. It will be a privilege to hear a speaker with your qualifications.[6] Sincerely yours, [124]

389 Mr. Frank: I have read with considerable interest your translation of the article on transistors that[1] appeared in a Japanese magazine. You have done a job that you can, with justification, be very[2] proud of.

I would like to send copies of this translation to our own engineers for their information. As I[3] am sure you will agree, the article contains many significant facts that our engineers should have. Before I[4] send them copies, though, would you be good enough to study the sections that I have indicated in red pencil. I[5] think these sections need revision, clarification, and simplification. James Green [115]

390 Gentlemen: You will be interested to know that on Friday, June 16, the Air Transportation Company[1] celebrates an anniversary, its tenth. We look with gratification upon the significant progress[2] we have made in those ten years; we feel we have every justification for being proud of it.

On this tenth[3] anniversary we want to acknowledge the contributions you have made to the success of the Air Transportation[4] Company and to thank you for the confidence you have shown in us.

It has been a privilege to serve[5] you, and we hope that we will have frequent opportunities to serve you in the future. Sincerely yours, [118]

391 Mr. Brown: The plans and specifications for our new building were transmitted to me several days ago by[1] your secretary. After studying them carefully, I find that several significant modifications[2] were made without my knowledge or permission.

Although there may actually be[3] some justification for making these modifications, there is no justification for your making them without letting me know.

I am[4] exceedingly reluctant to approve these plans and specifications in their present form. If it is convenient,[5] I would like to discuss them with you on Friday, June 15. Frank J. Smith [114]

392 Dear Miss Cummings: We are seeking a competent girl to fill the opening as secretary to the head of our[1] translation division. As your school has supplied us with fine girls in the past, we are hoping that you will be able to[2] help us again.

If you know of a girl who meets these qualifications, please have her submit her[3] application to us at her convenience. Very truly yours, [72]

393 Dear Mr. Green: I am returning for clarification your bill covering the cost of the transcript you[1] prepared for us in the case of the New York Transportation Company versus Transcontinental Airlines.

On the[2] bill you indicated that you transcribed 120 pages at the rate of $1 a page, making a[3] total of $120. Yet the transcript itself contains only 110 pages. Shouldn't[4] you, therefore, have billed us for $110?

Please let me know whether your bill is incorrect or whether[5] the difference of $10 represents a charge for some other service in connection with the transcript.[6] Very truly yours, [123]

394 Dear Mr. Smith: I have just learned with gratification that you have opened a charge account with us. I know you[1] will find your charge account a convenient, quick, and practical way to buy. I know, too, that you will enjoy shopping[2] in the friendly atmosphere of our store.

Our employees will consider it a privilege to serve you. Cordially[3] yours, [61]

LESSON 42

395 *Recall Chart*

1 Myself, yourself; security, authority; facility, nationality.

2 Improve, improvement; employ, employment; willingly, seemingly.

3 Submit, submission; relationship, friendship; introduce, introduction.

4 Entertain, entertainment; interest, interested; bearings, clippings.

5 Technical, technically; inform, informed; displace, misplace.

6 Alters, altered; steadily, speedily; actual, actually.

7 Procedure, procedures; careful, carefulness; express, expresses.

8 Enforce, enforcement, transport, transportation; gratification, notification.

9 Unpaid, unfair; contain, detain; comfort, comfortable.

10 Mother, further; perform, performance; personal, personally.

11 Debate, depress; purchase, purchased; become, before.

12 Rebate, replacement; reliable, terrible; mention, termination.

13 Special, especially; neatly, clearly; faculty, penalty.

14 Proficient, deficient; efficiency, deficiency; ourselves, themselves.

397 *How Is Your Vocabulary?*

If you want to get ahead in the business world, you must pay attention to your vocabulary. As many[1] tests have shown, good students almost always have a better working vocabulary and read faster than the weaker[2] students. Good students can recognize, define, and use more words than their weaker brothers.

This helps them read[3] faster because they understand the meaning of words at a glance. To become a fast reader, therefore, you must become a[4] master of the words you read. There are a number of ways you can do this.

Get the Dictionary Habit. Be[5] constantly on the lookout for new words. When you see a new word or encounter one that is only vaguely familiar[6] to you, don't pass it by, thinking you can get along without it. Often the meaning of a whole sentence may[7] hang on the new word. If you are going to read efficiently, you will need to know well all the words you read.

When[8] you come across a new word, the first thing to do is look it up in the dictionary. Have a good dictionary[9] handy at all times.

Successful writers, who probably have a better command of the language than most people,[10] usually have two or three dictionaries for different purposes where they can reach them readily.

Use New Words. Besides looking[11] up new words, take steps to add them to your working vocabulary. It is a good[12] idea to write down these new words on a card or on a piece of paper. During the course of a day in which you read[13] for perhaps an hour or two, you can probably compile a list of eight or ten new words. When a dictionary[14] is available later, look them up. Finally, try to use those words in your everyday conversation and[15] writing.

If it is your ambition to become a successful secretary, you must remember that you will[16] constantly be working with words. The more words you know and can use, the easier will your secretarial work[17] be and the more rapidly will you progress. [350]

398 *Economy*

The most economical person I ever knew was a big spender — "investor" would perhaps be a better[1] word. He never let his money lie idle but was always finding ways and means to make it earn more income.

This[2] man realized that economy is the careful use of anything. Many people think of economy[3] as refraining from spending. That is merely stinginess.

To be truly economical, you must learn to spend[4] wisely. Once you learn to do this, you are on the high road to becoming truly economical.

There are more[5] kinds of economy than economy of money. There is economy of time and economy of[6] energy. These are most important. If you do not use time and energy properly, you will have no money[7] on which to practice economy!

To economize on time means to use your time to best advantage. To do[8] this, you must economize on energy. In turn, this means that you must work on a plan and a schedule. [179]

Chapter 8

LESSON 43

405 Dear Mr. Billings: When our representative, Mr. Lyons, was in the office yesterday, he left with us[1] your order for our No. 16 postage meter and our Superior calculator. We were particularly[2] happy to get your order, for it is the first we have received from you. I hope, Mr. Billings, that this is[3] the beginning of a long business relationship.

Before we ship the postage meter and calculator, though,[4] we want to establish a credit rating for you. May we request, therefore, that you fill out our regular credit[5] form and return it to us in the postage-paid envelope that is enclosed. Sincerely yours, [117]

406 Dear Mr. Smith: Congratulations

on the stimulating speech you made before the National Supervisors[1] Association on Friday, May 10. It was superb! Your subject, "The Population Explosion," was a timely[2] one.

One of our people taped your speech, and I have had my secretary transcribe it.

May we have your permission[3] to print your speech in the bulletin that we issue each month to our supervisors, superintendents, and others[4] in supervisory positions?

A postage-paid envelope is enclosed for your convenience in letting[5] us know whether we may have your permission. Yours very truly, [111]

407 Dear Mr. Hughes: *The World of Business* is the only publication that supplies businessmen with the facts they must[1] have today in order to supervise their business properly.

We have on our staff more than 250[2] superior reporters, editors, and writers who accumulate and tabulate up-to-the-minute[3] information about population trends and other factors of interest to businessmen.

Our circulation is[4] more than 200,000, and it is growing steadily.

If you would like to subscribe to *The World of Business*,[5] return the enclosed convenient postcard. Don't postpone taking action; mail the postcard today. Yours very truly, [119]

408 Mr. Kelley: As I suggested to you yesterday, I believe that we should not postpone any longer the[1] appointment of Harry Nelson, my assistant, as supervisor of our magazine's circulation department.[2] He has done a superb job as acting supervisor. When he took over the job two years ago, our circulation[3] was 80,000. Our circulation today is more than 100,000.

I realize that you may feel[4] that Harry is too young for the position, but I am confident he will do a superior job for us.[5] Robert Lee [102]

409 Dear Mr. Drake: I was sorry to receive your letter telling me that you will be unable to have dinner with[1] us on June 15. I realize, though, that you have a busy schedule.

I hope that the next time you are in New York,[2] you will reserve a few hours for us. Sincerely yours, [50]

410 Dear Mr. Green: Here is what a Superior postage meter will do for you:

1. It will print postage on your[1] letters, circulars, and other mail.

2. It will give you close supervision over postage expenditures.

If[2] you have been postponing the purchase of a postage meter because of the expense, postpone no longer. You can[3] now purchase a Superior postage meter that exactly fits the needs of your office, and you can do so[4] at a surprisingly low cost.

After your staff has used the Superior postage meter for a few days, you[5] will congratulate yourself on the savings you will make. Cordially yours, [113]

411 Dear Mr. Casey: The postman just delivered your manuscript for the second edition of your book,[1] *Tabulation Made Easy*. May I congratulate you on a superlative job. You have justification to be[2] proud of its quality.

I want to congratulate you also on keeping to the schedule that we set up[3] last spring. I realize that it took superhuman effort on your part, and I appreciate it.

If my[4] calculations are accurate, next year we should sell at least 15,000 copies of *Tabulation Made Easy.*[5] Very cordially yours, [104]

LESSON 44

418 Mr. Jackson: This morning I had a call from Mr. J. C. Smith, a representative of the World Manufacturing[1] Company, regarding the calculator we sold them several weeks ago. In spite of three visits[2] by one of our servicemen, it is not yet working satisfactorily.

This company gave us over[3] $100,000 worth of business last year, and it is to our self-interest that they be completely satisfied.[4]

Under the circumstances I assume you will want to look into this situation personally. In[5] my opinion we should replace the calculator with our new, improved model if necessary. James Baker[6] [121]

419 Dear Miss Case: The girl who gets ahead is the one who has that poise that comes from self-confidence, self-assurance, and self[1]-reliance.

Do you have these qualities? If you do not, you can easily acquire them by taking the Wilson[2] Self-Study Personality Course. When you complete this course, you will know how to express yourself with clarity.[3] You will become an interesting, dynamic person.

If you would like a copy of our circular describing[4] our self-study course, fill out the enclosed form and return it to us in the postage-paid envelope that is also[5] enclosed. Very truly yours, [105]

420 Mr. Smith: As the January and February issues of the *National Consumer Reports* have not reached my[1] desk, I assume that we have let our subscription expire.

My supervisors and I have always read these consumer[2] reports as a matter of self-interest, and we would like to see our subscription resumed. Under the[3] circumstances will you please place an order for a two-year subscription to *National Consumer Reports* beginning[4] with the current issue. James C. Thomas [88]

421 Mr. Macy: When I was in New York recently, I learned of a manuscript for a modern, up-to-date book[1] entitled *Self-Teaching Course in Typing.* It occurred to me that *Self-Teaching Course in Typing* would be a fine[2] addition to our self-improvement and self-study series. Under the circumstances I asked the author to submit[3] the manuscript to us, which he has done.

I assume you will want to examine this manuscript yourself to[4] see whether it meets our specifications. Accordingly, I am transmitting it to you along with the author's[5] letter, which is self-explanatory. A. J. Taylor [111]

422 Dear Mr. Davis: If you are like most persons, we may assume that you wish you had more self-confidence and[1] self-assurance when you get up to address a gathering. You wish you could overcome the feeling of stage fright.

There[2] are two ways to defeat stage fright. One way is by striving for self-improvement by yourself. As I am sure you will[3] agree, this is a tedious, difficult way. A better way is to take the Johnson public-speaking course. In[4] this course you will dcvclop self-expression and self-confidence under the supervision of a skilled instructor.[5]

If you would like to have more information about our course, fill in and return the enclosed stamped, postage-paid[6] card. Yours very truly, [124]

423 Dear Reader: According to our records, your remittance for the book you ordered on May 15 is still outstanding.[1]

It may be that you have already sent us your check and that our letters have crossed in the mails. If that is the[2] case, please disregard this note.

If you have not yet sent us your remittance, I should appreciate your taking care[3] of this little detail.

A stamped, self-addressed envelope and a duplicate invoice are enclosed for your convenience.[4] Sincerely yours, [84]

LESSON 45

430 Gentlemen: The president of a big merchandising company found out one day that his employees were working[1] under great difficulties as a result of the noise in the general office. He consulted us, and[2] we sent one of our experienced representatives to make a survey.

After studying the situation,[3] our representative suggested that the ceiling be covered with special tiles. The tiles were put in at a[4] cost of a few hundred dollars, and the office workers became more efficient than ever before.

If you have[5] a noise problem, call us. We will send our representative in your neighborhood to your office for a free[6] consultation. Sincerely yours, [125]

431 Mr. Dexter: On Friday, October 8, I had a rewarding consultation with one of the engineers[1] of the Baker Heating Company about our heating problems. We went over them backwards and forwards.

As a result[2] of this consultation, we shall ultimately be able to cut our heating expenses by several hundred[3] dollars a year. All we have to do is install some new equipment that costs about $900. When I get[4] all the figures, I will forward to you a complete, detailed report. James Lyons [94]

432 Dear Mr. Baker: Frankly, I find myself in an awkward, uncomfortable situation. Unless I receive[1] your check for $500 by June 6, it will be my responsibility to turn your account over to[2] our attorneys.

As you know, this $500 covers your purchases on January 2 of 300[3] pounds of grass seed, 800 feet of lumber, and 500 feet of wire.

Under the circumstances,[4] Mr. Baker, won't you please help me out of this awkward situation by sending me your check for $500.

I[5] shall look forward to receiving your check without delay. I am enclosing a self-addressed, postage-paid[6] envelope for your convenience. Yours very truly, [129]

433 Gentlemen: For the past twelve weeks I have been teaching typing in the adult-education school in my neighborhood.[1] It has been a rewarding experience indeed, and I look forward to each session.

Most of these adults[2] are already typing 40 words a minute. I attribute these fine results in large part to your textbook, *Typing*[3] *for Adults.* I selected this book after examining, backwards and forwards, more than ten books on the market.[4]

Please offer the authors my congratulations for producing such a fine book. Yours very truly, [98]

434 Dear Sir: Over a million depositors of the Mutual Savings Bank increased their savings last year by more[1] than a billion dollars. As a result, they have on deposit at our bank almost two billion dollars.

These[2] depositors received in the neighborhood of forty million dollars in dividends last year.

If you do not have a[3] savings account, this is the time to open one. You will find it a rewarding experience to watch your[4] savings multiply from month to month.

Why not call at our branch in your neighborhood and let one of our officers[5] show you how simple it is to open an account. Very truly yours, [114]

435 Dear Mr. Weber: As you requested, we have reserved two large rooms for you for the week of April 28.[1] We are confident that you will find these rooms suitable for your purposes. The cost of these two rooms for one week is[2] $75.

If we can be of assistance to you in any other way, please do not hesitate[3] to let us know. Yours very truly, [67]

LESSON 46

443 Gentlemen: At 10 a.m. this morning we shipped you 500 copies of the convention program of the[1] National Electric Appliance Manufacturers to replace those in which the name of the speaker was misspelled. There[2] will, of course, be no charge for these programs.

I wish I could tell you how this mistake happened, but I cannot.[3] Ordinarily the proof of every program, circular, or booklet that we print is read twice. Someone[4] apparently released the program for printing without having it proofread by anybody.

I hope that the[5] Electric Appliance Manufacturers have a very successful, worthwhile convention. Sincerely yours, [119]

444 Mr. Harris: Within the next day or so I shall forward to you the diagram I prepared for the location[1] of furniture and equipment in our new quarters in the Chamber of Commerce Building.

After you and your[2] staff have had an opportunity to study the diagram, I would like to discuss with someone on your staff[3] the installation of electrical outlets for the electric typewriters and electric calculators[4] that we bought.

Any time between 11 a.m. and 3 p.m. on Wednesday, May 8, will be satisfactory[5] for me. A. J. Smith [104]

445 Dear Friend: Thanks to the miracle of electronics, you can now have an organ in your home for less than the price[1] of a fine piano. The science of electronics, which has already brought radio and television[2] within the reach of everyone, now brings you another delightful instrument, the Nelson electronic[3] organ.

This exciting electronic instrument develops far richer tones than are possible with other[4] types of organs. However, its cost is well within the reach of the average family budget.

Your neighborhood[5] dealer will welcome your visit. You will find your visit well worthwhile. Sincerely yours, [116]

446 Dear Friend: No doubt your lights went out on Saturday during the electrical storm that started at 10 a.m. and[1] lasted until about 5 p.m.

When this electrical storm hit us, we immediately alerted all[2] our repairmen, electricians, and supervisors. Notwithstanding the high winds, these men worked at great sacrifice[3] right through the storm.

In your neighborhood alone there were over a thousand breaks in transmission wires. Within twenty-four[4] hours, however, electricity had been brought back to more than 300,000 of our customers.

To the[5] thousands of customers like you who were without electricity, we extend our sincere, grateful thanks for[6] their patience. Very truly yours, [126]

447 Dear Mr. Abbey: Perhaps it has escaped your attention that your subscription to the *Radio Program Guide*[1] expired with the July issue. We are, however, sending you the August issue because we assume that you[2] will want to receive this program guide without interruption.

If you haven't yet sent us your renewal, why not do[3] so today. Cordially yours, [65]

448 Dear Tenant: It will be necessary for us to cut off your electric service from 11 a.m. until 1[1] p.m. on Thursday, June 16, while our electricians repair the electrical wiring on your floor of the Chamber[2] of Commerce Building. This is part of our general program of building improvement.

We are sorry to have[3] to deprive you of electric service for this period, but we are confident that you will be pleased with the more efficient[4] electric service you will receive as a result of this work. Yours very truly, [95]

LESSON 47

452 Dear Mr. Cunningham: Would it surprise you, Mr. Cunningham, if we told you that the next plant you build will be[1] worth more to the Pittsburgh Electric Company than it will be worth to you?

As you know, we sell electric power.[2] If you build your plant in our area, we will not sell electricity just to you. We will also sell it to[3] the home builders, to the merchants, and to the professional men your plant will attract.

You see, therefore, that the success[4] of your plant will be more important to us than one might think.

When you decide to build that new plant, let us tell[5] you about the fine sites that are available in the Pittsburgh area. Very truly yours, [118]

453 Dear Mr. Cummings: It is my pleasure, Mr. Cummings, to notify you that the board of directors has[1] authorized me to invite you to continue as a member of the Nashville Country Club during the coming year.[2]

The dues for the season have been set at $200. Please indicate on the enclosed card whether you wish[3] to accept this invitation, and return the card on or before April 5. If we do not hear from you by that[4] time, it will be our understanding that you wish to discontinue your membership in the Nashville Country Club.[5] Very truly yours, [103]

454 Dear Mr. Lexington: Sales letters, news releases, or any other materials that you duplicate will get better[1] attention if they are bright, clear, and easy to read.

You can make these messages more inviting by putting[2] them on Jacksonville duplicating papers, which are made especially for stencil work.

We would like to send you[3] our folder of duplicating papers. Once you have examined them, you will want to use one or more of them on[4] your next job. Cordially yours, [85]

455 Dear Mr. Wellington: You will find something new and convenient waiting for you the next time you drive to the Pittsburgh[1] National Bank. Our parking lot on Danville Place has been completely repaved, enlarged, and generally improved.[2]

No bank or business can solve the complicated parking problem for all of Pittsburgh, but we are doing our[3] utmost to make sure that the customers of the Pittsburgh National Bank will have plenty of free parking space while[4] they take care of their banking business.

Parking, Mr. Wellington, is part of the service of the Pittsburgh National[5] Bank, Pittsburgh's leading bank. Yours very truly, [109]

456 Dear Mr. Green: If you have not already made arrangements for moving from Pittsburgh to your new home on 18[1] Farmington Road, may we have the opportunity to send one of our representatives to give you an[2] estimate.

We are an established, well-known moving and storage firm.

Our representative, as well as our managers,[3] is looking forward to serving you. Cordially yours, [70]

457 Dear Mr. Buckingham: Don't run the risk of theft or loss by carrying around large sums of cash. Use a Nashville[1] Trust Company special checking account. You can open an account with any amount; no minimum balance[2] is required.

When you are in our neighborhood again, why not come in and open a special checking account. Cordially[3] yours, [62]

458 Dear Mr. Lexington: We have just learned that you have moved to Greensburg, and we would like to be among the first to[1] welcome you to our city.

We extend to you a cordial invitation to use the facilities of the[2] Greensburg National Bank whenever you need them. We would welcome the opportunity to meet you personally,[3] Mr. Lexington. We want to do all we can to help you get settled in Greensburg. Yours very truly,[4] [80]

LESSON 48

459 *Recall Chart*

1 Harm, becoming, justification, impending, exceedingly, checks.

2 Appears, called, qualify, misinform, encourages, young.

3 Program, furniture, consumed, names, skates, authorities.

4 Altogether, circulation, shown, amounts, utilities, subdividing.

5 Hopeless, savings, ounces, kingdom, ultimate, zealously.

6 Thin, pursued, terminations, childhood, family, earth.

7 Perplexing, respectful, forwarded, yelled, skillful, musical.

8 Confused, function, joining, threads, townships, costly.

9 Distribution, surest, distract, afternoon, privileged, desired.

10 Themselves, notify, conveniently, patiently, creative, encounter.

11 Exportation, quiet, including, dependable, whenever, electric wiring.

12 Scheduled, postponed, circumstantial, awakened, introduce, supervisor.

13 Self-made, compliance, entertain, investment, transportation, maintaining.

14 Louisville, emphatic, uncompromising, Washington, Birmingham, Nashville.

15 $3; $500,000; 3,000,000; 4 pounds; 3 o'clock; $8 billion.

16 To be, have been, has not been able, to know, to me, years ago.

17 Let us, to do, of course, at a loss, one of the, if you want.

461 *Faithful Servant*

The postman who puts the mail in your mailbox day after day is sort of a permanent soldier. He outwalks many[1] of the soldiers and marines in the armed services and keeps right on hiking along, rain or shine, day in and[2] day out. We know a postman who has been making his daily rounds for twenty-eight years, and in making those rounds he[3] has walked the equivalent distance of five times around the earth at the equator!

There are many people who[4] say that there is no indispensable man. But if there is one, it's the postman! He is our connecting link with[5] the rest of the world. Through the magic of his daily delivery of the mail, he brings minds and hearts closer together.[6] He speeds business, because more business is handled through letters than by any other way.

Postmen take millions[7] of footsteps each day to serve us. The mail, through the miracle of the postman's loyalty and spirit, always comes[8] through. [161]

462 *Self-Control*

One of the most important qualities a person must possess if he is to assume a position of[1] leadership in business is self-control. He must be able to control his temper even when others are losing[2] theirs. Before a person can control others, he must first learn to control himself.

If you will examine the traits[3] of men who have made good in business, you will find that they have also schooled themselves against making snap decisions.[4] They have made it a habit to consider things clearly, calmly, and carefully. In addition, they have kept their[5] personal feelings out of the picture.

A person is not born with this type of self-control. In fact, it is[6] contrary to the nature of most people. It takes practice to acquire it, but those who acquire it move ahead fast. There is[7] always a place at the top in business for them. [150]

463 *Pride*

Every one of us would like to be proud of himself. We all like to know that we really matter, that we[1] are needed, and that we are important to someone.

This will be an important fact for you to remember when[2] you rise to an executive position. If you can make people feel that they are really needed, wanted,[3] and important, they will always do their best for you.

The trouble with most of us is that we take too much for granted.[4] As long as others perform their jobs satisfactorily, we tend to forget how important they are to[5] us.

Who, for example, gives much thought to the people who do the cleaning in an office, in a factory, or[6] in a school? Yet the work that these people do is vital. If offices, factories, and schools were not cleaned, work would[7] come to a standstill.

When you stop to think about it, every employee, no matter how humble his position,[8] is important to the company. Do not forget it, and don't let him forget it. People never get tired[9] of hearing that they are important.

The person who takes pride in himself and in his work is a happy worker[10] and a productive worker. [205]

Chapter 9

LESSON 49

465 Mrs. Smith: Our store in Akron is doing so well that I am planning to add three people to my staff. I will[1] need two sales clerks, as well as a good typist.

Do you know of any girls who can fill these posts? If you do, please let me[2] know. James Church [42]

466 Dear Dad: Here is a nice surprise. I made a grade of 95 in French. As you know, I did not do so well in[1] French in the first semester. I did well in history, too. My grade is 90. In fact, I may make the dean's list.[2]

The last day of school is June 5, but I do not plan to arrive home till June 7. Can you meet my plane? It arrives[3] in Dallas at eight in the evening. Mary [68]

467 Mr. Baker: Last evening at home I read with pleasure the speech you plan to give at the May meeting of the[1] chemistry teachers of the East Side High School in Akron. Your speech is brief but not too brief. I am sure that the teachers[2] will like it.

I would make a minor change, though. I would omit the four lines that I have checked in blue pencil in the[3] margin of the last page. Harry J. Gates [67]

468 Dear Fred: As you know, since I moved to Dallas in 1970, I have had as my goal the opening of[1] my own car agency. I have at last reached that goal.

In March I am opening a Federal car agency[2] at 16 Church Road. I need not tell you, I am sure, that the Federal is the finest car made. In my two-story[3] showroom I will have the four cars in the Federal line that are making car history.

My staff of five people[4] will help you select the Federal car that will best serve your needs. Your neighbor [94]

469 Dear Mary: Do you realize that you left your red jacket in my living room last night? If you need the jacket,[1] let me know; I will mail it to you in a day or so. If you do not need it, I will keep the jacket here till I[2] see you again at Christmas. Helen [46]

470 To the Staff: I regret that I have to write you that Mr. Harry J. Harper has left our sales staff. He tells me[1] that he plans to go back to teaching school.

Mr. Harper did well in his territory; the whole staff will miss him.[2]

I do not have a man to take Mr. Harper's place. If you know of a man who you feel can sell our line of coats,[3] please let me know. James H. Smith [65]

471 Dear Neighbor: Do you have gas heat in your home? If you do not, you are missing a fine chance to lower your heating bills.[1] Gas is the best heat you can buy. It is the cleanest heat you can buy.

If you have a coal burner in your home, the[2] change to a gas burner is a simple matter.

Telephone or write your local gas dealer in Akron. He[3] will make a heating survey of your home that will show you the saving you can make if you change to gas. Yours, [79]

472 Mr. Gray: As you know, I plan to add two girls to my staff in April. Do you have two desks you can move to my[1] floor in a day or so to take care of these girls?

If you do not have two desks you can spare, please let me know. James[2] Bailey [41]

473 Dear Fred: If you have driven past my home, you have noticed, I am sure, the large hole in the middle of the road near[1] my gate. I wrote three letters to Mr. Baker, who is in charge of roads, advising him that the road is in bad[2] shape. I have not had an answer to any of my letters.

May I solicit your help as mayor to[3] get our road paved or at least patched. James R. Gibbs [68]

474 Dear Ned: May I ask a favor of you?

I am flying to Dallas late in May to take care of selling my dad's[1] home. That means that I cannot meet with my typing class at Baker School, as it meets each evening at seven. Can you[2] arrange to take the class in my absence?

If you can take it, please let me know so that I can mail you the class roll as[3] well as my set of lesson plans. George [66]

LESSON 50

477 Dear Madam: It was kind of you to write me that our staff rendered you special services on your last flight to the[1] Coast. Most people do not hesitate to write when they do not get the type of service to which they feel they are[2] entitled, but rarely do I hear from passengers who get fine service.

I will share your letter with the crew of your[3] flight. I am sure that they will be as pleased to read it as I was.

Should you have occasion to fly to the Coast again,[4] I sincerely hope that you will let our airline take you there. Sincerely yours, [94]

478 Dear Dr. Mild: You don't have to have any special talents to be able to fly a plane. The chances are that you can[1] learn to fly a plane in a matter of hours, especially if it is a National plane. Flying a National[2] plane is as easy as driving a car.

Let me prove this to you by giving you your first lesson for only[3] $5. If at the end of that first lesson I haven't proved to you that you can learn to fly, I will give you[4] back your $5.

Isn't that a fair offer? Sincerely yours, [92]

479 Dear Fred: I am sorry that it is necessary for me to write this letter, for I know the message I have to[1] give you will not make you happy. I am afraid that I shall not be able to keep my promise to talk to your sales[2] staff on June 15.

On June 7 my daughter was taken ill, and her doctor advised me to take her[3] to the Smith Clinic for a series of tests. I plan to drive her to the clinic and remain with her till she is[4] released.

I have asked my friend, Mr. James Gray, if he could take my place, and he said he would be happy to. I am[5] sure he would do a fine job for you.

If you would like to have Mr. Gray, please call him at 141-1166.[6] Yours very truly, [124]

480 Dear Sir: The bearer of this letter is my secretary, Miss Helen Green. Please show Miss Green your line of filing[1] cabinets. I am planning to buy a

cabinet for my private office, and I am asking Miss Green to select the[2] cabinet that will best meet our needs. Yours truly, [48]

481 Dear Friend: With the fall clothing season starting and with stocks at the Baker Clothing Mart at their peak, you couldn't[1] select a better occasion to choose your fall coat.

The chances are good that you will be able to find the coat that[2] really appeals to you in the large selection that our store provides. Our prices range from $60 to[3] $120.

If you prefer, you can pay for your coat on our special charge plan. Sincerely yours, [79]

482 Dear Sir: My secretary asked me, "Can't the Smith people pay their bills or at least answer our letters?"

I had to[1] admit that I did not know the answer. I need the answer badly, though, as I am getting ready to place the[2] matter in the hands of a collection agency.

That is a step I should be loath to take, but it is the[3] only course open for me if I do not hear from you by July 15.

Both you and I will be happier[4] when this matter has been settled. Yours very truly, [90]

483 Dear Sir: Mr. Harry Small, whom you are planning to hire as an official of the Akron Food Stores, has been with[1] me since 1967.

He was hired as a clerk and rapidly rose to the position of head buyer. Mr. Small[2] made a host of friends for our store, and I am sorry to lose his services.

I realize, though, that your offer is[3] a fine promotion for him; therefore, he leaves our store with our goodwill.

I know that Mr. Small will do a fine job[4] for you and that you will find him to be a real asset to the Akron Food Stores. Very truly yours, [99]

LESSON 51

486 Dear Joyce: You will recall that when I visited your home recently as a guest of your parents, you mentioned that[1] you would like to work in our manufacturing plant as a typist. I told you that I would be glad to let you[2] know when there was an opening.

Yesterday I learned that the manager of our order services, Mr. Quinn, needs[3] a typist.

If you still desire to work for us, stop in to see me on June 15 at 10 o'clock. I will see that[4] you meet Mr. Quinn, who will tell you all about the job. I think you would like working for him.

Please remember me to[5] your parents. Sincerely yours, [105]

487 Dear Friend: Thank you for visiting our store recently and purchasing a pair of our shoes. We know that the shoes will give[1] you many years of fine service.

We keep a permanent record of the type and size of shoes you purchase. When you again[2] need a pair of shoes, you can simply place an order for them by telephone or by mail.

Once again, thank you for your[3] business. Sincerely yours, [64]

488 Dear Friend: Thank you for your letter telling us that you plan to register in the Woods School of Business in the fall.[1] We were very glad to learn of your plans. We are sure that you will find your work here challenging.

We still have a number[2] of rooms

available in Smith Hall. Before we can assign one to you, though, we shall have to have your deposit of[3] $25 soon.

I am enclosing a brochure about our school that just came off the press. It lists many[4] reasons why we believe that the Woods School of Business is a leader in its field. Please read it. Sincerely yours,[5] [101]

489 Dear Friend: It has been more than six months since we have seen you in our store or had the pleasure of serving you in any[1] way.

We have always tried to keep our store a friendly place in which to shop. We are wondering if we have failed in[2] our aim or have not given you the service that you have a right to receive. If we have offended you in any[3] way, won't you please tell us.

As you know, your credit rating with us is high.

It is our sincere hope that you[4] will visit us soon so that we may show you the many fine bargains that we have on our racks. Yours very truly,[5] [100]

490 Dear Friend: This year's *Handbook of Business* will be available on March 15. This handbook will provide a wealth of valuable[1] financial and business statistics that are of great importance to you in the operation of your[2] manufacturing business.

If you will mail the enclosed card, we shall be glad to send you a copy. Cordially yours, [58]

491 Dear Sir: Perhaps you may think it strange that we should be talking about Christmas so early in the year, but just before[1] the holidays we are always faced with more orders for our products than we can fill. We are, therefore, writing[2] you today to be sure that we can take care of your needs.

As you know, we have many Christmas packages of candies,[3] attractively wrapped for the Christmas season, at prices ranging from $3 to $15.

If you will[4] mail us your gift list soon, we will enclose a name card with each gift. Sincerely yours, [94]

492 Dear Friend: There is nothing like getting your paper the first thing in the morning. That is why so many people have[1] us deliver the *Troy Post* to their door bright and early each morning. They find that this service helps them start their day[2] off right—and it costs only a few pennies a week.

There are two ways that you can order delivery service:[3]

1. Call 117-1414 and tell the operator that you would like the *Troy Post* delivered each morning.[4]

2. Mail the enclosed coupon, and we will take care of all the necessary details.

Why not call or write us to[5] begin this service for you at once. Very truly yours, [110]

LESSON 52

496 Dear Mr. Temple: I have delayed acknowledging your letter of August 10 for this reason: We were considering[1] the advantages of sending our representative to France to set up an agency to handle[2] our computers and other equipment on the continent of Europe. It was our thought that this man could stop in[3] London on his way to Paris and go over your questions with you in person. This would be a better way than trying[4] to answer them through correspondence.

We have now made a decision. Our representative, Mr. Fenton,[5] will arrive in London on Friday, September 30, and depart for Paris on Thursday, November 6. Will[6] you have an opportunity to see him during his stay in London? Sincerely yours, [136]

497 Dear Mr. Crowley: Nobody likes to fly in bad weather. Perhaps that is why so many big businessmen like flying[1] in a Hughes jet. No other plane gets up and over bad weather faster than a Hughes jet. With its pure jet motors the[2] Hughes develops more power than any other commercial airliner. It climbs rapidly and flys at the rate of[3] 500 miles an hour.

The Hughes jet sells for less than any other business jet that you can buy. For all the facts about[4] the Hughes jet, call us to arrange a demonstration flight. Yours truly, [93]

498 Dear Mr. Abbott: Are you in a spot where you must have cash immediately to pay off debts or for any other[1] good reason? If you are, we suggest that you stop in to see us without delay. Have a confidential talk with[2] an officer of our credit division. His job is to help you. He is paid to make things as easy as possible[3] for you to obtain a loan.

It costs very little to borrow at the County Trust Company. Our rates are listed[4] on the table that is enclosed.

It will be well worth your while to see us whenever you must have cash in a hurry.[5] Sincerely yours, [103]

499 Dear Mr. Hughes: At the present time we have no opening in our accounting division, and there seems little[1] chance that such an opening will occur before September or October.

If you would care to consider a[2] position with our company as a correspondent, I should be glad to have you fill out and mail to me the[3] enclosed application.

After I have had an opportunity to study your application, I will write[4] you about a possible conference with the head of the correspondence department. Cordially yours, [99]

500 Gentlemen: This is just a note to tell you how happy we are with our advertising in the *Times*.

Recently[1] we had an illustration of the value of advertising in the *Times*. In our last series of advertisements[2] we stressed our new paint-job service for automobiles, which we are offering for $80. The number[3] of replies has been very gratifying. Definite proof of the pulling power of the *Times* was provided by[4] the number of customers who came in with a copy of our advertisement in their hands.[5]

You may be sure that we shall continue to make provision for advertising in the *Times*. Cordially yours, [115]

LESSON 53

503 Dear Miss Dexter: The amount you owe us is, of course, small, but it means very much to us. The collection of small sums,[1] taken together, makes it possible for our organization to continue the publication of our[2] magazine.

I think you will agree that each week's *Magazine of Science* brings you a wealth of exciting and useful[3] material as well as creative ideas on many subjects.

Frankly, I would like to go on sending the[4] magazine to you regularly, but unless I receive your payment by next week, I shall have to drop your name from[5] our list.

I hope, therefore, that you will pay

the enclosed statement promptly. Sincerely yours, [115]

504 Dear Mr. Long: The purpose of this letter is to ask your help regarding a difficult problem that I am[1] facing.

I am responsible for obtaining a speaker to address a meeting of public relations[2] directors on June 16. I have extended invitations to six different people, but all of them said no[3] for one reason or another.

Can you suggest a speaker who can handle this assignment? We shall, of course, pay[4] him our regular speaker's fee of $150 as well as take care of his traveling expenses.[5] Yours very truly, [104]

505 Dear Mr. Underwood: Every investor today must consider the factor of progressive inflation.[1] If he is not careful, he may find that some of his investments are worth much less than he thinks.

The most satisfactory[2] way to protect your investments against inflation is to read *The Wall Street Bulletin* regularly. The[3] facts that this newspaper brings you daily will help you decide which stocks you should hold, which stocks you should buy, and which stocks[4] you should probably sell.

Ordinarily *The Wall Street Bulletin* sells for $12 a year, but we are making[5] you a special trial offer of six months for only $3.

Why not send us your order today. Sincerely[6] yours, [121]

506 Gentlemen: Our idea of a collection letter may be summarized as follows:

1. It should be brief.
2. It[1] should be friendly.
3. It should be successful.

This letter is brief; it is friendly. Whether it is successful[2] depends on whether you send us your check to take care of your unpaid invoices. Very truly yours, [58]

507 Dear Mr. Dexter: In 1910 the National Bank of New York was a successful pioneer in the field[1] of foreign banking.

Recently we added another country to the long list that we serve. On April 10 we[2] opened an office in Paris.

If you would like to have all the facts about the helpful services that this new[3] bank can render your organization, you can obtain them by writing to us. Yours very truly, [77]

508 Dear Mr. Banker: As a regular reader of the *Miami Times*, you will be particularly happy[1] to learn of a novel service we are starting next Monday. Beginning with that issue, the *Miami Times*[2] will publish daily a civil service section that will provide a complete list of positions that are open,[3] public examinations that will be held, and appointments that have been made in the civil service.

If you have[4] any suggestions on other ways in which we can increase the usefulness of our newspaper in the days ahead,[5] please be sure to let us know. Very truly yours, [109]

509 Dear Mr. Yale: No matter where you go on your vacation in this country, you can get your regular copy[1] of the *Miami Times*. If Uncle Sam can find you, we can see to it that you enjoy your regular newspaper[2] every day.

Before you get into the packing rush, mail the enclosed blank to us and let us be responsible[3] for all the details.

Do it now so that you won't miss a single issue. Cordially yours, [76]

LESSON 54

513 Dear Mr. Billings: Are you a sports fan? If you are, then the sports section of our newspaper, *The Daily Times,* is[1] for you. Have *The Daily Times* delivered to your home early each morning throughout the year. Every day in[2] every season, you will be informed about the happenings in the world of sports.

Our experienced editors[3] will bring you all sports news objectively reported and colorfully described. They will give you all the facts and[4] figures that every sports fan enjoys.

Call us at 414-3131 today between the hours of nine[5] and five and we will have tomorrow's *Daily Times* at your door early in the morning. Very truly yours, [118]

514 Dear Mr. Samuels: A short time ago you mentioned to me, Mr. Samuels, that you were planning to leave your[1] government job and that you wanted to get into some phase of merchandising in the near future.

If you have[2] not altered your plans since I saw you, you may be interested in the job described in the enclosed letter from[3] my former partner, Max Stern. You have the technical experience for that job, and I can certainly vouch for[4] the fact that you are capable, forceful, and hardworking.

You may, of course, use my name as a character reference[5] if you apply for the job. Sincerely yours, [109]

515 Dear Miss Brown: Have you seen the new Chester camera that makes taking pictures even more fun? With this practical camera,[1] you snap your picture, press a button, and a few seconds later lift out a beautiful print regardless of[2] the weather.

You will experience a real thrill when you see the picture shortly after you have taken it.

The Chester[3] camera takes pictures indoors as well as outdoors. It makes no difference whether the sun is shining, whether[4] it is cloudy, or whether it is raining.

If you would be interested in receiving our free descriptive[5] booklet, *Cameras Can Be Fun,* just return the enclosed card. Yours very truly, [113]

516 Dear Mr. Gates: If you are interested in buying modern furniture for your office, we invite you to[1] visit our showrooms on Railroad Avenue. In these showrooms, Mr. Gates, you will find sixty individual[2] office settings. We believe that the best way for a customer to obtain exactly what he wants is to see[3] our furniture in actual office settings.

In our showrooms you will also find a staff of technical[4] advisors ready to discuss your needs with you. These people, all of them recognized furniture experts, can answer[5] any questions you may have to ask.

You will find your dealings with us easy, pleasant, and profitable. You will never regret[6] having come to us. Sincerely yours, [127]

517 Dear Mr. Samuels: Thank you for the nice order we received from you a few days ago for a quantity[1] of our sporting goods.

I am sorry to report that our credit file on your organization is not complete.[2] We cannot, therefore, ship this merchandise to you on open account.

As time is short, Mr. Samuels, may we[3] suggest that on this order you send us your advance check for $480. Then after this merchandise[4] has been manufactured and we have the actual cost figures, we will immediately refund to you[5] the amount of any overpayment.

We shall, of course, continue our credit investigation in the[6] hope that we can offer you our regular terms on future orders. Cordially yours, [135]

518 *Car*

A father was objecting to the girl that his son was dating. He insisted that the son be more particular[1] about the company he kept. "I'm sorry, Dad," said the boy, "but that's the best girl I can get with the car[2] we've got." [41]

LESSON 55

522 Dear Mr. West: When visitors enter your office, what do they see? Do they see furniture that is shabby? Or[1] do they see furniture that gives the impression of comfort, success, and prosperity?

If your furniture was[2] purchased from the Empire Furniture Company, your visitors will be favorably impressed.

If you need new office[3] furniture, now is an exceedingly good time to visit us. Everything on our floors is on sale.[4] Consequently, you will be able to make substantial savings on your purchases.

While you are here, you can talk with one[5] of our interior decorators. He will be glad to help you select quality furniture that will[6] meet your requirements and specifications.

Convince yourself of the high quality of our furniture. Come in[7] to see us. Sincerely yours, [145]

523 Dear Mr. Green: Our records show that you used the facilities of the Transcontinental Hotel four times in[1] the last six months. We hope, Mr. Green, that you enjoyed yourself here every time.

As you stay with us so frequently,[2] wouldn't you enjoy the convenience of one of our credit cards? We want you to enjoy every[3] possible privilege and service that we offer. If you would like one of our cards, simply return the enclosed form.[4]

When your travels take you to Chicago again, please stop in to see me. My office is on the lobby floor. It will[5] be a genuine pleasure to meet you personally. Very truly yours, [113]

524 *Your Telephone Voice*

Have you ever "met" a person for the first time over the telephone? Usually you could tell by his voice[1] the kind of person he was. If his voice was pleasant and his tone friendly, he impressed you as a nice person to[2] know and to do business with. If his voice was gruff and unfriendly, you completed the call with the feeling that he[3] was probably a difficult person to get along with.

What impression do you give people over the[4] telephone? You cannot, of course, be seen. You can only be heard, and your voice must convey your personality.[5]

Do you speak with clarity? Are you logical in expressing your thoughts? Are you tactful? Do you have "the voice with[6] a smile"?

You will represent your company over the telephone. By speaking softly, by choosing words that convey[7] your thoughts clearly, and by giving the caller the feeling that you are sincerely interested in helping[8] him, you will make friends for your organization. [168]

525 Dear Mr. Abbey: A man is judged by his letters, and so is his company. After all, business letters are[1] the representatives he sends to speak for him and his company.

When your letters look sloppy, they make a[2] very poor impression. That is one good reason why you should trade in your old typewriters on new Nelsons.

Surprisingly[3] enough, new Nelsons will save you a great deal of money because they require very little servicing.

Our[4] representative in your locality, Mr. E. H. Green, will be glad to submit to you a plan that will tell[5] you just when it will pay you to trade in your old machines for more efficient Nelsons. Very truly yours, [118]

LESSON 56

529 Dear Mr. Wellington: Can women make good supervisors in your company? One way to find out is to try[1] several of your women employees in supervisory jobs, but this can be expensive. A better way[2] is to enroll promising young women in our practical, stimulating training program. This is the[3] economical way.

Employers in many large businesses are finding out that our program brings results, and they are sending[4] more and more women to us for supervisory training.

Our booklet, *Women as Supervisors,* gives the[5] complete story about our program. If you would like a copy, we shall be glad to forward one to you. Just fill out and[6] mail the enclosed stamped, self-addressed postcard. Sincerely yours, [130]

530 Dear Mr. Wellington: Buckingham self-service elevators have been in successful operation for many years[1] in office buildings throughout the country. Building owners are finding that the installation of Buckingham self-[2]service elevators results in substantial savings in overhead. Under the circumstances wouldn't it be worthwhile[3] for you to study the possibility of installing them in your building?

If you would like a list of[4] the buildings in your neighborhood that presently have Buckingham self-service elevators, return the enclosed stamped,[5] self-addressed postcard. When we receive it, we will forward the list to you promptly. Sincerely yours, [117]

531 Dear Mr. Rich: No two successful businessmen look alike, dress alike, or work alike. When you see a man who[1] fits a certain pattern, however, the chances are that you are looking at a superior executive.[2] Here are some of the ways to spot him:

1. He has self-confidence and does not shirk responsibility.

2. He[3] is able to supervise several jobs simultaneously without becoming flustered.

3. He has an office[4] that helps him to work efficiently.

It is in this last point, Mr. Rich, that our furniture helps. Our equipment[5] gives the executive or supervisor an office that looks attractive. An attractive, efficient office[6] helps him sell himself and his ideas.

When you are in the market for new office furniture, let us show you our[7] line. Cordially yours, [144]

532 Dear Mrs. Gates: When our grandparents were married, the only major appliance they had was probably a small[1] refrigerator. They never dreamed

of most of the electric appliances that today's young couples take for[2] granted.

Even twenty-five years ago who would have thought of electric washing machines, electric home air conditioners,[3] and television?

Of course, with more appliances in the house, more current is used. However, electricity[4] is more than ever a big bargain. With our new, economical rates, the more electricity you use, the[5] less your electricity costs per kilowatt hour.

To receive our booklet, *How Electricity Can Serve the*[6] *Consumer,* return the enclosed card. Very truly yours, [130]

533 Dear Mr. Jones: Without a doubt the most welcome and most appreciated check that reached my desk this morning was[1] yours for $200 covering your April, May, and June balances.

Thanks for working with us so thoughtfully[2] in setting up a payment program that met our requirements and yet did not ultimately place too great a[3] burden on your finances. May I congratulate you, too, on having overcome the trying circumstances[4] that made things so difficult for you during the past few months.

It was a pleasure cooperating with you, and[5] we look forward to serving you again when you need electrical appliances. Very truly yours, [119]

534 Dear Mrs. Harrington: Recently we forwarded to you a Maintenance Service Agreement for your electric[1] machines. As we have not received a signed copy from you, we again bring to your attention the benefits[2] that will accrue to you from our maintenance program.

The great majority of our customers now avail themselves[3] of the Maintenance Service Agreement, for they find that it reduces to a minimum the expense and[4] inconvenience caused by service calls.

We would appreciate it if you would return to us one signed copy and[5] retain the duplicate for your files. Cordially yours, [110]

Chapter 10

LESSON 57

537 Dear Mrs. Short: On September 19 we wrote you in regard to a new idea we had to encourage reading[1] on the part of students. We were going to organize a group called the Teen-age Book Club. The purpose of our[2] letter, Mrs. Short, was to put before you the general details of the program of publications we had[3] in mind.

The idea was presented to the public, and it gives promise of becoming an immediate success.[4] As you will see by the enclosed circular, we have already contracted for books on a wide variety[5] of subjects of interest to teen-agers.

We want to thank you and the other responsible men and women[6] who were generous with their encouragement, suggestions, and money in helping us organize the program.[7] Sincerely yours, [142]

538 Gentlemen: Your letter of Friday, June 16, expressing interest in the government's correspondence[1] practices and requesting a copy of the *Government Correspondence Handbook* has been referred to me.

Our correspondence[2] handbook has recently been revised, and at the present time it is in the hands of the printer. If everything[3] goes well, we will probably have copies in about ten days. When we receive a quantity at this office,[4] I will send you a copy.

If there is any other way in which we can help you, please let us know. Yours very truly, [99]

539 Dear Mr. Stone: How do you read your newspaper? Do you begin on the front page and read straight through, or do you turn[1] first to the amusement page?

In our judgment, reading a newspaper is a personal thing. No two people do[2] it the same way.

Yet as the publishers of the *Daily Sun,* one of the world's greatest newspapers, we recognize[3] that we have an important responsibility to improve people's newspaper reading habits.

To meet this[4] responsibility, our editors have written a leaflet that suggests ways to make your newspaper reading[5] more pleasurable, more profitable, and more interesting.

We shall be glad to send you a copy free upon request.[6] Sincerely yours, [123]

540 Dear Mr. Young: A friend once told us that for amusement he watches and speculates about people as he sees[1] them passing on the street or waiting in a railroad station. He says that many persons seem alike in general,[2] but somehow each is different.

We find that this is true with our customers. Each one is the same because each has[3] needs that must be supplied; yet no two persons seem to have identical needs. Some persons know exactly what they[4] want, and we serve them promptly. Others like to browse, and they are equally welcome.

You know, a hardware store is, actually,[5] a fascinating place. We suggest that you come to Allen's the next time you are in town and see[6] for yourself. Very truly yours, [125]

541 Dear Mr. Brown: Are those tires of yours becoming worn? If they are, here is your opportunity to dispose[1] of them at a worthwhile profit.

We must obtain a quantity of used tires to take care of an order from a foreign[2] government. If you are interested in selling your tires, fill out the enclosed form and return it in the[3] envelope that is also enclosed. Yours truly, [69]

542 Dear Mr. Lord: As you requested, we sent you yesterday one of our regular catalogs. You should receive[1] it shortly.

We are sure, Mr. Lord, that you will find this catalog helpful in selecting the things you need for[2] yourself and for your family.

Our popular time-payment plan is described in an advertisement on page 6[3] of the catalog. We shall be glad to have you take advantage of this plan.

Whenever we can be of further[4] service to you, please let us know. Very truly yours, [90]

543 Gentlemen: I have been asked to speak at the convention of the New York Business Teachers Association[1] on the subject of "Correspondence in Business." My purpose in writing you is to ask whether you still publish[2] a book entitled *The Correspondent's Manual* by E. H. Brown. If you do, please send me a copy as soon[3] as possible. My recollection is that it contains many stimulating ideas, and I would like to use[4] some of them in my speech.

I will, of course, send you my check as soon as I receive your bill. Yours very truly, [99]

LESSON 58

546 Dear Mr. Brown: Thank you for your order for one of our electric blankets. It will be shipped just as soon as you[1] let us know which color you prefer. This blanket is available in six colors; they are listed at the bottom of[2] this letter.

We want to be sure that your order is handled exactly the way you want it handled. We are,[3] therefore, checking with you before we make shipment. When we hear from you, we will fill your order promptly. Sincerely[4] yours, [81]

547 Dear Mr. Day: A hundred years ago most people could read at the rate of about 300 words a minute. A hundred[1] years ago that rate was adequate to keep up with what was happening in the world.

Today, however, our knowledge[2] is expanding so rapidly that some people who want to keep up to date are actually falling behind.[3] There is simply too much to read.

What is the solution? Learn how to read faster. During the past five years more than[4] 400,000 people have done this by taking our rapid reading course. Many of them have tripled their reading[5] speed.

If you would like to know more about our course, stop in at one of our twelve offices and let us tell you about it.[6] Very truly yours, [123]

548 Dear Mr. Best: A dollar doesn't go nearly so far as it did some years ago, does it? As our needs are the same[1] as they ever were, we must be very careful how we spend each dollar.

If you want to make your money give you the greatest[2] value, do your shopping from the pages of our catalog, a copy of which we sent you several weeks ago.[3] It contains several thousand items of all types of merchandise. No matter what your needs may be, you are sure[4] to find our catalog helpful.

A form is enclosed for your convenience in sending us your order. Sincerely[5] yours, [101]

549 Dear Mrs. Wilson: It is a pleasure to welcome you as one of our new credit customers, and we hope that[1] you will have many opportunities to use the special services that we offer to our credit customers.[2]

Your credit card is enclosed. This card will make your shopping in our store easy, quick, and convenient. All it needs[3] is your signature.

Thank you, Mrs. Wilson, for the confidence you have expressed in our store by opening an[4] account with us. Sincerely yours, [86]

550 Dear Mr. Johnson: As you requested, we sent you several days ago one of our brochures on air conditioning.[1] We hope that you found it helpful in answering your questions.

In about two or three weeks one of our[2] representatives, Mr. E. H. Green, will be in your city for a few days. When he arrives, he would like to[3] discuss your air-conditioning problems with you.

Mr. Green will telephone you as soon as he arrives in Westport[4] to inquire about a convenient time to see you. If there is any other information we can supply[5] you in the meantime, please be sure to let us know. Yours very truly, [112]

551 Dear Mr. Baker: We appreciate very much your order for stationery that you gave to our[1] representative, Mr. Brown, several days ago.

Since this is our first transaction with you, would you be good enough[2] to fill out and return the blank that is enclosed. Any information you give us will, of course, be kept confidential.[3] Very truly yours, [63]

LESSON 59

554 Gentlemen: In the past I was an extremely slow reader. I was considerably embarrassed whenever a person[1] handed me something to read and then waited until I had finished. Furthermore, I did not always comprehend[2] everything I read.

When I recently saw your ad describing your rapid reading kit, I decided[3] I had nothing to lose by purchasing it. That was the wisest investment I ever made.

After following the[4] suggestions in the kit for only two months, I can already read in a few moments what formerly took me[5] minutes to cover.

I cannot, of course, measure my improvement accurately, but I know that my reading speed[6] has increased substantially. Sincerely yours, [128]

555 Dear Mr. Casey: Thank you for your letter of Thursday, June 15, in which you reported to us the[1] inconvenience you experienced on your plane trip to Washington to attend a conference.

It was indeed unfortunate[2] that engine trouble delayed your flight and that as a result you missed your connection to Albany.

We[3] spare no effort, Mr. Casey, to maintain our planes in perfect mechanical condition. However, we occasionally[4] encounter minor difficulties that are beyond our control.

We are exceedingly sorry that[5] you incurred an additional expense in the amount of $3.80 in order to reach your destination.[6] A check for that amount is enclosed. Sincerely yours, [131]

556 Dear Mr. Harper: It is indeed a pleasure to give you complete, up-to-the-minute information about our[1] air travel plan.

This plan is a worldwide charge account arrangement for air travel. It requires a deposit of[2] $250, but it permits unlimited charge privileges over the routes of more than 80[3] scheduled airlines throughout the world.

The enclosed folder describes the plan. To take advantage of it, all you[4] need do is sign the enclosed form and return it with your check for $250. Cordially yours, [99]

557 Mr. Green: The past year was a very successful one for our organization, and I feel we have taken[1] very important steps forward. You and the people in your department have been of great assistance in refining,[2] extending, and improving service to our customers.

We must, of course, expect new problems in the days ahead.[3] I have complete confidence, however, that you and your staff will meet them in the same effective, commonsense way[4] that you met this year's problems.

Please convey my congratulations to all the members of your staff. James H. Brown [99]

558 Dear Mr. Baker: Thank you for sending us your financial statement so promptly. Let me congratulate you on[1] the fine credit record your concern has made for itself.

We have shipped your order of March 16 via express, and[2] you should receive the furniture early next week.

As we explained to you, we will bill you on the tenth of[3] each month for merchandise purchased the previous month. If you pay your invoice within 10 days, you are entitled[4] to a discount of 2 percent.

We hope that you will enjoy doing business with us. For our part we shall do[5] everything we can to deserve the confidence you have placed in us. Very truly yours, [116]

559 Dear Mr. Harper: Mr. Harry Brown, a former clerk in your concern, has submitted your name as a reference[1] and has indicated that you can tell us of his education, his experience, and his character.

We[2] would appreciate your replies to the following questions:

How long was Mr. Brown in your employ?

What was his[3] highest salary?

What were his duties?

We would also be grateful for any other information that might[4] be of assistance to us in our consideration of Mr. Brown as a prospective employee.

You have[5] our assurance, of course, that we shall keep this information confidential. Yours very truly, [117]

LESSON 60

562 Dear Mr. Stern: One of the scheduled domestic airlines has asked us to make an impartial study of its passenger[1] service to determine how it compares with that of other airlines.

Since you have been flying on commercial[2] airlines for many years, you are in the best possible position to give us answers to the questions on the enclosed[3] questionnaire. Won't you fill out that questionnaire now. You can easily do this in a few moments.

A self-addressed,[4] stamped envelope is enclosed for your convenience in returning the questionnaire.

We shall be extremely grateful[5] for your help. Very truly yours, [109]

563 Dear Mr. Miner: Summer will be with us shortly. With it will undoubtedly come many hot, humid, and[1] uncomfortable days and nights. This will not disturb you, however, if you have an efficient, dependable Mason[2] air conditioner in your home. This unit will maintain your house at an even, refreshing temperature[3] during the entire day.

What will this coming summer's comfort cost you? Depending on the type of air conditioner[4] you select, it will cost you between $150 and $200.

Come in without delay[5] to select your air conditioner, and be ready for the uncomfortable weather that summer brings. Yours[6] very truly, [123]

564 Dear Mr. Green: If you are capable of writing and want to sell what you write, be sure to read John Smith's book, *The*[1] *Writer's Manual.* The author's helpful, down-to-earth suggestions take you easily and efficiently through all[2] the steps of successful writing.

We shall be glad to send you a copy of the book on a special ten-day trial[3] basis. If after that time you have satisfied yourself that you cannot use the book profitably, repack it and[4] return it to us; we will assume the cost of mailing. If you feel that the book is exactly what you want, send[5] us your payment of $5.50. Very truly yours, [113]

565 Dear Mr. Jones: At the end of each year it is desirable for every businessman to inform himself about[1] the state of the economy if he is to run his business efficiently.

In *The Annual Business Review,*[2] which will come off the press on January 3, we bring you the whole complex picture of the country's business and[3] what is in store for it during the coming year. This useful volume discusses such fundamental questions as[4] these:

1. What is our present national debt, and is it possible to carry it indefinitely?
2. Are[5] taxes too high, or can we easily stand more?
3. What is our annual consumption of goods?

The[6] *Annual Business Review* sells for a special price of only $8. Cordially yours, [137]

566 Dear Mr. Harris: This is just a note to remind you that our special offer of 18 months of the *News*[1] *Magazine* for $10 will expire in a few days.

Here is a fine chance for you to start reading the *News Magazine,*[2] a custom that is shared by more than 250,000 busy, successful executives. These people[3] depend on us to keep their business information up to date, to supply them with a wealth of profitable[4] ideas, and to provide many hours of reading enjoyment.

Your subscription on this special offer can start[5] with the September issue if you sign and return the enclosed card within the next week. Cordially yours, [119]

567 Dear Mr. Green: Thank you for writing us about the two bank statements that were sent to you in unsealed envelopes.[1]

If there is one thing on which the Nashville Mutual Savings Bank and Trust Company prides itself, it is on its[2] effort to take every precaution to see that the financial affairs of our depositors are kept[3] confidential. I am, therefore, grateful to you for calling this matter to our attention and for your patience concerning[4] this annoying situation.

We have taken steps, Mr. Green, to see that this mistake will not recur. Sincerely[5] yours, [101]

568 *Doctor*

A father was asked by a friend how his son who was a doctor was getting along in his practice.

"Fine," said the[1] father. Then with a slight grin, he added, "He is doing so well that he can occasionally tell a patient[2] that there is nothing the matter with him." [47]

LESSON 61

571 Dear Mrs. Deems: Thank you for your letter telling us about the self-study units in employee supervision[1] that you developed.

We are always interested in seeing new materials in the areas in which we publish.[2] If you would care to send me a set of your self-study units, I will transmit them to the proper editor.[3] After he submits his report, I will write you whether we can publish them.

We appreciate your thoughtfulness,[4] Mrs. Deems, in giving us an opportunity to consider your self-study units in employee[5] supervision. Sincerely yours, [106]

572 Dear Mr. Andrews: On Friday, June 15, I was transferred to the New

York office of the International[1] Electric Company. This transfer was necessitated by the death of the manager of that office. I[2] left for New York on June 16.

I wish that I had had time to thank you personally for the business you gave me[3] during the years that I called on you. Because of the suddenness of my transfer, this was impossible.

My place[4] in Chicago will be taken by James Underwood, who presently has overall supervision of our electric[5] appliances division. I have asked Mr. Underwood to call on you as soon as possible and introduce himself.[6] Yours very truly, [124]

573 Dear Mr. Overmeyer: You will be interested to know that now any office can afford a postage[1] meter. There is a model for every office, whether it is large or small.

The Interboro postage meter [2] is electrically operated. It prints postage right on the envelope. It also prints a dated[3] postmark and, if you wish, a small advertisement of your goods.

Why not let us install an Interboro postage[4] meter in your office for a month's trial. If your mailing room supervisor is not happy with it at the end of[5] that time, you can return it at our expense. Cordially yours, [112]

574 To All Department Heads and Supervisors: When circumstances call for the transfer of an employee from one[1] city to another, the company will pay the cost of transportation for the employee and his family[2] from his former residence to his new permanent residence.

The company will pay all reasonable costs of[3] packing, insuring, and transporting the employee's furniture and household goods.

This new policy is intended[4] to make sure that no employee shall suffer a financial loss as a result of being transferred in the[5] best interests of the company. John H. Jones [109]

575 Gentlemen: Our company, which manufactures high-quality furniture, is considering expanding its[1] facilities and is thinking of Albany as a possible site for this expansion.

We would like to know,[2] therefore, about the advantages that Albany might have for an enterprise such as ours. Our proposed expansion[3] would involve a plant employing about 1,000 people, a substantial number of whom would have to be[4] recruited from the area in which we decide to locate.

May we expect a reply soon. Very truly yours,[5] [100]

576 Dear Mr. Allen: It seldom becomes necessary for us to transfer an account to a collection[1] agency. When circumstances leave us no alternative, we consider it in the interests of the customer[2] to tell him exactly what we intend to do.

If we do not hear from you by February 22,[3] we shall be compelled to transfer your account to a collection agency. Please use the enclosed envelope to[4] let us hear from you. Yours very truly, [87]

577 Dear Mr. Green: According to a recent survey, it costs the average business $1.25[1] to write a check.

Actually the cost of the check itself is a small item. A much larger cost factor is[2] the time consumed in checking invoices, preparing and signing checks, and similar activities.

Enterprising[3] companies have found that when they introduced a Superior electric check signer, they substantially[4] cut the overhead cost of issuing a check.

It is definitely to your interest to get the facts about[5] the Superior electric check signer. These facts are yours if you will fill out and return the enclosed card.[6] Sincerely yours, [122]

578 Dear Mr. Green: Thank you for your letter telling us of the report that you are making on electric typewriters.[1] As you know, we are manufacturers of the leading electric typewriter on the market. Naturally[2] we are interested in all developments in the field of electric[3] typewriting.

Enclosed is a folder[3] of reprints that describe the experiences of educators who have used the electric typewriter[4] for teaching beginning typing and advanced transcription.

We hope that this folder contains all the information you[5] need for your report. Yours very truly, [107]

LESSON 62

581 Dear Mr. Billings: May I offer you my congratulations on your promotion to the position of[1] president of the Electric Appliance Company. I know that you have outstanding technical qualifications[2] for this position, and I am sure that the Electric Appliance Company will enjoy great prosperity[3] under your leadership.

However, I offer you my congratulations with mixed feelings. I am exceedingly[4] happy for you, but I am sorry for our township. It will lose the benefit of your leadership in the[5] various programs of which you have been an important part.

I hope, Mr. Billings, that you will visit your old[6] neighborhood occasionally. Sincerely yours, [129]

582 Dear Mr. Cunningham: Perhaps you feel sure that the securities you own are the best securities you can[1] find. If that is the way you feel, that is fine. But if you would like to have an impartial, technically competent[2] person take a look at your security holdings, our advice is yours for the asking.

Just come in and talk[3] with us about your investment program. We will give you the best advice we can. If you wish, we will help you formulate[4] a new program. No appointment is necessary. Sincerely yours, [94]

583 Dear Mr. Birmingham: Your letter of April 16 asking whether we have a program to develop[1] executives was passed on to me by Mr. Green.

We do have a well-planned, comprehensive program in which we try[2] to develop leadership, responsibility, and other qualities in potential executives.

We[3] believe that the success of such a program depends upon the way the men who are invited to take the course[4] are selected. For that reason we have devised a list of qualifications that each man must meet before he[5] will be accepted. A copy of the list is enclosed.

If we can be of further assistance to you, please be sure[6] to let us know. Yours very truly, [126]

584 Dear Miss Davis: Thank you for your letter applying for a position as file clerk with our organization.[1]

Unfortunately, there are no openings at the present time in our filing department. When an opening[2] occurs, we shall certainly arrange an interview for you.

I am happy to tell you, Miss Davis, that we were[3] exceedingly impressed with your qualifications. Very truly yours, [73]

585 Dear Mr. Wilmington: May I express with all sincerity my gratification for the wonderful job[1] your staff did over the past weekend in repairing the fire damage to our telephone facilities. As you[2] know, your men willingly worked around the clock and did not stop until the job was done.

This was typical of your[3] company's tradition of providing service under the worst possible conditions.

If there is some way I[4] could personally express my feelings to each man who worked on the job, I would certainly like to do so.[5]

Congratulations, Mr. Wilmington, on a tremendous job well done. Yours very truly, [117]

586 Dear Mr. Buckingham: Thank you for the advertising contract that you forwarded to me covering your[1] sponsorship of a program on our radio station on Monday, April 15, from 8 to 9 p.m.

Because[2] of circumstances over which we have no control, that hour will not be available. We received a notification[3] to the effect that at 8 p.m. on that day the President will speak to the nation on the present[4] critical world situation. We have, of course, willingly made our facilities available to carry[5] his message.

Mr. Wellington, our advertising manager, will be in your neighborhood on Friday, April[6] 19, to attend a series of advertising meetings. I have asked him to stop in to see you about[7] the possibility of arranging a program for another day. Sincerely yours, [156]

587 Dear Mr. Wellington: I was exceedingly happy to learn that you have opened a savings account in your[1] neighborhood branch of the Chemical Trust Company. I congratulate you on your decision to establish[2] a regular program of savings.

It has been my experience that the majority of new depositors[3] do not realize the extent to which their bank can be of service to them. For that reason we have prepared[4] a folder that describes all the classifications of our services that might be of help to you. A copy[5] is enclosed.

We look forward to many opportunities to be of service to you. Cordially yours, [119]

LESSON 63

590 Dear Mr. Wilde: I seldom have time to write testimonial letters to the manufacturers of the[1] equipment we use in our offices. I feel, however, that I must take the time to tell you that the usefulness of[2] the Fenton computer has far exceeded our fondest hopes.

Since we installed the Fenton computer several[3] months ago, we have decreased our overhead costs considerably. While we have not been able to determine exactly the[4] labor savings that have resulted from the use of the Fenton, I am sure that they are substantial.

When we purchased[5] the Fenton, we made an excellent investment. Sincerely yours, [113]

591 Gentlemen: Today I received a second notice from your accounting department requesting me to pay my[1] bill for a one-year subscription to the *Business Monthly*. Apparently your accounting department has made a[2] mistake.

As soon as I received your first notice on October 5, I sent you my check for $6. The[3] canceled check was returned to me by my bank.

May I ask your cooperation in straightening out this situation[4] so that I will not continue to receive your collection letters.

You will be interested to know that[5] I have been a reader of the *Business Monthly* for many years, and I look forward to the arrival of each issue.[6] Sincerely yours, [124]

592 Dear Mr. Flint: We have missed your orders, and we are wondering whether we have offended you without realizing[1] it.

Your account and your friendship are important to us. We like to think that with our prompt, efficient service[2] and excellent merchandise we earn the goodwill of customers like you. If we haven't rendered the type of[3] service that you are entitled to receive, we would definitely appreciate your letting us know so that[4] we can do whatever is necessary to remedy the situation.

It has been a privilege to serve you[5] in the past, and we hope that we may continue to do so in the future. Yours very truly, [117]

593 Dear Mr. Temple: We are happy to be able to give you a very encouraging report on Fenton[1] Brothers.

This company has been banking with us since 1960, and we consider them a valuable account.[2] Our experience with them has been most pleasant, and at no time have they failed to make a payment on any loan promptly.[3]

The latest financial report in our files, dated May 31 of this year, indicates that the company[4] has a net worth of $2,000-000.

The men who run Fenton Brothers are dependable, progressive, and forward[5] looking. We regard them highly. Yours very truly, [110]

594 Dear Mr. Trent: I wonder whether you would be good enough to do me a favor.

You have been using Temple[1] paper towels for a year now, and I have every reason to believe that you have been pleased with them. If that is true[2] (and if it isn't, I want to know it), I would consider it a real kindness if you would drop me a note[3] telling me just what your experiences have been with Temple paper towels.

May I have your cooperation[4] in this matter. I assure you, Mr. Trent, that I will reciprocate your kindness should the opportunity[5] present itself. Yours very truly, [107]

595 Dear Mr. House: Some time ago I wrote you expressing regret that you had not placed any orders with us for[1] many months, and I requested that you tell me why. Thus far, however, I have not received a reply.

I know,[2] of course, that there are many reasons why a customer stops buying from an organization. Losing a good[3] customer's business is a serious matter to me, and I want to know the reason for it.

When you have a[4] moment, please drop me a note and tell me what happened. Cordially yours, [93]

596 Dear Mr. Mild: Welcome to our family of coffee dealers. For many years we have been welcoming new[1] customers and making new friends, and we are delighted to include you among them.

Since 1850 we have been[2] specializing in high-quality coffee. During that time we have learned many things about roasting and blending[3] processes. That experience is available to you.

Whenever you encounter any problem in selling[4] our coffee, please feel free to call on us. Cordially yours, [90]

597 Dear Mr. Grant: As I am sure you will agree, old friends are the best friends. That is the way we feel about the old[1] friends we have made in our thirty years of business. When we don't see an old friend for a long time, we are naturally[2] concerned.

That is why we are writing you. We are concerned that we may have unintentionally done something you[3] didn't like. If that is so, we want to know about it and to remedy the matter.

Won't you let us know why[4] we have not had the pleasure of filling any orders for you since June. Sincerely yours, [96]

LESSON 64

600 Dear Mr. Dunn: Now is the ideal time to renew your *News Week* subscription, even though it may not expire for some[1] months yet.

The reason why this is the ideal time, Mr. Dunn, is that we will soon raise our rates. Before we do so,[2] however, we are giving our regular customers an opportunity to extend their subscriptions for an[3] additional 65 issues at a special price of $8.

Send us your renewal without delay.[4] Once the price increase is announced, this offer cannot be repeated.

It is not necessary to[5] send any money with your renewal; we will bill you later. Sincerely yours, [111]

601 Dear Mrs. Brush: May we be among the first to welcome you to our neighborhood and to your new home.

You will find[1] the shopping center in our neighborhood a convenient, economical place to shop. As you may know, it is[2] situated only a few blocks from your new home.

When you and your family need clothes, we hope you will come to[3] Wilson Brothers, Westport's leading clothing store. When you are finally settled in your new home, come in, look around,[4] and talk to our efficient, courteous, and friendly clerks. You will be most welcome. Sincerely yours, [97]

602 Dear Mr. Dunn: I have carefully reviewed the summary of your personal qualifications and am[1] favorably impressed by the history of your business career. I am genuinely sorry, Mr. Dunn, that[2] we do not have an opening in which you could utilize your excellent background in the fields of accounting,[3] marketing, and management.

If a vacancy should occur later that we think would be suitable for you, we[4] will, of course, get in touch with you.

Meanwhile, thank you very much for your complimentary remarks about our[5] organization. Very truly yours, [106]

603 Dear Mr. Plumber: Last summer you expressed an interest in the Victory Hotel by writing us for our[1] rates and for a description of our accommodations. Apparently your plans did not permit you to visit[2] our part of the country.

Now that spring is just around the corner once again, perhaps you are giving some serious[3] thought to your customary summer vacation. Needless to say, we shall be delighted to have you spend some time with[4] us, Mr. Plumber.

The enclosed folder will serve to refresh your recollection of the various facilities[5] that will be at your disposal at the Victory. Cordially yours, [113]

604 Dear Mr. Brush: Would you like a prescription for that tired, listless feeling?

The best and most effective tonic is[1] a trip to Miami. March and April in Miami are beautiful. A great many doctors protect their own[2] health by taking trips to Miami. Why don't you follow their example?

Revive yourself after a hard winter.[3] Swim in our large pool, bask in the sun, enjoy the scenery, and have fun at your favorite sport. Get away from[4] it all for a time at the Victory, Miami's finest hotel.

Just fill out and mail the enclosed reservation[5] form, and then pack your bags. Yours very truly, [109]

605 Dear Mr. Rush: When the July issue of the *News Magazine* reaches you, it will be the last you will receive[1] on your present subscription.

You may not realize it, but during the past year our columns contained more than a[2] thousand pages of national and foreign news. To keep this information coming each week, it will be necessary[3] for you to renew your subscription without delay.

While you are thinking about your renewal, why not[4] consider giving each of your friends a subscription to the *News Magazine* as a Christmas present this year? As[5] you know, it makes an ideal gift. Yours very truly, [109]

606 Dear Mr. Wilson: A friend of mine is much happier today than he has been for a long time, and he has a[1] reason to be.

My friend says that for the first time he is genuinely comfortable about the future. If[2] something serious happens to him during the next 20 years, his wife will receive $200 a month[3] for a period of 20 years and an additional $20,000 in a lump sum. Previously,[4] such protection would have been far beyond his reach. Now he can afford it because of a new plan that our company[5] has made available.

I am going to get in touch with you sometime soon, Mr. Wilson, to see whether[6] you will invite me to give you more information about this new plan. Sincerely yours, [137]

LESSON 65

609 Dear Mrs. James: I am happy to be able to report that our Community Chest drive for Dade County has[1] already exceeded its goal by 10 percent.

As you will recall, the amount we hoped to reach in our drive was[2] $300,000. On Friday, May 15, our treasurer reported that we had received $330,000[3] in gifts and in pledges. We will probably receive an additional $6,000 or $7,000[4] before the drive is over. Consequently, the Community Chest will be about $337,000[5] richer!

May I express to you my gratitude, Mrs. James, for the part you played in making this year's[6] drive such a great success. Sincerely yours, [127]

610 Dear Mrs. Green: The National Bank and Trust Company has done away with the old-fashioned, confusing method[1] of computing checking account charges. Now we have only four simple plans:

1. If you maintain your balance at[2] $300 or more, there will be no service charge.

2. If you maintain your balance between $200[3] and $299, your monthly service charge will be $1.

3. If you maintain your balance[4] between $100 and $199, your monthly service charge will be $2.[5]

4. If your balance goes below $100, your monthly service charge will be $3.

Isn't this simple,[6] Mrs. Green? When you use one of our plans, you always know what your monthly service charge will be.

Come in soon and[7] open an account with us. Sincerely yours, [147]

611 *America's Cultural Growth*

Last year the sale of books in this country amounted to more than $500,000,000—an increase of more[1] than 50 percent over 1967. Approximately 600,000,000 juvenile books were sold[2] last year—an increase of 50 percent over 1967.

Almost every city with a[3] population of more than 100,000 now has a symphony orchestra.

There are 2,800[4] museums in this country today. In 1932 there were 1,400.

Some $800,000,000[5] worth of phonograph records are sold annually—30 percent of them classical.

More than 6,000,000[6] students were enrolled in colleges last year—30 percent more than in 1967. [137]

612 Mr. Jackson: I think I have located a storage house that is just what we have been looking for. The building[1] has the following desirable features:

1. It is 300 feet wide and 400 feet long.
2. It is on[2] a plot that is 450 feet by 600 feet.
3. It has a loading platform that will hold up to[3] 14,000 pounds of freight.

The owner is quite anxious to sell the building, but he has not been able to find a[4] buyer in the six months the building has been on the market. Consequently, I think we can get it at a[5] reasonable price, probably $250,000.

If you would like to see the building, I shall be[6] glad to make the necessary arrangements with the owner. Harry Smith [133]

613 Dear Mr. Clay: How far does the average worker in your plant have to walk to get a drink of water? Does he[1] walk 50 feet, 100 feet, or 200 feet? Unnecessary steps very often prove more costly than[2] the installation of additional water coolers.

With our new plan you can check your drinking facilities[3] quickly and easily. Why not call our representative for information about this plan. Yours truly, [78]

614 Dear Mr. Jennings: Five hundred people in your county will receive this letter. All 500 can profit by[1] answering it. Only about 2 percent of these 500, however, will reply.

How do we know this? For[2] one thing, only one or two persons out of a hundred are really ambitious enough to obtain important,[3] well-paying jobs. Only one out of a hundred is willing to prepare himself in his spare time.

If you are one[4] of the 2 percent who will reply, you will receive immediately a copy of our booklet, *Opportunities*[5] *in Accounting.* This booklet is much too valuable for us to use as a general mailing piece. It is yours, however,[6] if you will mail the enclosed card. Sincerely yours, [130]

LESSON 66

617 Dear Mr. Doyle: The enclosed card is your invitation to this year's automobile show, which opens on Monday,[1] September 18, in our State Street showrooms.

Our experienced, well-trained representatives will be on hand to answer[2] any questions you may have in regard to our new models. They will also be glad to explain to you the new and[3] important features that have been added to this year's cars.

Coffee and doughnuts will be served each day between the hours[4] of 11 a.m. and 4 p.m.

I hope, Mr. Doyle, that I may have the opportunity to greet you[5] personally during the show. Sincerely yours, [109]

618 Dear Mr. Jones: Because of the great public interest in the civil defense program in general and the[1] fallout shelter program in particular, we will display several government-approved fallout shelters in[2] our showrooms on State Street on Saturday, November 12.

Our organization does not sell shelters, and our only[3] purpose in presenting this display is to provide the public with information about the program.[4]

Representatives of the manufacturers of the shelters will be on hand to answer any questions you may have[5] regarding the shelters.

Don't miss this unusual public-service display. Cordially yours, [117]

619 Dear Mr. Edwards: I am very unhappy. You have not taken advantage of your charge account with us for[1] well over a year. Won't you take a moment to tell me why.

Your visits were always welcome, and we regarded[2] you as an important customer. The question in my mind, Mr. Edwards, is whether unsatisfactory[3] service on our part is responsible for your absence or whether there is some other reason why you have stayed[4] away. Won't you please use the reverse side of this letter to tell me where we have been remiss. Yours very truly, [98]

620 Gentlemen: When you ship your merchandise by United Airfreight, you gain time and also avoid unnecessary[1] shipping costs.

A progressive merchant who uses our service saved 73 percent on ordinary packing[2] and crating costs, 88 percent on insurance fees, and 90 percent on forwarding fees.

We will be glad[3] to make an objective comparison for you between the cost of shipping your particular line of goods by[4] air and the cost of shipping by sea. After you have gone over this comparison, you will have the complete picture[5] before you when you make a decision. Yours very truly, [110]

621 Dear Mr. Short: Have you ever been in a situation where you worked out a good idea to increase your[1] company's business but were unable to sell your idea to management? If you have experienced this[2] difficulty, here is important news for you.

We have just published a book that will tell you how to sell your[3] ideas—*The Art of Persuasion*. Mr. Smith, the author, is a former newspaperman, government official,[4] and businessman. In his book he presents the same modern methods that have won success for men and women in[5] advertising, in manufacturing, and in many other fields.

You can obtain a copy by returning[6] the postcard that is enclosed. Sincerely yours, [128]

622 Dear Mr. Bacon: If you do not plan to use your car this winter, why pay storage and other unnecessary[1] charges on it when you can sell it at a satisfactory profit?

There is still a big market for used[2] cars, and there is no better place to advertise your car than in the columns of our newspaper, the *Morning World*.[3] Very truly yours, [64]

623 Dear Mr. Myers: I am happy to be able to give you a favorable report on Mr. A. R. Green,[1] who is applying for a position with your organization as a correspondent.

Mr. Green joined our[2] company as a clerk, but he soon won several important promotions. He left us to enter the Army.[3] Upon his discharge we offered him his former position. He felt, however, that he would probably be[4] happier in a larger organization.

I am confident that Mr. Green will be an asset to your organization[5] in any capacity that you may employ him. Very truly yours, [114]

624 Dear Friend: We take pleasure in announcing that on or about July 1 the General Motor Company will[1] open a branch at 39 West State Street, right next to the White Plains railroad station.

This branch will be under the[2] supervision of Mr. L. R. Brown and will be staffed by experienced personnel to serve your sales and service[3] needs.

Please accept our thanks for your past business and our assurance that our organization will endeavor[4] in every way to merit the confidence of all owners of General Motor cars in this area.[5] Very cordially yours, [104]

LESSON 67

627 Dear Mr. Kelly: Thank you for letting us know about your plans to visit Omaha during the week of[1] February 6. We shall, of course, be glad to meet with you and discuss some of the ideas we talked about over[2] the phone a few weeks ago.

While you are here, I want you to get to know our comptroller, Mr. Hart. I hope,[3] too, that you will be able to spare an hour or so to go through our plant.

As soon as your travel plans are definite,[4] let us know when you will arrive. I will arrange to have one of our employees meet you at the airport.[5] Sincerely yours, [102]

628 Dear Mrs. Simmons: If you are like most women, you are proud of your cooking skill. Are you equally proud of your[1] kitchen? Is it up to date? Is it one of the most cheerful rooms in the house, a room in which other members of[2] the family enjoy living?

If you are not entirely satisfied with your kitchen as it is now, let us[3] help you modernize it and also save you many hours of work every day.

To arrange for a survey of your[4] kitchen by one of our representatives, sign and return the enclosed card. As soon as we receive it, we will[5] have one of our representatives get in touch with you. Yours very truly, [113]

629 Dear Mr. Hall: Do you want to get out more letters, invoices, and stencils each day? Do you want to free your typists[1] for other work? In short, do you want to solve one of the major problems of high office costs that have been[2] harassing business executives for a long time?

If you do, you should immediately investigate the[3] money-saving possibilities of the new Harper electric typewriter, which was placed on the market[4] several months ago.

If you will return the attached card

to me, I will send you full details about the Harper.[5] You will, of course, be under no obligation. Yours very truly, [112]

630 Dear Mrs. James: As you requested, we have closed your account. We want you to know, however, that we are sorry to[1] lose you as a depositor.

We are grateful for the business you have given us, and we hope that we may have[2] the pleasure of serving you again in the future. Cordially yours, [52]

631 Dear Mr. James: As you may have read in the newspapers a few days ago, the Jackson Hotel is now under[1] new management. It has been my good fortune to be appointed manager.

The many fine features of the Jackson[2] are, of course, familiar to you.

Naturally, we hope that you plan to be with us again this winter. In order[3] that we may reserve for you just the type of room you want, won't you make your reservations as soon as possible.[4] We have made it easy for you to do this. Simply fill out and return the enclosed card to let us know when we may[5] expect you. Cordially yours, [105]

632 Dear Mr. Barnes: As the Christmas season approaches, we want to take time to thank you, on behalf of our entire[1] staff, for your friendship to our organization.

As you know, the past year was not an easy one. Some of the[2] materials we needed were not easy to get, and prices kept rising steadily. Your patience with us in these[3] trying times was a source of comfort to us.

You may be sure that we shall do our best in the future to take care[4] of your needs at prices that will please you.

Let us take this opportunity to wish you a Merry Christmas and[5] a very happy, prosperous New Year. Sincerely yours, [110]

633 Dear Mr. Smith: Do you want people to listen when you speak? Do you want people to purchase your goods? Do you want[1] an increase in salary? Whatever you want from life, you can get it if you will learn those things that influence[2] people to act.

During the past ten years Mr. Frank H. Brown, one of the country's most successful salesmen, has been[3] able to convince thousands of people to act as he wants them to act. When he writes a sales letter, people sit[4] down and write orders.

How has he been able to do these things? You can learn his methods by reading his book, *How to*[5] *Convince People,* which was published two or three months ago.

Let us send you a copy on approval. Very[6] truly yours, [122]

LESSON 68

636 Dear Mr. Day: We shall be glad to change the address on your subscription to the *Advertiser's Weekly.* Before[1] we can do so, we shall need your complete former address. You see, Mr. Day, our files are arranged alphabetically[2] by state, city, and subscriber's name. A self-addressed card is enclosed for your convenience in giving us this[3] information.

We hope, Mr. Day, that you enjoy receiving the *Advertiser's Weekly* and that you find in[4] it many suggestions that are of assistance to you in planning your own advertising. Cordially yours, [98]

637 Dear Mr. Wilmington: Many men

shut themselves out of important, rewarding jobs because they do not sound important[1] when they speak. They are self-conscious about speaking in public.

Because they cannot express themselves convincingly,[2] they lack the ability to influence others.

Now thousands of people are learning how to speak effectively.[3] They are learning through a stimulating program of instruction that utilizes high-fidelity[4] recordings to help them discover their own shortcomings.

Our fascinating booklet describes the entire program. If[5] you would like to have a copy, we shall be glad to forward it to you on request. Sincerely yours, [117]

638 Dear Mr. Gates: One of my assistants tells me that you are planning to feature the complete line of Nelson suits[1] in your department store. We are confident, Mr. Gates, that you will be well pleased with the way these suits sell.

We are[2] looking forward to a relationship that will result in a steady, substantial profit to both of us.

If[3] there is anything that we can do to help you with your promotion of Nelson suits, please let us know. Sincerely yours,[4] [80]

639 Dear Mr. Smith: Thank you for the interest you expressed in your letter of Friday, June 16, concerning the way[1] in which we compensate our salesmen and supervisors. We are indeed flattered that a businessman as successful[2] as you should ask our advice. Unfortunately, we cannot divulge this information.

If we can be of[3] assistance to you in some other way, please feel free to write us. Yours very truly, [74]

640 Dear Mr. Casey: We are extremely sorry that the radio you purchased from us was unsatisfactory.[1] You have every right to expect merchandise from this store to be in perfect condition, and we appreciate[2] your telling us of your experience.

Our shipping department makes every effort to see that each[3] radio, television, or piece of furniture is thoroughly inspected before it is sent out.[4] Unfortunately, your radio was not inspected.

We expect to receive another shipment of Benson[5] radios tomorrow. When it arrives, we will send you a replacement. Very truly yours, [116]

641 Gentlemen: In our office the Baker typewriter has always been considered a superior machine. We[1] shall soon have to replace a number of our typewriters, and we are entertaining the idea of switching[2] to electric machines. Under the circumstances we would like to have answers to the following questions:

1. Is[3] it possible for an operator who is proficient on a standard machine to transfer to an[4] electric without a long period of training?
2. Are there any studies that prove that an operator can[5] obtain greater speeds on an electric than on a standard machine?

A self-addressed, postage-paid envelope is[6] enclosed for your convenience in replying. Very truly yours, [132]

642 Dear Mr. Ryan: Don't you agree that the Wilson franchise is worth a good deal to you as well as to us?[1] The longer you delay payment of your overdue account, however, the more difficult it will be to do[2] business with you in the future.

We have been patient; we have been

considerate. Now it is time for you, Mr.[3] Ryan, to do your part.

Won't you please send us a check for $200 as soon as possible. Very[4] truly yours, [82]

643 Dear Friend: Recently a woman in our neighborhood wrote us, "What justification does the Wellington Electric[1] Power Company have for advertising? I can't buy my electricity from anyone else, can I?"

True,[2] our customers cannot buy their electricity elsewhere. But unless we advertised, they could not learn about[3] our new electric appliances and our vast, forward-looking program designed to supply them with all the[4] electricity they want. Our advertising also aims to keep their friendship and to stimulate the sale of more[5] electricity.

When you have any questions about our facilities or services, never hesitate[6] to write us. Sincerely yours, [125]

LESSON 69

646 Dear Mr. Green: On making the customary room inspection after a guest's departure, our housekeeper[1] reported that two woolen blankets, replacement value $15 each, were missing from the room you occupied. May[2] we respectfully ask that should you discover these blankets on unpacking your luggage, you return them to us.[3]

Very often in their haste to catch a train or a plane guests unknowingly place such items in their bags. They return[4] them, of course, when they discover them in unpacking. Very sincerely yours, [93]

647 Dear Mr. Roy: I was desolated to learn, after reading your tactful letter of Friday, September 4,[1] that you have guests at your hotel who are so absent-minded as to check out and take such slight souvenirs as blankets[2] when packing their neckties. By the same token I suppose that passengers on some of our leading railroads are[3] apt to carry off a locomotive or a few hundred feet of rails when getting off the train on reaching their[4] destination. Or a visitor to a big city zoo might conceivably take away an elephant or[5] a rhinoceros, concealing it in a sack of peanuts—after removing the peanuts, of course.

In this[6] particular case, however, I may be able to assist you in running down your blankets. Because I had a lot of[7] luggage, I needed all the storage space you so thoughtfully provide in each room. The blankets in question occupied[8] the bottom drawer of the dresser. Because I wanted to place a few white shirts (replacement value $5.50[9] each) in that drawer, I removed the said blankets and placed them on a chair. When the maid came in later, I handed her[10] the blankets (same blankets and same replacement value), telling her in nice gentlemanly language to get them out[11] of the room. If you count all the blankets in your establishment, I predict that you will find that not a blanket[12] is missing. Yours very truly,

P.S. Have you counted your elevators lately? [254]

648 Dear Mr. Green: I wish to thank you for one of the most interesting, understanding, and delightful letters[1] it has been my pleasure to read in my entire business career. My sincere congratulations.

Yes, it is[2] essential that we do a lot of counting around here. I've counted the elevators, and they are right where they should be[3] and operating—every one of them. What I want to count now is more important to me. I want to[4] continue counting you as a friend of this hotel.

Twenty-five thousand dollars' worth of our finest silverware is[5] carried away annually by our "absentminded" guests. A similar total is cherished annually[6] by guests who like our linens as a souvenir of their visit. So it goes. We are sorry indeed, Mr. Green,[7] that you were bothered. Yours very truly, [147]

649 Dear Mr. Day: We were happy to receive your letter of Friday, October 16, expressing interest[1] in our line of insulating products.

We are enclosing a copy of our booklet, *Keeping Warm in the*[2] *Winter*. This booklet will explain to you how easy it is to install our insulation and how it will save[3] you a great deal of money in heating costs.

I am also asking our representative in your area,[4] Mr. Frank Brown, to arrange an appointment with you. He will be delighted to answer any questions that you[5] may have after you have read the booklet. Cordially yours, [110]

650 Dear Mrs. Brown: I wish to express our appreciation of your purchase of a new President. I understand[1] that your car was delivered several days ago by our local agency.

May I take this opportunity,[2] Mrs. Brown, to make two suggestions that will help you derive the greatest satisfaction from your car:

1.[3] Please look over very carefully the service policy that you will find in the glove compartment.

2. When your[4] car needs servicing, take it to your local President dealer. In our judgment, he is the man who can best keep[5] your car in good working order.

After you have driven your President for a short time, we think you will[6] agree without question that it is one of the finest cars ever manufactured. Sincerely yours, [137]

LESSON 70

653 *Names*

Do you have trouble remembering people's names? Unfortunately, many people do. You will be wise to[1] overcome that failing, however, if you hope to be successful in your business, professional, or social life.[2]

Actually, anyone who really tries can learn to remember names. It is simply a matter of exerting[3] the effort.

People who habitually forget names do so for one of two reasons:

1. They have not learned[4] to appreciate the importance of remembering names. Or,

2. They are not sufficiently interested[5] in people to make the effort to remember their names.

When someone forgets your name, how do you feel? You don't feel[6] very big, do you?

Here are two steps you can take to help you remember names:

1. When you are introduced to a[7] person, pay careful attention as his name is spoken. If you do not hear it clearly, ask to have his name[8] repeated. You might even ask how his name is spelled; he will be honored by your interest.

2. Try to find something[9] about a person to associate with his name, something that will automatically give you a clue to[10] his name each time you see him. The funnier the clue, the greater

the likelihood that it will help you to recall[11] his name.

The person who remembers names shows that he is genuinely interested in people. A person's[12] name is extremely important to him, and it is the last thing he wants you to forget. [256]

654 *Loyalty*

A young office worker was asked her definition of the term "loyalty." She offered this definition: "It[1] is the willingness to stick by someone through thick and thin, whether things are going well or badly."

This is a fair[2] definition, but loyalty is something more. As one employer put it: "I want to feel that my secretary[3] knows and appreciates the part I am playing in my organization. She knows my feelings, but she doesn't[4] let others know that she knows. She defends me, if necessary, to anyone who questions my motives or[5] my methods of working."

Another executive referred to loyalty in this way: "Loyalty also means[6] believing in the company as a whole. It includes a person's attitude and his dedication to the[7] job. A person who is really loyal wants the company to succeed and works at all times toward that goal."

So[8] you might say that the secretary who possesses the trait of loyalty "sells" her company, her boss, and her fellow[9] workers. She plugs hard to help make the office a better place for everyone. [196]

655 *Judgment*

Judgment is the rarest of qualities. It consists merely in deciding correctly. That sounds very simple,[1] but to judge a question correctly in business often requires sifting the most complex facts and considering[2] a large number of possibilities.

The beginning secretary is not ordinarily called upon[3] to exercise judgment on questions of great importance; nevertheless, the faculty of good judgment is one[4] that is invaluable to even the beginner in business.

Situations arise every day[5] in the business office that call for instant decisions. The secretary must be ready to meet these situations.[6] An analysis must be made of the known facts and circumstances. Each point must be weighed carefully.

Good[7] judgment comes from correct reasoning. It is not a matter of impulse or what is commonly called a "hunch." It[8] is almost an axiom in business that when one guesses, one guesses wrong.

Situations arise in which the[9] evidence is so evenly balanced that it is difficult to make a decision from the facts at hand, but[10] a decision is nevertheless necessary immediately. In such cases we can always fall back[11] on common sense. We cannot expect all our judgments to be correct, but our rating in the business office will[12] be the result of our average of successes. [250]

Appendix

RECALL DRILLS

Joined Word Endings

1 Treatment, alignment, supplement, amusement, compliment, experiment.
2 Nation, termination, station, operation, inflation.
3 Credential, confidential, essential, commercial, socially.
4 Greatly, namely, nicely, mainly, nearly.

5 Readily, speedily, easily, hastily, necessarily, family.
6 Careful, thoughtful, delightful, mindful, usefulness.
7 Assume, assumption, resume, resumption, presume, presumption, consumer, consumed.
8 Dependable, reliable, profitable, table, troubled.
9 Gather, gathered, together, rather, either, leather, bother, bothered, neither.
10 Actual, actually, gradual, schedule, annual, equally.
11 Furniture, picture, nature, stature, captured, miniature, failure, natural.
12 Yourself, myself, itself, himself, herself, themselves, ourselves, yourselves.
13 Port, sport, import, report, deportment.
14 Contain, retain, certain, container, contained.
15 Efficient, sufficient, deficient, efficiency, deficiency, proficiency.

Disjoined Word Endings

16 Childhood, motherhood, neighborhood, brotherhood.
17 Forward, backward, onward, afterward, rewarded.
18 Relationship, steamship, authorship, professorship, championship.
19 Radical, technical, political, article, chemically, periodically, logically.
20 Congratulate, regulate, stipulates, tabulated, congratulation, regulation, regulations, stipulations.
21 Willingly, exceedingly, knowingly, surprisingly, grudgingly.
22 Readings, mornings, sidings, dressings, savings, drawings, sayings, blessings, feelings.
23 Program, telegram, diagrams.
24 Notification, modification, specifications, classifications.
25 Personality, ability, reliability, facilities, utility, generalities.
26 Faculty, penalty, casualty.
27 Authority, sincerity, majority, minority, clarity, sorority, charity, seniority.

Joined Word Beginnings

28 Permit, perform, perfect, pertain, persist, purchase, pursue, pursued, purple, purse.
29 Employ, empower, embarrass, embody, empire, emphatic, embrace, emphasis.
30 Impress, impression, imply, impossible, impair, impel, imbue, impact.
31 Increase, intend, income, inform, inconsistent, indeed, inference, inferior.
32 Enlarge, enforce, enlist, encourage, encounter, encircle, enrich, enrage.
33 Unkind, unwritten, unwilling, unsuccessful, undo, unpleasant, untie, unpopular.
34 Refer, resign, receive, reform, reorganize.
35 Beneath, believe, belong, before, became.
36 Delay, deliver, deserve, diligent.
37 Dismiss, disappoint, discover, discuss, despite.
38 Mistake, misquote, misspell, misstate, misunderstand, misapplied, mistrust.
39 Explain, excite, extend, excuse, express.
40 Comprise, comfort, comply, completed.
41 Condition, consult, continue, confident, convey, confess.
42 Submit, substantiate, subdivide, sublease, suburban.
43 Almost, also, already, although, alteration.
44 Forget, forceful, performed, forecast, foreman.

45 Furnish, furnished, furnishings, furniture, furnace, further.
46 Turn, turned, term, attorney, determine.
47 Ultimate, ulterior, adult, culture, result.

Disjoined Word Beginnings

48 Postman, postage, postmaster, postponed, post office.
49 Interested, internal, interview, intercept, introduce, introduction, enterprise, entrances, entertain, entered.
50 Electricity, electrician, electrical, electric wire, electric fan, electric light, electric motor.
51 Supervise, supervision, supervisor, superhuman, superb.
52 Circumstance, circumstances, circumstantial, circumvent, circumspect.
53 Selfish, self-made, self-defense, self-respect, self-conscious.
54 Transit, transfer, transact, transplant, translation.
55 Understand, undertake, undergo, underpaid, undermine.
56 Overcome, overdue, overhead, overture, overpay, oversee.

KEY TO CHART ON INSIDE BACK COVER

Brief Forms of Gregg Shorthand in Order of Their Presentation

3 I, Mr., have, are-our-hour, will-well, a-an, am, it-at, in-not.
5 Is-his, the, that, can, you-your, Mrs., of, with, but.
8 For, shall, which, be-by, put, would, there-their, this, good.
11 And, them, they, was, when, from, should, could, send.
13 Glad, work, yesterday, very, thank, order, soon, enclose, were-year.
15 Value, than, one-won, what, about, great, thing-think, why, business.
17 Gentlemen, morning, important-importance, those, where, manufacture.
19 Present, part, after, advertise, company, wish, immediate, must, opportunity.
21 Advantage, use, big, suggest, such, several, correspond-correspondence, how-out, ever-every.
23 Time, acknowledge, general, gone, during, over, question, yet, worth.
25 Difficult, envelope, progress, satisfy-satisfactory, success, next, state, under, request.
27 Particular, probable, regular, speak, idea, subject, upon, street, newspaper.
29 Purpose, regard, opinion, circular, responsible, organize, public, publish-publication, ordinary.
31 Merchant, merchandise, recognize, never, experience, between, short, quantity, situation.
33 Railroad, railroads, world, throughout, object, objected, character, characters, govern, government.

Index of Gregg Shorthand

In order to facilitate finding, this Index has been divided into six main sections—Alphabetic Characters, Brief Forms, General, Phrasing, Word Beginnings, Word Endings.

The first figure refers to the lesson; the second refers to the paragraph.

INDEX OF BRIEF FORMS

The first figure refers to the lesson; the second to the paragraph.

INDEX OF BUILDING TRANSCRIPTION SKILLS

The first figure refers to the lesson; the second to the paragraph.

BRIEF FORMS OF GREGG SHORTHAND

IN ORDER OF PRESENTATION

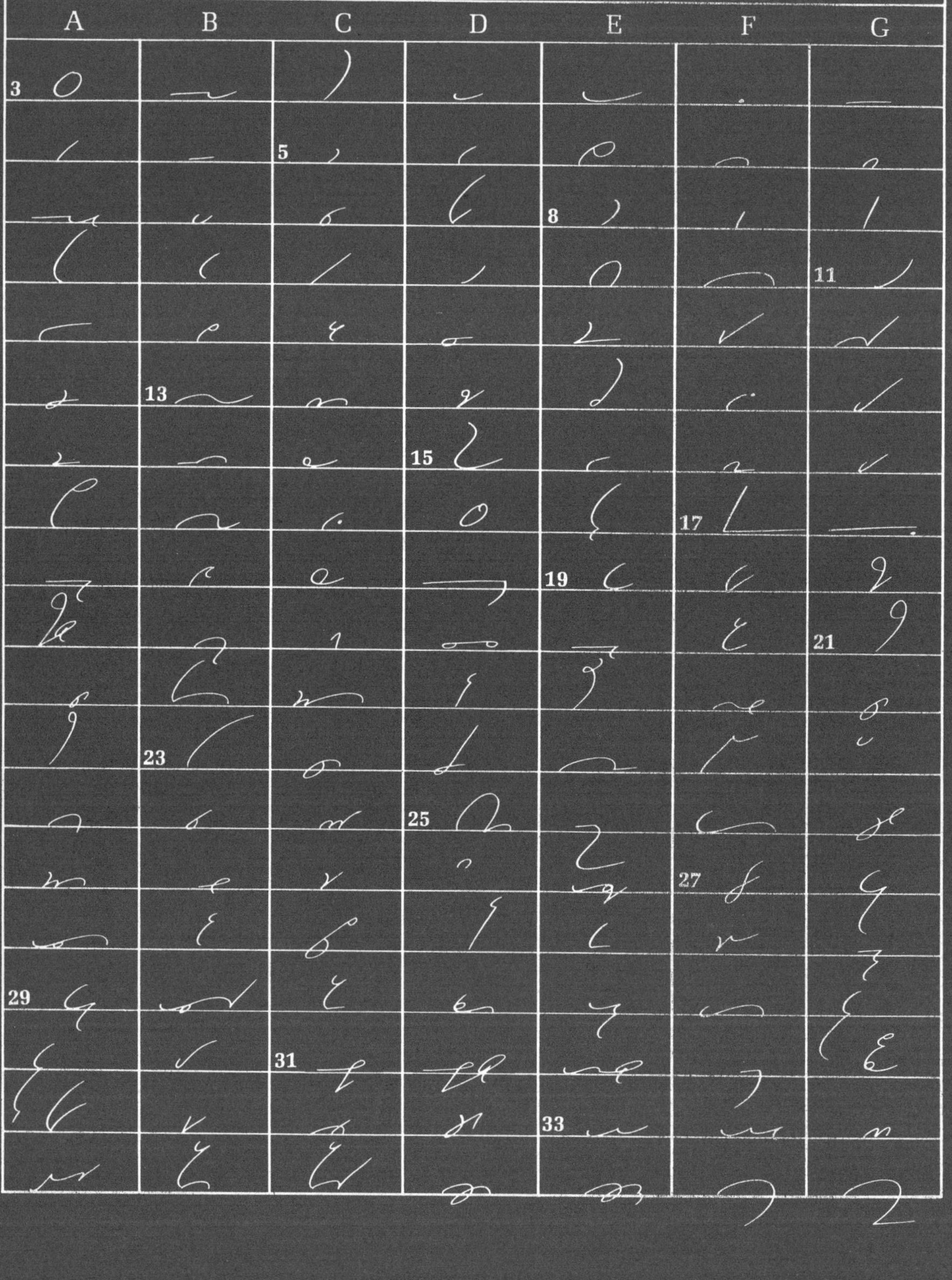

A
B
C
D
E
F
G
3
5
8
11
13
15
17
19
21
23
25
27
29
31
33